PLANNING AND CONTROL
USING
ORACLE® PRIMAVERA® P6
VERSIONS 18 to 23 PPM PROFESSIONAL

Planning and Progressing Project Schedules
With and Without Roles and Resources
in an
Established Database

BY

PAUL EASTWOOD HARRIS

© *Hyde Park Solutions Limited*

Oracle and Primavera are registered trademarks of Oracle and/or its affiliates.

Windows, Microsoft® Office Project Standard 2021, Microsoft®Office Project Professional 2021, Microsoft® Office Project Standard 2019, Microsoft®Office Project Professional 2019, Microsoft® Office Project Standard 2016, Microsoft®Office Project Professional 2016, Microsoft® Office Project Standard 2013, Microsoft® Office Project Professional 2013 Windows and Excel are registered trademarks of Microsoft Corporation.

Elecosoft Powerproject is a registered trademark of Elecosoft®.

Adobe® and Acrobat® are registered trademarks of Adobe Systems Incorporated.

All other company or product names may be trademarks of their respective owners.

Screen captures reprinted with authorization from Oracle Corporation.

This publication was created by Eastwood Harris Pty Ltd and is not a product of Oracle Corporation.

DISCLAIMER

The information contained in this publication is to the best of the author's knowledge true and correct. The author has made every effort to ensure the accuracy of this publication but may not be held responsible for any loss or damage arising from any information in this publication. Furthermore, Oracle Corporation reserves the right in their documentation to make changes to any products to improve reliability, function, or design. Thus, the application of Service Packs or the use of upgraded software may result in the software operating differently from the descriptions in this publication.

AUTHOR

Paul E Harris

PUBLISHER

Hyde Park Solutions Limited
2 Octavia Buildings, Kilmacolm, Renfrewshire, PA13 4AE, Scotland

e-mail: eastwood.harris@hydeparksolutions.com
Web: www.eastwoodharris.com
Tel: +44 20 3174 0070

Please send any comments on this publication to the author.

IISBN 978-1-925185-97-3 - Letter - Perfect

ISBN 978-1-925185-98-0 - Letter/A4 - Spiral

ISBN 978-0-6486355-3-6 - eBook

2 November 2024

INTRODUCTION

This publication is an upgrade of the authors original publication *Project Planning & Control Using Primavera P6 Version 7* and has been written to enable new users to learn the planning and scheduling functions of Primavera 18, 19, 20, 21, 22 and 23. Please note there are no versions 9 to 14 and Oracle changed their naming convention with the release of 15.1 so the name is the same as the year of the release.

Many users will have prior experience with Elecosoft (Asta) Powerproject or Microsoft Project and the author explains where there are differences in the products' functionality.

The author would appreciate any constructive comments on how this publication may be improved.

SUMMARY

The publication may be used as:

> ➢ A training manual for a three-day training course, or
>
> ➢ A self-teach book, or
>
> ➢ A reference manual.

The screen shots for this publication are mainly taken from Primavera Versions 18 or 19 or 20 or 21 or 22 or 23. Screen shots from earlier versions are used when required for demonstrating differences in versions.

One-day, two-day, or three-day training courses may be run using this publication and it includes exercises for the students to complete at the end of each chapter. After the course, students may use this publication as a reference book. Instructors' PowerPoint presentations are available from Eastwood Harris web sites.

This publication is ideal for people who would like to quickly gain an understanding of how the software operates and explains how the software differs from Elecosoft Powerproject and Microsoft Project, thus making it ideal for people who wish to convert from these products.

CUSTOMIZATION FOR TRAINING COURSES

Training organizations or companies that wish to conduct their own training may have this publication tailored to suit their requirements. This may be achieved by removing, reordering or adding content to the publication and by writing their own exercises. Please contact the author to discuss this service.

AUTHOR'S COMMENT

As a project controls consultant, I have used a number of planning and scheduling software packages for the management of a range of project types and sizes. The first publications I published were user guides/training manuals for Primavera SureTrak, P3 and Microsoft Project users. These were well received by professional project managers and schedulers, so I decided to turn my attention to Primavera Enterprise, which is now called Primavera P6. This publication follows the same proven layout of my previous publications. I trust this publication will assist you in understanding how to use Primavera P6 on your projects.

APPRECIATION

I would like thank Michael Jack for his assistance in writing this book and Thomas Grant for his assistance in proof reading parts of the book.

CURRENT BOOKS PUBLISHED BY EASTWOOD HARRIS

Create and Update an Unresourced Project Using Elecosoft (Asta) Powerproject Version 17
Planning and Control Using Oracle Primavera P6 Versions 18 to 23 PPM Professional
Planning and Control Using Microsoft Project 365 and 2021 - Including 2019, 2016 and 2013
99 Tricks and Traps for Microsoft Project 365 and 2021- A Casual User Guide Including 2019, 2016 and 2013
99 Tricks and Traps for Oracle Primavera P6 PPM Professional - The Casual Users Survival Guide Updated for Version 23

SUPERSEDED BOOKS BY THE AUTHOR

Project Planning Using SureTrak for Windows Version 2.0
Planning Using Primavera Project Planner P3 Version 2.0
Planning Using Primavera Project Planner P3 Version 3.0
Planning Using Primavera SureTrak Project Manager Version 3.0
Planning and Scheduling Using Microsoft Project 2000
Planning and Scheduling Using Microsoft Project 2002
Planning Using Primavera Project Planner P3 Version 3.1 Revised Text and Updated Workshops
Planning Using Primavera SureTrak Project Manager Version 3.0 Revised Text and Updated Workshops
Planning and Scheduling Using Microsoft Project 2002 Revised Text and Updated Workshops
Planning and Scheduling Using Microsoft Project 2003
Project Planning and Scheduling Using Primavera Enterprise - Team Play Version 3.5 None
Project Planning and Scheduling Using Primavera Enterprise - P3e & P3e/c Version 3.5 None
Project Planning and Scheduling Using Primavera Version 4.1 - For Engineering & Construction and Maintenance & Turnover
Project Planning and Scheduling Using Primavera Version 4.1 - For IT Project Office and New Product Development
Project Planning and Scheduling Using Primavera Contractor Version 4.1 - For the Construction Industry
PRINCE2 Planning & Control Using Microsoft Project
Planning and Control Using Microsoft Project and *PMBOK®* Guide Third Edition
Planning & Scheduling Using Primavera® Version 5.0 for Engineering & Construction
Planning & Scheduling Using Primavera® Version 5.0 for IT Project Office
Planning and Scheduling Using Microsoft Office Project 2007 - Including Microsoft Project 2000 to 2003
PRINCE2 Planning & Control Using Microsoft Project - Updated for Microsoft Office Project 2007
Planning and Control Using Microsoft Project and *PMBOK®* Guide Third Edition - Updated for Microsoft Office Project 2007
99 Tricks and Traps for Microsoft Office Project - Including Microsoft Project 2000 to 2007
Project Planning & Control Using Primavera® P6TM For all industries including Versions 3 to 6
Planning Using Primavera Project Planner P3 Version 3.1 - Revised 2006
Planning Using Primavera SureTrak Project Manager Version 3.0 - Revised 2006
Project Planning and Scheduling Using Primavera Contractor Version 6.1 - Including Versions 4.1, 5.0 and 6.1
Planning and Scheduling Using Microsoft Office Project 2007 - Including Microsoft Project 2000 to 2003 - Revised 2009
PRINCE2 Planning & Control Using Microsoft Project - Updated for PRINCE2 2009 and Microsoft Project 2007
Planning and Control Using Microsoft Project and *PMBOK®* Guide Fourth Edition
Project Planning & Control Using Primavera P6- For all industries including Versions 4 to 7
Planning and Scheduling Using Microsoft Project 2010
PRINCE2 2009 Planning and Control Using Microsoft Project 2010
Planning and Control Using Microsoft Project 2010 and *PMBOK®* Guide Fourth Edition
99 Tricks and Traps for Microsoft® Office Project 2010
Project Planning and Control Using Oracle Primavera P6 - Version 8.1 Professional Client and Optional Client
Project Planning and Control Using Oracle Primavera P6 - Version 8.1 & 8.2 Professional Client & Optional Client
Planificación y Control de Proyectos Usando Oracle Primavera P6 - Versiones 8.1 y 8.2 Cliente Profesional y Opcional
Project Planning and Control Using Oracle Primavera P6 - Version 8.2 EPPM Web
项目规划和控制 ORACLE PRIMAVERA P6 应用 - 版本 8.1 & 8.2 专业&可选客户端
Project Planning & Control Using Primavera P6 Version 7 - For all industries including Versions 4 to 7 Updated 2012
Planning and Scheduling Using Microsoft Project 2010 - Updated 2013 Including Revised Workshops
Project Planning and Control Using Oracle Primavera P6 - Versions 8.1, 8.2 & 8.3 Professional Client & Optional Client
Planificación y Control de Proyectos Usando Oracle Primavera P6 - Versiones 8.1, 8.2 y 8.3 Cliente Profesional y Opcional
项目规划和控制 ORACLE PRIMAVERA P6 应用 - 版本 8.1, 8.2 & 8.3 专业&可选客户端
Planning and Control Using Microsoft Project 2010 & PMBOK Guide Fifth Edition
Planning and Control Using Microsoft Project 2013 - No Subtitle
Planning and Control Using Microsoft Project 2013 & PMBOK Guide Fifth Edition - No Subtitle
Planning and Control Using Oracle Primavera P6 - Versions 8.2 & 8.3 EPPM Web
99 Tricks and Traps for Microsoft Project 2013
Project Planning and Control Using Oracle Primavera P6 - Versions 8.1 to 8.4 Professional Client & Optional Client
Planning and Control Using Oracle Primavera P6 - Versions 8.2 to 8.4 EPPM Web
Planificación y Control de Proyectos Usando Oracle Primavera P6 Versiones 8.1 a 8.4 Cliente Profesional & Cliente Opcional
规划和控制 ORACLE® PRIMAVERA® P6 应用 版本 8.1-8.4 专业&可选客户端
Oracle Primavera P6 Version 8 and 15 EPPM Web Administrators Guide
Planning and Control Using Oracle Primavera P6 Versions 8.1 to 15.1 PPM Professional
Planificación y Control Usando Oracle Primavera P6 Versiones 8.1 a 15.1 PPM Profesional
规划和控制 Oracle Primavera P6 应用 版本 8.1-15.1 PPM 专业版
Planning and Control Using Oracle Primavera P6 Versions 8.2 to 15.1 EPPM Web
Planning and Control Using Oracle Primavera P6 Versions 8.1 to 15.2 PPM Professional
Planning and Control Using Microsoft Project 2013, 2016 and 2019
99 Tricks and Traps for Microsoft Project 2013, 2016 and 2019
Planning and Control Using Oracle Primavera P6 Versions 8, 15 and 16 EPPM Web
Planning and Control Using Oracle Primavera P6 Versions 8, 15 and 16 PPM Professional
Oracle Primavera P6 Version 8, 15 and 16 EPPM Web Administrators Guide
Create and Update an Unresourced Project using Asta Powerproject
Planning and Control Using Oracle Primavera P6 Versions 8 to 17 PPM Professional
Planning and Control Using Oracle Primavera P6 Version 18 EPPM Web
Planning and Control Using Microsoft Project 2013 or 2016 and PMBOK Guide Sixth Edition
Create and Update an Unresourced Project using Asta Powerproject - 2nd Edition
Planning and Control Using Oracle Primavera P6 Versions 8 to 18 PPM Professional
Planning and Control Using Microsoft Project 2013, 2016 and 2019
99 Tricks and Traps for Microsoft Project 2013, 2016 and 2019
Planning and Control Using Microsoft Project 2013, 2016 or 2019 and PMBOK Guide Sixth Edition
99 Tricks and Traps for Oracle Primavera P6 PPM Professional
Create and Update an Unresourced Project using Asta Powerproject Version 15
Planning and Control Using Oracle Primavera P6 Versions 8 to 19 PPM Professional
Create and Update an Unresourced Project Using Elecosoft (Asta) Powerproject Version 15.2
Planning and Control Using Microsoft Project 365 - Including Microsoft Project 2010, 2013, 2016 and 2019
Planning and Control Using Oracle Primavera P6 Versions 8 to 20 PPM Professional
99 Tricks and Traps for Oracle Primavera P6 PPM Professional - The Casual Users Survival Guide Updated for Version 21
Planning and Control Using Oracle Primavera P6 Versions 8 to 21 PPM Professional
Create and Update an Unresourced Project using Asta Powerproject Version 16
99 Tricks and Traps for Oracle Primavera P6 PPM Professional - The Casual Users Survival Guide Updated for Version 22
Planning and Control Using Oracle Primavera P6 Versions 8 to 22 PPM Professional

1 INTRODUCTION

1.1 Purpose

The purpose of this book is to provide a method for planning, scheduling and controlling projects using Primavera P6 Version 18 to 23 **Professional Project Management (PPM)** which is a windows client and is connected to an established Enterprise Project database or a blank database. This book covers up to an intermediate level and may also be used for earlier versions of the software. Primavera P6 PPM may open up to three database types, a **PPM** database or a **Stand-Alone** database or an **EPPM** database. There are differences between how the **Professional** or **Windows Client** operate when opening these different databases and these differences are identified throughout the book:

- A **PPM** and a **Stand-Alone** database may only be opened with the Windows Client and
- A **EPPM** database may be opened with both the Windows and Web Clients.

The Windows Client was also referred to in the past as the **Optional Client** but this book uses the term **Windows Client** when referring to the PPM Professional Windows software.

This book covers the following topics:

- Understand the steps required to create a project plan and monitor a project's progress,
- Understand the Primavera P6 environment,
- Create a project and set up the preferences,
- Define calendars,
- Creating a Work Breakdown Structure and adding activities,
- Format the display,
- Add logic and constraints,
- Use Filters, Group, Sort and Layouts,
- Printing, reports and using Visualizer,
- Record and track progress of an un-resourced schedule,
- User and Administration Preferences and Schedule Options,
- Create and assign roles and resources,
- Resource optimization including leveling,
- Update a project containing resources,
- Other methods of organizing data and Global Change,
- Managing the enterprise environment including multiple project scheduling.

The book is not intended to cover every aspect of Primavera P6, but it does cover the main features required to create and update a project schedule. It should provide you with a solid grounding, which will enable you to learn the other features of Primavera P6 by experimenting with the software, using the help files and reviewing other literature.

This book was written to minimize superfluous text, allowing the user to locate and understand the information contained within as quickly as possible. If at any time you are unable to understand a topic in this book, it is suggested that you use the Primavera Help menu or User Manuals, which are available on the software downloads in pdf format, or the Oracle website to gain a further understanding of the subject.

The "What Is New" chapters identify the major changes in the software. If you are using this book with an older version, you may find some features do not exist, but I have tried to indicate in which version the new features were introduced and/or removed.

Oracle Corporation continually releases Service Packs for the software and there may be instances where the software operates differently due to the loading of a Service Pack.

1.2   Required Background Knowledge

This book does not teach you how to use computers or to manage projects. The book is intended to teach you how to use Primavera in a project environment. Therefore, to be able to follow this book you should have the following background knowledge:

- The ability to use a personal computer and understand the fundamentals of the operating system.
- Experience using application software, such as Microsoft Office, which would have given you exposure to Windows menu systems and typical Windows functions such as copy and paste.
- A sound understanding of how projects are managed, such as the phases and processes that take place over the lifetime of a project.

1.3   Purpose of Planning

The ultimate purpose of planning is to build a model that enables you to predict which activities and resources are critical to the timely completion of the project. Strategies may then be implemented to ensure that these activities and resources are managed properly, thus ensuring that the project will be delivered both **On Time** and **Within Budget**.

Planning aims to:

- Identify the total scope of the project and plan to deliver it,
- Evaluate different project delivery methods,
- Identify Products/Deliverables required to deliver a project under a logical breakdown of the project,
- Identify and optimize the use of resources and evaluate if target dates may be met,
- Identify risks, plan to minimize them and set priorities,
- Provide a baseline plan against which progress is measured,
- Assist in stakeholders' communication, identifying what is to be done, when and by whom and
- Assist management to think ahead and make informed decisions.

Planning helps to avoid or assist in evaluating:

- Increased project costs or reduction in scope and/or quality,
- Additional changeover and/or operation costs,
- Extensions of time claims against your customer or client,
- Loss of your client's revenue,
- Resolving contractual disputes with subcontractors and suppliers
- The loss of reputation of those involved in a project, and
- Loss of a facility or asset in the event of a total project failure.

1.4   Project Planning Metrics

The components that are normally measured and controlled using planning and scheduling software:

- Scope
- Time
- Resource Effort/Work (these are called Units in Primavera P6)
- Cost

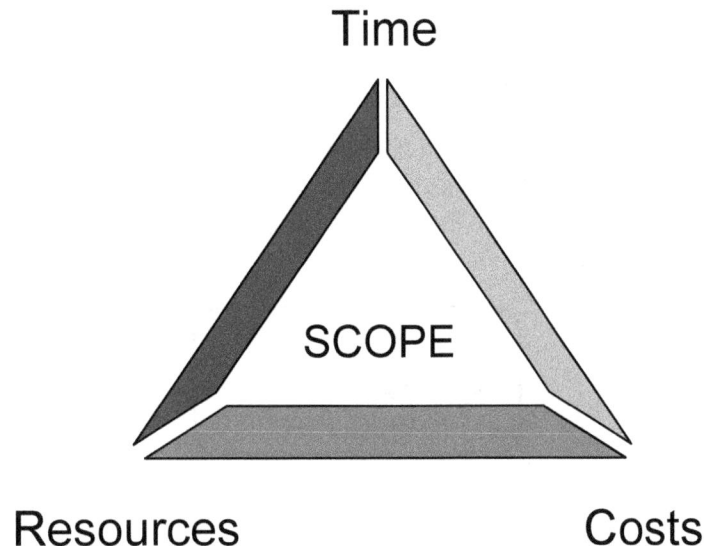

A change in any one of these components normally results in a change in one or more of the others.

Other project management functions that are not traditionally managed with planning and scheduling software but may have components reflected in the schedule include:

- Document Management and Control,
- Quality Management,
- Contract Management,
- Purchasing and Procurement,
- Issue Management,
- Risk Management,
- Industrial Relations, and
- Accounting.

The development of Enterprise Project Management systems has resulted in the inclusion of many of these functions in project planning and scheduling software. Primavera includes modules for:

- Issue Management,
- Risk Management, and
- Document Management.

1.5 Planning Cycle

The planning cycle is an integral part of managing a project. A software package such as Primavera makes this activity much easier.

When the original plan is agreed to, the **Baseline** or **Target** schedule is set. A P6 **Baseline** is a complete copy of the original plan and is used to compare progress of an updated schedule. Earlier P6 versions were limited to 50 baselines but this restriction has been removed in later versions, but you may only copy 50 Baselines when a project is copied.

After project planning has ended and project execution has begun, the actual progress is monitored, recorded and compared to the **Baseline** dates.

Progress is then reported and evaluated against a Baseline.

The plan may be changed by adding or deleting activities and adjusting Remaining Durations, Logic or Resources. A revised plan is then published as progress continues. A revised Baseline may be set if the original Baseline becomes irrelevant due to the impact of project scope changes, a change in methodology or excessive delays.

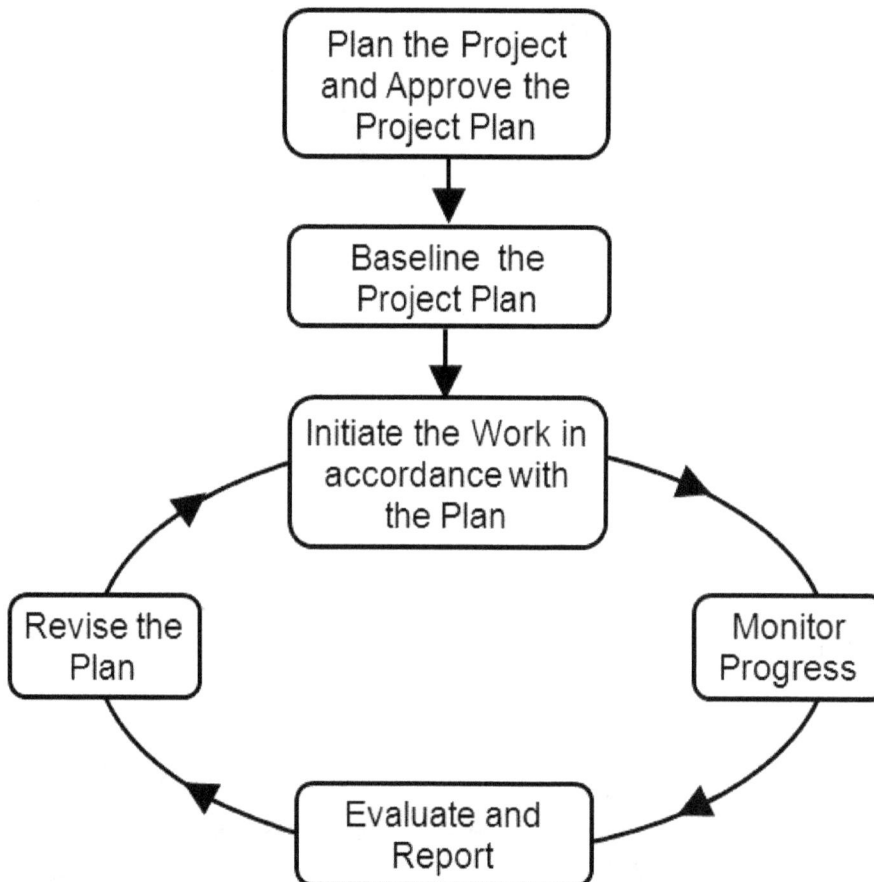

Updating a schedule assists in the management of a project by recording and displaying:

- Progress and the impact of project scope changes and delays as the project progresses,
- The revised completion date and final forecast of costs for the project,
- Historical data that may be used to support extension of time claims and dispute resolution, and
- Historical data that may be used in future projects of a similar nature.

1.6   Levels of Planning

Projects are often planned at a summary level and then at a later date detailed out before the work commences. Smaller projects may be scheduled in detail during project planning, but large or complex projects may require several iterations before the project plan is fully detailed out.

The main reasons for not detailing out a project early are that:

- There may not be enough information at that stage and
- Preparing detailed schedules wastes time, as they may be made redundant by unforeseen changes.

The following planning techniques discussed in other well-known project management books may be considered:

AACE International Publications

AACE International is the Association for the Advancement of Cost Engineering and has a number of publications including Total Cost Management Framework (TCM) and Recommended Practices (RPs)that should be considered when creating, developing and updating a project program.

The relevant scheduling practices that you may wish to review are:

ID	TITLE
14R-90	Responsibility and Required Skills for a Project Planning and Scheduling Professional
20R-98	Project Code of Accounts
21R-98	Project Code of Accounts – As Applied in Engineering, Procurement, and Construction for the Process Industries
23R-02	Identification of Activities
24R-03	Developing Activity Logic
27R-03	Schedule Classification System
32R-04	Determining Activity Durations
37R-06	Schedule Levels of Detail—As Applied in Engineering, Procurement, and Construction
38R-06	Documenting the Schedule Basis
39R-06	Project Planning – As Applied in Engineering and Construction for Capital Projects
45R-08	Scheduling Claims Protection Methods
48R-06	Schedule Constructability Review
49R-06	Identifying the Critical Path
52R-06	Prospective Time Impact Analysis – As Applied in Construction
61R-10	Schedule Design – As Applied in Engineering, Procurement, and Construction
70R-12	Principles of Schedule Contingency Management – As Applied in Engineering, Procurement and Construction
78R-13	Original Baseline Schedule Review - As Applied in Engineering, Procurement, and Construction
82R-13	Earned Value Management (EVM) Overview and Recommended Practices Consistent with EIA-748-C
84R-13	Planning and Accounting for Adverse Weather
89R-16	Management Summary Schedule
91R-16	Schedule Development
92R-17	Analyzing Near-Critical Paths
109R-19	Schedule Change Management - As Applied in Construction
128R-23	1Roles and Responsibilities of a Planning and Scheduling Practitioner

PMBOK® Guide

The *PMBOK® Guide*, which is a project management reference book published by the Project Management Institute, discusses the following techniques:

- The **Rolling Wave**. This technique involves adding more detail to the schedule as the work approaches. This is often possible, as more information is known about the scope of the project as work is executed. The initial planning could be completed at a high level in the **Work Breakdown Structure** (WBS). As the work approaches, the planning may be completed at a **WBS Component** and then to a **Work Package** level planning.

- The use of **Sub-projects**. These are useful in larger projects where more than one entity is working on the project schedule. This situation may exist when portions of projects are contracted out. A sub-project may be detailed out when the work is awarded to a contractor.

- The use of **Phases**. A Phase is different from a PRINCE2 Stage, as Phases may overlap in time and Stages do not. Phases may be defined, for example, as Design, Procure and Install. These Phases may overlap, as Procurement may commence before Design is complete. The Phase development of a schedule involves the detailing out of all the associated WBS elements prior to the commencement of that Phase.

- The *PMBOK® Guide* does not have strict definitions for levels of plans but assumes that this process is undertaken when decomposing the **Work Breakdown Structure** (WBS). There are some other models available that may be used as guidelines, such as the PMI "Practice Standard for Work Breakdown Structures."

PRINCE2 Plans

PRINCE2 is a project management methodology that was developed in the UK. This methodology defines the type of plans that a project team should consider.

Stages in PRINCE2 are defined as time-bound periods of a project, which do not overlap in time and are referred to as Management Stages. The end of a Stage may signify a major event, such as signing a major contract. Project Phases may overlap in time, but Stages do not. Under PRINCE2 a Project Plan is divided into Stages and a Stage plan is detailed out prior to its commencement. PRINCE2 defines the following levels of plans:

- **Programme Plan** – which may include Project Plans or one or more portfolios of multiple projects,

- **Project Plan** – this is mandatory and is updated through the duration of a project,

- **Stage Plan** – there is a minimum of two Stage Plans: An **Initiation Stage Plan** and **First Stage Plan**. There would usually be one Stage Plan for each Stage,

- **Exception Plan** – which is at the same level and detail as a Stage Plan and replaces a Stage Plan at the request of a Project Board when a Stage is forecast to exceed tolerances (contingent time), and

- **Team Plan** – which is optional and would be used on larger projects where Teams deliver Products that require detailed planning. A typical example is a contractor's plan, which would be submitted during the bid process.

1.7 Monitoring and Controlling a Project

After a plan has been produced, it should be executed and the work authorized in accordance with the plan. If there is to be a change in the plan, then the plan should be formally changed. If necessary, the client should be informed and, if required by the contract, approval should be sought.

It may be difficult to obtain approval for extension of time claims when the plan is not followed then and furthermore this will make dispute resolution more difficult.

Monitoring a project ensures the project provides management with historical data, trends and deviations from plan allowing them to make decisions and control the project. It should record the:

- Dates that work was started and completed,

- Hours and cost required to complete the work, and

- Deliverables/products produced.

Monitoring would also:

- Confirm the required quality is being met,

- Provide trends that may be used for forecasting the remainder of the project,

- Record historical data for use in assisting in planning future projects, and

- Obtain data required for preparing extension of time claims and for dispute resolution.

Controlling is the next level of management, analyzing the progress to date and trends to:

- Ensure that the project is being executed according to the plan,

- Compare the project's progress with the original plan,

- Review options in the case of deviations, and

- Forecast problems as early as possible, which enables corrective action to be taken as early as possible.

2   CREATING A PROJECT PLAN

The aim of this chapter is to give an understanding of what a plan is and some practical guidance on how a schedule may be created and updated during the life of a project.

2.1   Understanding Planning and Scheduling Software

Planning and scheduling software enables the user to:

- Enter the breakdown structure of the project deliverables or products into the software. This is often called a Work Breakdown Structure (WBS) or Product Breakdown Structure (PBS),

- Break a project down into the work required to create the deliverables and enter these into the software as Activities under the appropriate WBS,

- Assign durations, calendars, constraints, predecessors and successors of the activities and then calculate the start and finish date of all the activities,

- Assign resources and/or costs, which represent people, equipment or materials, to the activities and calculate the project resource requirements and/or cash flow,

- Optimize the project plan to make the best use of resources and meet predetermined target dates,

- Set Baseline to record the planned dates and budgets to compare progress against,

- Use the plan to approve the commencement of work,

- Record the actual progress of activities and compare the progress against the Baseline and amend the plan when required, allowing for scope changes, etc.,

- Record the consumption of resources and/or costs and re-estimate the resources and/or costs required to finish the project, and

- Produce management reports.

There are four modes or levels in which planning and scheduling software may be used.

	Planning	Tracking
Without Resources	LEVEL 1 Planning without Resources	LEVEL 2 Tracking progress without Resources
With Resources	LEVEL 3 Planning with Resources	LEVEL 4 Tracking progress with Resources

As the level increases, the amount of information required to maintain the schedule will increase and, more importantly, your skill and knowledge in using the software will increase. This book is designed to take you from Level 1 to Level 4.

2.2   Enterprise Project Management

Primavera is an Enterprise Project Management software package that enables many projects to be managed in one database. These projects may be summarized under a hierarchical structure titled the Enterprise Project Structure (EPS). This function is similar to summarizing activities of a project under a Work Breakdown Structure (WBS).

An EPS is used for the following purposes:

- To manage user access to projects within the database.

- To manage activities over multiple projects that have a common interest, such as a critical resource.

- Top-down budgeting of projects and resources that may later be compared to the bottom-up or detailed project estimates.

- To allow standardized reporting of all projects in the database.

Individual projects must be created within an EPS database. Primavera has not been designed as a single project planning and scheduling software package and there is an administrative overhead in managing projects in an EPS database.

Primavera has a function titled Portfolios that enables a limited number of projects to be viewed at a time. For example, Portfolio would enable you to view projects in a physical area, or of a specific type or client.

2.3   Understanding Your Project

Before you start the process of creating a project plan, it is important to have an understanding of the project and how it will be executed. On large, complex projects, this information is usually available from the following types of documents:

- Project charter or business case

- Project scope or contract documentation

- Functional specification

- Requirements baseline

- Plans and drawings

- Project execution plan

- Contracting and purchasing plan

- Equipment lists

- Installation plan

- Testing plan

- Historical data

Many project managers conduct a **Stakeholder Analysis** at the start of a project. This process lists all the people and organizations with an interest in the project and their interests or desired outcomes.

- Key success factors may be identified from the interests of the influential stakeholders.

- It is important to use the stakeholder analysis to identify all the stakeholder activities and include them in the schedule.

It is imperative to gain a good understanding of how the project is to be executed before entering any data into the software. It is considered good practice to plan a project before creating a schedule in any planning and scheduling software. These documents are referred to by many terms such as Project Execution Plan or Project Methodology Statement. You should also understand what level of reporting the project team requires, as providing either too little or too much detail will often lead to a discarded schedule.

It is also important to conduct a **Risk Analysis**, sometimes called a **Risk and Opportunity Analysis** to develop additional scope and activities created by any **Risk Mitigation** strategies that are selected.

There are three processes required to create or maintain a plan at each of the four levels:

- Collecting the relevant project data,
- Entering and manipulating the data in software, and
- Distributing, reviewing and revising the plan.

The ability of the scheduler to collect the data is as important as the ability to enter and manipulate the information using the software. On larger projects, it may be necessary to write policies and procedures to ensure accurate collection of data from the various people, departments, stakeholders/companies, and sites.

2.4   Level 1 – Planning Without Resources

This is the simplest mode of planning.

2.4.1   Creating Projects

To create a project in a Primavera database, you will need the following information:

- An EPS Node, OBS Node in the database to assign the project,
- A unique Project ID (a code assigned to the project) and the Project Name,
- The Project Start Date (and perhaps the Finish Date), and
- The Rate Type. Primavera has five rates per resource and this option enables you to select a rate as the default resources rate.

It would also be useful to know other information such as:

- Client name, and
- Project information such as location, project number and stakeholders.

2.4.2   Defining the Calendars

Before you start entering activities into your schedule, it is advisable to set up the calendars. These are used to model the working time for each activity in the project. For example, a 6-day calendar is created for those activities that will be worked for 6 days a week. The calendar should include any public holidays and any other exceptions to available working days, such as planned days off.

Primavera has three types of calendars:

- **Global** – which may be assigned to activities and resources in any project,
- **Project** – these are project-specific calendars assigned to activities, and
- **Resource** – that are assigned to resources.

Project and Resource calendars may be linked to Global calendars, enabling any changes to holidays made to a Global calendar to be inherited by the associated Project and Resource calendars.

2.4.3   Defining the Project Breakdown Structures

A **Project Breakdown Structure** (PBS) is a way of categorizing the activities of a project into numerous codes that relate to the project. The codes act as tags or attributes of each activity.

During or after the activities are added to the schedule, they are assigned their PBSs so that they may be grouped, summarized, and filtered in or out of the display.

Primavera has two principal methods of assigning a PBS to your project:

- The Work Breakdown Structure (WBS) function, which is comparable to the Elecosoft (Asta) Powerproject WBS function.
- The Activity Code function operates in a way similar to Elecosoft (Asta) Powerproject.

Before creating a project, you should design your PBSs by asking the following questions:

- Which phases are involved in the project (e.g., Design, Procure, Install and Test)?
- Which disciplines are participating (e.g., Civil, Mechanical and Electrical)?
- Which departments are involved in the project (e.g., Sales, Procurement and Installation)?
- What work is expected to be contracted and which contractors are to be used?
- How many sites or areas are there in the project?

Use the responses to these and other similar questions to create the PBSs.

2.4.4   Adding Activities

Activities must be defined before they are entered into the schedule. It is important that you carefully consider the following factors:

- What is the scope of the activity? (What is included and excluded?)
- How long is the activity going to take?
- Who is going to perform it?
- What are the deliverables or output for each activity?

The project estimate is usually a good place to start looking for a breakdown of the project into activities, resources, and costs. It may even provide an indication of how long the work will take.

Activities may have variable durations depending on the number of resources assigned. You may find that one activity that takes 4 days using 4 workers may take 2 days using 8 workers or 8 days using 2 workers.

Usually, project reports are issued on a regular basis such as every week or every month. It is recommended that, if possible, an activity should not span more than two reporting periods. That way the activities should only be **In-Progress** for one report. Of course, it is not practical to do this on long duration activities, such as procurement and delivery activities, that may span many reporting periods.

Good practice recommends that you have a measurable finish point for each group of activities. These may be identified in the schedule by **Milestones** and are designated with zero duration. You may issue documentation to officially highlight the end of one activity and the start of another, thereby adding clarity to the schedule. Examples of typical documents that may be issued for clarity are:

- Issue of a drawing package
- Completion of a specification
- Placing of an order
- Receipt of materials (delivery logs or tickets or dockets)
- Completed testing certificates for equipment or systems.

2.4.5 Adding the Logic Links

The logic is added to the schedule to provide the order in which the activities must be undertaken. The logic is designated by indicating the predecessors to, or the successors from, each activity. There are two methods that software uses to sequence activities:

- Precedence Diagramming Method (PDM), and
- Arrow Diagramming Method (ADM).

Most current project planning and scheduling software, including Primavera, uses PDM. You can create a PDM diagram using the Network Diagram function.

There are several types of dependencies that may be used:

1. **Mandatory dependencies**, also known as **Hard Logic** or **Primary Logic**, are relationships between activities that may not be broken. For example, a hole has to be dug before it is filled with concrete, or a computer delivered before software is loaded.

2. **Discretionary dependencies**, also known as **Sequencing Logic** or **Soft Logic** or **Secondary Logic,** are relationships between activities that may be changed when the plan is changed. For example, if there are five holes to be excavated and only one machine available, or five computers to be assembled and one person available to work on them, then the order of these activities could be set with sequencing logic yet changed at a later date.

   Both **Mandatory dependencies** and **Discretionary dependencies** are entered into Primavera as activity relationships or logic links. The software does not provide a method of identifying the type of relationship because notes or codes may not be attached to relationships. A **Note** may be added to either the predecessor or the successor activity to explain the relationship.

3. **External dependencies** are usually events outside the control of the project team that impacts on the schedule. An example would be the availability of a site to start work. This is usually represented in Primavera by a Milestone that has a constraint applied to it. This topic is discussed in more detail in the next section.

The software will calculate the start and finish dates for each activity. The end date of the project is calculated from the start date of the project, the logic amongst the activities, any **Leads**(often referred to as **Negative Lag**)or **Lags** applied to the logic and durations of the activities. The following picture shows the effect of a lag and a lead on the start of a successor activity:

An example of a **Finish to Start** with positive lag:

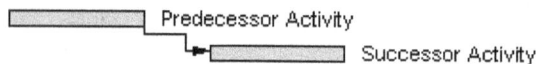

Predecessor Activity
Successor Activity

An example of a **Finish to Start** with a lead or negative lag:

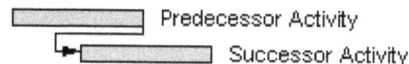

Predecessor Activity
Successor Activity

2.4.6 Developing a Closed Network

It is good practice to create a **Closed Network** with the logic. In a **Closed Network**, all activities have one or more predecessors and one or more successors except:

- The project start milestone or first activity, which has no predecessors, and
- The finish milestone or finish activity, which has no successors.

> When a closed network is not established then the Critical Path, Total Float and Free Float will not calculate correctly

The project's logic must not loop back on itself. Looping occurs if the logic states that A preceded B, B preceded C, and C preceded A. That is not a logical project situation and will cause the software to generate an error comment during network calculations.

Thus, when the logic is correctly applied, a delay to an activity will delay all its successor activities and delay the project end date when there is insufficient spare slippage time to accommodate the delay. This spare time is normally called **Float** but note that Microsoft Project uses the term **Slack** for **Float**.

2.4.7 Scheduling the Project

The software calculates the shortest time in which the project may be completed, Activities are moved forward in time until they meet a Relationship or Constraint or a calendar nonwork time. Un-started activities without logic or constraints are scheduled to start at the Project Start Date or as permitted by calendar nonwork times.

Scheduling the project will identify the **Critical Path(s)** when there is a **Closed Network**. The Critical Path is the chain(s) of activities that takes the longest time to accomplish; a delay to any activity in the chain will delay the end date of the project. The calculated completion date depends on the critical activities starting and finishing on time. If any of them are delayed, the whole project will be delayed.

2.4.8 Critical Path

The Critical Path is the shortest duration that a project may be completed in and a delay to any activity will delay the end date of the project, activities A1000 to A1030 and A1060 below also shown in red are on the critical path:

Activity ID	Activity Name	Orig Dur	Start	Finish
A1000	Start	0d	01-Sep-14	
A1010	Activity A	5d	01-Sep-14	05-Sep-14
A1020	Activity B	5d	08-Sep-14	12-Sep-14
A1030	Activity C	5d	15-Sep-14	19-Sep-14
A1040	Activity D	2d	01-Sep-14	02-Sep-14
A1050	Activity E	2d	08-Sep-14	09-Sep-14
A1060	Finish	0d		19-Sep-14

2.4.9 Total Float

Total Float is the amount of time an activity may be delayed without extending the project end date.

- An activity with Total Float may delay another activity,
- May be displayed in a column and in the Gantt Chart, as per the thin black bar below and
- May be negative.

Activity ID	Activity Name	Orig Dur	Start	Finish	Total Float
A1000	Start	0d	01-Sep-14		0d
A1010	Activity A	5d	01-Sep-14	05-Sep-14	0d
A1020	Activity B	5d	08-Sep-14	12-Sep-14	0d
A1030	Activity C	5d	15-Sep-14	19-Sep-14	0d
A1040	Activity D	2d	01-Sep-14	02-Sep-14	11d
A1050	Activity E	2d	08-Sep-14	09-Sep-14	8d
A1060	Finish	0d		19-Sep-14	0d

2.4.10 Free Float

The Free Float is the amount of time an activity may be delayed without delaying another activity.

- Displayed only in a column and
- Is never in the negative.

Activity ID	Activity Name	Orig Dur	Start	Finish	Total Float	Free Float
A1000	Start	0d	01-Sep-14		0d	0d
A1010	Activity A	5d	01-Sep-14	05-Sep-14	0d	0d
A1020	Activity B	5d	08-Sep-14	12-Sep-14	0d	0d
A1030	Activity C	5d	15-Sep-14	19-Sep-14	0d	0d
A1040	Activity D	2d	01-Sep-14	02-Sep-14	11d	3d
A1050	Activity E	2d	08-Sep-14	09-Sep-14	8d	8d
A1060	Finish	0d		19-Sep-14	0d	0d

i   P6 does not display Free Float as a bar.

2.4.11 Relationship Colors

Relationship colors in P6 may not be formatted as with most other software:

- Solid Red are Critical and normally do not have Total Float,
- Solid Black are Driving Non-Critical and their successors have Total Float,
- Dotted Black are Non-Driving Non-Critical and their predecessors have Free Float,
- Blue are selected relationships and may then be edited or deleted.

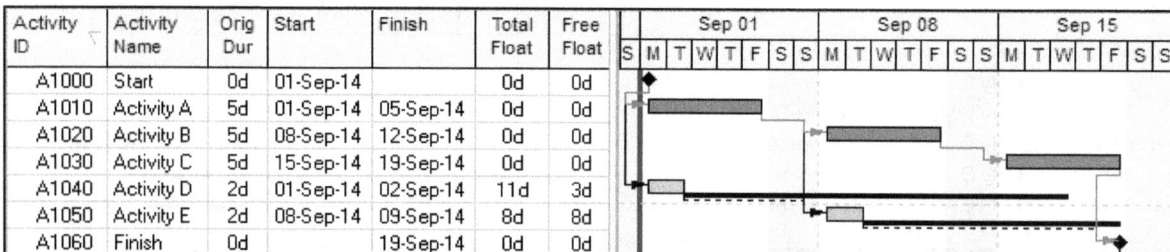

Activity ID	Activity Name	Orig Dur	Start	Finish	Total Float	Free Float
A1000	Start	0d	01-Sep-14		0d	0d
A1010	Activity A	5d	01-Sep-14	05-Sep-14	0d	0d
A1020	Activity B	5d	08-Sep-14	12-Sep-14	0d	0d
A1030	Activity C	5d	15-Sep-14	19-Sep-14	0d	0d
A1040	Activity D	2d	01-Sep-14	02-Sep-14	11d	3d
A1050	Activity E	2d	08-Sep-14	09-Sep-14	8d	8d
A1060	Finish	0d		19-Sep-14	0d	0d

2.4.12 Constraint Types

There are two types of constraints:

- **Project Constraints** which include the **Project Start Date** and optional **Project Finish Date**, and
- **Activity Constraints**; the two most common are **Start On or After** (Early Start) **and Finish On or Before** (Late Finish).

External dependencies are applied to a schedule using **Constraints** and these may model the impact of events outside the logical sequence of activities. A constraint would be imposed to specific dates such as the availability of a facility to start work or the required completion date of a project. Constraints should be cross-referenced to the supporting documentation, such as Milestone Dates from contract documentation, using the **Notebook Topics** function.

2.4.13 Project Constraints

A **Project Start Date** called **Project Planned Start** in P6 is the earliest date that any activity may be scheduled to start. An activity will start on the **Project Start Date** unless one of the following stop the activity starting on the **Project Start Date**:

- There is a Calendar Nonwork time, or
- A constraint, or
- A relationship.

A **Project Must Finish Date**s optional, but once set this controls Total Float (often referred to as Float in P6).

When a **Project Must Finish Date** constraint is assigned then Total Float is calculated to this date.

- The picture shows a project with a Project Finish date on Friday 26 September developing 5 days Total Float.

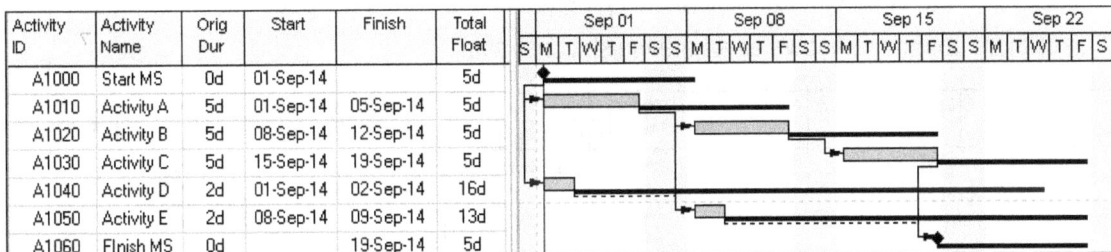

Activity ID	Activity Name	Orig Dur	Start	Finish	Total Float
A1000	Start MS	0d	01-Sep-14		5d
A1010	Activity A	5d	01-Sep-14	05-Sep-14	5d
A1020	Activity B	5d	08-Sep-14	12-Sep-14	5d
A1030	Activity C	5d	15-Sep-14	19-Sep-14	5d
A1040	Activity D	2d	01-Sep-14	02-Sep-14	16d
A1050	Activity E	2d	08-Sep-14	09-Sep-14	13d
A1060	Finish MS	0d		19-Sep-14	5d

- The picture shows a schedule with a Project Finish date of Friday 12,
- This is earlier than the calculated finish date, thus calculating 5 days Negative Float:

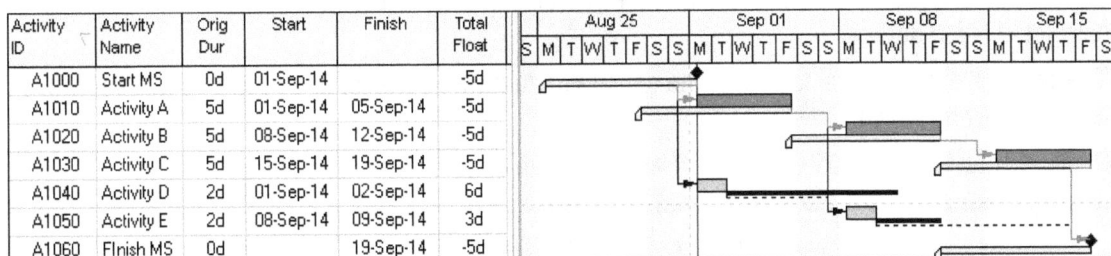

Activity ID	Activity Name	Orig Dur	Start	Finish	Total Float
A1000	Start MS	0d	01-Sep-14		-5d
A1010	Activity A	5d	01-Sep-14	05-Sep-14	-5d
A1020	Activity B	5d	08-Sep-14	12-Sep-14	-5d
A1030	Activity C	5d	15-Sep-14	19-Sep-14	-5d
A1040	Activity D	2d	01-Sep-14	02-Sep-14	6d
A1050	Activity E	2d	08-Sep-14	09-Sep-14	3d
A1060	Finish MS	0d		19-Sep-14	-5d

2.4.14 Activity Constraints

Typical examples of activity constraints would be:

- **Start on or After** for the availability of a site to commence work, and
- **Finish on or Before** for the date that a total project must be completed or handed over.

Activity Early Start Constraint

- An activity will no longer start on the Data Date when a **Start On or After** constraint is assigned
- This is more commonly known as an **Early Start** constraint.

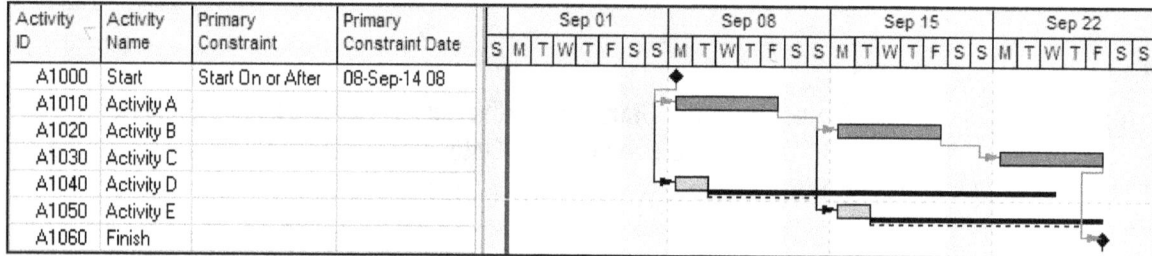

Activity ID	Activity Name	Primary Constraint	Primary Constraint Date
A1000	Start	Start On or After	08-Sep-14 08
A1010	Activity A		
A1020	Activity B		
A1030	Activity C		
A1040	Activity D		
A1050	Activity E		
A1060	Finish		

> *i* In P6 the time must always be displayed as P6 will often set constraints at 00:00hrs which is midnight and is not very often an appropriate time to set constraints.

Activity Late Finish Constraint

- This picture below shows a schedule with an additional **Finish Date On or Before** constraint assigned 4 days earlier than the calculated finish date,
- Thus, Negative Float is created, representing the amount of time that needs to be caught up.
- This is more commonly known as a Late Finish constraint:

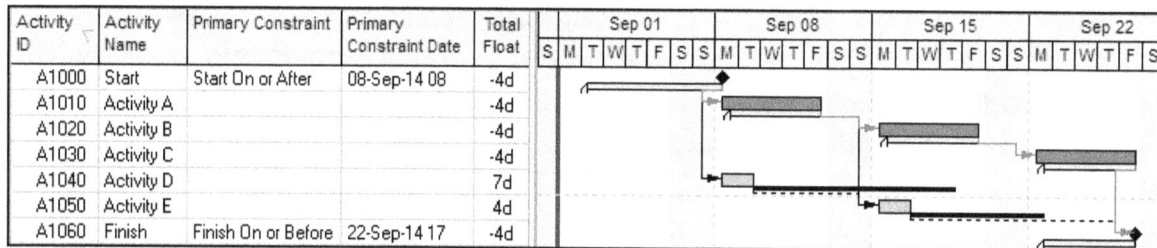

Activity ID	Activity Name	Primary Constraint	Primary Constraint Date	Total Float
A1000	Start	Start On or After	08-Sep-14 08	-4d
A1010	Activity A			-4d
A1020	Activity B			-4d
A1030	Activity C			-4d
A1040	Activity D			7d
A1050	Activity E			4d
A1060	Finish	Finish On or Before	22-Sep-14 17	-4d

- The picture below shows a schedule with a **Finish Date On or Before** constraint assigned after the calculated finish date,
- The Total Float is **NOT** calculated to the constraint date when the constraint date is **LATER** the calculated Early Finish.
- Positive Total Float is **NOT** created and a critical path of zero days float is maintained:

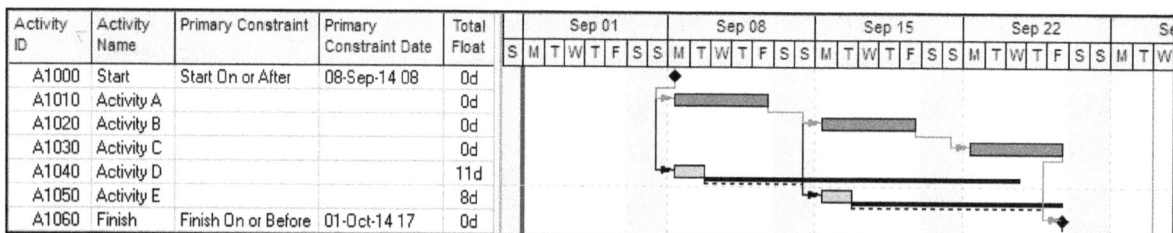

Activity ID	Activity Name	Primary Constraint	Primary Constraint Date	Total Float
A1000	Start	Start On or After	08-Sep-14 08	0d
A1010	Activity A			0d
A1020	Activity B			0d
A1030	Activity C			0d
A1040	Activity D			11d
A1050	Activity E			8d
A1060	Finish	Finish On or Before	01-Oct-14 17	0d

2.4.15 Risk Analysis

The process of planning a project may identify risks, so a formal risk analysis should be considered. A risk analysis may identify risk mitigation activities that should be added to the schedule before it is submitted for approval.

2.4.16 Contingent Time

The addition of contingent time should be considered when submitting a schedule for approval. Estimates usually have contingency and if this money is to be expended then an allowance for time to spend the contingent funds needs to be made. Contingent time may be added to a schedule in a number of ways:

- Insert one or more contingent time activities in the project. These would be adjusted in length as the project progresses to maintain the planned end date.
- Assign work days in the calendar nonwork days. For example, a building project could be scheduled on a 5-day per week basis, knowing that work will be undertaken on the Saturday.
- Increase the activity durations by a factor, this will affect either the resource Units per Time Period or total resource Units and should not be used on a resourced schedule.
- Assign positive lags between activities, although this is not recommended by the author.

2.4.17 Formatting the Display – Layouts and Filters

There are tools to manipulate and display the activities to suit the project reporting requirements. These functions are covered in the **Group, Sort and Layouts** and the **Filters** chapters.

2.4.18 Printing and Reports

There are software features that enable you to present the information in a clear and concise manner to communicate the requirements to all project members. These functions are covered in the **Printing and Reports** chapter.

2.4.19 Issuing the Plan

All members of the project team should review the project plan in an attempt to:

- Optimize the process and methods employed, and
- Gain consensus among team members as to the project's logic, durations, and Project Breakdown Structures.

Team members should communicate frequently with each other about their expectations of the project while providing each with the opportunity to contribute to the schedule and further improve the outcome.

2.5   Level 2 – Monitoring Progress Without Resources

2.5.1   Setting the Baseline

The optimized and agreed-to plan is used as a baseline for measuring progress and monitoring change. The software records the baseline dates for all activities for comparison against actual progress during the life of the project.

2.5.2   Tracking Progress

The schedule should be **Updated** (progressed) on a regular basis and progress recorded at that point. The date on which progress is reported is known by several different terms such as **Data Date**, **Update Date**, **Time Now** and **Status Date**. The **Current Data Date** is the field Primavera uses to record this date. The **Data Date** is **NOT** the date that the report is printed but rather the date that reflects when the update information was gathered.

Whatever the frequency chosen for updating, you will have to collect the following activity information in order to update a schedule:

- Completed activities:
  - ➢ Actual Start date
  - ➢ Actual Finish date
- In-progress activities:
  - ➢ Actual Start date
  - ➢ Percentage Completed
  - ➢ Remaining Duration or Expected Finish Date of the activity
- Un-started work:
  - ➢ Any revisions to activities that have not started
  - ➢ New activities representing scope changes
  - ➢ Revisions to logic that represent changes to the plan

The schedule may be updated after this information has been collected. The recorded progress is compared to the **Baseline** dates, either graphically or by using columns of data, such as the **Baseline Finish Variance** column:

Activity ID	Activity Name	Remaining Duration	Total Float	Free Float	Variance - BL Project Finish Date	Oct 31	Nov 07	Nov 14	Nov 21
	7 Activities Progr...	19	0	0	0				
A1000	Start Milestone	0			-1				
A1010	Activity 1	0			-1				
A1020	Activity 2	4	0	0	-1				
A1030	Activity 3	5	0	0	0				
A1040	Activity 4	0			0				
A1050	Activity 5	3	6	6	-3				
A1060	Finish Milestone	0	0	0	0				

2.5.3 Corrective Action

At this point, it may be necessary to further optimize the schedule to bring the project back on track by discussing the schedule with the appropriate project team members. The possible options are:

- Reduce the contingent time allowance.

- Allowing activities to overlap, say by assigning a negative lag on a Finish to Start relationship, which enables a successor to commence before a predecessor is completed.

- Change relationships to allow activities to be executed in parallel.

- Reduce the activity durations. In a resourced schedule, this could be achieved by increasing the number of resources assigned to an activity.

- Work longer hours per day or days per week by editing the calendars, or

- Reduce the scope and delete activities.

2.6 Level 3 – Scheduling with Resources, Roles and Expenses

2.6.1 Estimating or Planning for Control

There are two modes that the software may use at Level 3.

- **Estimating**. In this mode, the objective is to create a schedule with costs that are used only as an estimate. The schedule will never be updated. Activities may have many resources assigned to them to develop an accurate cost estimate and include many items that would never be updated in the process of updating a schedule.

- **Planning for Control**. In this mode, the intention is to assign actual units (hours) and costs to resources, then calculate units and costs to completion, and possibly conduct an Earned Value analysis. In this situation, it is important to ensure that the minimum number of resources are assigned to activities, and preferably only one resource assigned to each activity. The process of updating a schedule becomes extremely difficult and time consuming when a schedule has many resources per activity. The scheduler is then under threat of becoming a timekeeper and may lose sight of other important functions, such as calculating the forecast to complete and the project finish date.

2.6.2 The Balance Between the Number of Activities and Resources

When Planning for Control on large or complex schedules, it is important to maintain a balance between the number of activities and the number of resources that are planned and tracked. As a rule, the more activities a schedule has, the fewer resources should be created and assigned to activities.

When a schedule contains many activities and a large number of resources assigned to each activity, the result may be that no members of the project team are able to understand the schedule and the scheduler is unable to maintain it.

Instead of assigning individual resources, such as people by name, consider using "Skills" or "Trades," and on very large projects use "Crews" or "Teams."

This technique is not so important when you use a schedule for estimating the direct cost of a project (by assigning costs to the resources) or if you are not using the schedule to track a project's progress (such as a schedule that is used to support written proposals).

Therefore, it is more important to minimize the number of resources in large schedules that will be updated regularly, because updating every resource assigned to each activity at each schedule update is very time consuming.

2.6.3   Creating and Using Resources

First, one would usually establish a resource pool by entering all the required project resources into a hierarchical table in the software. The required quantity of each resource is assigned to the activities. In an Enterprise environment these resources may already be defined for you.

Entering a cost rate for each resource enables you to conduct a resource cost analysis, such as comparing the cost of supplementing overloaded resources against the cost of extending the project deadline.

Estimates and time-phased cash flows may be produced from this resource/cost data.

2.6.4   Creating and Using Roles

Primavera has an additional function titled **Roles**, which is used for planning and managing resources.

- A Role is a skill or trade or job description and may be used as an alternative to resources during the planning period of a project.
- Roles are defined in a hierarchical structure and hold a **Proficiency Level**.
- Roles may be assigned to activities in a way similar to assigning resources to activities. Roles can be replaced later by resources after it has been decided who is going to be assigned the work.
- Primavera Version 5.0 introduced a function allowing a Role to be assigned a rate.

2.6.5   The Relationship Between Resources and Roles

Primavera has the ability to define roles and associate them with resources. A role is a job title, trade or skill and may have many resources. A multi-skilled resource may have multiple roles. For example, a role may be a Clerical Assistant and there may be five clerical assistants in a company who would be assigned the Clerical Assistant Role. If one clerical assistant were also a data entry person, then this resource would be assigned two roles: Clerical Assistant and Data Entry.

2.6.6   Using Roles and Resources

Roles are used for long term planning and as the work approaches the activities are assigned to resources who would be created as specific individual people. Most construction projects do not use roles as they would never create resources as specific named people and resources, not roles, are used to represent trades, crews or construction equipment because resources have more functionality.

2.6.7   Activity Type and Duration Type

Activities may be assigned an **Activity Type** and **Duration Type**, which affect how resources are calculated. Additional software features enable the user to more accurately model real-life situations. These features are covered in the **Assigning Roles, Resources and Expenses** chapter.

2.6.8   Budgets

The Budget function enables Top-Down Budgeting at a summary level against each EPS Node in an accounting style. Budgets may be compared to the detailed estimates calculated after resources have been assigned to Activities. The Budget function is not covered in this book.

2.6.9 Resource Usage Profiles and Tables

These features enable the display and analysis of project resource requirements both in tables and graphs.

The data may be exported to Excel or reports run for further analysis and presentation.

2.6.10 Resource Optimization

The schedule may now have to be resource optimized to:

- Reduce peaks and smooth the resource requirements, or
- Reduce resource demand to the available number of resources, or
- Reduce demand to an available cash flow when a project is financed by a customer.

Leveling is defined as delaying activities until resources become available. There are several methods of delaying activities, and thus leveling a schedule, which are outlined in the **Resource Optimization** chapter.

2.7 Level 4 – Monitoring and Controlling a Resourced Schedule

2.7.1 Monitoring Projects with Resources

P6 by default will calculate the resource actual and remaining units and costs based on the activity remaining duration.

You may change the settings and enter the actual costs recorded in timesheet systems or accounting systems into P6 when you wish update a project with resource actual units and costs. In this situation you will need to collect some additional information:

- The quantities and/or costs spent to date per activity for each resource, and
- The quantities and/or costs required per resource to complete each activity.

You may then update a resourced schedule with this data.

After a schedule has been updated, then a review of the future resource requirements, project end date, and cash flows may be made.

Updating a resourced project is time consuming and requires experience and a good understanding of how the software calculates a schedule. Ideally, this should only be attempted by experienced users or by a novice under the guidance of an experienced user.

2.7.2 Controlling a Project with Resources

At this point, it is possible to undertake a great deal of analysis and often Earned Value Performance Measurement techniques are used.

3 STARTING UP AND NAVIGATION

There are two database options for P6 PPM, Oracle and Microsoft SQL, and either can use either PPM or EPPM database schema. The end user will see no difference when using either database option. There are three database types:

- **Enterprise Project Portfolio Management** (EPPM) database:
  - ➢ This database may be opened with either the **Web Client** or the **Windows Client** which in the past was referred to as the **Optional Client** when used to open an EPPM database.
  - ➢ Administration is completed in the Web Client,
  - ➢ Scheduling may be completed from the Web Client but the tool is weak scheduling tool,
  - ➢ Scheduling is normally undertaken in the Windows Client,
  - ➢ Allows integrations with many other Oracle tools,
  - ➢ Aimed at large corporations and has many reporting tools.

- **Professional Project Manager** (PPM) database:
  - ➢ One interface, **Windows Client**, also called the **Professional Client.**
  - ➢ Restricted integration,
  - ➢ Aimed at smaller companies and stand-alone installations.

- **Stand-Alone** this uses an SQLite database and has one user.

- **Primavera Cloud** is another Oracle tool which uses the EPPM database schema.

The **Windows Client** may open both databases and there is less functionality when an EPPM database is opened with the Windows Client:

- **PPM, Professional Project Management**, and this database may only be opened with the PPM **Windows Client** and administration of the database is undertaken in the **Windows Client** using the **Admin** menu. In this mode the software is referred to in this book as the **Windows Client**.

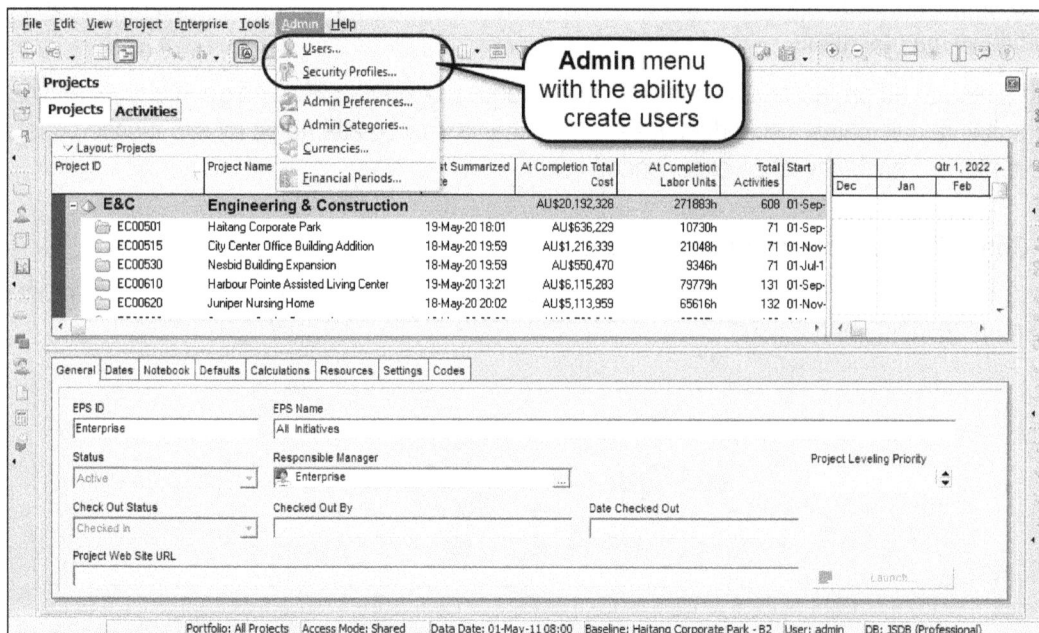

- **EPPM, Enterprise Portfolio Project Management** database that may be opened with either the PPM Windows Client or the EPPM Web Client. Database administration is only undertaken in the EPPM Web Client. Therefore, when you open a EPPM database with the Windows Client you will find the **Admin** menu and some **Enterprise** menu functions are removed and these functions are performed in the EPPM Web Client. In this mode the software is referred to in this book as the **Windows Client**:

- There is also a **Stand-Alone** load which is installed on a computer and only has the one user. This is suitable for consultants who do not need to share their data with other users and the ability to create users and security profiles has been removed.

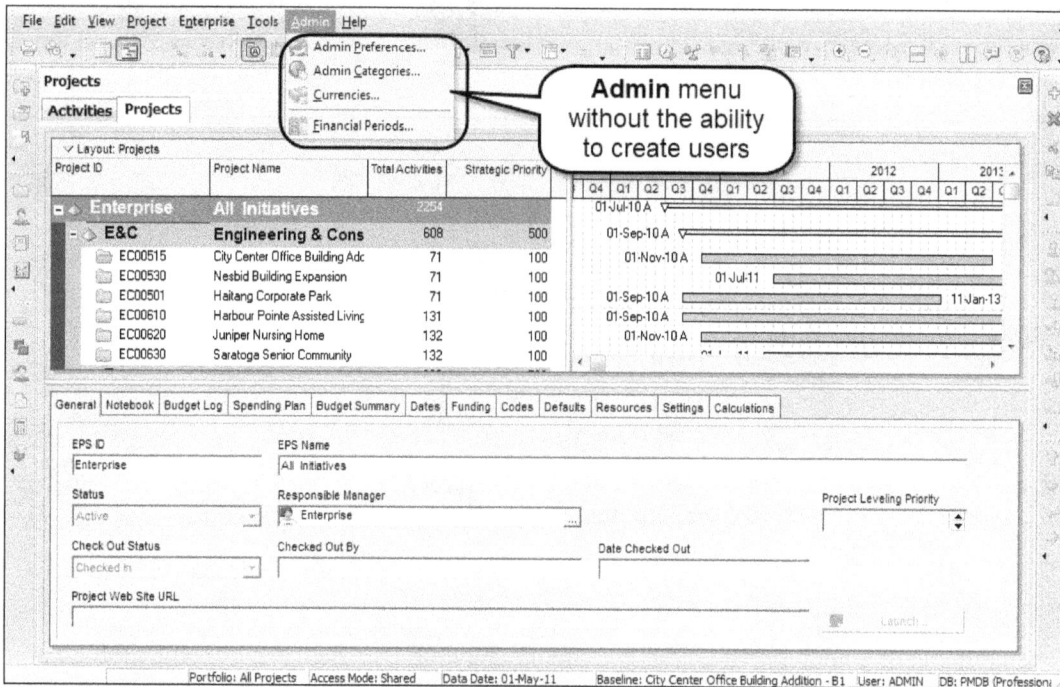

3.1   Logging In

After clicking on the icon or menu item on your desktop to start Primavera, you will be presented with the **Login** form, normally you would:

- Enter your **Login Name** and **Password**, which are case sensitive, and then

- Click **Connect** or **OK** in earlier versions to open the selected database.

When you have more than one database to select from, you may click on the drop down arrow in later versions which under **Advanced i**n Version 21 and later, or the [...] icon under **Database** in earlier versions. This allows you to select a different language where you may select a different database or **Edit Database Connections** form where you may select an alternative database to open:

- Select the required database from the list, then

- Enter your **Login Name** and **Password**, which are case sensitive, and then

- Click **Connect** or **OK** in earlier versions to open the selected database.

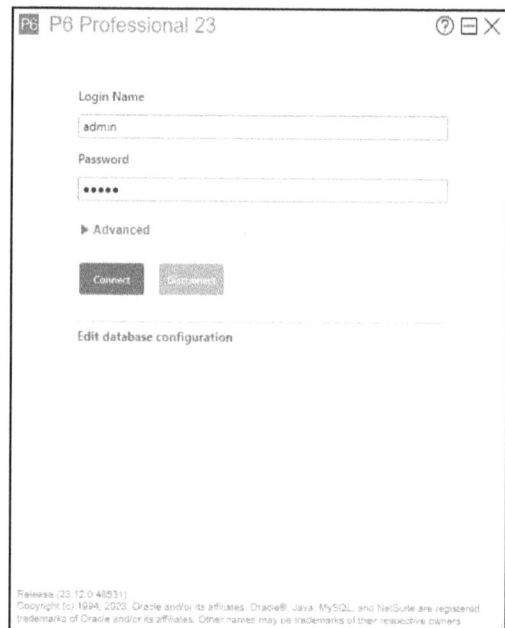

In P6 Version 20 the login screens were changed but the content remains unchanged:

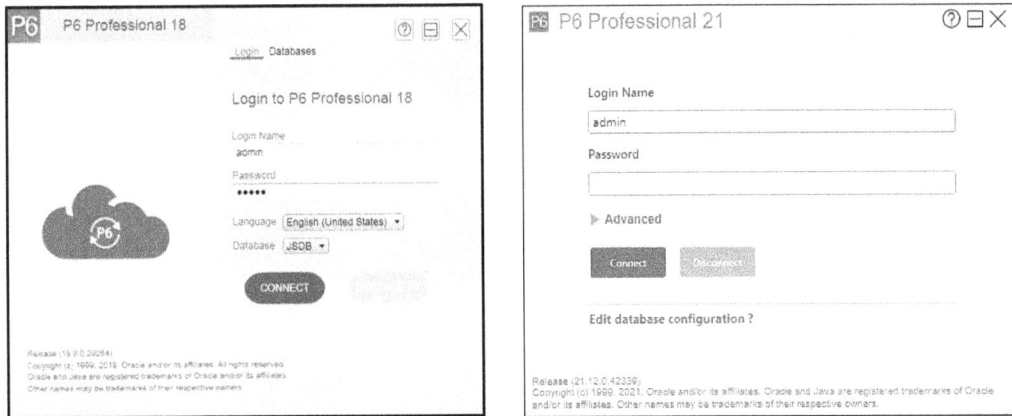

After logging in your screen may display data, or it may be blank and not show any data. What is displayed depends on the type of database you are opening, how your **User Profile** was set up and a number of other parameters.

If your screen is blank and does not display a list of projects under the Enterprise Project Structure (EPS) then select **Enterprise**, **Projects** to display the projects in the database under the EPS.

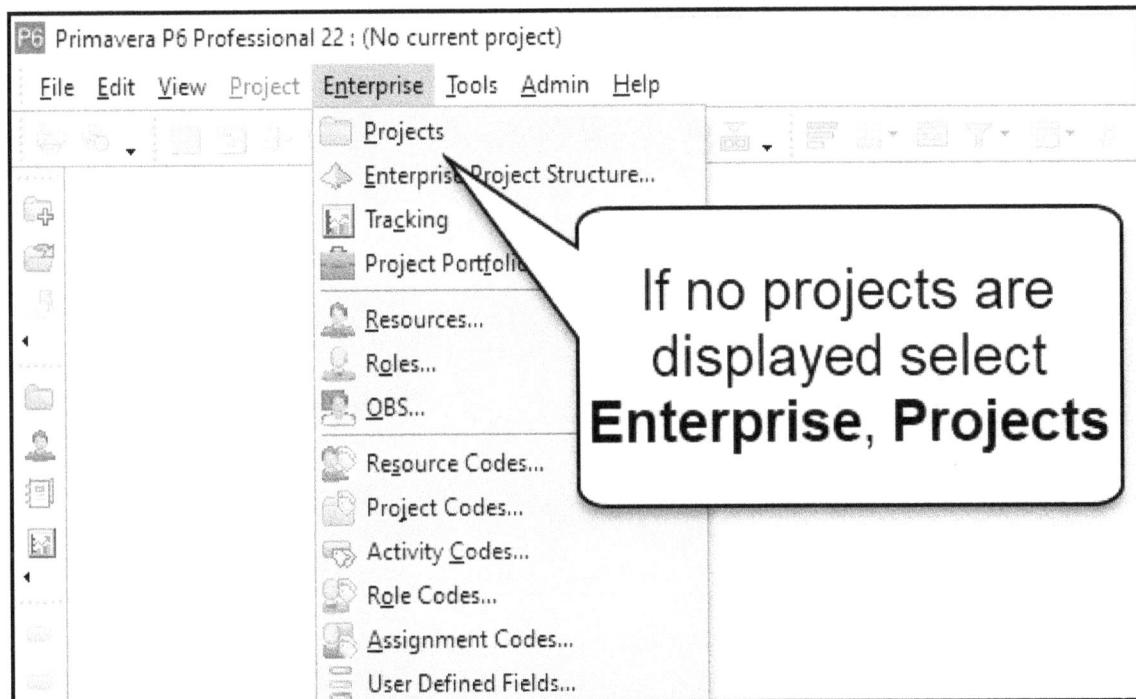

If no projects are displayed select **Enterprise, Projects**

To ensure that P6 will display the screen of your preference when you next start the software it is suggested that you select from the **User Preferences…**, **Application** tab your **Application Startup Window**:

- Select the **Projects** window if you work on different projects all the time and you will be presented with the **Project** window displaying the projects that you may open, or

- Select the **Activities** window if you work on the same project all the time and you will be displayed the project activities in the **Activities** window; as long as you do not close the project when you shut down P6.

3.2   The Projects Window

Select **Enterprise**, **Projects** or click on the ▢ **Projects** button to open the **Projects Window**.

3.2.1   Project Window Top Pane

The top window displays the **Enterprise Project Structure** (EPS):

- The ☐+☐ and ☐–☐ icons to the left of the EPS names are used to display or hide levels of the EPS. The picture shows that the **E&C** EPS Node has six projects.
  - ➤ Engineering and Construction, and
  - ➤ Energy Services.
- To add, delete or edit the EPS open the **Enterprise Project Structure (EPS)** form by selecting **Enterprise**, **Enterprise Project Structure...** from the menu.

- The menu commands **View**, **Expand All**, **Collapse All** and **Collapse To...** will summarize the bands to the required level in the EPS.

⚠ The project data displayed in columns will blank if projects have not been **Summarized** or is not open and incorrect if the project has been edited sine it was last **Summarized**. See para 24.10 for more information

3.2.2 Project Window Bottom Pane Details Tab

The bottom window **Details** tab may be hidden by clicking on the ⊞ icon or selecting **View, Show on Bottom**, **Details** and displayed by clicking on the ⊞ icon or selecting **View, Show on Bottom**, **Details**. The default load of P6 does not display the ⊞ icon and this will need to be added, this is demonstrated in the first workshop.

Information regarding an EPS Node or project assigned to an EPS Node is available at the bottom of the screen by selecting the EPS Node or Project and selecting tabs in the bottom window.

Many of the fields are grayed out which means they are calculated or summarized from other data or the project is not open and the data may not be edited.

Right-clicking on a tab name will display a menu and selecting **Customize Project Details....** will open the **Project Details** form and you may select which tabs are displayed and in what order:

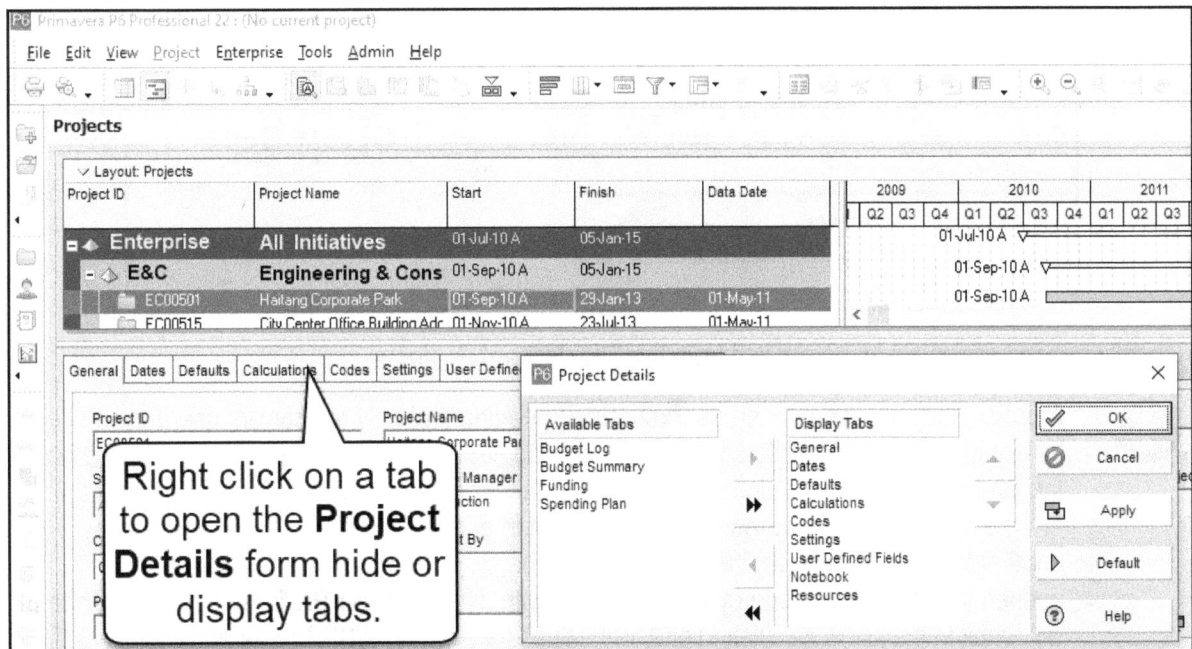

3.3 Opening One or More Projects

Enterprise and project data is accessed in the **Projects Window**.

To access project activity information such as activities, resources and relationships, a project must be opened and the **Activities Window** displayed.

One or more projects may be opened at the same time by

- Selecting:
  - ➢ One or more projects and/or
  - ➢ One or more EPS Nodes,
- Then, right-clicking and selecting **Open Project**, or
- Selecting **Ctl+O**.

Alternatively select **File**, **Open...** to open the **Open** form:

- The **Open** form displays the access options for opening a project as **Exclusive**, **Shared or Read Only** which are not available with the other methods of opening projects:

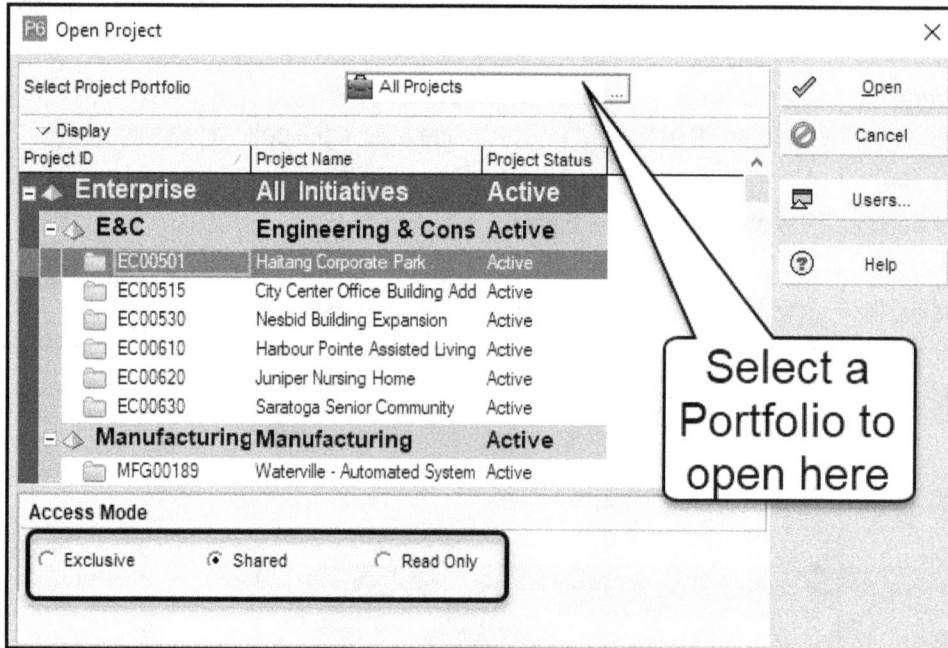

Recently opened projects may be opened from the **File, Recent Projects**.

A project may only be opened as **Exclusive** (meaning that only the current user may edit it) by using the **File**, **Open...**form. All other methods will result in the project being opened in the **Shared** mode and all users with access to the project may open and edit the project(s) at the same time. The **Shared** option may result in one user's edits being overwritten by another user's edits, depending on who saved the project and when. A project that is opened in the **Shared** mode by multiple users with different **User Preferences Time Units** will result in the users calculating different values for Activity, WBS Nodes and Project durations in days.

If more than one project is to be opened at a time, then it is **VERY IMPORTANT** that the **Multiple Project Scheduling** chapter is read and understood.

3.4　Displaying the Activities Window

To open the **Activities Window**:

- Select **Project**, **Activities**, or click on the ⬜ icon:

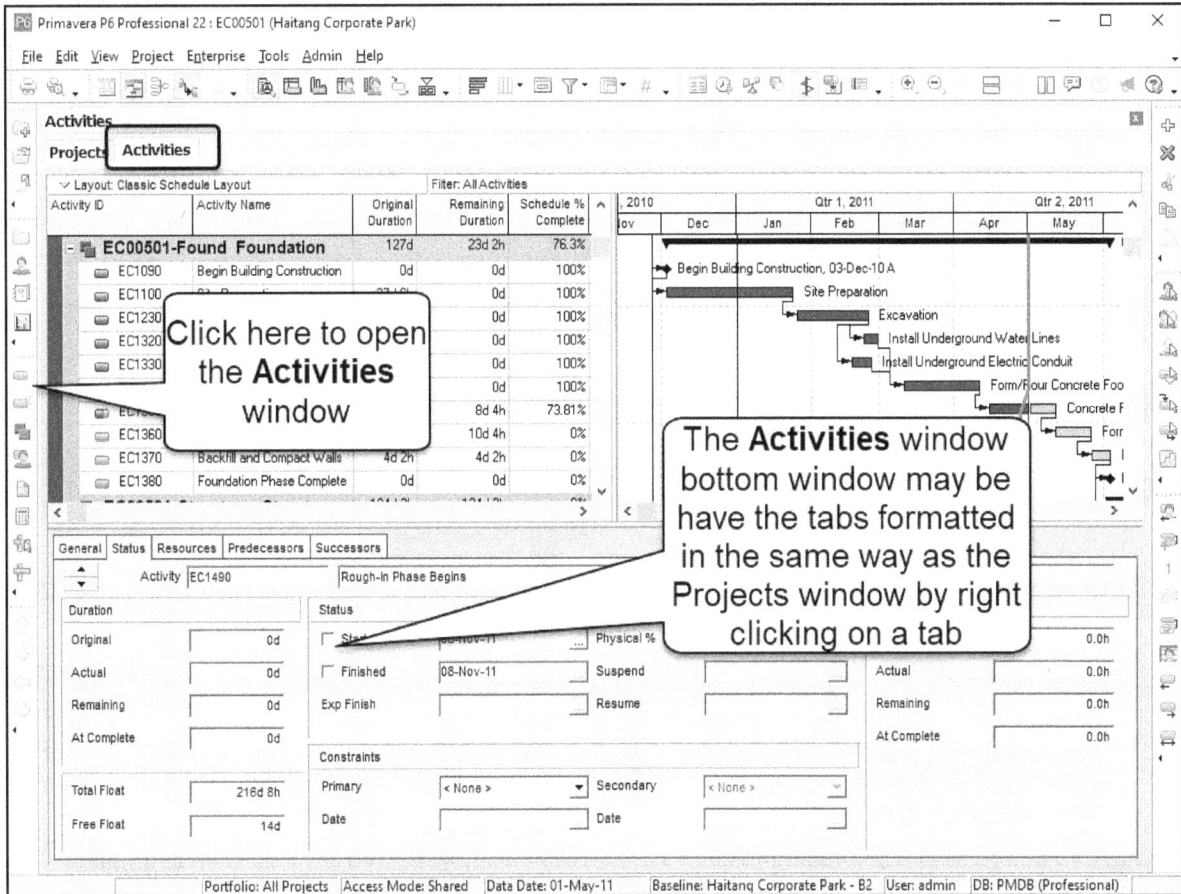

- There are now two tabs at the top; clicking on the Projects tab displays the **Projects Window**.

3.5   Opening a Portfolio

The **Portfolio** function reduces the number of Projects that are viewed in the **Projects Window**:

- To create a **Portfolio,** select **Enterprise**, **Project Portfolios…** and open the **Portfolio** form.

- Create a portfolio and add projects using the **Portfolio** form.

- A **Portfolio** may be **Global** and all users have access or **User** and just available to that user.

- The **File**, **Open…** (project) form also enables the selection of a **Portfolio** which reduces the number of projects that are displayed in the **Open** (project)form.

- After a **Portfolio** has been selected using **File**, **Select Project Portfolio…** only those projects in the Portfolio will be displayed in the **Projects Window**.

- Applying a **Portofino** speeds up opening P6 when a use has access to large number of projects.

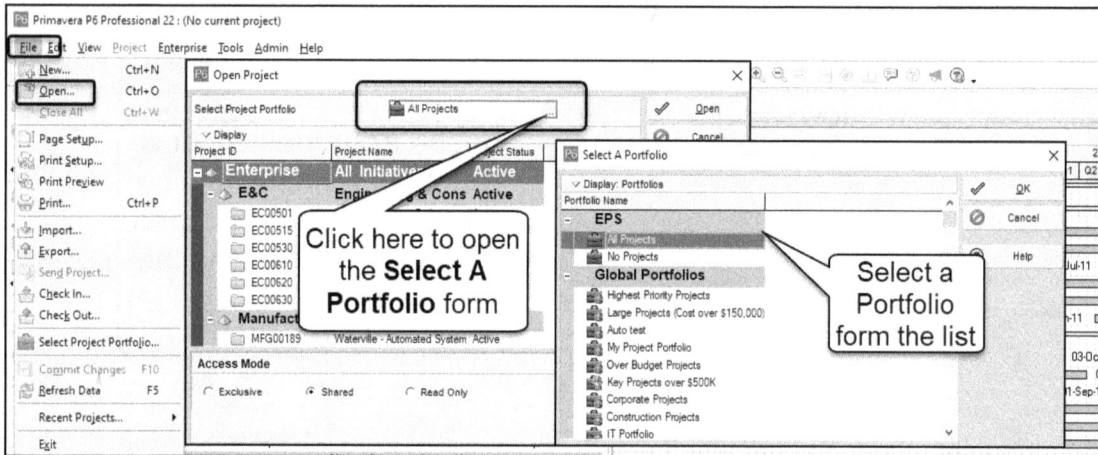

3.6   Introduction to Layouts

Layouts is a function in which the formatting of parameters such as the **Group and Sort**, **Columns**, **Timescale**, **Bars**, **Lower Pane** and **Print Settings** is saved and reapplied later. This function is similar to **Views** in Elecosoft (Asta) Powerproject and Microsoft Project. A **Layout** may be edited, saved, or reapplied at a later date and may have a **Filter** associated with it. Layouts contain the formatting for all options of both the top and bottom pane, such as columns, timescale and bars formatting.

NOTE: The date and duration formatting are not part of a Layout and are set in the **User Preferences**.

A standard load of Primavera is supplied with a number of predefined **Global Layouts**. The bar formatting of all of these Layouts are unsuitable for running training courses. This section introduces Activity Layouts with the aim of providing sufficient information for students to import an Activity Layout suitable for completing the workshops in this book. Layouts are covered in detail in the **Layouts** chapter.

A **Layout** may be copied or opened by either:

- Selecting **View**, **Layout** and selecting the appropriate command,

- Or clicking on the down arrow found under the Window tab name:

- The Open Layout command lists the available systems Layouts:

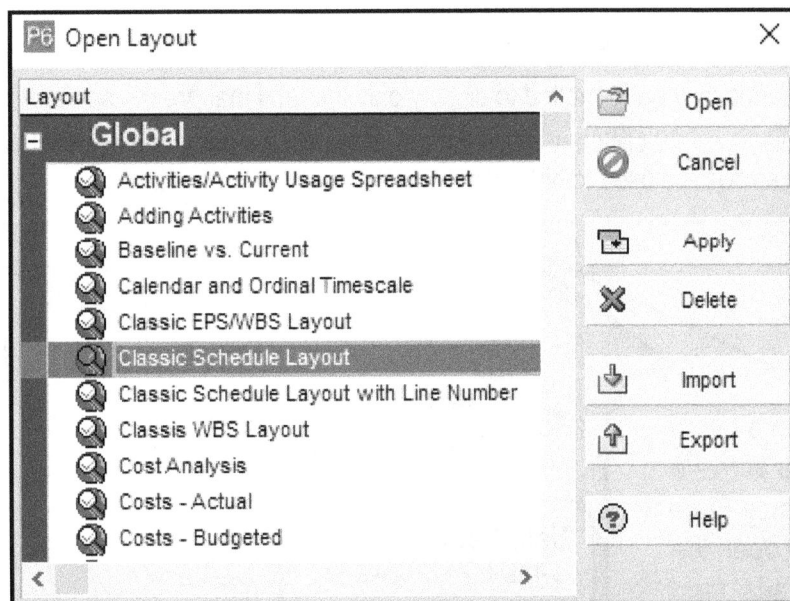

- The **Save As Layout** command allows Layouts to be saved as:

  > **All Users**, which makes them **Global Layouts** which are available to everyone,

  > **Another User**, which allows you to transfer your layout to someone else,

  > **Current User**, which allows a layout to be copied to create a new layout for the user, and

  > **Project** layout, which creates a layout that is available to anyone who opens the project.

The **Open Layout** form allows Layouts to be exchanged between P6 databases using the **Import** and **Export** commands. The Layout formatting is saved in a Layout file which has a *.plf extension. In the first workshop you will be asked to open a project, then download a layout, import it into your database and apply it to your project.

The following commands will enable you to hide and display the bottom panes; they are similar to the **Projects Window** discussed earlier.

- The bottom window **Details** tab may be hidden by clicking on the ☒ icon or selecting **View, Show on Bottom**, **No Bottom Layout**. You may need to add the buttons to your toolbar, see paragraph 3.7.1 for details on how to add buttons.

- The bottom window **Details** tab may be displayed by clicking on the ☒ icon or selecting **View, Show on Bottom**, **Details**.

- Right-clicking in the Gantt chart area and selecting **Activity Details** from the menu will display the **Bottom** pane, or

- Right-clicking in the **Bottom** pane and selecting **Hide Detail Window** from the menu will hide the

- Selecting **View, Show on Top** or **Show on Bottom** will show other display options for the top and bottom panes.

The following commands will enable you to format the top and bottom panes.

- Some **Details** forms may be formatted to display only the tabs that are of use to the scheduler.

- To format the display, right-click any tab in the top of the details pane and select **Customize Project Details...**. The arrows are used to hide and display tabs and reorder them.

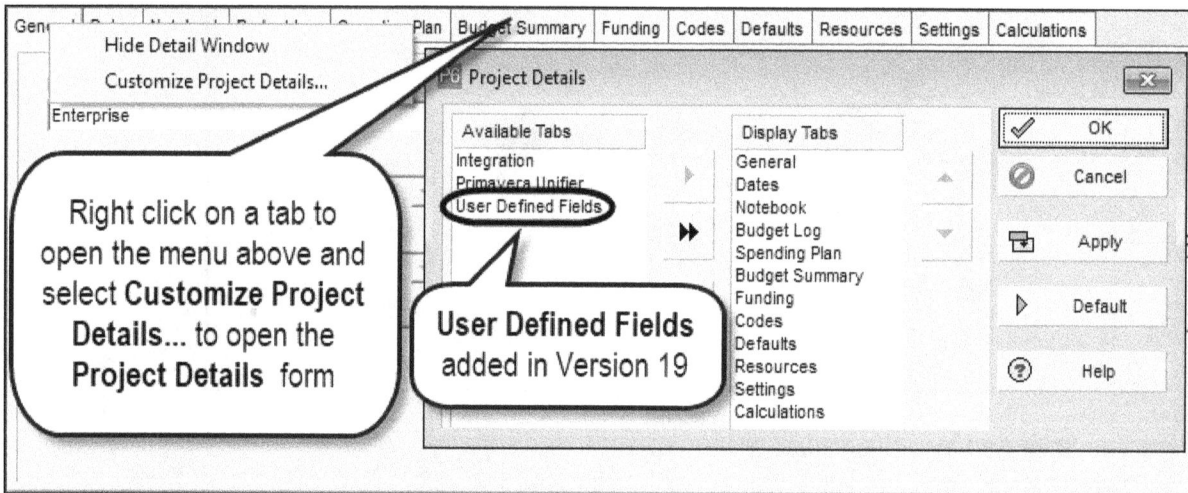

It is recommended that you remove all the tabs that you are not using so the screen is not so busy and it is simpler to find commands.

The columns of tabs such as the **Activity** window Predecessor, Successor, Relationships and Expenses may also be edited by right clicking on any column header:

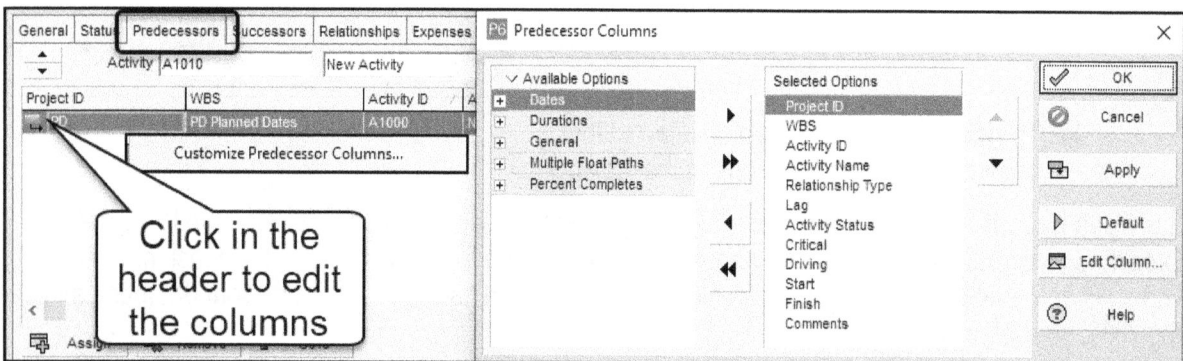

3.7   Customizing Toolbars

3.7.1   Customizable Toolbars

P6 toolbars operate in a similar way to Microsoft Office 2003.

Toolbars will not be covered in detail but significant productivity improvements may be made by ensuring that functions frequently used are available on a toolbar.

- There are many built-in toolbars in Primavera P6. These may be displayed or hidden by:
  - ➢ Using the command **View**, **Toolbars** or right-clicking in the toolbar area and then checking or un-checking the required boxes to display or hide the toolbars, or
  - ➢ Using the command **View**, **Toolbars**, **Customize...**, **Toolbars** tab and then un-checking the required boxes to display or hide the toolbars.

- Individual toolbar icons may be reset to default by selecting **View**, **Toolbars**, **Customize...**, **Toolbar** tab and clicking on [Reset...].

- Icons may be added to a bar by selecting **View**, **Toolbars**, **Customize...**, **Toolbar** tab **Commands** tab. **Toolbar Icons** may be selected from the dialog box and dragged onto any toolbar.

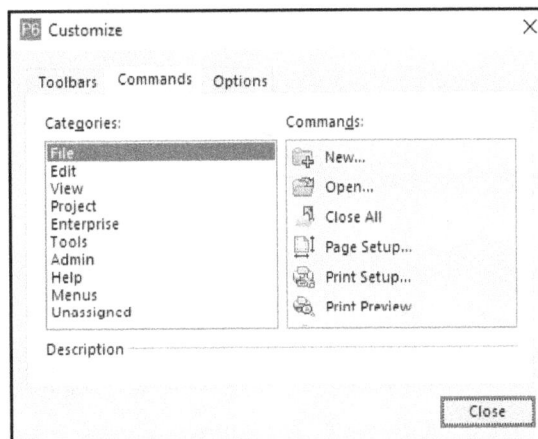

- Icons may be removed from the toolbars after the **Customize** (Toolbar) form is opened by holding down the left mouse button on the icon and dragging them off the toolbar.

- Icons may also be added or removed when a toolbar is dragged into the center of a window. This reveals a further menu for editing the icons:

- Icons may also be added or removed by clicking on the down arrow at the right-hand end of each toolbar:

The **No Bottom Layout** button is usually missing on a default load of P6 and should be manually added

Click here on the down arrow to open the **Add or Remove Buttons** menu to add or remove toolbar buttons

- All toolbar icons may be reset to default by selecting **View, Reset All Toolbars**.
- Toolbars may be locked so they may not be dragged by selecting **View, Lock All Toolbars**.
- Other toolbar display options are found under **View**, **Toolbars…**, **Customize** and then selecting the **Options** tab.

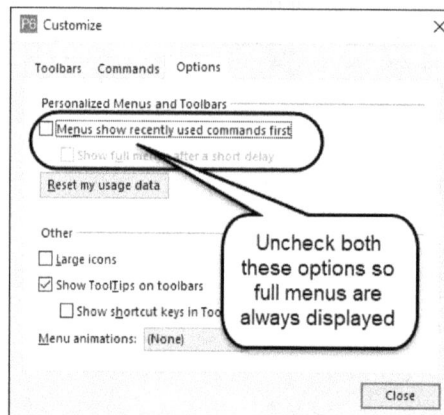

Uncheck both these options so full menus are always displayed

It is recommended **NOT** to check the **Show full menus after a short delay** or the **Menus show recently used commands first** options in the **View**, **Toolbars…**, **Customize**, **Options** tab to ensure full menus are always displayed. This saves time waiting for the menu item you require to be displayed.

3.7.2 Customizable menus

The menus may also be edited:

- Open the **Customize** form by selecting **View**, **Toolbars...**, **Customize**,

- Then with the **Customize** form open move the mouse to the menu on the top left-hand side of the screen,

- Right-click on a menu title to reveal a menu that allows you to rename menu commands:

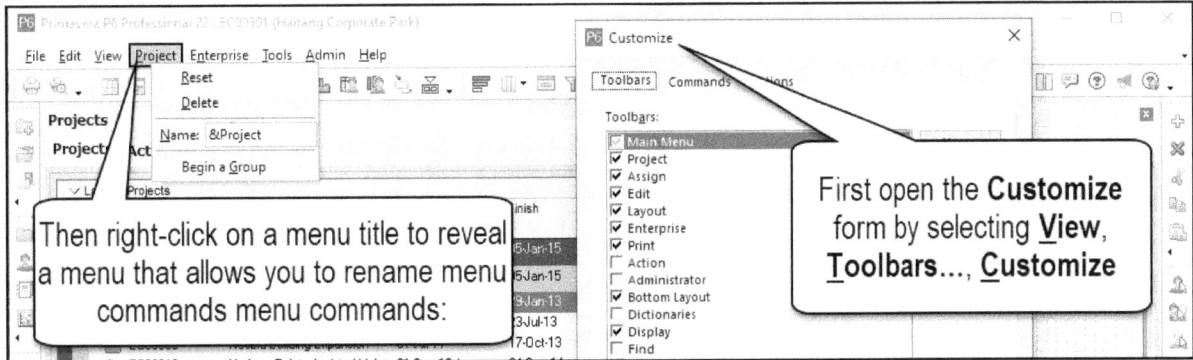

- You may also reorder menu line items by dragging them up or down when the **Customize** form is open:

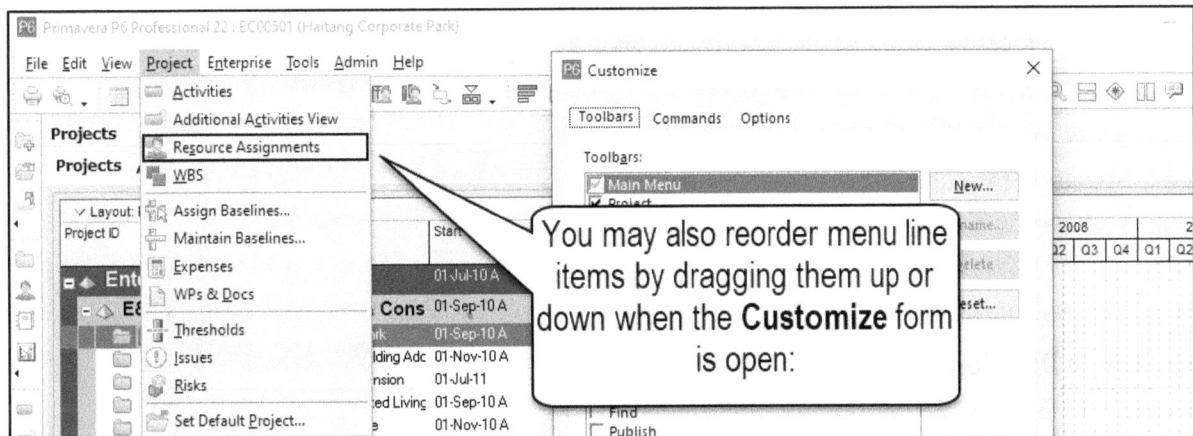

- You should consider selecting the **View**, **Toolbars...**, **Customize**, **Options** tab and uncheck the **Show full menus after a short delay** and the Menus show recently used commands first options in to ensure full menus are always displayed.

3.7.3 Status Bar

The Status bar is at the bottom of the screen and may be hidden or displayed by selecting **View**, **Status Bar**. It shows some useful information about the project you have open:

3.8   User Preferences

3.8.1   Time Unit Formatting

The **User Preferences** enable each user to select how some information is displayed or calculated. These are covered in detail in the **User and Administration Preferences and Advanced Schedule Options** chapter.

To adjust how the date and time are displayed:

- Select **Edit**, **User Preferences...**,

- Select the **Time Units** tab,

- The **Duration Format** section determines how the activity durations are displayed,

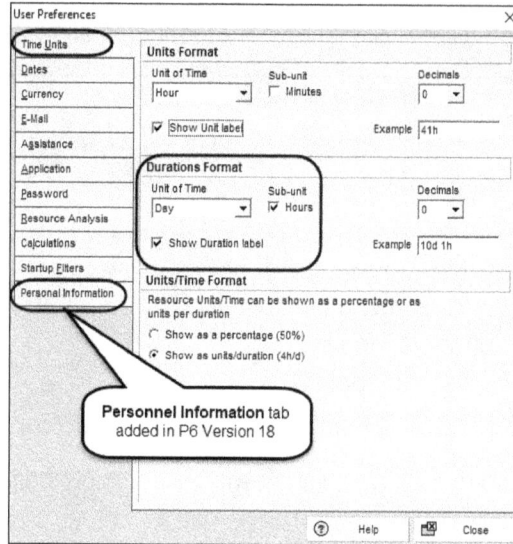

It is important that the **Show Duration label** and **Sub-units** are checked as you will see immediately when non round days for durations have been created.

3.8.2   Date Formatting

This is where you decide if the time is to be displayed:

- Select the **Dates** tab,

- Set the **Date Format**,

- Set the **Options**,

- Set the **Time** options.

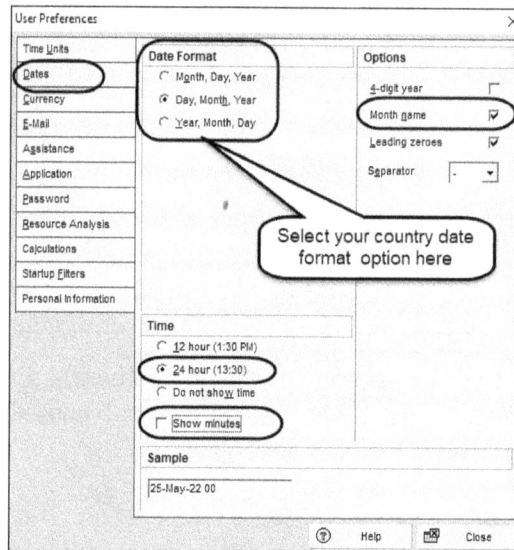

Date Format. It is strongly recommended using **Month name** on international projects so there is no confusion between the US mm/dd/yy format and the ROW (Rest of World) format of dd/mm/yy.

Time Units: It is **STRONGLY** recommended that the time is **ALWAYS** displayed in 24 hour format so the user knows the time of any selected date. This is because the software will often select 00:00, (the first minute of a day) when assigning dates. The author does not display minutes to keep the date column widths slightly narrower.

3.8.3 Users may See and Set Activity Start and Finish Times in the Date Picker box

P6 Version 20 and earlier the time is not available in the **Date Picker** box when hidden by the **User Preferences**, **Date Formatting**. In P6 Version 21 Users may see and set Activity Start and Finish times in the **Date Picker** box and operates even when the User Preferences are set only to show the date without the time.

This is a great enhancement for P6 Version 21 as P6 usually picks the wrong time when setting Actual dates, Constraints, Suspend and Resume dates when the time is not set to be displayed from the User Preferences.

- P6 Version 20 and earlier the time is not available from the **Date Picker** box.

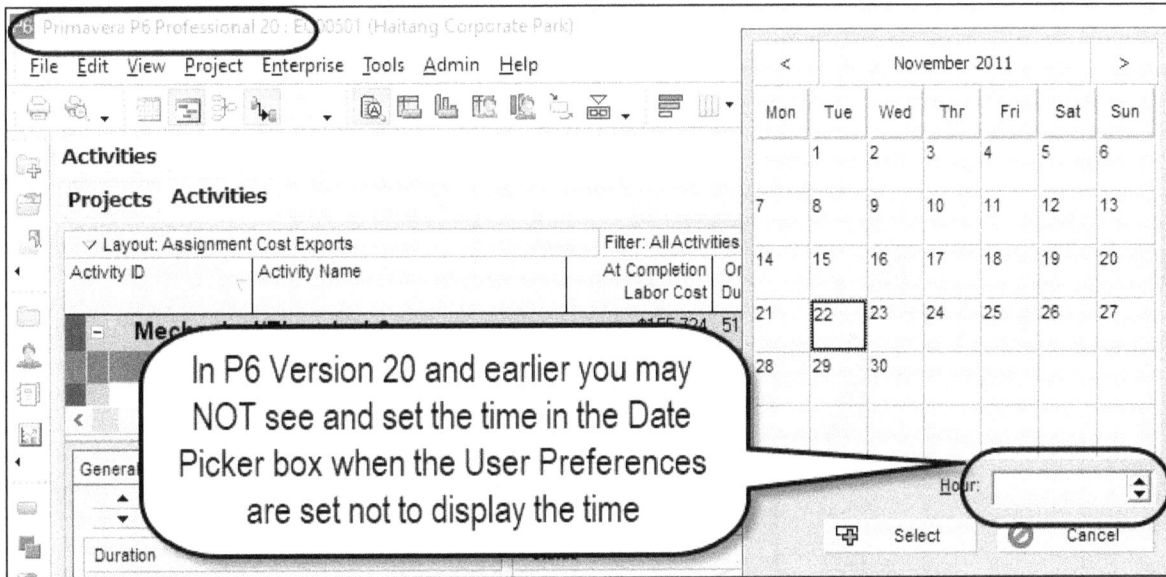

- P6 Version 21 the time may be seen and set from the **Date Picker** box.

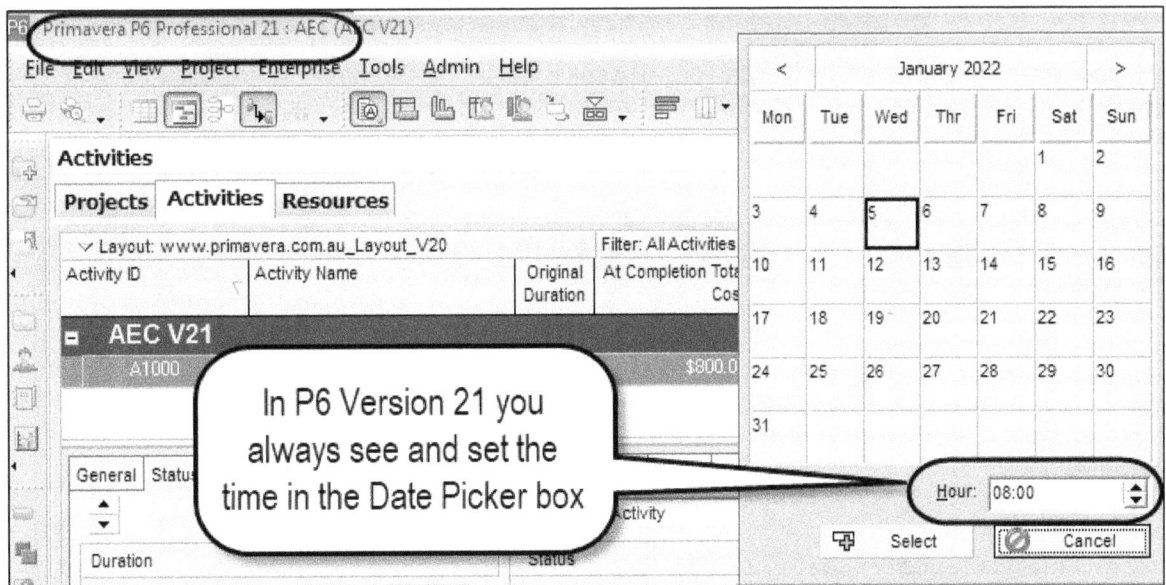

Even with this enhancement the author recommends always displaying the time with the date so the user can ensure that all tasks start and finish when it is intended for them to start and finish.

3.9   Starting Day of Week

The default **First day of week** on a default load of P6 is Sunday. Many people prefer to see Monday because the calendar date in the weekly view is then Monday and is a workday, as per the picture below:

The **Starting Day of Week** is set in the **Admin, Admin Preferences..., General** tab in P6 Professional:

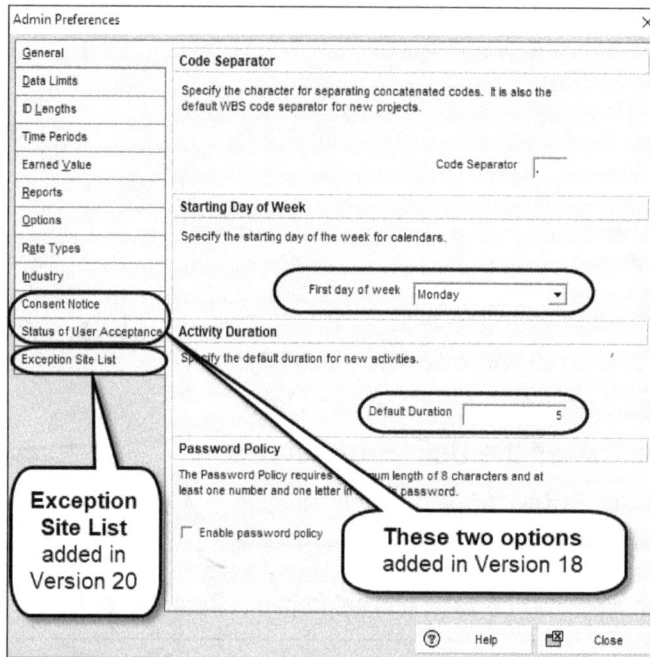

When you open a EPPM database the start day of week is set by the database administrator from **Administer**, **Application Settings**, **General**:

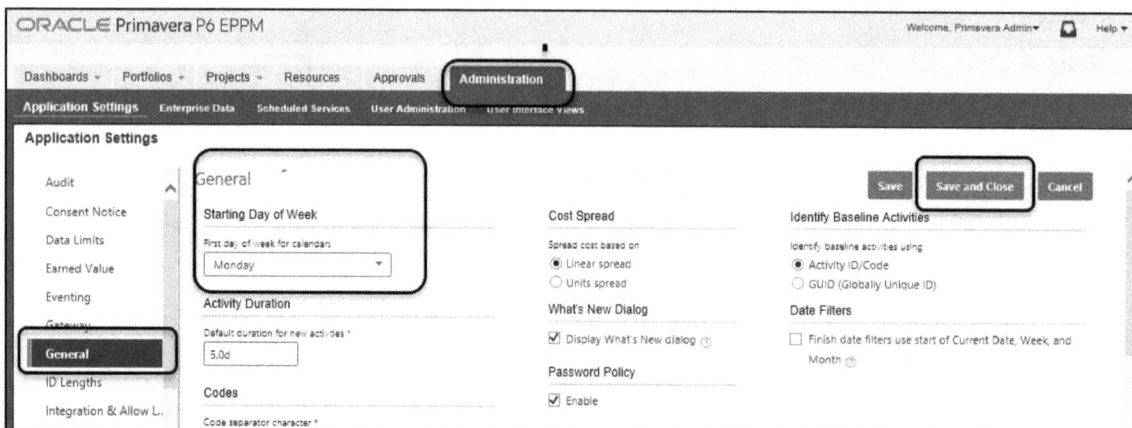

You must select **Save and Close** or your edits will be lost:

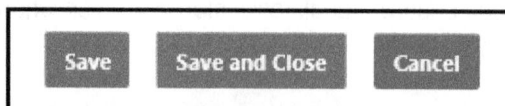

3.10   Admin Preferences – Set Industry Type

The **Industry Type** determines the terminology used in some fields and in earlier versions was set when the software was loaded. This now may be set in the P6 Professional by selecting **Admin**, **Admin Preferences...**, **Industry** tab:

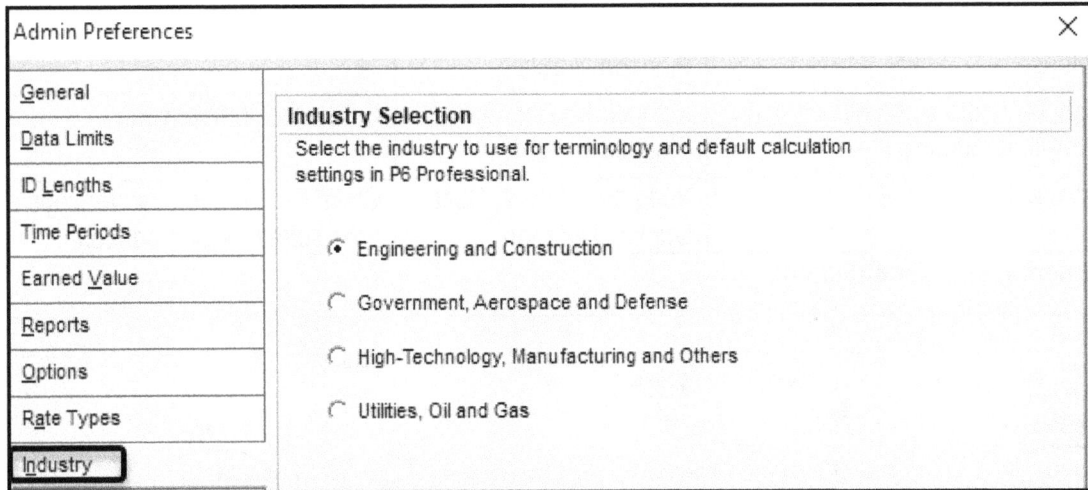

This is set in the Web Client in the **Administration**, **General**, **Industry Selection** drop-down box:

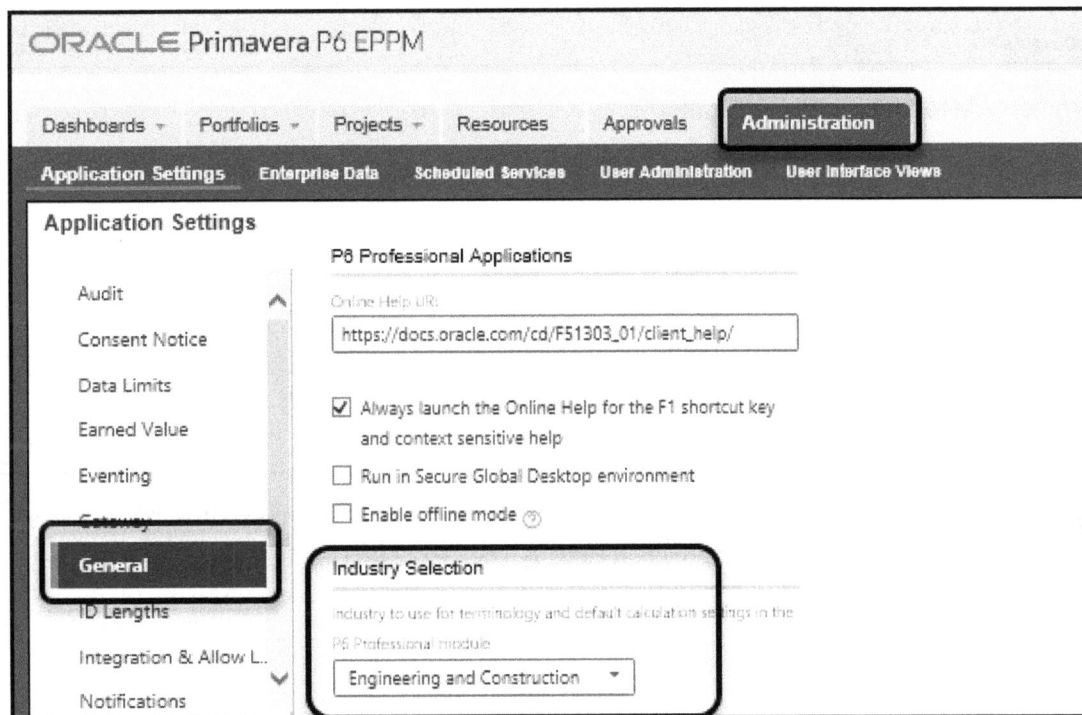

The following table displays the terminology:

Industry Type	Terminology	Name of Project Comparison Tool
Engineering and Construction	Budgeted Units & Cost Original Duration	Claim Digger in earlier versions and now Schedule Comparison
Government, Aerospace, and Defense	Planned Units & Cost Planned Duration	Schedule Comparison
High-Technology, Manufacturing and Other Industry	Planned Units & Cost Planned Duration	Schedule Comparison
Utilities, Oil, and Gas	Budgeted Units & Cost Original Duration	Claim Digger in earlier versions and now Schedule Comparison

Engineering and Construction:

Government, Aerospace, and Defense:

i If a different Industry Type is selected, then P6 must be restarted to see the changes. The EPPM Web Client only uses Planned Units & Cost, Planned Duration and Schedule Comparison.

3.11   Application of Options within Forms

Primavera is consistent in the way the data may be Grouped, Sorted and Filtered. After the basics are understood, then as these principles may be applied to most forms you will find it easier to navigate around the software.

After the format or options have been selected within forms such as Bars, Filters and Group and Sort, click:

- The [✓ OK] icon to apply the formatting and close the form, or

- The [🗔 Apply] icon to apply the format and leave the form open.

This is useful for checking if the option displays as required before closing the form.

Often there is an arrow [▽] in a box and this indicates that there is a menu that may be opened by clicking on the arrow. Data in a form may be formatted and filtered from this menu.

NOTE: The direction of this arrow was reversed in Version 22, and now the arrow pointing up sorts alphabetically down.

The picture on the right shows the **Enterprise, User Defined Fields...** form:

Sorting data within windows and forms such as Activities, Resources, OBS, may be achieved by clicking on the title above the first data item. Clicking on the **Resource ID** box will rotate the sort from hierarchical to alphabetical to reverse alphabetical.

If there is a filter applied, then this data may not be sorted.

3.12   Do Not Ask Me About This Again

Many forms have a check box **Do not ask me about this again**.

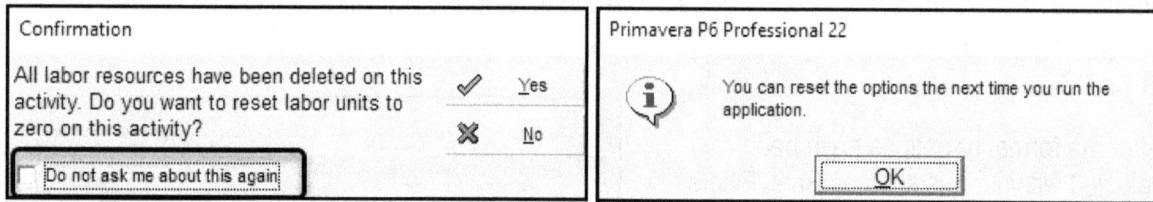

Confirmation	Primavera P6 Professional 22
All labor resources have been deleted on this activity. Do you want to reset labor units to zero on this activity? ✓ Yes ✗ No	ⓘ You can reset the options the next time you run the application.
☐ Do not ask me about this again	OK

This option will hide the form when the function is used the next time, thus saving time when a function is used multiple times.

3.13   Right-clicking with the Mouse

It is important that you become used to using the right-click function of the mouse as this is often a quicker way of operating the software than using the menus.

The right-click function will usually display a menu, which is often different depending on the displayed View and Active Pane selected. It is advised that you experiment with each view to become familiar with the menus.

3.14   Accessing Help

- The help file may be accessed by selecting **Help** menu or by clicking on the ⊙ icon on the **Display** toolbar.

- **Local Help**, if installed on earlier versions of P6, by pressing the Ctl+F1 key,
- **Online Help** takes you to an Oracle website, or by pressing Ctl+Alt+F1. This option will display the information in HTML format assisting people with disabilities who may access additional browser functions.
  NOTE: This is the only method of accessing Help with later versions of P6.
- Primavera P6 Version 22 introduced the **What's New** command that links to the **Oracle Primavera Cumulative Feature Overview** web site, where users may look up the changes between versions.

The **Contract Management URL** was removed in Version 19 to coincide with the termination for support for **Contract Management**, Version 20 introduced **Document Security** and **Cost Spread** in P6 Version 21:

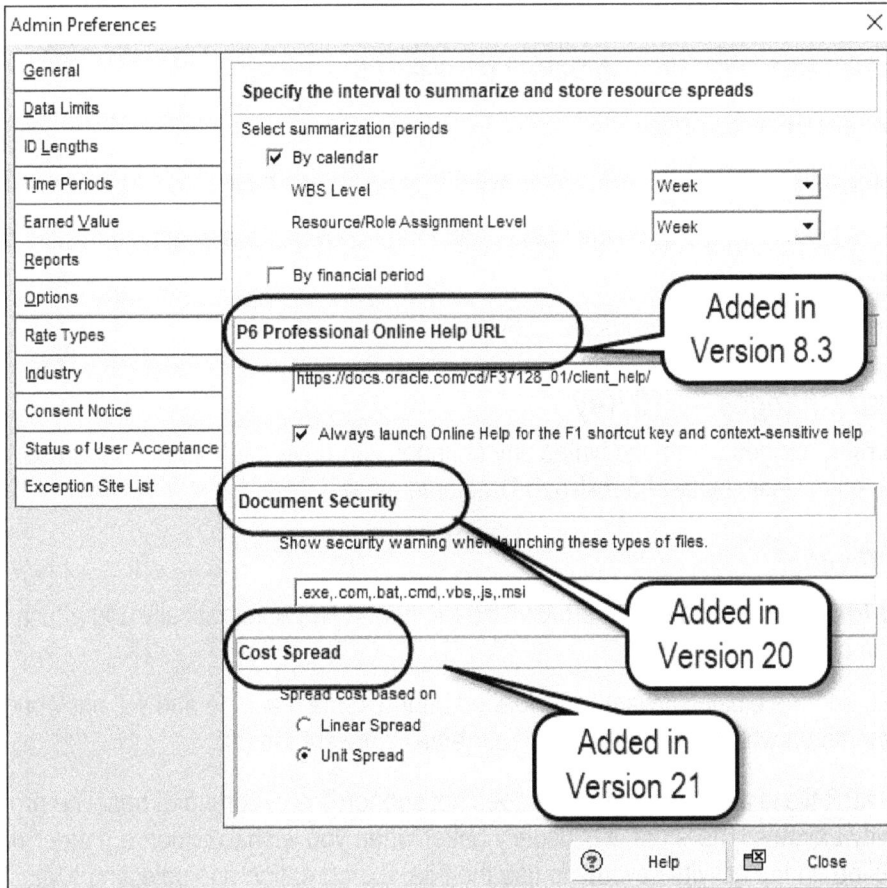

Selecting **View**, **Hint Help** will display information about a field when the mouse is moved over the field heading, as in the preceding picture. This is useful for understanding how the fields calculate. Selecting **View**, **Hint Help** a second time will hide the information.

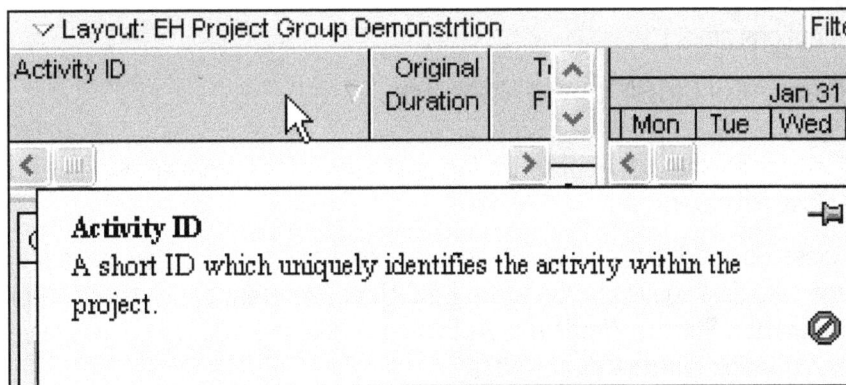

You may also log in to the Oracle Support web list, a link available from https://primavera.com.au/, and access the Oracle Support database.

Many articles are available at the author's web sites https://primavera.com.au/.

3.15   Refresh Data – F5 Key

The author found that sometimes changes made in one place would not be reflected somewhere else such as relationships added but not visible in columns, or WBS Nodes edited in the WBS Window but the changes not reflected in the Activities Window.

If this happens then select **File**, **Refresh Data** or press the **F5** key which:

- Writes your data to the database,

- Reads changes that other users who also have the project open have made to the schedule,

- Puts the Data Date vertical line on the Gantt chart in the correct place when the system does refresh correctly and

- Corrects other display issues discussed above.

3.16   Commit Changes – F10 Key

The **File**, **Commit Changes** command writes any changes you have made to the database. These may then be read by other users by the **F5 Refresh Data** command.

3.17   Send Project

The **File**, **Send Project...** should create an XER file (an export file) automatically and attach it as an attachment to an email.

This requires P6 and the email software to be loaded on the same machine and will not work in cloud or virtual environments on which you do not have your email software loaded.

> ⓘ The XER file is an older format that does not support the exporting of baseline projects and activity Layouts. Therefore, it is usually better when you wish to export a project with a baseline and/or activity Layouts to use the File, Export option and selecting XML. The downside of using XML files is that they may change the cost of the projects on import when the Resource rate in the Resource window is not the same as the activity resource rate.

3.18   Closing Down

The closing down options are:

- Select **File**, **Close All** or **Ctrl+W** to close all **Projects**.

- Select **File**, **Exit** or click the ⊠ icon in the top right side of the Primavera window to shut down all projects and close Primavera.

> ⓘ If you close down the system leaving one or more projects open, then these projects will be open the next time you log in. Go to the **Edit**, **User Preferences...**, **Application** tab and set the **Application Startup Window** to **Activities** so the software will open with your last project **Activities Window** displayed.

3.19 Workshop 1 – Navigating Around the Windows

Background

To become familiar with Primavera you will open your database and navigate around the windows.

Note: Your windows may look different from the ones used in this publication which uses a demonstration database provided by Oracle Primavera.

Assignment

1. Open your database. If a project is open then select **File**, **Close All** to close the project.

2. Close all open windows except the **Projects Window**. If the **Project Window** is not open then select **Enterprise**, **Projects** to open the **Projects Window**.

3. From the **Projects Window**, hide and display the bottom pane **Projects Details** form by clicking on the **View**, **Show on Bottom, No Bottom Layout** and **View, Show on Bottom, Details**.

4. Add the ⬇ button to the **Bottom Layout** toolbar and then use the and buttons on the **Bottom Layout** toolbar to hide and display the bottom pane **Projects Details** form. See para **Error! Reference source not found.** for details.

5. To ensure you see the full menus each time you select menu then right click on a Toolbar and select **Customize...** to open the **Customize** form, select the **Options** tab and uncheck **Menus show recently used command first**, as per the picture:

6. Scroll up and down and inspect the Enterprise Project Structure and the projects.

7. Expand and close the EPS structure using the + and - buttons to the left of the project descriptions and use the right mouse menu **Expand All**, **Collapse All** and **Collapse To....**

8. Explore the **EPS** by selecting **Enterprise, Enterprise Project Structure...**, click on the column headings and explore the menu options by clicking on the **Display: EPS** menu.

9. Double click in the Gantt Chart area in line with a project to bring the project bar into view. If no project bars are being displayed then your projects need to be **Summarized** so the latest project data is available in the **Projects** window.

10. Select the **View, Toolbars…, Customize, Options** tab and uncheck the **Show full menus after a short delay** and the **Menus show recently used commands first** options in to ensure full menus are always displayed.

11. Hide and display the **Status Bar** by using the **View, Status Bar** menu.

12. Open the **Projects Details** form, right-click on a tab in the **Projects Details** form and select **Customize Project Details...** then hide and display some tabs. Leave only the **General**, **Dates**, **Defaults** and **Notebook** tabs displayed. We will reveal the remainder as needed:

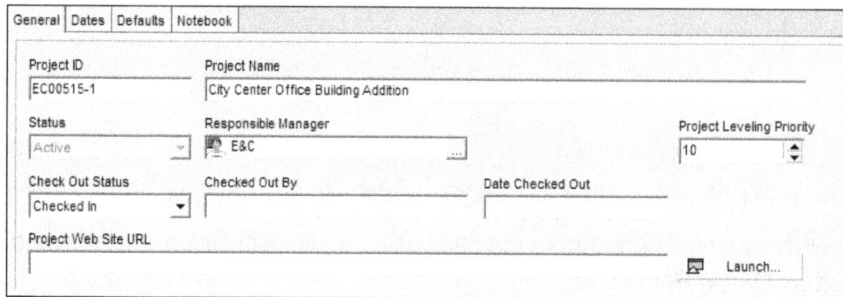

13. Select a project you have access to (possibly the City Center Office Building Addition project if you are operating in the Primavera Demonstration database) and open the **Project** by right-clicking on the project and selecting **Open Project**.

14. Click on the **Activities** tab or the [icon] icon on the right-hand side of the screen or select **Project**, **Activities** if the **Activities Window** does not open automatically and display the project activities.

15. You should now download a layout titled **www.primavera.com.au_Layout.plf** found at https://primavera.com.au/ under **Software and Downloads** page, unzip it and place it on your desktop. You may double click on the zip file to open it and then drag the file to your desktop. There are layouts exported from later P6 Versions are identified by the software version in the file name.

16. Import the Layout as a **User Layout** by selecting **View**, **Layout**, **Open Layout**.

17. Do not save your Layout.

18. Select [Import], select the layout from your desktop,

19. Set your options as per the picture and the Layout will be saved as a User Layout,

20. Select [Apply] to apply the layout and you will see the changes on the screen.

21. Now select [Open] to apply the Layout and close the **Open Layout** form.

22. Double-click in the Gantt Chart area in line with an activity to bring the activity bar into view.

23. Click on the Activity ID column title multiple times and see the activities reorder, then click on other column titles and see the activities reorder based on the column data. Leave the activities ordered by Activity ID.

24. Adjust the timescale using the [⊕ ⊖] buttons.

25. Move back to the **Projects Window** and then back to the **Activities Window** using the tabs at the top of the window.

26. From the **Activities Window** display the **Activity Details** form in the **Bottom** pane by selecting **View**, **Show on Bottom**, **Details** and then hide it by selecting **View**, **Show on Bottom**, **No Bottom Layout**.

27. From the **Activities Window** hide and display the bottom pane **Activity Details** form by clicking on the [icon] and [icon] buttons on the **Bottom Layout** toolbar.

28. Open the **Activity Details** form, right-click on a tab in the **Activity Details** form and select **Customize Activity Details...** then hide and display some tabs. Set the tabs as per the picture below:

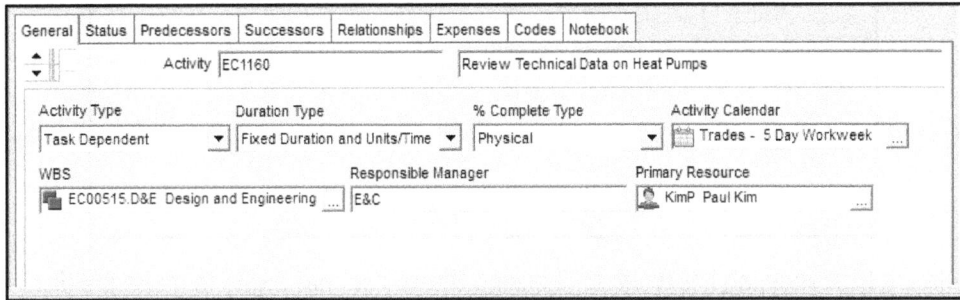

29. Close the project by selecting **File**, **Close All** and return to the **Projects Window**.

30. Open the **User Preferences** form by selecting **Edit**, **User Preferences...**and select the method you wish to display the date from the **Dates** tab and set your options as per below. People in the US may wish to use the **Month, Day, Year** option, but ensure you show the time in 24 hour format and do not select **Show minutes**:

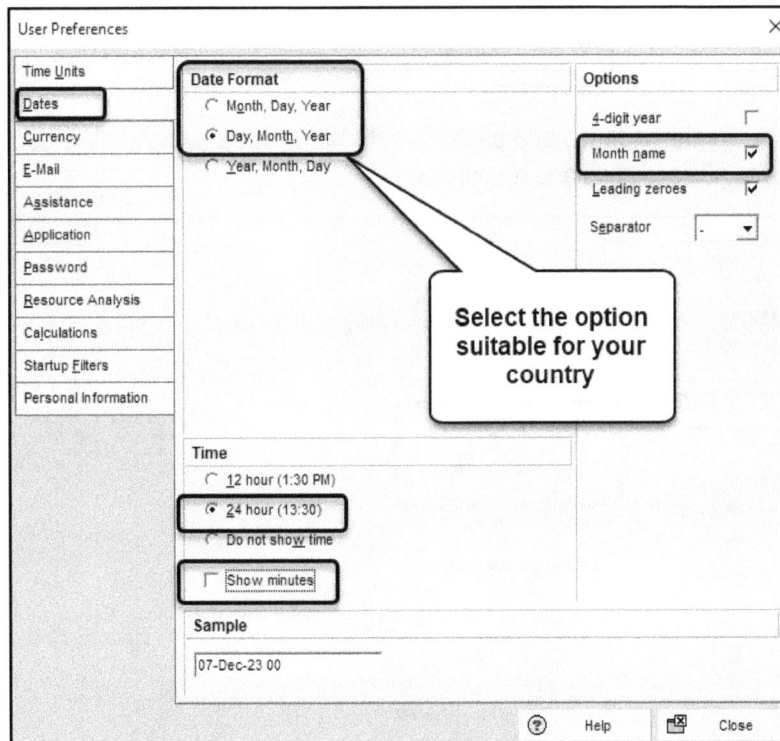

NOTE: It is strongly recommended that the time is always displayed as per the picture above so the user knows the time when Actual Start, Actual Finish and Constraints are applied because the software will often select 00:00, first minute of a day.

31. Select the **Time Units** tab and set your options as shown below:

32. In the **Currency** tab it is worth unchecking **Show decimal digits** to make the display of cashflow and cost columns narrower.

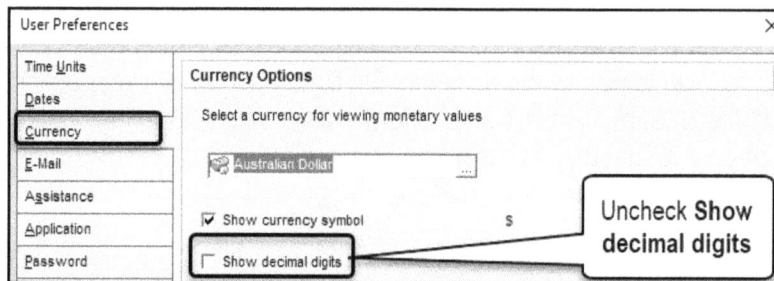

33. Select the **Assistance** tab and uncheck both **Wizards** as shown below because these make it slower to add activities and resources:

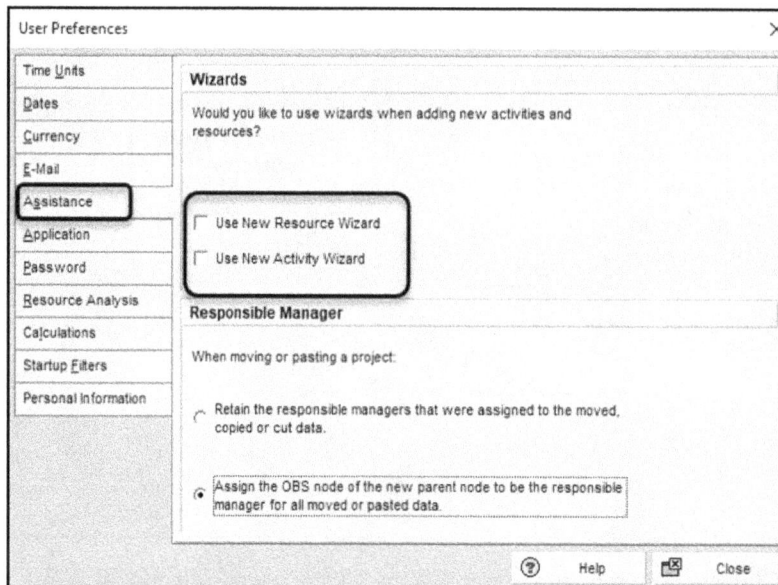

34. Select the **Application** tab and select the **Application Startup Window** as **Projects**. This will ensure the database opens at the **Project Window** each time you start up Primavera.

35. Select the **Startup Filters** and check **View all data (No Filter)** as this will ensure that when you open one of the windows you will see all the database data and not a blank screen.

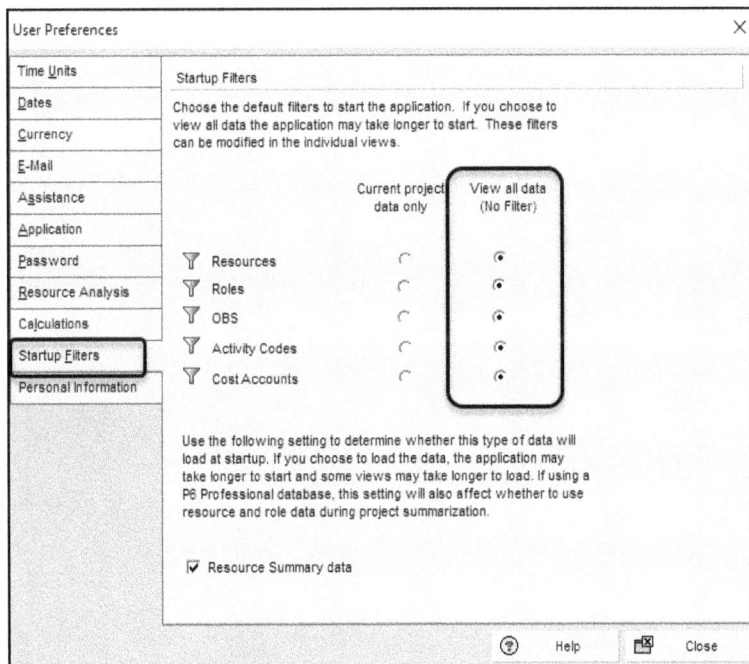

36. Close the **User Preferences** form.

37. Ensure all projects are closed by selecting **File**, **Close All**.

38. Restart P6 to lock in these options.

NOTES FOR TRAINING COURSE INSTRUCTORS AND/OR DATABASE ADMINISTRATORS:

1. Training course instructors and/or administrators may consider purchasing the instructor's PowerPoint presentation from https://primavera.com.au/. There is an option of a fully editable pdf of the slide show that may not be edited. A sample in pdf format may be downloaded from these web sites.

2. Completed workshops and layouts may be downloaded from https://primavera.com.au/.

3. This book is only available through bookshops in eBook format (Google, Kobo, Kindle and iTunes) and as paperback or spiral bound books. Training companies may consider buying the Google eBook for students as this format may be gifted, thus you may buy and supply this format to your students.

4. If you are a training organization and you wish to train multiple users in one database, please contact the author for a paper on how to set up your database.

5. In summary, when multiple users are working in a single database, the Database Administrator or Course Instructor should:

   - Create a unique EPS Node for each student to work in,

   - Assign a unique Project ID for each student to use,

   - Create a unique Resource for each student to use, and

   - Assign a protocol that the students use to create Project IDs and Resource IDs so that each student project, and their resources, all have a unique name.

4   CREATING A NEW PROJECT

There are several methods to create a new project from the **Projects Window**:

- Run the **Create New Project** wizard, or

- Copy and paste an existing project and edit it, or

- Import a project created from another Primavera database or created with another software program such as Microsoft Project, or Elecosoft (Asta) Powerproject.

Primavera P6 Enterprise Project Portfolio Management Web Client has project templates.

> ⓘ   The Templates available in the EPPM Web Client are not accessible in the PPM Windows Client, but a project created from an EPPM template is available.

4.1   Creating a Blank Project

You may create a new project at any point in time by selecting **File**, **New...** from the menu or clicking on the ⊕ icon on the **Edit** toolbar. You will be guided through the **Create a New Project** wizard which will require the following information:

- The **EPS Node** the project is to be assigned.

- The **Project ID**, a code to represent the project (which has been increased from 20 to a maximum of 40 characters and set in the **Admin Preferences**, **ID Lengths**), and **Project Name**.

- A **Planned Start** date, which is the earliest date any un-started activity will be scheduled to commence and an optional **Project Must Finish By** date.
  NOTE: Be sure to check the Start Time is compatible with the proposed calendars.

- When a **Project Must Finish By** date is set the project float will be calculated to this date and not to the latest activity finish.

> ⚠   It is even more important to check the finish time as it often defaults to 00:00 which is midnight of the Finish day, giving you one less day than planned:

- The **Responsible Manager** is selected from the OBS structure. Normally the default will be yours and should not be changed.

- The **Resource Rate Type**. Each resource may have five different rates. This is where the default rates are selected but may be changed after a resource has been assigned to an activity.

- **Note:** It is recommended that you close all other projects before you create a new one as this process does not close any existing projects.

> ⓘ   It is a normal practice to copy and paste projects to keep a copy of a project at a specific point in time, normally after each update. When copying projects, you should consider utilizing the Primavera default numbering system for the renumbering of the Project ID.

4.2 Copy an Existing Project

A Project or Projects may be copied in the **Projects Window** by:

- Highlighting the project, or projects, or EPS Node you wish to copy and select **Edit**, **Copy** or **Ctrl+C**,

- Highlighting the EPS Node that you wish to associate the new project with and select **Edit**, **Paste** or **Ctrl+V**,

- The first **Copy Project Options** form will then be displayed, enabling you to choose which Project data items you wish to copy with the project; select OK,

- Primavera Version 22 introduced the ability to copy **Visualizer Layouts when copying a project**.

- The second **Copy WBS Options** form will be displayed, allowing you to choose which WBS data items you wish to copy with the project;

- After making a selection, click OK.

- The third **Copy Activity Options** form will be displayed, allowing you to choose the Activity data items you wish to copy with the project; select OK,

- Open and edit the new project.

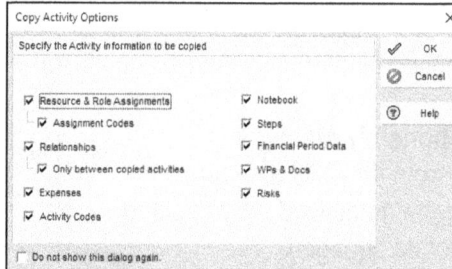

The copied projects and copied EPS Nodes will be assigned a new ID with a sequential number added to the Original ID.

Copying and pasting a project is a good way of deleting data before sending a project to a client.

An EPS Node may also be selected and copied in the **Projects Window** and pasted to another location which will copy the projects and add another EPS Node.

When opening an EPPM database projects are copied as a job service, thus working in the background, allowing you to continue working as projects are being copied. You will need to press F5 Refresh data to see the new project in the Projects window after P6 notifies that the process is complete.

4.3   Importing a Project and Project Data

Different Versions of Primavera run on different databases including Oracle and Microsoft databases. Primavera will only operate with the database format with which it has been installed and set up.

Primavera will not open a Stand-Alone project file, does not supply a reader, and all project data must be imported into a database before it may be opened.

You may be required to import a project that has been created in another program supplied by someone from within or outside your organization. Primavera is equipped with a set of tools for importing projects from other sources.

Depending on the version of your software and what type of database you are connected to there are different file format options for importing and exporting projects.

Unfortunately, there are very limited options for copying and pasting from other programs like Excel into P6.

4.3.1   Primavera File Types

There are several Primavera proprietary file formats that you need to be aware of:

- **XER** – Used to exchange one or more projects between Primavera databases regardless of the database type in which it was created and exports all project data. Earlier versions of **XER** files may be imported into later version databases. A layout (formatting) is not part of an XER file. Baselines are nor exported with an XER. The **Web Client** does not import or export XER files.

- **PLF** – Used to exchange **Layouts** between Primavera databases regardless of the database type in which it was created. PLF files may now be imported into Visualizer.

- **ANP** – Used to save the position of activities in an **Activity Network**.

- **ERP** – Used to exchange **Reports** between Primavera databases regardless of the database type in which it was created.

- **XML** – Used to import and export projects.

    ➢ Supported by the web client whereas an XER is not.

    ➢ This function supports the ability to import and export Baseline projects and Activity Layouts, and XER does not.

    ➢ This is the same software language but a different format to a Microsoft Project XML file so be careful with the naming of your files, so you do not confuse MSP and P6 XML files.

A P6 XML file may recalculate the cost of an imported project when the resource rate in the Resource window of either the source or target project are different to the rate assigned to an activity, thus an imported XML file may change the project costs. See para 26.11 for a full explanation.

- **PCF** – Used to exchange **Global Changes** between Primavera databases.

- **VLF** – Visualizer Layout File allows the import and export of Visualizer Layouts between users.

4.3.2   Non Primavera File Types

Select **File**, **Import…** to open a wizard that will guide you through the process of importing projects into your database.

Primavera will import and export to the following non Primavera file types using the wizards found under the menu commands **File**, **Import…** and **File**, **Export…**:

- Microsoft Project **XML** format is supported in Version 6.2 and later. This allows import of a file created by Microsoft Project 2000 and later without the installation of Microsoft Project. The file needs to be saved from Microsoft Project in XML format.

- **XLS**. Primavera Version 5.0 introduced a function allowing the import and export of data in Excel format. It is best to export some sample data first and then update the data and import it. See the UTILITIES chapter for more information.

    > Read the Administrators Guide carefully before importing a project as this is a very complex operation and may import unwanted data into your database. It is recommended that you establish a sacrificial database into which you import projects so that corporate databases are not filled up with unwanted data.

- **MPX (*.mpx)**. This is a text format created by Microsoft Project 98 and earlier versions. MPX format was once a popular format to import and export data and used by many other project scheduling software packages but is less frequently used these days and does not support task calendars. This option has been removed in later versions of P6.

Formats removed from later P6 versions:

- **Project (*.mpp)**.This is the default file format that Microsoft Project uses to create and save files. Microsoft Project 2010 – 2019, Microsoft Project 2007 and Microsoft Project 2000 – 2003 are three different formats. Earlier versions of P6 would import a *.mpp file when MSP 2003 or earlier was installed but later versions do not support the import of a *.mpp file and Microsoft Project files have to be saved in XML format in order to be imported into P6.

- **Primavera Project Planner P3** and **SureTrak** files saved in **P3** format. A SureTrak project in SureTrak format should be saved in Concentric (P3) format before importing. The option of importing P3 files was removed in later versions of P6.

Primavera P6 will only export to the following file formats:

- **UN/CEFACT Format 6 – (XML)**. This format is mandated by many US Government agencies.

- **IPMDAR Export Format**. P6 Version 21 introduced the support of format from the **File**, **Export** menu. IPMDAR is a project export format required by the US Department of Defence. In P6 Version 21 this option was only available when you open an EEM database and when exporting from a PPM database the option is greyed out. P6 Version 22 PPM may now export IPMDAR format from SQLite and PPM databases.

- **CPP Export Format** introduced in P6 Version 22 and enhanced in P6 Version 23. The US Department of Energy had mandated that the current CSV, and MDB upload formats for PPD (Project Performance Data) upload will be migrated to the JSON (JavaScript Object Notation) format in early 2023. Primavera P6 Version 22 had to be connected to an EPPM to export to a CPP format, now using P6 Version 23 a user may export in CPP format from P6 Professional connected to any database. The mapping for a CPP format must be manually created.

4.4   Setting Up a New Project

To review or modify some of the basic Project or EPS information entered when a project was created, ensure that the **Project Details** form is displayed in the bottom of the screen:

- Highlight a project or EPS Node,

- The project must be open in order to edit some project data,

- You must also have the appropriate access rights to edit data,

- Select <u>V</u>iew, Sho<u>w</u> on Bottom, **Details** and click on the **General** tab:

- The **Project Leveling Priority** is used when leveling a project to reduce peaks in resource requirements. The value of 1 is the highest and 100 the lowest.

- **Check Out Status** enables the user to determine if the project is checked in or checked out. **Checked Out By** and **Date Checked Out** enables the user to establish if the project is currently checked out.

- Additional functionality was added in P6 Version 20 allowing different projects to have different **Financial Periods** and the function was renamed **Financial Period Calendars**.

4.5   Project Dates

At this point, a project would not have normally started and you would set the project start date sometime in the future using the **Planned Start** field in the **Projects Window**, **Details** form, **Dates** tab. To open this form:

- Highlight your new project,

- Select **View**, **Show on Bottom**, **Details** and click the **Dates** tab:

- **Scheduled Dates**
  - ➤ The **Planned Start** is the date before which no activity will be scheduled to start.

  - ➤ The **Must Finish By** date is an optional date. When this date is entered, it is used to calculate the **Late Finish** of activities, thus all **Total Float** will be calculated to this date. This topic is covered in the **Adding Relationships** chapter.

  - ➤ The **Finish date** is a calculated date and is the date of the completion of the last activity.

  - ➤ The **Data Date** is used when updating a project. This topic is covered in the **Tracking Progress** chapter. Unlike Microsoft Project, all incomplete work is scheduled to take place after this date.

  - ➤ The **Actual Start** date is inherited from the earliest started activity.

  - ➤ The **Actual Finish** date is inherited from the latest completed activity when all activities are complete.

- **Anticipated Dates**
  - ➤ The **Anticipated Start** and **Anticipated Finish** dates may be assigned before a WBS structure and Activities have been created. The start and finish dates columns and bars at the EPS level adopt these dates when there are no activities. After Activities have been created, they may remain as a historical record only and are not displayed or inherited anywhere else.

  - ➤ **Anticipated Dates** may also be assigned to **WBS Nodes** in the **WBS Window**.

4.6   Saving Additional Project and EPS Information – Notebook Topics

Often additional information about a Project or EPS Node is required to be saved with the project such as location, client and type of project. This data may be saved in the **Projects Window**, **Details** form, **Notebook** tab.

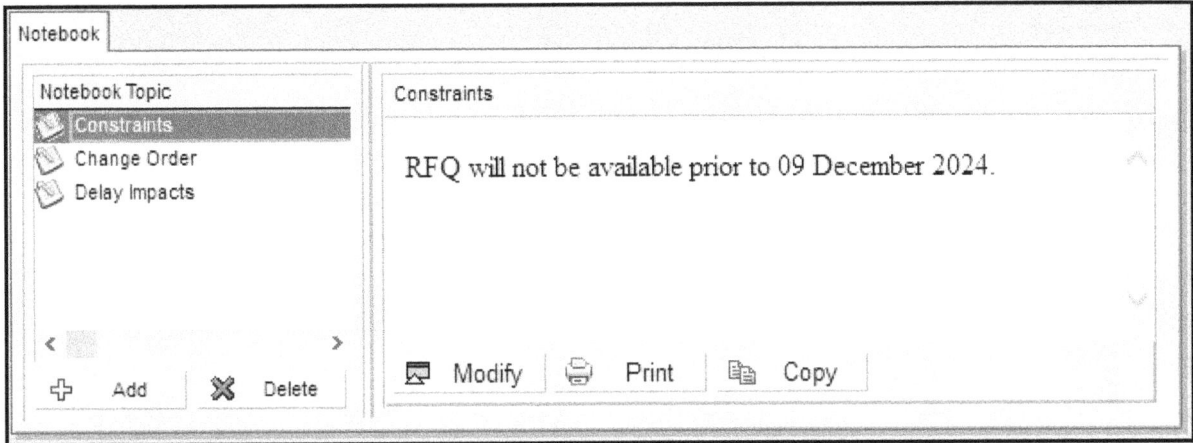

To add a **Note** to a Project:

- Click `Add` to open the **Assign Notebook Topic** form.

- Select a **Topic** from the list by clicking on the **Notebook Topic** you wish to select and click on the ⊞ icon to add the topic to the Notebook.

- Close the form by clicking on the ⊠ icon.

- You may now add notes to the selected **Project Notebook Topic** by clicking on the `Modify` **Modify** button,

- Notes may be added to **EPS** Nodes, **Activities** and **WBS Nodes** in the same way as Projects.

- Primavera version 6.0 introduced the search facility when assigning Notes.

To create a new **Notebook Topic** in a PPM or Stand Alone database:

- Select **Admin**, **Admin Categories...** to open the **Admin Categories** form and select the **Notebook Topics** tab.

- The check boxes make the Categories available to EPS Nodes and/or Projects.

When opening an EPPM database then the **Notebook Topics** are in the Administration area.

4.7   *Workshop 2 – Creating Your Project*

Background

You are an employee of Wilson International and are responsible for planning the Bid preparation required to ensure that a response to an RFQ (Request for Quote) from OzBuild Pty Ltd is submitted on time. While short-listed, you have been advised that the RFQ will be available on 09 December 2024 at 8:00 hrs (8:00 am) and you will be required to submit 3 bound copies of the proposal before 27 January 2025 at 16:00 hrs (4:00 pm).

NOTE: When multiple users are working in a single Professional database or using the Windows Client then:

- The Database Administrator or Instructor should create a unique EPS Node for each student to create their projects under.

- Each student should also be assigned a unique Project ID to use when creating their projects.

Assignment

1.   Close any open projects.

2.   Create a new project with the following information by selecting **File**, **New…** to open the **Create a New Project** wizard:

   - Select an appropriate EPS Node in your database to create the project or your nominated node when working in a shared database.

   - Project ID – OZB.

     NOTE: This Project ID may not be accepted if you are working in a shared database when there is another project with this Project ID. You may need to use another Project ID in this situation, such as OZB plus your initials.

   - Project Name – Bid for Facility Extension

   - Planned Start Date – 09 December 2024 at 08:00

     NOTE: Ensure that the time of 08:00 (8:00 AM) is added in this step. Forgetting to check and, if required, setting the time when assigning dates may lead to the schedule not calculating correctly.

   - Must Finish By – Leave Blank

   - Responsible Manager – Accept the default

   - Rate Type – Accept the default which is usually Price/Unit or Standard Rate

   - Click ▓ Finish to create the project.

3.   The project should now be open. Check the text in the top left side of the screen; the project name should be displayed.

4.   Ensure you are in the **Projects Window**.

5.   Ensure the project is selected by clicking on it.

---

6. Add the following project information in **Project Details** in the **Bottom Pane**:

    - Select your project in the **Project Window** by clicking on it.

    - In the **General** tab set the **Status** to **What-if**. The project needs to be open to change the **Status**.

    - **Dates** tab

        ➢ Set the Data Date to 09 December 2024 at 08:00

        ➢ Anticipated Start 09 December 2024 at 08:00

        ➢ Anticipated Finish 27 January 2025 at 16:00

        You should now see a bar in the Bar Chart above spanning these dates although there are no activities in the schedule. If no bar is displayed double-click in the Gantt Chart area level with the project.

    - Add a Notebook Topic using a suitable topic such as Constraints, Project Status or Issues stating, "RFQ will not be available prior to 09 December 2024."

7. Your project should look like this:

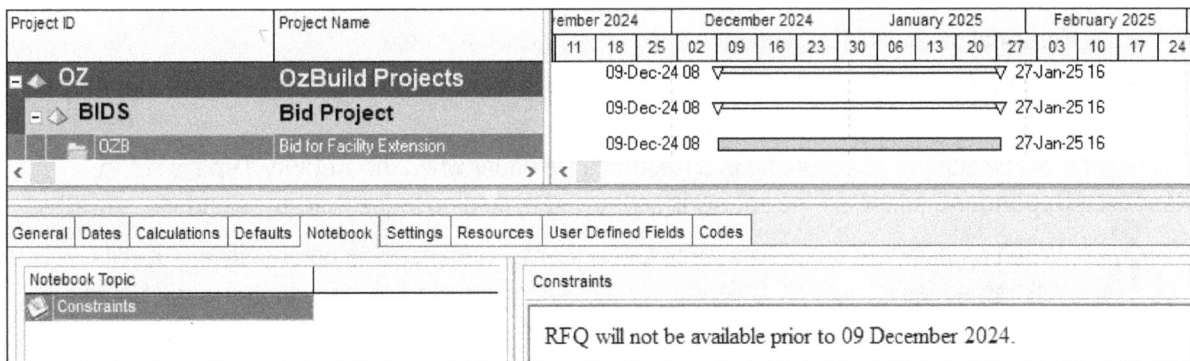

NOTES:

The date format will be displayed according to the **User Preferences** settings by selecting **Edit**, **User Preferences…** and selecting the **Dates** tab. Your date format should display the time as per the picture above.

The **First day of week** dates are displayed in the Timescale are normally a Sunday or Monday. This display option is set by the Administrator and applies to all projects and users in a database. By default, this is a Sunday but, in the picture above and below the Start of week has been set as Monday as Monday is usually a work day and Sunday is normally not a working day:

5   DEFINING CALENDARS

The finish date (and time) of an activity is calculated from the start date (and time) plus the duration of the calendar associated with the activity. Therefore, a five-day duration activity that starts at the start of the workday on a Wednesday and is associated with a five-day workweek calendar (with Saturday and Sunday as nonwork days) will finish at the end of the workday on the following Tuesday.

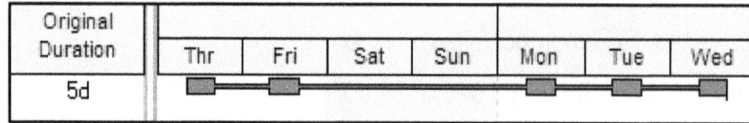

Original Duration		Thr	Fri	Sat	Sun	Mon	Tue	Wed
5d								

Primavera has three categories for calendars:

- **Global** – These calendars are available to all Projects and Resources.

- **Project** – These calendars are only available to the projects they are created in. These may only be created for a project when that project is open.

- **Resource** – There are two types of resource calendars: **Personal** and **Shared**, which is the same as the earlier Resource calendar.

  ➢ A **Personal** calendar is created for a specific individual resource.

  ➢ A **Shared** Resource calendar may be assigned to one or more Resources, which in turn may be assigned to an activity in any project.

A Resource will be scheduled according to a Resource Calendar when the **Activity Type** is set to **Resource Dependent**; otherwise the activity is scheduled according to the Activity calendar.

When an activity is made **Resource Dependent**, unlike in some other software, it still acknowledges the Activity Calendar for calculating the start of the resource work. Some software ignores the Activity Calendar and ONLY acknowledges the resource calendars when an activity is made resource-driven. You may wish to consider placing resource-driven activities on a 24-hour, 7-day per week calendar in circumstances when resource calendars have start times that are earlier in the day than the activity calendar start times. This prevents a delay to start of resource-driven activities by an Activity Calendar.

You may create a new, or edit an existing, calendar to reflect your project requirements, such as adding holidays or additional workdays or adjusting work times. For example, some activities may have a 5-day per week calendar and some may have a 7-day per week calendar.

This chapter covers the following topics:

Topic	Menu Command
• Database **Default Calendar**	Select **Enterprise**, **Calendars**…and select the database **Default Calendar** from the **Default** column.
• Assigning the **Default Activity/Project Calendar**	This calendar is assigned to new activities. From the **Projects Window**, click the **Defaults** tab in the **Details** form.
• Creating, copying, editing or deleting calendars	**Enterprise**, **Calendars**…, select the **Global**, **Project**, or **Resource** button then click [▯ Add] (to create a new calendar by copying an existing calendar) or [▤ Modify…], or [✗ Delete].
• Renaming an existing calendar	**Enterprise**, **Calendars**…,select **Global**, **Project**, or **Resource**, click the description and then modify it.

5.1 Database Default Calendar

The **Database Default Calendar** is selected in the **Enterprise, Calendars...** form and is used to display the Nonworking times for all users in all layouts and for all projects in a database.

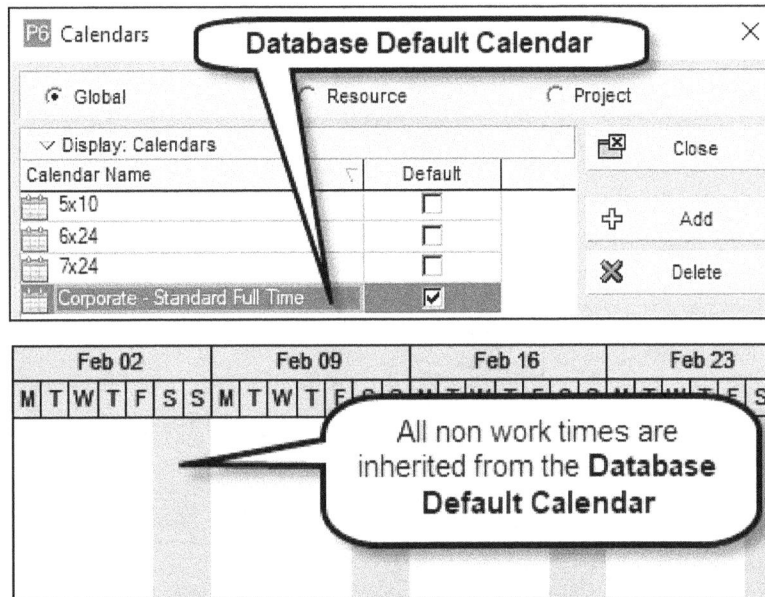

It is not possible for users to display different nonwork periods for different projects or views, as in most other scheduling software packages, without affecting all other projects in a database. This may become an issue with projects that have different work periods and may be solved by creating another database with a different **Database Default Calendar**.

5.2 Accessing Global and Project Calendars

Calendars may be accessed from the **Calendars** form for copying, editing and deleting by selecting **Enterprise, Calendars....**

The following rules dictate when you are able to access the calendars:

- **Global** and **Resource Calendars** may be accessed with or without any projects open.
- A **Project Calendar** may only be copied, edited, and deleted when the project has been opened.
- To list, create, and edit more than one existing **Project Calendar** at the same time all the projects in question must be open.

5.3 The Project Default Calendar

5.3.1 Understanding the Project Default Calendar

A project is assigned a **Default Project Calendar** which may be either a **Global** or **Project** calendar:

- All new activities are assigned the project **Default Project Calendar** when they are created, like Powerproject. Unlike in Microsoft Project, changing the P6 **Default Project Calendar** will **NOT** affect the calendar assigned to any activities.
- The **Default Project Calendar** may be selected for calculating leads and lags in the **Tools...,** **Schedule..., Options** form.

5.3.2 Assigning a Default Project Calendar

To assign or change the **Default Project Calendar** a project must be open:

- Open the **Projects Window** by selecting **Enterprise**, **Projects** and highlight the project,

- Click on the **Defaults** tab in the **Details** form; you will see the current **Default Project Calendar** in the **Calendar** box.

- Click the ⊡ icon to the right of the heading **Calendar** to open the **Select Default Project Calendar** form:

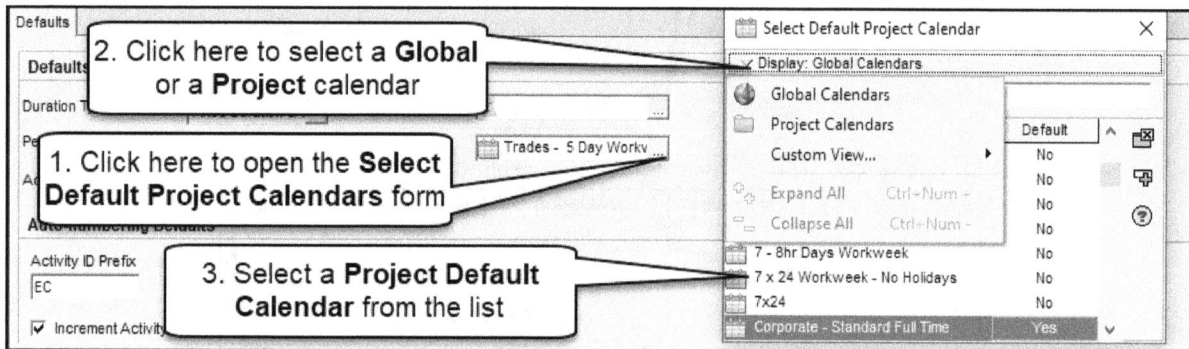

- Select either the **Global Calendars** or **Project Calendars** menu item from the drop-down box under the ⌄ Display: Project Calendars heading,

- Select the calendar to be the **Default Project Calendar**,

- Click the 🔲 icon or **Double-Click** on the calendar to assign the new calendar.

5.4 Creating a New Global or Project Calendar

A project must be active to create a **Project Calendar**. You can create a new **Project Calendar** by copying an existing Global Calendar. You **MAY NOT** copy an existing Project or Personal Resource calendar to create a **Project Calendar**.

To create a new calendar:

- Select **Enterprise**, **Calendars…**,

- Select the **Global**, or **Project** button, depending on the type of calendar required,

- Then click on the ⊕ Add icon to create a new calendar, or

- Select an existing Global calendar to copy. You may not copy an existing Project or Personal Resource calendar,

- Assign a name. It is best to keep these short as they are then easily displayed in a column.

5.5 Resource Calendars

A **Resource** or a **Global** calendar may be assigned to one or more resources. This is different from the philosophy of Microsoft Project and Elecosoft (Asta) Powerproject where each resource has its own calendar based on a project calendar and many resources are not able to share one calendar.

ⓘ A Resource will be scheduled according to the assigned **Resource Calendar** when the **Activity Type** is set to **Resource Dependent**; otherwise, the activity is scheduled according to the **Activity Calendar**. When the activity is a **Task Dependent** then the **Resource Calendars** are ignored and the task and resources are scheduled according to the **Activity Calendar**.

Resource availability is displayed in **Resource Usage Profiles** and is based on the Resource Calendar even when it is assigned to a **Task Dependent** activity.

5.5.1 Creating a New Shared Resource Calendar

To create a new Shared Resource calendar:

- Select **Enterprise**, **Calendars…**,
- Select the **Resources** button,
- Click on an existing Shared Resource Calendar,
- Then click either the [⊹ Add] icon to create a new calendar, or
- Select an existing Global or Shared calendar to copy. You may not copy an existing Project or Personal Resource calendar,
- Assign a name. It is best to keep these short as they are then easily displayed in a column.

A Personal Calendar may also be made into a Shared Calendar by:

- Opening the **Calendar** form,
- Selecting the **Resource** button,
- Selecting an existing **Personal Calendar** and clicking on the [To Shared] **To Shared** icon.

5.5.2 Creating New Personal Resource Calendars

These may be created from the **Calendars** form by:

- Selecting **Enterprise**, **Calendars…**,
- Clicking on **Personal Resource Calendars**,
- Clicking on [⊹ Add] to open the **Select Resource** form,
- Select the resource to be assigned the calendar, and

- Clicking on [🖼 Modify...] to modify the calendar in the normal way.

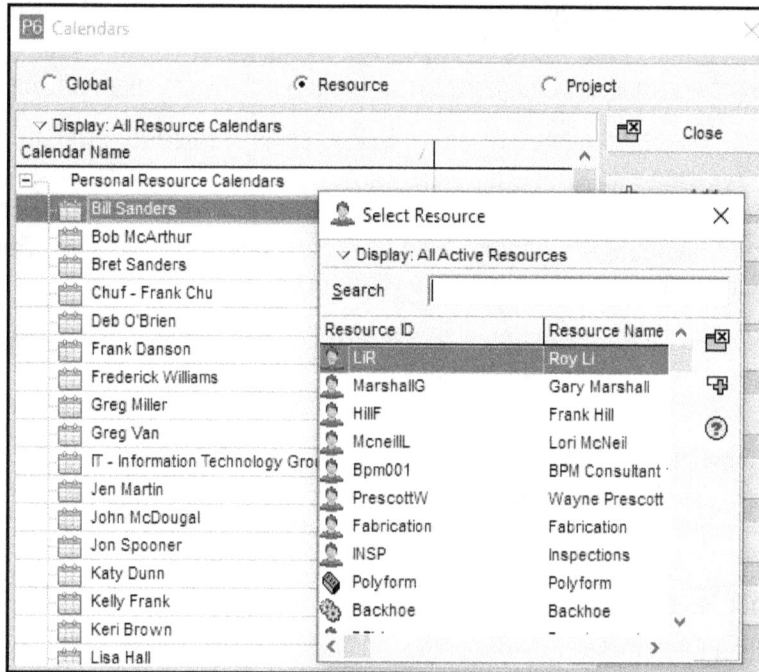

A Shared Calendar may also be made into a Personal Calendar by:

- Opening the **Calendar** form, **Resource** button,

- Selecting an existing **Shared Calendar** and clicking on the [To Personal] **To Personal** icon.

Or from the **Resources Window** by

- Opening the **Resources Window**, **Details** tab and select the resource,

- Clicking on the [Create Personal Calendar] icon to open the **Resource Calendar** form and edit the calendar in the normal way.

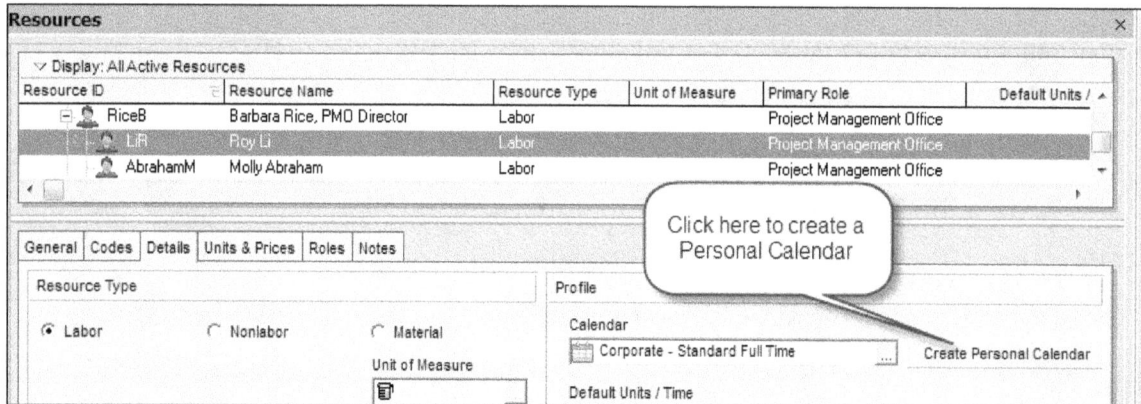

5.5.3   Personal and Shared Calendars Calculation and Display

The picture below displays three activities each 5 days long:

- A1000 is **Task Dependent** and acknowledges the 5-day per week activity calendar and ignores all resource calendars,

- A1010 and A1020 both acknowledge their respective **Personal** or **Shared Resource Calendars** for scheduling the work, but

- A1010 and A1020 both ignore **Resource Calendars** for **Bar Necking**:

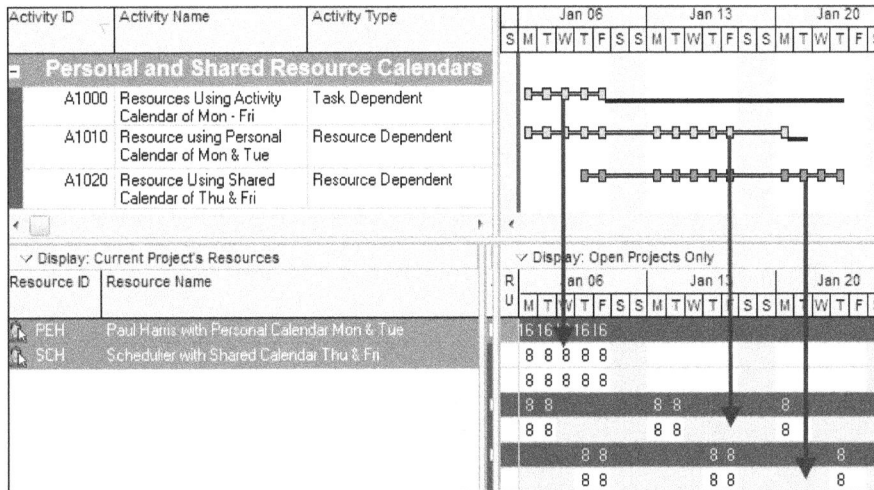

You will observe from the picture above that Bar Necking is based on Activity Calendar not resource working times.

When an activity is made **Resource Dependent**, unlike in some other software, it still acknowledges the Activity Calendar for calculating the start of the resource work.

This activity is scheduled to start on the project start date ONLY when both the resource and activity are assigned 24x7 calendars

5.6   Move, Copy, Rename and Delete a Calendar

5.6.1   Moving a Project Calendar to Global

A **Project Calendar** or **Resource Calendar** may be copied only moved to become a **Global Calendar**:

- Open the project that the calendar currently resides in,

- Select **Enterprise**, **Calendars…**,

- Select the **Project** button and highlight the calendar to be copied, and

- Click the [To Global] icon.

- The calendar will no longer be a Project calendar so this function is not a copy function.

- **NOTE:** A calendar may be copied in an EPPM database with the Web Client.

5.6.2 Copy a Calendar from One Project to Another

To copy a calendar from one project to another:

- Move the **Project Calendar** to be a **Global Calendar** as detailed above, and
- Create a new **Project Calendar** in both projects by copying the new **Global Calendar**.
- You will then have to assign the newly created calendars to any existing activities as they will now be assigned the original Calendar that will now be a Global Calendar.

NOTE: The web module does allow the copying of project and resource calendars.

5.6.3 Renaming a Calendar

To rename a calendar:

- Select **Enterprise**, **Calendars…**,
- Double-click the calendar description to edit in the same way as renaming a directory in Explorer.

5.6.4 Deleting a Calendar

To delete a calendar:

- Select **Enterprise**, **Calendars…**,
- Select the calendar and click the [✖ Delete] icon.

5.7 Editing Calendar Working Days

Prior to editing a calendar, particularly if it is a global calendar, click the [🖳 Used By…] icon to open the **Calendar Used By** form to determine which other Projects and Resources also use the calendar.

To edit a calendar:

- Select **Enterprise**, **Calendars…**,
- Select the **Global**, **Project**, or **Resource** button,
- Then click [🖳 Modify…] to open the **Calendar** form and modify an existing calendar:

Click on the month to view a monthly calendar

Click on a day to select a column of days

- Click in the month name to change the calendar view to monthly. This makes it quicker to navigate around the calendar and works in the other calendar view:

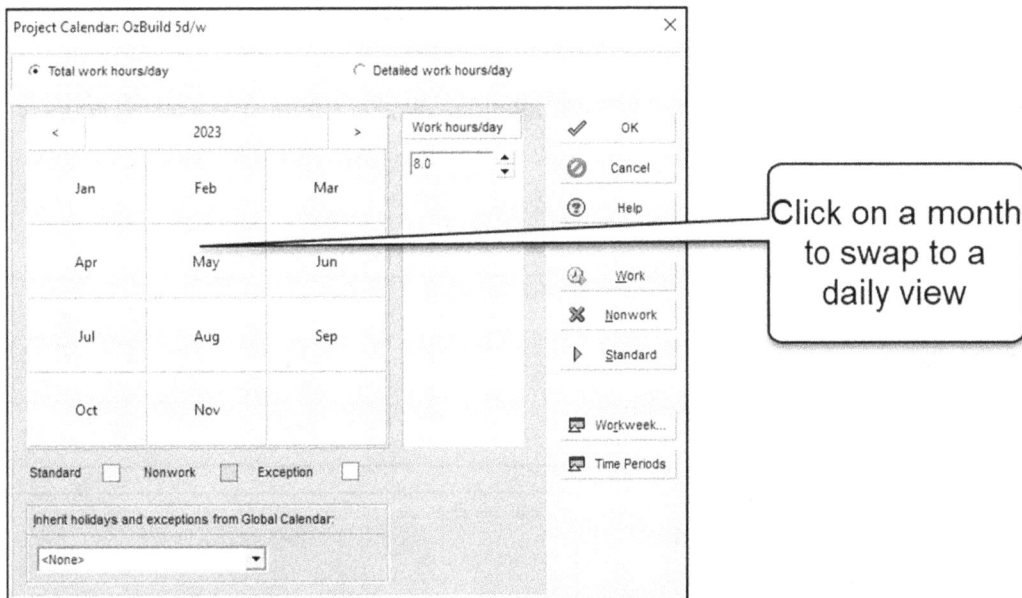

Click on a month to swap to a daily view

- To make **Nonwork Days** into **Work Days**, highlight the day(s) you want to edit by:
  - ➢ Clicking on an individual day, or
  - ➢ Ctrl-clicking to select multiple days, or
  - ➢ Clicking on a column or columns of days by clicking the day of the week box, which is located below the month and year. Ctrl-click will allow multiple columns to be selected.
  - ➢ Then click the ⊞ Work icon to make these days working and **CHECK THE HOURS**.

  ⚠️ When making a **Nonwork Day** into **Work Day** ensure you check that the working hours are the same as the rest of the calendar working days as the default is 08:00 to 16:00 which does not suit every calendar.

- To make **Work Days** into **Nonwork Days**, highlight the day(s) you want to edit as described in the paragraph above and then click the ✕ Nonwork icon to make these days nonworking days.

- To return individual days to the default setting, select the day and click the ▷ Standard icon.

5.8   Inherit Holidays and Exceptions from a Global Calendar

When creating a new Project or Resource calendar, a Global Calendar may be selected from the drop-down box and this function will link the calendar holidays from the selected Global Calendar into the displayed calendar.

The Global and the new Project or Resource calendars will remain linked and a change to a Global calendar holiday will be reflected in a calendar with Inherited Holidays.

ⓘ It is suggested that this option is never used and each calendar should be created as Stand-Alone without inheriting holidays from another calendar, and therefore will not change when another calendar has holidays changed.

5.9 Adjusting Calendar Working Hours

It is strongly recommended that the working hours per day are all the same and have the same start and finish time; otherwise, one-day activities may span two days and two-day activities may span three days, etc.

The working hours of a standard week are termed **Calendar Weekly Hours**. The working hours of selected individual days may be edited.

5.9.1 Editing Calendar Weekly Hours

There are two methods of editing the hours of every weekday of a calendar:

- From the **Calendar** form:
  - ➤ Select **Total work hours/day** and then,
  - ➤ Click [📅 Workweek...] to open the **Calendar Weekly Hours** form.
  - ➤ See warning below.
- Or from the **Calendar** form:
  - ➤ Select **Detailed work hours/day** and then,
  - ➤ Click [📅 Workweek...] to open the second Calendar Weekly Hours form.
  - ➤ Individual days of the week may be selected using Ctrl-click and then the work hours for multiple days edited simultaneously.

- Adjust the hours for the selected days in this form and click [✓ OK] to accept the changes.

⚠️ It is suggested that the **Total work hours/day** is not used as you will not know what start and finish time the software has selected for you.

5.9.2 Editing Selected Days Working Hours

To edit the working hours of individual days using **Total work hours/day**:

- Select the days you wish to edit by Shift-clicking, Ctrl-clicking individual days, or selecting one or more columns,

- Adjust the hours in the box below the title **Work hours/day**.

- The edited days will now adopt the color of the **Exception** days.

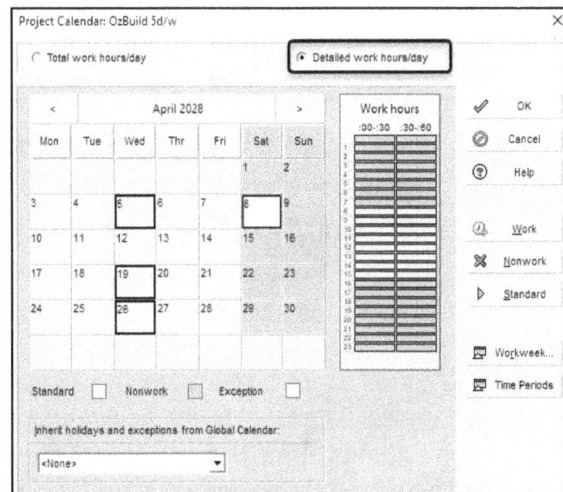

- Nonwork days may be made into Workdays by selecting the day and clicking on **Standard** or **Work**.

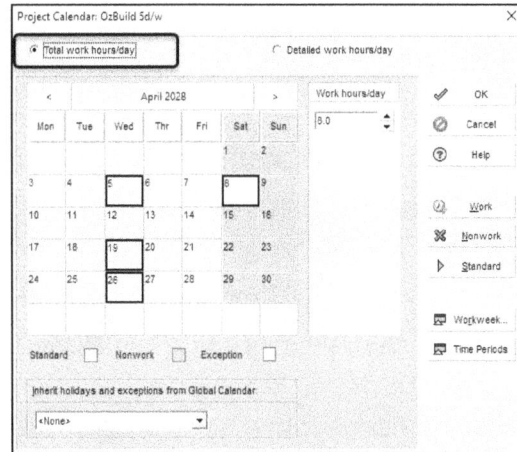

Use the **Work** button with care with calendars that do not have 8 hours a day as this will always set the day to 8 working hours.

Ensure you check that the working hours are the same as the rest of the calendars' working days when making a **Nonwork Day** into **Work Day**. This is because P6 uses the default hours (08:00 to 16:00) which may be different from the calendar you are editing.

5.9.3 Editing Detailed Work Hours/Day

To edit the **Detailed work hours/day** of individual days:

- Select the days to edit by Shift-clicking, Ctrl-clicking individual days, or selecting one or more columns,

- Click the **Detailed work hours/day** radio button,

- Adjust the hours to the nearest half hour by double-clicking on the table below the title **Work hours** to change them from working to nonworking.

- The edited days will now adopt the color of the **Exception** days.

When any calendar is changed or edited, the end date of all activities assigned with the calendar will be recalculated based on the new calendar. This may make a considerable difference to your project schedule dates.

When calendars have different start and end times some activities will span one day more than the duration of the activity because, for example, the last hour of the activity will roll into the next day.

It is recommended that the **Total work hours/day** form not be used as there is no control over the start and finish time of the day. It has been the author's experience that the software will assign some unpredictable start times, such as on the half hour. Users should use the **Detailed work hours/day** form.

When using the [Work] function, the hours per day are set to the Database Calendar hours per day and this function does not use the hours set in the Workweek form of the calendar being edited. Therefore, nonwork days made into working days with this function may have different working hours than other working days.

5.10 Calculation of Activity Durations in Days, Weeks or Months

P6 records durations in hours and the display of durations in days, weeks, or months of activities is a mathematical calculation that may be made by one of two methods:

- Individually for each Calendar – **RECOMMENDED METHOD**, or
- Globally for All Calendars – **NOT RECOMMENDED** (this was the only method used by P6 Version 6.2 and earlier).

In P6 Professional the option for the Global calculation of the durations in days, weeks, and months for all calendars is set by the Administrator in the **Admin**, **Admin Preferences…**, **Time Periods** tab.

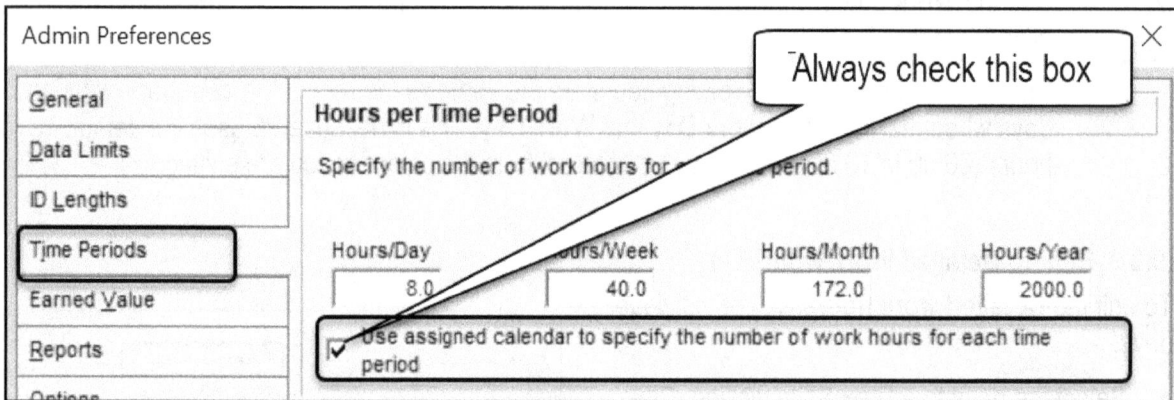

Un-checking the **Use assigned calendar to specify the number of work hours for each time period** check box disables individual calendar settings and therefore the activity durations in days weeks, months and years calculate incorrectly when the calendar **Hours per Time Period** do not conform to the settings in the **Admin**, **Admin Preferences…**, **Time Periods** tab. It is recommended that this never left unchecked.

In the P6 Windows Client the option for the Global calculation of the durations in days, weeks, and months for all calendars is set by the Administrator through the Web Interface by selecting **Administer**, **Application Settings**, **Time Periods** and un-checking the **Use assigned calendar to specify the number of work hours for each time period** check box:

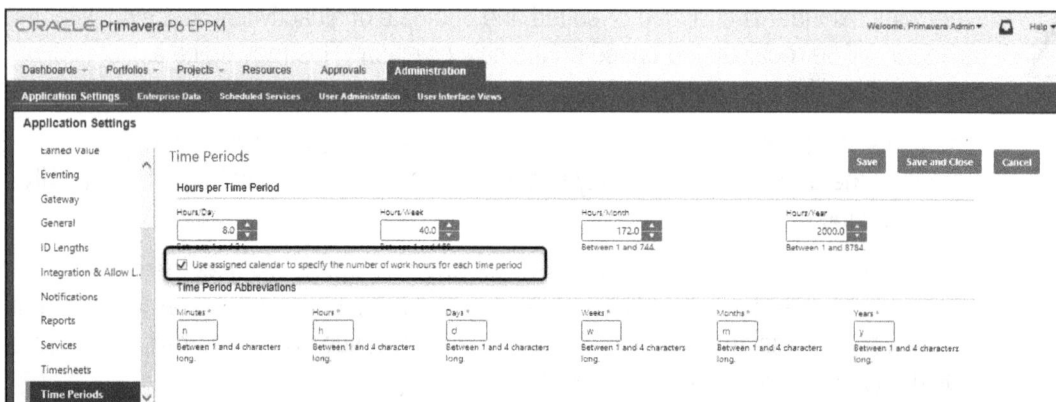

Individually for each Calendar – RECOMMENDED

In this situation the **Use assigned calendar to specify the number of work hours for each time period** box is checked and each calendar has its own set of parameters which are set in the **Hours per Time Period** tab when creating or editing a calendar. To set these parameters:

- Select **E**nterprise, **C**alendars…,

- Select the calendar to be edited,

- Click on the [🖵 Modify…] icon to open the **Calendar** form,

- Click on the [🖵 Time Periods] icon to open the **Hours per Time Period** form:

Hours per Time Period					
Specify the number of work hours for each time period.				✔	OK
Hours/Day	Hours/Week	Hours/Month	Hours/Year	⊘	Cancel
8.0	40.0	172.0	2000.0	?	Help

- This form allows the definition of the number of hours per day for each calendar, which in turn will enable the activity durations in days to be calculated and displayed correctly as long as the number of hours per day is the same for each work day in the calendar.

i This is not an automated system and you will need to calculate each cell manually based on how your calendar is defined.

⚠ For the **Hours/Day** parameters to work it is advisable that each working day in a calendar has the same number of hours per day.

Therefore, in the situation where a project is working a different number of hours per day it is recommended that you use an average hours per day and set both the **Work Hours per Day** in the **Hours per Time Period** form for every work day and the **Hours/Day** in the **Hours per Time Period** form to the one average number of hours per day.

For example; if you have a project that works 10 hours per day for Monday through Thursday, 8 hours on Friday and 6 hours on Saturday then each working day should be set to 9 hours per day.

Globally for All Calendars – NOT RECOMMENDED

With this option all calendars use the same parameters and these are set by the database administrator, in the **Hours per Time Periods** form which in turn sets the calculation for all calendars in the database to the same values.

This is **NOT** recommended unless all calendars in a database have exactly the same number of hours per day, days per week, and weeks per year which is very unusual.

⚠ When all the calendars do not have exactly the same number of hours per day, days per week, etc. then the durations in days, weeks, or months will not calculate correctly for calendars that do not comply with the setting in the **Admin Preferences**, **Time Periods** form. It is strongly recommended that this option is **NEVER UNCHECKED**.

5.11 Calendars for Calculating Project, WBS and Other Summary Durations

Summary durations of bands projects in the **Projects Window** are calculated based on the **Database Default Calendar** from the first activity Start to the last activity Finish from all the project in that band.

The summary duration of WBS bands and other bands created by Grouping activities by User Defined Fields or Activity Codes are calculated by:

- When all the activities in a band share the same calendar then the summary duration is calculated on the calendar of the activities in the band and the calendar name is displayed in the Calendar column, and

- When the calendars for the activities are different the summary duration is calculated on the Project Default calendar and the calendar field is blank.

The picture below has the Project Default calendar set as the 8hr/d & 5d/w and shows that when the calendars are different then the Project Default calendar is used to calculate the summary duration for WBS Nodes, Projects etc.:

5.12 Tips for Mixed Calendar Schedules

When a project has mixed calendars, say an 8- and 10-hour per day, then a change of calendar from a predecessor on an 8-hour per day calendar to successor on a 10-hour calendar, the successor activity may have one hour of work on the same day as the predecessor and span 2 days. This situation leads to interesting Float calculations and confusion to schedulers.

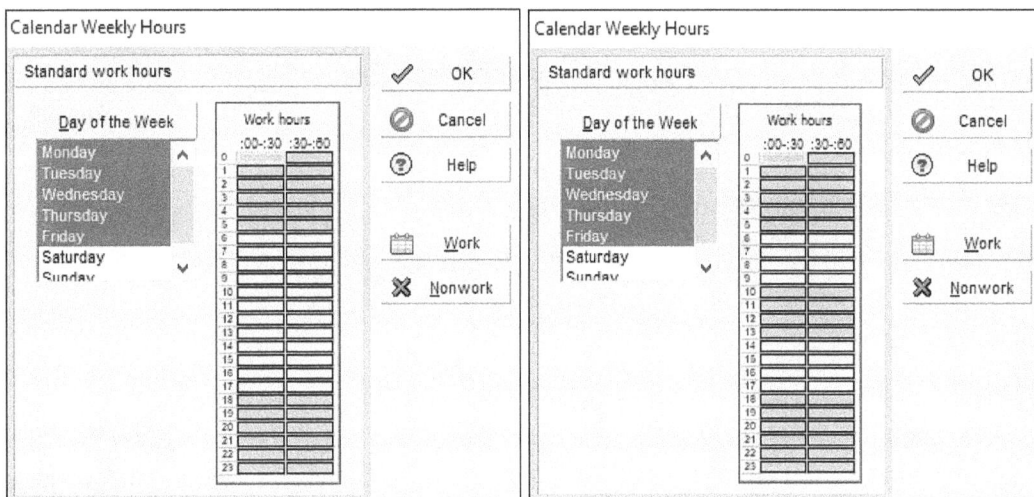

Primavera P6 does not have a "Start on a New Day" function found in other products such as Elecosoft (Asta) Powerproject, but which in itself brings on a new set of calculation issues. Techniques that may be considered to ensure one-day activities span one day and two-day activities span two days, etc. are:

- Apply an appropriate lag to the relationship, or

- Ensure all calendars have the same finish time but different start times thus giving the activities a different number of hours per day. Then as long as the activity durations are whole days, they will be scheduled to start at the start of the day according to their calendar and will end at the same time at the end of the day, or

- When the Start and Finish Times are not an important scheduling consideration then assign all the calendars the same Start and Finish time but adjust the duration of the lunch break so the days have the desired number of hours. For example, a 10-hour day calendar could start at 07:00 and finish at 17:00 without any lunch break and an 8-hour calendar could start at 07:00 and finish at 17:00 and be assigned a 2-hour lunch break.

The picture below shows how 8-hour a day and 12-hour a day calendars in the same project may be set up to ensure all activities start and finish on the same day:

The important issue using the method above is that all Activity Calendars finish at the same time.

5.13 Elapsed Duration Activities

Activities like "concrete curing" and "process testing" that take place 24 hours per day may be modeled using a 24 hour per day calendar. The disadvantage of this option is that if the predecessor ends at 17:00 then a 5-day curing activity will start and finish at 17:00 and will have float when the successor starts the following morning. To prevent this, I recommend putting these types if activities on calendars with the same hours per day as the other work, but on a 7 day/week basis without weekends or nonwork days, but this still has an issue when the curing activity ends on a weekend and the critical path is then lost:

Activity ID	Calendar	Activity Name	Start	Org Dur	Finish	Total Float	
Elapsed Durations							
All activities on 5d/w 8h/d calendar - No curing over weekends and project end date is delayed							
A1000	5 day/week 8 hours/day	Prepare and pour concrete	01-Apr-24 08:00	5d	05-Apr-24 16:00	0d	
A1010	5 day/week 8 hours/day	Cure concrete	08-Apr-24 08:00	6d	15-Apr-24 16:00	0d	
A1020	5 day/week 8 hours/day	Stip formwork	16-Apr-24 08:00	5d	22-Apr-24 16:00	0d	
Curing on 7d/w 24h/d calendar- Curing activity always has float and critical path lost							
A1030	5 day/week 8 hours/day	Prepare and pour concrete	01-Apr-24 08:00	5d	05-Apr-24 16:00	0d	
A1040	7 day/week 24 hours/day	Cure concrete	05-Apr-24 16:00	6d	11-Apr-24 16:00	0d 16h	
A1050	5 day/week 8 hours/day	Stip formwork	12-Apr-24 08:00	5d	18-Apr-24 16:00	0d	
Curing on 7d/w 8h/d calendar - Curing does not have float and critical path maintained							
A1060	5 day/week 8 hours/day	Prepare and pour concrete	01-Apr-24 08:00	5d	05-Apr-24 16:00	0d	
A1070	7 day/week 8 hours/day	Cure concrete	06-Apr-24 08:00	6d	11-Apr-24 16:00	0d	
A1080	5 day/week 8 hours/day	Stip formwork	12-Apr-24 08:00	5d	18-Apr-24 16:00	0d	
Curing on 7d/w 8h/d calendar - Curing finished on the weekend, has float and critical path lost							
A1090	5 day/week 8 hours/day	Prepare and pour concrete	01-Apr-24 08:00	5d	05-Apr-24 16:00	0d	
A1100	7 day/week 8 hours/day	Cure concrete	06-Apr-24 08:00	7d	12-Apr-24 16:00	2d	
A1110	5 day/week 8 hours/day	Stip formwork	15-Apr-24 08:00	5d	19-Apr-24 16:00	0d	

> *i* If the curing activity ends on Friday or Saturday evening, then it will normally still have Total Float as the successor may not start till the following Monday.

5.14 P6 Calendar Issues

Users who are moving from other products will find that Primavera Calendars do not have the following functions:

- Ability to print calendars, there are some third-party products listed on https://primavera.com.au/ that have the ability to print calendars,
- Time increments less than 30 minutes,
- Start and Finish times that are not on the hour or ½ hour,
- Notes/descriptions for nonwork days/periods,
- Gantt Chart background colouring for nonwork periods,
- Start on new day function,
- Working day numbering, which is very useful for claims analysis,
- The ability to display different nonwork periods for different Layouts and projects. Only the Global Default Calendar is displayed as nonwork time in all Project windows and Activity windows for all projects.

5.15 Workshop 3 – Maintaining the Calendars

Background

The normal working week at OzBuild Pty Ltd is Monday through Friday, 8 hours per day excluding public holidays. The installation staff works Monday through Saturday, 8 hours per day and the company observes the following holidays:

	2024	2025	2026	2027
New Year's Day	1 January	1 January	1 January	1 January
Easter	29 March- 1 April	18 - 21 April	3 - 6 April	26 - 29 March
Christmas Day	25 December	25 December	25 December	27 December*
Boxing Day	26 December	26 December	28 December*	28 December*

* These holidays occur on a weekend and the dates have been moved to the next weekday.

NOTE: Boxing Day is a holiday the day after Christmas celebrated in many countries.

Assignment

We will create two new calendars for this project, although we could use a standard calendar.

1. Ensure your new OzBuild Bid project is open.
2. Select **Enterprise**, **Calendars…** to open the **Calendars** form,
3. Select the **Project** radio button,
4. Create a new Project Calendar titled "OzBuild 5d/w" by clicking on the [🕂 Add] button and copying a calendar, if available, with 8 working hours per day and 5 working days per week.
5. Click on the [🖳 Modify…] button to open the **Calendars** form.
6. Select the **Detailed work hours/day** radio button.
7. Click on the [🖳 Workweek…] button to open the **Calendar Weekly Hours** form.
8. Make the work hours from 08:00 to 16:00 without a lunch break from Monday to Friday and close the form.
9. Select **<None>** for **Inherit holidays and exceptions from Global Calendar**.
10. Click on the [🖳 Time Periods] button and check the Hours per Time Period are the same as in the diagram below, if not then edit them and then close the form:

This publication is only sold as a bound book, no parts may be reproduced by any means, e.g., electronic, video or print.

Hours per Time Period

Specify the number of work hours for each time period.

Hours/Day	Hours/Week	Hours/Month	Hours/Year
8.0	40.0	172.0	2000.0

OK
Cancel
Help

11. As the project starts in 2024 you only need to add holidays in 2024 and 2025 from the table above.
12. Check there are no pre-existing holidays in the source calendar that should be made into work days.

Project Calendar: OzBuild 6d/w

⊙ Total work hours/day   ○ Detailed work hours/day

<	December 2024	>	Work hours/day

Mon	Tue	Wed	Thr	Fri	Sat	Sun
						1
2	3	4	5	6	7	8
9	10	11	12	13	14	15
16	17	18	19	20	21	22
23	24	25	26	27	28	29
30	31					

Work hours/day: 8.0

OK
Cancel
Help
Work
Nonwork
Standard
Workweek...
Time Periods

Standard ☐   Nonwork ☐   Exception ☐

Inherit holidays and exceptions from Global Calendar:

OzBuild 6d/w ▼

13. Create a new calendar titled "OzBuild 6d/w" for the 6-day week by copying the same Global calendar.
14. Make the work hours from 8:00 to 16:00 from Monday to Saturday and close the form.
15. Select **<None>** for **Inherit holidays and exceptions from Global Calendar**.
16. Click on the [⊞ Time Periods] button and check the Hours per Time Period are the same as in the diagram below, if not then edit them and then close the form:

Hours per Time Period

Specify the number of work hours for each time period.

Hours/Day	Hours/Week	Hours/Month	Hours/Year
8.0	48.0	206.0	2400.0

OK
Cancel
Help

17. Add the holidays above in 2024 and 2025 only.
18. Ensure Easter Saturdays are made into Nonwork days.
19. Check there are no pre-existing holidays in the source calendar that should be made into work days.
20. Should you wish to make the first day of the week a Monday then select **Admin**, **Admin Preferences**, **General** tab and change the Starting Day of Week to Monday.

6 CREATING A PRIMAVERA PROJECT WBS

This chapter outlines how to create a WBS structure to enable activities to be assigned to a WBS Node so a schedule may be created.

The **Project WBS** function is designed to record a hierarchical WBS that has been developed on a traditional basis as outlined in many project management documents. A well-structured WBS should:

- Include all the project deliverables, and
- Be set at the appropriate level for summarizing project activities and reporting project progress.

The **Project WBS** function is used to group and summarize activities under a hierarchical structure in the same way as the WBS function Elecosoft (Asta) Powerproject and the Custom Outline Codes in Microsoft Project. It is also similar to Outlining in all versions of Microsoft Project; however, in Primavera the Activities are assigned to a hierarchical WBS Node and are not demoted under a Parent task as with Outlining with Microsoft Project. The WBS structure is used to organize and summarize your project activities, including costs and resources during the planning, scheduling, and updating of Projects.

The project should be granulated (broken down) into manageable areas by using a project breakdown structure based on attributes of the project such as the Phases or Stages, Systems and Subsystems, Processes, Disciplines or Trades, and Areas or Locations of work. These headings are normally the basis of the project breakdown structure and are used to create the Primavera WBS structure, and the WBS should present the primary view of your project.

Defining the project breakdown structure may be a major task for project managers.

Primavera also has an **Activity Code** function similar to the **Codes** function in Elecosoft (Asta) Powerproject and the Custom Outline Codes in Microsoft Project. This feature enables the grouping of activities under headings other than the "WBS Structure." They are covered in the **Activity Codes and Grouping Activities** chapter.

Topic	Menu Command
• Creating and Deleting a WBS Node	The menu commands **Add**, **Delete**, **Copy**, **Cut** and **Paste** all work to create, delete, move, and copy WBS Nodes.
• WBS Categories	WBS Categories are created in Professional P6 using the **Admin**, **Admin Categories...**, **WBS Categories** tab and are assigned to WBS Nodes by inserting the **WBS Categories** column in the **WBS Window**.

The following AACE RPs are applicable to this chapter:

- 20R-98 Project Code of Accounts
- 21R-98 Project Code of Accounts – As Applied in Engineering, Procurement, and Construction for the Process Industries

A **WBS Node** is a term used by Primavera that is often called a **WBS Code** and is a single point in the WBS structure that activities are assigned to. A Primavera WBS Node may record more information than Elecosoft (Asta) Powerproject WBS Node:

- **Anticipated Dates**, which are used to create a bar in the **WBS Window** when there are no activities under the WBS Node, but do not summarize in the **Projects Window**.

- **Notes**, which are recorded under **Notebook Topics**,

- **Budget**, **Spending Plan** and **Budget Change Log**,

- **WBS Milestones**, which may be used for assigning progress at WBS Node,

- **WP & Docs** that provide links to documents, and

- The rules for calculating **Earned Value** for each WBS Node.

- **User Defined Fields**, a new function introduced with P6 Version 19, enabling users to see the UDF fields that have been assigned to a WBS Node.

The start and finish dates of a WBS Node are adopted from the earliest start date and latest finish date of the detailed activities under that WBS Node and use the **WBS Anticipated Dates** to create a bar when there are no activities assigned to a WBS Node.

The duration of a WBS Node is calculated from the start and finish dates, the database **Default Calendar** and the **User Options**.

> A WBS Node may not have costs or resources assigned directly to the node. All costs and quantities are calculated from the activities associated with the WBS Node.

6.1 Opening and Navigating the WBS Window

To view, edit, or create a **WBS** structure:

- The project must be open.

- The **WBS Window** is displayed by selecting **Project**, **WBS** or by clicking on the 🔲 **WBS** icon on the **Project** toolbar.

- The following picture is of the City Center Office Building Addition project showing the WBS Nodes on the left side of the screen and the WBS bars on the right side of the screen.

- The 🔲 icons in the **Top Layout** toolbar enable different views of the WBS. Click on each icon to see its purpose.

6.2   Creating and Deleting a WBS Node

To create a new WBS Node:

- Select a WBS Code or Name and right-click to display the menu, or

- Select the **Edit** menu command, or

- Use the icons from the **Edit** toolbar,

- Use the [⇧ ⇩ ⇦ ⇨] icons on the **Move** toolbar to put the WBS Nodes at the right level or to reorder them.

The commands **Add**, **Delete**, **Copy**, **Cut** and **Paste** all work to create, delete, move, and copy WBS Nodes.

- **Add** will add a new WBS Node under the level currently highlighted.

- **Delete** will delete the WBS Node. When a WBS Node has been assigned activities, you will be given the option from the **Merge or Delete WBS Element(s)** form to either:
  - ➢ Delete the activities by selecting **Delete Element(s),** or
  - ➢ Reassign the activities to the next lower level WBS Node by selecting **Merge Element(s):**

- **Copy** copies a WBS Node and the associated activities.

- **Cut** prepares to move a WBS Node and the associated activities to another location.

- **Paste** pastes a **Cut** or **Copied** WBS Node. After selecting **Paste**, the **Copy WBS Options** form, **Copy Activity Options** form, and **Renumber Activity IDs** form may be presented which enables the selection of the data to be pasted with the WBS Node. You will also be asked to renumber activities.

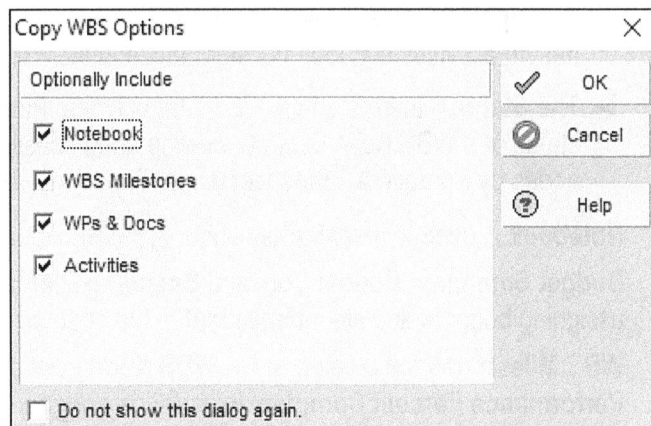

6.3   WBS Node Separator

There may be a requirement to use a specific WBS Node separator for contractual or system requirements:

- The default WBS Node Separator is assigned in the **Admin**, **Admin Preferences…**, **General** tab.

- Each individual project WBS Node separator is defined in the **Projects Window**, **Project Details** form, **Settings** tab and overrides the default set in the **Admin Preferences** form, **General** tab.

Settings	
Summarized Data	**Project Settings**
Last Summarized On	Character for separating code fields for the WBS tree

6.4   Work Breakdown Structure Lower Pane Details

The lower pane has several tabs that may be hidden or displayed.

General	Notebook	Budget Log	Spending Plan	Budget Summary	WBS Milestones	WPs & Docs	Earned Value	User Defined Fields

General

WBS Code
EC00610

WBS Name
Harbour Pointe Assisted Living Center

Status
Active

Responsible Manager
E&C

Anticipated Dates

Anticipated Start

Anticipated Finish

- **General** – in this tab you may assign:

  - The **WBS Code** must be unique for each project.

  - **WBS Name** is the description for the WBS Node, which also has to be unique.

  - The **Responsible Manager** is an interesting function as it enables access to data to be controlled at the WBS Node level. When a User has access to change data in one WBS Node only then they are able to see the whole project but may only change data in the one node.

  - **Anticipated Dates**, as with the Project Anticipated Dates, will display a bar when the WBS Node has no activities but does not summarize in the **Projects Window**.

  - The **Status** – there are four WBS Status types: **Planned**, **Active**, **Inactive**, and **What-if**. The status of a WBS Node controls viewing and access to the Nodes and Activities assigned to the nodes by Primavera Timesheet users. These may be used in filtering and reporting.

- **Notebook** is used to record notes about the WBS Node.

- **Budget Summary**, **Budget Log**, and **Spending Plan** are used together as a top-down method of assigning budgets and are independent of the costs assigned at the activity level.

- **WBS Milestones** are created at the **WBS Node** level and provide a summary method of assigning a **Performance Percent Complete** to activities assigned to that node. For this function to operate there must be at least one activity assigned to a **WBS Node**.

- **Earned Value** is where the rules for calculating the Estimate to Complete (ETC) and other Earned Value parameters are set.

- **WPs & Docs** enables the assignment of documents to a WBS Node and operates in the same way as the activities **WPs & Docs** tab.

- **User Defined Fields**, a new function introduced with P6 Version 19, enabling users to see the UDF fields that have been assigned to a WBS Node.

- **Planning Resources**, this tab is only available in the **Projects** and **WBS** windows when connecting to an EPPM database and any data is only available read from P6 Professional.

6.5 WBS Categories

WBS Nodes may be assigned categories, which enable WBS Nodes to be grouped and sorted in different ways. WBS Categories are to WBS Nodes as Activity Codes are to Activities. In earlier P6 versions these were referred to as **Project Phases**.

- WBS Categories are created using:
  - ➤ In the Windows Client by selecting **Admin**, **Admin Categories…**, **WBS Categories** tab, and
  - ➤ In the Web Client by selecting **Administer**, **Enterprise Data, Projects BS Categories**.

- WBS Categories are assigned to and removed from WBS Nodes by inserting the **WBS Categories** column into the **WBS Window**.

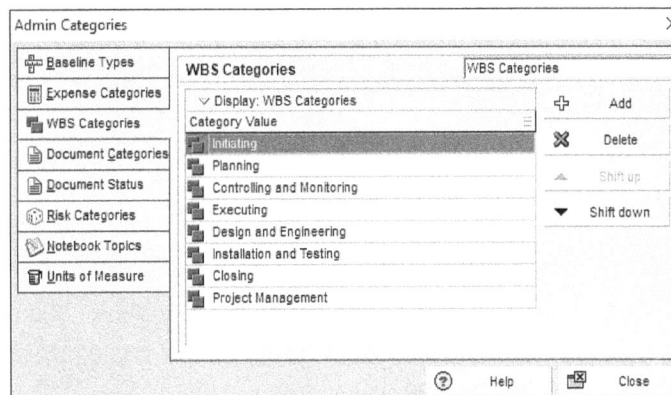

One use of a WBS Category could be, for example, to tag the WBS Nodes with the phases such as Design, Procure and Install and then the Activities may be grouped by WBS Category and then by WBS or some other Activity Code.

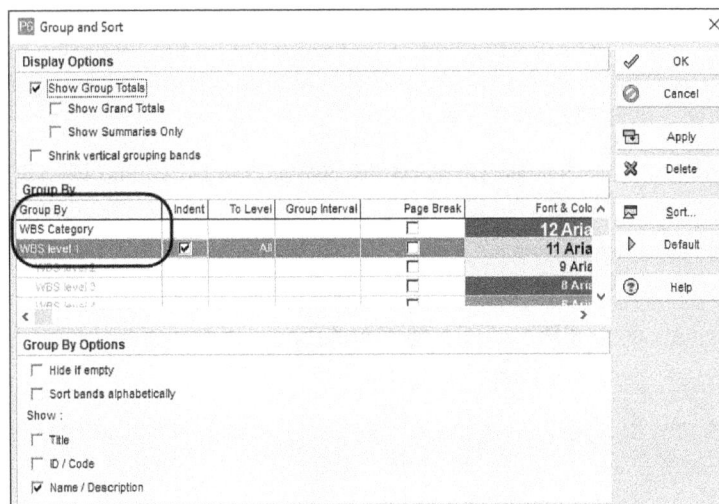

This topic is covered in more detail in the **Grouping, Sort and Layouts** chapter.

> **WBS Categories** may also be used in the **Tracking Window**.

6.6   Displaying the WBS in the Activity Window

On moving back to the Activity window, the WBS may be displayed if an applicable Layout is selected of formatted correctly. If the WBS in not displayed then select **View**, **Group and Sort by** and ensure:

- The Layout is **Grouped By WBS** and
- **Hide if empty** is not checked:

The author has found that after closing the Group and Sort form that the WBS bands were not displayed correctly and the user should press the F5 key to refresh the screen allowing the bands to be correctly displayed

6.7   Why a Primavera WBS is Important

People converting from Microsoft Project and Elecosoft (Asta) Powerproject will be used to using Summary Tasks and Outlining which Primavera P6 does not support.

You may be tempted to ignore the WBS and use Activity Codes instead. This paragraph will explain the main purposes of the WBS function:

- **User Access** may be assigned at this level, so two schedulers may open the same project and one may only change activities in WBS Nodes that have been assigned to that user.

- Progress at the WBS level may be measured with the use of **WBS Milestones**, which in turn may be used with the Earned Value calculations,

- **Earned Value** calculations and **Project Performance** may be measured at this level.

- WBS Activities are very useful as summary activities.

- **Anticipated Dates** may be assigned at the WBS level to provide a bar when no activities have been added to a WBS Node.

- The **Tracking Window** operates down to WBS Node level.

- There are several standard **Reports** that function at WBS Node level,

- WBS filters are very useful but only work in the project they are created in because they contain the Project ID which is unique.

6.8 Workshop 4 – Creating the Work Breakdown Structure

Background

A review of the scope identifies three deliverables:

- Technical Specification
- Delivery Plan
- Bid Document

Assignment

1. With your OzBuild project open click on the ▦ button to open the **WBS Window**.

2. Click in the WBS field header until the sort indicator is displayed as three horizontal bars, as displayed in the picture below. The WBS will now be displayed hierarchically now:

WBS Code	WBS Name
⊟ 🗂 OZB	Bid for Facility Extension

Three Horizontal bars

3. Select the Project Node and press the **Ins** key, or right-click and select **Add** to add the WBS Nodes and continue to add all three WBS Nodes for the three Phases above.

4. If the WBS Nodes are not indented, click the **WBS Code** heading as described in paragraph 2, until they are indented.

5. Use the arrows on the **Move** toolbar (right side of screen) to put them in the correct order and indent.

6. Your result should look like the following picture:

WBS Code	WBS Name
⊟ 🗂 OZB	Bid for Facility Extension
🖿 OZB.1	Technical Specification
🖿 OZB.2	Delivery Plan
🖿 OZB.3	Bid Document

7. Move to the **Activities Window** by clicking on the ▭ icon on the **Project** toolbar or clicking on the **Activities** tab. Your screen may look like this:

Activity ID	Activity Name	Original Duration	Start	Finish	Total Float		Dec 09					
						Sat	Sun	Mon	Tue	Wed	Thr	Fri
⊟ **Bid for Facility Extension**		0d			0d							
Technical Specification		0d			0d							
Delivery Plan		0d			0d							
⊟ **Bid Document**		0d			0d							

NOTE: Users may have to press the F5 key to refresh their data if the WBS is displayed incorrectly.

8. Your view may look different when you have not used the https://primavera.com.au/.

9. The WBS will not be displayed for two reasons, in the **Group and Sort** form:

    - The **Group By** must be set to **WBS level 1** and **To Level** set to **All**, and/or
    - **Hide if empty** must not be checked.

10. If the WBS is not displayed correctly select **V**iew, **G**roup and Sort by to open the **Group and Sort** form and set it as per the picture below:

    - **Group By** WBS and
    - **Hide if empty** NOT checked.

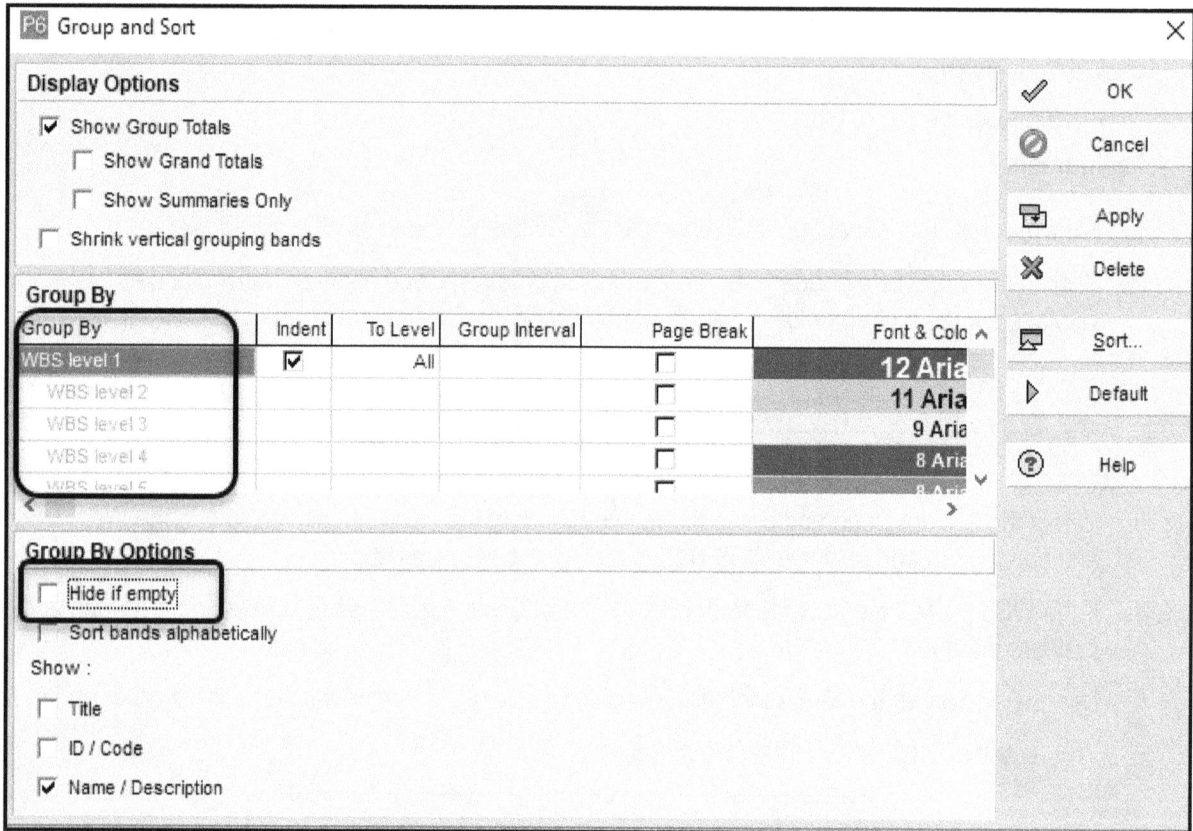

7   ADDING ACTIVITIES AND ORGANIZING UNDER THE WBS

Activities should be well-defined, measurable pieces of work with a measurable outcome. Activity descriptions containing only nouns such as "Bid Document" have confusing meanings. Does this mean read, write, review, submit or all of these? Adequate activity descriptions always have a verb-noun structure to them. A more appropriate activity description would be "Write Bid Document" or "Review and Submit Bid Document." The limit for activity names is 120 characters but try to keep activity descriptions meaningful yet short and concise so they are easier to print.

When activities are created, they are normally added under a WBS Node but may be organized under other coding structures such as Activity Codes or User Defined Fields.

This chapter will cover the following topics:

Topic	Menu Command
• Setting **Auto-numbering Defaults** and other defaults for new Activities	Select the **Defaults** tab from the **Bottom** pane in the **Project Window**.
• **Adding New Activities**	Select a line in the schedule and strike the **Ins (Insert Key)** or right-click and select the **Add** menu item.
• **Activity Details** form	May be displayed in the bottom pane by selecting **View**, **Show on Bottom**, **Details**.
• **Copying** activities in **Primavera**	Select the activities and copy and paste to the required location.
• **% Complete Type**	Use the **% Complete Type** drop-down box in the **General** tab of the **Activity Details** form.
• **Milestones**	Use the **Activity Type** drop-down box in the **General** tab of the **Activity Details** form.
• Assigning **WBS Nodes** to activities	• Create an activity in an existing WBS band, • Drag one or more activities into the desired band, • Display the WBS column and click the WBS cell to display the **Select WBS** form, or • Open the **General** tab in the lower window.

The following AACE RPs are applicable to this chapter:

- 23R-02 Identification of Activities
- 32R-04 Determining Activity Durations
- 37R-06 Schedule Levels of Detail—As Applied in Engineering, Procurement, and Construction

7.1 New Activity Defaults

After creating a new project and before adding activities it is important to set the defaults such as the Activity ID Numbers and Calendars. By setting them correctly before adding activities you will save a significant amount of time because you will not have to change several attributes against all activities at a later date. These defaults are set in the **Defaults** tab of the **Project Details** form:

```
┌─────────────────────────────────────────────────────────────────────┐
│ Defaults                                                              │
│ ┌─────────────────────────────────────────────────────────────────┐ │
│ │  Defaults for New Activities                                      │ │
│ │                                                                   │ │
│ │  Duration Type      [Fixed Duration & Units ▼]   Cost Account  [§        ...] │ │
│ │                                                                   │ │
│ │  Percent Complete Type [Duration          ▼]    Calendar   [▦ OzBuild 5d/w  ...] │ │
│ │                                                                   │ │
│ │  Activity Type      [Task Dependent        ▼]                     │ │
│ │                                                                   │ │
│ │  Auto-numbering Defaults                                          │ │
│ │                                                                   │ │
│ │   Activity ID Prefix      Activity ID Suffix      Increment       │ │
│ │   [OZ            ]         [        1000  ]        [        10  ]  │ │
│ └─────────────────────────────────────────────────────────────────┘ │
└─────────────────────────────────────────────────────────────────────┘
```

7.1.1 Duration Type

None of the **Duration Type** options affects how the schedule calculates until one or more resources is assigned to an Activity. The following options are available:

- **Fixed Units**
- **Fixed Duration & Units/Time**
- **Fixed Units/Time**
- **Fixed Duration & Units**

If you do not plan to add resources to Activities, then you do not need to assign a **Duration Type** and it may be left as the default.

This topic will be covered in detail in the **Assigning Roles and Resources Expenses** chapter.

7.1.2 Percent Complete Type

The **Percent Complete** type should be understood if it is intended to be used to update (status or progress) the schedule. This option may be set for each activity individually in Primavera and the default for new activities is set in the **Percent Complete Type** drop-down box. Primavera has many Activity Percent Complete fields that may be displayed in columns and we will discuss four of them now:

Activity % Complete, which may be linked to only one of the three following % Complete fields and is always linked to the % Complete displayed on the Gantt Chart bars:

- **Physical % Complete**, which is independent of activity resources and durations,
- **Duration % Complete**, which is linked to activity durations, and
- **Units % Complete**, which is linked to resource units.

There are three percent complete options; each new activity is assigned the project default **Percent Complete Type** and then this may be edited for each activity as required.

Therefore, for example, when the option of **Physical % Complete** is selected for an activity then the **Activity % Complete** and the **Physical % Complete** are linked and a change to one will change the other and this value would be displayed on the Gantt Chart.

Default Percent Complete Type

The **Default Percent Complete Type** for each new activity in each project is assigned in the **Defaults** tab of the **Details** form in the **Project Window**:

- The **Percent Complete Type** of a new activity is set to the Default Percent Complete when created and may be changed at any time.

Percent Complete Types

- **Physical % Complete** – This field enables the user to enter the percent complete of an activity and this value is independent of the activity durations and no summary values are calculated.

- **Duration % Complete** – This field is calculated from the proportion of the **Original Duration** and the **Remaining Duration** and they are linked. A change to one value will change the other. When the **Remaining Duration** is set to greater than the **Original Duration** this percent complete is always zero.

- **Units % Complete** – This is where the percent complete is calculated from the resources' Actual and Remaining Units of Labor and Non Labor resources only. A change to one value will change the other and when more than one resource is assigned then all the Actual Units for all resources will be changed proportionally. This will be covered further in the **Updating Resources** chapter. This is similar to the Microsoft Project % Work Complete.

Activity % Complete

The **Activity % Complete** field is linked to the **% Complete Type** field assigned to an activity in the **General** tab of the **Details** form in the **Activities Window** or the **% Complete Type** column:

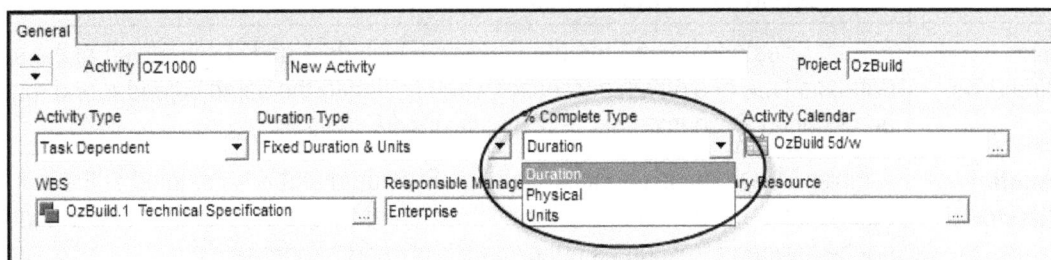

The **Activity % Complete** is also linked the **% Complete Bar** and this value is represented on the **% Complete** Bar.

Percent Complete Type	Orig Dur	Rem Dur	Activity % Complete	Duration % Complete	Physical % Complete	Units % Complete	Actual Labor Units	At Completion Labor Units	Jan 05	Jan 12
Duration	10d	6d	40%	40%	12%	0%	0	0		
Physical	10d	6d	12%	40%	12%	0%	0	0		
Units	10d	6d	60%	40%	12%	60%	12	20		

7.1.3 Activity Types and Milestones

An Activity may be assigned one of the following default Activity Types using the drop-down box in the Project Defaults tab:

- **Finish Milestone**
- **Level of Effort**
- **Resource Dependent**
- **Start Milestone**
- **Task Dependent**
- **WBS Summary**

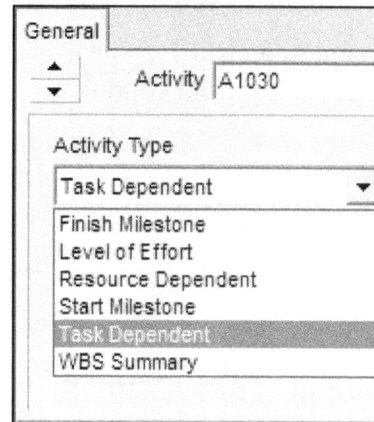

Activity Type	Description
• **Task Dependent**	These Activity Types have a duration and will only calculate the duration using the assigned calendar even when one or more resources are assigned to an activity.
• **Resource Dependent**	These Activity Types have a duration and will calculate the finish date using the calendar assigned to the activity when NO resources are assigned to the activity.
	When resources are assigned, the resources durations are calculated on their own calendars and do not require to be available at the same time to work. The activity end date is taken from the longest resource.
	They acknowledge the Activity calendar to calculate the Early Start date.
• **Level of Effort – LOE**	It spans from the start or finish of one or more predecessor activities to the start or finish of one or more successor activities which are linked by relationships. A LOE activity may span from the end of one activity to the start of another and may be used to fill a gap, for example for between two crane tasks to represent when the crane is on standby and a lower rate could be assigned in this period. Elecosoft (Asta) Powerproject has Hammocks and Buffer tasks with similar functionality.
	i If you schedule a LOE activity without relationships then it will mark its self as complete on the Data Date and you will have to reverse the status of the activity to Not Started before it will calculate.
• **Start Milestone**	A Start Milestone has a Start date and no Finish date and is scheduled at the same date and time of a driven successor when assigned the same calendar and may not be assigned Resources but may be assigned Expenses.
• **Finish Milestone**	A Finish Milestone has a Finish date, no Start date and is scheduled at the same date and time of a Driving predecessor when assigned the same calendar and may not be assigned Resources but may be assigned Expenses.
	Changing a milestone from Start to Finish would not affect a schedule when all the activities are on one calendar but would move the milestone from the start of a day to the finish of the previous day.
• **WBS Summary**	This Activity type calculates in the same way as Elecosoft (Asta) Powerproject and Microsoft Project Summary activities and they span all activities with the same WBS code, but without relationships that are used with LOEs.

A Milestone has zero duration and is used to mark the start or finish of a major event. Primavera differentiates between **Start** and **Finish Milestones** in the same way as Elecosoft (Asta) Powerproject. A P6 Start Milestone has a start date and no finish date and a P6 Finish Milestone has a finish date and no start date. This is unlike Microsoft Project, which only has one type of Milestone and later versions of Microsoft Project allow milestones with durations. Microsoft Project Milestones are calculated like P6 Finish Milestones but are normally imported as Start Milestones.

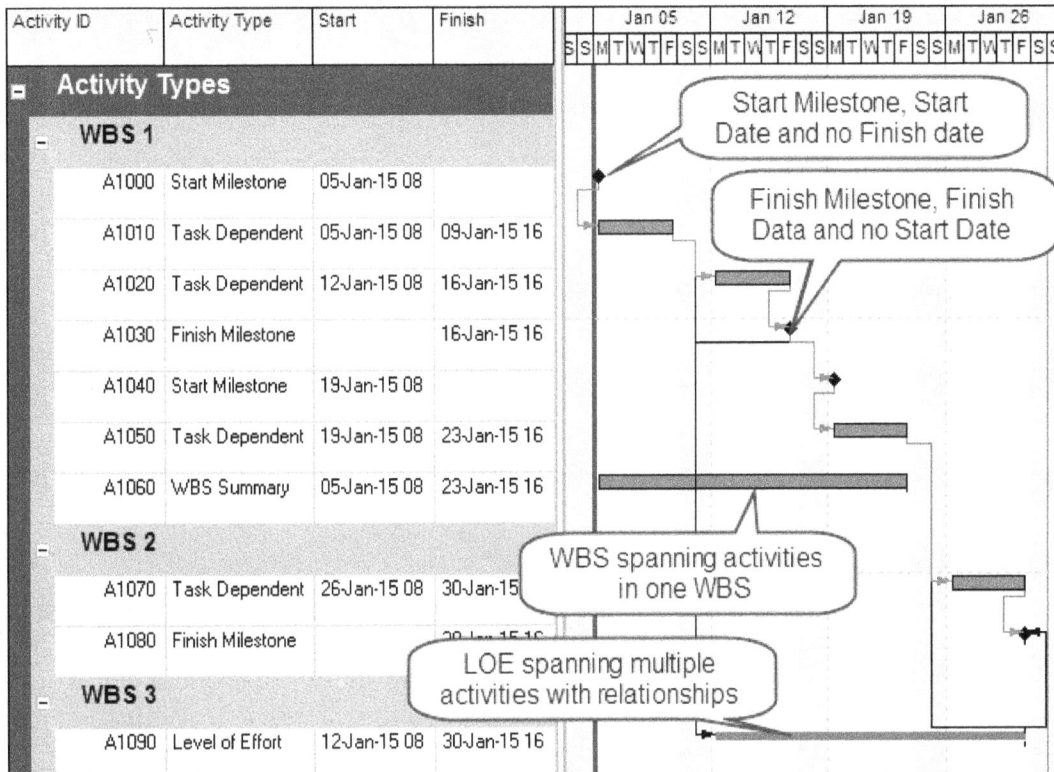

Activity ID	Activity Type	Start	Finish	Jan 05	Jan 12	Jan 19	Jan 26
Activity Types							
WBS 1							
A1000	Start Milestone	05-Jan-15 08		Start Milestone, Start Date and no Finish date			
A1010	Task Dependent	05-Jan-15 08	09-Jan-15 16	Finish Milestone, Finish Data and no Start Date			
A1020	Task Dependent	12-Jan-15 08	16-Jan-15 16				
A1030	Finish Milestone		16-Jan-15 16				
A1040	Start Milestone	19-Jan-15 08					
A1050	Task Dependent	19-Jan-15 08	23-Jan-15 16				
A1060	WBS Summary	05-Jan-15 08	23-Jan-15 16				
WBS 2							
A1070	Task Dependent	26-Jan-15 08	30-Jan-15	WBS spanning activities in one WBS			
A1080	Finish Milestone		30-Jan-15 16				
WBS 3				LOE spanning multiple activities with relationships			
A1090	Level of Effort	12-Jan-15 08	30-Jan-15 16				

7.1.4 Cost Account

This selects the default Cost Account for all new Resources and Expenses and is blank by default. They are problematic as the default Cost Account is assigned to the project and not the resource; thus every resource in a project is assigned the same Cost Account which generally not how cost accounts are used. Cost Accounts are covered in detail in the **Other Methods of Organizing Activities** chapter.

7.1.5 Calendar

This topic was covered in detail in the **Calendars** chapter. This drop-down box is used to select the default calendar for an activity. A **Default Project Calendar** is assigned to each project from the **Global** or **Project** calendar list.

All new activities are assigned the project **Default Project Calendar** when they are created; however, individual calendars may be assigned for each activity.

Changes may be made to multiple calendar assignments by:

- The **Edit**, **Fill Down** command, or
- Creating and running a Global Change.

7.1.6   Auto-numbering Defaults

The **Auto-numbering Defaults** decides how new activities are numbered. The first activity added to a new project will be based on the defaults set in this form.

- The **Increment Activity ID based on selected activity** check box controls which of the **Auto-numbering Defaults** rules are acknowledged after the first activity is added:

  - ➢ When checked, new activities will inherit the number of the highlighted activity plus the **Increment** number, and

  - ➢ When unchecked, new activities will always use the **Activity ID Prefix,** plus the **Activity ID Suffix** plus the Increment from the last activity.

> ⓘ   All Activity IDs are unique to a project but two projects may have the same Activity ID.
>
> There are no Activity ID Codes allowing logic to be automatically embedded into the Activity IDs, which were a powerful feature in both P3 and SureTrak.
>
> Activity IDs do not change when activities are reordered as with Microsoft Project Task IDs.
>
> An increment of 100 is recommended for large projects to allow many new activities to be inserted between two original activities.

7.2   Adding New Activities

It is often quicker to create a schedule in a spreadsheet and import the data into the scheduling software. Primavera offers a spreadsheet import function found under **File**, **Import...** which is very user friendly. This is covered in detail in **Utilities** chapter.

> ⚠   Some data associated with an imported activity must exist before the activity is imported from Excel otherwise it will not be imported. This includes items such as Roles, Resources, and Activity Codes. The P6 import function will not import this data but there are some third party software packages that will do this. A list of these software packages is maintained at https://primavera.com.au/.

To add an Activity to a project in the **Activities Window** you must first open the project, select the appropriate WBS Node and then:

- Select **Edit**, **Add**, or
- Press the **Insert** key on the keyboard, or
- Click on the ⊞ Add icon on the **Edit** toolbar.

7.3 Default Activity Duration

The default activity duration for newly created activities is specified in the **Admin**, **Admin Preferences...**, **General** tab **Activity Duration cell**.

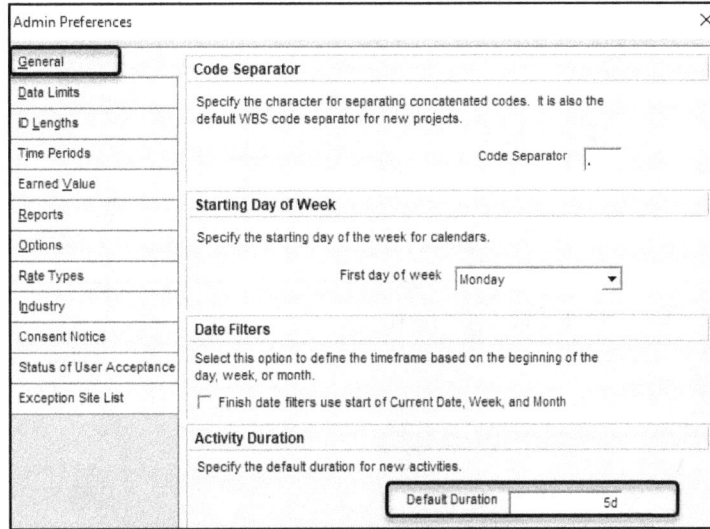

In the Windows Client in the **Administrations**, **Application Settings**, **General**, **Activity Duration** section:

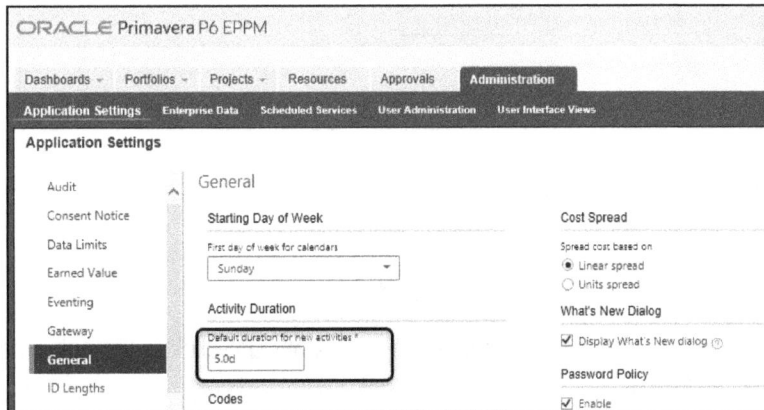

7.4 Copying Activities from other Programs

Activity data may NOT be copied from or updated from other programs (such as Excel) by cutting and pasting.

7.5 Copying Activities in P6

Activities may be copied from another project when both projects are open at the same time or copied from within the same project using the normal Windows commands **Copy** and **Paste**, by using the menu commands **Edit, Copy** and **Edit, Paste**, or by using **Ctrl+C** and **Ctrl+V**.

One or more activities may be selected to be copied by:

- **Ctrl**-clicking, or
- Holding the **shift** key and clicking on the first and last activity in a range, or
- Dragging a range with the mouse. With this operation be sure to select the whole activity or activities, not just a cell.

The **Copy Activity Options** form will be displayed. These options are self-explanatory:

The **Renumber Activity IDs** form is displayed next:

7.6   Renumbering Activity IDs

To use this function:

- Select the activities that are to be renumbered,

- Select from the menu **Edit**, **Renumber Activity IDs** or right-click in the columns area and select **Renumber Activity IDs**,

- This opens the **Renumber Activity IDs** form, displayed above, allowing renumbering of the activity IDs.

The P6 Renumbering function does not renumber the project Activity IDs in the order displayed on the screen unless you go into **Group and Sort** form, select **Sort** and delete all the Sorts in this form. Then P6 will renumber all the activities from top to bottom.

7.7   Elapsed Durations

An activity may NOT be assigned an **Elapsed** duration as in Microsoft Project. The activity should be scheduled on a 24-hour per day and 7-day per week calendar.

7.8   Finding the Bars in the Gantt Chart

At times you will find there are no bars displayed in the Gantt Chart because the Timescale has scrolled too far into the past or future. Double-click in the Gantt Chart in line with an activity and the Timescale will scroll to display the activity bar.

7.9   Activity Information – Bottom Layout

The Bottom Layout has several tabs where information about the highlighted activity may be viewed and edited. (These are not in any specific order as the tabs may be reordered on the screen.)

General	This form displays the: • **Activity ID** and **Activity Description**. • **Project** and **Responsible Manager**, these may not be edited here. It also displays activity attributes including some which were set as defaults in the **Project Window**: • **Activity Type, Duration Type, % Complete Type, Activity Calendar, WBS,** and **Primary Resource**.
Status	This is where the following data is displayed/edited: • The **Durations**, • The **Status**, where Actual Dates and % Complete may be entered, • Where **Constraints** are entered, and • By selecting from the drop-down box, the **Labor** and **Nonlabor Units** or **Costs** and **Material Costs** may be displayed. **NOTE:** It is possible to assign resource Units in the **Status** tab without a resource being assigned to the activity and the rate will be taken from the **Project Properties Calculations** tab.
Summary	This form displays summary information about the activity. It has three buttons that select which data will be displayed: • **Units** or **Costs** or **Dates**.
Resources	**Resources** and **Roles** may be assigned to activities and assignment information displayed.
Expenses	**Expenses** may be added and edited here. These are intended for one-off costs that do not require a resource to be created. **NOTE:** These are often used for material costs on construction and maintenance projects to prevent clogging up the **Resource Window**.
Notebook	Notes about activities may be made here by adding a **Notebook Topic** and then adding notes about the topic.
Steps	This function enables an activity to be broken down into increments titled **Steps** that may be marked as complete as work on the Activity progresses.

Feedback	This is where comments made in the timesheet module may be viewed.
WPs & Docs	This is where files that have been listed in the **Work Products and Documents Window** may be associated with activities and then opened from this form.
Codes	Activity Codes are assigned to activities assigned in this form. These codes are similar to Elecosoft (Asta) Powerproject Codes and Microsoft Project Custom Fields. But in P6 and Microsoft Project only one Code Value from each Code may be assigned to an activity but with Elecosoft (Asta) Powerproject a task may have multiple Code Values assigned; this is very useful as for example a column may have three floors assigned to it but in P6 and Microsoft Project you may only select one floor.
Relationships, Predecessors & Successors	This is where the activity's predecessors and successors are added, edited, and deleted. This is covered in the **Adding the Relationship** chapter.
Discussion	Users may create an Activity Discussion thread for each activity.
Risks	This is where users may view information on Risks assigned to an activity. **NOTE:** This is only available when a PPM database is opened.
Used Defined Fields	This is a new function in P6 Version 19 allowing users to easily see which UDF Fields have been assigned values to activities. The user must add the UDF Field to the **User Defined Fields** tab and this is saved as part of the View, so the user will not automatically see which UDFs a Project as utilized.
Tasks	Tasks are a function is Primavera Cloud where an activity may be broken down into Tasks which do not drive dates but allow a further granulation of an activity into more detailed work, but they are different to Steps. This is a new function in P6 Version 19 allowing users to **VIEW ONLY** of Tasks created in Primavera Cloud when a project imported from Primavera Cloud to an EPPM database.

7.10   Assigning Calendars to Activities

Activities often require a different calendar from the default **Project Calendar** assigned in the **Project Information** form. Primavera enables each activity to be assigned a unique calendar. An **Activity Calendar** may be assigned by the **General** tab of the **Bottom Layout** or from the **Calendar** column.

7.10.1   Assigning a Calendar Using General Tab of the Bottom Layout Form

- Select one activity that you want to assign to a different calendar. Multiple activity selection may not be used. Open the **General** tab of the **Bottom Layout**,
- Click on the ⬚ icon in the **Activity Calendar** box to open the **Select Activity Calendar** form,
- Select either **Global** or **Project** from the drop-down list in the top left menu, and

Select an **Activity Calendar** by clicking the ⊞ icon.

7.10.2 Assigning a Calendar Using a Column

You may also display the **Calendar** column and edit the activity calendar from this column. The process of displaying a column is covered in the **Formatting the Display** chapter.

Edit, **Fill Down** or a **Global Change** may be used to assign a new calendar to multiple selected activities.

Activity ID	Activity Name	Calendar
Bid for Facility Extension		
OZ1000	Approval to Bid	OzBuild 5d/w
OZ1010	Bid Document Submitted	OzBuild 5d/w
Technical Specification		OzBuild 5d/w
OZ1020	Determine Installation Requirements	OzBuild 5d/w
OZ1030	Create Technical Specification	OzBuild 5d/w
OZ1040	Identify Supplier Components	OzBuild 5d/w
OZ1050	Validate Technical Specification	OzBuild 5d/w

7.11 Assigning Activities to a WBS Node

Activities are assigned to a WBS Node from the Activities Window. They may be assigned using the following methods:

- A new activity will inherit the WBS Node that is highlighted when an activity is created.

- A new activity will inherit the WBS Node of a selected existing activity when the project is organized by WBS Nodes and an activity is created.

- Select the activity and click the WBS box in the **General** tab in the lower window. This will open the **Select WBS** form where you may assign the WBS Node.

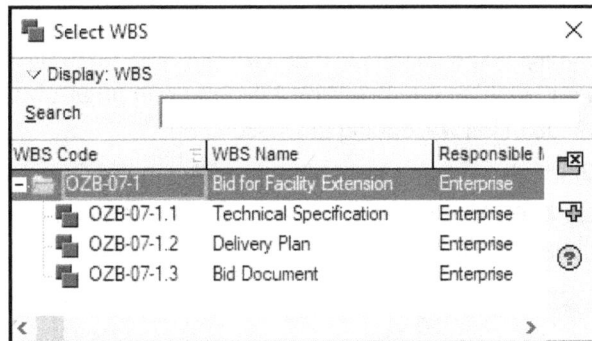

- The [+] and the [-] are used to expand or roll up the WBS structure. Click on the [⊞] icon to assign the node.

- Select one or more activities and move the mouse to the left of the activity description and the mouse will change into the shape displayed in the following picture. You may then drag the activities to another WBS Node.

Be sure the mouse pointer changes to this shape before dragging

- Insert the WBS column by clicking on the [▥▼] icon and selecting WBS from the Columns form under General. Clicking in the WBS column of an activity will open the Select WBS form.

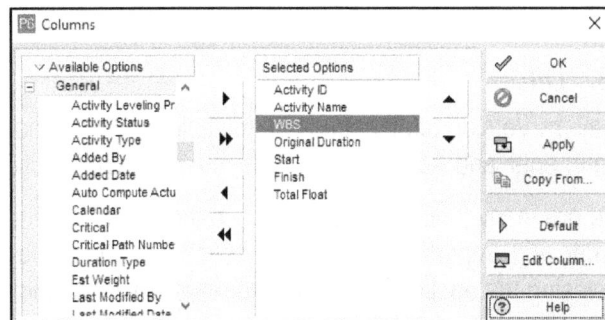

7.12 Reordering or Sorting Activities

The sort order of activities within a band is set by an order from one or more columns and you may not drag activities up or down the schedule in the same way as other products.

There are two principal methods of ordering activities after they have been added:

- Using the **Sort** function. To open the **Sort** form:

  ➤ Select **View**, **Group and Sort by**, **Customize...** and click the [Sort...] icon, or

  ➤ Click on the [icon] icon and click the [Sort...] icon to open the **Sort** form.

Sort				
Field Name	Sort Order		✓	OK
Start	Ascending		⊘	Cancel
Finish	Ascending		⊹	Add
Total Float	Ascending		✗	Delete
			▲	Move Up
			▼	Move Down
			⑦	Help

⚠ It is unfortunate that with Primavera, as soon as you use the option below to sort activities by clicking in a column header, then without any warning, the sorting fields entered into the **Sort** form above are overwritten by the column that has been used to sort the activities.

- Highlighting a column title and clicking with the mouse. The activities within a band will be reordered within that band in the order indicated with an arrow in the right side of the column header. The order will be either Ascending or Descending.

- Although not listed as an enhancement in the Oracle documentation the arrow in a column header has been reversed in P6 Version 22 and now when it points up when the column is sorted alphabetically down, as in the EPPM Web tool:

Activity ID ▽	Activity Name
City Center Office Buil... ...dition	
Design and Engineer...	
EC1000	D...
EC1010	St...
EC1030	R...
EC1050	As...
EC1160	Review Technical Data on Heat Pumps

P6 Version 21 and earlier

Activity ID △	Activity Name
Haitang Corporate Pa...	
Design and Engineer...	
EC1000	D...
EC1010	S...
EC1030	R...
EC1050	Assemble Technical Data for Heat Pump
EC1160	Review Technical Data on Heat Pumps

P6 Version 22

NOTE: This change in arrow direction operates in all windows and on all data items.

- This function changes all the settings made in the **Sort** form on a permanent basis.

ⓘ The Activities IDs are not renumbered when they have been reordered as they are with Microsoft Project Task IDs.

7.13 Undo

Primavera Version 5.0 introduced a multiple **Undo** function that operates on Resources, Resource Assignments, and Activities Windows, but no **Redo** function.

There are many functions that will erase the **Undo** memory in older versions, such as scheduling, summarizing, importing, opening a project, opening Code forms, opening User and Admin Preferences and closing the application, but in later versions less functions erase the undo memory.

7.14 Summarizing Activities Using WBS

The WBS bands may be summarized in the same way as in other project planning and scheduling software. The following picture shows the activities displayed under the WBS Nodes:

Activity ID	Activity Name	Original Duration	Remaining Duration	Schedule % Complete	October 2002	November 2002	December 2002	January 2
	Office Building Addition	248d	80d	72.58%				07-Jan-0
	Structure	64d	0d	100%				
BA702	Begin Structural Phase	0d	0d	100%	Begin Structural Phase			
BA710	Erect Structural Frame	20d	0d	100%	Erect Structural Frame			
BA712	Floor Decking	14d	0d	100%	Floor Decking			
BA720	Erect Stairwell and Elevator Walls	10d	0d	100%		Erect Stairwel		
BA730	Concrete First Floor	15d	0d	100%		Concrete First Floor		
BA731	Concrete Basement Slab	10d	0d	100%		Concrete Bas		
BA732	Structure Complete	0d	0d	100%		Structure Con		
BA735	Concrete Second Floor	15d	0d	100%		Concret		
	Design and Engineering	45d	0d	100%				
BA400	Design Building Addition	23d	0d	100%				

The following picture shows the activities summarized under the WBS Nodes:

Activity ID	Activity Name	Original Duration	Remaining Duration	Schedule % Complete	October 2002	November 2002	December 2002	January 2
	Office Building Addition	248d	80d	72.58%				07-Jan-0
	Structure	64d	0d	100%				
	Design and Engineering	45d	0d	100%				
	Foundation	60d	0d	100%	09-Oct-02 A, Foundation			
	Mechanical/Electrical Systems	201d	78d	62.86%				
	Exterior Finishes	153d	17d	19.47%				

WBS Nodes may be summarized or expanded by:

- Double-clicking any WBS band description. The band will either roll up when expanded or expand when rolled up.

- Selecting **View, Expand All** or **View, Collapse All** from the menu.

- Right-clicking and selecting **Expand All** or **Collapse All** from the menu.

- Clicking on the ⊟ or the ⊞ to the left of the WBS Node description to expand or collapse the WBS Node.

WBS Nodes may be reordered by clicking the arrow icons in the **Command** toolbar to the right side of the WBS Window.

7.15 Spell Check

To spell check a project, select a cell in the column you wish to spell check on and open the **Spell Check** form:

- Select **Edit**, **Spell Check**, or

- Hit the **F7** key.

This form is simple to use and does not use the operating system dictionary.

The spell checker may be configured for languages other than English through Oracle and organizations may configure the spell checker with their own additional words.

> *i* Ensure you have selected a cell in the column you wish to be spell checked. Then the column will not be reordered and the data in that column spell checked.

7.16 Workshop 5 – Adding Activities

Background

We need to set up the defaults and add the activities to the schedule.

Assignment

1. Go to the **Projects Window**, highlight the OzBuild project and select the **Defaults** tab in the **Activity Details** pane. If required, adjust all the following parameters.

2. Open the **Activities Window** and add the following activities under the appropriate WBS.

NOTE: If the **New Activity** wizard appears select the "do not show this wizard again."

3. Click on the Activity ID column header if the activities become out of order.

Activity ID	Activity Name	Orig Dur	Calendar	Activity Type
	Technical Specification			
OZ1000	Approval to Bid	0d	OzBuild 5d/w	Start Milestone
OZ1010	Determine Installation Requirements	4d	OzBuild 5d/w	Task Dependent
OZ1020	Create Technical Specification	5d	OzBuild 5d/w	Task Dependent
OZ1030	Identify Supplier Components	2d	OzBuild 5d/w	Task Dependent
OZ1040	Validate Technical Specification	2d	OzBuild 5d/w	Task Dependent
	Delivery Plan			
OZ1050	Document Delivery Methodology	4d	OzBuild 5d/w	Task Dependent
OZ1060	Obtain Quotes from Suppliers	8d	OzBuild 5d/w	Task Dependent
OZ1070	Calculate the Bid Estimate	3d	**OzBuild 6d/w**	Task Dependent
OZ1080	Create the Project Schedule	3d	**OzBuild 6d/w**	Task Dependent
OZ1090	Review the Delivery Plan	1d	OzBuild 5d/w	Task Dependent
	Bid Document			
OZ1100	Create Draft of Bid Document	6d	OzBuild 5d/w	Task Dependent
OZ1110	Review Bid Document	4d	OzBuild 5d/w	Task Dependent
OZ1120	Finalise and Submit Bid Document	2d	OzBuild 5d/w	Task Dependent
OZ1130	Bid Document Submitted	0d	OzBuild 5d/w	Finish Milestone

4. Assign the **Activity Calendar** a **6-day per week calendar** to Activity IDs OZ1070 and OZ1080 in the **General** tab of the **Activity Details** form.

5. Reschedule by pressing **F9** and check that the Data Date is set at 9 December 2024 at 08:00.

6. Your answer should look like the following picture, but you may have different columns displayed and there may be different text on the bars.

7. Ensure the sort order is by Activity ID by clicking on the Activity ID Heading:

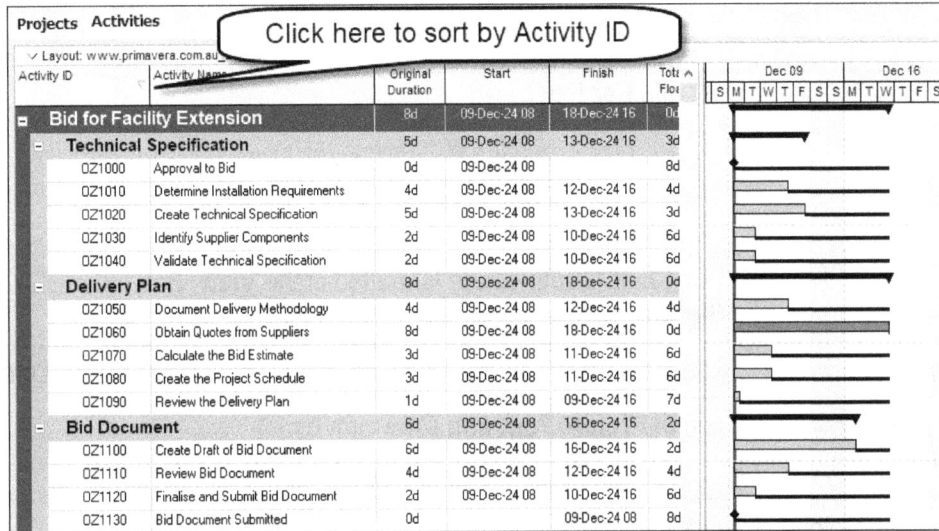

Activity ID	Activity Name	Original Duration	Start	Finish	Total Float	
Bid for Facility Extension		8d	09-Dec-24 08	18-Dec-24 16	0d	
Technical Specification		5d	09-Dec-24 08	13-Dec-24 16	3d	
OZ1000	Approval to Bid	0d	09-Dec-24 08		8d	
OZ1010	Determine Installation Requirements	4d	09-Dec-24 08	12-Dec-24 16	4d	
OZ1020	Create Technical Specification	5d	09-Dec-24 08	13-Dec-24 16	3d	
OZ1030	Identify Supplier Components	2d	09-Dec-24 08	10-Dec-24 16	6d	
OZ1040	Validate Technical Specification	2d	09-Dec-24 08	10-Dec-24 16	6d	
Delivery Plan		8d	09-Dec-24 08	18-Dec-24 16	0d	
OZ1050	Document Delivery Methodology	4d	09-Dec-24 08	12-Dec-24 16	4d	
OZ1060	Obtain Quotes from Suppliers	8d	09-Dec-24 08	18-Dec-24 16	0d	
OZ1070	Calculate the Bid Estimate	3d	09-Dec-24 08	11-Dec-24 16	6d	
OZ1080	Create the Project Schedule	3d	09-Dec-24 08	11-Dec-24 16	6d	
OZ1090	Review the Delivery Plan	1d	09-Dec-24 08	09-Dec-24 16	7d	
Bid Document		6d	09-Dec-24 08	16-Dec-24 16	2d	
OZ1100	Create Draft of Bid Document	6d	09-Dec-24 08	16-Dec-24 16	2d	
OZ1110	Review Bid Document	4d	09-Dec-24 08	12-Dec-24 16	4d	
OZ1120	Finalise and Submit Bid Document	2d	09-Dec-24 08	10-Dec-24 16	6d	
OZ1130	Bid Document Submitted	0d		09-Dec-24 08	8d	

Click here to sort by Activity ID

NOTE:

1. The picture above was created using the **www.primavera.com.au_Layout**, you will see different colors and columns when you use a different Layout. If you are unable to import this Layout, try selecting a different layout using the command **View**, **Layouts**, **Open Layout...**and select another layout from the list, such as the **Classic** or **Default WBS** Layout. If this does not solve your problem, then refer to the Layouts and Formatting sections of this book.

2. If your timescale week start date is different to the one above, for example the first day in the timescale is Sunday 10 Dec 24 whereas the first day above is Monday 9 Dec 24, then you may change this for all projects in the database if you have the access rights:

   - From the **Windows Client** (PPM database) select **Admin**, **Admin Preferences** form, **General** tab, **Starting Day of Week** section and select Monday:

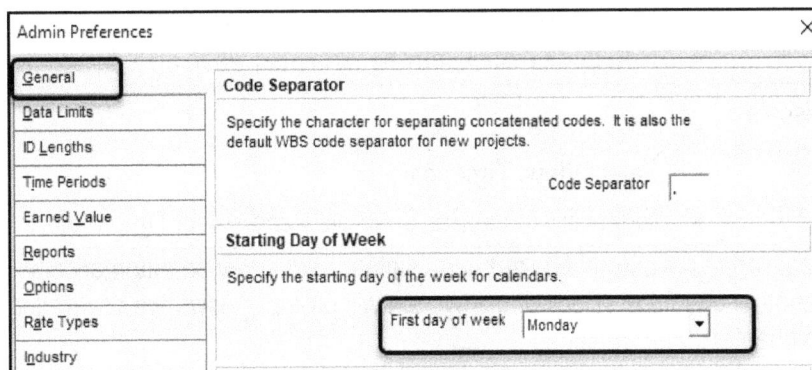

Admin Preferences	✕
General	**Code Separator**
Data Limits	Specify the character for separating concatenated codes. It is also the default WBS code separator for new projects.
ID Lengths	
Time Periods	Code Separator: .
Earned Value	
Reports	**Starting Day of Week**
Options	Specify the starting day of the week for calendars.
Rate Types	First day of week: Monday
Industry	

   - From the Web Client (EPPM database) for the Windows Client, log into the web and select **Administer**, **Application Settings**, **General** tab, **Starting Day of Week** section.

8   FORMATTING THE DISPLAY

This chapter shows you how to set up the on-screen presentation so that the schedule will be easier to read and more consistent. This chapter covers the following display and customizing topics:

Topic	Menu Command
• Formatting Columns	Open the **Column** form: • Select **View, Columns, Customize…,** or • Click on the [⬚▾] icon.
• Formatting Activity Bars	Open the **Bar** form: • Select **View, Bars,** [Options…], or • Click on the [⬚] icon.
• Format Gridlines	**Bar Chart Gridlines** are formatted in the **View, Bar,** [Options…] form, **Sightlines** tab.
• Format Data Date	The **Data Date** is formatted in the **Bar Chart Options** form, **Data Date** tab.
• Formatting Row Height	Open the **Table, Font and Row** form by: • Selecting **View, Table Font and Row.**
• Formatting Colors	There are limited options for formatting colors: • **Text** colors are formatted in the **Color** form accessed from the **Table, Font and Row** form which is opened by selecting **View, Table Font and Row,** [AaBbYyZz] icon. • **Bar Colors** are covered in the **Formatting the Bars** paragraph of this chapter. • **Band** colors are selected as part of the formatting of the layout by selecting **View, Group and Sort by** or clicking on the [⬚] icon.
• Formatting Fonts	There are limited options for formatting fonts: • **Text** fonts are formatted in the **Font** form accessed from the **Table, Font and Row** form which is opened by selecting **View, Table Font and Row,** [AaBbYyZz] icon. • **Notebook** entries may be formatted when edited.
• Format Timescale	• Click on the [⬚] icon, or • Select **View, Timescale,** or • Right-click in the Bar Chart area and select **Timescale.**

The formatting is applied to the current **Layout** and this formatting may be automatically saved as part of the Layout when another Layout is selected; the system will prompt. Views are covered in the **Group, Sort and Layouts** chapter.

⚠ Beware of clicking the [▷ Default] button in any form; this does not save your edits, but re-sets the form back to the Primavera defaults, destroying your hard work.

8.1 Formatting the Project Window

The formatting of the Project Window is very similar to the formatting of the **Activities Window** and will not be covered separately. Formatting, Filters and Layouts all work in the same way, except one is dealing with projects and not activities.

8.2 Understanding Forms

Unlike many software packages, Primavera has sorting and filtering functions in most forms and the principles are the same in most forms. This section will demonstrate some of the functions but you must be prepared to experiment with each form to see how they operate.

- Clicking in the **Resource ID** column of the **Resources Window** takes the formatting from hierarchical to alphabetical to reverse alphabetical and back to hierarchical. This function works in other forms with a hierarchical structure.

- The **Assign Successors** form has **Filter By** and **Group and Sort By** options that affect how data is grouped.

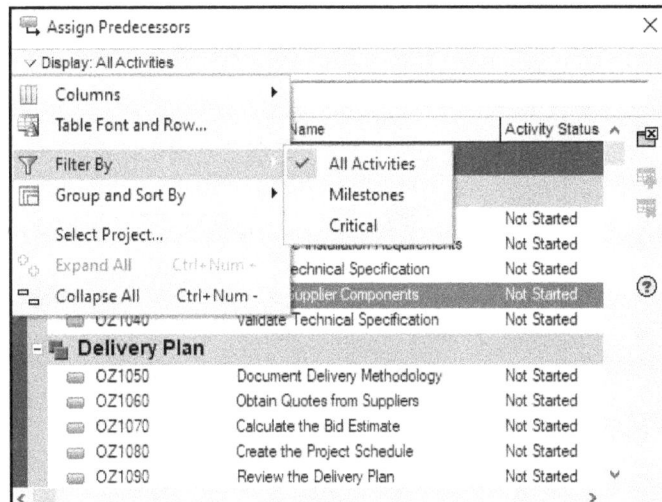

- The **Assign Resource** form has **Columns**, **Filter By**, and **Group and Sort By** options that affect what data is available.

- Ctl+F will also allow you to search for Resources matching a specific criterion.

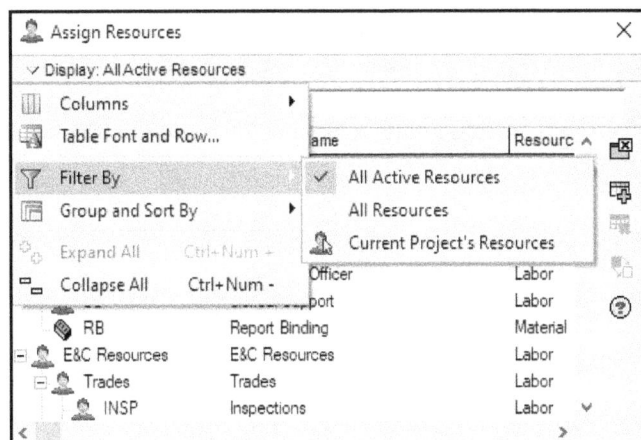

8.3 *Formatting the Bars*

- The bars in the Gantt Chart may be formatted to suit your requirements for display. Primavera does not have the option to format individual bars as in Microsoft Project and Elecosoft Powerproject. The coloring of specific activities may be achieved by creating a bar style (with the desired colors) with a filter to assign the bar style to select the activities requiring specific formatting, or using Visualizer,

At the time of writing this book the author had placed a layout on https://primavera.com.au/ *under the **Technical Papers** page that has the bar formatting issues discussed below fixed. It is suggested that downloading this layout will save users a significant amount of formatting time.*

8.3.1 Formatting Activity Bars

To format all the bars you must open the **Bar** form:

- Select **View, Bars**, or

- Click on the icon, or

- Right-click in the bars area and select **Bars** from the menu.

The following notes are the main points for using this function. Detailed information is available in the Help facility by searching for "Bar styles dialog box."

- Each bar listed in the table may be displayed on the bar chart by checking the box in the **Display** column.

- New bars may be added by clicking on the ⊹ Add icon and deleted by clicking on the ✖ Delete icon.

- The bar at the top of the list is placed on the screen and the one below drawn over the top of it, so it would be simple to hide one bar with a second. The ▲ Shift up and ▼ Shift down icons are used to move the bars up or down the list and therefore determine which bar is drawn on top of the next.

- The **Name** is the title assigned to the bar and may be displayed in the printout legend.

- The **Timescale** option is similar to the **Show For ...**, **Tasks** option in the Microsoft Project **Bar Styles** form and enables the nomination of a predefined bar which is selected from the drop-down box.

- Double-clicking on a cell in the **Filter** column opens the **Filters** form where you are able to select the filter/s which will determine which activities are displayed with the assigned bar format. Filters will be covered in detail in the **Filters** chapter.

- **Negative Float** is displayed in a similar way as in Microsoft Project and requires another bar in addition to the **Positive Float** bar with both the **Timescale** and **Filter** selected as Negative Float.

- The **Float** bar shows **Total Float**; there is no **Free Float** bar available, as in Elecosoft (Asta) Powerproject and Microsoft Project.

- The **% Complete** bar is linked to the **Activity % Complete**.

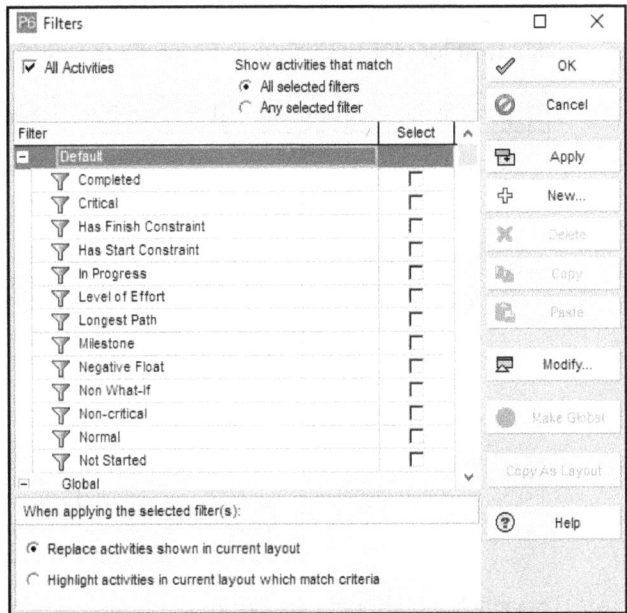

8.3.2 Formatting Bars Issues

There are a number of issues with the Primavera standard bar formatting that need to be understood so the user may display the activity bars logically:

Actual, Remaining Critical and Remaining Critical Bars

It is recommended that you use the Primavera default bar display options displaying the **Actual Work** (this bar is displayed from the **Start** date to the **Data Date**), **Remaining Work** and **Critical Remaining Work** bars (these bars are displayed from the **Data Date** to the **Finish** date with the appropriate filter). This is because the **Early** bar will not display actual progress as in other software packages. Please read the **Understanding Dates** section in the **Tracking Progress** chapter to understand how the dates are calculated that are used to draw each bar.

Total Float Bar

The Total Float Bar is called the Float Bar in the Bars form which is inconsistent terminology.

By default, a Total Float bar is displayed on a completed activity but the Float value is set to "Null" (which is displayed as a blank). It is not logical to display a float bar when there is no float value:

Activity ID	Activity Name	Start	Finish	Total Float	September 2014				October 2014				November 2014				De
					25	01	08	15	22	29	06	13	20	27	03	10	17	24	01
A1010	Activity A	29-Aug-14 08 A	30-Sep-14 17 A																
A1020	Activity B	22-Sep-14 08 A	31-Oct-14 17	5d															
A1030	Activity C	03-Nov-14 08	28-Nov-14 17	5d															

- To prevent this from happening you should edit the total **Float Bar Filter** in the **Bars** form so it is only displayed for Not Started or In Progress activities:

Display	Name	Timescale	User Start Date	User Finish Date	Filter	Preview
☑	Float Bar	Float Bar			Not Started or In Progress	▬▬▬

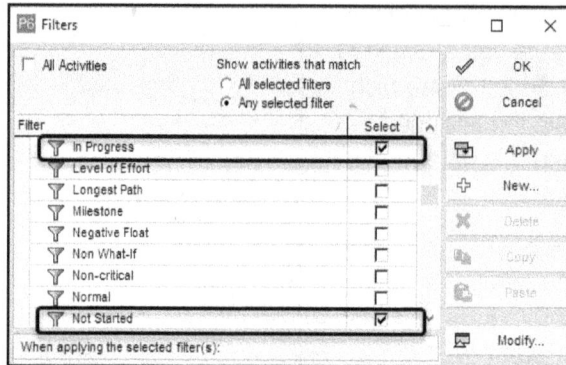

- This is what it should look like now:

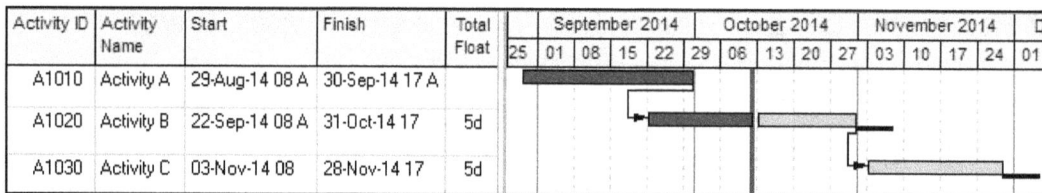

Free Float Bar

This may not be easily displayed.

A Baseline Bar is Displayed when NO Project Baseline set.

A Project Baseline Bar and Primary User Baseline Bar is displayed when a Baseline has not been assigned in the **Assign Baseline** form. The Planned Dates are displayed as the Baseline Bar. Therefore, you must ensure you have a Baseline set before displaying a Baseline Bar. The Secondary and Tertiary Baselines bars are not displayed until a baseline has been assigned.

Relationships displayed on Baseline Bars

By default, the relationships are displayed on the Baseline Bar, this is not the normal method:

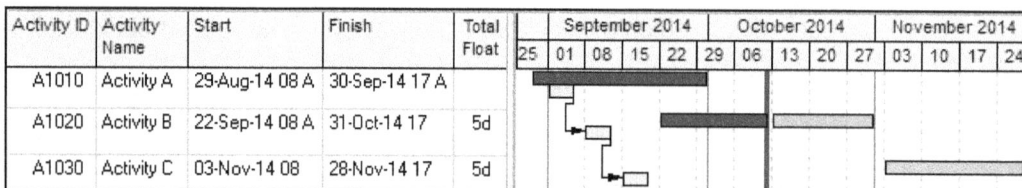

To remove relationships from the Baseline Bar and put them on the current bars, move all the Baseline Bars and Baseline Milestones to the bottom of the Bars form:

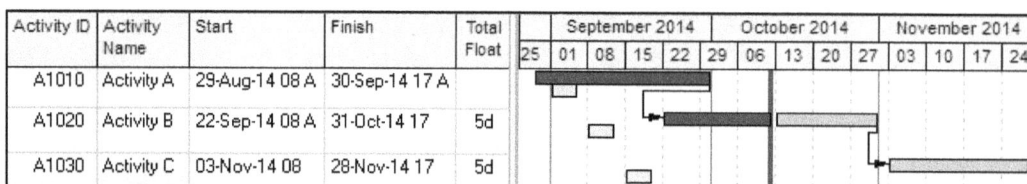

Remaining Level of Effort and Actual Level of Effort Bars

These are by default hidden and when these Activity Types are used then the activity bar will disappear. You should check both these bars so they are always displayed.

Baseline Bar Formatting

After you have moved all the baseline bars to the bottom:

- There is no **Project Baseline Milestone**; this will need to be added,

- The **Project Baseline** and **Primary Baseline** bars are both narrow yellow bars, the same as the Negative Float,

  - It is suggested you make them a different color and put them as thicker bars on the top and bottom of row 2,
  - Then change the **Baseline Milestone** colors to match,
  - Change the shape so one may be seen behind the other, and
  - Change the descriptions so they make sense,

- There are no **Secondary Baseline** or **Tertiary Baseline Milestones**. If you are not using these then delete the **Secondary Baseline** or **Tertiary Baseline** bars:

Display	Name	Timescale	User S	User F	Filter	Preview
☐	Project Baseline Bar	Project Baseline Bar			Normal	▭
☐	Project Baseline Milestone	Project Baseline Bar			Milestone	▽ ▽
☐	Primary Baseline	Primary Baseline Bar			Normal	▭
☐	Primary Baseline Milestone	Primary Baseline Bar			Milestone	△ △

Text on Bars

There is text on many bars and it is difficult to add or remove text from bars with the current configuration.

It is suggested that text be removed from all bars, except from the **Current Bar Labels** bar by:

- Clicking on the **Bar Labels** tab at the bottom,

- Clicking on one bar at a time and using the [✄ Delete] button at the bottom (NOT SIDE) of the screen to delete the text line,

- Changing the **Current Bar Labels** bar filter to read All Activities.

Now if you display the **Current Bar Labels** bar then text will be displayed on all bars and when this bar is hidden then all text will be removed from bars, thus making it simpler to add or remove bar text:

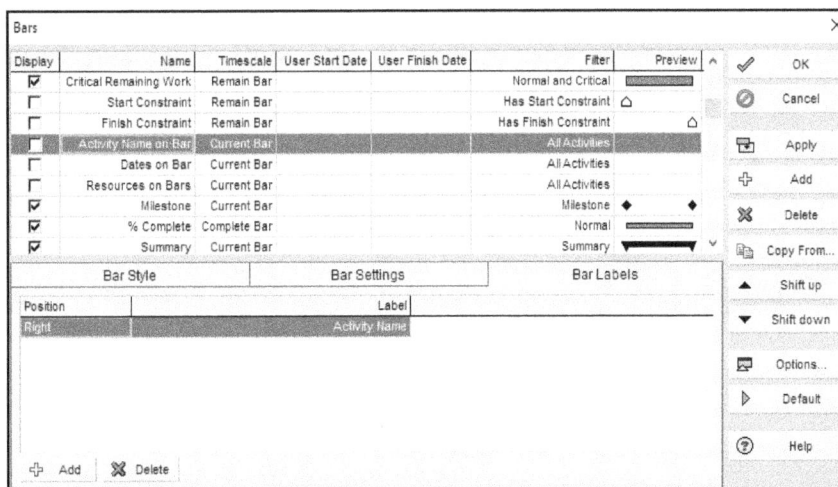

Suspend Date Display

To ensure a **Suspend** date is displayed on the bar the Activity nonwork intervals should be checked:

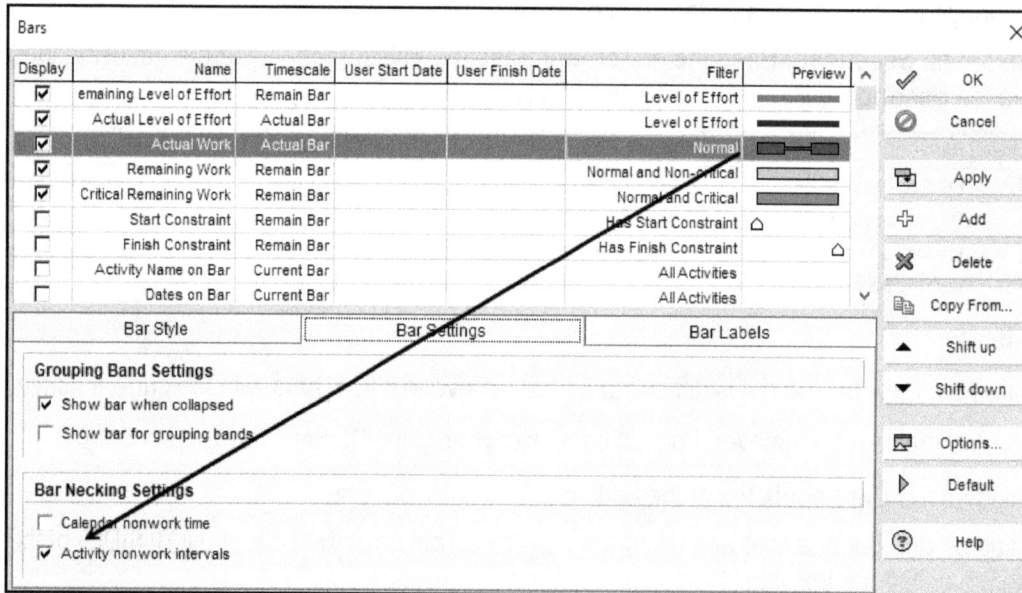

Creating a Summary Baseline Bar

The default formatting also has no bar to display a Baseline Summary bar. To create a Summary Baseline bar, you must add and format a bar as per the picture below:

Display	Name	Timescale	Filter	Preview
☐	Primary Baseline	Primary Baseline Bar	Summary	▭

Creating a Summary Bar

It is not obvious how to create a Summary Bar:

- To create a new Summary Bar you will see that you may not select **Summary** from the filter drop-down box,

- You must check the **Bar Settings** tab, **Show bar for grouping bands** to create a Summary Bar:

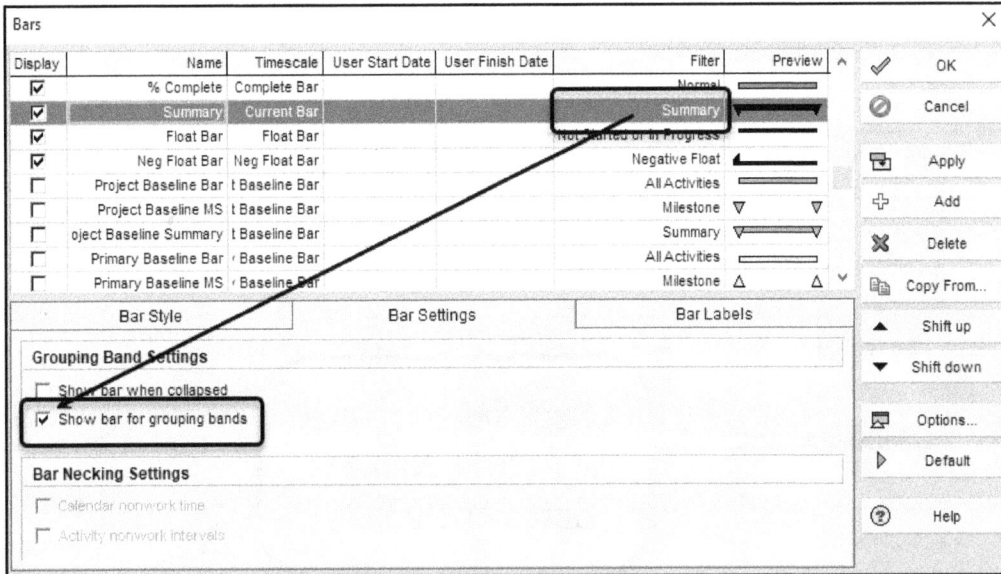

> ℹ️ At the time of writing this book the author had placed a layout on https://primavera.com.au/ under Technical Papers that has these bar formatting issues fixed. It is suggested that downloading this layout will save users a significant amount of formatting time.
>
> The formatting of any existing layout may be set to the same as another layout, such as the **www.primavera.com.au_layout, by** using the **Copy From...** function.

Baseline Bar Disappearing when an Activity is made an LOE

Often after a Baseline has been set, it is required to add more detail to a baselined activity but retain a view of the original Baseline bar. This may be achieved by converting the original Activity to an LOE and adding the detailed activities below the LOE and linking the new activities to it. If the original Baseline activity disappears the you need to open the bars form and set the filter to **All Activities** and the Baseline bar will be displayed:

---

www.primavera.com.au_Layout

This layout may be downloaded from https://primavera.com.au/ under **Software and Downloads** page, unzip it and place it on your desktop. Layouts created from later software versions may be identified from the file name.

A layout has been exported from each later version in order for new fields that have been added to database to be displayed, the version number is in the layout name.

This layout has the bars formatted as per the pictures below and resolves all the issues with the Primavera P6 defaults discussed above:

Display	Name	Timescale	Filter	Preview
☑	Remaining Level of Effort	Remain Bar	Level of Effort	▬▬▬▬
☑	Actual Level of Effort	Actual Bar	Level of Effort	▬▬▬▬
☑	Actual Work	Actual Bar	Normal	▬▭▬
☑	Remaining Work	Remain Bar	Normal and Non-critical	▭▭▭
☑	Critical Remaining Work	Remain Bar	Normal and Critical	▬▬▬
☐	Start Constraint	Remain Bar	Has Start Constraint	△
☐	Finish Constraint	Re	nstraint	△
☐	Activity Name on Bar	C		
☐	Dates on Bar	C		
☑	Milestone	C		◆ ◆
☑	% Complete	%		▭▭▭
☑	Summary	Current Bar	Summary	▬▬▬
☑	Float Bar	Float Bar	Not Started or In Progress	▬▬▬
☑	Neg Float Bar	Neg Float Bar	Negative Float	◀▬
☐	Project Baseline Bar	Project Baseline Bar	All Activities	▭▭▭
☐	Project Baseline MS	Project Baseline Bar	Milestone	▽ ▽
☐	Project Baseline Summary	Project Baseline Bar	Summary	▽▬▽
☐	Primary Baseline Bar	Primary Baseline Bar	All Activities	▭▭▭
☐	Primary Baseline MS	Primary Baseline Bar	Milestone	△ △
☐	Primary Baseline Summary	Primary Baseline Bar	Summary	△▬△
☐	Secondary Baseline Bar	Secondary Baseline Bar	All Activities	▬▬▬
☐	Secondary Baseline MS	Secondary Baseline Bar	Milestone	▼ ▼
☐	Secondary Baseline Summar	Secondary Baseline Bar	Summary	▼▬▼
☐	Tertiary Baseline Bar	Tertiary Baseline Bar	All Activities	▭▭▭
☐	Tertiary Baseline MS	Tertiary Baseline Bar	Milestone	△ △
☐	Tertiary Baseline Summary	Tertiary Baseline Bar	Summary	△▬△
☐	Late Bar	Late Bar	All Activities	◀▬▶

*Check these to place the **Activity Name** or **Dates** on the Bars*

Later version also have a resource bar added but not displayed.

⚠️ Later versions of P6 format the **Name** column to the left and the picture above is from an earlier version of P6 and shows the **Name** column formatted to the right. Administrators must check all their P6 Layouts to ensure the bars formatting is good and ensure all users are aware of the issues of using the **Bars** form **Default** button. One option is to just replace all the Oracle bar formatting with the formatting from the **www.primavera.com.au_Layout**.

8.3.3 Bar Style Tab

The appearance of each bar is edited in the lower half of the form. The bar's start, middle, and end points may have their color, shape, pattern, etc., formatted.

The bars may be placed on one of three rows numbered from 1 to 3, from top to bottom, one bar above the other. If multiple bars are placed on the same row, the bar at the top of the list will be drawn first and the ones lower down the list will be drawn over the top.

8.3.4 Bar Settings Tab

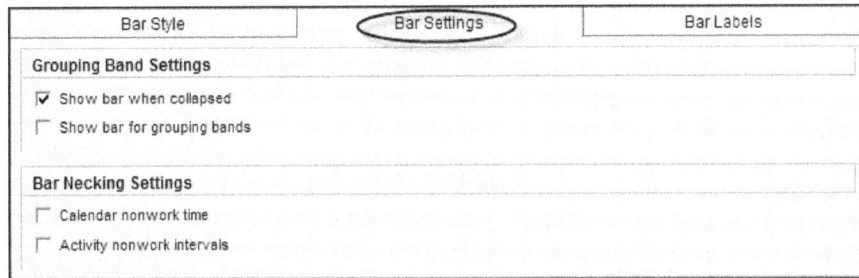

Show bar when collapsed

- **Show bar when collapsed** option displays the detailed bars on a single line when the WBS Node has been summarized; see the two pictures following:

  ➢ Before summarizing:

  ➢ After summarizing:

This is similar to the Microsoft Project **Always roll up Gantt bars** option in the **Layout** form.

Show bar for grouping bands

This shows a summarized bar all the time and converts the filter automatically to "Summary" bars only.

> **i** When formatting the **Bar Settings** for Milestones it is important to take note of the checked boxes and Filter format. If the box **Show bar for grouping bands** is checked, Milestones will appear at the ends of Summary Bars and not in line with the actual activities they belong to. The filter in this case will read **Summary** and not **Milestone**.

Bar Necking Settings

Bar Necking displays a thinner bar during times of inactivity such as weekends and holidays and applies only to the Current Bar setting column in the **Bars** form:

Un-necked bars   Necked bars

- **Calendar nonwork time** necks the bar based on the activity's calendar.
- **Activity nonwork intervals** necks the bar when Out of Sequence Progress options of Actual Dates or Retained Logic causes a break in the work. See the **Advanced Schedule Options** paragraph.

> **i** There is no Resource Bar available and Primavera will not neck on the resource calendar. When an activity is Resource Dependent and the resource is on a calendar different from the activity, then the bar may neck when the resource is working or not neck when the resource is not working.

8.3.5 Bar Labels Tab

This tab enables the placement of text with a bar above, below, to the left, and to the right. The following pictures show how the start and finish dates are formatted and displayed on the bar chart:

- Select the bar that you wish to add the label to.
- Click on the [✛ Add] and the [✖ Delete] icons at the bottom of the **Bars** form to add and delete a **Label** item.

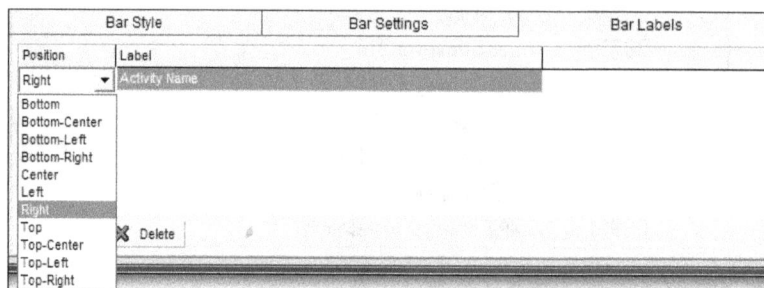

- Select the **Position** and **Label** from the drop-down boxes in the **Bar Labels** tab.

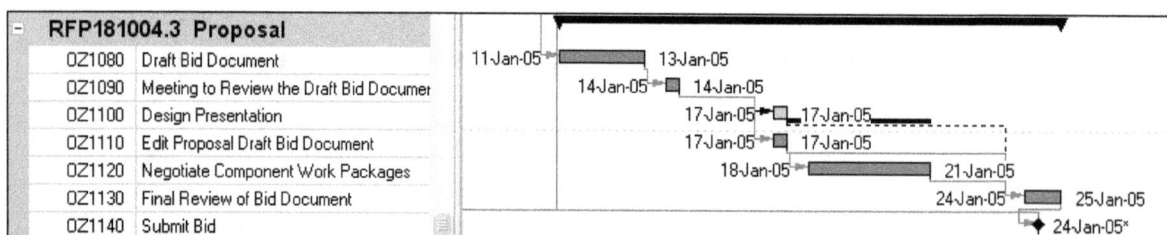

- The dates on the bar chart are adopted from the **User Preferences** and may not be formatted separately.

  ⓘ It is often useful to create a bar that only displays the text. This bar may be displayed or not displayed as required, which is much simpler than reformatting a bar to show text.

- Each **Notebook Topic** may be displayed on a bar one at a time by selecting the topic in the **Bar Labels** tab. After the box containing the label is displayed on the screen it may be adjusted in size by dragging.

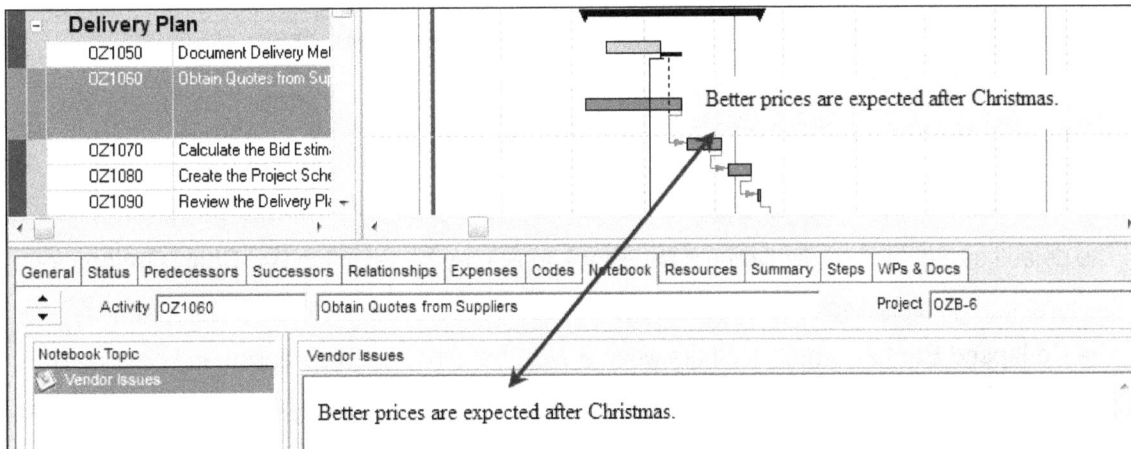

8.3.6 Bar Chart Options Form

- The **Bar Chart Options** form is displayed by:
  - ➢ Clicking on the [Options...] icon from the **Bars** form, or
  - ➢ By selecting **View, Bar,** [Options...], or
  - ➢ Right-clicking in the Gantt Chart area and selecting **Bar Chart Options...**:

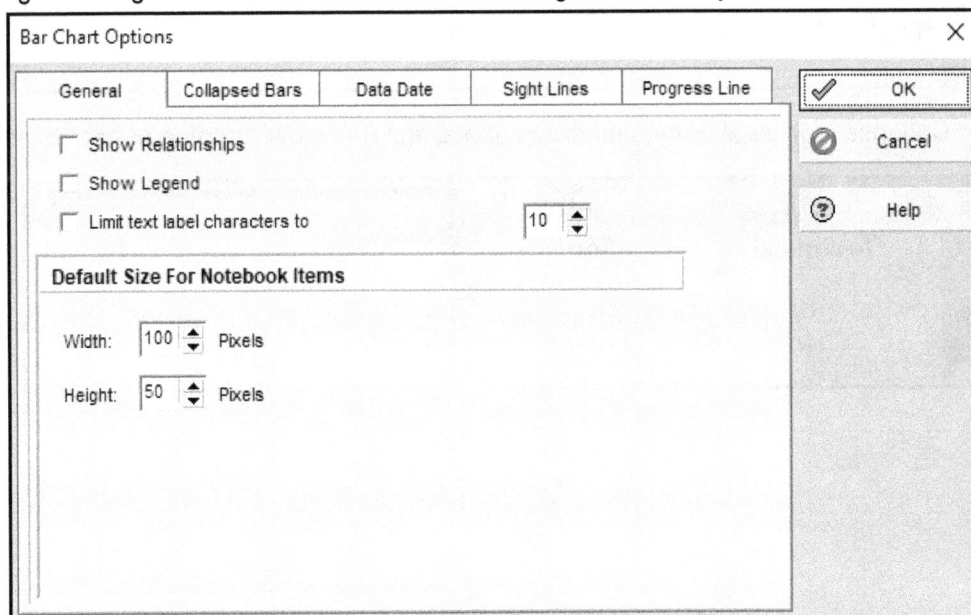

- The **General** tab has a variety of options for formatting the bar chart which are mainly self-explanatory.

  ➢ **Show Relationships** has the same result as clicking on the ⬛ icon and displays the relationships.

  ➢ **Show Legend** displays a legend on the bar chart in the Activities View; see the following picture:

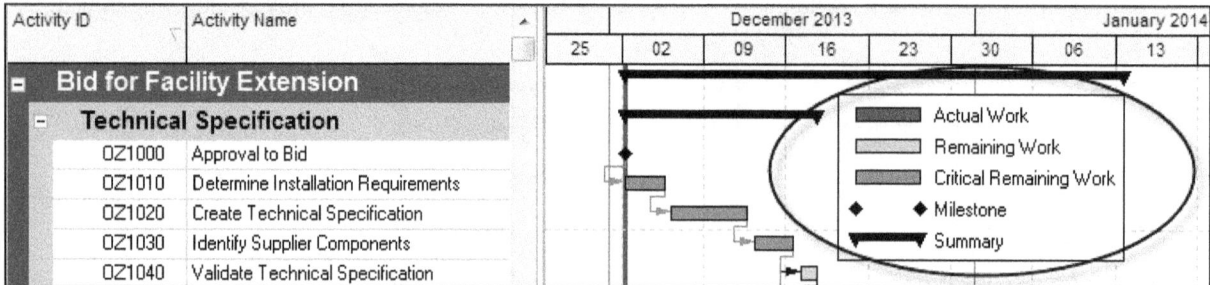

- The default size of the box displaying a **Notebook** topic may be set in the **Bar Chart Options** form, **General** tab, which is displayed by clicking on the ⬛ Options... icon from the **Bars** form.
- The **Collapsed Bar** tab formats the bars when a WBS band has been collapsed and displays a summarized bar.

  ➢ **Collapse to grouping bars**:

  ➢ **Collapse individual bars to minimize space**:

  ➢ **Collapse individual bars to minimize space** and **Allow overlapping of bar labels**:

- The **Data Date** tab formats the Data Date, its style, color and size:

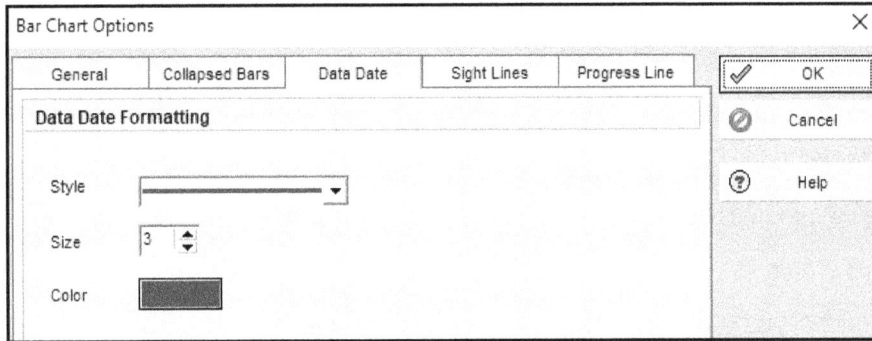

- Primavera Version 5.0 introduced the **Sight Lines** tab which enables the specification of both Major and Minor vertical and horizontal Sight Lines, which brings this functionality up to match Microsoft Project, but nowhere near the graphical functionality of Elecosoft (Asta) Powerproject.

- **Progress Line** Display on the Gantt Chart which is covered in detail in the next paragraph.

8.4   Progress Line Display on the Gantt Chart

A progress line displays how far ahead or behind activities are in relation to the Baseline. Either the Project Baseline or the Primary User Baseline may be used and there are four options:

- Difference between the Baseline Start Date and Activity Start Date,

- Difference between the Baseline Finish Date and Activity Finish Date,

- Connecting the progress points based on the Activity % Complete,

- Connecting the progress points based on the Activity Remaining Duration.

There are several main components of displaying a Progress Line in P6:

- First the progress line is formatted using the **View, Bar,** [Options...], form, **Progress Line** tab, which may also be opened by right-clicking in the Gantt Chart area:

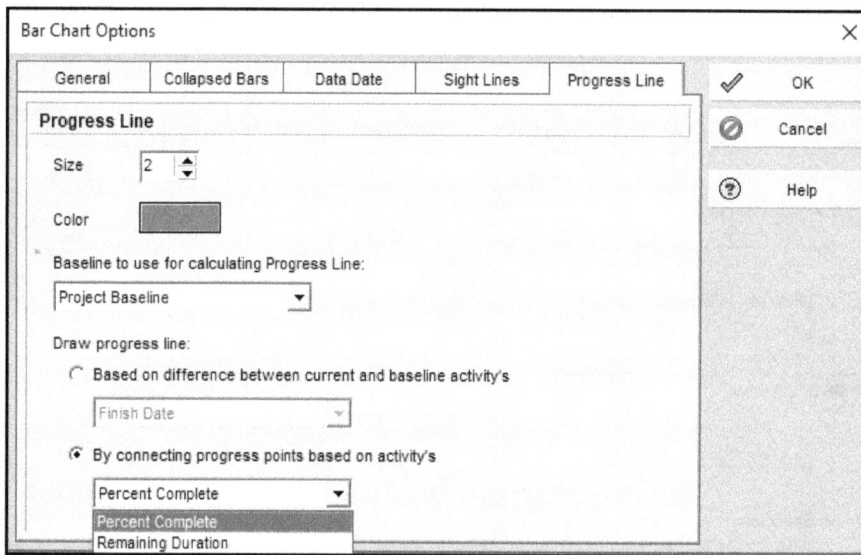

- Selecting **View, Progress Line** to hide or display the **Progress Line**.

- If you use either of the options of Percent Complete or Remaining Duration then you must display the appropriate Baseline Bar that has been selected as the **Baseline to use for calculating Progress Line:**

- The picture below shows the option highlighted above of **Percent Complete**:

8.5 Formatting Columns

8.5.1 Selecting the Columns to be Displayed

The columns are formatted through the **Columns** form which may be opened by:

- Select **View, Columns, Customize**, or

- Click on the ▥▾ icon, **Customize**, or

- Right-click in the Columns to open a menu and select **Columns**:

The columns may be sorted by **List** of **Category** and they may be added or deleted either by:

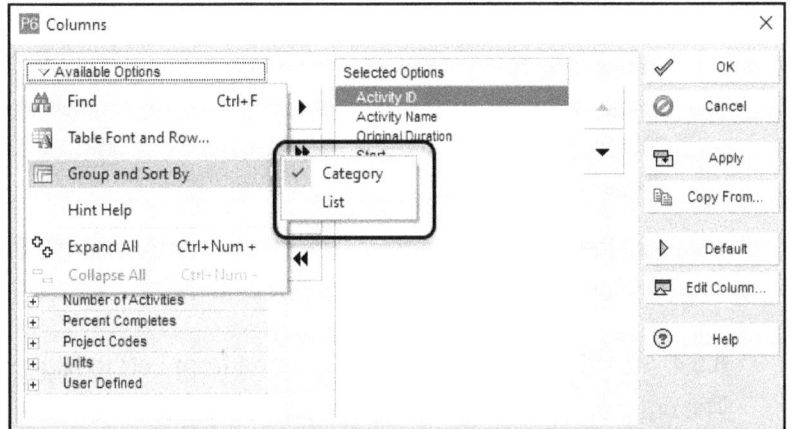

- Using the black arrows or

- By dragging the description left of right and up or down.

- When a Baseline is set then many more Baseline schedule column fields become available.

The **Column** form may be resized by dragging the edges.

- The available columns are displayed in the left window and may be listed under **Categories** or as a single **List**.

- To select how the column titles are displayed, click the **Available Options** drop-down box and then select **Group and Sort By** to choose either **List** or **Categories**, as per the picture above.

- The columns to be displayed are listed in the right **Selected Options Window** and are copied from **Available Options** to and from **Selected Options** using:

  ➢ The icons ⏪ ⏩ ▶ ◀ , or

  ➢ Dragging, or

  ➢ Double-clicking.

- The ▷ Default icon sets the columns back to the Primavera default column display.

8.5.2 Column Header Alignment

- Select **View, Columns, Customize**, or

- Click on the ▥▾ icon, **Customize**, then

- Select the ▦ Edit Column... option which opens the **Edit Column** form and enables a user definable column title to be created in the **New Title:** cell and the **Column Title Alignment** to be set to Left, Center, or Right.

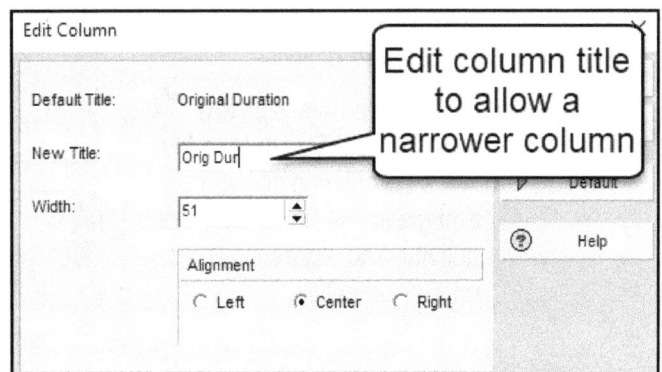

Edit column title to allow a narrower column

8.5.3 Adjusting the Width of Columns

You may adjust the width of the column in two ways:

- By dragging the column title separator: move the mouse pointer to the nearest vertical line of the column. A ↔ mouse pointer will then appear and enable the column to be adjusted by click, hold and dragging.

Activity Name		Original Duration
Install Door and Window Frames		1d
Install Exterior Doors and Windows		2d
ishes		216d

- From the **Column** form select [📷 Edit Column...] to open the **Edit Column** form and enter the width of the column in pixels.

8.5.4 Setting the Order of the Columns from Left to Right on the Screen

The order of the columns on the screen, from left to right, is the same as the order in the **Columns** form **Selected Options Window** from top to bottom. The order of the columns may be altered:

- Highlight the column in the **Columns** form **Selected Options Window** and use the [▲] and [▼] icons, or

- Click and hold the column title in a window and drag the column.

8.6 Row Height and Show Icon

Row heights may be adjusted to display text that would otherwise be truncated by a narrow column.

- The height of all rows may be formatted by selecting **View, Table Font and Row** to open the **Table, Font and Row** form. The options in this form are self-explanatory.

- The **Show Icons** option will display a different icon in front of the Activity and WBS.

  ➢ In the **Projects Window** 🖭 indicates a **What-if** project, 🗀 a **Unopened** project, and 🗁 an **Opened** project.

  ➢ In the **Activities Window** 🖿 indicates a WBS Node, a blue ▬ a complete activity, a blue and green ▬ an in-progress activity, and a green ▬ an un-started activity.

Table, Font and Row form:

Font and Color — Font: AaBbYyZz, Color: [ ]

Row Height — ☑ Keep Current Row Heights; ○ Optimize height by row content; ☑ Do not exceed [1] lines per row; ○ Select height for all rows [20]; ☐ Show Icons

OK, Cancel, Apply, Default, Help

	BA840	Rough-In Plumbing/...	1d	1d
	BA810	Set Mechanical and Electrical Equipment	15d	0d
⊟	**Exterior Finishes**		**153d**	**17d**
	BA800	Building Enclosed	0d	0d

- The height of a single row may be manually adjusted in a similar way to adjusting row heights in Excel. Click the row; the pointer will change to a double-headed arrow ↕; then drag the row with the mouse. These manually adjusted rows are not saved with a Layout.

8.7 Format Timescale

8.7.1 Moving and Rescaling the Timescale

To display hidden parts of the schedule the timescale may be grabbed and moved by placing the cursor in the top half of the Timescale. The cursor will turn into a 🖑; left-click and drag left or right.

The timescale may be rescaled, therefore increasing or decreasing the length of the bars and displaying more or less of the schedule, by placing the cursor in the bottom half of the Timescale. The cursor will turn into a 🔍 ; click, hold and drag left to make the bars shorter and right to make the bars longer.

When there are no bars in view when you are viewing a time ahead or behind the activity dates, you may double-click in the **Gantt Chart** area to bring them back into view.

8.7.2 Format Timescale Command

The **Timescale** form provides a number of options for the display of the timescale, which is located above the Bar Chart. To open the **Timescale** form:

- Click on the ▥ icon, or

- Select **View**, **Timescale**, or

- Right-click in the Bar Chart area and select **Timescale**.

The options available in the **Timescale** form are:

- **Timescale Format** has the options of:
  - ➢ Two lines, or
  - ➢ Three lines

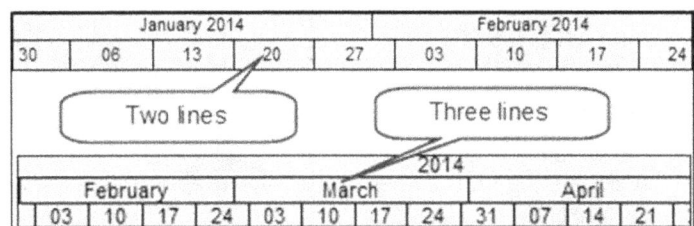

- **Font and Color**
  - ➢ The AaBbYyZz icon opens the **Edit**, **Font and Color** form which enables the timescale and column headers font and color to be changed.
  - ➢ By clicking on the Default Font icon all changes will be reversed.

Date Format

- **Type**
  - ➤ **Calendar** displays a normal calendar.
  - ➤ **Fiscal Year** displays the fiscal year in the year line. The Fiscal Year Start Month is set in the **Settings** tab of the **Project Details** form in the **Projects Window**.
  - ➤ **Week of the Year** displays the week of the year starting from "1" for the first week in January and is often termed **Manufacturing Week**.

- **Date Interval** sets the timescale and has the options in the picture to the right:
  - ➤ The **Week/Day 1** displays the days like this:

  - ➤ The **Week/Day 2** displays the days like this:

  - ➤ The **Date Interval** may also be adjusted by clicking on the ⊕ or the ⊖, which moves the timescale setting up and down the list shown above.

- **Shift Calendar** breaks the day into time intervals to suit the shift intervals when the **Day/Shift** option has been selected.

- Show Ordinal Dates displays the timescale to be counted by the unit selected in the Date Interval. This is useful for displaying a schedule when the start of the project is unknown. Ordinal dates display the timescale by counting in the selected units starting from a user definable start date. When 3 lines are displayed the ordinal dates and calendar dates may be displayed:

8.7.3 Nonwork Period Shading in Timescale

The nonwork period shading behind the bars is set by the database **Default Calendar** and is selected by:

- In the Professional Version selecting **Enterprise**, **Calendars...**and checking a calendar in the **Default Column**, and

- In the Windows Client this is set through the Web under **Administer**, **Enterprise Data**.

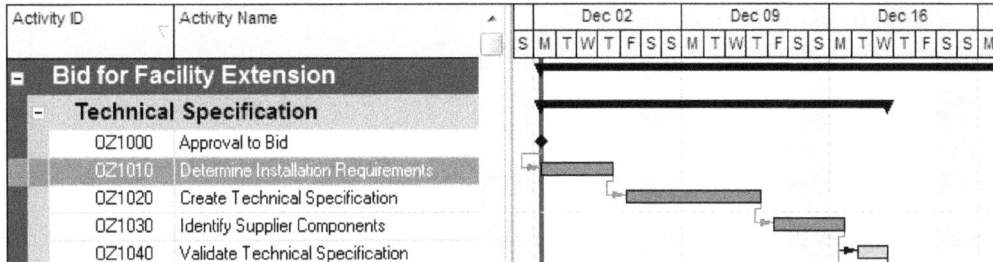

8.8 *Inserting Attachments – Text Boxes and Curtain*

8.8.1 Adding and Deleting a Text Box

A text box may be inserted in a bar chart area:

- Select the Activity which the new Text Box is to be associated with, either

  ➢ Right-click in the Bar Chart to open the menu, select **Attachments**, **Text**, Or:

  ➢ Select **View, Attachments**, **Text**, and

  ➢ The **Text Attachment** form will be displayed.

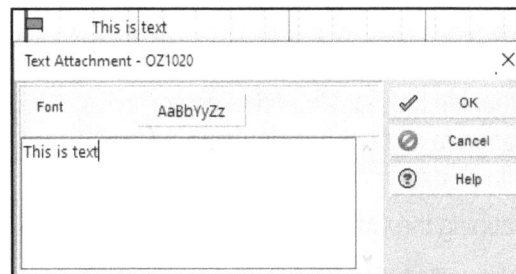

Then:

- Type in the text and format the font by clicking on the [AaBbYyZz] icon.

- A **Text Box** may be repositioned by clicking on the text and using the cursor to drag the corners and sides.

To delete a Text box, position the cursor over the text box until it transforms into a **✛** then click and you may now hit the **Delete** key.

8.8.2 Adding and Deleting a Curtain

Primavera Version 5.0 introduced a function allowing the placing of multiple curtains on the Gantt Chart which may be all hidden or displayed. A **Curtain**, used to highlight periods of time over part of the bar chart.

Select **View, Attachments** to display the **Curtain** menu or right-click a bar and select **Attachments, Curtain**:

- **Add Curtain** opens the **Curtain Attachment** form used to create a curtain,

- **Show All** shows all the curtains,

- **Hide All** hides all the curtains, and

- Double Clicking on a curtain in the Gantt Chart also opens the **Curtain Attachment** form where individual curtains may be deleted or hidden.

- Using the **Start Date** and **Finish Date** boxes, or

- Grabbing the left or right edge of the Curtain in the Bar Chart (the cursor will change to a ✧↔) and dragging the start or finish date, or

- Grabbing the Curtain in the center (the cursor will change to a ✧) and dragging the whole Curtain.

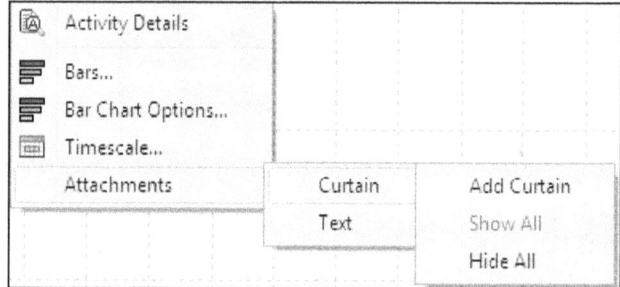

A curtain is deleted by double clicking on the curtain to open the **Curtain Attachment** form and clicking on the ☒ Delete button.

8.9 Format Fonts and Font Colors

The format font options are:

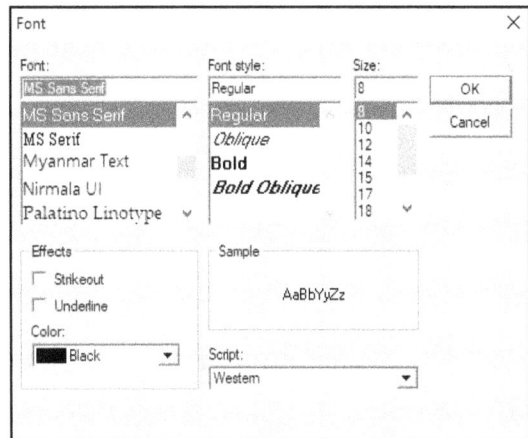

- The **Activity Data** fonts are formatted in the **Table, Font and Row** form (displayed in the paragraph above) by selecting **View, Table Font and Row**.

  - Clicking on [AaBbYyZz], the **Font** icon will open the font form where normal Windows functions are available.

  - Clicking on the **Color** icon will enable the selection of a color for the text.

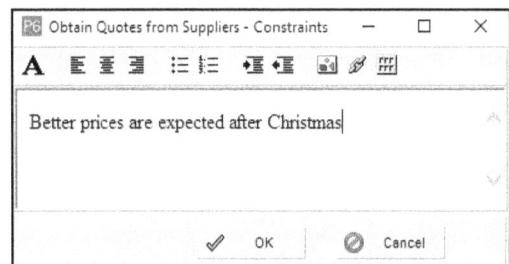

- The **Notebook Topics** may be formatted using the formatting features above where the Notebook items are entered in the lower pane.

- Some forms may have the fonts for displaying data edited when there is a menu on the top left side with the **Table Font and Row** menu item.

- The text in a **Text Box** that has been inserted onto the Bar Chart may be formatted when the box is created.

8.10 Format Colors

These are the main options for formatting colors:

- **Band** colors in layouts are formatted in the **Group and Sort** form by clicking on the [icon] icon or selecting **View, Group and Sort by**.

- **Text** colors are covered in the **Format Font and Colors** paragraph.

- **Bar Colors** are covered in the **Formatting the Bars** paragraph.

- **Timescale** and **Column Headers** are covered in the **Format Timescale Command** paragraph.

- **Sight Lines (Gridline)** colors may not be formatted.

- The **Progress Line** color is selected in the **Bar Chart Options** form, **Progress Line** tab.

- The **Data Date** is formatted in the **Bar Options** form, **Data Date** tab.

- The **Relationship Lines**, also known as **Dependencies**, **Logic**, or **Links**, may not be formatted and are displayed with the following characteristics:

  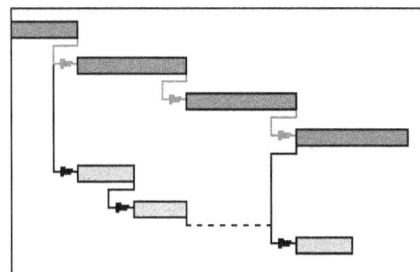

  - Solid Red for Critical,

  - Solid Black for Driving,

  - Dotted Black for Non-driving, and

  - Blue when selected and may be deleted.

8.11 Line Numbers

Select **View**, **Line** Number to display or hide the Line Number.

#	Activity ID	Activity Name
1	EC00515	City Center Office Building Addition
2	EC00515.D&E	Design and Engineering
3	EC1000	Design Building Addition
4	EC1010	Start Office Building Addition Project
5	EC1030	Review and Approve Designs
6	EC1050	Assemble Technical Data for Heat Pump
7	EC1160	Review Technical Data on Heat Pumps
8	EC00515.Found	Foundation
9	EC1090	Begin Building Construction
10	EC1100	Site Preparation
11	EC1230	Excavation
12	EC1320	Install Underground Water Lines
13	EC1330	Install Underground Electric Conduit
14	EC1340	Form/Pour Concrete Footings
15	EC1350	Concrete Foundation Walls
16	EC1360	Form and Pour Slab

i This is a very useful feature for reviewing a schedule to ensure that everyone in a meeting is looking at the same activity.

But as in Microsoft Project and Elecosoft (Asta) Powerproject this is an activity order and the number will change if the schedule is reordered.

8.12 *Workshop 6 – Formatting the Bar Chart*

Background

Management has received your draft report and requests that some changes be made to the presentation.

Assignment

Format your schedule as follows, but depending on the default settings, your Gantt Chart View may differ from that shown, e.g., there may be no summary bars:

1. You will not have to complete the Step 2 of this workshop if you have internet access and are able to download a **www.primavera.com.au_Layout.plf** layout from https://primavera.com.au/. There are layouts for later P6 Versions which are identified by the software version in the file name.

    *   If you have downloaded and applied a **www.primavera.com.au_Layout.plf** move to Step 3, DO NOT COMPLETE Step 2.

    *   If you have NOT downloaded and applied a **www.primavera.com.au_Layout.plf** complete Step 2.

2. Format Bars, only if you are unable to download a **www.primavera.com.au_Layout.plf** layout then:

    *   To format the bars, open the **Bars** form,

    *   Click on the ▷ Default button to set the bars to the Primavera default settings,

    *   Edit the **Float Bar** Filter (**Total Float** bar) so it only shows float for Not Started or In Progress activities. Ensure you select the **Any selected filter** in the **Filters** form:

Display	Name	Timescale	User Start Date	User Finish Date	Filter	Preview
☑	Float Bar	Float Bar			Not Started or In Progress	▬▬▬▬

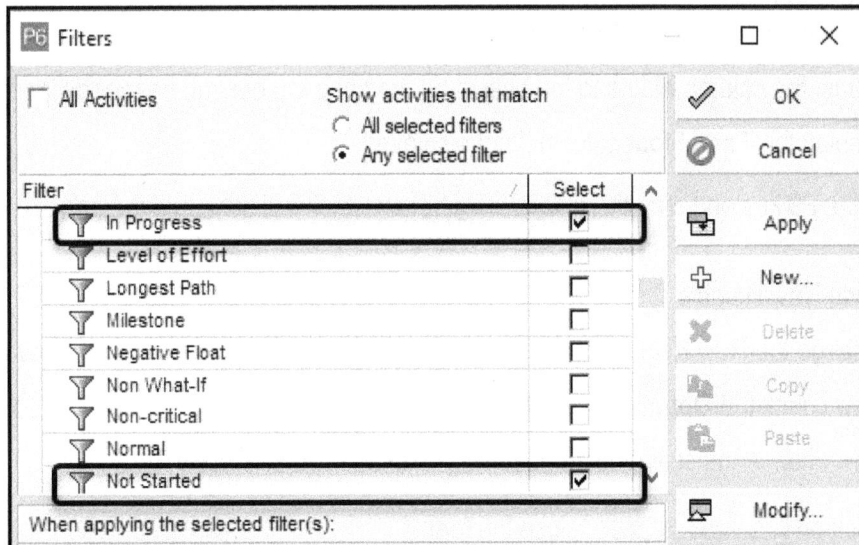

    *   Delete the **Secondary Baseline** & **Tertiary Baseline** bars,

---

- Move the Baseline bars and Baseline Milestones to the bottom of the Bars form to remove relationships on the Baseline bars,
- Add missing Project Baseline Milestone and format the Baseline bars as per the picture below, making them different colors:

Display	Name	Timescale	User S	User F	Filter	Preview
☐	Project Baseline Bar	Project Baseline Bar			Normal	▭
☐	Project Baseline Milestone	Project Baseline Bar			Milestone	▽ ▽
☐	Primary Baseline	Primary Baseline Bar			Normal	▭
☐	Primary Baseline Milestone	Primary Baseline Bar			Milestone	△ △

- Remove all text from all bars, except from the **Current Bar Labels** bar, by:
  - ➤ Clicking on the **Bar Labels** tab at the bottom,
  - ➤ Clicking on one bar at a time and using the [✄ Delete] button at the bottom (NOT SIDE) of the screen to delete the text line,
  - ➤ Change the **Current Bar Labels** bar filter to read All Activities and do not display.

3. Display the following bars:

- Remaining Level of Effort
- Actual Level of Effort
- Actual Work
- Remaining Work
- Remaining Critical Work
- Milestones
- % Complete
- Summary Bar
- Float Bar (Total Float)
- Negative Float Bar

4. Adding Columns:

- Add **Calendar** and **Activity Type** columns, from the **General** section of the **Columns** form, to the right of the Activity Name column.
- Adjust the column widths to the best fit by dragging the column header divider lines.
- Display the **Total Float** column if not displayed.

5. Press the **F9** key and click the [▷ Schedule] button which will schedule the project and calculate the float.

6. Adjusting Row Heights:

- Change the Row Height to 30 points by selecting **View, Table Font and Row** and apply,
- Now check the **Optimize height by row content** box, not exceeding 1 line per row and apply,
- Now change the setting to 18 point height for all rows and apply.
- Click on [✓ OK] to close the form.

7. Format Timescale to Year and Month, then Week and Day (two options), then Month and Week by using the [⊕ ⊖] buttons.

8. Format the Vertical lines with a solid Major line every month and a Minor line every week by selecting **View**, **Bars** and clicking on the [🖳 Options...] button and selecting the **Sight Lines** tab, or right-clicking in the Gantt Chart area and selecting **Bar Chart Options...** and selecting the **Sight Lines** tab.

9. Expand and contract the timescale and adjust it so that all the bars are visible.

10. See below for the expected results:

Activity ID	Activity Name	Calendar	Activity Type	Original Duration	Start	Finish	Total Float
— **Technical Specification**		OzBuild 5d/w		5d	09-Dec-24 08	13-Dec-24 16	3d
OZ1000	Approval to Bid	OzBuild 5d/w	Start Milestone	0d	09-Dec-24 08		8d
OZ1010	Determine Installation Requirements	OzBuild 5d/w	Task Dependent	4d	09-Dec-24 08	12-Dec-24 16	4d
OZ1020	Create Technical Specification	OzBuild 5d/w	Task Dependent	5d	09-Dec-24 08	13-Dec-24 16	3d
OZ1030	Identify Supplier Components	OzBuild 5d/w	Task Dependent	2d	09-Dec-24 08	10-Dec-24 16	6d
OZ1040	Validate Technical Specification	OzBuild 5d/w	Task Dependent	2d	09-Dec-24 08	10-Dec-24 16	6d
— **Delivery Plan**				8d	09-Dec-24 08	18-Dec-24 16	0d
OZ1050	Document Delivery Methodology	OzBuild 5d/w	Task Dependent	4d	09-Dec-24 08	12-Dec-24 16	4d
OZ1060	Obtain Quotes from Suppliers	OzBuild 5d/w	Task Dependent	8d	09-Dec-24 08	18-Dec-24 16	0d
OZ1070	Calculate the Bid Estimate	OzBuild 6d/w	Task Dependent	3d	09-Dec-24 08	11-Dec-24 16	6d
OZ1080	Create the Project Schedule	OzBuild 6d/w	Task Dependent	3d	09-Dec-24 08	11-Dec-24 16	6d
OZ1090	Review the Delivery Plan	OzBuild 5d/w	Task Dependent	1d	09-Dec-24 08	09-Dec-24 16	7d
— **Bid Document**		OzBuild 5d/w		6d	09-Dec-24 08	16-Dec-24 16	2d
OZ1100	Create Draft of Bid Document	OzBuild 5d/w	Task Dependent	6d	09-Dec-24 08	16-Dec-24 16	2d
OZ1110	Review Bid Document	OzBuild 5d/w	Task Dependent	4d	09-Dec-24 08	12-Dec-24 16	4d
OZ1120	Finalise and Submit Bid Document	OzBuild 5d/w	Task Dependent	2d	09-Dec-24 08	10-Dec-24 16	6d
OZ1130	Bid Document Submitted	OzBuild 5d/w	Finish Milestone	0d		09-Dec-24 08	8d

11. Check the following:

- Click on Activity ID to make sure they are ordered correctly,

- The dates and times of all activities should start and finish at the same time of the day,

- Activity OZ1060 bar should be colored red as it is the Critical activity representing the shortest duration that the project may be completed,

- All other activities should have Float.

9   ADDING RELATIONSHIPS

The next phase of a schedule is to add logic to the activities. There are two types of logic:

- **Relationships** (**Dependencies** or **Logic** or **Links** between activities), and
- Imposed **Constraints** to activity start or finish dates. These are covered in the **Constraints** chapter.

The Primavera Help file and other texts use the terms **Relationships** and **Logic** for **Relationships** but do not use the terms **Dependencies** or **Links**.

We will look at the following techniques in this chapter:

Topic	Notes for creating a SF Relationship
• Graphically in the Bar Chart.	Drag the ↳ mouse pointer from one activity to another to create a dependency.
• By opening the **Activity Details** form.	Predecessor and Successors may be added and deleted from the **Relationships**, **Predecessor** or **Successor** tabs.
• By editing or deleting a dependency using the **Edit Relationship** form.	Double-click an activity link in the **Bar Chart** or **Activity Network** View.
• Opening the **Assign Predecessor** form or the **Assign Successor** form from the menu.	• Select **E**dit, **Ass**ign, **P**redecessors..., or • Select **E**dit, **Ass**ign, **S**uccessors....
• By displaying the **Predecessor** and/or **Successor** columns.	Double-clicking in the Predecessor or Successor cells will open the **Assign Predecessor** form or the **Assign Successor** form.
• Chain Linking or Automatically Linking activities with a Finish-to-Start relationship.	Select the activities in the order they are to be linked using the **Ctrl** key, right-click and select **Link Activities**.

Relationships

There are two types of dependencies that are discussed in scheduling:

- **Hard Logic**, also referred to as **Mandatory** or **Primary Logic**, are dependencies that may not be avoided: for example, a footing excavation has to be prepared before concrete may be poured into it.
- **Soft Logic**, also referred to as **Sequencing Logic**, **Discretionary Logic**, **Preferred Logic**, or **Secondary Logic**, may be changed at a later date to reflect planning changes: for example, determining in which order the footing holes may be dug.

There is no simple method of documenting in Version 19 and earlier which is hard logic and which is soft logic as notes may not be attached to relationships. Version 20 has a new function title **Relationship Comments** that solves this issue.

A schedule with a large amount of soft logic has the potential of becoming very difficult to maintain when the plan is changed. As a project progresses, soft logic converts to hard logic due to commitments and commencing activities.

Microsoft Project allows one relationship between two activities, P6 four relationships between two activities and Elecosoft (Asta) Powerproject an unlimited number plus partial Critical Path calculation.

The AACE RP 24R-03 Developing Activity Logic is applicable to this chapter.

9.1 Understanding Logic

The next phase of a schedule is to add logic, there are two types of logic:

- Imposed Constraints that operate on activity start or finish dates. These will be covered in the Constraints module, and

- Relationships (Dependencies or Logic or Links) between activities, which we will cover now,

There are two types of Relationships that are discussed in Project Management books:

- **Hard Logic**, also referred to as **Mandatory** or **Primary Logic**, are dependencies that may not be avoided,

- **Soft Logic**, also referred to as **Sequencing Logic**, **Discretionary Logic**, **Preferred Logic**, or **Secondary Logic**, these may often be changed at a later date to reflect planning changes,

9.2 Understanding Relationships

There are four types of dependencies available in Primavera P6:

- Finish-to-Start (**FS**) (also known as conventional)
- Start-to-Start (**SS**)
- Start-to-Finish (**SF**)
- Finish-to-Finish (**FF**)

Two other terms you must understand are:

- **Predecessor**, an activity that controls the start or finish of another immediate subsequent activity.

- **Successor**, an activity where the start or finish depends on the start or finish of another immediately preceding activity.

The following pictures show how the dependencies appear graphically in the **Bar Chart** and **Activity Network** (also known as PERT, Network Diagram and Relationship Diagram Views):

The **FS** (or conventional) dependency looks like this:

The **FS** (or conventional) dependency looks like this:

A1000	A1010
Predecessor Activity	**Successor Activity**

While the **SS** dependency is like this:

A1020	A1030
Predecessor Activity	**Successor Activity**

The **SF** dependency looks like:

A1040	A1050
Predecessor Activity	- Successor Activity

The **FF** dependency would be:

A1060	A1070
Predecessor Activity	**Successor Activity**

9.3 Understanding Lags and Leads

A **Lag** is a duration that is applied to a dependency to make the successor start or finish earlier or later.

- A successor activity will start later when a positive **Lag** is assigned. Therefore, an activity requiring a 3-day delay between the finish of one activity and start of another will require a positive lag of 3 days.

- Conversely, a lag may be negative when a new activity may be started before the predecessor activity is finished. This is called a **Lead** or **Negative Lag**.

- **Leads** and **Lags** may be applied to any relationship type.

- Unlike Powerproject or Microsoft Project **Leads** and **Lags** MAY NOT be assigned a **% Lag** thus you should not complete a Monte Carlo Simulation with a P6 program when it has Leads or Lags.

An example of a **FS** with positive lag:

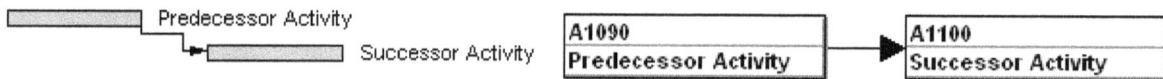

An example of a **FS** with negative lag:

Here are some important points to understand about Lags:

- The lag duration is calculated on the lag as in Microsoft Project and other Primavera products. A lag is not assigned to one or both of the Predecessor and Successor activities as in Elecosoft (Asta) Powerproject.

- Lags may be assigned one of four calendars from the **Calendar for Scheduling Relationship lag** drop-down box in the **General Schedule Options** form. This form is opened by selecting **Tools**, **Schedule...** and clicking on the [Options...] tab. The four Lag Calendar options are:

  - ➤ Predecessor Activity Calendar,
  - ➤ Successor Activity Calendar,
  - ➤ 24-Hour Calendar, and
  - ➤ Project Default Calendar.

i Microsoft Project 2003 and later use the Successor Calendar or may have an Elapsed Duration Lag. Earlier versions of Microsoft Project used the Project Calendar. Powerproject assigns the lag to either or both the predecessor or successor thus allowing either the Predecessor or Successor Calendar to be selected for each relationship.

⚠ You must be careful when using a lag to allow for delays such as curing concrete when the Lag Calendar is not a seven-day calendar. Because this type of activity lapses nonwork days, the activity could finish before Primavera calculated finish date.

You must be extremely careful when opening multiple projects when the Lag Calendar option is different for each project. see para17.5.3 and 25.3.2 for details about the **Project, Set Default Project** and the **Tools, Schedule, Options, Use scheduling options from** option.

The picture below shows various options for the assignment of leads and lags:

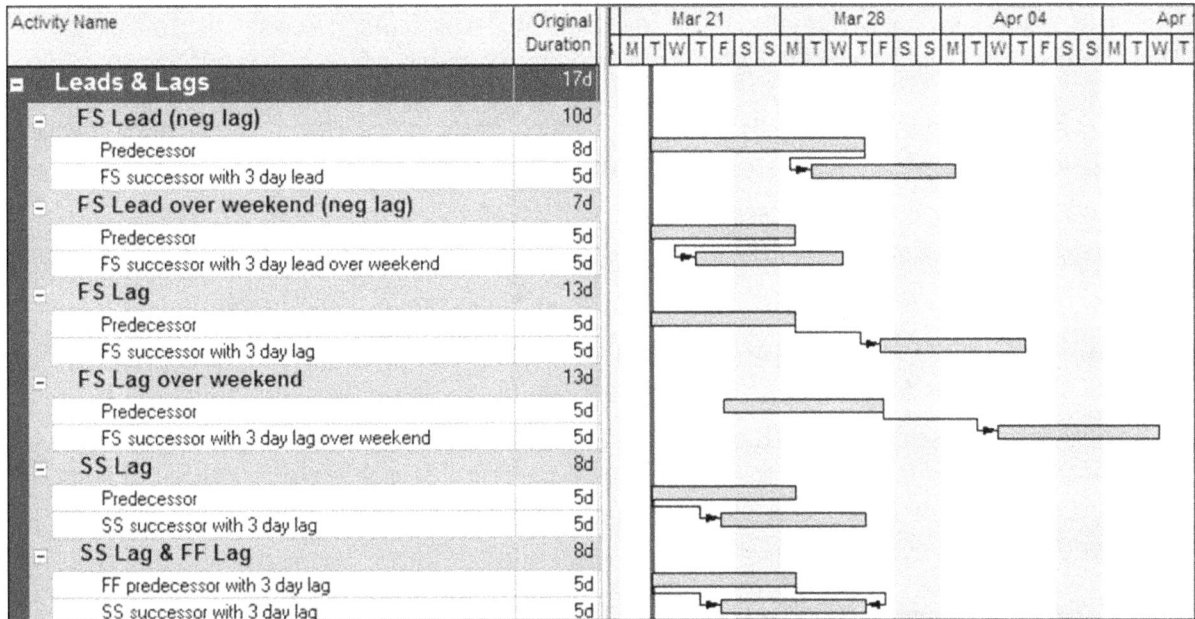

When the activity calendar changes from one activity to another then the elapsed duration of the lag may change, see the two examples below:

- The in both pictures below is 5 days or 40 hours:
- **Predecessor Activity Calendar**, which is the default, or

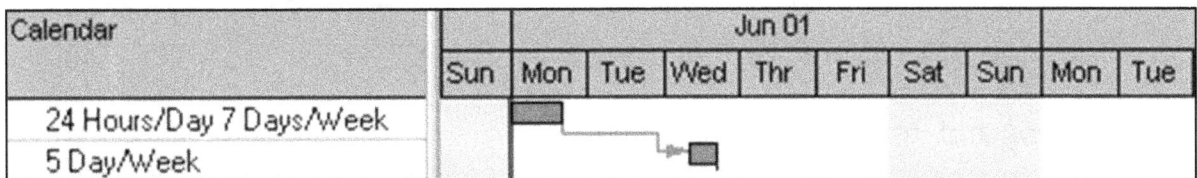

- **Successor Activity Calendar**, or

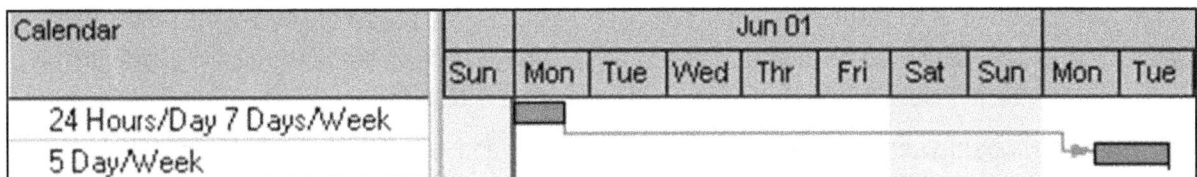

It is recommended that you do not change calendars between activities with lags.

© **Hyde Park Solutions Limited**   129

9.4   Formatting the Relationships

Relationships lines may not be formatted like in SureTrak, or Elecosoft (Asta) Powerproject but unlike Microsoft Project they do not adopt the color of the predecessor activity which is often misleading.

- The relationships may be displayed or hidden by clicking the **Activity** toolbar icon or by checking and un-checking the box in the **Bar Chart Options** form, **General** tab.
- The color of the relationship represents:
  - ➢ Red - Critical and therefore a Driving relationship,
  - ➢ Solid Black - Non-Critical Driving relationship and therefore has Total Float,
  - ➢ Dotted Black - Non-Critical Non-Driving relationship and has Free Float, and
  - ➢ Blue - a selected relationship and may be deleted.
- A relationship is displayed on the **Baseline** bar, as discussed in paragraph 8.3, when the Baseline bar is above the Actual and Remaining bars in the **Bars** form. To place the relationships onto the Early bar, which is more logical, you should move the Baseline bars in the **Bars** form to below the Actual and Remaining bars in the **Bars** form.

Relationships on the Baseline Bar   Relationships on the Current Bar

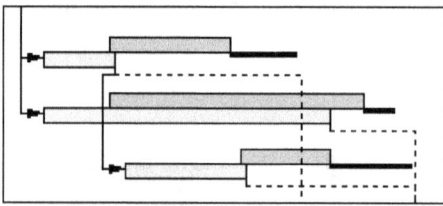

9.5   Adding and Removing Relationships

9.5.1   Graphically Adding and Deleting a Relationship

To add a FS, SS, FF or SF relationship, move the mouse pointer to appropriate end of the predecessor activity bar, which will change the mouse arrow to a ⮮, then hold down the left mouse key, drag to the appropriate end of the successor activity and release the mouse button.

The **Edit Relationship** form may be opened to edit, delete or add lag after a link has been added,

- Select a relationship line by clicking and it will turn to blue and an arrow ↑ will appear, then
- Double-click to open the **Edit Relationship** form:

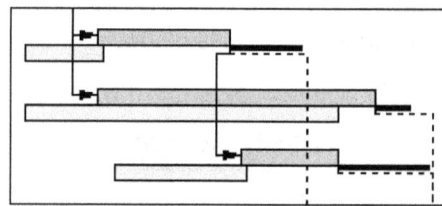

- Click on [❌ Delete] to delete a relationship.

9.5.2 Graphically Deleting a Relationship

Select a relationship and when it turns blue strike the **Delete** key to delete it and select ⬚ Yes .

Another relationship may turn blue and if you wish to delete this relationship then you may strike the **Delete** key again and select ⬚ Yes .

Multiple relationships may be deleted by striking the **Delete** key and select ⬚ Yes multiple times. Once the last relationship has been deleted then you will start deleting activities, so be careful!

9.5.3 Adding and Deleting Relationships with the Activity Details Form

The **Activity Details** form in the lower pane may be used for adding and deleting relationships.

Opening the Form

- Select either the **Predecessor,** or **Successor** or the **Relationship** tab (they all operate in a similar way). The **Successor** tab is displayed in the following picture:

Editing the Form

- The **Predecessor** and **Successor** tabs may both be formatted and the columns you require may be displayed:
  - ➤ Right-click in the **Predecessor** or **Successor** tab, and
  - ➤ Select ⬚ Customize Successor Columns… to open the **Predecessor** or **Successor Columns** form.
  - ➤ The following picture displays the fields that are available:

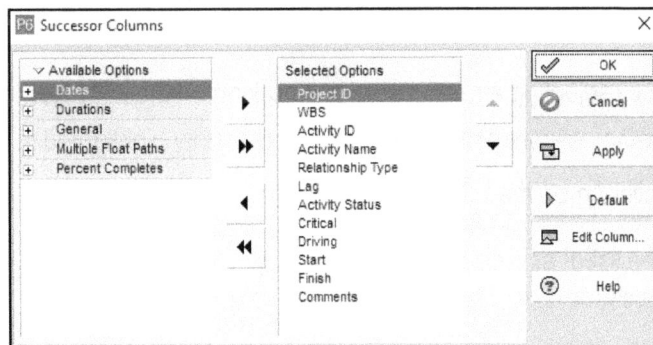

  - ➤ The data fields you require are added, deleted, and reordered using the arrows.
  - ➤ The title may also be edited using the **Edit Column Titles** form by clicking on the ⬚ Edit Column… icon.

Adding a Relationship

- To **Add** a predecessor or successor:

  - ➤ Click on the 🔲 icon **Assign Predecessor** in the **Assign Predecessor** form, or 🔲 icon **Assign Successor** in the **Assign Successor** form, or

  - ➤ Format the form as required by clicking on the [∨ Display: All Activities] icon,

  - ➤ Then select the relationship from the list:

  - ➤ You may use the **Search** function and type in the first characters of either the Activity ID or the Description to narrow down your search.

  - ➤ Double-click the Activity or click the 🔲 icon to assign the predecessor or successor.

- Enter the Relationship Type from the **Relationship Type** drop-down list and the lag, if required, from the **Lag** drop-down list.

- To enter another relationship, click the next activity line. The **Assign Predecessor** or **Successor** form will remain open.

- **Delete** a relationship by selecting a relationship and clicking on the 🔲 **Remove** icon.

- It is possible to follow the network path by jumping to an activity highlighted in the **Predecessor** or **Successor** form by clicking on the [▪⁺ GoTo] icon.

- Move up and down the list of activities by clicking on the [▲ ▼] icons in the top left side of the **Predecessor** or **Successor** tabs. This icon exists in every lower pane tab.

9.5.4   Adding and Deleting Relationships Using Columns

To assign relationships using columns:

- Display the Predecessor and/or Successor columns,

- Double-click in the Predecessor or Successor column of an activity to open the **Assign Predecessor** or **Successor** form, and

- Proceed as above.

9.5.5   Chain Linking

Activities may also be linked by selecting two or more activities using the Ctrl key in the order you wish them to be linked, right-click and select **Link Activities:**

- This option will only create Finish-to-Start relationships.
- This option does not enable the user to Chain Unlink.

9.5.6   Using the Assign Toolbar Icons to Assign Relationships

The **Assign Predecessors** icon 🖹 may be used to open the **Assign Predecessors** form and the **Assign Successors** icon 🖹 may be used to open the **Assign Successors** form.

9.6   Dissolving Activities and Retain Lag

When an activity is deleted then a chain of logical activities is broken. The **Edit**, **Dissolve** command and the right-click **Dissolve** command will delete an activity and links the predecessors and successors with a Finish-to-Start relationship.

P6 Version 19 introduced the ability to retain lag when dissolving activities. When **Retain Lag** is selected from the **User Preferences**, **Calculations** tab, the dissolved activities predecessor and successor lags will be added together to calculate the lag in the new relationship:

- Before Dissolving Activity 2:

- After Dissolving Activity 2 in P6 Version 19 without **Retain Lag** checked or in earlier versions of P6:

- After Dissolving Activity 2 in P6 Version 19 with **Retain Lag** checked:

Activity Name	Orig Dur	Predecessor Details	Mar 31 T W T F S S	Apr 07 M T W T F S S	Apr 14 M T W T F S S	Apr 21 M T W T F S S	Apr 28 M T W T F S S	May 05 M T W T F
Activity 1	5d							
Activity 3	5d	A1000: FS 10d						

NOTE: The predecessor and successor lag are added together.

9.7   Circular Relationships

A **Circular Relationship** is created when a loop is created in the logic. When you reschedule you will be presented with the **Circular Relationships** form, which identifies the loop. If a loop is detected when scheduling a project, the **Circular Loop** form is displayed identifying any loops:

To remove a circular relationship either select the first activity in the list and remove the offending predecessor, which is the last Activity in the list, or go to the last activity in the list and remove the offending successor, which is the first activity in the list.

If you have not made your **Schedule Options**, **When scheduling progressed activities use**: setting **Retained Logic** and an activity in a loop is complete then this function will not operate.

9.8 Scheduling the Project

After you have your activities and the logic in place, Primavera calculates the activities' dates/times. More specifically, Primavera **Schedules** the project to calculate the **Early Dates**, **Late Dates**, **Free Float** and the **Total Float**. This will enable you to review the **Critical Path** of the project. (Microsoft Project uses the term **Slack** instead of the term **Float**.) To schedule a project:

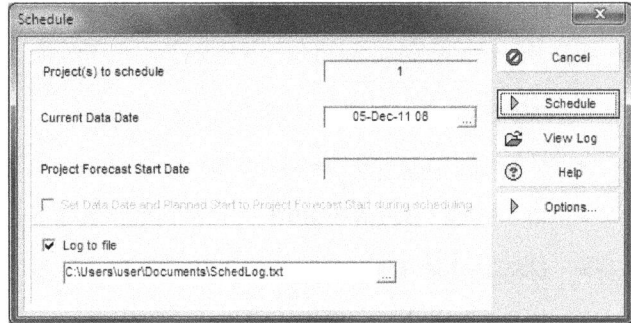

- Select **Tools**, **Schedule...**, or

- Strike the **F9** key to open the **Schedule** form:

- Check the **Current Data Date**, which before a schedule is progressed should be the start date of the project.

- Version 20 added an additional option:

  ➢ All **Projects use their own data dates** which is how Version 19 and earlier versions calculated, or

  ➢ **Apply selected data date to all open projects** for Version 20 and later and all projects will have their **Data Date** permanently changed to the selected date.

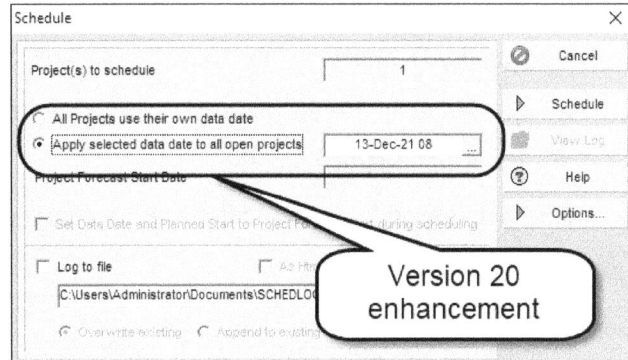

- Click on the ▷ Schedule icon.

i   Ensure the "Log to file" check box is checked to display the scheduling log report. After scheduling a project, reopen the scheduling form and click the "View Log" to review the log report.

To turn on automatic calculation, select **Tools**, **Schedule...**, ▷ Options... icon. Select **Schedule automatically when a change affects dates**.

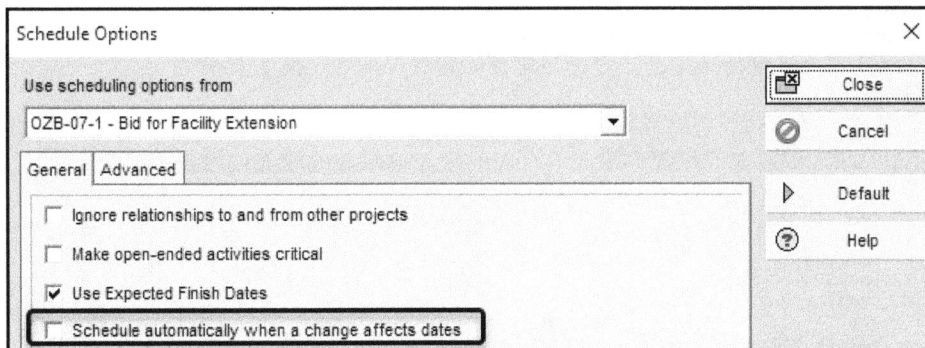

Sometimes it is preferable to have the software recalculate the schedule each time an edit is made to an activity which affects any activity dates. Often the response time with large schedules running on remote servers through Citrix or Terminal Server respond slowly and this option is best schedule left unchecked.

The default calculation setting for Microsoft Project Automatic Calculation, in Elecosoft (Asta) Powerproject it is dependent on your template and manual Primavera P6.

9.9 Reviewing Relationships, Leads and Lags

Relationships may be viewed in the following methods:

- Relationships **WITHOUT** lags may be viewed by:
  - ➤ By displaying the **Predecessor** or **Successor** column,
  - ➤ In the "**Schedule Report - Predecessors & Successors**",
  - ➤ Display the relationships on bars,
  - ➤ In the **Activity Network** view,

- Relationships **WITH** lags may be viewed by:
  - ➤ **Activity Details** form tabs displays with lags,
  - ➤ Displaying the **Predecessor Details** and **Successor Details** columns,
  - ➤ The **Relationships** report,
  - ➤ As an export to Excel and this is a place where the leads and lags may be displayed and filtered on in columns:

	A	B	C	L	M
1	pred_task_id	task_id	pred_type	lag_hr_cnt	delete_record_flag
2	Predecessor	Successor	Relationship Type	Lag(d)	Delete This Row
3	SH2002	SH2010	FS	-5	
4	SH2010	SH2020	FS	-5	
5	SH2020	SH2030	FS	-5	

9.10 Lag and Relationship Type Displayed in the Activity Table

These columns display the relationship type and leads or lag in the Activity Table, in a similar way to Microsoft Project and Elecosoft (Asta) Powerproject, as per the picture below:

A filter may be created to filter for specific relationship types. So, it will be simple to find all the activities which for example have a SS, FF or SF relationship with the filter displayed below:

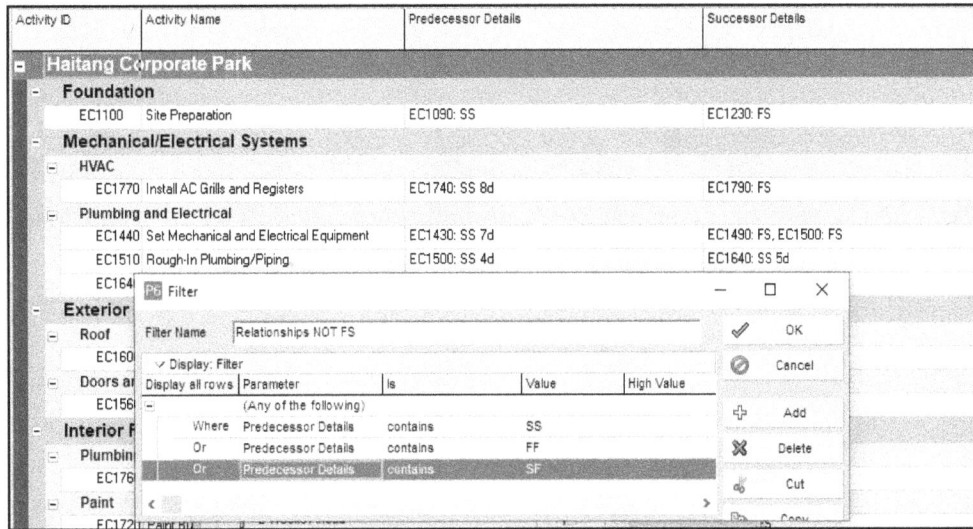

9.11 Ladder Scheduling

Large negative lags are often considered unacceptable and Ladder Scheduling is a technique used to link a set of activities that have substantial overlap, such as pipe laying operations. As seen from the picture below the activities are linked with SS + a lag and FF + a lag relationship.

Some contracts specifically specify that negative lags are not to be used in a contract program.

Most products, except Microsoft Project, allow multiple relationships between two activities, as per the P6 example below, where the activities are linked using two relationships, a SS+3d and a FF+3d:

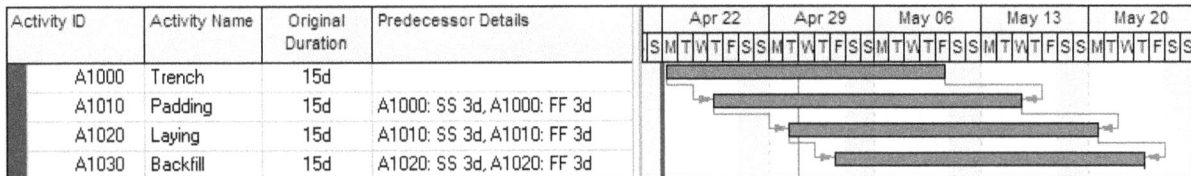

Activity ID	Activity Name	Original Duration	Predecessor Details	Apr 22	Apr 29	May 06	May 13	May 20
A1000	Trench	15d						
A1010	Padding	15d	A1000: SS 3d, A1000: FF 3d					
A1020	Laying	15d	A1010: SS 3d, A1010: FF 3d					
A1030	Backfill	15d	A1020: SS 3d, A1020: FF 3d					

9.12 Relationship Comments

P6 Version 20 introduced a **Comments** column that may be added to the **Activities** window **Relationships**, **Predecessor** and **Successor** tabs:

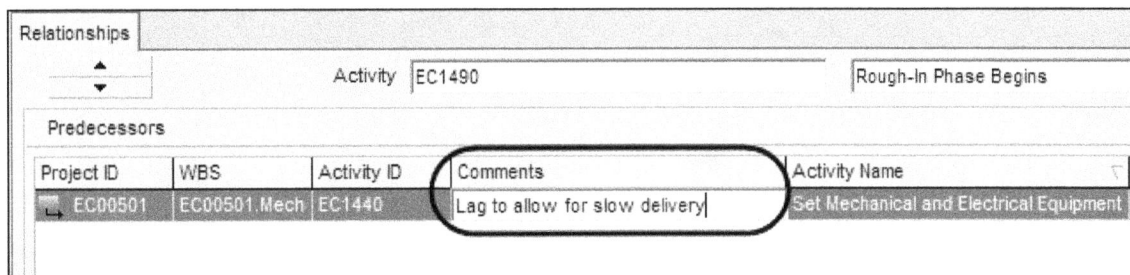

The comment is seen in both the Predecessor and Successor window of each relationship assigned a comment:

Successors						
▲ ▼		Activity	EC1440		Set Mechanical and Electrical Equipment	
Project ID	WBS	Activity ID	Activity Name	Comments	Relations	Lag
EC00501	EC00501.Mech	EC1500	Install HVAC Ducts		FS	0
EC00501	EC00501.Mech	EC1490	Rough-In Phase Begins	Lag to allow for slow delivery	FS	10

This is a very useful function and in the past one had to either use a Note or a UDF assigned to either the predecessor or successor activity to record notes about a relationship.

This function is also useful for recording changes to relationships.

The **Comments** column is available in the **Activity Relationship** report but not in Activity window columns:

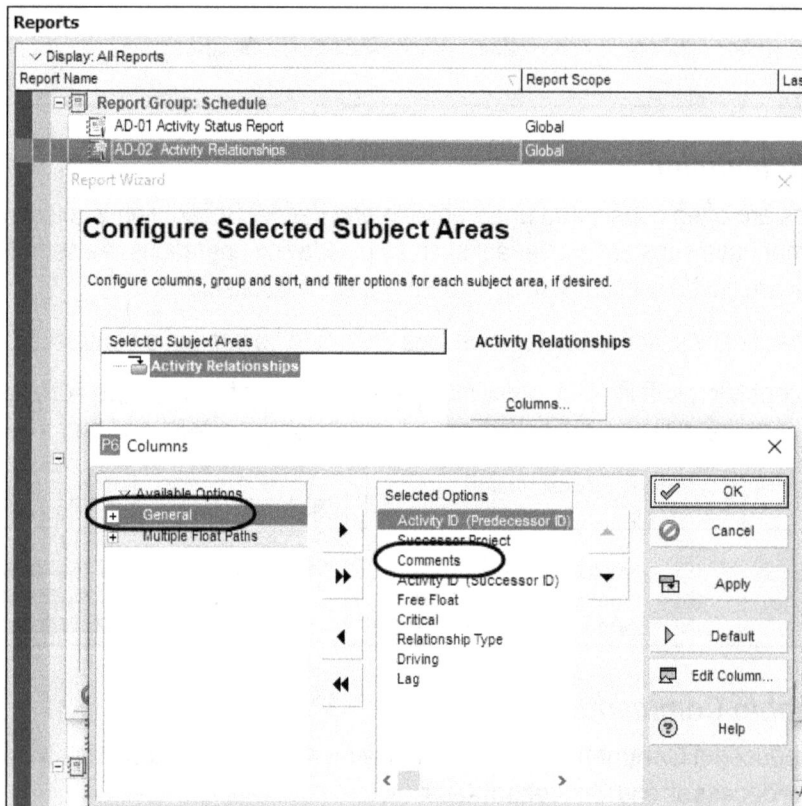

This publication is only sold as a bound book, no parts may be reproduced by any means, e.g., electronic, video or print.

9.13 Milestone Reduced Relationship Types

P6 Version 20 and earlier supports more relationship types than P6 Version21.

	Start Milestone Predecessors	Start Milestone Successors	Finish Milestone Predecessors	Finish Milestone Successors
P6 Version 20 & earlier	FS and SS	FS, SF and SS	FF, FS and SF	FF and FS
P6 Version21	FS and SS	SF and SS	FF and SF	FF and FS

Thus, in Version 21 Chain Linking does not result in all the predecessors and successors being a FS relationship and some people would say that this is no longer a critical path program:

- P6 Version 20 Chain Linking

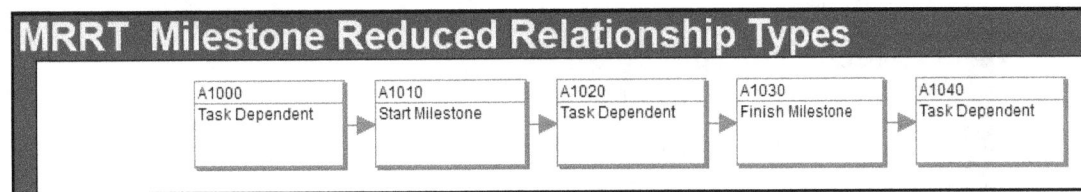

- P6 Version 21 Chain Linking

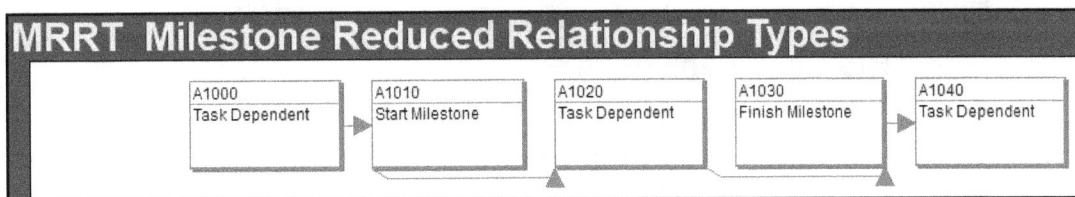

Projects imported into P6 Version 21 from earlier versions bring in and acknowledge the old relationship types, but these Start Milestone FS and Finish Milestone FF cannot be set in Version21.

> ℹ️ Should you wish your Milestones to be linked with FS relationships then just add the Milestones with an **Activity Type** of **Task Dependant**, add the relationships and then change the task to a Milestone.

9.14 Workshop 7 – Adding the Relationships

Background

You have determined the logical sequence of activities, so you may now create the relationships.

Assignment

1. Display the **Predecessor** column from the **Lists** section of the **Columns** form, to the right of the Activity Name.

2. Input the logic below using several of the methods detailed in this chapter:

Activity ID	Activity Name	Predecessors
Bid for Facility Extension		
Technical Specification		
OZ1000	Approval to Bid	
OZ1010	Determine Installation Requirements	OZ1000
OZ1020	Create Technical Specification	OZ1010
OZ1030	Identify Supplier Components	OZ1020
OZ1040	Validate Technical Specification	OZ1030
Delivery Plan		
OZ1050	Document Delivery Methodology	OZ1040
OZ1060	Obtain Quotes from Suppliers	OZ1030
OZ1070	Calculate the Bid Estimate	OZ1050, OZ1060
OZ1080	Create the Project Schedule	OZ1070
OZ1090	Review the Delivery Plan	OZ1080
Bid Document		
OZ1100	Create Draft of Bid Document	OZ1050
OZ1110	Review Bid Document	OZ1090, OZ1100
OZ1120	Finalise and Submit Bid Document	OZ1110
OZ1130	Bid Document Submitted	OZ1120

3. Press **F5 – Refresh Data** if the relationships do not appear in columns.

4. Press **F9** or click on the [▷ Schedule] button to schedule.

5. Hide and display the Logic Links using the icon. Leave them displayed.

continued…

Answer to Workshop 7

6. Format the columns as per the following picture:

Activity ID	Activity Name	Predecessors	Successors	Original Duration	Start	Finish	Total Float	Free Float
Bid for Facility Extension				31d	09-Dec-24 08	23-Jan-25 16	0d	0d
Technical Specification				13d	09-Dec-24 08	27-Dec-24 16	2d	0d
OZ1000	Approval to Bid		OZ1010	0d	09-Dec-24 08		0d	0d
OZ1010	Determine Installation Requirements	OZ1000	OZ1020	4d	09-Dec-24 08	12-Dec-24 16	0d	0d
OZ1020	Create Technical Specification	OZ1010	OZ1030	5d	13-Dec-24 08	19-Dec-24 16	0d	0d
OZ1030	Identify Supplier Components	OZ1020	OZ1040, OZ1060	2d	20-Dec-24 08	23-Dec-24 16	0d	0d
OZ1040	Validate Technical Specification	OZ1030	OZ1050	2d	24-Dec-24 08	27-Dec-24 16	2d	0d
Delivery Plan				14d	24-Dec-24 08	15-Jan-25 16	0d	0d
OZ1050	Document Delivery Methodology	OZ1040	OZ1070, OZ1100	4d	30-Dec-24 08	03-Jan-25 16	2d	0d
OZ1060	Obtain Quotes from Suppliers	OZ1030	OZ1070	8d	24-Dec-24 08	07-Jan-25 16	0d	0d
OZ1070	Calculate the Bid Estimate	OZ1050, OZ1060	OZ1080	3d	08-Jan-25 08	10-Jan-25 16	0d	0d
OZ1080	Create the Project Schedule	OZ1070	OZ1090	3d	11-Jan-25 08	14-Jan-25 16	0d	0d
OZ1090	Review the Delivery Plan	OZ1080	OZ1110	1d	15-Jan-25 08	15-Jan-25 16	0d	0d
Bid Document				14d	06-Jan-25 08	23-Jan-25 16	0d	0d
OZ1100	Create Draft of Bid Document	OZ1050	OZ1110	6d	06-Jan-25 08	13-Jan-25 16	2d	2d
OZ1110	Review Bid Document	OZ1090, OZ1100	OZ1120	4d	16-Jan-25 08	21-Jan-25 16	0d	0d
OZ1120	Finalise and Submit Bid Document	OZ1110	OZ1130	2d	22-Jan-25 08	23-Jan-25 16	0d	0d
OZ1130	Bid Document Submitted	OZ1120		0d		23-Jan-25 16	0d	0d

P6 Version 20 and earlier will join Milestones with a FS relationship:

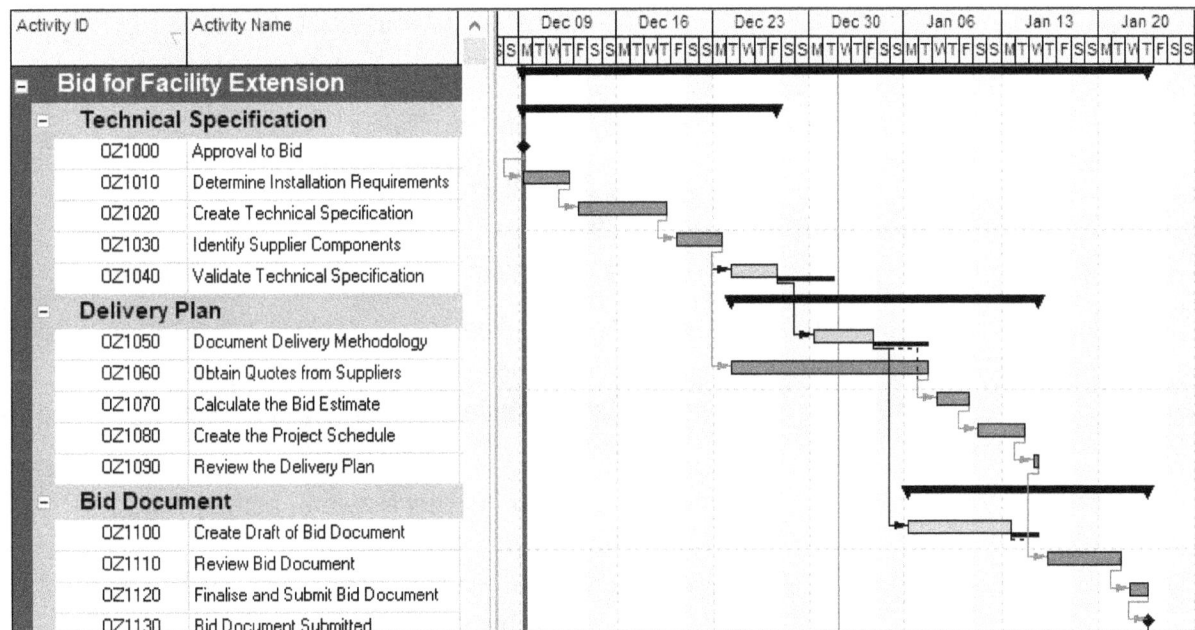

P6 Version 21 and later will NOT join Milestones with a FS relationship and your answer will look like the picture below:

Finish Milestone joined with a FF relationship

10 ACTIVITY NETWORK VIEW

The **Activity Network**, also known as the **PERT View**, displays activities as boxes connected by the relationship lines. See the following picture:

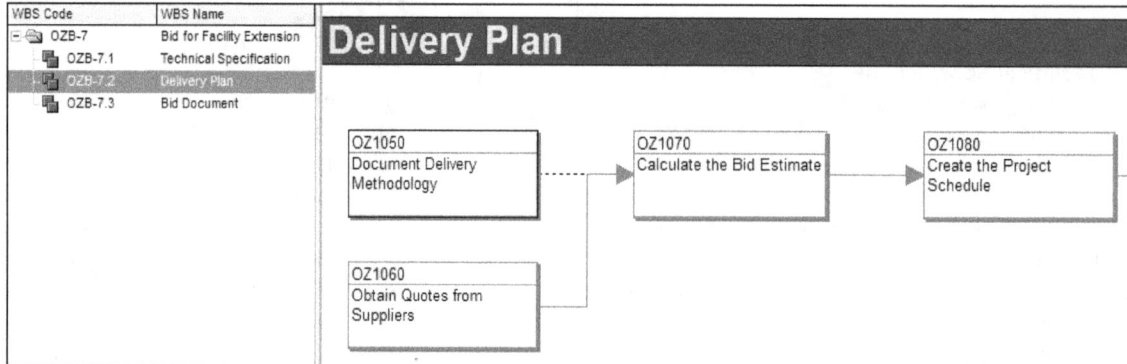

This chapter will not cover this subject in detail but will introduce the main features.

Many features available in the **Gantt Chart View** are also available in the **Activity Network View**, including:

Topic	Menu Command
• Viewing a Project Using the **Activity Network View**.	• Click on the **Top Layout** toolbar ⊞ button, or • Select **View, Show on Top, Activity Network**.
• Adding and Deleting Activities in the **Activity Network** View.	• Use the **Insert** and **Delete** keys, or • Use the **Edit** toolbar, **Add** ⊞ and **Delete** ☒ buttons, or • Use the menu commands **Edit, Add** and **Delete**.
• Adding, Editing and Deleting Relationships.	• Graphically drag from one activity to another, or • Use the **Predecessor**, or **Successor**, or **Relationship** tabs in the **Activities Window, Details** form.
• Formatting the Activity Boxes.	• Select **View, Activity Network, Activity Network Options...**, or • Right-click in the **Activity Network** area and select **Activity Network Options....**

10.1 Viewing a Project Using the Activity Network View

To view your project in the **Network View** either:

- Click on the **Top Layout** toolbar [⊞] button, or
- Select **View, Show on Top**, **Activity Network**.

10.2 Adding and Deleting Activities

10.2.1 Adding an Activity

A **New Activity** may be created without a relationship by:

- Using the **Insert** key, or
- Use the **Edit** toolbar, **Add** [✛] button, or
- Selecting **Edit**, **Add**.

10.2.2 Deleting and Activity

Activities may be deleted by:

- Using the **Delete** key, or
- Use the **Edit** toolbar, **Delete** [✕] button, or
- Selecting **Edit**, **Delete**.

10.3 Adding, Editing and Deleting Relationships

Relationships may be added, deleted or edited using the following methods:

10.3.1 Graphically Adding a Relationship

- To create a FS relationship, move the mouse to the right side of the predecessor activity box (the pointer will change to a ↳) and drag to the left side of the successor activity. Selecting the left or right side of the predecessor and successor activity box will determine the type of relationship that is created.
- To edit the relationship, select the relationship (it will change to blue), double-click to open the **Edit Relationship** form, and edit the relationship.

10.3.2 Using the Activity Details Form

Open the **Relationships** tab in the **Activity Details** form:

- When the **Activity Details** form is not displayed, select **View, Show on Bottom**.
- Then add, edit, and delete activities in the same way as with the Gantt Chart.

10.4 Formatting the Activity Boxes

Activity Boxes may be formatted from the **Activity Network Options** form, which may displayed when an Activity Network View is displayed. The formatting affects both the **Trace Logic** and **Activity Network Window** formatting for the layout that is being formatted:

- Select **View, Activity Network**, **Activity Network Options…**,or

- Right-click in the PERT area and select **Activity Network Options…**:

  ➢ A selection of box templates are available from the drop-down box under the Activity Box Template title. These templates display different data in the box.

  ➢ Click on **Font & Colors…** to format the text font and colors,

  ➢ Click on **Box Template…** to edit the template or add and remove data items from the activity boxes.

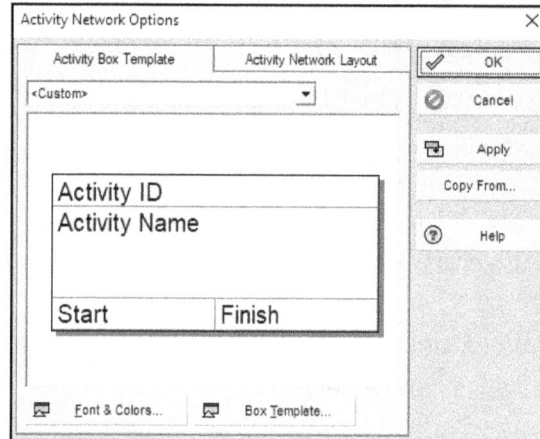

NOTE: This option also formats the **Trace Logic** boxes with the same format.

- Click on the **Activity Network Layout** tab to display further options which are self-explanatory:

  ➢ **Show progress** will place a diagonal line through an in-progress activity and a cross through a completed activity.

  ➢ The **spacing factors** are a percentage of the box sizes.

10.5 Reorganizing the Activity Network

Activities in the **Activity Network** view may be repositioned by dragging. There are two functions available when right-clicking in the **Activity Network** view:

- **Reorganize** will reposition activities that have not been manually positioned, and

- **Reorganize All** will reposition all activities including those that have been manually positioned.

10.6 Saving and Opening Activity Network Positions

When activities are manually dragged into new positions on the screen for presentation purposes, it is possible to save and reload these positions at a later date, they are not saved when you exit the view:

- **View, Activity Network**, **Save Network Positions…** will create an *.anp file, and

- **View, Activity Network**, **Open Network Positions…** will enable an *.anp file to be located and loaded which will reposition the activities as they were saved.

10.7 Early Date, Late Date and Float Calculations

To help understand the calculation of late and early dates, float and critical path, we will now manually work through an example. The boxes below represent activities.

ES = Early Start	EF = Early Finish
DUR = Duration	TF-Total Float
LS = Late Start	LF = Late Finish

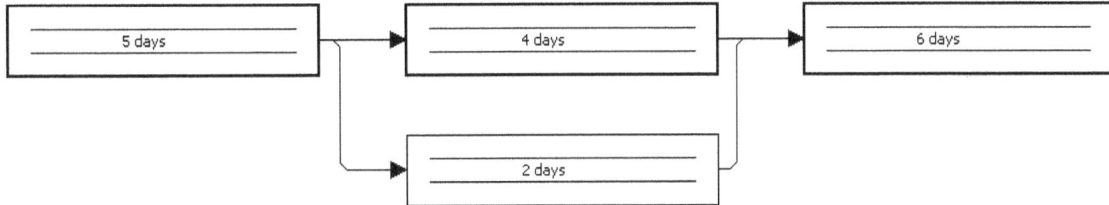

5 days	4 days	6 days
	2 days	

- The forward pass calculates the early dates: EF = ES + DUR – 1

  Start the calculation from the first activity and work forward in time.

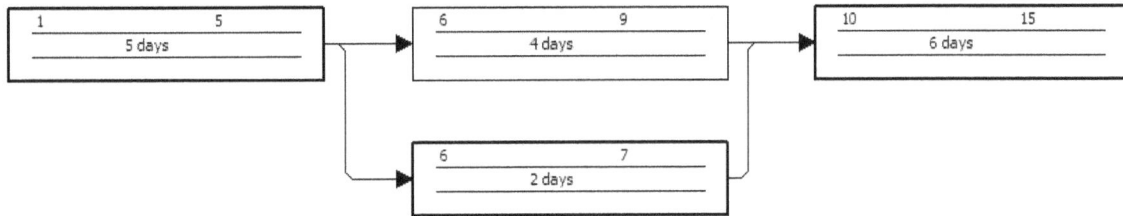

1 ___ 5	6 ___ 9	10 ___ 15
5 days	4 days	6 days
	6 ___ 7	
	2 days	

- The backward pass calculates the late dates: LS = LF – DUR + 1

  Start the calculation at the last activity and work backwards in time.

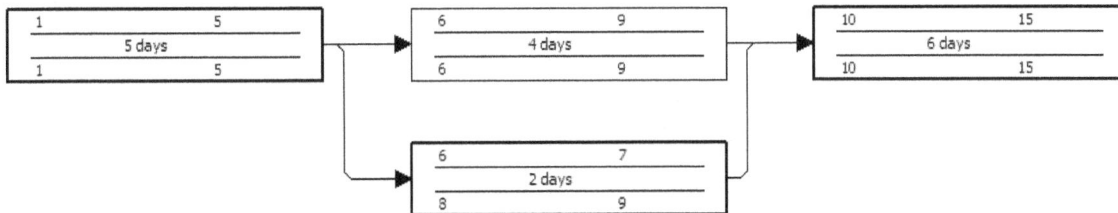

1 ___ 5	6 ___ 9	10 ___ 15
5 days	4 days	6 days
1 ___ 5	6 ___ 9	10 ___ 15
	6 ___ 7	
	2 days	
	8 ___ 9	

Total Float is the difference between either the **Late Finish** and the **Early Finish** or the difference between the **Late Start** and the **Early Start** of an activity. The lower 2 days' activity has float of 9 – 7 = 2 days. None of the other activities has float.

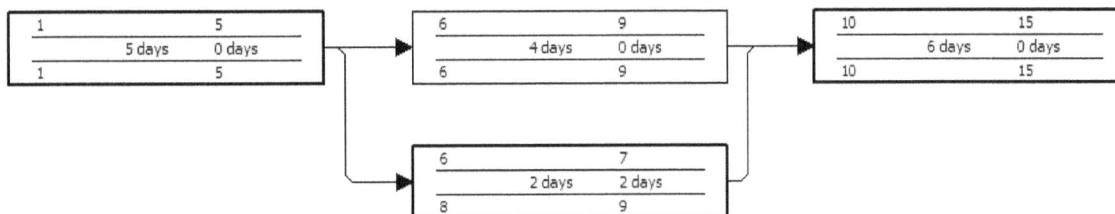

1 ___ 5	6 ___ 9	10 ___ 15
5 days 0 days	4 days 0 days	6 days 0 days
1 ___ 5	6 ___ 9	10 ___ 15
	6 ___ 7	
	2 days 2 days	
	8 ___ 9	

The **Critical Path** is the path where any delay causes a delay in the project and runs through the top row of activities. **Free Float** is the difference between the Predecessor Early Finish and the Successor Early Start.

i An activity may not be on the Critical Path and may have more than one predecessor. A **Driving Relationship** is the predecessor that determines the Activity Early Start.

10.8   Workshop 8 – Scheduling Calculations and Activity Network View

Background

We want to practice calculating early and late dates with a simple manual exercise.

Assignment

1. Apply the Activity Network View of your OzBuild schedule by clicking on the ⊞ icon.

2. Click on each node of the WBS and notice how only activities assigned to each node are displayed.

3. Click on the three Zoom icons ⊕ ⊖ ⊙ and notice their effect on the schedule.

4. Calculate the Early Dates, Late Dates, and Total Float for the following activities, assuming a Monday-to-Friday working week and the first activity starting on 1 April.

ES = Early Start	EF = Early Finish
DUR = Duration TF - Total Float	
LS = Late Start	LF = Late Finish

<		April				>
Sun	Mon	Tue	Wed	Thr	Fri	Sat
	1	2	3	4	5	6
7	8	9	10	11	12	13
14	15	16	17	18	19	20
21	22	23	24	25	26	27
28	29	30				

5. See over the page for the answer:

Answer to Workshop 8

<	April					>
Sun	Mon	Tue	Wed	Thr	Fri	Sat
	1	2	3	4	5	6
7	8	9	10	11	12	13
14	15	16	17	18	19	20
21	22	23	24	25	26	27
28	29	30				

Early Start	Early Finish
Duration	Float
Late Start	Late Finish

Forward Pass   EF = ES + DUR – 1

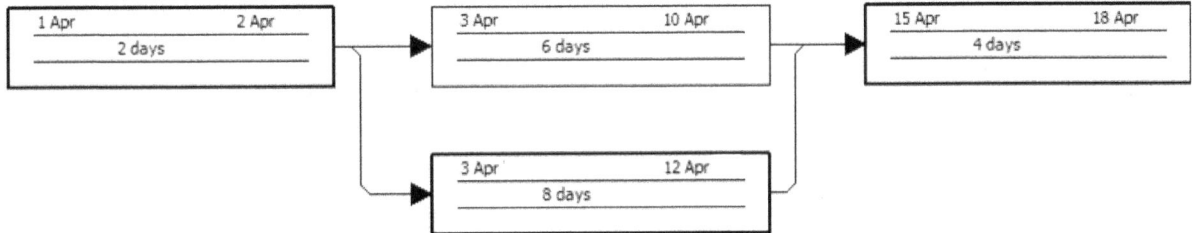

Backward Pass   LS = LF – DUR + 1

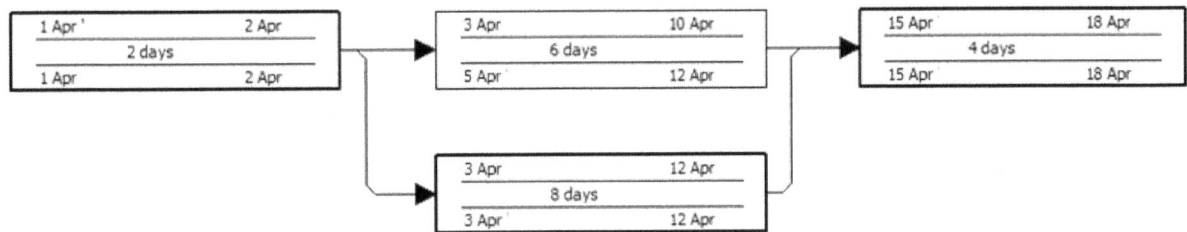

Float Calculation   TF = LS – ES

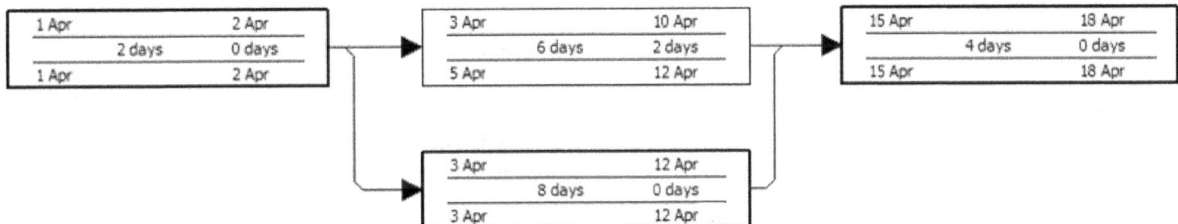

The Early Bar is the upper bar, the Late Bar the lower bar and the end of the Total Float bar, which is the thin bar, ends at the Late Finish date.

Original Duration	Total Float	Mar 31	Apr 07	Apr 14
2d	0d			
6d	2d			
8d	0d			
4d	0d			

11 CONSTRAINTS

Constraints are used to impose logic on activities that may not be realistically scheduled with logic links. This chapter will deal with the following constraints in detail:

- **Start On or After**
- **Finish On or Before**

These are the minimum number of constraints that are required to effectively schedule a project.

Start On or After (also known as an "Early Start" or "Start No Earlier Than" constraint as it only affects the Early dates calculation) is used when the start date of an activity is known and does not have a predecessor. Primavera will not calculate the activity's early start date prior to this date.

Finish On or Before (also known as "Late Finish" or "Finish No Later Than" constraint as it only affects the Late dates calculation) is used when the latest finish date is stipulated. Primavera will not calculate the activity's late finish date after this date.

The following table summarizes the methods used to assign Constraints to Activities or how to add notes to activities:

Topic	Notes for Creating a Constraint
• Setting a **Primary** and **Secondary** constraint with the **Activity Details** form.	Open the **Status** tab on the **Activity Details** form.
• Setting Constraints using columns.	The following columns may be displayed and the constraints assigned or edited: • Primary Constraint • Primary Constraint Date • Secondary Constraint • Secondary Constraint Date • Expected Finish Date
• Dragging an Activity in the Gantt Chart.	Dragging an Activity in the Gantt Chart will open the **Confirmation** form where the user is able to confirm the setting of a **Start On or After** constraint.
• Adding Notes, these could be about constraints or other activity information.	The **Activity Details** form has a **Notebook** tab, which enables Notes to be assigned to **Notebook Topics**.

The AACE RP 24R-03 Developing Activity Logic is applicable to this chapter.

i Primavera will permit two constraints to be assigned to each activity. Microsoft Project only permit one constraint except when a Deadline constraint is applied in Microsoft Project. Elecosoft (Asta) Powerproject allows only one constraint but the **Work Between** constraint is similar to applying two constraints.

A full list of **constraints** available in Primavera:

- **<None>** This is the default for a new activity. An activity by default is scheduled to occur **As Soon As Possible** and does not have a Constraint.

- **Start On** Also known as **Must Start On,** sets the activity start date, has no float. The early start and the late start dates are set to the Constraint Date.

- **Start On or Before** Also known as **Start No Later Than** or **Late Start**, this constraint sets the late date after which the activity will not start.

- **Start On or After** Also known as **Start No Earlier Than** or **Early Start**, this constraint sets the early date before which the activity will not start.

- **Finish On** Also known as **Must Finish On**, sets the activity will finish date, has no float as the early finish and the late finish dates are set to be the same as the Constraint Date.

- **Finish On or Before** Also known as **Finish No Later Than** or **Late Finish**, this sets the late date after which the activity will not finish.

- **Finish On or After** Also known as **Finish No Earlier Than** or **Early Finish**, this sets the early date before which the activity will not finish.

- **As Late As Possible** Calculates as a Zero Free Float constraint, NOT as an As Late As possible constraint. Thus an activity delay only consumes Free Float, will not delay any other activity and is not assigned Constraint Date. In Microsoft Project an As Late As Possible constraint will consume Total Float and delay all successor activities with Total Float.

- **Mandatory Start** This constraint prevents float being calculated through this activity and effectively breaks a schedule into two parts. This is also sometimes called a Hard Constraint.

- **Mandatory Finish** This constraint prevents float being calculated through this activity and effectively breaks a schedule into two parts. This is also sometimes called a Hard Constraint.

- **Expected Finish** An **Expected Finish** sets the Early Finish to the Expected Finish constraint date and calculates the Remaining Duration from the Early Start date for an un-started activity, or Data Date if the activity is in-progress to the Expected Finish date.

Earlier Than constraints operate on the **Early Dates**, and **Later Than** constraints operate on **Late Dates**. The following picture demonstrates how constraints calculate Total Float on activities without links:

Activity ID	Primary Constraint	Primary Constraint Date	Total Float	Free Float	Feb 02	Feb 09	Feb 16
A1000			10d	5d			
A1010	As Late As Possible		5d	0d			
A1020	Finish On	14-Feb-25 16	0d	0d			
A1030	Finish On or After	14-Feb-25 16	5d	0d			
A1040	Finish On or Before	14-Feb-25 16	5d	5d			
A1050	Mandatory Finish	14-Feb-25 16	0d	0d			
A1060	Mandatory Start	10-Feb-25 08	0d	0d			
A1070	Start On	10-Feb-25 08	0d	0d			
A1080	Start On or After	10-Feb-25 08	5d	0d			
A1090	Start On or Before	10-Feb-25 08	5d	5d			

i An activity assigned an **As Late as Possible** constraint in Primavera P6 and Elecosoft (Asta) Powerproject (as **Placement**) will schedule the activity so it absorbs only **Free Float** and will not delay the start of any successor activities, this is normally called a **Zero Free Float** constraint. In Microsoft Project, an activity assigned with an **As Late as Possible** constraint will be delayed absorbing the Total Float and delay all its successor activities which have float, not just the activity with the constraint. Thus, a project imported from Microsoft project may calculate differently when it has n **As Late as Possible** constraints.

11.1 Assigning Constraints

⚠ When setting constraints sometimes the constraint time will not be set at the start or finish of the activity calendar but set at 00:00 or some other irrelevant time. Therefore, when setting constraints, you should always display the time by selecting **Edit**, **User Preferences ...**, **Dates** tab to ensure the constraint time is compatible with the activity calendar.

11.1.1 Number of Constraints per Activity

Two constraints are permitted against each activity. They are titled Primary and Secondary Constraint. After the Primary has been set, a Secondary may be set only when the combination is logical and therefore a reduced list of constraints is available from the Secondary Constraint list after the Primary has been set.

11.1.2 Setting a Primary Constraint Using the Activity Details Form

To assign a constraint using the **Activity Details** form:

- Select the activity requiring a constraint,
- Open the **Status** tab on the **Activity Details** form,
- Select the **Primary Constraint** type from the **Date** drop-down list to the right of **Primary Date**:

Constraints			
Primary	Start On or After ▼	Secondary	< None > ▼
Date	02-Jan-25 08 ...	Date	...

11.1.3 Setting a Secondary Constraint Using the Activity Details Form

To assign a constraint using the **Activity Details** form:

- Select the activity requiring a constraint,
- Open the **Status** tab on the **Activity Details** form,
- Select the **Secondary Constraint** type from the **Date** drop-down list to the right of **Secondary Date**:

Constraints			
Primary	Start On or After ▼	Secondary	Finish On or Before ▼
Date	02-Jan-25 08 ...	Date	13-Jan-25 16 ...

The picture above shows that after a **Primary Start On or After** constraint is set there are only two Secondary Constraints available. After a constraint is set the date will have an asterisk "*" next to it.

- Start Constraints will have the "*" next to the Start Date, and
- Finish Constraints will have the "*" next to the Finish Date.

11.1.4 Expected Finish Constraint

This constraint is set in the dates **Status** area above the **Constraints** area and will only work if the **Tools**, **Schedule…**, ▷ Options… , **Use Expected Finish dates** check box is checked.

Status				
☐ Started	02-Jan-25 08	…	Physical %	0%
☐ Finished	13-Jan-25 16	…	Suspend	
Exp Finish	13-Jan-25 16	…	Resume	

This constraint is set in the **Status** section of the **Activity Details** form, **Status** tab, not under the **Constraints** section as one would expect:

An **Expected Finish** constraint recalculates the **Remaining Duration** on a permanent basis.

An **Expected Finish** constraint in the past will always set the **Remaining Duration** to zero.

> *i* The author uses an Expected Finish constraint as a tool to calculate the Remaining Duration when the planned finish date is known, but then removes it after calculation. This is because when the Expected Finish constraint date is in the past it will zero out the Remaining Duration.

11.1.5 Setting Constraints Using Columns

The following constraint columns may be displayed and the Constraints edited or assigned using these columns:

- Primary Constraint
- Primary Constraint Date
- Secondary Constraint
- Secondary Constraint Date
- Expected Finish

Activity ID	Activity Name	Primary Constraint	Primary Constraint Date	Secondary Constraint	Secondary Constraint Date	Expected Finish
Bid for Facility Extension						
Technical Specification						
OZ1000	Approval to Bid	Start On or After ▼	02-Jan-14 08			
OZ1010	Determine Installation Requirements	< None >				
OZ1020	Create Technical Specification	As Late As Possible				
OZ1030	Identify Supplier Components	Mandatory Start / Start On				
OZ1040	Validate Technical Specification	Start On or After				
Delivery Plan		Start On or Before				
OZ1050	Document Delivery Methodology					
OZ1060	Obtain Quotes from Suppliers					
OZ1070	Calculate the Bid Estimate					

11.1.6 Typing in a Start Date

A **Start On or After** constraint may be assigned from the **Activity Status** tab or the **Start Date** column by typing a date into the **Start** field:

Confirmation		
Do you want to add a Start On or After constraint on 16-Dec-24 to hold the activity in place?	✓	Yes
	✗	No
☐ Do not ask me about this again		

- A **Start On or After** constraint is assigned by overtyping the Start date. The **Confirmation** form will confirm this action.

> *i* A date typed into the finish date will not assign a Finish Date constraint but will adjust the duration of the activity. In Microsoft Project, a date typed into either the Start or the Finish field will set a constraint; Primavera does not operate in this way.

⚠️ Beware of clicking **Do not ask me about this again** as you will be unable to turn this option back on again using the user interface with earlier versions of P6.

11.2   External Dates

In summary:

- **External Dates** are created where there are inter-project relationships in a source database that you are importing a P6 project from.
- When you import the project into your database that had **External Relationships** in the source database then these relationships are not imported then **External Dates** are created that represent the missing relationships and calculate like constraints.
- You must always search for **External Dates** when you import a project from an unknown source.
- Check this in the **Tools**, **Schedule…**, **Options** form and check **Ignore relationships to and from other projects** to disable **External Dates,** but I do not recommend this option.
- **External Dates** may be located by displaying the columns **External Early Start** (which works as an Early Start Constraint) and the **External Late Finish** (that works like a Late Finish Constraint) or look for Start and Finish dates that have an "*" but no normal constraint.

Activity ID	Original Duration	External Early Start	External Late Finish	Start	Finish	Total Float	2026 16	23	30	April 2026 06	13
A1000	5d	20-Mar-26 16		23-Mar-26 08*	27-Mar-26 16	-5d					
A1010	10d			30-Mar-26 08	10-Apr-26 16	-5d					
A1020	5d		13-Apr-26 08	13-Apr-26 08	17-Apr-26 16*	-5d					

⚠️ These dates can be very confusing if one is not aware that they have been created or how they operate. The negative float in the picture below is created by these dates after Activity A101 duration was increased by 5 days:

11.3   Project Must Finish By Date

An absolute finish date may be imposed on the project using the **Project Window**, **Dates** tab, **Must Finish By** date:

Dates

Schedule Dates

Project Planned Start	Must Finish By
09-Dec-24 08	24-Jan-25 16

Data Date	Finish
09-Dec-24 08	27-Jan-25 16

Anticipated Dates

Anticipated Start
09-Dec-24 08

Anticipated Finish
27-Jan-25 16

Imposing a **Must Finish By** date makes Primavera calculate the late dates from the **Must Finish By** date rather than the calculated early finish date. This will introduce positive float to activities when the calculated **Early finish** date is prior to the **Must Finish By** date:

Activity ID	Activity Name	Original Duration	Total Float	Free Float	Oct 31	Nov 07	Nov 14	Nov 21
7 Activities		120h	16h	0h				
A1000	Start Milestone	0h	16h	0h				
A1010	Activity 1	40h	16h	0h				
A1020	Activity 2	40h	16h	0h				
A1030	Activity 3	40h	16h	0h				
A1040	Activity 4	16h	104h	24h				
A1050	Activity 5	16h	80h	64h				
A1060	Finish Milestone	0h	16h	0h				

This will also create negative float when the activity's calculated early finish date is after the **Must Finish By** date, but it is not obvious where the negative float is being driven from as there are no constraints assigned to activities:

Activity ID	Activity Name	Original Duration	Total Float	Free Float	Oct 24	Oct 31	Nov 07	Nov 14
7 Activities		120h	-16h	0h				
A1000	Start Milestone	0h	-16h	0h				
A1010	Activity 1	40h	-16h	0h				
A1020	Activity 2	40h	-16h	0h				
A1030	Activity 3	40h	-16h	0h				
A1040	Activity 4	16h	72h	24h				
A1050	Activity 5	16h	48h	64h				
A1060	Finish Milestone	0h	-16h	0h				

When opening multiple projects some further issues need to be considered when a **Project Must Finish By** date is set and these are covered in the **Multiple Project Scheduling** chapter.

To remove a **Project Must Finish By** date, highlight the date, press the **Delete** key and then the **Enter** key or tab out of the cell to ensure the date is removed.

> **i** It is not obvious where the float is being generated after a **Must Finish By** date is imposed on a project. This is often confusing to people new to scheduling and it is recommended that you do not use a **Must Finish By** date. Instead, tie all activities to a **Finish Milestone** which has a **Late finish** constraint.

11.4   Activity Notebook

It is often important to note why constraints have been set. Primavera has functions that enable you to note information associated with an activity, including the reasons associated for establishing a constraint.

The **Activity Details** form has a **Notebook** tab, which enables Notes to be assigned to **Notebook Topics** and has some word processing-type formatting functions.

11.4.1 Creating Notebook Topics

Notebook Topics are created by selecting **Admin**, **Admin Categories…** in the Professional Version, and through the Web tool for the Windows Client and then selecting the **Notebook Topics** tab. After a topic has been created this topic may be made available to the following data fields by checking the appropriate box:

- EPS
- Project
- WBS
- Activities

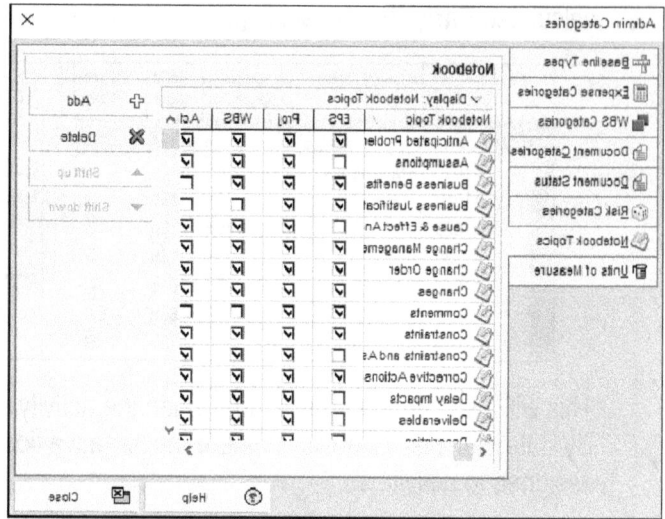

-

11.4.2 Adding Notes

To add a note to an activity:

- Select the **Notebook** tab in the **Activity Details** form,

- Click ⊹ Add to open the **Assign Notebook Topic** form,

- Assign a Notebook topic using the 🔣 icon, and

- Click 🖻 Modify… to open a form where you may type in your note:

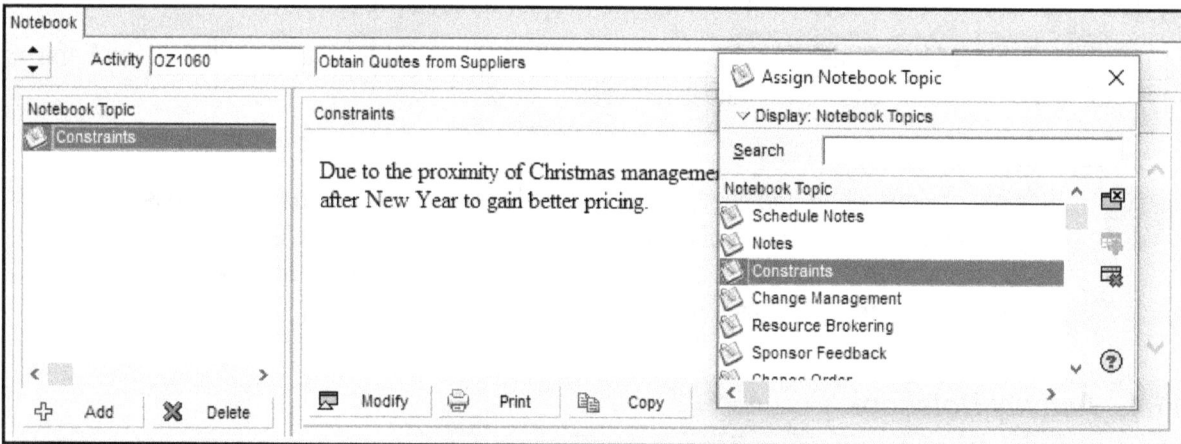

⚠ Notebook fields may not be displayed in columns, therefore if you wish to display note in a column then you should create a UDF for this purpose.

The Relationship Comments column should be use for notes about relationships.

11.5 Check Schedule Report

The **Tools**, **Check Schedule Report** option allow the user to conduct a **Quantitative Check** on a schedule which is becoming more popular with a number of organisations:

The report is aligned to documents such as the US Defense Contract Management Agency (DCMA) 14 Point Assessment.

Running the command allows the user to change the analysis settings in the form below:

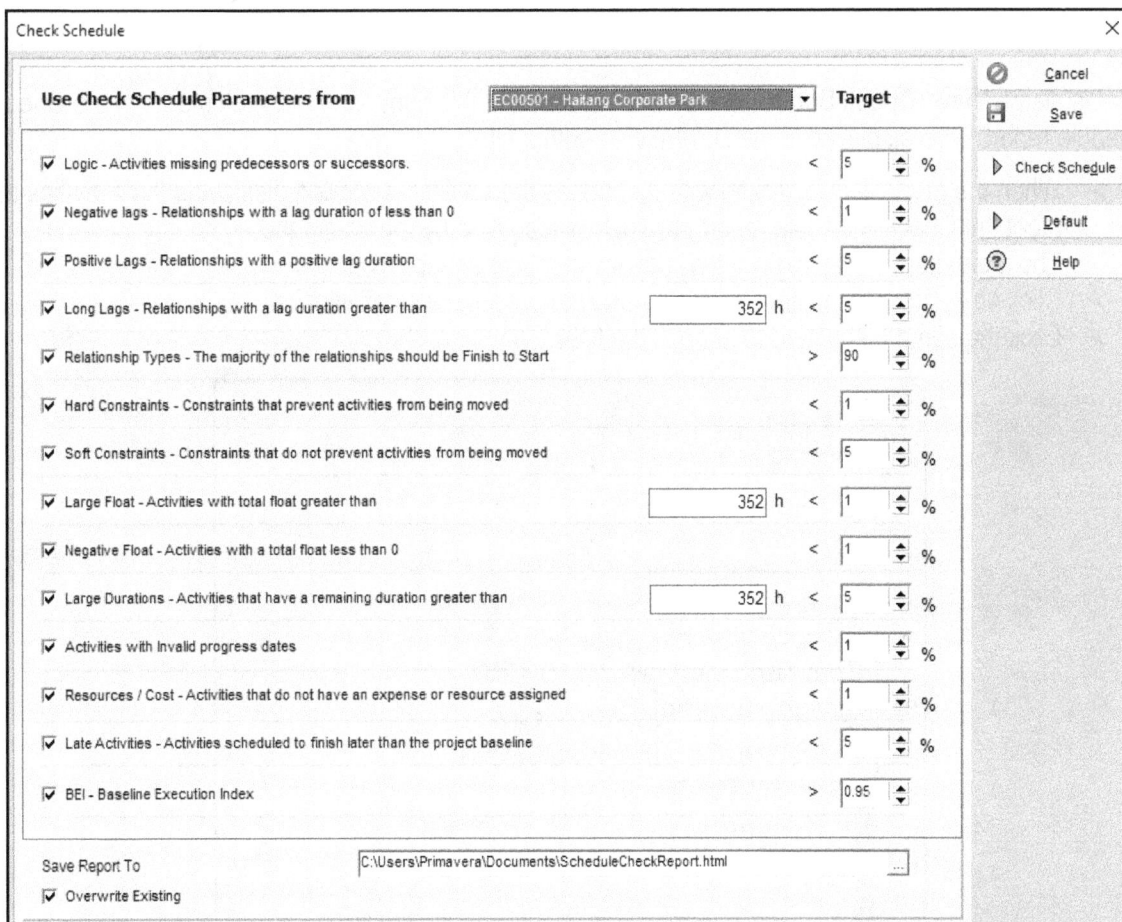

If you make changes to the **Default** setting you may save them with the **Save** button, but it is not possible to save different profiles and setting will need to be changed manually for each different scenario that may be required.

You may the run a report by clicking on the **Check Schedule Report** button which will be displayed in a browser:

There is also a **View**, **Check Schedule** menu command and this command allow elements of the Check Schedule report to be displayed in the current view with a filter.

➢ When the menu item is clicked with the mouse then a filter is applied displaying the activities that meet the Check Schedule report parameters identified by the command,
➢ The menu item will be highlighted grey when a filter is applied,
➢ Click on another menu item to display another parameter's activities, or
➢ Click the same menu item to remove the filter.

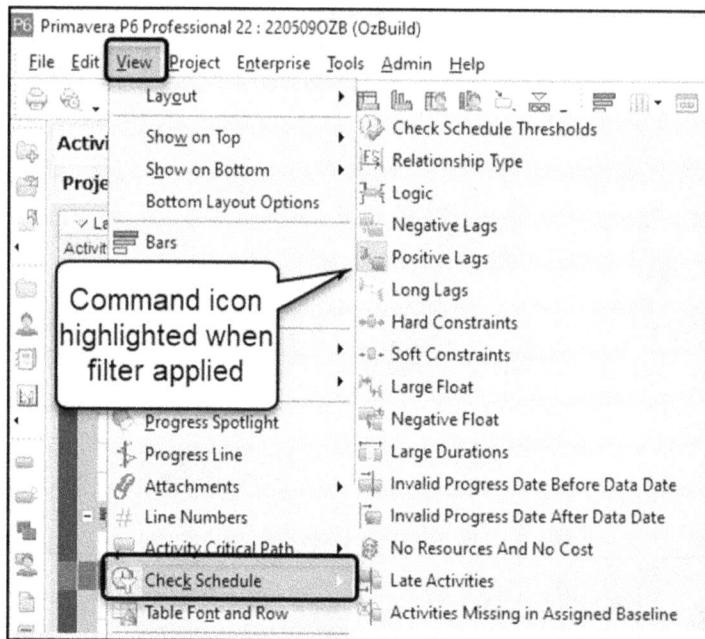

NOTE: Do not run a **Check Schedule Report** unless a **Qualitative Check** as outlined in the next paragraph has been completed.

11.6   Completed Schedule Check List

Users must remember that it is more important to complete a **Qualitative Check** before running a **Quantitative Check** such as the P6 **Check Schedule Report** and ensure that all the normal checks are made to a schedule integrity which include but not limited to the following types of checks:

- Check the full scope of the project has been captured.

- Ensure all contract or customer requirements have been considered by reading the contract or scope of works.

- Check all calendars and holidays are correct and that the holidays are set well into the future so any delayed activity will calculate correctly. Typically, this would be twice the project duration.

- Ensure there is a closed network with all activities having a start predecessor and finish successor. This may be achieved by displaying the predecessor and successor columns.

- Check all relationships are valid.

- Check all constraints are valid and cross referenced to contract documentation.

- Have inappropriate Schedule Options been assigned?

- Review float. Activities with excessive float should be assigned dummy successors or delayed if they are not scheduled in a realistic timeframe with sequencing logic or Early Start constraints.

- Ensure all stakeholders are represented and agree to their scope or work.

- Ensure all risk mitigation activities have been added.

- Check the Critical Path is realistic and aligned with what project personnel consider critical.

- A resourced schedule should be optimized by checking the histograms and tables.

- Evaluate the contingent time.

- Ensure all project personnel agree with the schedule.

> ℹ️ There are many other check lists available and one of the more popular ones is the US Defense Contract Management Agency (DCMA) 14-point schedule assessment which has been incorporated into software tools such as Acumen Fuse and the Primavera P6 Schedule Check report.

11.7 Workshop 9 – Constraints

Background

Management has provided further input to your schedule as the client has said that they require the submission on or before 27 January 2025.

Assignment

1. Go to the **Activities Window** and observe the calculated finish date and the critical path of the project before applying any constraints.

2. Bars – Display the **Float Bar** (**Total Float Bar**) and **Neg Float Bar** (**Negative Float Bar**).

3. Columns – display the columns as per the picture below.

4. The client has said that they require the submission on 27 January 2025. Apply a **Finish On or Before** constraint and assign a constraint date of 27 January 2025 16:00 to the **Bid Document Submitted** activity from the **Status** tab.

   NOTE: The author has in the past found that constraint times have not always matched the activity calendar start times (e.g., 08:00) and finish times (e.g., 16:00) and have been set to 00:00. Therefore ensure the **User Preferences** form, **Dates** tab is set to display the time.

5. Schedule the project. There should be no change in the Total Float as a **Finish On or Before** constraint will not develop Positive Float.

6. Remove the **Finish On or Before** constraint from the **Bid Document Submitted** activity.

7. Now move to the **Project Window**, **Dates** tab and assign a **Project Must Finish By** constraint of 27 January 2025 16:00. Return to the **Activities Window** and reschedule.

8. All activities now have their Total Float calculated to a **Project Must Finish By** constraint date, all have positive Total Float and the Critical Path has disappeared, which is not useful.

Activity ID	Activity Name	Original Duration	Start	Finish	Total Float	Free Float	Dec 2024 / Jan 2025 Gantt
	Bid for Facility Extension	31d	09-Dec-24 08	23-Jan-25 16	2d	0d	
	Technical Specification	13d	09-Dec-24 08	27-Dec-24 16	4d	0d	
OZ1000	Approval to Bid	0d	09-Dec-24 08		2d	0d	
OZ1010	Determine Installation Requirements	4d	09-Dec-24 08	12-Dec-24 16	2d	0d	
OZ1020	Create Technical Specification	5d	13-Dec-24 08	19-Dec-24 16	2d	0d	
OZ1030	Identify Supplier Components	2d	20-Dec-24 08	23-Dec-24 16	2d	0d	
OZ1040	Validate Technical Specification	2d	24-Dec-24 08	27-Dec-24 16	4d	0d	
	Delivery Plan	14d	24-Dec-24 08	15-Jan-25 16	2d	0d	
OZ1050	Document Delivery Methodology	4d	30-Dec-24 08	03-Jan-25 16	4d	0d	
OZ1060	Obtain Quotes from Suppliers	8d	24-Dec-24 08	07-Jan-25 16	2d	0d	
OZ1070	Calculate the Bid Estimate	3d	08-Jan-25 08	10-Jan-25 16	2d	0d	
OZ1080	Create the Project Schedule	3d	11-Jan-25 08	14-Jan-25 16	2d	0d	
OZ1090	Review the Delivery Plan	1d	15-Jan-25 08	15-Jan-25 16	2d	0d	
	Bid Document	14d	06-Jan-25 08	23-Jan-25 16	2d	0d	
OZ1100	Create Draft of Bid Document	6d	06-Jan-25 08	13-Jan-25 16	4d	2d	
OZ1110	Review Bid Document	4d	16-Jan-25 08	21-Jan-25 16	2d	0d	
OZ1120	Finalise and Submit Bid Document	2d	22-Jan-25 08	23-Jan-25 16	2d	0d	
OZ1130	Bid Document Submitted	0d		23-Jan-25 16	2d	0d	

---

9. Remove **Project Must Finish By** constraint of 27 January 2025 16:00 (by highlighting the date and pressing the **Delete** key and tab out of the cell to ensure the date has been deleted.

10. Schedule the project and the Critical Path should return.

11. Apply a **Finish On or Before** constraint and assign a constraint date of 27 January 2025 16:00 to the **Bid Document Submitted** activity and schedule, the Critical Path will remain.

Activity ID	Activity Name	Original Duration	Start	Finish	Total Float	Free Float	December 2024 / January 2025
Bid for Facility Extension		31d	09-Dec-24 08	23-Jan-25 16	0d	0d	
Technical Specification		13d	09-Dec-24 08	27-Dec-24 16	2d	0d	
OZ1000	Approval to Bid	0d	09-Dec-24 08		0d	0d	
OZ1010	Determine Installation Requirements	4d	09-Dec-24 08	12-Dec-24 16	0d	0d	
OZ1020	Create Technical Specification	5d	13-Dec-24 08	19-Dec-24 16	0d	0d	
OZ1030	Identify Supplier Components	2d	20-Dec-24 08	23-Dec-24 16	0d	0d	
OZ1040	Validate Technical Specification	2d	24-Dec-24 08	27-Dec-24 16	2d	0d	
Delivery Plan		14d	24-Dec-24 08	15-Jan-25 16	0d	0d	
OZ1050	Document Delivery Methodology	4d	30-Dec-24 08	03-Jan-25 16	2d	0d	
OZ1060	Obtain Quotes from Suppliers	8d	24-Dec-24 08	07-Jan-25 16	0d	0d	
OZ1070	Calculate the Bid Estimate	3d	08-Jan-25 08	10-Jan-25 16	0d	0d	
OZ1080	Create the Project Schedule	3d	11-Jan-25 08	14-Jan-25 16	0d	0d	
OZ1090	Review the Delivery Plan	1d	15-Jan-25 08	15-Jan-25 16	0d	0d	
Bid Document		14d	06-Jan-25 08	23-Jan-25 16	0d	0d	
OZ1100	Create Draft of Bid Document	6d	06-Jan-25 08	13-Jan-25 16	2d	2d	
OZ1110	Review Bid Document	4d	16-Jan-25 08	21-Jan-25 16	0d	0d	
OZ1120	Finalise and Submit Bid Document	2d	22-Jan-25 08	23-Jan-25 16	0d	0d	
OZ1130	Bid Document Submitted	0d		23-Jan-25 16*	0d	0d	

12. Due to the proximity to Christmas, management has requested that you delay the **Obtain Quotes from Suppliers** until first thing in the New Year (02 January 2025). Consensus is that a better response and sharper prices will be obtained after the Christmas rush.

   ➤ To achieve this, set a **Start On or After** constraint date of 02 January 2025 08:00 on the **Obtain Quotes from Suppliers** activity.

   ➤ Now reschedule. Observe the impact on the critical path and end dates.

Activity ID	Activity Name	Original Duration	Start	Finish	Total Float	Free Float	December 2024 / January 2025
Bid for Facility Extension		35d	09-Dec-24 08	29-Jan-25 16	0d	0d	
Technical Specification		13d	09-Dec-24 08	27-Dec-24 16	4d	0d	
OZ1000	Approval to Bid	0d	09-Dec-24 08		2d	0d	
OZ1010	Determine Installation Requirements	4d	09-Dec-24 08	12-Dec-24 16	2d	0d	
OZ1020	Create Technical Specification	5d	13-Dec-24 08	19-Dec-24 16	2d	0d	
OZ1030	Identify Supplier Components	2d	20-Dec-24 08	23-Dec-24 16	2d	0d	
OZ1040	Validate Technical Specification	2d	24-Dec-24 08	27-Dec-24 16	4d	0d	
Delivery Plan		16d	30-Dec-24 08	21-Jan-25 16	-2d	0d	
OZ1050	Document Delivery Methodology	4d	30-Dec-24 08	03-Jan-25 16	4d	0d	
OZ1060	Obtain Quotes from Suppliers	8d	02-Jan-25 08*	13-Jan-25 16	-2d	0d	
OZ1070	Calculate the Bid Estimate	3d	14-Jan-25 08	16-Jan-25 16	-3d	0d	
OZ1080	Create the Project Schedule	3d	17-Jan-25 08	20-Jan-25 16	-3d	0d	
OZ1090	Review the Delivery Plan	1d	21-Jan-25 08	21-Jan-25 16	-2d	0d	
Bid Document		18d	06-Jan-25 08	29-Jan-25 16	0d	0d	
OZ1100	Create Draft of Bid Document	6d	06-Jan-25 08	13-Jan-25 16	4d	6d	
OZ1110	Review Bid Document	4d	22-Jan-25 08	27-Jan-25 16	-2d	0d	
OZ1120	Finalise and Submit Bid Document	2d	28-Jan-25 08	29-Jan-25 16	-2d	0d	
OZ1130	Bid Document Submitted	0d		29-Jan-25 16*	-2d	0d	

13. The Finish Constraint on the **Bid Document Submitted** activity has created some negative float, which is displayed in the **Total Float** column and the **Negative Float** bar.

14. Notice that activities with constraints have an "*" by their dates.

15. Activity OZ1070 and OZ1080 have 3 days Negative Float because they are on a 6 day/week calendar, but the other Critical activities have 2 days Negative Float because they are on a 5 day/week calendar.

---

16. Display the Notebook tab in the **Activities Window**.

17. Add a **Notebook Topic** against the **Obtain Quotes from Supplier** activity indicating why there is a constraint on 02 January 2025.

Activity ID	Activity Name	Original Duration	Start	Finish	Total Float	Free Float
Bid for Facility Extension		35d	09-Dec-24 08	29-Jan-25 16	0d	0d
Technical Specification		13d	09-Dec-24 08	27-Dec-24 16	4d	0d
OZ1000	Approval to Bid	0d	09-Dec-24 08		2d	0d
OZ1010	Determine Installation Requirements	4d	09-Dec-24 08	12-Dec-24 16	2d	0d
OZ1020	Create Technical Specification	5d	13-Dec-24 08	19-Dec-24 16	2d	0d
OZ1030	Identify Supplier Components	2d	20-Dec-24 08	23-Dec-24 16	2d	0d
OZ1040	Validate Technical Specification	2d	24-Dec-24 08	27-Dec-24 16	4d	0d
Delivery Plan		16d	30-Dec-24 08	21-Jan-25 16	-2d	0d
OZ1050	Document Delivery Methodology	4d	30-Dec-24 08	03-Jan-25 16	4d	0d
OZ1060	Obtain Quotes from Suppliers	8d	02-Jan-25 08*	13-Jan-25 16	-2d	0d

General | Status | Predecessors | Successors | Relationships | Expenses | Codes | Notebook | Resources | Summary | Steps | WPs & Docs | User Defined Fields

Activity OZ1130   Bid Document Submitted   Project OZB-09

Notebook Topic
Constraints

Constraints

Due to the proximity of Christmas management has requested that the quotes are obtained after New Year to obtain better prices.

18. Open the **Group and Sort** form by clicking on the [icon] icon and group by **Total Float** and close the form.

P6 Group and Sort ✕

Display Options
☑ Show Group Totals
   ☐ Show Grand Totals
   ☐ Show Summaries Only
☐ Shrink vertical grouping bands

✔ OK
⊘ Cancel
⊡ Apply
✕ Delete

Group By

Group By	Indent	To Level	Group Interval	Page Break	Font & Colo
Total Float			<None>	☐	12 Aria
					11 Aria
					9 Aria
					8 Aria

🖼 Sort...
▷ Default
❓ Help

Group By Options
☐ Hide if empty
☐ Sort bands alphabetically
Show :
☐ Title
☐ ID / Code
☑ Name / Description

19. Sort on duration (by clicking in the **Original Duration** column) to bring the longest activity to the top. It is normally the longest activity that may be shortened.

Activity ID	Activity Name	Original Duration	Start	Finish	Total Float	Free Float
▣ **-3d**		6d	14-Jan-25 08	20-Jan-25 16	-3d	0d
OZ1070	Calculate the Bid Estimate	3d	14-Jan-25 08	16-Jan-25 16	-3d	0d
OZ1080	Create the Project Schedule	3d	17-Jan-25 08	20-Jan-25 16	-3d	0d
▣ **-2d**		20d	02-Jan-25 08	29-Jan-25 16	-2d	0d
OZ1060	Obtain Quotes from Suppliers	8d	02-Jan-25 08*	13-Jan-25 16	-2d	0d
OZ1090	Review the Delivery Plan	1d	21-Jan-25 08	21-Jan-25 16	-2d	0d
OZ1110	Review Bid Document	4d	22-Jan-25 08	27-Jan-25 16	-2d	0d
OZ1120	Finalise and Submit Bid Document	2d	28-Jan-25 08	29-Jan-25 16	-2d	0d
OZ1130	Bid Document Submitted	0d		29-Jan-25 16*	-2d	0d
▣ **2d**		11d	09-Dec-24 08	23-Dec-24 16	2d	0d
OZ1000	Approval to Bid	0d	09-Dec-24 08		2d	0d
OZ1010	Determine Installation Requirements	4d	09-Dec-24 08	12-Dec-24 16	2d	0d
OZ1020	Create Technical Specification	5d	13-Dec-24 08	19-Dec-24 16	2d	0d
OZ1030	Identify Supplier Components	2d	20-Dec-24 08	23-Dec-24 16	2d	0d
▣ **4d**		12d	24-Dec-24 08	13-Jan-25 16	4d	0d
OZ1040	Validate Technical Specification	2d	24-Dec-24 08	27-Dec-24 16	4d	0d
OZ1050	Document Delivery Methodology	4d	30-Dec-24 08	03-Jan-25 16	4d	0d
OZ1100	Create Draft of Bid Document	6d	06-Jan-25 08	13-Jan-25 16	4d	6d

20. After review, it is agreed that 2 days may be deducted from **Review Bid Document** activity. Change the duration of this activity to 2 days, reschedule:

Activity ID	Activity Name	Original Duration	Start	Finish	Total Float	Free Float
▣ **0d**		18d	02-Jan-25 08	27-Jan-25 16	0d	0d
OZ1060	Obtain Quotes from Suppliers	8d	02-Jan-25 08*	13-Jan-25 16	0d	0d
OZ1070	Calculate the Bid Estimate	3d	14-Jan-25 08	16-Jan-25 16	0d	0d
OZ1080	Create the Project Schedule	3d	17-Jan-25 08	20-Jan-25 16	0d	0d
OZ1090	Review the Delivery Plan	1d	21-Jan-25 08	21-Jan-25 16	0d	0d
OZ1110	Review Bid Document	2d	22-Jan-25 08	23-Jan-25 16	0d	0d
OZ1120	Finalise and Submit Bid Document	2d	24-Jan-25 08	27-Jan-25 16	0d	0d
OZ1130	Bid Document Submitted	0d		27-Jan-25 16*	0d	0d
▣ **4d**		11d	09-Dec-24 08	23-Dec-24 16	4d	0d
OZ1000	Approval to Bid	0d	09-Dec-24 08		4d	0d
OZ1010	Determine Installation Requirements	4d	09-Dec-24 08	12-Dec-24 16	4d	0d
OZ1020	Create Technical Specification	5d	13-Dec-24 08	19-Dec-24 16	4d	0d
OZ1030	Identify Supplier Components	2d	20-Dec-24 08	23-Dec-24 16	4d	0d
▣ **6d**		12d	24-Dec-24 08	13-Jan-25 16	6d	0d
OZ1040	Validate Technical Specification	2d	24-Dec-24 08	27-Dec-24 16	6d	0d
OZ1050	Document Delivery Methodology	4d	30-Dec-24 08	03-Jan-25 16	6d	0d
OZ1100	Create Draft of Bid Document	6d	06-Jan-25 08	13-Jan-25 16	6d	6d

21. Now organize by WBS and sort by Activity ID:

Activity ID	Activity Name	Original Duration	Start	Finish	Total Float	Free Float
▣ **Bid for Facility Extension**		33d	09-Dec-24 08	27-Jan-25 16	0d	0d
▣ **Technical Specification**		13d	09-Dec-24 08	27-Dec-24 16	6d	0d
OZ1000	Approval to Bid	0d	09-Dec-24 08		4d	0d
OZ1010	Determine Installation Requirements	4d	09-Dec-24 08	12-Dec-24 16	4d	0d
OZ1020	Create Technical Specification	5d	13-Dec-24 08	19-Dec-24 16	4d	0d
OZ1030	Identify Supplier Components	2d	20-Dec-24 08	23-Dec-24 16	4d	0d
OZ1040	Validate Technical Specification	2d	24-Dec-24 08	27-Dec-24 16	6d	0d
▣ **Delivery Plan**		16d	30-Dec-24 08	21-Jan-25 16	0d	0d
OZ1050	Document Delivery Methodology	4d	30-Dec-24 08	03-Jan-25 16	6d	0d
OZ1060	Obtain Quotes from Suppliers	8d	02-Jan-25 08*	13-Jan-25 16	0d	0d
OZ1070	Calculate the Bid Estimate	3d	14-Jan-25 08	16-Jan-25 16	0d	0d
OZ1080	Create the Project Schedule	3d	17-Jan-25 08	20-Jan-25 16	0d	0d
OZ1090	Review the Delivery Plan	1d	21-Jan-25 08	21-Jan-25 16	0d	0d
▣ **Bid Document**		16d	06-Jan-25 08	27-Jan-25 16	0d	0d
OZ1100	Create Draft of Bid Document	6d	06-Jan-25 08	13-Jan-25 16	6d	6d
OZ1110	Review Bid Document	2d	22-Jan-25 08	23-Jan-25 16	0d	0d
OZ1120	Finalise and Submit Bid Document	2d	24-Jan-25 08	27-Jan-25 16	0d	0d
OZ1130	Bid Document Submitted	0d		27-Jan-25 16*	0d	0d

22. This is the end of the Workshop.

12 GROUP, SORT AND LAYOUTS

Group and Sort enables data such as activities in the **Activities Window**, WBS Nodes in the **WBS Window**, projects in the **Project Window**, and many other data items to be sorted and organized under other parameters such as **Dates** and **Resources** or user defined **Activity** and **Project Codes**. This function is similar to **Grouping** in Microsoft Project and Elecosoft (Asta) Powerproject.

Layouts is a function in which the formatting of parameters such as the **Group and Sort**, **Columns** and **Bars** is saved and reapplied later. This function is similar to **Views** in Elecosoft (Asta) Power Project and Microsoft Project. A **Layout** may be edited, saved, or reapplied at a later date and may have a **Filter** associated with it. Layouts contain the formatting for all options of both the top and bottom pane.

Layouts do not save the Date, Time and Duration formatting, these are set in the **User Preferences** form.

Although Group and Sort is available in many forms, Layouts are only available in a few places including the following Windows:

- Projects
- WBS
- Activities
- Tracking

Users must be aware that when they open a new project that the Layout applied to the old project will still be applied and used to format the new project's data on the screen and in printouts. There is a high probability that printouts will have the incorrect header and footers for the new project that you have opened, especially if the project is for a different client and you have client logos in your headers or footers. User need to check when they have opened a new project that the layout that is in use is still applicable to the newly opened project.

This chapter will concentrate on how **Group and Sort** and **Layouts** are applied in the **Activities Window** but the same principles apply to the other windows. This chapter covers the following topics:

Topic	Notes on the Function
• Open the **Group and Sort** form reformat data in the **Projects Window** or **Activities Window**	• Click on the [icon] icon, or • Select **View**, **Group and Sort by**, **Customize**.
• Create, save or edit a Layout	Select either: • From the menu **View**, **Layout**, **Save Layout As…**, or • By clicking the down arrow in the **Layout** bar:

12.1 Group and Sort Activities

The **Group and Sort** function has been used in this publication to group activities under WBS bands.

To Group and Sort activities open the **Group and Sort** form by:

- Clicking the [icon] toolbar icon, or

- Selecting **View**, **Group and Sort by**, **Customize**.

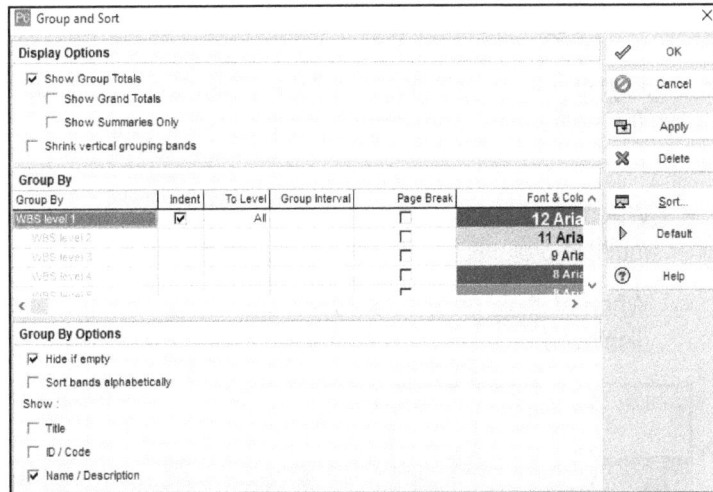

12.1.1 Display Options

Show Group Totals

Show Group Totals is a new function in Primavera Version 6.0 which when unchecked hides the summary data in the bands, which prevents the truncating of Band titles.

Summary Data Displayed

Activity ID	Original Duration	Start	Finish	Total Float
▣ **Bid for Fac**	139d	08-Dec-09 A	22-Jan-10	0d
▣ **Research**	31d	08-Dec-09 A	21-Dec-09	6d
OZ1000	0d	08-Dec-09 A		
OZ1010	1d	08-Dec-09 A	08-Dec-09 A	
OZ1020	8d	09-Dec-09 A	21-Dec-09	2d
▣ **Estimate**	52d	22-Dec-09	08-Jan-10	3d
OZ1070	2d	07-Jan-10	08-Jan-10	0d

Summary Data Hidden

Activity ID	Original Duration	Start	Finish	Total Float
▣ **Bid for Faciliity Extension**				
▣ **Research**				
OZ1000	0d	08-Dec-09 A		
OZ1010	1d	08-Dec-09 A	08-Dec-09 A	
OZ1020	8d	09-Dec-09 A	21-Dec-09	2d
▣ **Estimate**				
OZ1070	2d	07-Jan-10	08-Jan-10	0d

Show Grand Totals

Show Grand Totals provides a total of all the activities in a band at the top of a view and is similar to displaying a Project summary task in Microsoft Project or Elecosoft (Asta) Powerproject.

This displays a Summary band for multiple projects and adds up all the costs and hours for a project, displays the earliest and latest dates and a summary duration for all the data displayed. This feature is very useful:

- When the project is not organized by WBS and therefore has no project total line, or when multiple projects have been opened to calculate all the projects' values, and

- When multiple projects are open and thereby enables the total for multiple projects to be displayed.

Activity ID	Activity Name	BL Project Total Cost	BL Project Labor Units
Total		A$6,899,980.56	10039
Nesbid Building Expansion		A$550,470.40	9346
Haitang Corporate Park		A$636,980.80	10735
City Center Office Building Addition		A$1,162,028.80	20110
Harbour Pointe Assisted Living Center		A$4,550,500.56	60201

Show Summaries Only

Show Summaries Only hides all the activities and displays only the WBS or Codes that have been used to summarize the activities:

Activity ID	Activity Name	Early Start	Early Finish	BL Budgeted Labor Cost
1-5 OzBuild Bid		01-Dec-03	29-Jan-04	$22,830
1-5.1 Research		01-Dec-03	17-Dec-03	$6,640
1-5.2 Estimation		12-Dec-03	15-Jan-04	$8,150
1-5.3 Proposal		15-Jan-04	29-Jan-04	$8,040

Shrink Vertical Grouping Bands

Shrink vertical grouping bands is new to Primavera Version 6.0 and narrows the Vertical Bands on the left of the screen. This is useful in projects with a number of levels in the WBS as this provides more usable screen space and paper width for printing.

Option Unchecked

Activity ID	Activity Name	Original Duration
Bid for Faciliity Extension		
Research		
OZ1000	Bid Request Docume...	0.0d
OZ1010	Bid Strategy Developed	1.0d
OZ1020	Technical Feasibility S...	8.0d
Estimate		

Option Checked

Activity ID	Activity Name	Original Duration
Bid for Faciliity Extension		
Research		
OZ1000	Bid Request Docume...	0.0d
OZ1010	Bid Strategy Developed	1.0d
OZ1020	Technical Feasibility S...	8.0d
Estimate		

12.1.2 Group By

The **Group By** box has several options:

- **Group By and Indent**

When a hierarchical code such as a **WBS** and the **Indent** are selected, the subsequent bands are completed by the software and there are no other banding options available. The WBS is then displayed hierarchically:

Group By	Indent	To Level	Group Interval	Font & Color
WBS level 1	☑	All		12 Arial
WBS level 2				11 Arial
WBS level 3				9 Arial
WBS level 4				8 Arial

Activity ID	Activity Name	Early Start	Early Finish
⊟ Bid for Facility Ext...		06-Dec-04	24-Jan-05
⁻ Research		06-Dec-04	21-Dec-04
OZ1010	Bid Strategy M...	06-Dec-04	06-Dec-04
OZ1020	Investigate Te...	07-Dec-04	16-Dec-04
OZ1030	Document Inst...	17-Dec-04	21-Dec-04
OZ1000	Bid Request D...	06-Dec-04	
⁻ Estimation		17-Dec-04	10-Jan-05
OZ1040	Request Comp...	04-Jan-05	06-Jan-05

When a hierarchical code such as a **WBS** is selected and the **Indent** is **NOT** selected on a line then the subsequent bands are **NOT** completed by the software and other bands may be selected. The WBS is not displayed hierarchically:

Group By	Indent	To Level	Group Interval	Font & Color
Early Start			Week	12 Arial
WBS	☐	All		11 Arial
Resources				9 Arial
				8 Arial

Activity ID	Activity Name	Early Start	Early Finish
⊟ 01-Dec-03		01-Dec-03	11-Dec-03
⁻ Research		01-Dec-03	11-Dec-03
⁻ Sales Engineer, System Engin...		01-Dec-03	01-Dec-03
A1010	Bid Strategy Meeting	01-Dec-03	01-Dec-03
⁻ System Engineer		02-Dec-03	11-Dec-03
A1020	Investigate Techni...	02-Dec-03	11-Dec-03
⊟ 08-Dec-03		12-Dec-03	15-Jan-04
⁻ Research		12-Dec-03	17-Dec-03
⁻ Sales Engineer, System Engin...		12-Dec-03	17-Dec-03
A1030	Document Installati...	12-Dec-03	17-Dec-03

- **To Level**

The **To Level** option decides how many levels of the hierarchical code structure such as the WBS will be displayed. All activities are displayed under the lowest level of WBS, as chosen from the **To Level** drop-down box.

This option enables other banding below the select level which is not permitted with the **All** option.

Group By

Group By	Indent	To Level	Group Interval	Font & Color
WBS	☐	2 ▾		12 Arial
		All		11 Arial
		1		9 Arial
		2		8 Arial

Group By

Group By	Indent	To Level	Group Interval	Font & Color
WBS	☐	2		12 Arial
Resources				11 Arial
				9 Arial
				8 Arial

- **Group Interval**

  This option is available with some fields such as **Total Float**, where the interval may be typed in, and **Date** fields, where a drop-down box enables the selection of the time interval used to group activities:

- **Font and Color**

  Double-click these boxes to open the <u>E</u>dit **Font and Color** form to change the font and color of each band.

12.1.3 Group By Options

- **Sort Banding Alphabetically**, this means sort by the Code value.

  When unchecked they are sorted naturally per the picture above:

  When this is checked the bands are sorted by the code assigned to the Activity Code or WBS Code:

  i This function is extremely useful for providing two sort orders for coding structures such as the WBS when the coding is entered, but only operates when the coding in the WBS Window is not in a natural sort order.

- **Hide if empty**

  Check this box to hide bands that:

  ➢ Have not been assigned an activity, or

  ➢ When activities have been filtered out and only the bands remain.

  > **_i_** This function is useful when you have filtered on a couple of activities and the screen is filled with blank bands. This will remove all the blank bands.

- **Show Title**, **Show ID/Code** and **Show Name/Description**

  These options format the display of the band title. It is not possible to uncheck all the options as there then would not be a title in the band. The options change depending on the data displayed in the band:

With All Options Checked	With Only Description Checked

Activity ID	Original Duration	Start	Finish	Total Float
■ Project: REF101206 Bid for Faciliity Extension				
⊟ WBS: REF101206.1 Research				
OZ1000	0d	07-Dec-09		4d
OZ1010	1d	07-Dec-09	07-Dec-09	4d
OZ1020	8d	08-Dec-09	17-Dec-09	4d
⊟ WBS: REF101206.2 Estimate				
OZ1070	2d	07-Jan-10	08-Jan-10	0d

Activity ID	Original Duration	Start
■ Bid for Faciliity Extension		
⊟ Research		
OZ1000	0d	07-Dec-09
OZ1010	1d	07-Dec-09
OZ1020	8d	08-Dec-09
⊟ Estimate		
OZ1070	2d	07-Jan-10

NOTE: These options are set for each band individually.

12.1.4 Sorting

The [⊟ Sort...] icon opens the **Sort** form where the order of the activities in each band may be specified.

Move Up and **Move Down** was added in Version 22.

The order shown in the picture provides a good natural "Waterfall" order to activities:

> ⚠️ This order may be easily overridden by clicking on the column titles to reorder activities and therefore the use of this option is problematic as clicking on the column header is very simple and will override options set here.

Sort		×
Field Name	Sort Order	✓ OK
Start	Ascending	
Original Duration	Ascending	⊘ Cancel
Total Float	Ascending	
		⊹ Add
		✖ Delete
		▲ Move Up
		▼ Move Down
		? Help

Added in P6 Version 22

This publication is only sold as a bound book, no parts may be reproduced by any means, e.g., electronic, video or print.

© **Hyde Park Solutions Limited**   **167**

12.1.5 Auto-Reorganization

This function reorganizes data based on the current **Group and Sort** order when an activity's attributes are changed.

For example, when an activity's WBS code is re-assigned in the Activity Details pane, then the activity will automatically be moved to the newly assigned WBS band where the activities are grouped by WBS when this option is turned on.

This has now been moved to the menu and may be turned on and off and is uniquely set for each window. To activate or de-activate this function:

- Select **T**ools, **Disable Auto-Reorganization**, or

- Click on the ⬚ **Tools** toolbar icon.

> ⚠ When the icon is a dark shade then the function is disabled and the command on the menu erroneously still states **Disable Auto-Reorganization** when it actually means **Enable Auto-Reorganization.**
>
> When a new Layout or Filter is applied then the data is also automatically reorganized.

12.1.6 Set Page Breaks in the Group and Sort Form

In earlier versions of P6 page breaks could only be set at the first band in the **Group and Sort** form from the **Page Setup**, **Options** tab.

Select **V**iew, **Group and Sort by**, **Customize** or click on the ⬚ icon and select **Customize** to open the **Group and Sort** form:

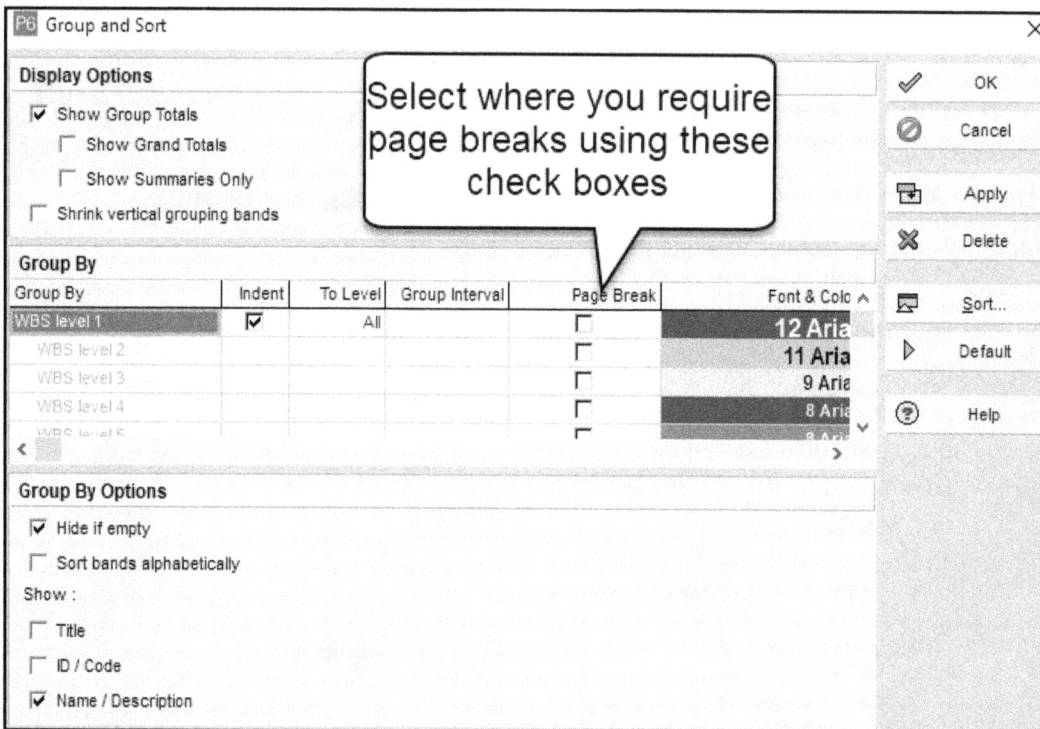

12.1.7 Group and Sort Projects at Enterprise Level

Projects in the **Projects Window** may be Grouped and Sorted in a similar way to the Grouping and Sorting of activities.

The main difference is that a predefined group is created for each Project Code in the drop down list.

When a database is opened, the projects are by default displayed under the Enterprise Project Structure (EPS) in the **Projects Window**.

The projects may be Grouped and Sorted under a number of different headings by:

- Selecting **Layout**, **Group and Sort by**, **Customize**, or

- Right-clicking in the columns area and selecting **Group and Sort ...**, or

- Selecting **View**, **Group and Sort By**

Then selecting the option from the drop-down list.

The **Customize**... option will open the project's **Group and Sort** form which operates in a similar way to the Activity's **Group and Sort** form.

12.2 Understanding Layouts

A standard load of Primavera is supplied with a number of predefined Layouts for some of the windows which are defined by default as **Global Layouts** and any user on the system may apply these. These layouts may be copied and shared with other users or be available to the current user in a similar way as filters.

Primavera Version 6.0 introduced Project Layouts available from the Activities Window. Project Layouts are only available when a project is open and may be exported with a project and therefore minimizes the need for Global Layouts.

In large databases with many users and projects there becomes a need to code layouts so they may easily be found in long lists of filters. Prefixing them with the project number may be considered.

The following types of Layouts are available in the **Activities Window**:

- **Global** which are normally managed by the Database Administrator and are available to all users and all projects,

- **User** that a user may apply to any project that the user has open, and

- **Project** that may only be applied when a project is open.

> Layouts are not exported with an XER file in but may be exported using a PLF file. Therefore, to send a person a complete project schedule you may need to include the layout as a PLF file so the other user may easily reproduce your view of the data.

12.2.1 Applying an Existing Layout

Layouts may be applied from the **Open Layout** form by:

- Selecting the **Open** option from the **Layout Options** bar:

- Or, by selecting **View**, **Layout**, **Open Layout**....

When a Layout has been edited by changing any parameter, such as column formatting, a form will be displayed allowing the confirmation of the changes that have been made to the layout.

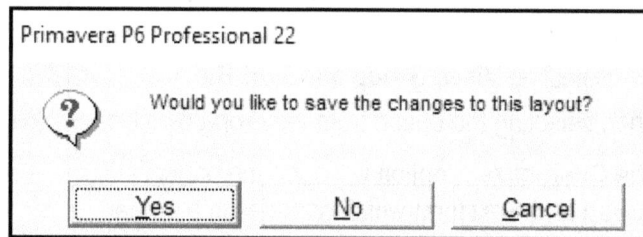

The **Open Layout** form will be displayed and an alternative layout may be selected from the list. The list has three headings after a project layout has been created, **Global**, **User**, and **Project**:

- ➤ Click on the [Apply] icon to apply the layout. This will leave the form open but allow the effect to be viewed, or

- ➤ Click on the [Open] icon to apply the layout and close the form:

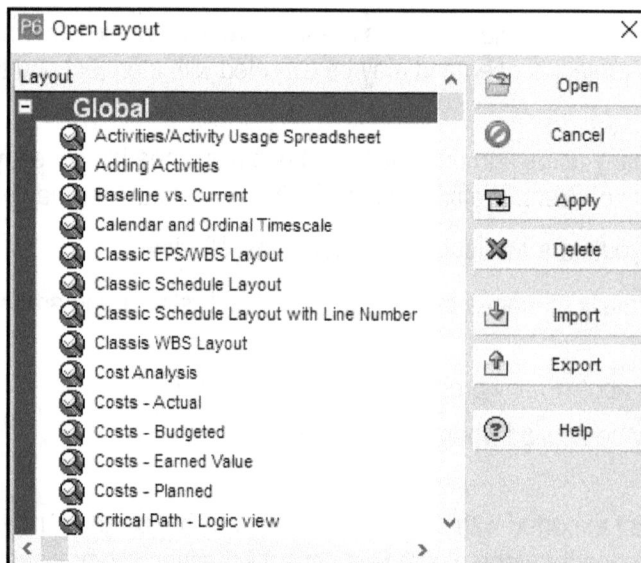

Click on the [Layout] icon to reorder the Layouts.

12.2.2 Creating a New Layout

A new layout may be created by saving an existing layout with a new name and editing it:

- Apply the layout that closely matches the requirements of the new layout and apply.

- Select either:
  - ➢ From the menu **View, Layout, Save Layout**, or
  - ➢ From the Layout Options bar **Layout, Save As...**:

- Type in a new **Layout Name** and select to whom you wish the layout to be available.
  - ➢ **All Users** will make the layout Global and therefore available to all users and you will need the appropriate security access to be able to create a Global Layout.

  - ➢ **Another User** will make the layout available to a nominated user.

  - ➢ **Current User** will make a copy for your own use.

  - ➢ **Project** will make the layout available to anyone who has the project open. This option is useful to reduce the number of Global Layouts in a database with a number of projects requiring a number of layouts each.

- Click on the 🖫 save toolbar icon.

12.2.3 Saving a Layout after Changes

This layout may now be edited and the edits saved by selecting:

- ➢ From the menu **View, Layout, Save Layout As**, or
- ➢ From the Layout bar **Layout, Save**.

12.2.4 Layout Types

A layout is comprised of a **Top Pane** and a **Bottom Pane**. Each **Pane** may be assigned a **Layout Type**. This is a list of **Layout Types** and the panes that may be applied to the **Activities Window**:

Layout Name	Available in Top Pane	Available in Bottom Pane
• Gantt Chart	Yes	Yes
• Activity Details		Yes
• Activity Table	Yes	Yes
• Activity Network	Yes	
• Trace Logic		Yes
• Activity Usage Profile		Yes
• Resource Usage Spreadsheet		Yes
• Resource Usage Profile		Yes
• Activity Usage Spreadsheet	Yes	Yes

ⓘ The available layouts vary depending on the window open. This chapter will predominately discuss the Activities Window but experimentation will show the options available in the other windows.

12.2.5 Changing Activity Layout Types in Panes

The **Toolbars** have icons for the display options in the top and bottom pane. Placing the mouse over each icon will display the function of each:

- are the **Top Layout** toolbar icons, and

- 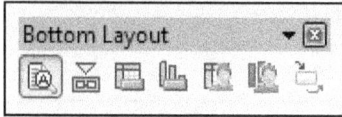 are the **Bottom Layout** toolbar icons.

To change a **Layout Type** in a pane, select from the menu:

- **View, Show on Top**, or

- **View, Show on Bottom**.

Then select the Layout Type required from the list.

12.2.6 Activities Window Layout Panes

Each Layout Type has a number of options and the formatting of these has been discussed in earlier chapters.

Gantt Chart

The Gantt Chart has two sides:

- The left side where the columns are displayed may be formatted with the **Columns**, **Sorting** and **Grouping** functions.

- The right side may be formatted using the **Timescale**, **Bars** and **Gridlines** functions.

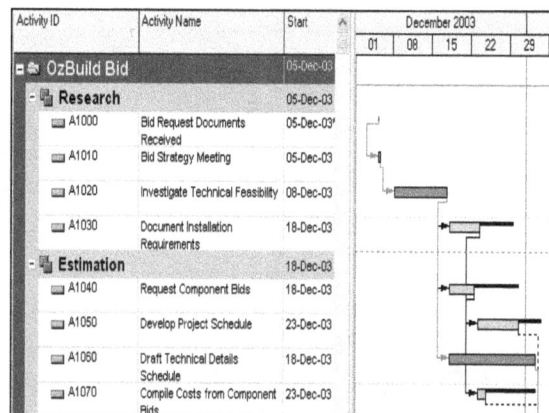

Activity Details

These may be displayed at any time in the Bottom Pane with any of the tabs hidden or displayed.

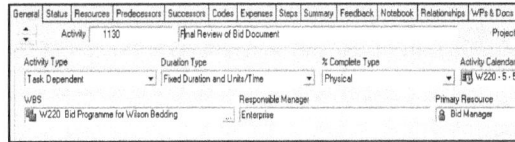

Activity Table

This layout is the same as the left side of the Gantt Chart and has no Bars and Timescale on the right side.

Activity Network

Like the Gantt Chart it has two panes:

- The **left** pane displays the WBS:
  - ➢ This side may not be formatted except by adjusting the width of the columns.

  - ➢ The selection of a WBS Node acts like a filter and will only display activities that are associated with the selected WBS Node and lower level member WBS Nodes. This enables the relationships between activities within one WBS Node to be checked.

- The **right** pane displays the activity data in boxes and is organized under headings:
  - ➢ The Activity Boxes may be formatted as described in the **Activity Network** chapter.
  - ➢ The activities may be Grouped, which is covered in the **Grouping** section of this chapter.

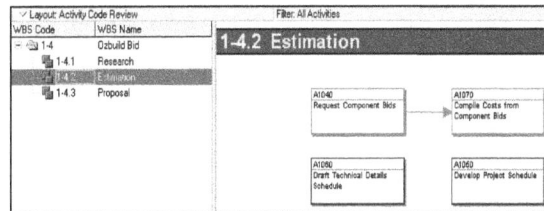

Trace Logic

The Trace Logic options allow the selection of the number of predecessor and successor levels.

This is achieved by selecting **View, Show on Bottom, Trace Logic**.

To select the number of levels of predecessors to be displayed you are required to open the **Trace Logic Options** form.

The form is then opened by right-clicking in the lower pane and selecting **Trace Logic Options...**.

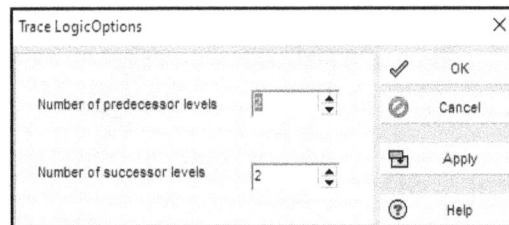

Formatting Trace Logic and Activity Network

Formatting of these boxes in both of these panes is linked to the formatting in the **Activity Network**. The boxes are formatted by right-clicking in the right screen of the **Activity Network** pane and selecting **Activity Network Options**....

Resource Analysis Panes

The **Activity Usage Profile**, **Resource Usage Spreadsheet**, **Resource Usage Profile**, **Activity Usage Spreadsheet** views display resource information and will be discussed in the **Resource Optimization** chapter.

12.2.7 WBS and Projects Window Panes

The WBS and Projects Windows have three icons for the top pane:

- ▣ shows a table without bars,

- ▥ shows a table with bars, and

- ▦ displays a Chart View of the WBS and the boxes may also be formatted by right-clicking and selecting **Chart Box Template**:

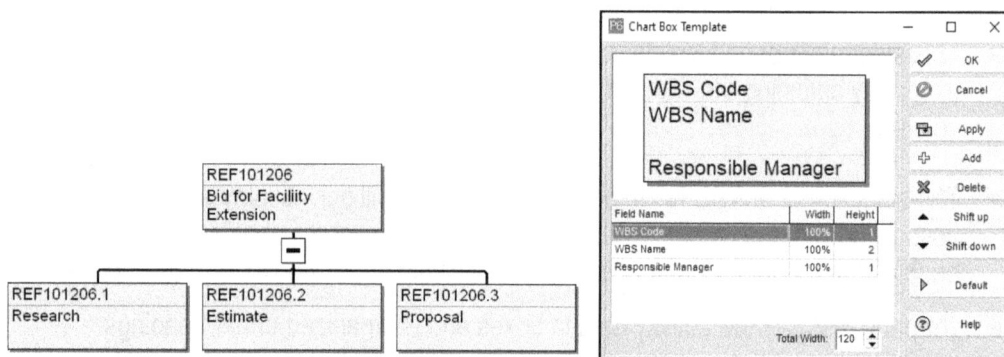

12.3 Copying a Layout To and From Another Database

A layout from any **Window** may be copied to another database by using the Import and Export functions from the **Open Layout** form. The layout is saved in a **Primavera Layout File (*.PLF)** format as a stand-alone file and is then imported into another database.

Activity Layouts may be exported and imported when exporting a file in *.XML format.

Layouts may also be imported into Visualizer using the **More**, **Manage**, **Import** option.

i   Layouts that include User Defined Fields and Codes may not display the UDF or Code information or display incorrect information when a project and layout are imported because the UDFs and Codes are assigned a different database index number on import and these index fields are used to display the UDF data.

12.4 Workshop 10 – Organizing Your Data

Background

Having completed the schedule, you may report the information with different Layouts.

Assignment

Display your project in the following formats, noting the different ways you may represent the same data.

1. Hide and display the relationships, use the ▦ icon.

2. Display the **Activity Network**, use the ▦ icon.

3. Select **Zoom in**, **Zoom out** and **Best fit** using the ▦ icons.

4. Scroll up and down or click the **WBS** Nodes on the left side of the screen. You will notice that only the Activities associated with the highlighted WBS are displayed.

5. Ctrl-click and select two WBS Nodes and you will see the relationships between the activities in each WBS Node.

6. Display the **Activity Table** by clicking on the ▦ icon.

7. Now display the Gantt Chart by clicking on the ▦ icon

8. Hide and display the **Bottom** pane by clicking on the ▦ and ▦ icons; you may need to add these icons to your toolbar.

9. With the bottom pane displayed click the ▦ icon to show the **Trace Logic** form.

10. Right-click in the **Trace Logic** form, select **Trace Logic Options...** and change the number of Predecessor and Successor Levels displaying 1, 2 and 3 levels and note the change in the layout.

11. Click on the predecessors and successors in each option and observe the changes.

12. Click on different activities in the upper pane and see the effect on the **Trace Logic** form.

13. Click on the ▦ icon to display the **Activity Details** form.

continued....

14. Create a new layout titled **OzBuild Workshop 10 – Without Float**, making it a **User Layout**, displaying the columns and formatting the bars per the following picture; the Total Float and Negative Float bars are not displayed:

Activity ID	Activity Name	Original Duration	Start	Finish
Bid for Facility Extension		33d	09-Dec-24 08	27-Jan-25 16
Technical Specification		13d	09-Dec-24 08	27-Dec-24 16
OZ1000	Approval to Bid	0d	09-Dec-24 08	
OZ1010	Determine Installation Requirements	4d	09-Dec-24 08	12-Dec-24 16
OZ1020	Create Technical Specification	5d	13-Dec-24 08	19-Dec-24 16
OZ1030	Identify Supplier Components	2d	20-Dec-24 08	23-Dec-24 16
OZ1040	Validate Technical Specification	2d	24-Dec-24 08	27-Dec-24 16
Delivery Plan		16d	30-Dec-24 08	21-Jan-25 16
OZ1050	Document Delivery Methodology	4d	30-Dec-24 08	03-Jan-25 16
OZ1060	Obtain Quotes from Suppliers	8d	02-Jan-25 08*	13-Jan-25 16
OZ1070	Calculate the Bid Estimate	3d	14-Jan-25 08	16-Jan-25 16
OZ1080	Create the Project Schedule	3d	17-Jan-25 08	20-Jan-25 16
OZ1090	Review the Delivery Plan	1d	21-Jan-25 08	21-Jan-25 16
Bid Document		16d	06-Jan-25 08	27-Jan-25 16
OZ1100	Create Draft of Bid Document	6d	06-Jan-25 08	13-Jan-25 16
OZ1110	Review Bid Document	2d	22-Jan-25 08	23-Jan-25 16
OZ1120	Finalise and Submit Bid Document	2d	24-Jan-25 08	27-Jan-25 16
OZ1130	Bid Document Submitted	0d		27-Jan-25 16*

15. Save this layout.

16. Make a copy of it titled **OzBuild Workshop 10 – With Float**, making it a User Layout, displaying the columns and formatting the bars per the following picture; this is displaying the **Total Float** and **Negative Float** bars:

17. Save this layout.

Activity ID	Activity Name	Original Duration	Start	Finish	Total Float	Free Float
Bid for Facility Extension		33d	09-Dec-24 08	27-Jan-25 16	0d	0d
Technical Specification		13d	09-Dec-24 08	27-Dec-24 16	6d	0d
OZ1000	Approval to Bid	0d	09-Dec-24 08		4d	0d
OZ1010	Determine Installation Requirements	4d	09-Dec-24 08	12-Dec-24 16	4d	0d
OZ1020	Create Technical Specification	5d	13-Dec-24 08	19-Dec-24 16	4d	0d
OZ1030	Identify Supplier Components	2d	20-Dec-24 08	23-Dec-24 16	4d	0d
OZ1040	Validate Technical Specification	2d	24-Dec-24 08	27-Dec-24 16	6d	0d
Delivery Plan		16d	30-Dec-24 08	21-Jan-25 16	0d	0d
OZ1050	Document Delivery Methodology	4d	30-Dec-24 08	03-Jan-25 16	6d	0d
OZ1060	Obtain Quotes from Suppliers	8d	02-Jan-25 08*	13-Jan-25 16	0d	0d
OZ1070	Calculate the Bid Estimate	3d	14-Jan-25 08	16-Jan-25 16	0d	0d
OZ1080	Create the Project Schedule	3d	17-Jan-25 08	20-Jan-25 16	0d	0d
OZ1090	Review the Delivery Plan	1d	21-Jan-25 08	21-Jan-25 16	0d	0d
Bid Document		16d	06-Jan-25 08	27-Jan-25 16	0d	0d
OZ1100	Create Draft of Bid Document	6d	06-Jan-25 08	13-Jan-25 16	6d	6d
OZ1110	Review Bid Document	2d	22-Jan-25 08	23-Jan-25 16	0d	0d
OZ1120	Finalise and Submit Bid Document	2d	24-Jan-25 08	27-Jan-25 16	0d	0d
OZ1130	Bid Document Submitted	0d		27-Jan-25 16*	0d	0d

13 FILTERS

This chapter covers the ability of Primavera to control which activities are displayed, both on the screen and in printouts, by using **Filters**.

13.1 Understanding Filters

Primavera has the ability to display activities that meet specific criteria. You may want to see only the incomplete activities, or the work scheduled for the next couple of months or weeks, or the activities that are in-progress. Primavera defaults to displaying all activities.

There are a number of pre-defined filters available that you may use or edit. You may also create one or more of your own. A filter may be applied to display or to highlight only those activities that meet a criterion.

There are four types of filters:

- **Default** filters which are supplied with the system which may not be edited or deleted but may be copied and then edited or modified and are often used in conjunction with the display of bars.

- **Global** filters which are made available to anyone working in the database,

- **User Defined** filters which are defined by a user and available only to that user unless it is made into a **Global** filter, and

- **Layout** filters which make a copy of the filter which is only available the layout is applied to.
  NOTE: If the current layout is a **Project** layout, then this effectively makes the **Layout** filter a project filter.

In addition:

- The **Group and Sort** function **Show Summaries Only** also works as a filter and displays only summaries (Bands), and no activities.

- The **View**, **Check Schedule** and **Activity Critical Path** options are both in effect predefined filters.

The following types of filters are not available:

- Drop-down or Auto filters as in Excel and Microsoft Project.

- Interactive filters as available in SureTrak, Elecosoft (Asta) Powerproject and Microsoft Project. This is when a filter is applied and the user is offered choices from a drop-down list. The lack of this function may result in an excessive quantity of filters being generated or the user continually editing frequently used filters.

- Project filters but copying all the filters used in a project to all the Project Layouts effectively creates Project filters but this is a lot of administration.

On the other hand, P6 does allow multiple filters to be applied at the same time.

> **i** There are no dedicated project filters (except by creating a Layout filter that have issues covered later) available in Primavera, so you might consider placing the project name or number at the start of a filter name so you may identify which filters belong to which projects. This is especially helpful when you have a number of **User Filters** or there are a number of **Global Filters**.

Topic	Menu Command
• To apply, edit, create, or delete a filter open the **Filters** form.	• Click on the 🔽 icon, or • Select **View, Filter By..., Customize**, or • Right-click in the columns area and select **Filters....**

13.2 Applying a Filter

13.2.1 Filters Form

Filters are applied from the **Filters** form which may be opened by:

- Clicking on the ⊽ icon, or

- Selecting **View, Filters...**, Customize...or

- Right-clicking in the columns area and selecting **Filters...**

NOTE: If the **All Activities** check box is not checked then there is a filter applied.

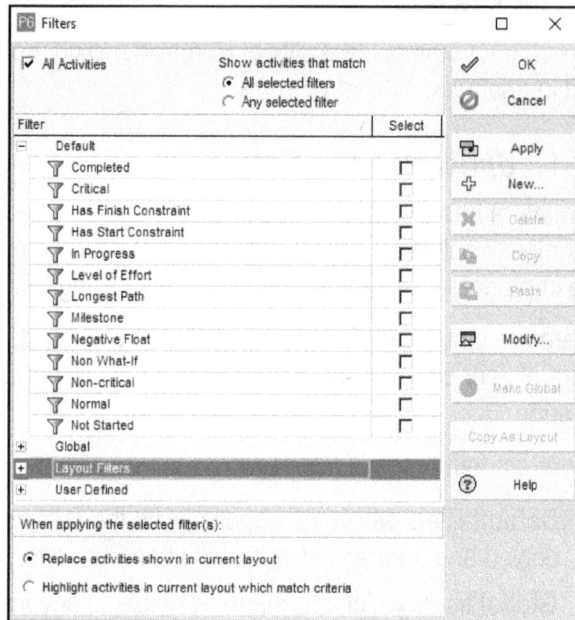

13.2.2 Applying a Single Filter

A single filter is applied by:

- Checking the **Select** check box beside one filter, and

- Clicking on the [🔲 Apply] icon to apply the filter and not close the form. If the result is undesirable another option may be selected, or

- Clicking on [✓ OK] to apply the filter and close the form.

- When applying the selected filter(s):

  ➢ Only activities that comply to the filter criteria will be displayed when the **Replace activities shown in the current layout** button is checked.

  ➢ These activities will be highlighted in the **Select Activity** color when the **Highlight activities in current layout which match criteria** button is checked.

13.2.3 Applying a Combination Filter

A combination filter has two or more filters selected and has two options under **Show activities that match**:

- **All selected filters** where an activity to be displayed or highlighted has to match the criteria of **ALL** the filters, or

- **Any selected filters** where an activity to be displayed or highlighted has to match the criteria of **ONLY ONE** filter.

i In many places in the software there will be an option of either clicking on the [✓ OK] icon or the [🔲 Apply] icon:

- The [🔲 Apply] icon applies the format yet leaves the form open.

- The [✓ OK] icon applies the format and closes the form.

13.3 Creating and Modifying a Filter

13.3.1 Creating a New Filter

Filters may be created from the **Filters** form by:

- Clicking on the [⊹ New...] icon in the **Filter** form and create a new filter, or

- Copying an existing filter using the [🗋 Copy] and [🗋 Paste] icons and then editing the new filter.

New filters will be created in the **User Defined** filter area at the bottom of the list.

There are a large number of options available to create a filter and from the following examples you should be able to experiment and add your own filters. To modify an existing filter, select it from the **Filters** form and click the [🖻 Modify...] icon.

13.3.2 One Parameter Filter

The following example is a filter to display incomplete activities:

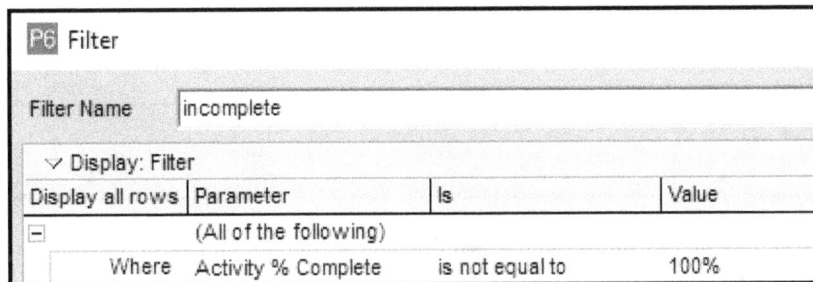

Filter Name	incomplete		
∨ Display: Filter			
Display all rows	Parameter	Is	Value
⊟	(All of the following)		
Where	Activity % Complete	is not equal to	100%

- **Parameter** is used to select any of the available database fields:

  - Select one of the options from the **Is** drop-down box:
  - The parameter selected in the **Is** box determines if:
    - ➤ Only one **Value** is required, which is entered into the **Value** field, or
    - ➤ A range is required and two values are to be entered; then the **Value** and **High Value** are entered.

equals
is not equal to
is less than
is less than or equals
is greater than
is greater than or equals
is within range of
is not within range of

The following example is a filter to display in-progress activities using the **is not within range of** and **Value** and **High Value** options:

Display all rows	Parameter	Is	Value	High Value
	(All of the following)			
Where	Physical % Complete	is within range of	0.1%	99.9%

P6 Filter — Filter Name: Physical % In Progress — Display: Filter

And this example uses the **equals** parameter and only the **Value** field is completed:

Display all rows	Parameter	Is	Value	High Value
	(Any of the following)			
Where	Activity Status	equals	In Progress	

P6 Filter — Filter Name: In Progress — Display: Filter

13.3.3 Two Parameter Filter

The following example is a filter to display all critical path activities and activities assigned the PM resource:

Display all rows	Parameter	Is	Value	High Value
	(All of the following)			
Where	Critical	equals	Yes	
And	Resource IDs	contains	PM	

P6 Filter — Filter Name: Critical and Contains PM — Display: Filter

- The drop-down box under **Parameter** has two options:
  - ➤ **(All of the following)**. This is used when an activity must meet all of the parameters selected below.
  - ➤ **(Any of the following)**. This is used when an activity must meet any of the parameters selected below.

When the first parameter is change to **All of the following** the **Display all rows** option changes to an **AND**. Therefore, with the filter below there would normally be fewer activities displayed as the activities have to be critical and assigned the resource PM:

Display all rows	Parameter	Is	Value	High Value
	(All of the following)			
Where	Critical	equals	Yes	
And	Resource IDs	contains	PM	

P6 Filter — Filter Name: Critical or Contains PM — Display: Filter

13.3.4 Multiple Parameter Filter

The following example is a filter to display incomplete activities on the critical path with resources PEH and SEH:

Display all rows	Parameter	Is	Value	High Value
	(All of the following)			
Where	Activity Status	equals	In Progress	
And	Critical	equals	Yes	
And				
	Resource IDs	contains	PEH	
	Resource IDs	contains	SEH	

P6 Filter

Filter Name: Incomplete, Critical, PEH & SEH Resource

Display: Filter

- In this example, **(All of the following)** was selected from the **Parameters** drop-down box which enables a nesting effect of filter parameters.

13.3.5 Editing and Organizing Filter Parameters

Lines in a filter are added, copied, pasted, and deleted using the appropriate icons in the **Filters** form.

The arrows allow the filter lines to be moved up and down and indented to the left and outdented to the right in a similar way to indenting and outdenting tasks in Microsoft Project.

A filter may be optimized to delete the redundant filter lines using the **Optimize** command:

		Is	Value	High Value
Optimize				
Print Preview	following)			
	Status	equals	In Progress	
And	Critical	equals	Yes	
And				
	Resource IDs	contains	PEH	
	Resource IDs	contains	SEH	

P6 Filter

Filter Name: Incomplete, Critical, PEH & SEH Resource

Display: Filter

13.3.6 Understanding Resource Filters

NOTE: THIS IS A VERY IMPORTANT POINT FOR RESOURCE FILTERING

When filtering on resources, the filter must use the option of **contains** in the **Is** column and not **equals**. This is because when an activity has been assigned more than one resource, then the activity will not be selected with a filter using the **equals** parameter.

13.4 Activity Critical Path Visibility

There is a new function and toolbar in Version 21 titled **Activity Critical Path** which may be used to examine both the Critical Path and other chains of non-critical activities.

- The new toolbar is displayed by right clicking on any toolbar and checking the **Activity Critical Path** option:

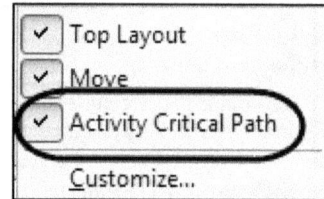

- This will display the toolbar:

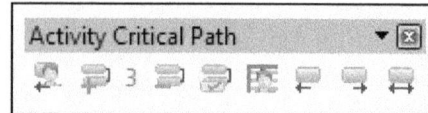

- There is also a new menu item on the **View** menu:

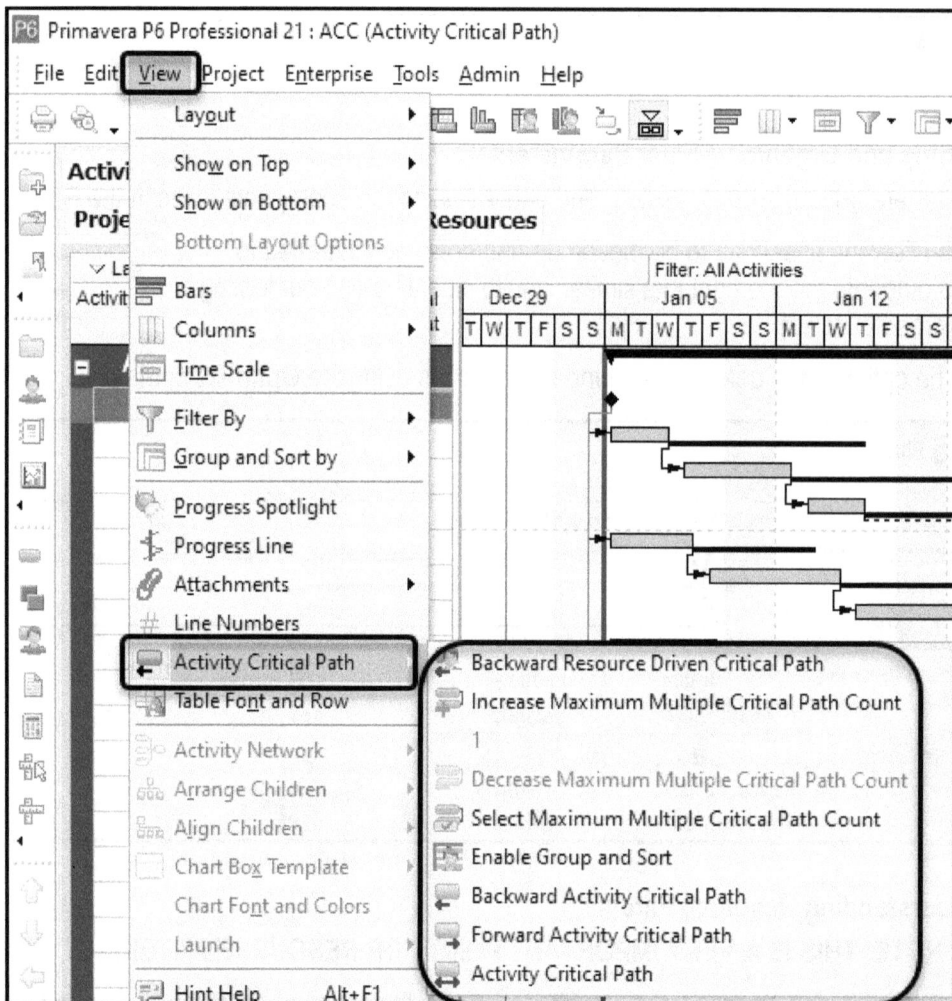

- **IMPORTANT NOTE**: Clicking on a button will activate the command and clicking again will deactivate the command.

The Oracle Cumulative Feature Overview file states:

To aid in the resolution of delayed critical paths before they become project over-runs, P6 Professional can show:

- Activities on up to 30 activity-driven critical paths, calculated on the forward pass, backward pass, or forward and backward passes (with or without resource leveling).

- The activities on up to 30 resource driven critical paths, calculated on the backward pass with resource leveling.

This Oracle description is not clear and we will work through the icons one at a time and explain how the functions work.

The schedule we will work with is as per below where Activity A1100 is preceded and succeeded by three chains of events with differing Total Float Values:

Users should also consider using the **Activity Critical Path** function in conjunction with the **Float Path Order** function to provide a clear view of view of the **Float Paths**:

Command	Function
Backward Activity Critical Path	This option displays the chain of events before a selected activity that has the least amount of Float. If there is a critical path it will display this and if there is not, then it will find the chain of events with the lease amount of float to the start of the project and display this as the **Backward Activity Critical Path**. The picture below displays the **Backward Activity Critical Path** from activity A1100 which is a chain of events that is on the schedule Critical Path.
Forward Activity Critical Path	This option displays the chain of events after a selected activity that has the least amount of Float. If there is a critical path it will display this path and if there is not, then it will find the chain of events with the least amount of float to the end of the project and display this as the **Forward Activity Critical Path**. The picture below displays the **Forward Activity Critical Path** from activity A1100 which is a chain of events that is on the schedule Critical Path.
Activity Critical Path	This option displays the chain of events before and after a selected activity that has the least amount of Float. Thus, the picture below shows both the **Forward Activity Critical Path** and **Backward Activity Critical Path** from Activity A1100.

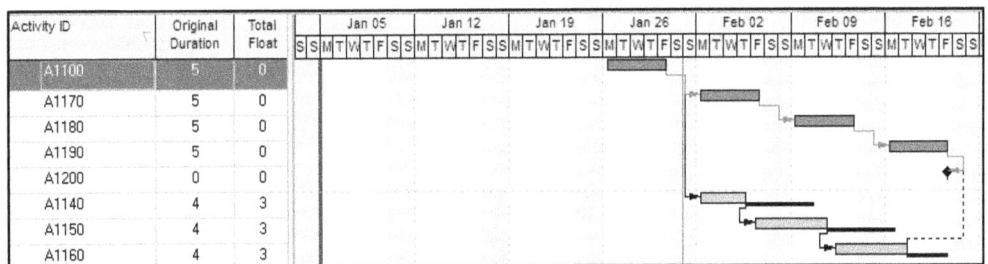

Increase Maximum Multiple Critical Path Counts	This increases the value of the **Maximum Multiple Critical Path Counts** which is displayed in the button below.
2 **Maximum Critical Path Count**	This button is not a command button but displays the number of **Maximum Critical Paths** that has been set by the user. Selecting one as **Maximum Critical Path Count:**
	Selecting two as **Maximum Critical Path Count:**
	Selecting three as **Maximum Critical Path Count:**
	Thus, this command determines how many chains of events will be displayed, consider also using the **Float Path Order** here.
Decrease Maximum Multiple Critical Path Counts	This decreases the value of the **Maximum Multiple Critical Path Counts** which is displayed in the button above.

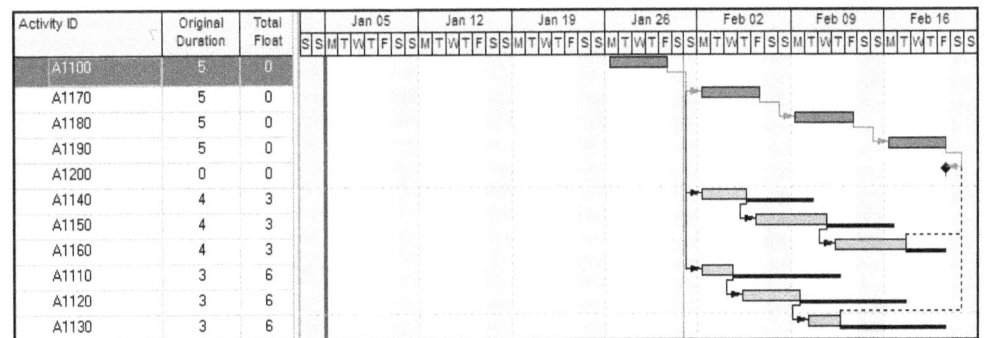

Select Maximum Multiple Critical Path Counts	This opens a form allowing the setting of the **Maximum Multiple Critical Path Counts**: Select Maximum Multiple Critical Path Count 2 Select 1 2 3 4 5 6 7 8 9 10 11 12 13 14 15 16 17 18 19 20
Enable Group and Sort	Clicking this button hides and displays the current applied **Group and Sort bands**. Hiding the bands enables the user to see the chain of events as an uninterrupted single chain of activities: **Group and Sort** enabled: **Group and Sort** disabled: This single Float Path is not on the critical path.

Backward Resource Driven Critical Path

The schedule below has no relationships between activities and have been levelled.

When selecting A1040 and **Backward Activity Critical Path** you will see the result below:

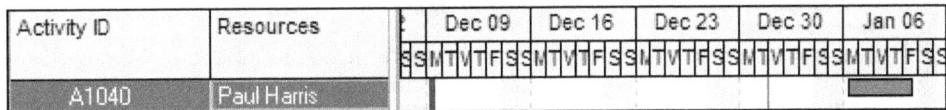

When selecting A1040 and **Backward Resource Driven Critical Path** you will see the result below:

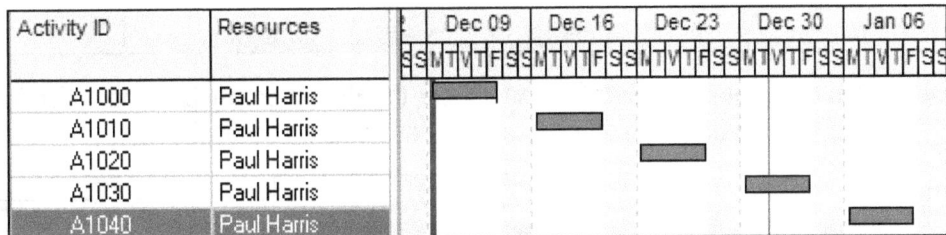

13.5 Workshop 11 – Filters

Background

Management has asked for reports on activities to suit their requirements.

Assignment

Ensure your **OzBuild Bid** project is open.

1. Apply the **OzBuild Workshop 10 – With Float** layout.

2. They would like to see all the critical activities.

   ➢ Ensure a column showing the **Total Float** is displayed, and

   ➢ Apply the **Critical** activities filter.

3. You will see only activities that are on the critical path.

Activity ID	Activity Name	Original Duration	Start	Finish	Total Float	Free Float
	Bid for Facility Extension	18d	02-Jan-25 08	27-Jan-25 16	0d	0d
	Technical Specification	0d			0d	0d
	Delivery Plan	14d	02-Jan-25 08	21-Jan-25 16	0d	0d
OZ1060	Obtain Quotes from Suppliers	8d	02-Jan-25 08*	13-Jan-25 16	0d	0d
OZ1070	Calculate the Bid Estimate	3d	14-Jan-25 08	16-Jan-25 16	0d	0d
OZ1080	Create the Project Schedule	3d	17-Jan-25 08	20-Jan-25 16	0d	0d
OZ1090	Review the Delivery Plan	1d	21-Jan-25 08	21-Jan-25 16	0d	0d
	Bid Document	4d	22-Jan-25 08	27-Jan-25 16	0d	0d
OZ1110	Review Bid Document	2d	22-Jan-25 08	23-Jan-25 16	0d	0d
OZ1120	Finalise and Submit Bid Document	2d	24-Jan-25 08	27-Jan-25 16	0d	0d
OZ1130	Bid Document Submitted	0d		27-Jan-25 16*	0d	0d

4. Open the **Group and Sort** form and check the **Hide if empty** box and notice the **Technical Specification** band is hidden because it has no activities displayed.

Activity ID	Activity Name	Original Duration	Start	Finish	Total Float	Free Float
	Bid for Facility Extension	18d	02-Jan-25 08	27-Jan-25 16	0d	0d
	Delivery Plan	14d	02-Jan-25 08	21-Jan-25 16	0d	0d
OZ1060	Obtain Quotes from Suppliers	8d	02-Jan-25 08*	13-Jan-25 16	0d	0d
OZ1070	Calculate the Bid Estimate	3d	14-Jan-25 08	16-Jan-25 16	0d	0d
OZ1080	Create the Project Schedule	3d	17-Jan-25 08	20-Jan-25 16	0d	0d
OZ1090	Review the Delivery Plan	1d	21-Jan-25 08	21-Jan-25 16	0d	0d
	Bid Document	4d	22-Jan-25 08	27-Jan-25 16	0d	0d
OZ1110	Review Bid Document	2d	22-Jan-25 08	23-Jan-25 16	0d	0d
OZ1120	Finalise and Submit Bid Document	2d	24-Jan-25 08	27-Jan-25 16	0d	0d
OZ1130	Bid Document Submitted	0d		27-Jan-25 16*	0d	0d

5. Now apply some other filters such as the **Milestone**, **Has Start Constraint** and **Has Finish Constraint**.

6. There are two activities with 6 days Total Float, OZ1040, OZ1050 and OZ1100, see the picture below:

Activity ID	Activity Name	Original Duration	Start	Finish	Total Float	Free Float	December 2024 / January 2025
Bid for Facility Extension		33d	09-Dec-24 08	27-Jan-25 16	0d	0d	
Technical Specification		13d	09-Dec-24 08	27-Dec-24 16	6d	0d	
OZ1000	Approval to Bid	0d	09-Dec-24 08		4d	0d	
OZ1010	Determine Installation Requirements	4d	09-Dec-24 08	12-Dec-24 16	4d	0d	
OZ1020	Create Technical Specification	5d	13-Dec-24 08	19-Dec-24 16	4d	0d	
OZ1030	Identify Supplier Components	2d	20-Dec-24 08	23-Dec-24 16	4d	0d	
OZ1040	Validate Technical Specification	2d	24-Dec-24 08	27-Dec-24 16	6d	0d	
Delivery Plan		16d	30-Dec-24 08	21-Jan-25 16	0d	0d	
OZ1050	Document Delivery Methodology	4d	30-Dec-24 08	03-Jan-25 16	6d	0d	
OZ1060	Obtain Quotes from Suppliers	8d	02-Jan-25 08*	13-Jan-25 16	0d	0d	
OZ1070	Calculate the Bid Estimate	3d	14-Jan-25 08	16-Jan-25 16	0d	0d	
OZ1080	Create the Project Schedule	3d	17-Jan-25 08	20-Jan-25 16	0d	0d	
OZ1090	Review the Delivery Plan	1d	21-Jan-25 08	21-Jan-25 16	0d	0d	
Bid Document		16d	06-Jan-25 08	27-Jan-25 16	0d	0d	
OZ1100	Create Draft of Bid Document	6d	06-Jan-25 08	13-Jan-25 16	6d	6d	
OZ1110	Review Bid Document	2d	22-Jan-25 08	23-Jan-25 16	0d	0d	
OZ1120	Finalise and Submit Bid Document	2d	24-Jan-25 08	27-Jan-25 16	0d	0d	
OZ1130	Bid Document Submitted	0d		27-Jan-25 16*	0d	0d	

7. Management would like to see all the activities with float less than or equal to 5 days:

> Create a new filter titled: **Total Float Less Than or Equal to 5 Days**, and

> Add the condition to display a total float of less than 5 days.

Display all rows	Parameter	Is	Value	High Value
∨ Display: Filter				
−	(All of the following)			
Where	Total Float	is less than	5d	

> Close the **Filter** form,

> Click on the **All Activities** check box to ensure all activities are displayed,

> Apply the new filter **Total Float Less Than or Equal to 5 Days**,

> You should find that three activities with more than 6 days float are hidden:

Activity ID	Activity Name	Original Duration	Start	Finish	Total Float	Free Float	December 2024 / January 2025
Bid for Facility Extension		33d	09-Dec-24 08	27-Jan-25 16	0d	0d	
Technical Specification		11d	09-Dec-24 08	23-Dec-24 16	4d	0d	
OZ1000	Approval to Bid	0d	09-Dec-24 08		4d	0d	
OZ1010	Determine Installation Requirements	4d	09-Dec-24 08	12-Dec-24 16	4d	0d	
OZ1020	Create Technical Specification	5d	13-Dec-24 08	19-Dec-24 16	4d	0d	
OZ1030	Identify Supplier Components	2d	20-Dec-24 08	23-Dec-24 16	4d	0d	
Delivery Plan		14d	02-Jan-25 08	21-Jan-25 16	0d	0d	
OZ1060	Obtain Quotes from Suppliers	8d	02-Jan-25 08*	13-Jan-25 16	0d	0d	
OZ1070	Calculate the Bid Estimate	3d	14-Jan-25 08	16-Jan-25 16	0d	0d	
OZ1080	Create the Project Schedule	3d	17-Jan-25 08	20-Jan-25 16	0d	0d	
OZ1090	Review the Delivery Plan	1d	21-Jan-25 08	21-Jan-25 16	0d	0d	
Bid Document		4d	22-Jan-25 08	27-Jan-25 16	0d	0d	
OZ1110	Review Bid Document	2d	22-Jan-25 08	23-Jan-25 16	0d	0d	
OZ1120	Finalise and Submit Bid Document	2d	24-Jan-25 08	27-Jan-25 16	0d	0d	
OZ1130	Bid Document Submitted	0d		27-Jan-25 16*	0d	0d	

8. They would like to see all the activities that are critical or contain the word "Bid".

> Copy the **Critical** filter,

> Edit the filter title to read: **Critical or Contains "Bid"**,

> Edit the top line to read **(Any of the following)**,

➢ Add the condition: **Or** Name (Activity Name) contains **Bid**, and

Filter Name	Critical or Contains "Bid"			
∨ Display: Filter				
Display all rows	Parameter	Is	Value	High Value
⊟	(Any of the following)			
Where	Critical	equals	Yes	
Or	Activity Name	contains	bid	

➢ **Note:** The text is not case sensitive,

➢ Apply the filter.

Activity ID	Activity Name	Original Duration	Start	Finish	Total Float	Free Float	
Bid for Facility Extension		33d	09-Dec-24 08	27-Jan-25 16	0d	0d	
Technical Specification		0d	09-Dec-24 08	09-Dec-24 08	4d	0d	
OZ1000	Approval to Bid	0d	09-Dec-24 08		4d	0d	
Delivery Plan		14d	02-Jan-25 08	21-Jan-25 16	0d	0d	
OZ1060	Obtain Quotes from Suppliers	8d	02-Jan-25 08*	13-Jan-25 16	0d	0d	
OZ1070	Calculate the Bid Estimate	3d	14-Jan-25 08	16-Jan-25 16	0d	0d	
OZ1080	Create the Project Schedule	3d	17-Jan-25 08	20-Jan-25 16	0d	0d	
OZ1090	Review the Delivery Plan	1d	21-Jan-25 08	21-Jan-25 16	0d	0d	
Bid Document		16d	06-Jan-25 08	27-Jan-25 16	0d	0d	
OZ1100	Create Draft of Bid Document	6d	06-Jan-25 08	13-Jan-25 16	6d	6d	
OZ1110	Review Bid Document	2d	22-Jan-25 08	23-Jan-25 16	0d	0d	
OZ1120	Finalise and Submit Bid Document	2d	24-Jan-25 08	27-Jan-25 16	0d	0d	
OZ1130	Bid Document Submitted	0d		27-Jan-25 16*	0d	0d	

9. All the activities are either Critical or contain the word Bid.

10. Copy the filter and rename it **Critical and Contains "Bid"**,

Filter Name	Critical and Contains "Bid"			
∨ Display: Filter				
Display all rows	Parameter	Is	Value	High Value
⊟	(All of the following)			
Where	Critical	equals	Yes	
And	Activity Name	contains	bid	

11. Now change the **(Any of the following)** option to **(All of the following)** apply the filter and see the effect.

Activity ID	Activity Name	Original Duration	Start	Finish	Total Float	Free Float	
Bid for Facility Extension		10d	14-Jan-25 08	27-Jan-25 16	0d	0d	
Delivery Plan		3d	14-Jan-25 08	16-Jan-25 16	0d	0d	
OZ1070	Calculate the Bid Estimate	3d	14-Jan-25 08	16-Jan-25 16	0d	0d	
Bid Document		4d	22-Jan-25 08	27-Jan-25 16	0d	0d	
OZ1110	Review Bid Document	2d	22-Jan-25 08	23-Jan-25 16	0d	0d	
OZ1120	Finalise and Submit Bid Document	2d	24-Jan-25 08	27-Jan-25 16	0d	0d	
OZ1130	Bid Document Submitted	0d		27-Jan-25 16*	0d	0d	

12. There should be fewer activities and it is now displaying activities that meet both conditions of being Critical and contain the word Bid.

13. Now apply the **All Activities** filter to display all the activities.

14 PRINTING, REPORTS AND VISUALIZER

This is the stage at which the schedule is printed so people may review and comment on it. This chapter will examine some of the options for printing your project schedule.

There are several tools available to output your schedule:

- The **Printing** function prints the data displayed in the current Layout.

- The **Reporting** function prints reports, which are independent of the current Layout. Primavera supplies a number of predefined reports that may be tailored to suit your own requirements. Reports will not be covered in detail in this publication.

- The **Project Web Site Publisher** to publish the schedule to a web site.

- **Visualizer** includes **Timescaled Logic Diagram**, **Gantt** and **Schedule Analyzer** modules.

- You may also copy and paste text data from columns and some tables into Excel and other products.

> ⓘ It is recommended that you consider using a product such as Adobe Acrobat to output your schedule in pdf format. You then will be able to e-mail high quality outputs that recipients may print or review on screen without needing a copy of Primavera.

14.1 Printing

When a Layout is split, the lower pane may be printed with the upper pane, with the exception of the **Activity Details** pane. This is similar to Elecosoft (Asta) Powerproject, but different from Microsoft Project where only the Activity View may be printed. Other products, such as Elecosoft (Asta) Powerproject and Tilos, allow multiple resource histograms to be printed in one printout, which is not possible in P6.

Print settings, such as headers and footers, are applied to the individual Layouts and the settings are saved with that Layout.

The following normal print commands may be used when printing:

- **File**, **Page Setup...**
- **File**, **Print Setup...**
- **File**, **Print Preview**
- **File**, **Print...** or **Ctrl+P**

Each of these functions will be discussed only for printing the Gantt Chart. Printing all other Layouts is a similar process. Some Layouts will have different options due to the nature of the data being displayed. These other options should be easily mastered after the basics covered in this chapter are understood.

> ⓘ Each time you report to the client or management, it is recommended that you save a copy of your printout or report and a pdf file is an excellent method of saving this data. In conjunction with a robust file-naming convention that includes the project title and Data Date, a pdf file will enable you to reproduce these reports at any point in time in the future and have available a copy of the project schedule for dispute resolution purposes.
>
> It is good practice to keep a copy of the project after each update, especially if litigation is a possibility. A project may be copied either by creating a Baseline, by exporting the project as an XML file (which will also save any Baseline) or XER (without a Baseline) or by using the project copy function, then making the **Status** inactive in the **General** tab of the **Projects Window**. It is important to note that although the project may be marked as inactive it may still be opened and modified.

14.1.1 Print Preview

To preview the printout, use the Primavera **Print Preview** option. Select **File**, **Print Preview** or click the icon on the **Print** toolbar:

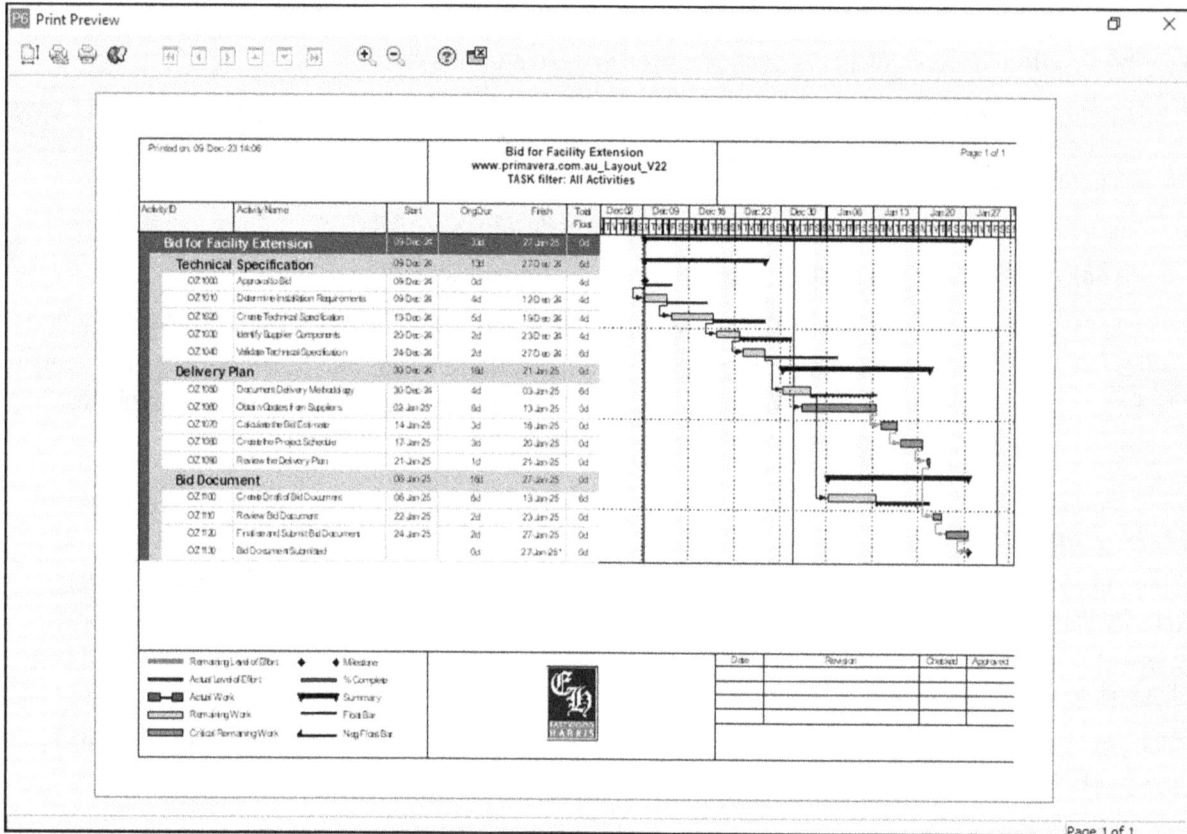

- The following paragraphs describe the functions of the icons at the top of the **Print Preview** screen from left to right:

- The [icon] icon opens the **Page Setup** form to be covered in the next paragraph.

- The [icon] icon opens the **Print Setup** form where the printer and paper size, etc., may be selected.

- The [icon] icon opens the **Print** form where the printer, the pages to be printed, and the number of copies to be printed may be selected.

- The [icon] icon opens the **Publish to HTML** form and saves the view in HTML format where both the tables and bar charts are converted.

- The first six icons on the left, [icons], allow scrolling when a printout has more than one page.

- The magnifying glass [icons] icons zoom in and out. You may also click in the **Print Preview** screen to zoom in.

- The [icon] button opens the Help file.

- The [icon] icon closes the **Print Preview** screen.

14.1.2 Page Setup

To open the **Page Setup...** form:

- Click the ⬚ **Page Setup** icon on the **Print** toolbar, or
- Select **File**, **Page Setup...** to display the **Page Setup** form:

The **Page Setup** form contains the following tabs: Page, Margins, Header, Footer and Options.

When changes are made to a header or footer then the icons on the right side may be used:

- [Apply] – Applies the changes so they are visible without closing the form.
- [Default] – Resets the Page Setup settings to default.
- [OK] – Accepts the changes and closes the form.
- [Cancel] – Cancels the changes and closes the form.

Page Tab

The Primavera options in the **Page** tab are:

- **Orientation** enables the selection of **Portrait** or **Landscape** printing.
- **Scaling** enables you to adjust the number of pages the printout will fit onto:
  - ➤ **Adjust to:**– enables you to choose the scale of the column text and then the horizontal scale of the bars is adjusted to fit the remaining space.
  - ➤ **Fit to:** – enables you to choose the number of pages across and down and Primavera should scale the printout to fit.
  - ➤ **Fit timescale to:** – enables the user to select the number of pages the Gantt Chart is scaled over but leaves the font of the columns un-scaled. This will often be the best setting with 1 page(s) wide selected.

> *ⓘ* These options work in conjunction with each other and can get quite difficult to operate. The author recommends that a good starting point for print options is to first set the **Adjust to:** to 100% so the text is printed out in a legible size and then set the **Fit timescale to:** is set to 1 page wide.

- Pages are numbered first across and then down, and does not follow the Microsoft Project convention of numbering pages down and then across.

Margins Tab

With this option, you may edit the margins around the edge of the printout.

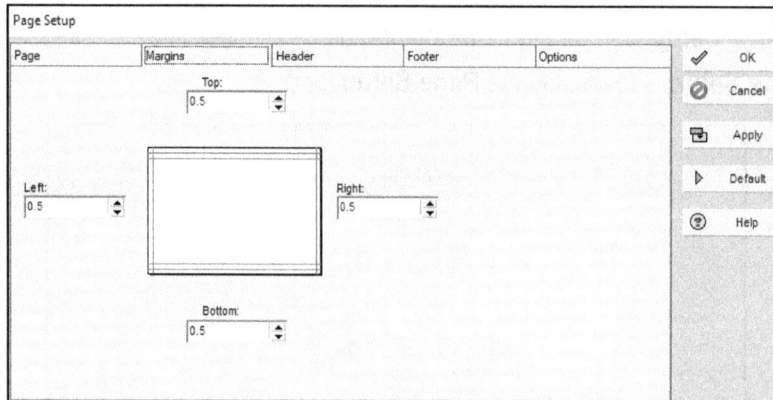

Type in the margin size around the page. It is best to allow a wider margin for an edge that is to be bound or hole punched – 1" or 2.5cm is usually sufficient.

Header and Footer Tabs

Headers appear at the top of the screen above all schedule information and footers are located at the bottom. Both the headers and footers are formatted in the same way. We will discuss the setting-up of footers in this chapter.

Click on the **Footer** tab from the **Page Setup** form. This will display the settings of the default footers and headers. You should modify the output to suit your requirements.

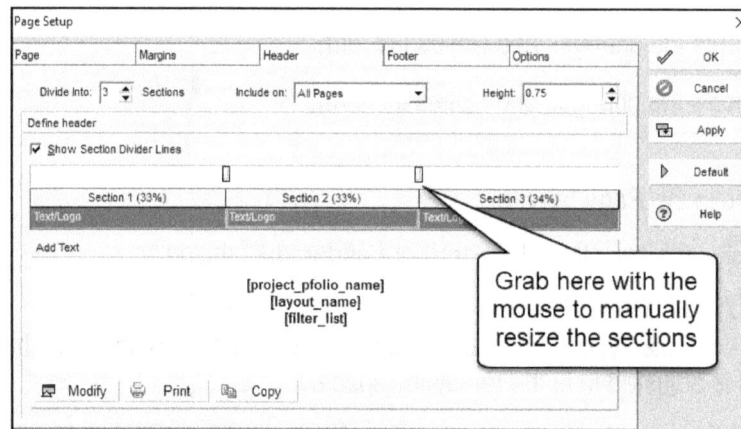

- **Divide Into:** – determines the number of sections the Header/Footer is divided into from 1 to 5 sections.

- **Include on:** – determines on which pages the Header/Footer is to appear: First Page, Last Page, All Pages, or No Pages.

- **Height:** – enables the user to select the height of the Header/Footer.

- **Define Footer**

  ➢ **Show Section Divider Lines** check box – hides or displays divider lines between the sections.

  ➢ The sections may be sized by manually moving the divider lines with the mouse and the slide underneath the **Show Section Divider Lines**.

- **Modify** ⊠ Modify allows editing and formatting of the section content.

- **Section Content**

  This may be selected by clicking on the ▾ icon under the **Section** title and a subject type to be displayed selected.

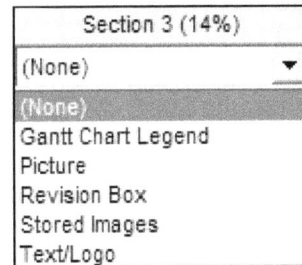

Section 3 (14%)
(None) ▾
(None)
Gantt Chart Legend
Picture
Revision Box
Stored Images
Text/Logo

  ➢ **(None)** – leaves the section blank.
  ➢ **Gantt Chart Legend** – displays all the bars checked in the display column of the **Bars** form and only the fonts may be edited by clicking on the little ⎣ Font ⎦ icon at the bottom.

  ➢ **Picture** – enables a picture to be placed in the footer and it may be manually adjusted to fit the space or automatically adjusted by checking the **Resize picture to fit the selection** box.

  ➢ **Revision Box** has a **Revision Box Title:** – the following information may be entered manually: Date, Revision, Checked, Approved.

  ➢ **Stored Images** – New to P6 Version 18. Up to 20 pictures at a max of 500x500 dpi may be saved in a database and are available for any user to access. This solved the issue of when one user had embedded a picture in a Layout Header and a second user did not have access to the same directory and was thus unable to display the same picture when applying the same Layout. Version 19 introduced the ability to upload multiple images at one time. Pictures are uploaded using **Enterprise, Store Image....**

  ➢ **Text/Logo** – enables many types of data to be displayed including text, a data item selected from the drop-down box, fonts formatted by clicking on the formatting icons **A ≡ ≡ ≡ ≔ ≔ ⫶ ⫶**, a Logo inserted by clicking on the ⊡ icon, Tables added by clicking on the ⊞ icon, and a Hyperlink added by clicking on the link icon ✎ which opens the **Hyperlink** form.

  NOTE: When you are editing text in a header or footer and a line return created by using the **Enter** Key will result in a paragraph break and a large gap between the lines. This may be prevented by using a **soft return** using the **Shift & Enter** command:

  > **Small gap created using Shift Enter** → [project_pfolio_name] [layout_name] ← **Large gap created using Enter key only**
  >
  > [filter_list]

- The ⊞ Add button allows the insertion of database fields from the drop-down list which automatically update with from the current project. The following fields may be set for the whole organization: **Custom Label 1 to 3**, **Footer Label 1 to 3**, and **Header Label 1 to 3** and defined in P6 Professional in the **Admin, Admin Preferences..., Reports** tab and in the Primavera EPPM Windows Client **NOT FROM THE WEB** but from **Tools, Reports, Report Preferences**.

  ⓘ The ⊞ Add button is a very useful feature as it allows for standard layouts to be created that update automatically from database fields such as Project ID and Project Name and therefore are always valid when you open a different project.

Options Tab

The Options tab has three sections:

- **Timescale Start:** and **Timescale Finish:** These options enable the **start and finish** point of the timescale to be set. Click on the ☐ icon and select a date from the drop-down list. A **Custom Date...** may be selected from the menu and a calendar is opened to select the date.

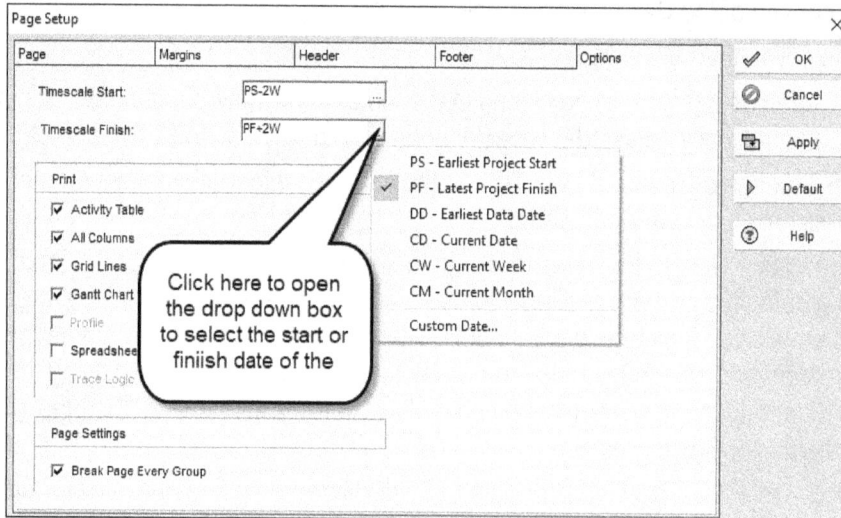

- A lag from the nominated dates may be specified, see the picture above where the timescale starts 10 days before the Project Start date and ends 10 days after the Project Finish date.

- The **Print** options alter depending on the Layout. The check boxes allow a selection of the data to be printed.

  i   Only one resource histogram or a resource table may be printed at a time.

- The **Break Page Every Group** puts a page break at each change of heading in the first group in the **Group and Sort** form. The option in this form only works when there are more than one level 1 band in the Group and Sort form and would not work for a WBS when Indented to All Levels but would work when activities are grouped by a Start or Finish date.

  The **Group and Sort** form allows a page break at any select level in Grouping of activities which in a way make this option redundant:

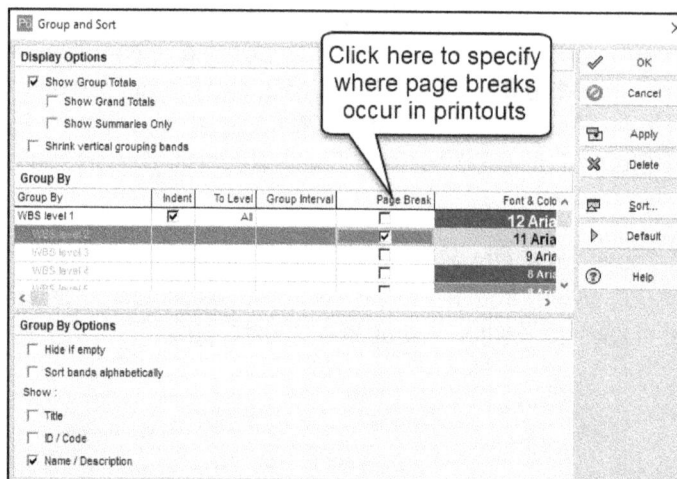

14.1.3 Print Form

The **Print** form is be opened by:

- Selecting **File**, **Print...**, or

- Executing the keystrokes **Ctrl+P**, or

- Clicking on the 🖨 print icon in the **Print Preview** screen.

14.1.4 Print Setup Form

The **Print Setup** form is be opened by:

- Selecting **File**, **Print Setup...**, or

- Clicking on the 🖨 print icon in the **Print Preview** screen.

14.2 Reports

Click the 📇 icon on the **Enterprise** toolbar or select **Tools**, **Reports**, **Reports** to open the **Reports Window**:

Report Name	Report Scope	Last Run Date
▬ 📑 **Report Group: Standard Construction Reports**		
📑 AD-01 Activity Status Report	Global	
📑 LA-01 Two Week Lookahead	Global	
📑 LG-01 Logic Report, By Project	Global	
📑 Notebook Topics	Global	
📑 RC-01 Resource Control Report	Global	
➕ 📑 **Report Group: Schedule**		
▬ 📑 **Report Group: Resource**		
▬ 📑 **Report Group: Control**		
📑 RC-01 Resource Control - Detail by Activity	Global	
📑 RC-02 Resource Control - Summary by Resource	Global	

- The reports are grouped under a hierarchical structure that may be modified by opening the **Tools**, **Reports, Reports Groups** form or right-clicking and using the menu.

14.2.1 Running Reports

- A single report may be run by right-clicking on a report and selecting **Run**, **Report…** or clicking the [icon] icon on the **Reports** toolbar. This will open the **Run Report** form:

- Selecting the option of **ASCII Text File** will allow the report to be opened and edited in Excel. The default Field Delimiter and Text Qualifier are usually suitable for Excel.

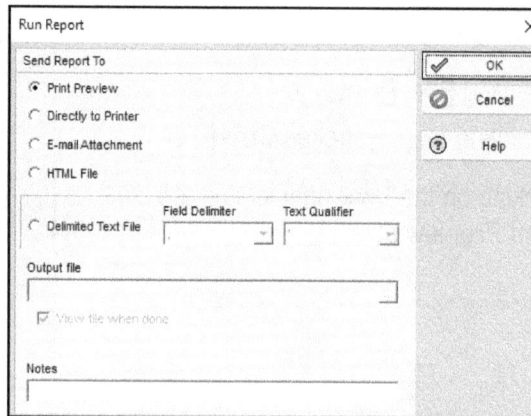

- **Batches** are groups of reports that are run at the same time:

  ➢ **Batches** are created and edited by using the **Tools**, **Reports, Batch Reports**…form, and

  ➢ Run by clicking the [icon] icon in the **Reports** toolbar.

14.2.2 Editing Reports

- Reports may be cut, copied, and pasted using the **Edit** toolbar icons or right-clicking.

- They may be renamed by clicking on the description.

- Some reports may be edited with the **Report Wizard** and all may be edited with the **Report Writer**.

  ➢ Reports that have a [icon] icon by the report name may be edited with the **Report Wizard**, which is the simplest method of editing these reports. **Note:** These reports may also be edited with the **Report Writer**.

  ➢ Reports that have a [icon] icon by the report name may only be edited with the **Report Writer** and this is quite complex. There are basic instructions in the Help file.

- To create a new report or modify an existing report that was created with the **Report Wizard**, run the **Report Wizard** by clicking the [icon] icon on the **Reports** toolbar, or selecting **Tools**, **Report Wizard**….

14.3 Publish to a Web Site

Primavera has several functions that enable a project to be published to a web site which is effectively the only "Free Reader" that Oracle Primavera provides with P6 and is a great way of sharing your project schedule with a number of other organizations.

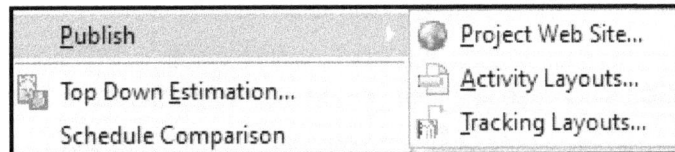

The **Tools**, **Publish**, menu has three options for creating a web site for a currently opened project:

- **Project Web Site...** creates a complete web site with any Reports or Layouts that have been created. This is a very useful function if it is required to publish a large amount of data:

- **Activity Layouts...** creates a web site with the selected Activity Layouts.
- **Tracking Layouts...** creates a web site with the selected Tracking Layouts.

14.4 Visualizer

14.4.1 Understanding Visualizer

A standalone windows software that reads your Oracle Primavera database and allows a higher level of Gant Chart customization than available from the Activities Window in either Professional or Web Client.

The screen dumps used in this section of the book are mainly taken from P6 Versions 22 and 23, but as Visualized evolves, the menus changed and your version may not be the same as these pictures.

P6 Version 23 introduced the option for adding a Curtains to a Gantt Chart and Timescaled Logic Diagram.

Visualizer may be run from within P6 or from the Windows Start Menu and will create either:

- **Timescaled Logic Diagram** (**TSLD**), similar to a Gantt Chart but allowing multiple activities per line,
- **Gantt Charts**, and
- **Schedule Comparison**, also known as **Claim Digger** in earlier versions and is used to compare one schedule with another schedule or a baseline.

It includes the following functions:

- Printing of Layouts imported from P6 and the creation of new Visualizer layouts,
- Notebook Topics and Steps may be displayed as fields in the activity table or as bar labels,
- Show Lead or Lag on relationships,
- Stack columns and use word wrapping in the Gantt chart,
- Show Multiple Activities on one row in the TSLDs, thus reducing the number of rows,
- Formatting of fields and labels,
- Use functions such as Baseline Bar display, Filters, Group and Sort,
- The Enterprise, Activity Code form allows Activity Codes colors to be defined. These colors may be assigned to bars, bar Start and Finish points in Visualizer, but these colors may not be assigned to bars in the Activity window Bars form.
- More shape choices and other formatting options for bars,
- Run reports in batches using programs like Windows Scheduler,
- The ability to import and export PLF Layout files which are created in P6 Professional.
- A user may exchange Visualizer Layouts using the import and export of a VLF file.

Understanding how Visualizer operates:

- It is a separate piece of Windows Client software that is installed on a PC,
- It uses the same security as PPM,
- It may not be used to manipulate data; therefore it is just for presentation,
- The user is required to select an existing layout or create a new layout which will either display a Gantt Chart or TSLD, before selecting the project to report,
- Then the projects to report on are selected,
- The layout is formatted and saved, if required,
- Visualizer layouts may be created and saved as Global, Project or User layouts, and
- Visualizer uses P6 Admin Preferences for Calendar Start Day of the week, and on line help settings.

14.4.2 Starting Visualizer

To start Visualizer:

- From P6 select **Tools**, **Visualizer**, and Visualizer will start without the need to log in again, or
- From the Windows Start Menu without opening P6 and using your P6 login name and password:

There are some buttons at the top of the screen and an additional printing button was available on earlier versions of Visualizer and removed in later versions:

- - to create a Schedule Comparison, TSLD or Gantt (chart)
- More ▼ - to Manage the import and export of layouts and to exit.

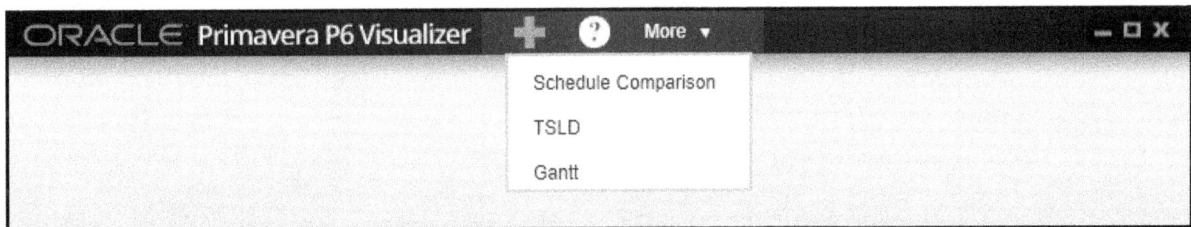

14.4.3 Create a New TSLD – Timescaled Logic Diagram

To create a new TSLD select ![plus icon], **New TSLD**:

- You will then select which projects to report on, the picture below displays the options available to create a new TSLD:

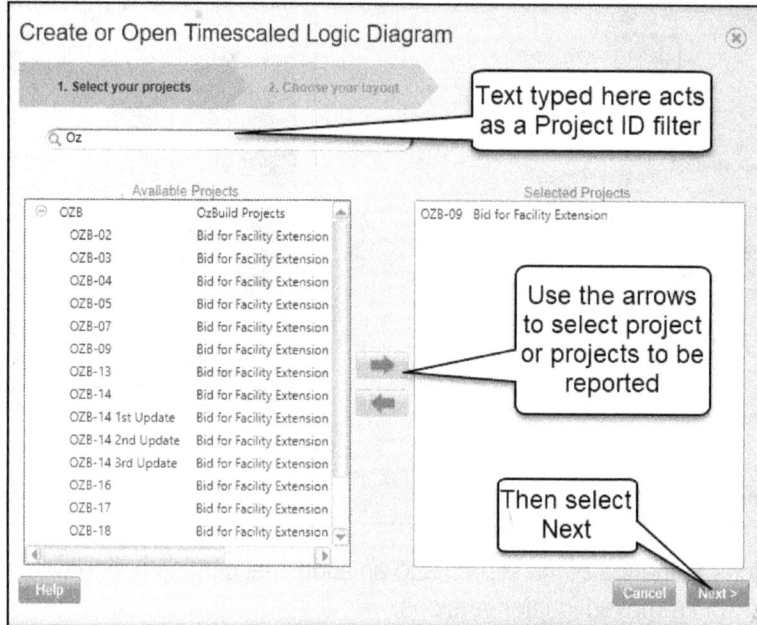

- Name the layout with an appropriate name,
- Use the radio buttons to either:
  - ➤ Select to copy an existing TSLD and select from the list below, or
  - ➤ To create a new TSLD,
- Select **Draw** to see the result or click **Options** to edit the layout:

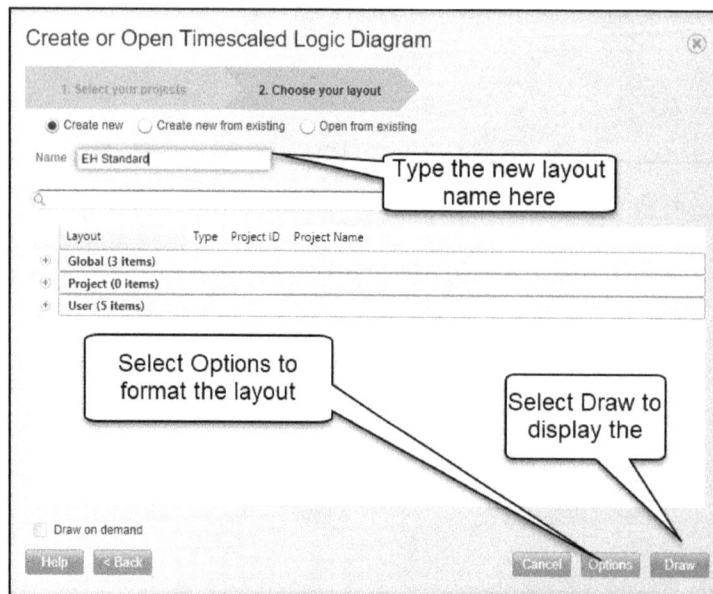

The **Options** form allows a large number of formatting options, which are similar to other P6 formatting functions, but graphically richer:

- **Timescale** is for formatting all aspects of the timescale, plus the gridlines on the body of the diagram:

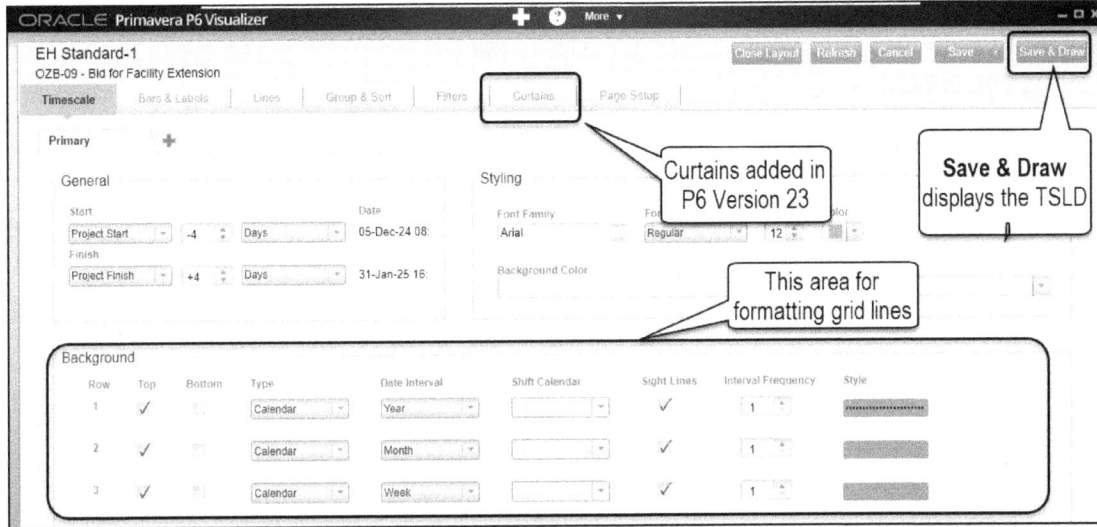

The **Bars & Labels** form is where bars are added, edited and deleted. This area is not intuitive so follow these instructions carefully:

- The **Available Bars** form is where bars are added, edited and deleted.
- You must name the bar with a name that makes sense, Visualizer does not name bars,
- The bar at the top of the list is drawn first and the second one in the list is drawn on top of the first, when it is on the same line,
- A bar selected under **Available Bars** is then formatted in the options on the right hand side,
- The middle top bar shows how the selected bar will be formatted and the bars in the middle bottom shows how all the bars will look:

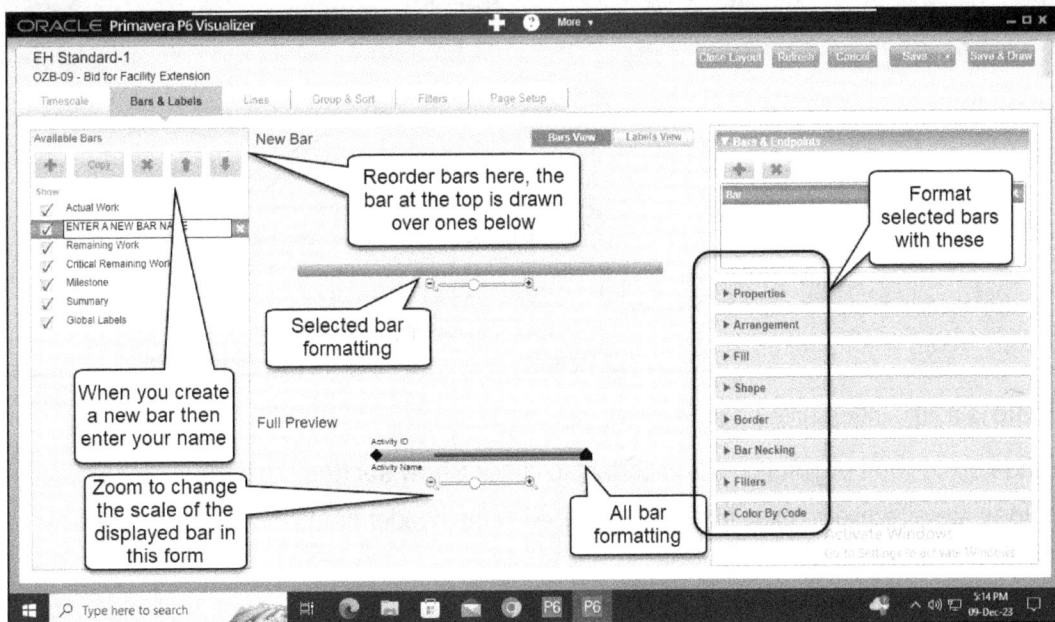

Lines tab is where the Relationships, Data Date and Activity Group bands are formatted:

> ➢ **Relationships** tab is where the relationships to be displayed are selected,
>
> ➢ **Connections** tab is where Lead and Lag may be displayed,
>
> ➢ **Data Date** allows formatting of the Data Date,
>
> ➢ **Activity Group** allows the placing of a line around a group of bars that are associated with one activity:

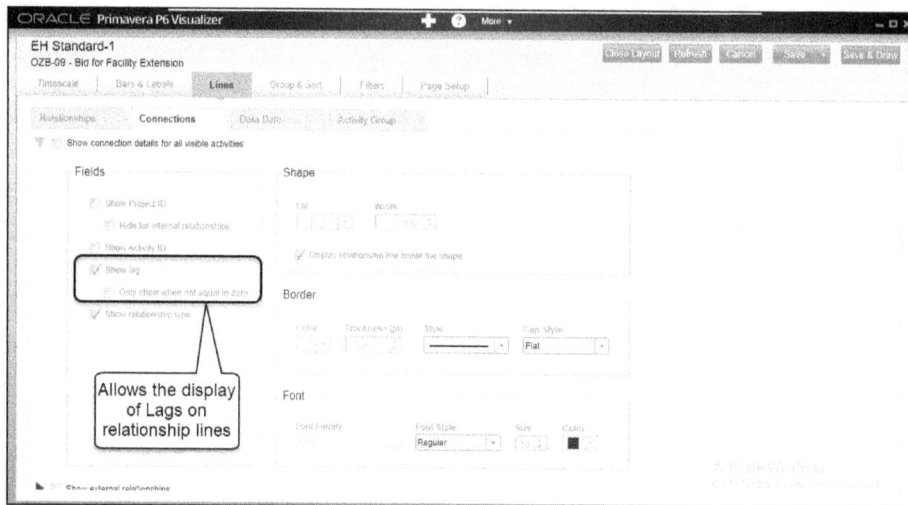

Group & Sort and **Filters Page Setup forms** work in the same way as other P6 products, but still does not allow grouping on single resource when multiple resources are assigned to an activity.

Filters with the normal filtering functions,

Curtains function was added in P6 Version 23 did not operate with the authors system and as reported to Oracle. This should operate in due course with a patch. The author made this function in a Gantt Chart work by importing a plf Layout.

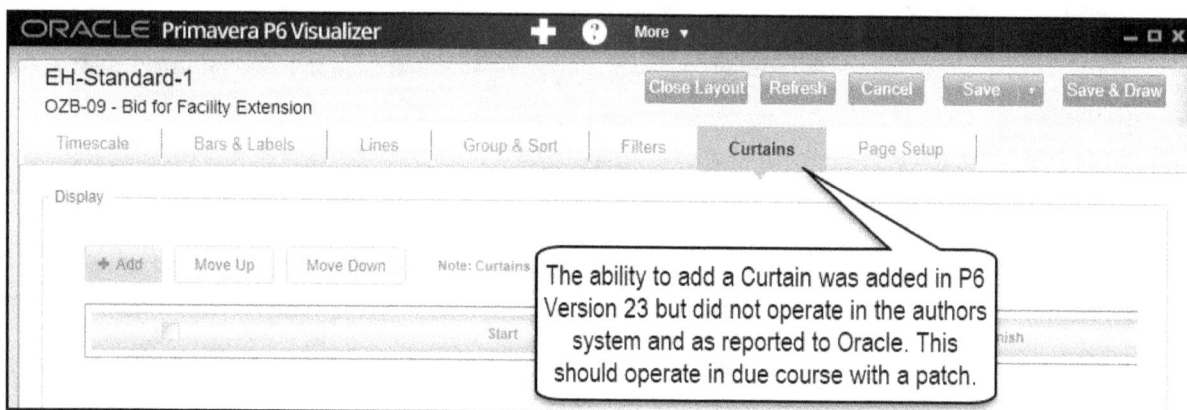

Page Setup is a little different to other P6 products:

- To understand what is going on it is important to check **Show section borders**,

- **Sections** are effectively boxes that may be placed in the header or footer and project data may be typed in or read from the P6 database,

- Sections may be added deleted or adjusted in size,

- Headers and Footers are formatted the same way:

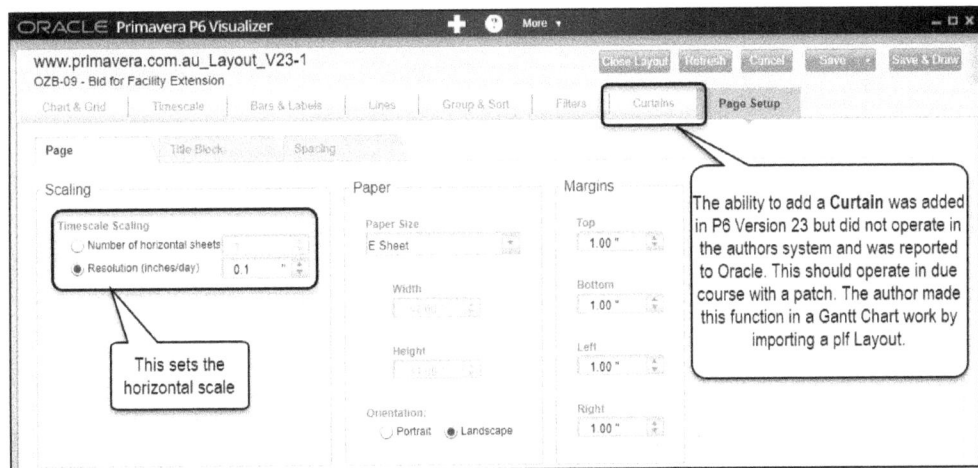

This is the result of selecting Save & Draw, note more than one activity per line.

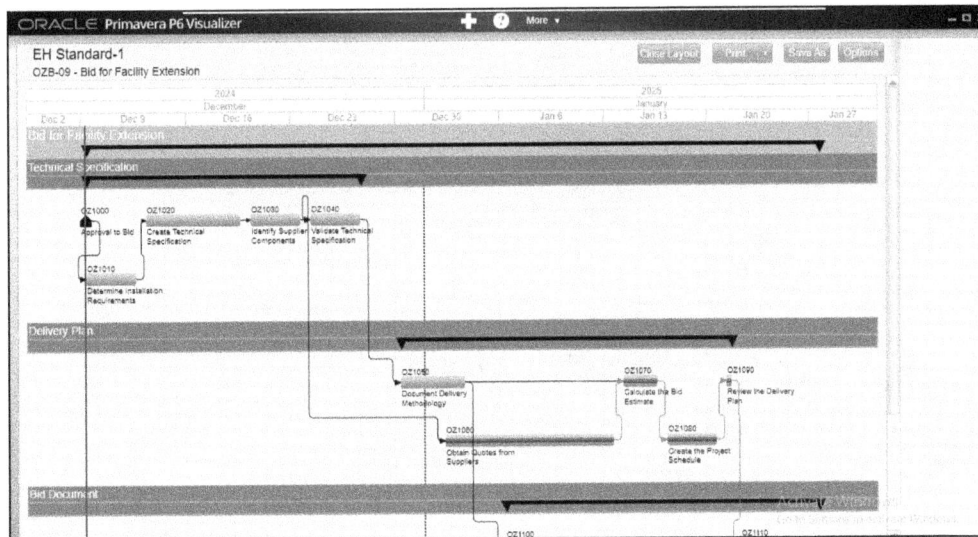

14.4.4 Create a New Gantt Diagram

Most of the options in the tabs are self-explanatory and the Gantt Diagram layout functions are similar to formatting in PPM and EPPM.

To create a new Gantt Chart select ✚, **New Gantt**:

- You will then select which projects to report on, the picture below displays the options available to create a new Gantt Chart:

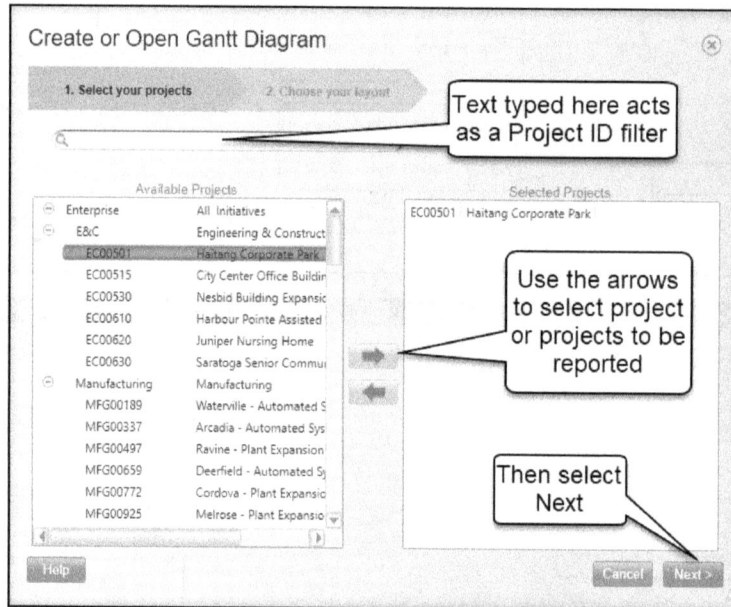

- Name the layout with an appropriate name,
- Use the radio buttons to either:
  - ➢ Select to copy an existing Gantt Diagram and select from the list below, or
  - ➢ To create a new Gantt Diagram, or
  - ➢ Open an existing layout,
  - ➢ The new Gantt Diagram is created as a User Layout.

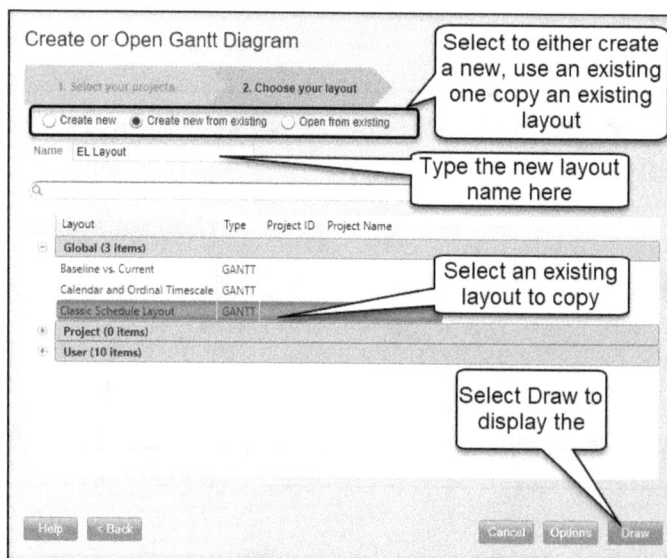

- Select **Draw** to see the result or click **Options** to edit the layout:

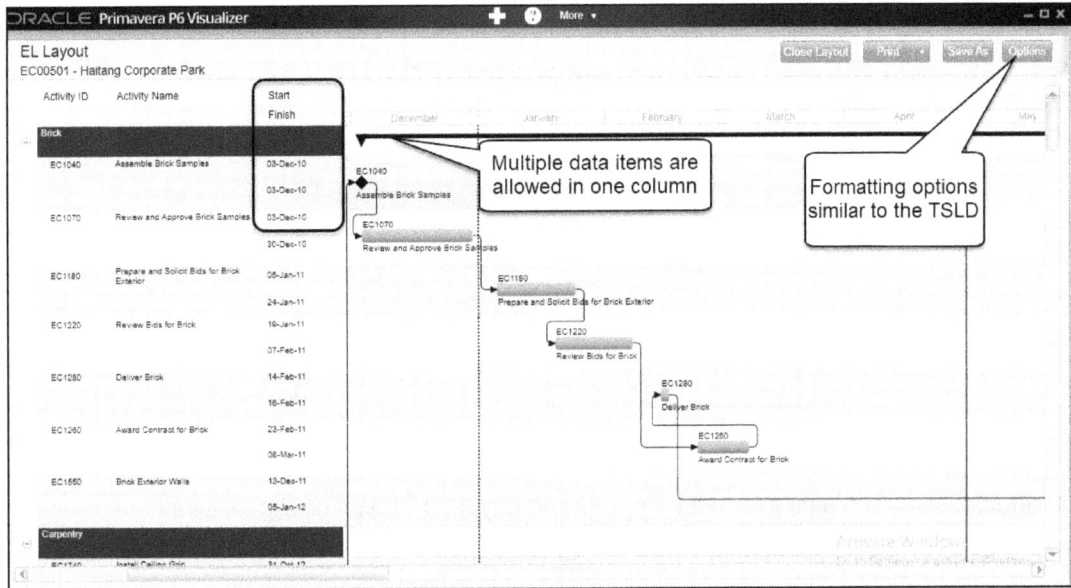

The **Options** form allows a large number of formatting options which are similar to other P6 formatting functions, but graphically richer:

- **Chart & Grid**
  - ➤ **Content** tab allows formatting of the columns and text.

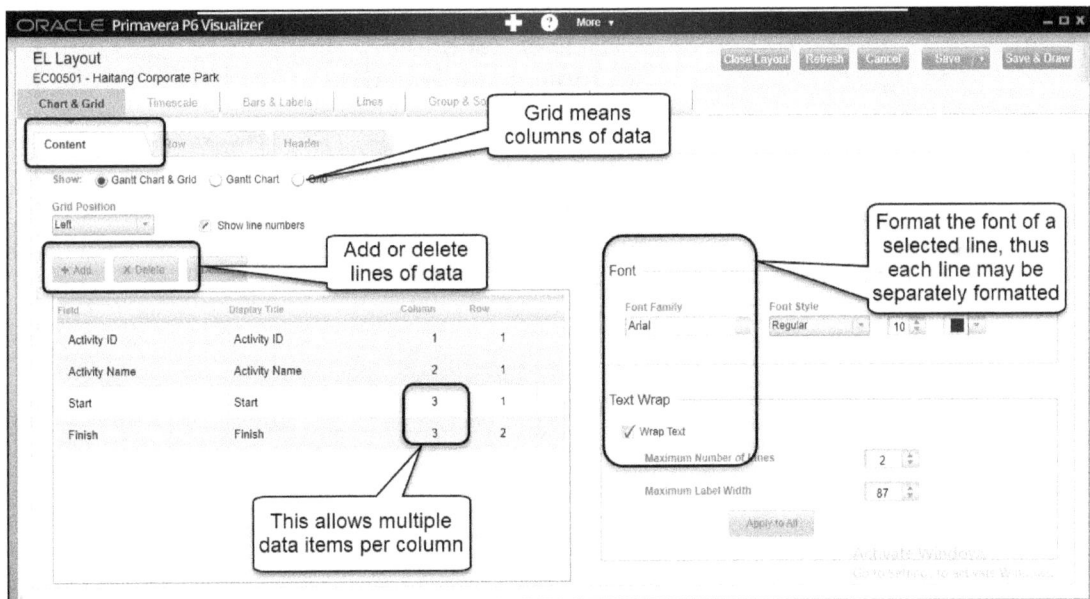

  - ➤ **Row** allows alternate coloring of rows,
  - ➤ **Header** is used to format the column headers.
- **Timescale**, **Bars** & **Labels Lines**, **Group & Sport**, **Filters**, and **Page Setup** tabs all work in the same way as the TSLD and will not be covered a second time.
- **Curtains** function was added in P6 Version 23 did not operate with the authors system and as reported to Oracle. This should operate in due course with a patch. The author made this function in a Gantt Chart work by importing a plf Layout.

14.4.5 Manage Layouts

This is where you import, copy and delete layouts.

The **More** menu has options for managing Layouts but the **Import** function was moved to the **Manage Layouts** form in later versions of Visualizer:

A New Gantt Chart or TSLD is created as a User Layout.

The **Manage** option allows a user to make any existing Layout a Project or Global layout:

- **Filter** allows the selection of **Gantt Chart** or **TSLD** layouts,
- Layouts may be copied and pasted to and from Global, Project and User.
- **Renaming** a layout is achieved by clicking on a Layout name and this will allow editing of the name:

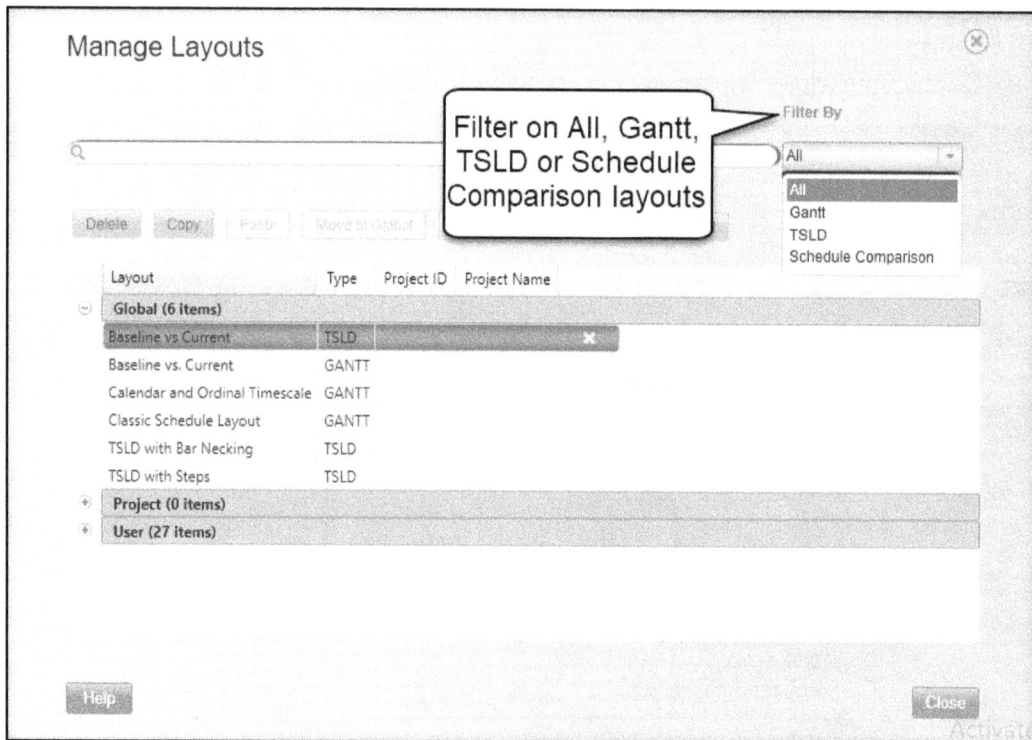

- **Exporting** a Visualizer Layout in VLF format is achieved by:
  - ➤ Selecting the layout,
  - ➤ Clicking the Export button,
  - ➤ Selecting a destination directory.

The **Import** function allows the import of:

- An existing Professional View that has been exported from the Windows Client as a *.PLF or
- A Visualizer report that may have been exported from another system.

To import a layout:

- Select **More**, **Import**,
- In the first screen select the PLF or VLF file:

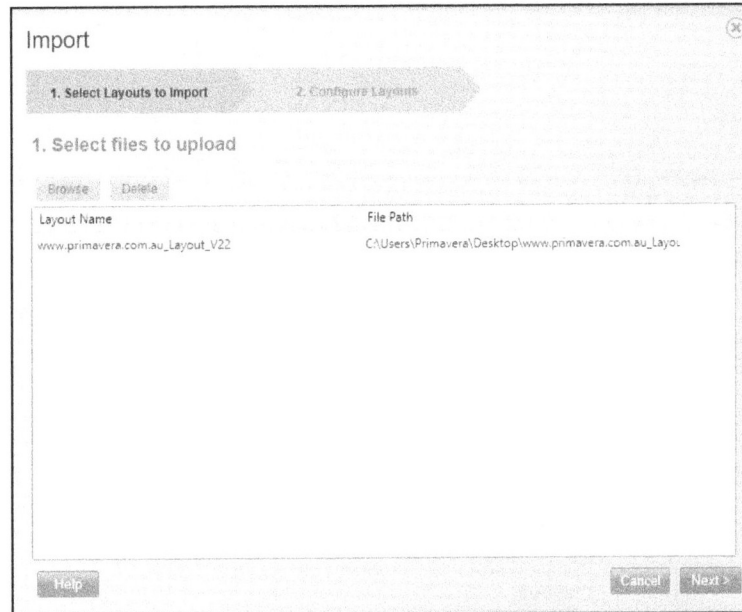

- In the second screen select from the options Global, Project or User.

- You should then check the **Options** to optimize the layout in Visualizer.

14.5   Claim Digger – Schedule Comparison

Schedule Comparison enables a user to compare two schedules and evaluate what changes have been made to another version and is often used in claims analysis. Every piece of schedule data is compared in a table, that may be printed out or exported to Excel as a CVS file and variances calculated.

From P6 select **Tools**, **Visualizer** to open **Visualizer** and select **Schedule Comparison**, or open **Visualizer** from the system start menu:

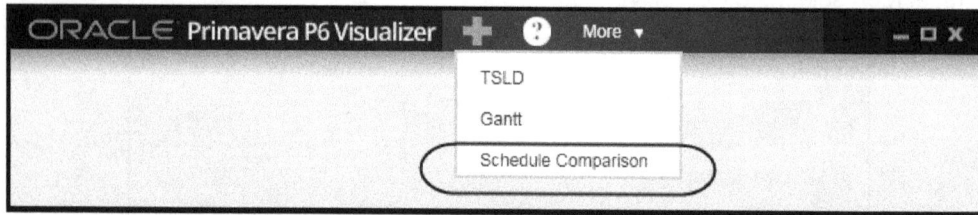

As with TSLD or Gantt in Schedule Comparison you will need to create a View and then add the projects or project and a baseline for comparison.

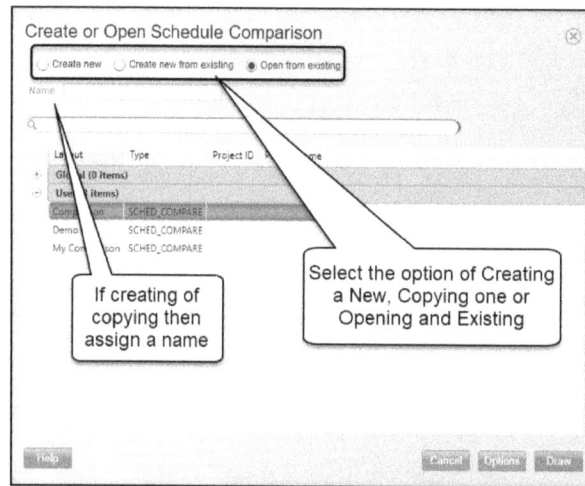

Select **Options**, **Project** to select the projects to be compared:

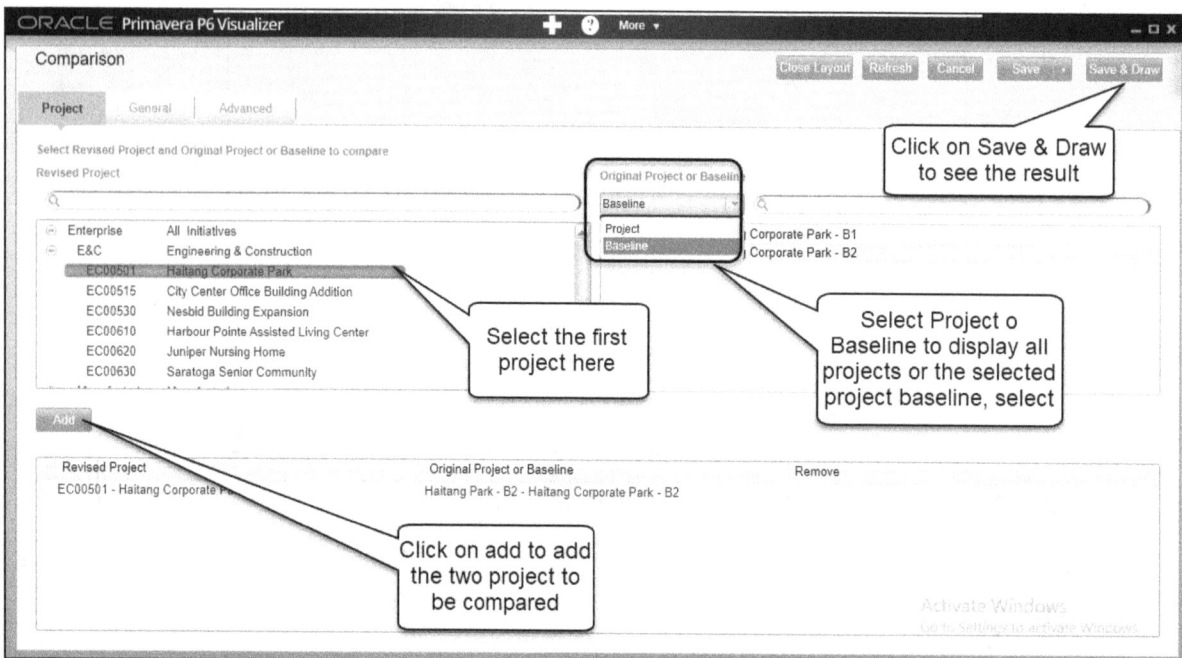

Select **Options**, **General** to select the output format, the author normally selects ASCII so it cane be opened in Excel and the differences and variances may be calculated as these are not calculated in the tool:

Select **Options**, **Advanced** to select the data that is compared:

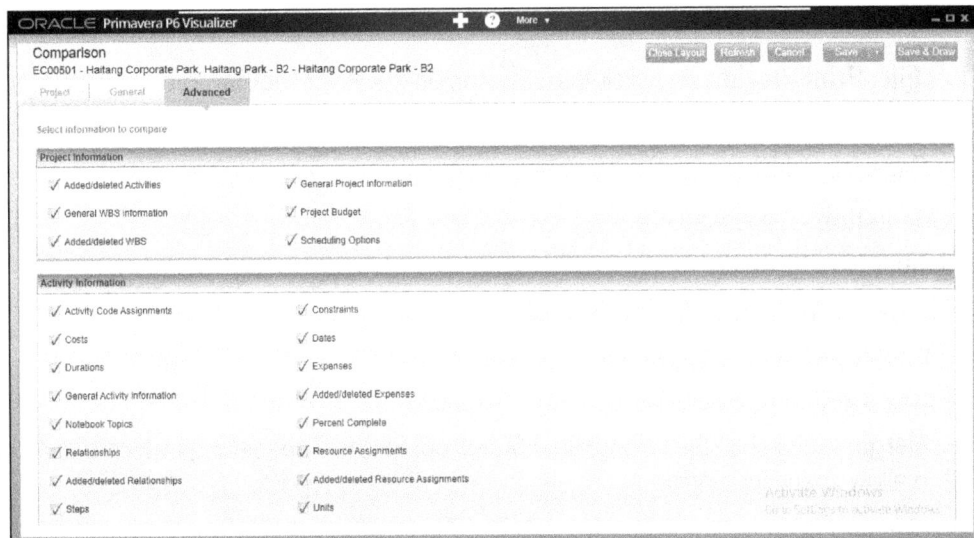

Then a table with all the projects data will be displayed:

14.6 Workshop 12 – Printing

Background

We want to issue a report for comment by management.

Assignment

Open your **OzBuild Bid** project from the previous workshop and complete the following steps:

1. Remove any filter.

2. Apply the **OzBuild Workshop 10 – With Float** layout.

3. From the **User Preferences**, **Dates** tab select **Do not show time**. It is not normal to display the time when submitting a schedule for review, but it must be displayed when manipulating a schedule.

4. Select **File**, **Print Preview** and click the ⬚ icon on the **Print toolbar** to open the **Page Setup** form.

5. In the **Page** tab select:

    ➢ **Orientation** – Landscape

    ➢ **Adjust to** – 100%

    ➢ **Fit to** – 0 page(s) wide by 0 pages tall

    ➢ **Fit timescale to:** – 1 page wide

    ➢ **Paper size:** – A4 or Letter

6. In the **Margins** tab set all the settings to 0.5", except for the **Top:** settings which should be set to 0.75" to allow space for binding.

7. In the **Header** tab:

    ➢ Divide Into: 3 Sections

    ➢ Include on: All Pages, so this will repeat on every page

    ➢ Height: 0.5

    ➢ Section 1, insert as Text/Logo – **Printed on: [date] [time]** – Arial Regular 8 to the left

    ➢ Section 2, insert as Text/Logo – **[project_name]** or **[project_pfolio_name]** – Arial Bold 12 in the middle

    ➢ Section 3, insert as Text/Logo – **Page [page_number] of [total_pages]** – Arial Regular 8, aligned to the right

8. In the **Footer** tab:

    ➢ Divide Into: 4 Sections

    ➢ Include on: First Page, so this will only be printed on the first page

    ➢ Height: 1.25

➢ Section 1 – Gantt Chart Legend

➢ Section 2 – Picture – Find a suitable picture to display

➢ Section 3 – Import a **Stored Image** and display

➢ Section 4 – Revision Box, edit as you wish

➢ Adjust widths as required.

9. In the **Options** tab:

➢ Set the Timescale Start: from the Project Start minus 5 days and Timescale Finish: to the Project Finish plus 5 days,

➢ Show the Activity Table, All Columns, Grid Lines and Gantt Chart.

10. Apply the Layout and click OK,

11. Compare your result with the picture below:

12. From the **User Preferences**, **Dates** tab select **24 hour (13:00)** and do not check **Show minutes**. This will ensure you know the time that activities will start and finish when you assign progress.

15 SCHEDULE OPTIONS AND SETTING A BASELINE

Tracking Progress is used after you have completed the plan or have completed sufficient iterations to reach an acceptable plan, and the project may be progressing. Now the important phase of regular monitoring and control begins. This process is important to help catch problems as early as possible, and thus minimize their impact on the successful completion of the project. The main steps for monitoring progress are:

- Saving a **Baseline** schedule, also known as a **Target**, holds the dates against which progress is compared. The current project may be copied and used as a baseline or an existing project may be assigned as a baseline. **The Baseline** is often considered as the Contract Baseline.

- A baseline may be used as the contract or revised contract program, last periods status of a copy of a program before delay activities are added or deleted.

- Recording or marking-up progress as of a specific date, titled the **Data Date**. This date is also known as the **Status Date**, **Update Date**, **Current Date**, **Report Date**, and **As-Of-Date**.

- **Updating** or **Progressing** the schedule.

- Scheduling the project and at the same time moving the **Data Date** to the new **Data Date** and recalculating all the activities dates.

- Comparing and reporting actual progress against planned progress and revising the plan and schedule, if required.

Comparing the status of an activity against more than one baseline is useful; for example:

- The original plan could be represented as one of the Baselines, to see the slippage against the original plan.

- Last Period, which could be another Baseline, to see the changes since the last update.

Primavera has the following functions:

- Primavera allows an unlimited number of baseline project files to be saved with a project.

- A baseline project may not be opened and viewed. It must be restored to the database to open and edit where it will no longer be a baseline.

- Up to four Baselines may be shown against a current schedule at one time either as bars on the Gantt Chart or in columns of data.

- Baseline comparison is displayed at Activity level in the **Activities Window**, not at resource level. Resource level comparison is available in resource views such as the **Resource Assignments Window**.

Shortcuts:

	Topic	Menu Command
•	Saving and Deleting and Setting a **Baseline**	To save a Baseline, select **P**roject, **Maintain Baselines…** to display the **Maintain Baselines** form
•	Setting a Baseline project	The baselines are assigned from the **P**roject, **Assign Baselines…** form
•	Update a Baseline	• Select **P**roject, **Maintain Baselines…**and select the ▷ Update icon to open the **Update Baseline** form.

The AACE RP 78R-13 Original Baseline Schedule Review - As Applied in Engineering, Procurement, and Construction is applicable to this chapter.

15.1 Understanding Date Fields

Primavera has many more date fields for the current schedule than Elecosoft (Asta) Powerproject or Microsoft Project. This section explains how these date fields are calculated.

There is very little documentation available on how these dates are calculated and the author has ascertained the information contained in this chapter by trial using an unresourced schedule.

After you understand these date fields, you should look again at the **Bar Timescale** options in the **Bars** form and it will be easier for you to understand how the bar formatting works.

15.1.1 Early Start and Early Finish

These are always the earliest dates that un-started activities or the incomplete portions of in-progress activities may start or finish based on calendars, relationships and constraints.

- The **Early Start** of the completed activity A1010 is set to the **Data Date** and time after the activity has commenced, not to the **Actual Start**, as in most other software,
- The **Early Finish** of the completed activity A1010 is set to the **Data Date** and time when the activity is complete, not to the **Actual Finish**, as in most other software,
- The **Early Start** of an in-progress activity is set to the **Remaining Early Start**, not to the **Actual Start**, as in other software, it is effectively the **Remaining Early Start**.

NOTE: Look carefully at the activity A1010 Early Start and Early Finish dates and then look at the Actual Start and Finish of the bar; they are very different:

Activity ID	Activity Name	Early Start	Early Finish	September 2014	October 2014	November 201
A1010	Activity A	12-Oct-14 00	12-Oct-14 00			
A1020	Activity B	13-Oct-14 08	24-Oct-14 17			
A1030	Activity C	27-Oct-14 08	21-Nov-14 17			

Thus, the Early Start and Early Finish dates of completed activities and Early Start of in-progress activities is not displayed in other software in this way and often leads to confusion when converting from other software. Thus, the **Early Bar** is not displayed by default in the Gantt Chart, as the **Early Bar** will not display Actual progress in the same way as other software.

15.1.2 Late Start and Late Finish

- These are the latest dates that **Un-started** activities or the incomplete portions of **In-progress** activities may start or finish based on calendars, relationships, and constraints. It is effectively the **Remaining Late Start**.
- The **Complete** activity has the **Late Dates** set the date that is equivalent to the latest point in time that the activity could be restarted.
- The **Total Float** on the Complete Activity is "Null" but the default Layout displays a Float Bar.

NOTE: The Total Float bar finish is the same as the Late Finish and used to calculate Total Float.

Activity ID	Activity Name	Late Start	Late Finish	Total Float	September 2014	October 2014	November 2014
A1010	Activity A	20-Oct-14 08	20-Oct-14 08				
A1020	Activity B	20-Oct-14 08	31-Oct-14 17	5d			
A1030	Activity C	03-Nov-14 08	28-Nov-14 17	5d			

15.1.3 Actual Start and Finish

These dates are manually applied, representing when an activity started or finished, and override constraints and relationships. These dates should be set in the past in relation to the **Data Date**.

Activity ID	Activity Name	Actual Start	Actual Finish	September 2014				October 2014				November 20		
				25 01 08 15 22				29 06 13 20				27 03 10 17		
A1010	Activity A	01-Sep-14 08	26-Sep-14 17											
A1020	Activity B	29-Sep-14 08												
A1030	Activity C													

⚠ Actual dates should never change after they are assigned but both the **Apply Actuals** when activities are set to **Auto Compute Actuals**, and **Update Progress** functions may change Actual Dates. These functions must be used with extreme caution.

15.1.4 Start and Finish

The **Start** is set to the **Early Start** when the activity has not started and the **Actual Start** when it has started.

The **Finish** is set to the **Early Finish** when the activity has not started or is in-progress and the **Actual Finish** when it is complete.

- An "A" is placed after the date when an **Actual Start** or **Actual Finish** has been set,
- An "*" is placed after the date when a constraint has been applied to the activity,
- These date fields allow the Early and Actual Start and Finish dates to be displayed as expected when the activity has not started, is in-progress, or complete:

Activity ID	Activity Name	Start	Finish	September 2014				October 2014				November 20		
				25 01 08 15 22				29 06 13 20				27 03 10 17		
A1010	Activity A	01-Sep-14 08 A	26-Sep-14 17 A											
A1020	Activity B	29-Sep-14 08 A	24-Oct-14 17											
A1030	Activity C	27-Oct-14 08	21-Nov-14 17											

⚠ Users converting from Elecosoft (Asta) Powerproject or Microsoft Project will be used to displaying the Early Start and Early Finish dates, but the Early Start and Early Finish dates should not be displayed when a schedule has progress, as this will give misleading information. The Start and Finish dates should always be displayed under normal scheduling conditions.

15.1.5 Planned Dates

The **Planned Finish** is calculated from the **Planned Start** plus the **Original Duration**. The **Original Duration** is labeled **Planned Duration** in some Industry Versions. These fields are always linked, therefore:

- A change to the **Planned Start** will change the **Planned Finish** via the **Original Duration**,
- A change to the **Planned Finish** will change permanently the **Original Duration,** and
- A change to the **Original Duration** will change the **Planned Finish**.

When an activity has **NOT** started:

- The **Planned** dates **ARE** normally linked to the **Start** and **Finish**.

  (i) The **Original** and **At Completion** durations are **ONLY** linked when an activity has not started and when **Link Budget and At Completion for not started activities** box in the **Projects Window**, **Calculations** tab is checked.

- They are **NOT** linked to the Early Dates.

Start	Planned Start	Finish	Planned Finish	Jan 09	Jan 16
				M T W T F S S	M T W T F S
09-Jan-23 08	09-Jan-23 08	20-Jan-23 16	20-Jan-23 16		

- A **Planned Start** may be manually edited and as the **Start** date is linked it is also changed, but the **Early Start** is **NOT** changed. The **Planned Start** and **Start** are reset to the Early Dates when a project is scheduled.

- The **Planned Finish** may be edited and is linked to the **Finish** date and the **Original Duration**. A change to the **Planned Finish** will change the **Finish** date and **Original Duration**. Rescheduling will recalculate the schedule using the new **Original Duration** and set the **Planned Finish**, **Finish**, and **Early Finish** to the same date.

- Thus, a change to the **Planned Start** is reversed by rescheduling, but a change to the **Planned Finish** affects the **Original Duration** and is not reversed by rescheduling.

When an activity is in-progress:

- The **Planned Start** date remains unchanged when an **Actual Start** date is set that is different to the **Planned Start**.

- Therefore, the **Planned Start** remains the same as the **Start Date** before the **Actual Start** was set:

Start	Planned Start	Finish	Planned Finish	Jan 02	Jan 09	Jan 16
				S M T W T F S	S M T W T F S	S M T W T F S
02-Jan-23 08 A	09-Jan-23 08	13-Jan-23 16	20-Jan-23 16			

- The **Planned Finish** is calculated from the **Planned Start Date** plus the **Original Duration**.

- A started activity **Remaining Duration** may be edited independently from the **Original Duration**. The **Planned Finish** may have a different date than the **Finish**, which is now set to the **Early Finish**.

When an activity is complete:

- The **Planned Dates** are unlinked from all other date fields.

15.1.6 Planned Dates Issues

⚠ This is one of the most important paragraphs in this book and you must be certain that you understand the Planned dates and how to avoid the issues associated with them.

The Planned Dates are very complex to explain and understand, so please read carefully, in summary:

- When an activity has **Not Started** the Planned Dates match the Early Start and Early Finish.

- When an activity is **Complete** or **In-progress** the Planned Dates match the status of the activity immediately before it was marked as Started.

In the situation where a schedule is in the process of being updated:

- Assume the Data Date has been moved to the new Data Date and the project scheduled,
- Now all un-started activities will have their Start and Finish dates in the future,
- At this point every activity that is marked In-progress by assigning an Actual Start (which should be in the past in relation to the **Data Date**) will have **Planned Dates** that neither:
  - ➤ Match the status of the activity before the activity was marked as Started, nor
  - ➤ Match the status of the activity after the activity was marked as Started and possibly finished.

  ⚠ Thus, in this situation and at this point in time the Planned Dates are now holding irrelevant dates that should never be displayed or used for any purpose.

Unfortunately, the Planned Dates are used by default in several places and Database Administrators and Users must be aware of where they are used and how to avoid displaying them.

- The Planned dates are displayed as the **Project Baseline** bars and **Primary User Baseline** bars when no baseline has been assigned,

  ⚠ Never display a Baseline Bar or columns unless a baseline project has been created and assigned, otherwise the Baseline bar and columns may represent irrelevant data.

- These Planned dates are used by the **Apply Actuals** function, when activities are set to **Auto Compute Actuals**, and the **Update Progress** function. Thus, **Actual Start** dates and **Early Finish** dates of in-progress activities will be changed to the Planned Date values without warning.

  ⚠ Ensure you never ever use the **Update Progress** function on a schedule that has been progressed, otherwise **Actual Start** dates and **Early Finish** dates of in-progress activities will be changed to the Planned Date values without warning.

- Ina PPM database the **Planned Dates** from a Baseline schedule will be displayed as the Baseline Bars when the **Admin**, **Admin Preferences...**, **Earned Value** tab is set to **Budget values with planned dates**. Thus, the Baseline Bars from an in-progress schedule will be incorrect.
- The recommended setting is **At Completion values with current dates:**

- In a EPPM database the recommended setting is At Completion values with current dates the **Planned Dates** from a Baseline will be displayed as the Baseline Bars when the **Administer**, **Application Settings**, **Earned Value** tab is set to the default of **Planned values with planned dates.**

- The recommended setting is **At Completion values with current dates:**

Ensure **A**dmin, **A**dmin **P**references…, **Earned Value** tab has this value set as **At Completion values with current dates** or **Budget Values with current dates**. When the schedule is not resource- or cost-loaded it does not matter which of these two you use. More details on these settings in paragraph 17.3.6.

15.1.7 Remaining Early Start and Finish

These are the earliest dates that the incomplete portions of un-started or in-progress activities may start and finish.

- They are blank when an activity is complete.
- They may be edited in the same way as Planned Dates.
    - When a **Remaining Early Start** is edited to a later than scheduled date, there is an option for constraining the **Remaining Early Start** with a **Start on or After Constraint**. If this is not set, then the activity will move forward to its original position when scheduling.
    - When a **Remaining Early Finish** is edited, the **Remaining Duration** is also edited and the change is permanent. Scheduling does not take the schedule back to the original position.

15.1.8 Remaining Late Start and Finish

These are the latest dates that the incomplete portions of activities may start and finish.

- They are blank when an activity is complete and may not be edited,
- They may not be displayed as a bar,
- They are set to equal the **Late Dates**.

15.2 Schedule Options – General Tab

When a project is rescheduled, there are some options available in the **Schedule Options** form which is opened by selecting **Tools**, **Schedule…**, **Options** which control how the schedule calculates:

- Pressing the ☐ ▷ Default ☐ will set the options back to the P6 defaults, it does not save yours as the default as in other products.

- The default options are good but some need to be changed to suit specific situations.

- These options apply to all activities in the currently opened schedule.

- When more than one schedule has been opened then you should carefully read the **Multiple Project Scheduling** chapter to understand how:

  ➤ The **Set Default Project** function operates in Version 19 and earlier, and

  ➤ Selecting a project from the **Schedule Options** form, **Select Default Project from** overrides the project selected in the **Project**, **Set Default Project** form, but does not change the **Project**, **Set Default Project** form setting,

  ➤ When more than one schedule has been opened the **Default Project Schedule options** are used to schedule all projects and other open projects' **Schedule options** are changed permanently the **Default Project** and may not calculate the same in future,

  ➤ This is covered in more detail in para 25.3.2.

- If you export a schedule to another database, it is prudent to send a copy of the project **Schedule Options** so they may be checked when imported into another database, especially if the schedule is to be opened with other projects. Again, you should read carefully the **Multiple Project Scheduling** chapter to understand how the **Default Project** function operates.

- Changing the **Schedule Options** may change the way the schedule calculates and users must be very careful if considering changing any of them. You may wish to copy the schedule, baseline it, and then change to options to see what the effect is on the schedule calculation.

  ⓘ The Primavera **Schedule Options** defaults are good and it is suggested that they should not be changed unless the user has good reason to change them.

15.2.1 Ignore relationships to and from other projects

Relationships may be created between two projects when:

- Two or more projects are opened together, or

- When assigning a relationship another project is opened and a relationship is created to an activity in another project.

Check the **Ignore relationships to and from other projects** in the **Tools**, **Schedule…**, **Options** form to:

- Ignore relationships with other projects that are currently not open, or
- To ignore **External Dates** that may be created when a P6 project is imported from another database and the imported project has interproject relationships.

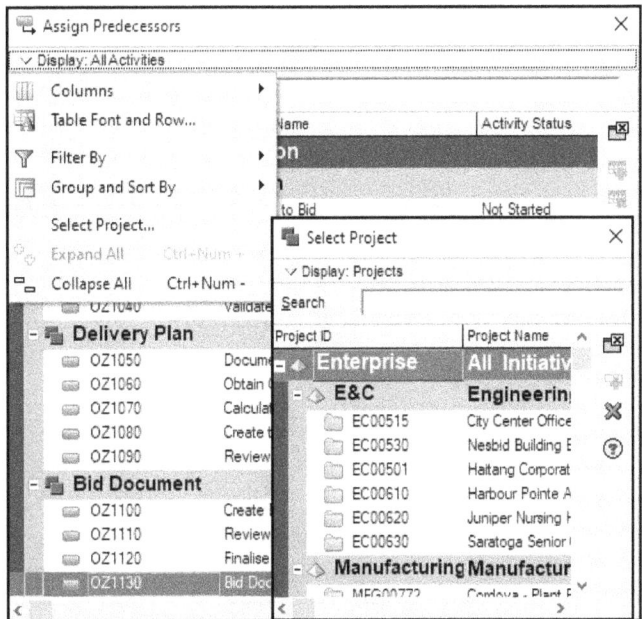

This option will also ignore **External Dates**, which are the **External Early Start** and **External Late Finish** dates.

External Dates are constraints created when a project is exported from Primavera Contractor and/or another P6 database and imported into P6. They act like Early Start and Late Finish Constraints and are used to represent the relationships that would have originally provided the Early Start and Late Finish dates to the Critical Path calculations of the imported schedule.

These dates can be very confusing if one is not aware that they have been created or how they operate. The negative float in the picture below is created by these dates after an activity's duration was increased by 34 days:

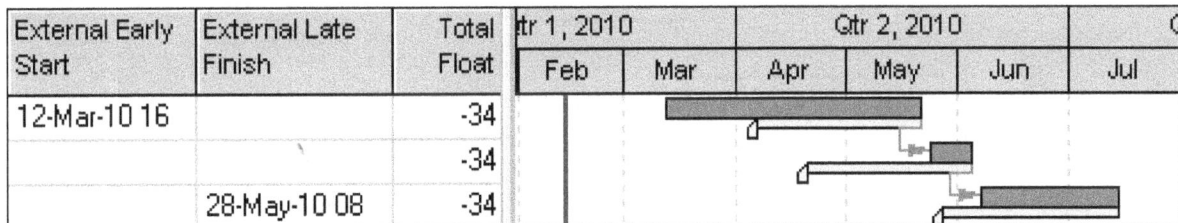

When you import a project from another database ensure you **ALWAYS** check for External Dates and understand how they operate.

If you export and then import back into the same database, then External dates are not normally created but the relationships are re-established with the original schedule they were linked with.

On the other hand, if the original schedules have been deleted then these External Dates may be created.

15.2.2 Make open-ended activities critical

An open-ended activity is an activity without a successor and which has float to the end of the project. Checking the box makes these activities critical with zero total float when they do not have a successor.

- Open-ends Not Critical:

- Open-ends Critical:

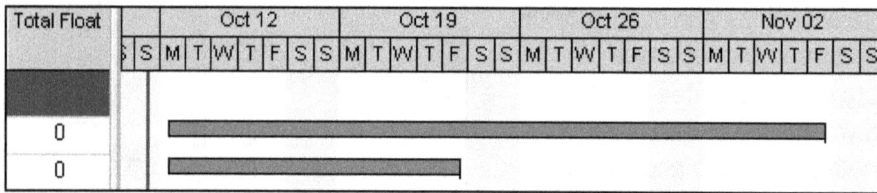

This also allows the user to display multiple critical paths in one project without the use of constraints and is useful should you wish to see the individual critical paths for each area of a project. In order for this function to work the last activity in each chain or events must not have a successor:

- Open-ends Not Critical:

- Open-ends Critical:

15.2.3 Use Expected Finish Dates

The intention of this option is for people using timesheets to be able to set an Expected Finish constraint for an activity.

Once an Expected Finish date is set then the software calculates the Remaining Duration from:

- The Early Start when an activity has not started, or
- The Data Date when an activity has started, or
- A Resume date if a Suspend and Resume date has been set.

Therefore, Expected Finish dates may be assigned from the Timesheets module and this option allows the project manager to ignore these dates submitted with the timesheets.

This is always checked by default and will disable or enable Expected Finish constraints assigned in the **Status** tab of the **Activities Details** tab or from a column.

This is usually not turned off and the pictures below show the effect of this constraint before and after scheduling an activity with an Expected Finish Constraint assigned:

- Before scheduling:

Activity ID	Original Duration	Remaining Duration	Expected Finish	Finish	Jan 26							Feb 02						
					un	Mon	Tue	Wed	Thr	Fri	Sat	Sun	Mon	Tue	Wed	Thr	Fri	Sat
A1000	4	4		31-Jan-14 16														
A1010	4	4	07-Feb-14 16	31-Jan-14 16														

- After scheduling:

Activity ID	Original Duration	Remaining Duration	Expected Finish	Finish	Jan 26							Feb 02						
					un	Mon	Tue	Wed	Thr	Fri	Sat	Sun	Mon	Tue	Wed	Thr	Fri	Sat
A1000	4	4		31-Jan-14 16														
A1010	9	9	07-Feb-14 16	07-Feb-14 16														

15.2.4 Schedule automatically when a change affects dates

This is similar to automatic recalculation in other products and this recalculates the schedule when data that affects the timing of the schedule is changed.

P6 is a database product and Schedule Automatically will result in the schedule recalculating every time you make a change. This may slow down your work significantly; this option is usually left off.

15.2.5 Level resources during scheduling

Leveling a schedule delays activities until resources become available. This is a form of resource optimization and this option levels the project resources each time it is scheduled. Resource leveling is covered in paragraph 20.6.

> ℹ️ This is **NOT** recommended as it slows down the schedule calculation and the schedule often change each time it is scheduled.

15.2.6 Recalculate assignment costs after scheduling

Resource Unit Rates may be set to change over time in the **Units & Prices** tab of the **Resources Window**:

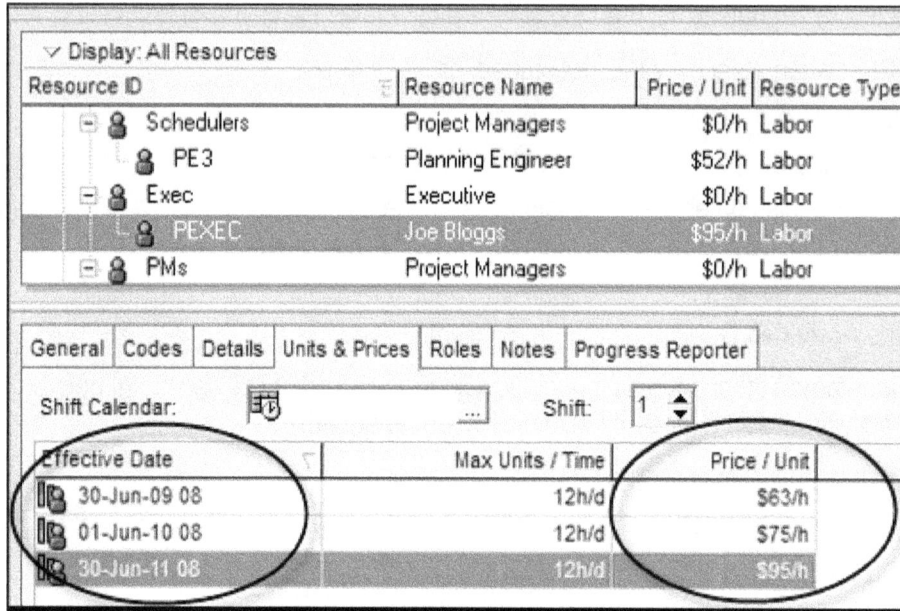

This option recalculates a resource cost when a resource is scheduled into a different cost rates time bracket.

Also, when the resource **Price / Unit** has been changed in the **Resource** window it will also recalculate the activity assigned resource cost.

15.2.7 When scheduling progressed activities use

"Out of Sequence Progress" occurs when an activity starts before a predecessor defined by a relationship has finished. Therefore, the relationships have not been acknowledged and the successor activity has started out of sequence. There are three options in P6 for calculating the finish date of a successor when the successor activity has started before the predecessor activity is finished:

- Retained Logic
- Progress Override
- Actual Dates

The selected option is applied to all activities in a schedule when it is calculated. Open the **Schedule Options** form by selecting **Tools**, **Schedule…** and clicking on the [▷ Options…] icon where the options are found under **When scheduling progressed activities use**:

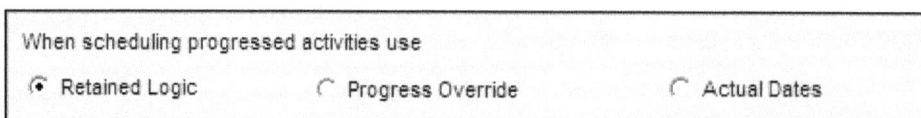

The picture below represents the status of the activities before updating the schedule:

- **Retained Logic**.
  In the example following, the relationship is maintained between the predecessor and successor for the unworked portion of the activity (the Remaining Duration) and continued after the predecessor has finished. The relationship forms part of the critical path and the predecessor has no float.
  NOTE: This is the recommended option as a more conservative schedule is produced and any relationships may be changed as required:

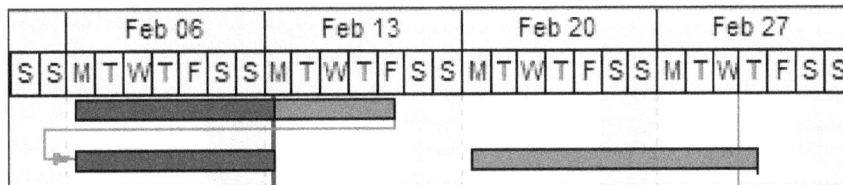

- **Progress Override**.
  In the example following, the Finish-to-Start relationship between the predecessor and successor is disregarded, and the unworked portion of the activity (the Remaining Duration) continues before the predecessor has finished.
  NOTE: The relationship is not a driving relationship and DOES NOT form part of the critical path in the example below and the predecessor has float:

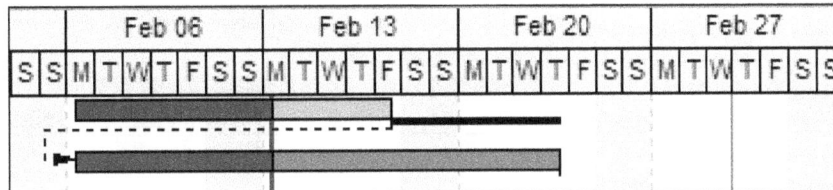

- **Actual Dates**.
  This function operates when there is an activity with Actual Start Dates in the future, which is not logical. With this option the remaining duration of an in-progress activity is calculated after the activity with actual start and finish in the future:

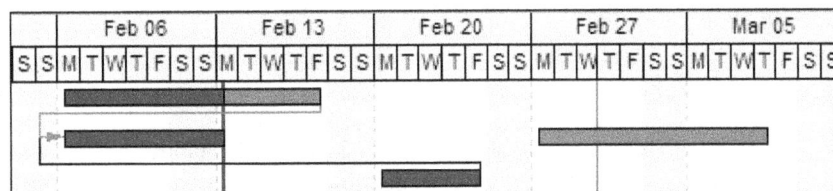

When there are no Actual Dates in the future this option calculates as Retained Logic.

This situation with Actuals in the future may happen when two projects are opened together and have different Data Dates. This situation is best avoided and it is best to make the Data Dates of all projects the same.

i Retained Logic and Progress Override are not terms used by Microsoft Project or Elecosoft (Asta) Powerproject. Microsoft Project uses the term **Split in progress** and Elecosoft (Asta) Powerproject uses two functions titled **Move part completed tasks** and **Relink around completed tasks** and these functions operate in a similar in Primavera P6. Retained Logic produces a more conservative schedule (a longer duration schedule) and is more likely to place an out-of-progress relationship on the critical path and adjustments may be made as required.

If your schedule has Actual dates in the future of the Data Date (which may occur when the update information is collected at different times and the earlier date is used as the Data Date or multiple projects are open) then the use of Actual Dates would calculate the most conservative schedule.

15.2.8 Calculate start-to-start lag from

The successor of an activity with a Start-to-Start and positive lag would start after the lag has expired. When the predecessor commences out of sequence the lag may be calculated from the predecessor calculated Early Start or the Actual Start.

- The Actual Start gives a less conservative schedule:

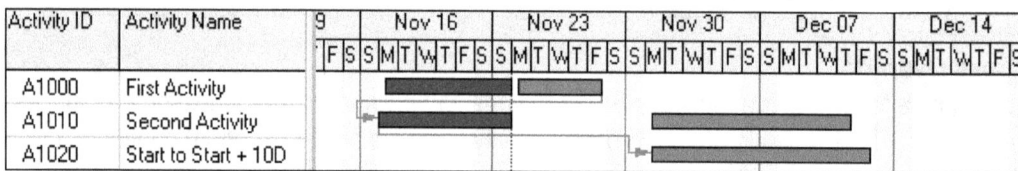

- The Early Start gives a more conservative schedule:

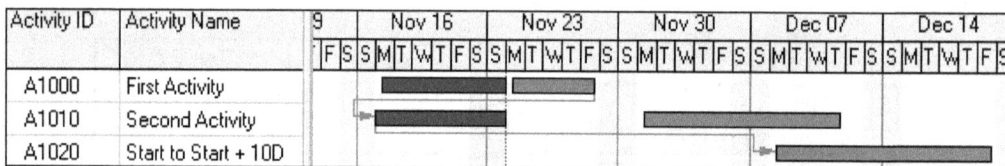

15.2.9 Define critical activities as

Critical Activities Definition criteria is defined in the **Projects Window**, **Project Details**, **Settings** tab:

These options are used for analyzing schedules that utilize multiple calendars which may result in activities on the critical path possessing float.

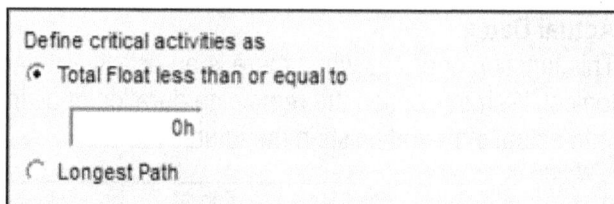

- **Total Float less than or equal to** – Activities may be marked as critical and with a chosen float value. Sometimes a small positive value is used to isolate the near critical activities on schedules or displaying the full critical path on multiple calendar schedules.

- **Longest Path** – This option isolates the longest chain of activities in a schedule and should be used when multiple calendars are in use and some activities, which form part of the critical path, still have float when the successor is assigned a calendar with fewer or different working days.
  Oracle define Longest Path in their Help File as "*In a multicalendar project, the longest path is calculated by identifying the activities that have an early finish equal to the latest calculated early finish for the project and tracing all driving relationships for those activities back to the project start date.*"

- In the example below the Total Float has been set to **Total Float less than or equal to zero** and the critical path has disappeared, with only the third activity critical:

- When the Total Float is then set to less than or equal to 1 day results in the picture below with the second and third activity critical:

- When the Total Float is then set to **Longest Path** results in the picture below with all activities critical:

ACTION: Longest path is recommended for projects with multiple calendars.

The following pictures give a more interesting view of how these options work, there are three chains of activities with different calendars, some 5 day per week, some 6 days per week and some 7 days per week:

- **Total Float** less than or equal to zero, with the critical path going from activity D, B, E:
  Note: This does not show a logic linked chain of activities.

- **Total Float** less than or equal to 1 day, with two chains of critical activities A, B, C and D, E, F:

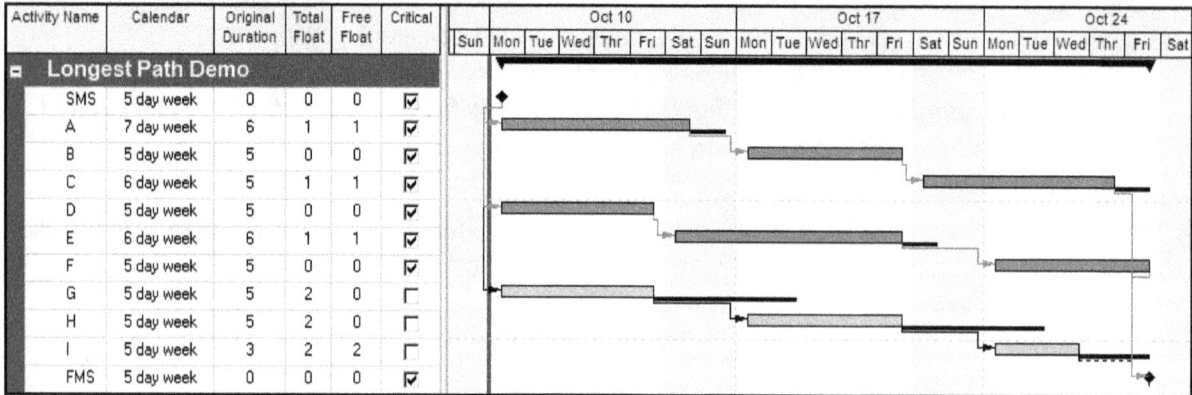

Activity Name	Calendar	Original Duration	Total Float	Free Float	Critical	
Longest Path Demo						
SMS	5 day week	0	0	0	☑	
A	7 day week	6	1	1	☑	
B	5 day week	5	0	0	☑	
C	6 day week	5	1	1	☑	
D	5 day week	5	0	0	☑	
E	6 day week	6	1	1	☑	
F	5 day week	5	0	0	☑	
G	5 day week	5	2	0	☐	
H	5 day week	5	2	0	☐	
I	5 day week	3	2	2	☐	
FMS	5 day week	0	0	0	☑	

- **Longest Path** recommended for projects with multiple calendars, the critical path now is a single chain of activities D, E, F:

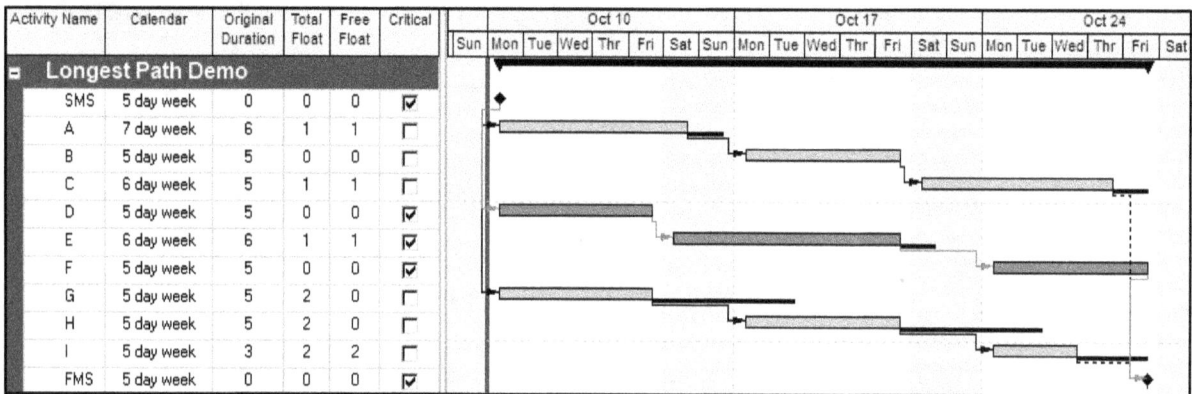

Activity Name	Calendar	Original Duration	Total Float	Free Float	Critical	
Longest Path Demo						
SMS	5 day week	0	0	0	☑	
A	7 day week	6	1	1	☐	
B	5 day week	5	0	0	☐	
C	6 day week	5	1	1	☐	
D	5 day week	5	0	0	☑	
E	6 day week	6	1	1	☑	
F	5 day week	5	0	0	☑	
G	5 day week	5	2	0	☐	
H	5 day week	5	2	0	☐	
I	5 day week	3	2	2	☐	
FMS	5 day week	0	0	0	☑	

15.2.10 Calculate float based on finish date

This is a new function to Version 6.2. When more than one project is opened the Total Float may be calculated based on each individual project or the longest project:

- Each project – used when each project's critical path is required:

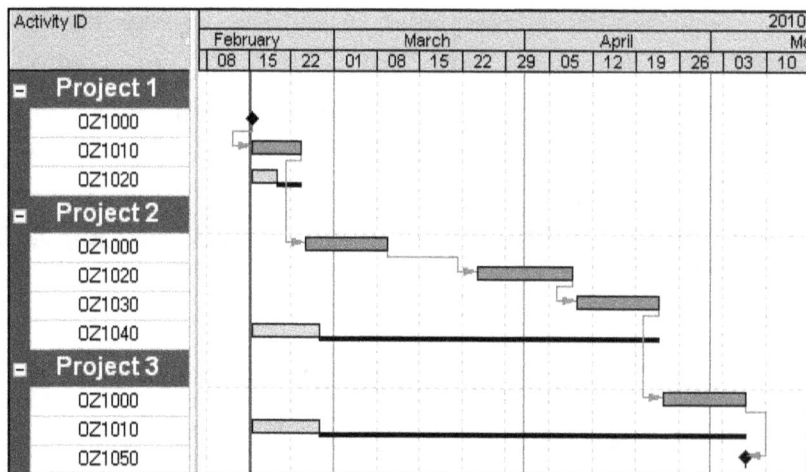

- Opened projects – used when all the P6 projects are related and float is required to be based on the longest project:

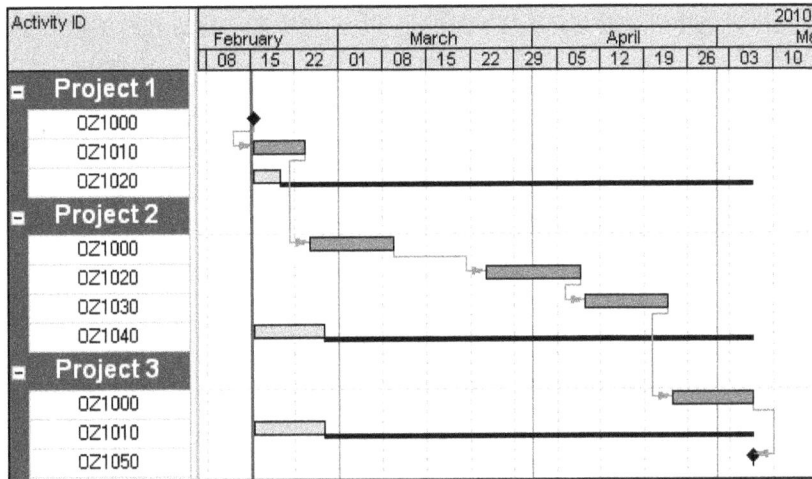

⚠️ The issue with the **Opened projects** setting is that, depending on what projects are opened, the **Total Float** will calculate differently and is therefore not recommended.

15.2.11 Compute Total Float as

There are three options for the calculation of the Float value displayed in the Total Float column of WBS and LOE activities only:

- Start Float = Late Start – Early Start

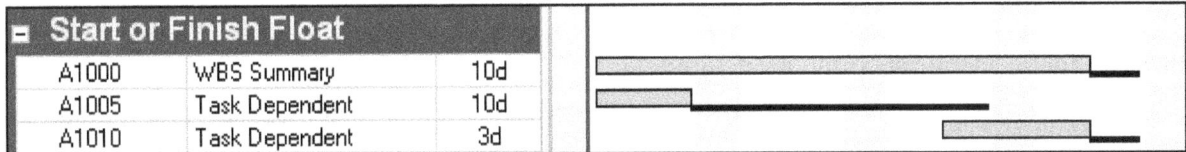

- Finish Float = Late Finish – Early Finish

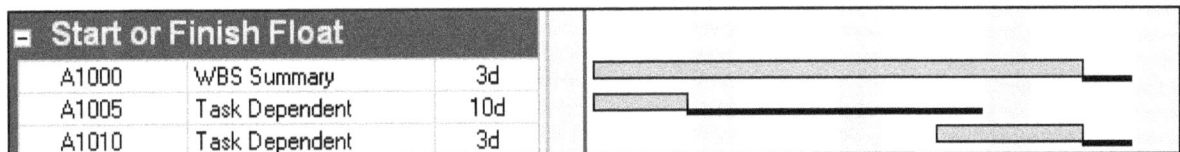

- Smallest of Start Float and Finish Float

ℹ️ It can be seen from the pictures above that the Total Float bar only displays the Finish Float. The Smallest of Start Float and Finish Float is the most conservative but the Finish Float will always give an answer that is the same as the Total Float bar.

15.2.12 Calendar for scheduling Relationship Lag

- There are four calendar options for the calculation of the lag for all activities:

  1. **Predecessor Activity Calendar** is the default, the example below has a 40-hour lag, or

Calendar		Jun 01								
	Sun	Mon	Tue	Wed	Thr	Fri	Sat	Sun	Mon	Tue
24 Hours/Day 7 Days/Week										
5 Day/Week										

  2. **Successor Activity Calendar**. note the change in the successor start, or

Calendar		Jun 01								
	Sun	Mon	Tue	Wed	Thr	Fri	Sat	Sun	Mon	Tue
24 Hours/Day 7 Days/Week										
5 Day/Week										

  3. **24-Hour,** or

  4. **Project Default Calendar**.

> ℹ️ **Microsoft Project** 2003 to 2019 uses the successor calendar for lag calculations. Microsoft Project also has the option of an Elapsed lag duration and % Duration lag.
>
> **Elecosoft (Asta) Powerproject** does not assign lags to the relationship but a lag is assigned to the predecessor or successor activity thus allowing an unlimited number of relationships between two activities and a partial Critical Path, plus it also has a % Duration lag.

15.2.13 Schedule Options – Advanced Tab

This tab selects the options for calculating multiple critical paths and is covered in detail in the **Utilities** chapter.

15.3 Setting the Baseline

Setting the Baseline makes a complete copy of a project, including relationships, notebook entries and codes. You are then able to compare the current project's progress against the baseline.

There are three types of Baselines that are often saved with scheduling software such as P6 – Management, Last Period Status and Claims Analysis to record the status before applying a delay or acceleration to a schedule:

Management Baselines

These are usually a copy of an original unprogressed schedule that has been contractually agreed to as the Baseline or Target schedule and are used to:

- Evaluate progress and report progress to a client or customer,
- Provide a base for Extension of Time claims and other contractual claims that may be made based on these Baseline schedules.

Last Period Status Baselines

These are copies of a schedule at a point in time and are used for the management of a project:

- Usually, they are used to measure the loss in time from one reporting period to another,
- They allow management to ascertain performance and make decisions on how to manage the project,
- They are displayed in exactly the same way as Management Baselines with the software,
- These Baselines usually, after the first period update, have progress.

Claims Analysis

- This is used to record the status before applying a delay or acceleration to a schedule.
- Delays may be added by adding activities, changing durations or editing calendars.

Up to 50 baselines per project may be saved in a database in earlier versions but in Version 6.0 and later an unlimited number may be saved.

There is still a restriction of a maximum of 50 Baselines when copying a project.

- The number of baselines that may be saved is set in the **Admin Preferences** form by selecting **Admin, Admin Preferences…, Data Limits** and setting the number in the **Maximum baselines per project** box.
- The number of baselines that may be copied when copying a project is set in the **Admin Preferences** form by selecting **Admin, Admin Preferences…, Data Limits** and setting the number in the **Maximum baselines copied with project** box.
- Up to four baselines, one **Project Baseline** and three **User Baselines**, may be displayed and compared to the current project.

  If another user opens the project, they will only see the one **Project Baseline** and not the other **Users Baseline**.

- A baseline project may be restored back into a database as a normal project. Then it may be edited and resaved as a baseline project.

After the Baseline is set, it is possible to compare the progress with the original plan. You will be able to see if you are ahead or behind schedule and by how much. The Baseline schedule should be established before you update the schedule for the first time.

15.3.1 Creating a Baseline

To create a Baseline, ensure the project is open and select **P**roject, **Maintain Baselines…** to display the **Maintain Baselines** form:

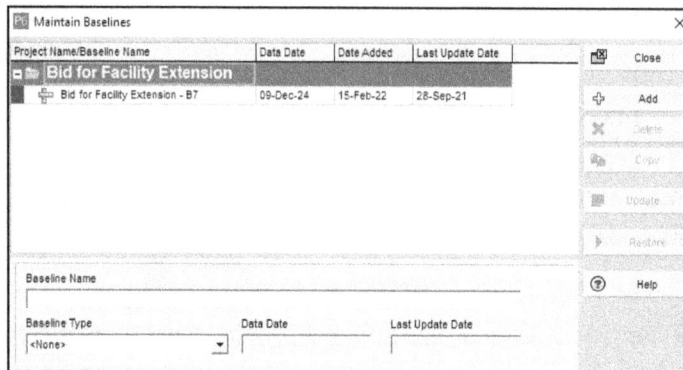

- To create a new baseline, click the ⊕ **Add** icon to open the **Add New Baseline** form:

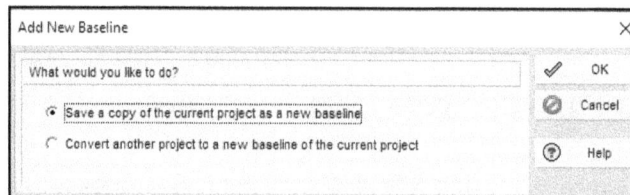

- Select either of the two options in the form:
  - ➢ **Save a copy of the current project as a new baseline** will make a copy of the currently open project. P6 adds B1, B2, etc., after the name and returns you to the **Baselines** form, or
  - ➢ **Convert another project to a new baseline of the current project** will open the **Select Project** form where another project may be selected to be a baseline. This project will then move from the current projects window into the **Maintain Baselines** form and is not available to be opened from the **Projects Window**.
- Assign a **Baseline Type** from the drop-down box. Baseline Types are defined in the **A**dmin, **Admin Categories…** form, **Baseline Type** tab.

15.3.2 Deleting a Baseline

To delete a project baseline from the database:

- Open the **Maintain Baselines** form by selecting **P**roject, **Maintain Baselines…**,
- Select the baseline project to be deleted, and
- Click on the ✖ **Delete** icon.

15.3.3 Restoring a Baseline to the Database as an Active Project

To restore a project back to the database so it may be edited or used as a current project:

- Open the **Maintain Baselines** form by selecting **P**roject, **Maintain Baselines…**,
- Ensure the baseline is not assigned as any baseline in the **Baselines** form,
- Select the baseline project to be restored, and
- Click on the ▷ **Restore** icon.

15.3.4 Update Baselines

The new Primavera Version 5.0 **Update Baseline** function enables the Baseline schedule to be updated with data from the current schedule or deleting activities that are no longer in the current schedule without restoring the Baseline schedule:

- Select **Project**, **Maintain Baselines…**and select the [Update…] icon to open the **Update Baseline** form:

- When **Run Optimized** is not checked then an error log is kept during the updating process.

- **Ignore Last Update Date** may be used when a project is updated at different times and the last Baseline Update may not be valid for the current schedule although the Baseline has been updated with more recent data.

- Select [Update Options…] to open the **Update Baseline Options** form to select which data items are updated.

This is a very powerful feature but it is the opinion and experience of the author that the Update Baseline is often the fastest way to destroy a good baseline. A backup of the baseline should be taken before using this function. Furthermore, it is probably best to open edit and review the changes to a Baseline rather than risk using the Update Baseline function.

15.3.5 Copying a Project with Baselines

Primavera Version 6.0 introduced the option of being able to copy baselines when a project is copied in the **Projects Window** using Copy and Paste.

(i) You must manually reassign the baselines after the project has been copied.

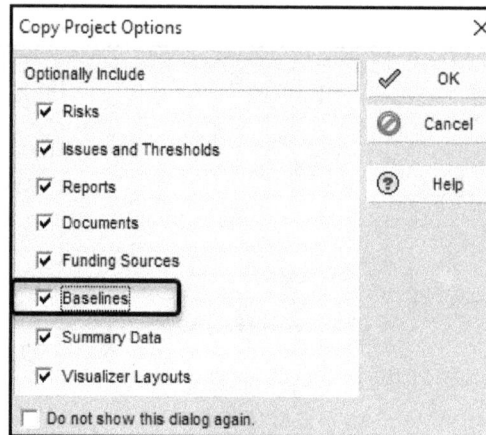

15.3.6 Setting the Baseline Project

The baselines are assigned from the **Project**, **Assign Baselines…** form:

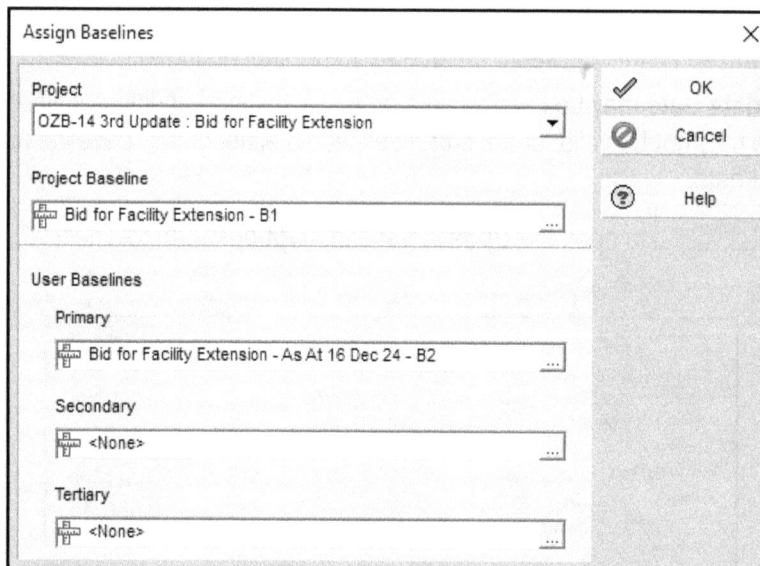

- Select from the drop-down box under **Project** which of the open projects is to have a baseline set.

- The **Project Baseline** may be used for calculating **Earned Value**. See **Admin**, **Admin Preferences…**, **Earned Value** tab for other Earned Value options. This Baseline is seen by any User who opens the project.

- Select which other baseline projects are required to be displayed using the drop-down boxes under **User Baselines**, the options are **Primary**, **Secondary** and **Tertiary** User Baselines.

⚠️ User Baselines are only seen by the User who has set the Baseline. So other users who open a project and apply, for example, a Project Layout that displays a User Baseline, will have to also make sure that they set the same baseline as the original user.

- Primavera P6 Version 22 introduced customizable columns in the **Project**, **Assign Baseline**, **Select Project Baseline** form allowing the user to see more information about a baseline when selecting a baseline project:

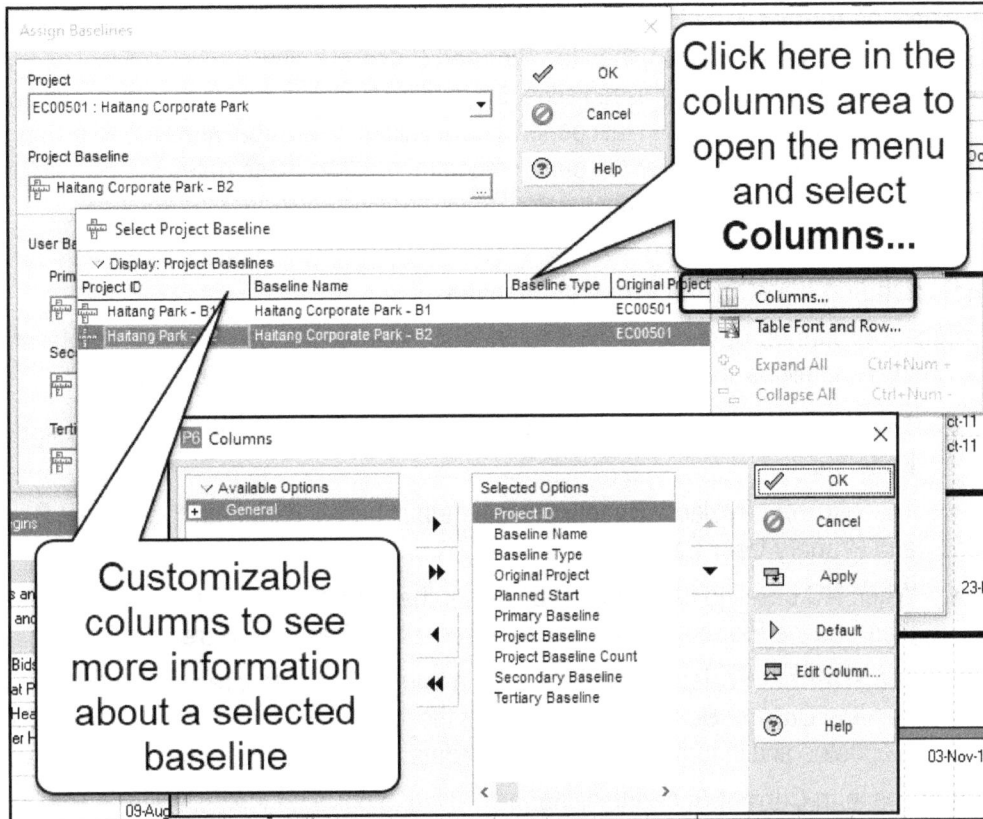

- Earned Value calculations may be performed using either the **Primary Baseline** values or the **Baseline** values from the current project. Select the **Settings** tab in the **Projects Window**.

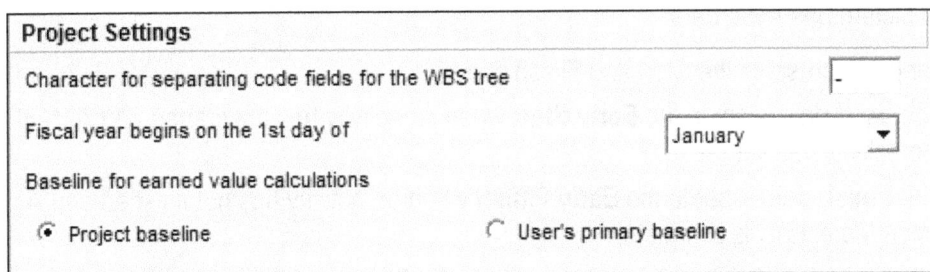

- The **Admin**, **Admin Preferences...**, **Earned Value** tab, **Earned value calculation** section has three options. These options decide which Baseline schedule values are read to calculate the Earned Value fields and which dates are selected and used to display the Baseline Bars. The **At Completion values with current dates** is the author's preferred option when resources are assigned.

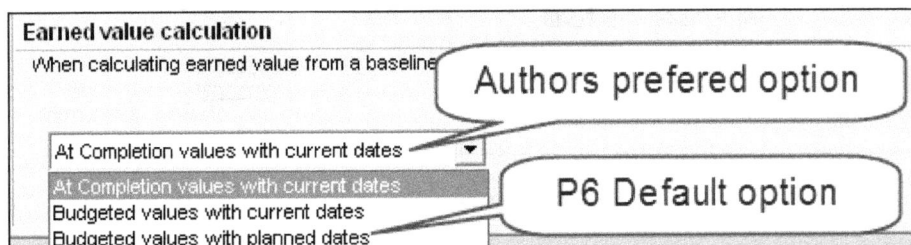

The Planned Dates from a Baseline will be displayed as the Baseline Bars in an EPPM database when the **Administer**, **Application Settings**, **Earned Value** tab is set to the default of **Budget values with planned dates**.

> ⚠️ When the **Budget values with planned dates** is selected, which is often the default value when the software is loaded, then the **Planned Dates** are displayed as a baseline bar. This is undesirable when a progressed schedule is displayed as a Baseline, say, for comparing this period's date values with last period's date values. This is because the **Planned Dates** often hold irrelevant data and the author recommends that these dates are ignored by not using P6 functions that read these dates.

15.3.7 Understanding the <Current Project> Baseline

> ⚠️ Because **Planned Dates** are difficult to understand and may lead to misinterpretation of the schedule baselines, it is important that you understand the following points:

- The **Planned Dates** are used by the <**Current Project**> **Baseline** in the **Assign Baseline** form.

- The <**Current Project**> **Baseline** is the default baseline for both the **Project Baseline** and **Primary User Baseline**.

- When **NO** baseline has been set by a user then the <**Current Project**> **Baseline** and therefore the **Planned Dates** are displayed as the **Baseline Bars**.

- The <**Current Project**> **Baseline** is not a true baseline, as it reads the **Planned Dates** from the **Current Schedule** and some of these dates will change each time a schedule is updated and in turn will hold irrelevant data in a schedule that has been updated.

- The term **Current Schedule** is normally used to describe the activities as they are currently scheduled, and the term <**Current Project**> **Baseline** is confusing as it is not the **Current Schedule** but the **Planned Dates**, which may be different from the **Current Schedule**.

The following picture has three bars:

- The upper bar represents the Start and Finish dates:
  - ➤ The **Start** date is set to the **Early Start** when an activity has not started and **Actual Start** when the activity has started.
  - ➤ The **Finish** date is set to the **Early Finish** when an activity has not finished and **Actual Finish** when the activity is complete.

- The middle bar is the <**Current Project**>baseline, the **Planned Dates**, and

- The lower bar is a proper baseline made by copying the un-progressed project.

With no progress all bars are the same, see picture below:

Activity ID	Activity Name	Original Duration	Start	Finish	February 2010			
					31	07	14	21
A1010	Activity 1	5d	01-Feb-10	05-Feb-10	▬			
A1020	Activity 2	5d	08-Feb-10	12-Feb-10		▬		
A1030	Activity 3	5d	15-Feb-10	19-Feb-10			▬	

Activity 1 has been marked complete and the Data Date moved. The Planned Dates equal the Start and Finish date before the activity was marked as started. The un-started activities, Activity 2 and 3, in the **<Current Project> baseline** have changed their dates to equal the Start and Finish, see picture below:

Activity 2 has been marked in-progress and the Data Date moved, delaying Activity 3. Activity 2 Planned Dates (represented by the **<Current Project> baseline**) match the status of the activity before it was marked Started, not a Baseline. Activity 3 Planned Dates represented by the **<Current Project> baseline** bars have changed a second time and match the new Start and Finish:

When no Baseline is set by the user, the project will **DISPLAY** the **<Current Project>** (from the Planned Dates, not the Current Schedule Start and Finish dates) as the Baseline bars and, in effect:

- All un-started activities are "re-baselined" at each update, and

- Started and Complete activities Planned Dates match the Start and Finish dates of the activity just before an activity was marked as started. Therefore, the Planned Dates of these activities could contain irrelevant data. This happens when a project has been rescheduled and the Data Date moved forward and then activities marked as Started. At this point the Planned Dates now do not represent either a Baseline, or the last period status or the next period status of an activity. They contain irrelevant data that should never be displayed.

There are some significant issues here that need to be carefully managed:

- If no Baseline is set and a layout that displays a baseline bar is applied, then a baseline bar that the user did not set and may contain irrelevant dates from the Planned Dates will be displayed. This may create confusion and these bars may change on each schedule update.

- If one user sets a Primary Baseline, which is a User Baseline and therefore only seen by that user, and a different user opens a project, then this second user will see only the **<Current Project> baseline** and not the other user's Primary Baseline. This will result in one user seeing something different from another user when two users open a project.

You may wish to restrict the access (see paragraphs 0 and 24.4) to a project schedule to prevent the **<Current Project> baseline** being displayed inadvertently.

15.3.8 Displaying the Baseline Data

The Baseline Dates may be displayed by:

- Displaying the **Baseline** columns; there are fewer predefined columns for the **Secondary User Baseline** and **Tertiary User Baseline**:
  - ➢ BL is the **Project Baseline**
  - ➢ BL1 is the **Primary User Baseline**
  - ➢ BL2 is the **Secondary User Baseline**
  - ➢ BL3 is the **Tertiary User Baseline**

Activity ID	Activity Name	Start	Finish	BL Project Finish	BL Project Start	BL1 Finish	BL1 Start
Bid for Facility Extension		02-Dec-13	27-Jan-14	27-Jan-14	02-Dec-13	27-Jan-14	02-Dec-13
Technical Specification		02-Dec-13	18-Dec-13	18-Dec-13	02-Dec-13	18-Dec-13	02-Dec-13
OZ1000	Approval to Bid	02-Dec-13			02-Dec-13		02-Dec-13
OZ1010	Determine Installation Req...	02-Dec-13	05-Dec-13	05-Dec-13	02-Dec-13	05-Dec-13	02-Dec-13
OZ1020	Create Technical Specific...	06-Dec-13	12-Dec-13	12-Dec-13	06-Dec-13	12-Dec-13	06-Dec-13
OZ1030	Identify Supplier Compone...	13-Dec-13	16-Dec-13	16-Dec-13	13-Dec-13	16-Dec-13	13-Dec-13
OZ1040	Validate Technical Specifi...	17-Dec-13	18-Dec-13	18-Dec-13	17-Dec-13	18-Dec-13	17-Dec-13
Delivery Plan		19-Dec-13	21-Jan-14	21-Jan-14	19-Dec-13	21-Jan-14	19-Dec-13

- Showing a baseline bar on the Bar Chart by selecting the appropriate bars in the **Bars** form:

Display	Name	Timescale	Filter	Preview
☐	Project Baseline Bar	Project Baseline Bar	All Activities	
☐	Project Baseline MS	Project Baseline Bar	Milestone	
☐	Project Baseline Summary	Project Baseline Bar	Summary	
☐	Primary Baseline Bar	Primary Baseline Bar	All Activities	
☐	Primary Baseline MS	Primary Baseline Bar	Milestone	
☐	Primary Baseline Summary	Primary Baseline Bar	Summary	
☐	Secondary Baseline Bar	Secondary Baseline Bar	All Activities	
☐	Secondary Baseline MS	Secondary Baseline Bar	Milestone	
☐	Secondary Baseline Summar	Secondary Baseline Bar	Summary	
☐	Tertiary Baseline Bar	Tertiary Baseline Bar	All Activities	
☐	Tertiary Baseline MS	Tertiary Baseline Bar	Milestone	
☐	Tertiary Baseline Summary	Tertiary Baseline Bar	Summary	

15.4 Limitations on Viewing Baseline Data

The following types of data may **NOT** be read from an **Activity** window column, table or histogram from a **Project Baseline** and **Primary User Baseline**:

- Relationships,
- Constraints,
- Critical Path,
- Late resource data, or late Baseline bar, but Late Baseline Dates are available,
- Individual resource or individual Expense costs or units. You may only see:
  - ➤ The value of Labor and Non Labor resource costs or units added up to their type, and
  - ➤ Material and Expense costs only added up to their type, and
  - ➤ You may not see any Material Resource and Expense Units.

The following types of data may NOT be read from a Secondary User and Tertiary User Baseline:

- Actual and Remaining Durations,
- Total and Free Float,
- % Complete,
- Any Resource or Expense data.

15.5 Workshop 13 – WBS, LOEs and Setting the Baseline

Background

We will first look at how WBS and LOE activities work and then set a Baseline.

Assignment - WBS Activity

Open your **OzBuild Bid** project file and complete the following steps:

1. Apply the **OzBuild 10 – With Float** layout.

2. From the **User Preferences**, **Dates** tab select **24 hour** and do not check **Show minutes**.

3. Create a new activity under the **Bid Document** WBS Node:

   ➢ Activity ID OZ1140

   ➢ Titled **WBS Activity** and

   ➢ Assign it an Activity Type of **WBS Summary** using the **Activities Window**, **General** tab.

4. Schedule to see how it calculates.

Activity ID	Activity Name	Original Duration	Start	Finish	Total Float	Free Float	December 2024	January 2025
Bid for Facility Extension		33d	09-Dec-24 08	27-Jan-25 16	0d	0d		
Bid Document		16d	06-Jan-25 08	27-Jan-25 16	0d	0d		
OZ1100	Create Draft of Bid Document	6d	06-Jan-25 08	13-Jan-25 16	6d	6d		
OZ1110	Review Bid Document	2d	22-Jan-25 08	23-Jan-25 16	0d	0d		
OZ1120	Finalise and Submit Bid Document	2d	24-Jan-25 08	27-Jan-25 16	0d	0d		
OZ1130	Bid Document Submitted	0d		27-Jan-25 16"	0d	0d		
OZ1140	WBS Activity	16d	06-Jan-25 08	27-Jan-25 16	0d	0d		

5. Drag the WBS activity to the **Delivery Plan** WBS Node and schedule to see how it operates.

Activity ID	Activity Name	Original Duration	Start	Finish	Total Float	Free Float	December 2024	January 2025
Bid for Facility Extension		33d	09-Dec-24 08	27-Jan-25 16	0d	0d		
Delivery Plan		16d	30-Dec-24 08	21-Jan-25 16	0d	0d		
OZ1050	Document Delivery Methodology	4d	30-Dec-24 08	03-Jan-25 16	6d	0d		
OZ1060	Obtain Quotes from Suppliers	8d	02-Jan-25 08"	13-Jan-25 16	0d	0d		
OZ1070	Calculate the Bid Estimate	3d	14-Jan-25 08	16-Jan-25 16	0d	0d		
OZ1080	Create the Project Schedule	3d	17-Jan-25 08	20-Jan-25 16	0d	0d		
OZ1090	Review the Delivery Plan	1d	21-Jan-25 08	21-Jan-25 16	0d	0d		
OZ1140	WBS Activity	16d	30-Dec-24 08	21-Jan-25 16	0d	4d		

6. Drag the WBS activity to the **Technical Specification** WBS Node and schedule:

Activity ID	Activity Name	Original Duration	Start	Finish	Total Float	Free Float	December 2024	January 2025
OZB-09 Bid for Facility Extension		33d	09-Dec-24 08	27-Jan-25 16	0d	0d		
OZB-09.1 Technical Specification		13d	09-Dec-24 08	27-Dec-24 16	6d	0d		
OZ1000	Approval to Bid	0d	09-Dec-24 08		4d	0d		
OZ1010	Determine Installation Requirements	4d	09-Dec-24 08	12-Dec-24 16	4d	0d		
OZ1020	Create Technical Specification	5d	13-Dec-24 08	19-Dec-24 16	4d	0d		
OZ1030	Identify Supplier Components	2d	20-Dec-24 08	23-Dec-24 16	4d	0d		
OZ1040	Validate Technical Specification	2d	24-Dec-24 08	27-Dec-24 16	6d	0d		
OZ1140	WBS Activity	13d	09-Dec-24 08	27-Dec-24 16	6d	20d		

7. Apply the **OzBuild 10 – Without Float** Layout

---

8. Change the **Activity Type** of the WBS Activity to a **Level of Effort** and rename it to **LOE Activity**,

9. Drag activity OZ1140 to the **Delivery Plan** WBS Node and sort on Activity ID,

10. Open the Bars form and ensure LOE bars are displayed,

11. **Note:** If you reschedule before adding the relationships then the LOE activity bar will disappear because it will be marked as complete on the Data Date and you will need to take of progress from the **Status** tab in the lower pane by unchecking **Finished** and **Started** before you may see it again to add the relationships.

12. Add OZ1060 SS OZ1140 and OZ1140 FF OZ1070 relationships and reschedule to see how it calculates.

Activity ID	Activity Name	Start	Finish	Total Float	Free Float
Bid for Facility Extension		09-Dec-24 08	27-Jan-25 16	0d	0d
Delivery Plan		30-Dec-24 08	21-Jan-25 16	0d	0d
OZ1050	Document Delivery Methodology	30-Dec-24 08	03-Jan-25 16	6d	0d
OZ1060	Obtain Quotes from Suppliers	02-Jan-25 08*	13-Jan-25 16	0d	0d
OZ1070	Calculate the Bid Estimate	14-Jan-25 08	16-Jan-25 16	0d	0d
OZ1080	Create the Project Schedule	17-Jan-25 08	20-Jan-25 16	0d	0d
OZ1090	Review the Delivery Plan	21-Jan-25 08	21-Jan-25 16	0d	0d
OZ1140	LOE Activity	02-Jan-25 08	16-Jan-25 16	0d	0d

13. Add OZ1050 SS OZ1140 and OZ1140 FF OZ1110 relationships and see how it calculates.

Activity ID	Activity Name	Start	Finish	Total Float	Free Float
Bid for Facility Extension		09-Dec-24 08	27-Jan-25 16	0d	0d
Delivery Plan		30-Dec-24 08	23-Jan-25 16	0d	0d
OZ1050	Document Delivery Methodology	30-Dec-24 08	03-Jan-25 16	6d	0d
OZ1060	Obtain Quotes from Suppliers	02-Jan-25 08*	13-Jan-25 16	0d	0d
OZ1070	Calculate the Bid Estimate	14-Jan-25 08	16-Jan-25 16	0d	0d
OZ1080	Create the Project Schedule	17-Jan-25 08	20-Jan-25 16	0d	0d
OZ1090	Review the Delivery Plan	21-Jan-25 08	21-Jan-25 16	0d	0d
OZ1140	LOE Activity	30-Dec-24 08	23-Jan-25 16	0d	0d
Bid Document		06-Jan-25 08	27-Jan-25 16	0d	0d
OZ1100	Create Draft of Bid Document	06-Jan-25 08	13-Jan-25 16	6d	6d
OZ1110	Review Bid Document	22-Jan-25 08	23-Jan-25 16	0d	0d
OZ1120	Finalise and Submit Bid Document	24-Jan-25 08	27-Jan-25 16	0d	0d
OZ1130	Bid Document Submitted		27-Jan-25 16*	0d	0d

14. Delete the LOE activity.

Assignment - Setting a Baseline

15. **Earned value calculation** settings:

    ➤ If you are using a PPM database you should check that the **Admin**, **Admin Preferences...**, **Earned Value** tab has the **Earned value calculation** set to **At Completion values with current dates** or **Budget Values with current dates**. You may not be able to change this if you do not have the necessary access.

    ➤ If you are using aa EPPM database you should find out what the **Earned value calculation** option is set to. It should be set to **At Completion values with current dates** or **Budget Values with current dates**.

    ➤ If the **Earned value calculation** is set to **Budget values with planned dates** or **Planned values with planned dates** the Baseline has progress, then the Planed Dates will be read and the Baseline bars may be wrong.

16. Select **Project**, **Maintain Baselines...** and save a copy of the current project as a Baseline and title it **Bid for Facility Extension – Baseline**.

17. Assign an appropriate **Baseline Type**, such as **Customer Sign-Off**, (the options may vary depending on your database) and close the form.

18. Select **Project**, **Assign Baselines...** and make this your **Project Baseline** and **Primary Baseline** and close the **Assign Baselines** form. This ensures that any baseline bar will show a real baseline and not the Planned Dates.

19. Apply the **OzBuild 10 – With Float** layout, do not save the current layout, and save this as a new layout titled **OzBuild Workshop 13 – Baseline**.

20. Create, if required, and display the following bars:

    ➤ All current schedule bars which are Actual Work, Remaining Work and Critical Remaining Work, Milestones and Summary,

    ➤ % Complete Bar,

    ➤ Float Bar (Total Float) and Neg Float Bar (Negative Float),

    ➤ The Project Baseline Bar and Project Baseline MS (Milestones),

    ➤ For clarity ensure no text is displayed and adjust the row height if required.

21. Display the following columns:

    ➤ Activity ID

    ➤ Activity Name

    ➤ Activity % Complete

    ➤ Original Duration

    ➤ Remaining Duration

    ➤ Start

    ➤ Finish

    ➤ Total Float

    ➤ Variance - BL Project Finish Date

22. Make sure the Timescale is daily or weekly and sorted by Activity ID.

23. Show the time in 24-hour format, but do not show the minutes by selecting **Edit**, **User Preferences...**, **Dates** tab.

24. Save your layout.

25. Check your answer against the pictures below:

Activity ID	Activity Name	Activity % Complete	Original Duration	Remaining Duration	Start	Finish	Total Float	Free Float	Variance - BL Project Finish Date
Bid for Facility Extension			33d	33d	09-Dec-24 08	27-Jan-25 16	0d	0d	0d
Technical Specification			13d	13d	09-Dec-24 08	27-Dec-24 16	6d	0d	0d
OZ1000	Approval to Bid	0%	0d	0d	09-Dec-24 08		4d	0d	0d
OZ1010	Determine Installation F	0%	4d	4d	09-Dec-24 08	12-Dec-24 16	4d	0d	0d
OZ1020	Create Technical Spec	0%	5d	5d	13-Dec-24 08	19-Dec-24 16	4d	0d	0d
OZ1030	Identify Supplier Compc	0%	2d	2d	20-Dec-24 08	23-Dec-24 16	4d	0d	0d
OZ1040	Validate Technical Spe	0%	2d	2d	24-Dec-24 08	27-Dec-24 16	6d	0d	0d
Delivery Plan			16d	16d	30-Dec-24 08	21-Jan-25 16	0d	0d	0d
OZ1050	Document Delivery Me	0%	4d	4d	30-Dec-24 08	03-Jan-25 16	6d	0d	0d
OZ1060	Obtain Quotes from Su	0%	8d	8d	02-Jan-25 08*	13-Jan-25 16	0d	0d	0d
OZ1070	Calculate the Bid Estim	0%	3d	3d	14-Jan-25 08	16-Jan-25 16	0d	0d	0d
OZ1080	Create the Project Sch	0%	3d	3d	17-Jan-25 08	20-Jan-25 16	0d	0d	0d
OZ1090	Review the Delivery Pl	0%	1d	1d	21-Jan-25 08	21-Jan-25 16	0d	0d	0d
Bid Document			33d	33d	09-Dec-24 08	27-Jan-25 16	0d	0d	0d
OZ1100	Create Draft of Bid Doc	0%	6d	6d	06-Jan-25 08	13-Jan-25 16	6d	6d	0d
OZ1110	Review Bid Document	0%	2d	2d	22-Jan-25 08	23-Jan-25 16	0d	0d	0d
OZ1120	Finalise and Submit Bid	0%	2d	2d	24-Jan-25 08	27-Jan-25 16	0d	0d	0d
OZ1130	Bid Document Submitte	0%	0d	0d		27-Jan-25 16*	0d	0d	0d

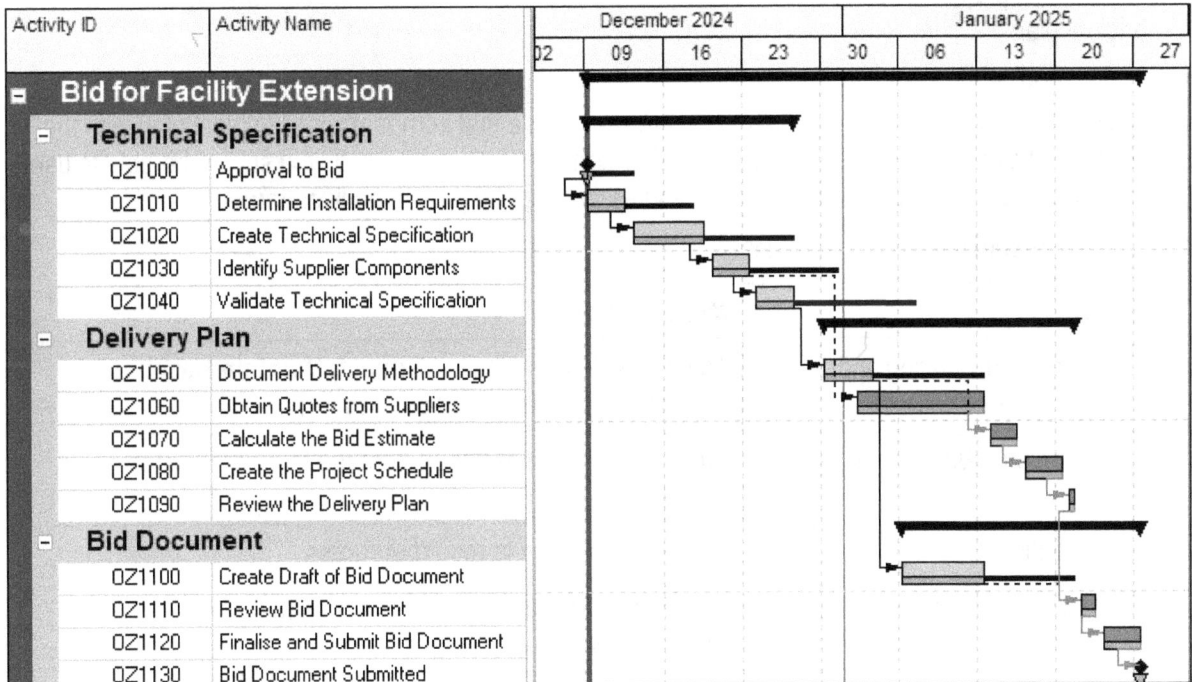

16 UPDATING AN UNRESOURCED SCHEDULE

Now that the Baseline has been set, we can start tracking progress and the important phase of regular monitoring and control begins. This process is important to help catch problems as early as possible, and thus minimize their impact on the successful completion of the project. The main steps for monitoring progress are:

- Saving a **Baseline** schedule, covered in the last chapter,
- Recording or marking-up progress at the **Data Date**.
- **Update** or **Assign Progress** to the schedule:
  - ➢ Completed activities are assigned **Actual Start** and **Actual Finish** dates, in the past in relation to the **Data Date**,
  - ➢ In-progress activities are assigned **Actual Start** dates, in the past in relation to the **Data Date**, and the activity's **Remaining Durations** and **Percent Completes** are adjusted,
  - ➢ Adjustments are made to un-started work based on the productivity to-date, and
  - ➢ Project scope changes should be added as new activities.
- Scheduling the project and at the same time moving the **Data Date** to the new **Data Date** and recalculating all the activities dates. The **Data Date** may also be moved before updating the activities from the **Project Window**, **Dates** tab.
- Comparing and reporting actual progress against planned progress and revising the plan and schedule, if required.

Comparing the status of an activity against more than one baseline is useful; for example:

- The original plan could be represented as one of the Baselines, to see the slippage against the original plan.
- Last Period, which could be another Baseline, to see the changes since the last update.

By the time you get to this phase you should have a schedule that compares your original plan with the current plan, showing where the project is ahead or behind. If you are behind, you should be able to use this schedule to plan appropriate remedial measures to bring the project back on target.

This chapter covers the following topics:

Topic	Menu Command
• Saving and Deleting and Setting a **Baseline**	To save a Baseline, select **Project**, **Maintain Baselines…** to display the **Maintain Baselines** form.
• Assigning a Baseline project	The baselines are assigned from the **Project**, **Assign Baselines…** form.
• Recording Progress	Guidelines on how to record progress.
• **Retained Logic** and **Progress Override**	Open the **General Schedule Options** form by selecting **Tools**, **Schedule……** and clicking the ▷ Options… icon.
• Setting the **Current Data Date** and **Scheduling** the project	Open the **Schedule** form by: • Selecting **Tools**, **Schedule…**, or • Pressing the **F9** key, or • Clicking the ⏲ icon.

16.1 Practical Methods of Recording Progress

Normally a project is updated once a week, bi-weekly, or monthly. Very short projects could be updated daily or even by the shift or hour. As a guide, a project would typically be updated between 12 and 20 times in its lifetime. A high-risk project should be updated more often than a low risk project. Progress is recorded on or just after the **Data Date** and the scheduler updates the schedule upon the receipt of the information.

The following information is typically recorded for each activity when updating a project:

- The activity start date and time if required,
- The number of days or hours required to complete the activity or the date and time the activity is expected to finish,
- The percentage complete, and
- If complete, the activity finish date and time.

A printout of the schedule may be used for recording the progress of the current schedule and is often produced prior to updating the project. Ideally progress should be recorded by a physical inspection of the work or by a person who intimately knows the work, although that is not always possible. It is good practice to keep this marked-up record for your own reference. Ensure that you note the Data Date of the mark-up and, if relevant, the time.

Often a Status Report or mark-up sheet, such as the following illustration, which has a 4-week look-ahead filter applied, is distributed to the people responsible for marking up the project progress. The marked-up sheets are returned to the scheduler for data entry into the software and then filed for dispute resolution.

A page break could be placed at each responsible person's band in the **Group and Sort** form, and when the schedule is printed each person could have their own page of activities that are either in-progress or due to commence. This is particularly useful for large projects.

Activity ID	Activity Name	Rem Dur	Orig Dur	Phy % Comp	Start	Actual Start	Suspend Date	Resume Date	Finish	Actual Finish
Bid for Facility Ext...		34d	38d		03-Dec-13 08 A	03-Dec-13 08			27-Jan-14 16	
Technical Specific...		9d	13d		03-Dec-13 08 A	03-Dec-13 08			18-Dec-13 16	
OZ1000	Approval to Bid	0d	0d	100%	03-Dec-13 08 A	03-Dec-13 08				
OZ1010	Determine Ins...	0d	4d	100%	03-Dec-13 08 A	03-Dec-13 08			05-Dec-13 16 A	05-Dec-13 16
OZ1020	Create Techni...	5d	3d	40%	05-Dec-13 08 A	05-Dec-13 08			12-Dec-13 16	
OZ1030	Identify Suppli...	2d	2d	0%	13-Dec-13 08				16-Dec-13 16	
OZ1040	Validate Tech...	2d	2d	0%	17-Dec-13 08				18-Dec-13 16	

Other electronic methods, discussed next, may be employed to collect the data. Irrespective of the method used, the same data needs to be collected.

There are several methods of collecting data for the project status:

- By sending a printed sheet to each responsible person to mark up by hand.
- By cutting and pasting the data from Primavera into another document, such as Excel, and E-mailing the document to them as an attachment.
- By giving the responsible party direct access to the schedule software to update it. This approach is not recommended unless the project is broken into sub-projects. By using multiple projects with one scheduler accessing each project, or assigning access through WBS Nodes, only one person updates each part of the schedule.
- When the Primavera timesheets are implemented this process may be used to update the activities.

Some projects involve a number of people. In such cases, it is important that procedures be written to ensure that the update information is collected:

- In a timely manner,
- Consistently,
- Completely, and
- In a usable format.

> **i** It is important for a scheduler to be aware that some people have great difficulty in comprehending a schedule. When there are a number of people with different skill levels in an organization, it is necessary to provide more than one method of updating the data. You even may find that you have to sit down with some people to obtain the correct data, yet others are willing and comfortable to E-mail you the information.

16.2 Understanding the Concepts

There are some terms and concepts used in scheduling and some that are specific to Primavera that must be understood before updating a project schedule.

> **i** Users must always display the time when updating a project, otherwise the time of 00:00 is sometimes selected by P6 as the Start or Finish time which is usually not desirable.

16.2.1 Activity Lifecycle

There are three stages of an activity lifecycle:

- **Not Started** – The **Early Start** and **Early Finish** dates are calculated from the **Predecessors**, **Constraints**, and **Activity Duration**.
- **In-Progress** – The activity has an **Actual Start** date but is not complete.
  - ➤ Assigning an **Actual Start** date overrides the **Start Constraints** and **Start Relationships** which are used to calculate the **Early Start**.
  - ➤ The **Finish Date** may be calculated from the **Data Date** or **Resume Date** and the **Remaining Duration**, or an **Expected Finish Constraint**, or a **Finish Relationship**.
- **Complete** – The activity is in the past, the **Actual Start** and **Actual Finish** dates have been entered into Primavera, and they override all logic and constraints.

16.2.2 Assigning an Actual Start Date and Time of an Activity

This section will explain how Primavera assigns the **Actual Start** of a **Complete** or an **In-Progress** activity.

- **Actual Start** date is assigned in the **Actual Start** field by checking the **Started** check box, or
- Entering a date in the **Actual Start** column.

This date overrides the **Early Start date**.

- The activity **Actual Start** date is set to equal the **Start** date when this box is checked.

- The **Actual Start** date calendar is opened by clicking on the 🔲 icon to the right of the **Started** check box and a different start date may be assigned. This date should not be in the future of the project Data Date. It would not be logical to have an activity assigned a start date in the future.

- An **Actual Start** may also be assigned in an **Actual Start** column.

16.2.3 Assigning an Actual Finish Date and Time of an Activity

This is assigned in the same way as an Actual Start and this should be in the past. An **Actual Finish** date overrides an **Early Finish** date and finish date constraints and finish relationships are ignored.

16.2.4 Calculation of Durations of an In-Progress Activity
Duration Fields

The Primavera has many duration fields, we will discuss four duration fields below:

- An activity **Original Duration** (**Planned Duration**) in some Industry Versions) is the duration from the **Early Start** to the **Early Finish** calculated over the **Activity Calendar** and is calculated when an activity has not yet started. When an **Actual Start** is entered, this duration is no longer recalculated or directly used for scheduling but may be edited.

- The **Actual Duration** is the activity's worked duration and is either the duration from:
    - ➢ The **Actual Start** to the **Data Date** of an **In-progress** activity, or
    - ➢ The **Actual Start** to the **Suspend Date** of a suspended **In-progress** activity, or
    - ➢ The **Actual Start** to the **Actual Finish** of a **Completed** activity.

- The **Remaining Duration** is the unworked duration of an **In-progress** activity and is the duration from the **Data Date** or **Resume Date** to the **Early Finish** date of an activity.

- The **At Completion Duration**= Actual Duration + Remaining Duration. Before an activity has started, the **Actual Duration** is zero and the **Remaining Duration** equals the **Original Duration**.

- The **Original Duration** is linked to the **Remaining Duration** when an activity is un-started and **Link Budget and At Completion for not started activities** box in the **Calculations** tab of the **Projects Window** is checked.

- The Remaining bar is based on the **Remaining Duration**, and the Remaining Duration may commence a period of time after the **Data Date** so there is often a gap between the **Data Date** and the **Remaining Start** of an in-progress activity.

Percent Complete

As discussed in the **Adding Activities and Organizing Under the WBS** chapter, this section is repeated for completeness of this chapter.

The **Percent Complete** type should be understood if it is intended to update (status or progress) a schedule. In Primavera this option may be set for each activity individually and the default for new activities is set in the **Percent Complete Type** drop-down box. Primavera has many Activity Percent Complete fields that may be displayed in columns and we will discuss four of them now:

Activity % Complete, displayed on the **% Complete Bar**, may be linked to only one of the three % Complete following three fields:

- **Physical % Complete**
- **Duration %Complete**
- **Units % Complete**

There are three Percent Complete options; each new activity is assigned the project default **Percent Complete Type** and then this may be edited for each activity as required.

Therefore, if the option of **Physical % Complete** is selected for an activity then the **Activity % Complete** and the **Physical % Complete** are linked and a change to one will change the other.

Default % Complete

The **Default % Complete Type** for each new activity in each project is assigned in the **Defaults** tab of the **Details** form in the **Project Window**:

- Each new activity **Percent Complete Type** is set to the **Default Percent Complete** and may be changed at any time.

Percent Complete Types

- **Duration % Complete** – This field is calculated from the proportion of the **Original Duration** and the **Remaining Duration** and they are linked and a change to one value will change the other. When the **Remaining Duration** is set to greater than the **Original Duration** this percent complete is always zero.

- **Physical % Complete** – This field enables the user to enter the percent complete of an activity and this value is independent of the activity durations.

- **Units % Complete** – This is where the percent complete is calculated from the resources Actual and Remaining Units. A change to one value will change the other and when more than one resource is assigned then all the Actual Units for all resources will be changed proportionally. This will be covered further in The **Updating Resources** chapter. This is similar to the Microsoft Project % Work Complete.

> The Units % Complete is calculated from the value of all the Labor and Non-Labor Resources, so be careful when more than one type of resource is assigned to an activity. For example, the software could be adding concrete volumes with labor hours and excavator hours.

Activity % Complete

The **Activity % Complete** field is linked to the **% Complete Type** field assigned to an activity in the **General** tab of the **Details** form in the **Activities Window** or the **% Complete Type** column:

The **Activity % Complete** is also linked the **% Complete Bar** and this value is represented on the **% Complete** Bar.

16.2.5 Summary Bars Progress Calculation

Summary bars such as WBS Node bars may not be updated, as in Microsoft Project, as they are virtual activities with their data created from summarizing the activities in the band.

16.2.6 Understanding the Current Data Date

The **Current Data Date** is also known as the **Data Date**, **Update Date**, **Status Date**, **Progress Date**, **As At Date**, **Time Now**, **Report Date** and the **Project Data Date**. Primavera has one **Data Date**, titled **Current Data Date,** which operates differently to both the Microsoft Project **Status Date** and Elecosoft (Asta) **Powerproject Report** date.

The Primavera **Current Data Date** is displayed as a vertical line on the schedule; this Data Date vertical line may be formatted in the **Bar Chart Options** form.

In P6 the function of the **Current Data Date** is to:

- Separate the completed parts of activities from incomplete parts of activities.

- Calculate or record all costs and hours to-date before the **Current Data Date**, and to forecast costs and hours to go after the **Current Data Date**.

- Calculate the **Finish Date** of an in-progress activity from the **Current Data Date** plus the **Remaining Duration** over the **Activity Calendar**, when the Suspend and Resume function has not been used.

16.3 Updating the Schedule

The next stage is to update the schedule by entering the mark-up information against each activity.

When dealing with large schedules it is normal to develop a look-ahead schedule by creating a filter to display incomplete and un-started activities commencing in the near future only.

The schedule may be updated using the following methods:

- Using the fields in the **Status** tab of the **Details** form in the lower pane, or
- Displaying the appropriate tracking columns by:
  - ➢ Creating your own layout, or
  - ➢ Inserting the required columns in an existing layout.

16.3.1 Updating Activities Using the Status Tab of the Details Form

Ensure you are showing the time and then open the **Status** tab:

Updating a Complete activity:

- Check the **Started** box and enter the actual **Start Date and Time** if different from the displayed date.
- Check the **Finished** box and enter the actual **Finish Date and Time** if different from the displayed date.

Updating an In-progress activity:

- Check the **Started** box and enter the actual **Start Date and Time** if different from the displayed date.
- When the **Duration Type** is **% Duration** the **% Duration Complete** and **Remaining Duration** are linked, then either:
  - ➢ The **Remaining Duration** is edited and the **% Complete** is calculated, or
  - ➢ The **% Complete** is entered and the software calculates the **Remaining Duration**, or
  - ➢ A **Remaining Duration** greater than the **Original Duration** may be entered and the **% Duration** will remain at zero, until the **Remaining Duration** is less than the **Original Duration**.

Irrespective of the method used to calculate the **Remaining Duration**, after the schedule is recalculated the end date of the activity is calculated from the **Current Data Date** plus the **Remaining Duration** over the **Activity Calendar**.

Be careful that the % Duration Complete does not change the Remaining Duration to a non-round day and that activity then finishes halfway through a day. This results in all the successor activities starting and finish in the middle of the day.

Updating an Un-started activity:

- The **Original Duration**, **Relationships** and **Constraints** of an un-started activity should be reviewed.

16.3.2 Updating Activities Using Columns

Another method of updating activities is by displaying the data in columns. This may be achieved by:

- Inserting the required columns in an existing layout, or better,

- Creating a Layout with the required columns and updating the schedule using these columns,

> ⚠ The issue with using columns to update a schedule is the date will always be at 00:00 every date will need the time set appropriately and can be very time consuming, thus the author prefers to use the **Status** tab.

16.4 Progress Spotlight and Update Progress

Primavera Version 5.0 introduced a new function for highlighting the activities that should have progressed in the update period and is titled **Progress Spotlight**.

The user then has the option of selecting some or all of the activities that should be updated and updating them using the **Update Progress** function as if they progressed exactly as they were Planned. It is sometimes easier to **Automatically update** a project with functions like **Progress Spotlight** and then adjust the Actual dates and Remaining Durations as a second step in the updating process, especially if the project is going to plan.

> ⚠ The **Update Progress** function must be used with caution on schedules with progress as it does not work as one would expect and may change actual dates without warning. This topic is covered in detail later in this chapter.

The Spotlight may be moved to reflect the new Data Date by either:

- Dragging the Data Date, or

- Using the **Tools** toolbar, **Spotlight** icon ▣.

16.4.1 Highlighting Activities for Updating by Dragging the Data Date

To highlight activities that should have been progressed in the last period by dragging the Data Date:

- Hold the mouse arrow on the Data Date line and display the double-headed arrow ↔ , and

- Press the left mouse and drag the Data Date line to the required date.

- All the activities that should have been worked in the time period are highlighted:

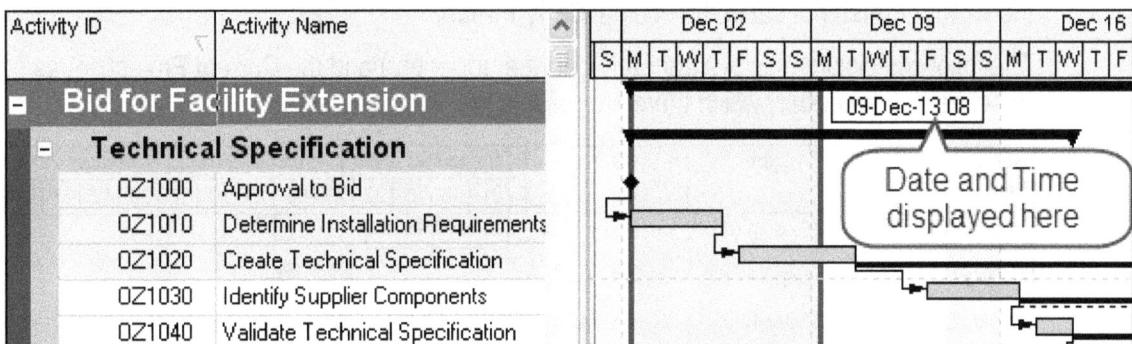

16.4.2 Spotlighting Activities Using Spotlight Icon

The Spotlight facility highlights all activities that should have progressed in one minor time period of the timescale settings. To use **Progress Spotlight**:

- Set the Timescale to be the same as your Update Periods. If you are updating weekly, then set the time period to weeks in the **Timescale** form.

- Select **View, Progress Spotlight** or click the [icon] icon and the next period of time (one week if your scale is set to one week) will be highlighted.

- Click the **Progress Spotlight** [icon] icon a second time to return the Spotlight back to the Data Date.

You are now ready to update progress.

16.4.3 Updating a Project Using Update Progress

To update a schedule using the **Update Progress** form, select **Tools**, **Update Progress**:

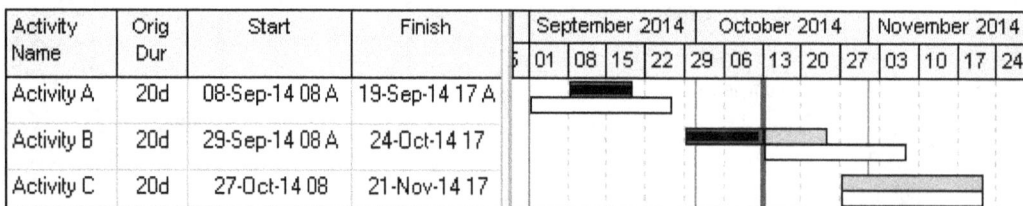

Unlike Microsoft Project **Update Project** function, this Primavera **Update Progress** facility uses the **Planned Start** and **Planned Finish** dates (not the **Early Start** and **Early Finish**) for setting the **Actual Start** and **Actual Finish** dates of in-progress activities.

Thus, when the **Planned Dates** of an in-progress activity are different from the **Actual Start** and **Early Finish** dates and the activity is Automatically updated to be complete, then both these dates are set to the **Planned** dates and the **Actual Start** may be changed and the **Actual Finish** not set to the original **Early Finish**.

The following picture displays the Early bar (the upper bar) and the Current Project set as a Baseline (the lower bar) which therefore reflects the Planned Dates:

Activity Name	Orig Dur	Start	Finish	September 2014				October 2014				November 2014			
				01	08	15	22	29	06	13	20	27	03	10	17	24
Activity A	20d	08-Sep-14 08 A	19-Sep-14 17 A													
Activity B	20d	29-Sep-14 08 A	24-Oct-14 17													
Activity C	20d	27-Oct-14 08	21-Nov-14 17													

continued...

The following picture shows the effect of applying **Update Progress** to the schedule above. The Actual Start of Activity 2 has been changed and the Actual Finish of Activity 2 set to the Planned Dates, which is not the same as the original Early Finish:

Activity Name	Orig Dur	Start	Finish	September 2014				October 2014				November 2014			
				01	08	15	22	29	06	13	20	27	03	10	17	24
Activity A	20d	08-Sep-14 08 A	19-Sep-14 17 A													
Activity B	20d	13-Oct-14 08 A	07-Nov-14 17 A													
Activity C	20d	27-Oct-14 08 A	21-Nov-14 17													

NOTE: You should not use this facility on a schedule with progress when you wish your activities to be Automatically updated to the Early dates (as in Microsoft Project) and not the Planned dates.

You may consider using a Global Change to set the Planned Dates to the Start and Finish dates before running Progress Spotlight, but this will also change the Original Duration and the % Duration will not calculate correctly.

There are several options for setting the **New Data Date**:

- Select a new Data Date in the **Project Window, Dates** tab,
- Select a new Data Date when scheduling from the **Schedule** form,
- You may use the **Progress Spotlight** facility before opening the **Update Progress** form and the **New Data Date** will be set to the highlighted Data Date, or
  - ➤ You may select the **New Data Date** when opening the form.
  - ➤ Either all the activities that are Spotlighted may be updated or if some were selected before opening the form then just the selected ones may be updated.
  - ➤ To update all the activities, select the **All highlighted activities** button, or
  - ➤ To update selected activities, highlight the activities (hold the **Ctrl** key and click the ones you wish to select) before selecting **Tools, Update Progress...** and then clicking on the **Selected activities only** button in the **Update Progress** form.

The option **When actuals are applied from timesheets, calculate activity remaining durations:** decides how the Remaining Duration is calculated:

- **Based on the activity duration type** will take into account activity type and hours to-date and reschedule the Remaining Duration in accordance with the activity Duration Type.
- **Always recalculate** will override the activity Duration Type and calculate the activity Remaining Durations and Hours as if the activity were a Fixed Units and Fixed Units/Time activity.
- Click [🖫 Apply] and the schedule will be updated as if all activities were completed according to the schedule.

16.5   Suspend and Resume

The Primavera Version 5.0 Suspend and Resume function enables the work to be suspended and the activity resumed at a later date. Open the **Activity Details** form **Status** tab and enter the **Suspend** and **Resume** dates. This function only one break in an activity unlike Elecosoft (Asta) Powerproject and Microsoft project that both allow multiple breaks in the past and future.

The following example shows an activity with a Suspend date and Resume date set:

- This feature works when an activity has commenced and normally the Suspend date is in the past and the Resume date in the future.

- The activity must have an actual start date before you can record a Suspend date.

- Only Resource Dependent and Task Dependent activities may be suspended and resumed.

- The suspended period is not calculated as part of the activity duration and resources are not scheduled in this period.

- The Actual bar has been necked for **Activity nonwork intervals** to show the nonwork in the past.

The Suspend and Resume time may be set at the incorrect time of the day. The author has found that the Suspend is usually set at the start of the day and Resume usually at the end of the day; therefore, the defaults for both are illogical. Therefore, you **SHOULD ALWAYS** display the time when setting Suspend and Resume dates to ensure that they are correct.

16.6 Scheduling the Project

At any time, usually after some or all the activities have been updated, the project is scheduled:

- Open the **Schedule** form:
  - ➤ Select **Tools**, **Schedule…**, or
  - ➤ Press the **F9** key, or
  - ➤ Click on the 🕐 icon.

- Select the revised **Current Data Date and Time** from the box and click the ▷ Schedule icon.

- The software will recalculate all the early finish dates from the remaining durations and the new **Current Data Date**, considering the relationships and the **Schedule Options**.

- Version 20 added an additional option:
  - ➤ All **Projects use their own data dates** which is how Version 19 and earlier versions calculated, or

  - ➤ **Apply selected data date to all open projects** for Version 20 and later and all projects will have their **Data Date** permanently changed to the selected date.

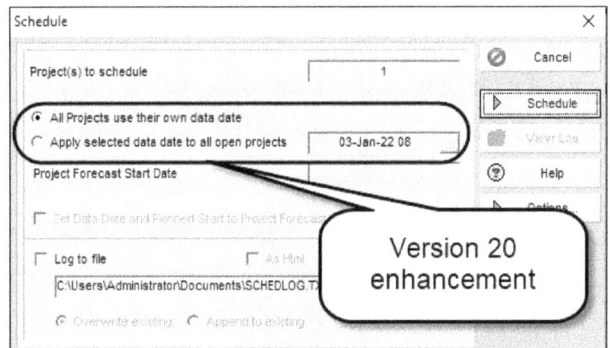

16.7 Comparing Progress with Baseline

There will normally be changes to the schedule dates and more often than not there are delays. The full extent of the change is not apparent without having a Baseline bar to compare with the updated schedule.

To display one or more of the **Baseline Bars** in the **Bar Chart** you must open the **Bars** form and check the **Display** box of one or more baseline bars.

Activity ID	Activity Name	Variance - BL Project Duration	Variance - BL Project Finish Date	Variance - BL Project Start Date	Dec 06	Dec 13	Dec 20
☐ **Bid for Facility Extension**		1d	0d	-1d			
☐ **Technical Specification**		2d 4h	1d 4h	-1d			
0Z1000	Approval to Bid	0d	-1d	-1d			
0Z1010	Determine Installation Requirements	1d	0d	-1d			
0Z1020	Create Technical Specification	0d 4h	1d 4h	1d			
0Z1030	Identify Supplier Components	0d	1d 4h	1d 4h			
0Z1040	Validate Technical Specification	0d	1d 4h	1d 4h			

If you want to see the Start and Finish Date variances, they are available by displaying the **Variance – BL Project Start Date**, **Variance – BL Finish Date**, **Variance – BL1 Start Date**, and **Variance – BL1 Finish Date** columns.

ℹ️ Variance columns for Secondary and Tertiary Baseline Dates are not standard columns but could be calculated with a Global Change.

⚠️ As discussed earlier in this chapter, when a **Project Baseline** or a **Primary User Baseline** bar is displayed without a baseline being set and the **<Current Project>** (which is based on the **Planned Dates**) will be displayed. The **<Current Project>/Planned Dates** of an in-progress projects are not Baselines and may hold irrelevant data.

16.8 Progress Line Display on the Gantt Chart

A progress line displays how far ahead or behind activities are in relation to the Baseline. Either the Project Baseline or the Primary User Baseline may be used and there are four options:

- Difference between the **Baseline Start Date** and **Activity Start Date**,

- Difference between the **Baseline Finish Date** and **Activity Finish Date**,

- Connecting the progress points based on the **Activity % Complete**,

- Connecting the progress points based on the **Activity Remaining Duration**.

There are several components to displaying a Progress Line:

- Firstly, the progress line is formatted using the **View, Bar,** [Options...] form, **Progress Line** tab, which may also be opened by right-clicking in the Gantt Chart area:

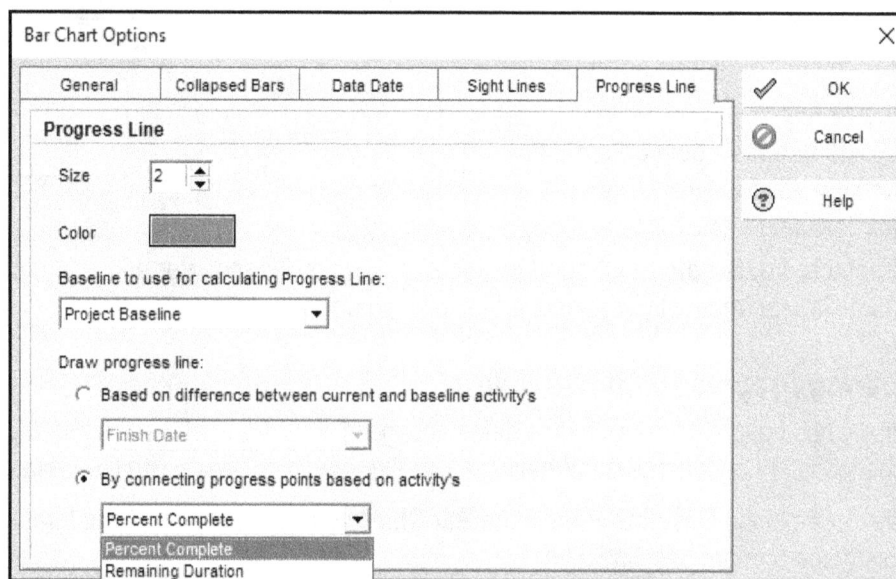

- Selecting **View, Progress Line** to hide or display the **Progress Line**.

- If you use either of the options of Percent Complete or Remaining Duration, then you must display the appropriate Baseline Bar that has been selected as the **Baseline to use for calculating Progress Line:**

- The picture below shows the option highlighted above of **Percent Complete**:

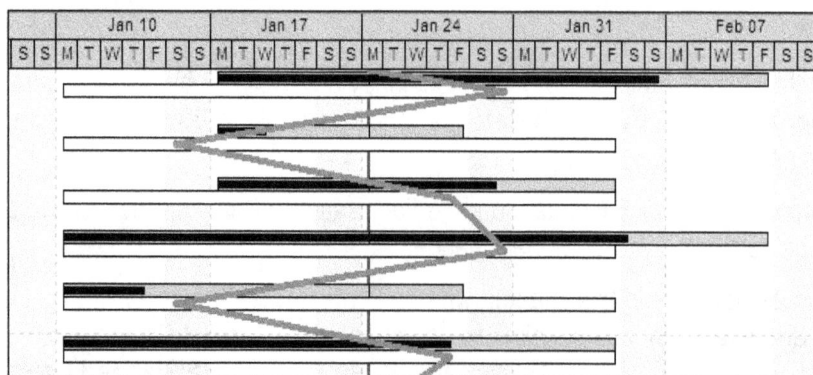

16.9 Check List before Updating a Schedule

You should check the following items before updating a schedule:

- Ensure you are showing the time from the **Edit**, **User Preferences…**, **Dates** tab and check that all Start and Finish dates and times are logical. You can see that these times make sense when you are updating a project.

- Check the **% Complete Type** for all the activities; the author recommends **Physical**.

- Check the **Tools**, **Schedule…**, **Options….** The defaults are usually good, but if you have multiple calendars, you should consider using the **Longest Path** option and is you wish to display **Multiple Critical Paths** then select **Make open-ended activities critical**.

- Check that the **Admin**, **Admin Preferences…**, **Earned Value** tab is **NOT** set to **Budget values with planned dates**, so you will not read the **Planned Dates** from a Baseline Schedule, **At Completion with Current Dates** is the recommended setting,

- After creating a Baseline, ensure that you have not left a **<Current Project>** as the Project or Primary Baseline.

- Ensure all **Actual Dates** are in the past as they are assigned.

- **NEVER EVER** use **Update Progress** on a schedule with progress, as this will change your Actual Start dates and Finish dates of in-progress activities to the Planned Dates.

- Take a complete copy of your schedule including all Baseline projects after update for claim analysis at a later date.

16.10 In-Progress Schedule Check List

The following check list may be used to check an in-progress schedule.

Complete Activities

- All activities have an Actual Start and an Actual Finish before the Status Date.

In-Progress Activities

- Actual Start dates should all be in the past and Early Finish dates in the future.

- Check activities with Constraints, are the constraints still valid?

- Do all activities have Finish successors?

- Are there any activities with progress greater than planned and require the duration shortened?

- Are there any activities that have progressed slower than planned and require the duration lengthened or split.

Not Started Activities

- All Start dates should be in the future.

- Check that all the constraints on these activities are still valid.

- All activities should have Finish successors except the Project Finish Milestone(s).

Open Ends and Total Float

- Confirm that all activities have successors and review float. Activities with excessive float should be assigned dummy successors or delayed if they are not scheduled in a realistic timeframe with sequencing logic or Early Start constraints.

Critical and Near Critical Path

- Check the Critical Path is realistic and aligned with what project personnel consider critical.

Scope Changes

- Ensure that all project changes have been reflected in the schedule.

- It is good practice to add new activities for new work and cross reference the activity to the change documentation using the Notes or a Text column.

Performance

- Has the performance of complete and in-progress activities been reflected in un-started activities, thus revising the un-started work durations based on achievements to date.

Baseline Comparison

- Review the Baseline dates with the current schedule and confirm that any delays are legitimate.

- Have there been many changes and delays and therefore should the schedule be re-baselined?

16.11 Corrective Action

Date slippage occurs when an activity is rescheduled to finish later than originally planned. There are two courses of action available:

- The first is to accept the slippage. This is rarely acceptable, but it is the easiest answer.

- The second is to examine the schedule and evaluate how you could improve the end date.

Solutions to return the project to its original completion date must be authorized by a responsible person.

Suggested solutions to bring the project back on track include:

- Reducing the durations of activities on, or near, the critical path. When activities have applied resources, this may include increasing the number of resources working on the activities. Changing longer activities is often more achievable than changing the length of short duration activities.

- Providing more work time and changing calendars, say from a five-day to a six-day calendar, so that activities are being worked on for more days per week.

- Reducing the project scope and deleting activities.

- Changing activity relationships so activities take place concurrently. This may be achieved by introducing negative lags to Finish-to-Start relationships, which maintains a Closed Network. A negative lag will allow the successor activity to start before the predecessor is complete, which is often what happens in reality.

- Replacing Finish-to-Start relationships with Start-to-Start relationships. Activities are now progressing in parallel and therefore at the same time. This has the potential of creating an open network as the predecessor activity may no longer have a finish successor and an extension in the duration of this activity may not affect the critical path. To maintain the critical path then this option should be avoided or a Finish-to-Finish successor added to complete a closed network.

- Changing the plan and therefore changing the logic to reduce the overall length of the critical path.

16.12 Workshop 14 – Progressing and Baseline Comparison

Background

At the end of the first week, you have to update the schedule and report progress and slippage.

Assignment

1. We are now going to update the schedule as at the end of the first week.

2. Check that all activities are **Physical % Complete**.

3. Update the activities in the **Activities** with the following information using the either:

   ➢ The bottom pane **Status** tab or

   ➢ By adding the **Actual Start**, **Actual Finish**, **Activity % Complete** and **Remaining Duration** columns:

Activity ID	Activity Name	Actual Start	Actual Finish	Activity % Complete	Remaining Duration
OZ1000	Approval to Bid	10-Dec-24 08:00		100%	0d
OZ1010	Determine Installation Requirements	10-Dec-24 08:00	12-Dec-24 16:00	100%	0d
OZ1020	Create Technical Specification	12-Dec-24 08:00		60%	6d

4. Reschedule the project by pressing **F9** to open the **Schedule** form:

   ➢ When using Version 20 or later, select **Apply selected data date to all open project**,

   ➢ Change the **Current Data Date** to 16-Dec-24 08:00, that will be Monday morning,

   ➢ Click on the [▷ Schedule] to reschedule,

   ➢ Check the answer in the following pictures.

Activity ID	Activity Name	Activity % Complete	Remaining Duration	Original Duration	Start	Finish	Total Float	Free Float	Variance - BL Project Finish Date
Bid for Facility Extension			28d	33d	10-Dec-24 08 A	27-Jan-25 16	0d	0d	0d
Technical Specification			10d	15d	10-Dec-24 08 A	31-Dec-24 16	4d	0d	-2d
OZ1000	Approval to Bid	100%	0d	0d	10-Dec-24 08 A				-1d
OZ1010	Determine Installation Requirements	100%	0d	4d	10-Dec-24 08 A	12-Dec-24 16 A			0d
OZ1020	Create Technical Specification	60%	6d	5d	12-Dec-24 08 A	23-Dec-24 16	2d	0d	-2d
OZ1030	Identify Supplier Components	0%	2d	2d	24-Dec-24 08	27-Dec-24 16	2d	0d	-2d
OZ1040	Validate Technical Specification	0%	2d	2d	30-Dec-24 08	31-Dec-24 16	4d	0d	-2d
Delivery Plan			14d	14d	02-Jan-25 08	21-Jan-25 16	0d	0d	0d
OZ1050	Document Delivery Methodology	0%	4d	4d	02-Jan-25 08	07-Jan-25 16	4d	0d	-2d
OZ1060	Obtain Quotes from Suppliers	0%	8d	8d	02-Jan-25 08*	13-Jan-25 16	0d	0d	0d
OZ1070	Calculate the Bid Estimate	0%	3d	3d	14-Jan-25 08	16-Jan-25 16	0d	0d	0d
OZ1080	Create the Project Schedule	0%	3d	3d	17-Jan-25 08	20-Jan-25 16	0d	0d	0d
OZ1090	Review the Delivery Plan	0%	1d	1d	21-Jan-25 08	21-Jan-25 16	0d	0d	0d
Bid Document			14d	14d	08-Jan-25 08	27-Jan-25 16	0d	0d	0d
OZ1100	Create Draft of Bid Document	0%	6d	6d	08-Jan-25 08	15-Jan-25 16	4d	4d	-2d
OZ1110	Review Bid Document	0%	2d	2d	22-Jan-25 08	23-Jan-25 16	0d	0d	0d
OZ1120	Finalise and Submit Bid Document	0%	2d	2d	24-Jan-25 08	27-Jan-25 16	0d	0d	0d
OZ1130	Bid Document Submitted	0%	0d	0d		27-Jan-25 16*	0d	0d	0d

---

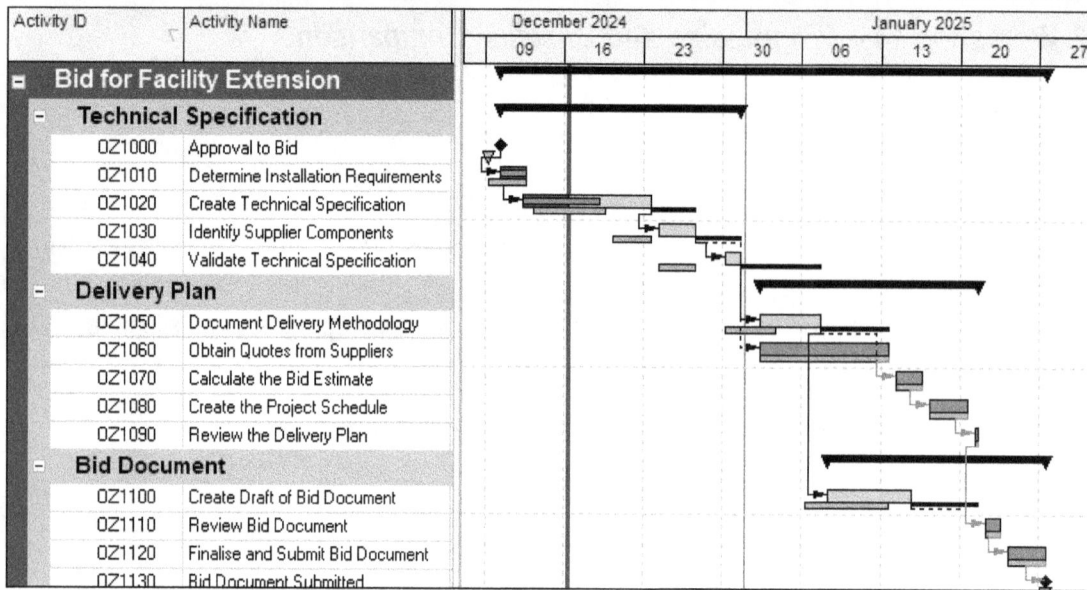

Activity ID	Activity Name	December 2024				January 2025			
		09	16	23	30	06	13	20	27
⊟	**Bid for Facility Extension**								
⊟	**Technical Specification**								
OZ1000	Approval to Bid								
OZ1010	Determine Installation Requirements								
OZ1020	Create Technical Specification								
OZ1030	Identify Supplier Components								
OZ1040	Validate Technical Specification								
⊟	**Delivery Plan**								
OZ1050	Document Delivery Methodology								
OZ1060	Obtain Quotes from Suppliers								
OZ1070	Calculate the Bid Estimate								
OZ1080	Create the Project Schedule								
OZ1090	Review the Delivery Plan								
⊟	**Bid Document**								
OZ1100	Create Draft of Bid Document								
OZ1110	Review Bid Document								
OZ1120	Finalise and Submit Bid Document								
OZ1130	Bid Document Submitted								

NOTE: The lower bar is the Baseline and delays to activities created by the late scheduling of the **Create Technical Specification** activity is clear in the picture above.

5. If you do not receive the same answer then check that all your activities are Physical % Complete.

6. We will update the schedule once more. Before we update it, we will set a second baseline to represent the status as at 16 Dec 24 and then we may see the change from both the original baseline and the last period status.

7. Create a second Baseline by:

    a. Selecting **Project**, **Maintain Baselines**,

    b. Click on **Add** and **Save a copy of the current project as a new baseline**,

    c. Name it as **Bid for Facility Extension - As at 16 Dec 24**,

    d. Set the **Baseline Type** as **Mid Project Status Baseline**:

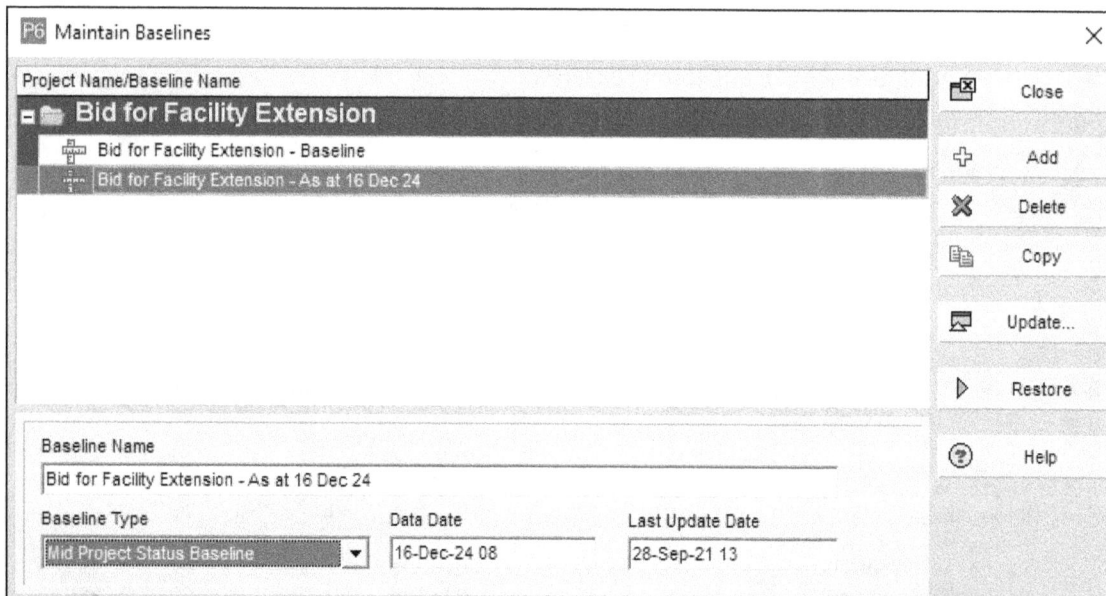

8. Show a second Baseline Bar by for the Last Period Status by:

    a. Selecting **Project Assign Baselines**, set the **Primary User Baseline** as the **Bid for Facility Extension - As at 16 Dec 24** and select OK,

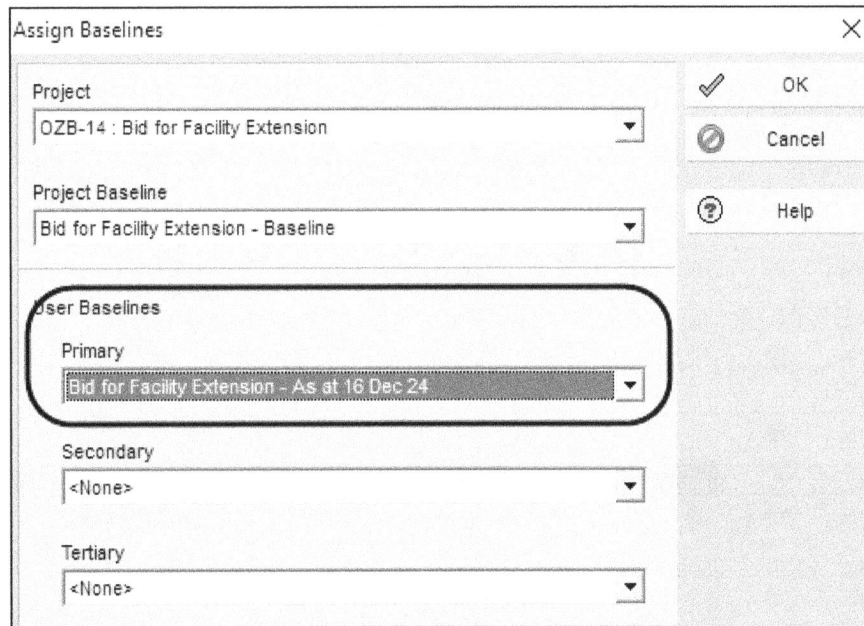

    b. Open the bars form and display the **Primary (User) Baseline** Bar and **Primary Baseline MS (Milestones)**:

    c. Use the **View**, **Table Font and Row** command and set the row height to ensure all the bars are clearly visible, the picture below has them set to 23,

    d. The picture below now displays two baseline bars:

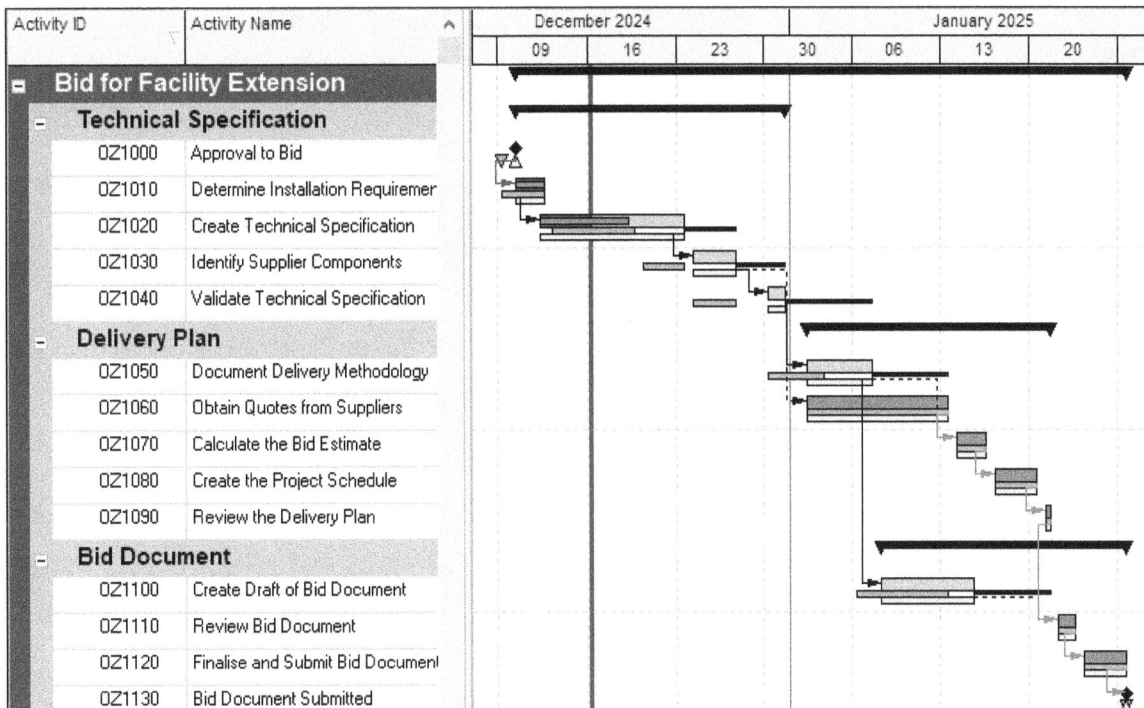

9. Now update the schedule with the information below:

Activity ID	Activity Name	Actual Start	Actual Finish	Activity % Complete	Remaining Duration
OZ1020	Create Technical Specification	12-Dec-24 08:00	20 Dec 24 16:00	100%	0d
OZ1030	Identify Supplier Components	19-Dec-24 08:00		50%	2d
OZ1040	Validate Technical Specification	20-Dec-24 08:00		10%	9d

10. **Reschedule** with a new **Data Date** of 23 Dec 24 08:00:

   a. OZ1040 has split because of the **Retained Logic setting** and

   b. The project is two days late, see the **Variance – BL Project Finish date**:

Activity ID	Activity Name	Activity % Complete	Remaining Duration	Original Duration	Start	Finish	Total Float	Free Float	Variance - BL Project Finish Date
Bid for Facility Extension			25d	35d	10-Dec-24 08 A	29-Jan-25 16	0d	0d	-2d
Technical Specification			11d	15d	10-Dec-24 08 A	09-Jan-25 16	-2d	0d	-8d
OZ1000	Approval to Bid	100%	0d	0d	10-Dec-24 08 A				-1d
OZ1010	Determine Installation Requirements	100%	0d	4d	10-Dec-24 08 A	12-Dec-24 16 A			0d
OZ1020	Create Technical Specification	100%	0d	5d	12-Dec-24 08 A	20-Dec-24 16 A			-1d
OZ1030	Identify Supplier Components	50%	2d	2d	19-Dec-24 08 A	24-Dec-24 16	-2d	0d	-1d
OZ1040	Validate Technical Specification	10%	9d	2d	20-Dec-24 08 A	09-Jan-25 16	-2d	0d	-8d
Delivery Plan			16d	16d	02-Jan-25 08	23-Jan-25 16	-2d	0d	-2d
OZ1050	Document Delivery Methodology	0%	4d	4d	10-Jan-25 08	15-Jan-25 16	-2d	0d	-8d
OZ1060	Obtain Quotes from Suppliers	0%	8d	8d	02-Jan-25 08*	13-Jan-25 16	0d	2d	0d
OZ1070	Calculate the Bid Estimate	0%	3d	3d	16-Jan-25 08	18-Jan-25 16	-2d	0d	-2d
OZ1080	Create the Project Schedule	0%	3d	3d	20-Jan-25 08	22-Jan-25 16	-2d	0d	-2d
OZ1090	Review the Delivery Plan	0%	1d	1d	23-Jan-25 08	23-Jan-25 16	-2d	0d	-2d
Bid Document			10d	10d	16-Jan-25 08	29-Jan-25 16	0d	0d	-2d
OZ1100	Create Draft of Bid Document	0%	6d	6d	16-Jan-25 08	23-Jan-25 16	-2d	0d	-8d
OZ1110	Review Bid Document	0%	2d	2d	24-Jan-25 08	27-Jan-25 16	-2d	0d	-2d
OZ1120	Finalise and Submit Bid Document	0%	2d	2d	28-Jan-25 08	29-Jan-25 16	-2d	0d	-2d
OZ1130	Bid Document Submitted	0%	0d	0d		29-Jan-25 16*	-2d	0d	-2d

OZ1040 is split

Project is 2 days late

11. Now select **Tools**, **Schedule**, **Options** and select **Progress Override** and reschedule,

    a. OZ1040 is no longer split because of the **Progress Override** setting and

    b. The project is now on time:

12. Open the **General** tab of the **OZ1030 Identify Supplier Components** activity:

    a. Change the **% Complete Type** to **Duration**.

    b. **Reschedule** and the **% Complete** will change to 0%.

    c. A link is now established between the **% Complete** and **Remaining Duration** and therefore the **% Complete** and **Remaining Duration** may not be entered independently from the **Activity % Complete**.

    d. The **Activity % Complete** Value is zero when the **Remaining Duration** is greater or equal to the **Original Duration**.

13. Enter 25% Complete against the **OZ1030 Identify Supplier Components** activity in the **Status** tab, the **Remaining Duration** will reduce to 1days 4 hours and you will notice the link between the **Activity % Complete**, **Original Duration** and **Remaining Duration**.

14. Now select **Tools**, **Schedule**, **Options** and select **Retained Logic** and reschedule,

15. Ensure you are showing the **Duration Sub-unit** of **Hours** by opening the **Edit**, **User Preferences... Time Unit** tab and check the **Duration Format**, **Sub-unit Hours** box and check **Show Duration label**.

16. This has resulted in the Remaining Duration no longer being expressed in whole days and activities which are two days long. For example: Activity OZ1070 which is 3 days long is now spanning 4 days because it starts and finishes at midday.

Activity ID	Activity Name	Activity % Complete	Remaining Duration	Original Duration	Start	Finish	Total Float	Free Float
Bid for Facility Extension			24d 4h	34d 4h	10-Dec-24 08 A	29-Jan-25 12	0d	0d
Technical Specification			10d 4h	15d	10-Dec-24 08 A	09-Jan-25 12	-1d 4h	0d
OZ1000	Approval to Bid	100%	0d	0d	10-Dec-24 08 A			
OZ1010	Determine Installation Requirements	100%	0d	4d	10-Dec-24 08 A	12-Dec-24 16 A		
OZ1020	Create Technical Specification	100%	0d	5d	12-Dec-24 08 A	20-Dec-24 16 A		
OZ1030	Identify Supplier Components	25%	1d 4h	2d	19-Dec-24 08 A	24-Dec-24 12	-1d 4h	0d
OZ1040	Validate Technical Specification	10%	9d	2d	20-Dec-24 08 A	09-Jan-25 12	-1d 4h	0d
Delivery Plan			15d 4h	15d 4h	02-Jan-25 08	23-Jan-25 12	-1d 4h	0d
OZ1050	Document Delivery Methodology	0%	4d	4d	09-Jan-25 12	15-Jan-25 12	-1d 4h	0d
OZ1060	Obtain Quotes from Suppliers	0%	8d	8d	02-Jan-25 08*	13-Jan-25 16	0d	1d 4h
OZ1070	Calculate the Bid Estimate	0%	3d	3d	15-Jan-25 12	18-Jan-25 12	-1d 4h	0d
OZ1080	Create the Project Schedule	0%	3d	3d	18-Jan-25 12	22-Jan-25 12	-1d 4h	0d
OZ1090	Review the Delivery Plan	0%	1d	1d	22-Jan-25 12	23-Jan-25 12	-1d 4h	0d
Bid Document			10d	10d	15-Jan-25 12	29-Jan-25 12	0d	0d
OZ1100	Create Draft of Bid Document	0%	6d	6d	15-Jan-25 12	23-Jan-25 12	-1d 4h	0d
OZ1110	Review Bid Document	0%	2d	2d	23-Jan-25 12	27-Jan-25 12	-1d 4h	0d
OZ1120	Finalise and Submit Bid Document	0%	2d	2d	27-Jan-25 12	29-Jan-25 12	-1d 4h	0d
OZ1130	Bid Document Submitted	0%	0d	0d		29-Jan-25 12*	-1d 4h	0d

17. The situation of having durations that are not round days is often not desirable and may be prevented by using Physical % Complete and entering the Remaining Duration in whole days.

18. Save the layout as **OzBuild Workshop 14 –Baseline Comparison**.

17 USER AND ADMINISTRATION PREFERENCES

This chapter will look at the following topics:

- User Preferences
- Admin menu, these are not displayed when opening an EPPM database
- Admin Preferences, these are not displayed when opening an EPPM database
- Admin Categories, these are not displayed when opening an EPPM database
- Miscellaneous Defaults, **Set Default Project** and Language

Functions that are not displayed when opening an EPPM database are accessed with the EPPM Web tool.

17.1 User Preferences

Select **Edit**, **User Preferences…** to open the **User Preferences** form. This form is used to set up a number of user defined parameters, which will determine how data is displayed.

The **User Preferences** form may also be opened by right-clicking in the right side of the bottom views when the **Resource Usage Spreadsheet** or **Resource Usage Profile** are displayed.

The **Stand-Alone** version does not have the **Personal Information** tab as it does not have users.

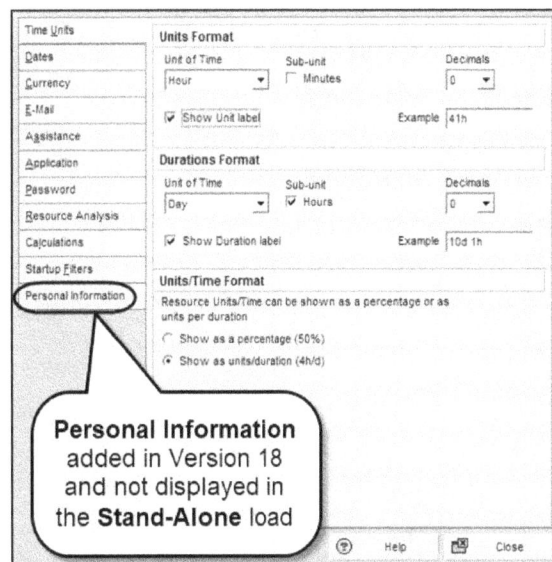

Personal Information added in Version 18 and not displayed in the **Stand-Alone** load

17.1.1 Time Units Tab

The **Units Format** section of the tab is used to define the **Unit of Time** format that resource information and resource assignments are displayed with, e.g., days or hours.

The **Durations Format** section of the tab is used to define the **Unit of Time** format that activity durations are displayed with, e.g., days or hours.

i The picture to the right shows the author's recommended settings.

© **Hyde Park Solutions Limited**   265

The **Units/Time Format** section of the form enables the Microsoft Project-type formatting options of **Resource/Time Format** to show Resource utilization as a percentage (50%) or as units per duration (4h/d). Therefore, there are several options here; for example, three people assigned to an activity may be displayed in many formats including:

- 300%
- 24h/d
- 3d/d
- 3h/h

17.1.2 Dates Tab

The **Dates** tab is self-explanatory and is used to format the display of dates and time.

NOTE: It is not possible to hide the year and there always has to be a date separator, thus leading to wider date columns than otherwise could be achieved. It is also not possible to display the days in characters such as Mon or Monday with the date.

i The picture to the right shows the author's recommended settings. People in the US may wish to use their local **Date Format**.

⚠ The author recommends that the **Time** should always be displayed so a user may see what time Primavera has selected when assigning Actual dates, Constraint dates, Suspend and Resume dates. Often Primavera selects 00:00, which is midnight on the morning of the selected date.

The author recommends that the **Month** name should always be displayed to avoid confusion between the US date format of mm/dd/yy and the ROW (Rest of World) format of dd/mm/yy.

17.1.3 Currency Tab

The **Currency Options** tab selects the currency symbol and exchange rate used to display with costs.

It is usually best NOT to **Show decimal digits**, this will reduce table column widths allowing more data to be displayed.

The **Currencies** form, available from the **Admin** menu item, is used to define the Base Currency. All costs are stored in the **Base Currency** and all other **Currencies** are calculated values using the **Base Currency** value and conversion rate.

⚠ It is possible to have two currencies with the same symbol and if a user selects a different currency then all costs displayed by the user will be converted to a different value.

This option must be carefully monitored and if you do not need multiple currencies then it is suggested that you should delete all but one currency, to avoid any possible problems. If you are using multiple currencies, then make sure that all have a different sign so there is no confusion.

17.1.4 E-Mail Tab

The **E-mail Protocol** tab sets up the current user's E-mail system.

This was updated with P6 Version 22, as per the picture, with more options allowing users to specify the SMTP port, and whether to use SSL, TLS, or no security for authentication with the mail server.

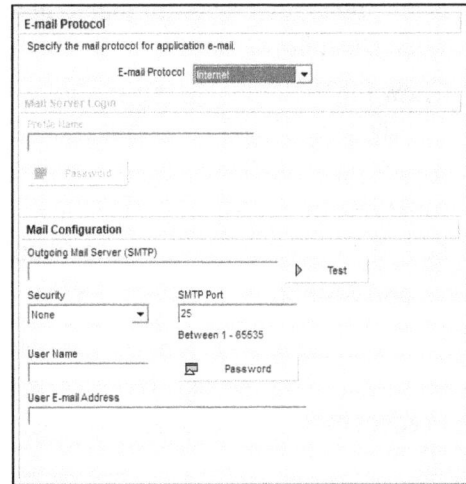

17.1.5 Assistance Tab

- **Wizards** specifies which wizards are run when creating Resources and Activities.
  NOTE: It is suggested to turn both off as it is quicker to type the information straight into the required fields when you know how to use the software.

- P6 Version 22 introduced a new **Responsible Manager** option for the assignment of the **OBS** to a copied project, allowing each user to two options for the OBS Node to be assigned to a project when it is copied and passed to a new EPS Node.

- **NOTE:** The parent code may not be logical and the option to select a new code is not available.

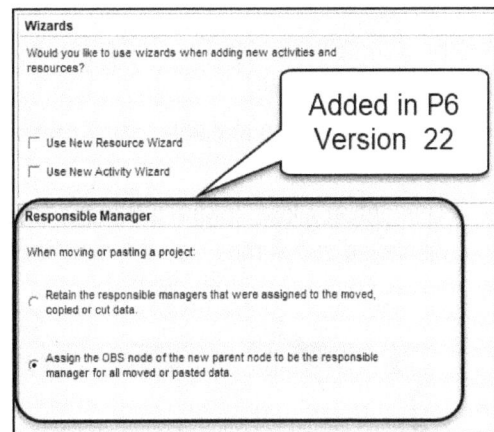

17.1.6 Application Tab
Application Startup Window

- **Application Startup Window** specifies which Primavera window is displayed when the software is started.

  ➢ If you work on the same project all the time, then set this to **Activities** and do not close the project when closing Primavera. The next time you open Primavera you will be taken to your project in the **Activities Window**.

  ➢ If you work in different projects all the time, then select **Projects** and you will be taken to the **Projects Window**.

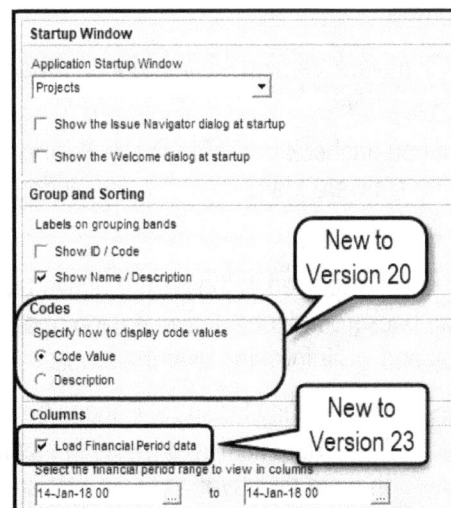

- **Show the Issue Navigator dialog at startup** should only be checked if you wish to view the Issues when the software starts.

- **Show the Welcome dialog at startup** displays a Welcome dialog box on startup and would not usually be displayed as it slows down the user's access to the software.

- **Application Log File** – Removed from later versions of P6 and when the **Write trace of internal functions to log file** is checked P6 creates a log of all data entries titled ERRORS LOG. This would be used by support staff and should not be turned on unless requested by support staff.

Group and Sorting

- This specifies what information is displayed in the bands; one or both options of Description or Code may be selected. This setting is effective in situations where a Group and Sort form is not available, such as the **Predecessor** and **Successors** forms.

Codes

This option was introduced in Version 20.

- P6 normally displays the **Code Value** in columns and the **Code Description** in the bands, as per the picture on the left.

- P6 has an option to display the **Code Value** in bands from the **Group and Sort** form, as per the picture on the right.

- This option allows for the either the **Code Value**, see the picture on the left, or **Code Description** to be displayed in columns, see the picture on the right:

Activity ID	Activity Name	OzBuild Department		Activity ID	Activity Name	OzBuild Department
OzBuild Department				**OZD OzBuild Department**		
OZ1000	Approval to Bid	OZD		OZ1000	Approval to Bid	OzBuild Department
OZ1130	Bid Document Submitted	OZD		OZ1130	Bid Document Submitted	OzBuild Department
Project Support				**OZD.PS Project Support**		
OZ1040	Validate Technical Specification	OZD.PS		OZ1040	Validate Technical Specification	Project Support
OZ1080	Create the Project Schedule	OZD.PS		OZ1080	Create the Project Schedule	Project Support
OZ1090	Review the Delivery Plan	OZD.PS		OZ1090	Review the Delivery Plan	Project Support
OZ1100	Create Draft of Bid Document	OZD.PS		OZ1100	Create Draft of Bid Document	Project Support
OZ1110	Review Bid Document	OZD.PS		OZ1110	Review Bid Document	Project Support
OZ1120	Finalise and Submit Bid Document	OZD.PS		OZ1120	Finalise and Submit Bid Document	Project Support
Engineering				**OZD.EN Engineering**		

- Unfortunately, the option to show both Code Value and Code description is not available.

Columns

- Primavera Version 5.0 introduced **Financial Periods** where the periods that may be displayed in columns is specified.

- If you uncheck **Load Financial Period Data** then this data is not loaded when the application starts and the software loads more quickly, added in Version 23.

Job Alert Polling

This is not displayed in the picture above but some operations like copy and paste a project are now carried out as background jobs and when you open an EEPM database this option sets how often the database is check and will inform the user if a process has finished or failed.

> *i* When many Financial Periods have been created, you may have to scroll down hundreds of rows to find a data field in forms such as the **Filter** form. You should limit the number of Financial Periods that are displayed to those that are currently being used.

17.1.7 Password Tab

The **User Password** tab is used to change the user password. It is not available to the Administrator. The **Admin**, **Admin Preferences...**, **General** tab has an option for your corporate Password Policy.

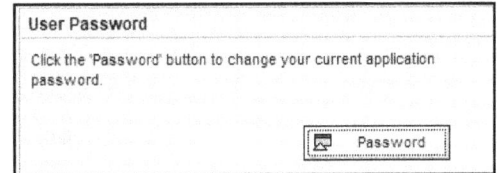

User Password
Click the 'Password' button to change your current application password.
☐ Password

17.1.8 Resource Analysis Tab

The **Resource Analysis** tab has two sections:

All Projects

- The **All Projects** option specifies which projects are used to calculate the Resources Remaining Values in **Resource Usage Profiles**.
  NOTE: Projects must be Summarized for this function to operate.

Time-Distributed Data

- It is possible to drag a project forward or backwards in time in the **Tracking Window**. This action creates a new set of dates titled **Forecast dates**. The **Resource Usage Profile** and **Resource Usage Spreadsheet** may be calculated using either the Current Schedule **Remaining Early Dates** or the revised **Forecast dates**.

All Projects box:
When All Projects are shown in the Resource Usage Profile and Spreadsheet, all opened projects are included as well as the closed projects specified below.
○ All closed projects (except what-if projects)
○ All closed projects with a leveling priority equal/higher than 10
● Opened projects only

This option must be set to hours to see Time-Distributed data in hours

Time-Distributed Data
In the Resource Usage Profile and Spreadsheet, display time-distributed Remaining Early data using
● Remaining Early dates
○ Forecast dates

Interval for time-distributed resource calculations: Day ▼
Hour / Day / Week / Month

Display the Role Limit based on
○ Custom role limit
● Calculated primary resources' limit
☐ Exclude inactive resources

Added in Version 23

Help   Close

- **Interval for time-distributed resource calculations:** This option determines the time increment for displaying the Resource Usage Profile and Resource Usage Spreadsheet data.

  When this is set to days and you display time-distributed data in hours, all the hours will be displayed on the first hour:

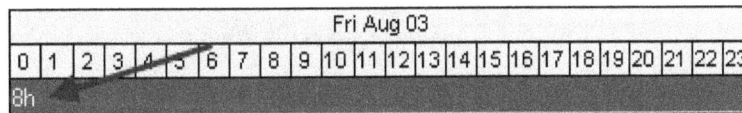

Fri Aug 03
0 1 2 3 4 5 6 7 8 9 10 11 12 13 14 15 16 17 18 19 20 21 22 23
8h

Selecting hours will spread the resource where they are scheduled but this consumes computer resources.

Fri Aug 03
0 1 2 3 4 5 6 7 8 9 10 11 12 13 14 15 16 17 18 19 20 21 22 23
1h 1h 1h 1h   1h 1h 1h 1h

i The **Interval for time-distributed resource calculations:** must be equal to or smaller than the timescale or the resource data will be displayed in the first time increment of the timescale and not distributed over the whole time period.

- **Display the Role limit based on** – Primavera introduced **Role Limits** in Version 6.0 and this enables options for displaying the **Role Limits** in **Resource Profiles**. For example, a role may have been defined a limit of six resources but only have four Resources assigned to the Role. This option allows you to decide if you wish to display a limit of four based on the resources available or six based on the limit assigned to the Role. The ability to **Exclude inactive resources** was added in P6 Version 23.

- The **Exclude inactive resources** was added in P6 Version 23 and this option a allows a user to conduct a resource analysis without the inclusion of **Inactive Resources** allowing more accurate reporting when **Inactive Resources** are being used.
  Note: This is a User Preference and thus different users may have different results if they use different Resource Analysis settings.

17.1.9 Calculations Tab

⚠ **IT IS IMPORTANT TO UNDERSTAND THIS OPTION.**

The **Resource Assignments** section **Calculations** tab, has two options:

- **Preserve the Units, Duration, and Units/Time for existing assignments**. With this option, as Resources are added or deleted the total number of hours assigned to an activity increases or decreases. The hours assigned for each resource are calculated independently.

- **Recalculate the Units, Duration, and Units/Time for existing assignments based on the activity Duration Type**. The total number of hours assigned to an activity will stay constant as second and subsequent resources are added or removed from an Activity, except when the Duration Type is **Fixed Duration and Units/Time**.

  Recalculate the Units, Duration, and Units/Time for existing assignments based on the activity Duration Type is similar to making an activity Effort Driven in Microsoft Project.

Resource Assignments

  When adding or removing multiple resource assignments on activities

  ⦿ Preserve the Units, Duration, and Units/Time for existing assignments

  ○ Recalculate the Units, Duration, and Units/Time for existing assignments based on the activity Duration Type

  Assignment Staffing

  When assigning a resource to an existing activity assignment:

  ⦿ Always use the new resource's Units per Time and Overtime factor
  ○ Always use current assignment's Units per Time and Overtime factor
  ○ Ask me to select each time I assign

  When a resource and role share an activity assignment:

  ○ Always use resource's Price per Unit
  ○ Always use role's Price per Unit
  ⦿ Ask me to select each time I assign

  Dissolving Activities

  ☑ Retain Lag   *New to Version 19*

⚠ With this option, as you assign or remove resources to or from an activity the total number of hours of work stays constant and the work is divided amongst all the resources.

Thus, assigning resources will reduce the work for each resource and either the activity duration will reduce or the Units per Time Period for each resource assignment will reduce. This calculation is dependent on the Duration Type.

The author prefers as a default **Preserve the Units, Duration, and Units/Time for existing assignments**. In this situation each resource work is independent on other resources assigned to an activity.

- **Assignment Staffing** are new functions to Primavera Version 5.0 options available on the **Calculations** tab of the **User Options** form allowing the user to set the defaults for:
  - ➢ Selecting the Units per Time when assigning a substitute resource to an existing resource assignment.
  - ➢ Selecting the Price per Unit for a resource which is being assigned to a Role.

The options are to select the existing resource, the new resource, or to be prompted each time a resource/role is substituted.

- **Dissolving Activities**, **Retain Lag** was new to P6 Version 19 and this function introduced the ability to retain lag when dissolving activities. When **Retain Lag** is selected from the **User Preferences**, **Calculations** tab, the dissolved activities predecessor and successor lags are added to the new relationship. This is covered in detail para 9.10.

17.1.10 Startup Filters Tab

The **Startup Filters** option enables the selection of filters for Resources, Roles, OBS, Activity Codes and Cost Accounts, which may be applied to the current project or to all data.

You may find when you open up a window, such as the **Resources Window**, that no data is displayed. This may be due to the settings in this tab.

ACTION: The author recommends selecting **View all data (No Filter)** so you will not end up with a blank screen when you open windows such as the **Resources Window**.

Resource Summary data should be checked if a user wishes to view summarized resource spread data after a project is Summarized. This data is viewed in the **Tracking** window.

17.1.11 Personal Information Tab

The **Personal Information** tab is new to P6 Version 18 and displays your personally identifiable information (PII) that the administrator enters when the user was created.

This is information is available from the **Admin** menu when a PPM database is opened. The **Admin** menu has been removed when the user opens an EPPM database and this tab enables users to see their Personal Information without requiring access to the Web Client.

This personal information may be exported with project data and this function was introduced at the same time as **Admin Preferences**, **Consent Notice** functions.

17.2   Admin Menu- Create Users

The links between Users, OBS, and Projects is covered in more detail in the **Managing the Enterprise Environment** chapter. This module is an introduction to the contents of the Admin Menu.

The **Admin** menu is available in P6 Professional but has been removed from the P6 Windows Client and has to be accessed through the Web module when using the Windows Client.

A **Stand-Alone** version does not have the ability to create users and thus does not have **Users** and **Security Profiles** menu items.

P6 PPM Professional Database

The **Admin** command opens the **Admin** form.

Depending on how Primavera has been installed and your access rights set, you may or may not have access to some or all of these menus.

EPPM Database

A EPPM database has more functions than a PPM database and the **Administration** tab in the Web Client allows access to all administration commands but the menu is completely different:

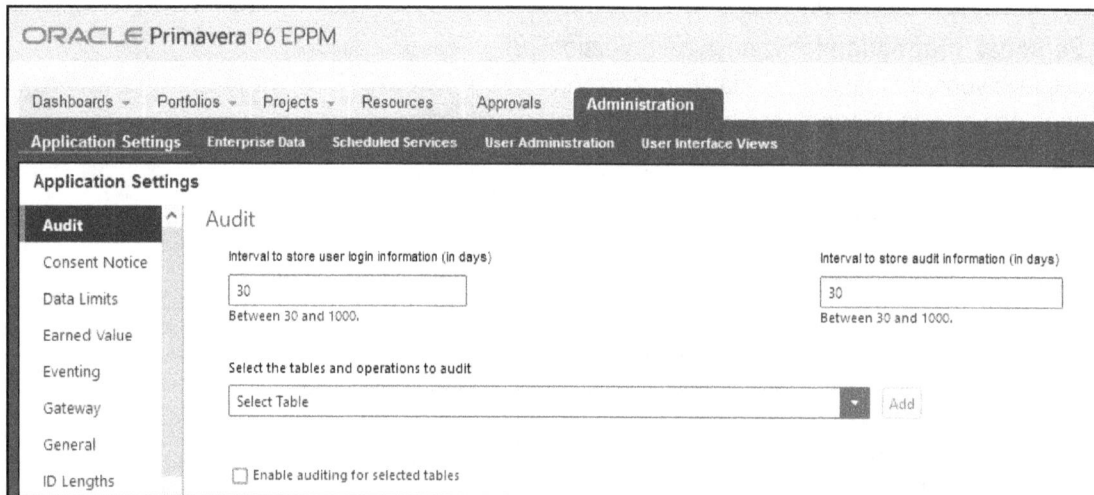

17.2.1 Users

The **Users** form is used to add and delete system users. The following information may be recorded:

- **General** tab: The Personal Name (the person's name), Login Name, Password and the Users Resource ID in the **Resources Window**.

- **Contact** tab: The person's telephone number and e-mail.

- **Global Access** tab: The Global information a user may change is specified here by assigning a **Global Profile**.

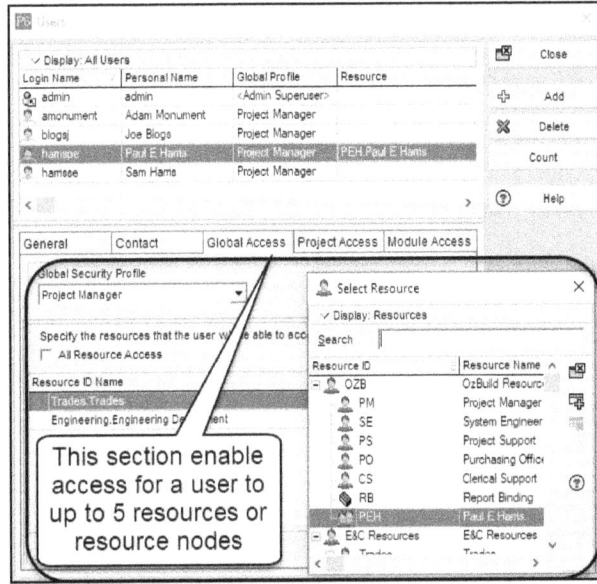

This section enable access for a user to up to 5 resources or resource nodes

The **Global Access** tab is the location where user access to resources may be restricted. P6 Version 18 and earlier only allowed either all resources or one resource or one resource node to be assigned to a user. P6 Version 19 introduced the ability to allow a user to be assigned up to five resources or resource nodes when defining resource access. A user may view and assign the selected resources and the child resources from resources assigned here:

- **Project Access** tab: This is where the **User** is assigned to one or more OBS Nodes and may only access Projects associated with those OBS Nodes. The level of user access to projects is controlled by the designated **Security Profile**.

- **Module Access** tab: This is where a person is assigned a license. A license needs to be assigned before the person may operate the system.

The User may also be assigned to an OBS Node in the **Organizational Breakdown Structure** form.

A **Global Security Profile**	This allows access to **Global data** such as EPS, OBS etc.
A **Project Security Profile** for each assigned **OBS Node**	This allows access to **one or more Projects**
	This allows access to one or more **Project WBS Nodes**
Access to one resource node in Version 18 and earlier and up to 5 **Resource Nodes** in Version 19 and later	Allows the **assigning of Resources** under this Node
A **software license**	Allows the software to be started
A optional **Resource ID**	This allows **Timesheeting**
A **Resource ID** may be assigned as a **Timesheet approval Manager**	This allows **Timesheet approval**

A **person** is created as a **User** and is assigned a **Password** that the user may change and is assigned:

A **Role** may be assigned to one or more Resources

17.2.2 Security Profiles

The **Security Profiles** form is used to set up security.

- **Global Profile** and **Project Profiles** may be established in this form.

- **Global Profiles** are created and/or edited to enable access to specific Enterprise functions and are assigned to users.

- **Project Profiles** are created and/or edited to enable access to specific Project functions.

- A **Project Profile** is assigned to a user when they are assigned to one or more **Organization Breakdown Structure** Nodes.

- A different **Project Profile** may be assigned to each user for each OBS Node, but an EPS Node and Projects may only be assigned to one OBS Node.

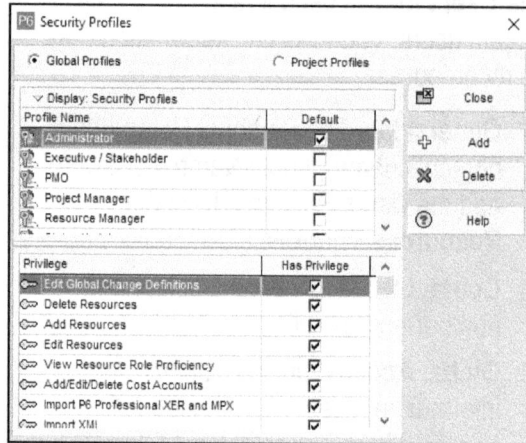

  It is critical that the **Security Profiles** be carefully evaluated and each person assigned an appropriate level.

  No one except the Administrator/s should be able to delete critical data such as project and EPS Nodes.

17.3 Admin Preferences

This form sets the default preferences for Primavera.

The **Admin Preferences** form has a number of tabs, which will be covered in more detail in the next section of this chapter.

If you do not have access to the **Admin Preferences**, then these options would have been set up by the system administrator for your organization.

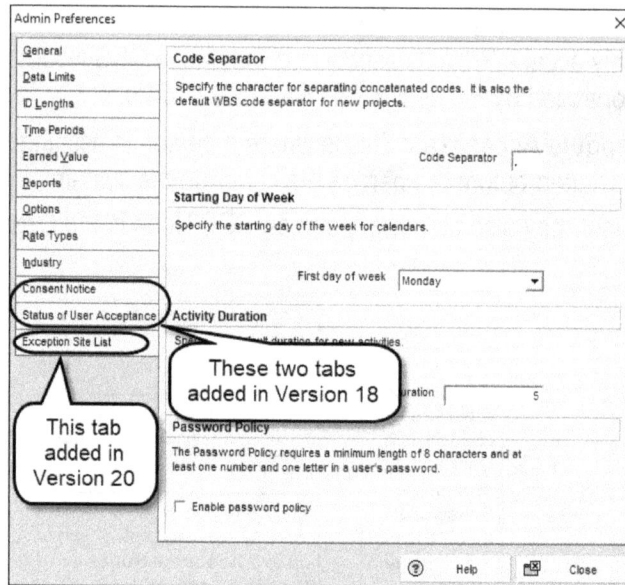

Some preferences may only be changed in this form. Items described as **defaults** may also be changed in other windows.

Select **Admin**, **Admin Preferences...** to open the **Admin Preferences** form.

17.3.1 General Tab

- **Code Separator** sets the default separator for new project WBS Codes and other codes such as Cost Accounts. The **Code Separator** may also be set for each project in the **Project Window**, **Setting** tab.

- **Starting Day of Week** sets the **First day of week** that is shown on the timescale and the left column of calendars.

- **Date Filters** added in Primavera P6 Version 22 and is explained below.

- **Activity Duration** sets the default Activity duration for new activities.

- **Password Policy**, introduced in Version 6.2, allows the requirement for a password of a minimum of 8 characters including a letter and number.

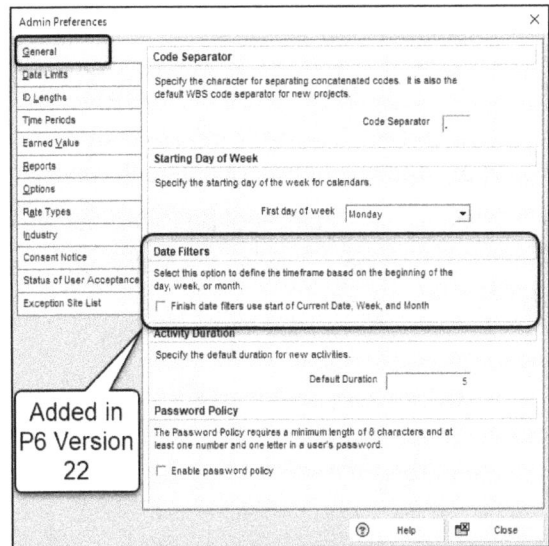

> *i* The default is usually Sunday and should be changed to a Monday, which results in the calendar day in the timescale representing a working day, which is often a lot more useful than a nonwork day date.

- When a **Finish Date** filter has been created the user may select **Current Date**, **Current Week** etc.

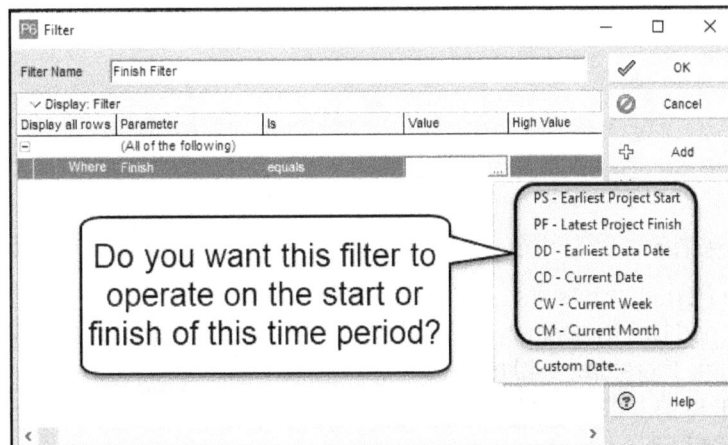

- Version 20.4 changed the way the filter operated to select the end of the time period, whereas earlier versions used the start of the time period. With this option the Administrator may make the software compatible with earlier versions.

- **NOTE:** It would appear more logical to have the filter operate on the end of the selected time period and I would not switch it on unless there was a demand to be compatible with earlier versions.

17.3.2 Timesheets Tab

The **Timesheets** tab was removed in Version 8.1 Professional but is available in the Web application.

17.3.3 Data Limits Tab

The **Data Limits** tab specifies:

- The maximum number of levels allowed in all hierarchical code structures,
- The maximum number of Activity Codes per project, and
- The maximum number of Baselines per project.

Primavera Version 6.0 added the **Maximum baselines copied with project**.

17.3.4 ID Lengths Tab

The **ID Lengths** tab specifies the maximum number of characters in the Code ID fields, not the Code Description.

17.3.5 Time Periods Tab

- **Hours per Time Period** values are used to convert from one time period Unit to another, for example, from days to hours. Therefore, a 40 hour activity would be calculated as 5-day with the setting displayed in the picture.
- **NOTE:** It is important that these conversions are understood. Please refer to the **Calendar** chapter for more details.

- Checking **Use assigned calendar to specify the number of work hours for each time period** enables users to edit the **Hours per Time Period** in each calendar.

> It is very important when multiple calendars with different hours per day are being used that this check box is checked and the user correctly sets the **Hours per Time Period** in each calendar.

- **Time Period Abbreviations** are used to indicate the display durations.

17.3.6 Earned Value Tab

See the **Earned Value** chapter for more information.

This tab sets the WBS defaults for calculating Earned Value and may be changed individually for each WBS and applies to all activities within each WBS Node.

Note: It is not possible to set the method for calculating the ETC or Performance % Complete for individual activities.

- The **Technique for computing performance percent complete** selects the formula for calculating the Earned Value.

- The **Technique for computing Estimate to Complete (ETC)** selects the formula for calculating the ETC. The ETC is a calculated field and is independent of the **At Completion Fields** but may contain the same value.

- **Earned value calculations** selects some options for calculating the Earned Value and displaying the Baseline Bar. The Primavera default is usually set to **Budgeted Values with Planned Dates**. This setting must never be used and please read the warning below.

⚠ It is very important that users read the sections on Planned Dates as leaving the setting at **Budgeted Values with Planned Dates** will result in the risk that all in-progress Baselines may display irrelevant dates as Baseline dates.

Technique for computing performance percent complete

- ○ Activity % Complete   ◉ 50/50 % Complete
- ○ Use WBS Milestones   ○ Custom % Complete
- ○ 0/100 % Complete   `4` ⬍

Technique for computing Estimate to Complete (ETC)

◉ ETC = remaining cost for activity

or

ETC = PF * (Budget at Completion - Earned Value), where:

- ○ PF = 1
- ○ PF = 1 / Cost Performance Index
- ○ PF = 1 / (Cost Performance Index * Schedule Performance Index)
- ○ PF = `0.88`

Earned value calculation

When calculating earned value from a baseline use

`At Completion values with current dates` ▼

17.3.7 Reports Tab

The **Report Headers and Footers** form sets the default labels for reports.

These may also be accessed in printouts.

Report Headers and Footers

Specify three sets of header, footer, and custom labels to place on application reports

◉ First Set   ○ Second Set   ○ Third Set

Header Label 1
`Header 1`

Footer Label 1
`# Oracle Primavera`

Custom Label 1
`User Variable 1`

17.3.8 Options Tab

- The **Specify the interval to summarize and store resource spreads** tab sets the time period, such as week or month, for storing Summarized activity data at WBS and Resource/Role Assignment Levels vied in the **Tracking window**.

- The **Project Architect** and **Web Access Server URL** check boxes were removed from the **Windows Client**.

- **Enable Link to Contract Management** Module (originally called Expedition) enables linking to this module when installed, removed in Version 19.

- **Professional Online Help URL** sets the URL for accessing help and should not normally be changed unless your company has produced its own help files.

- In P6 Version 20 **y**ou may prevent people from down loading harmful files in the **Admin Preferences**, **Options**, **Document Security** by listing the file types users may not download.

- P6 Version 21 introduced **Cost Spread** which is covered in the **Resource Analysis** chapter in para 18.2.2.

Version 18

Version 21

17.3.9 Rate Types Tab

Primavera has five resource rate types and the **Resource Rate Types** form enables you to rename the titles of the rates. You may have, for example, rates for:

- Internal consulting,
- External consulting,
- Preparing evidence, and
- Giving evidence.

i   In the building and construction industries a resource pool is created for each project and only one resource rate is used. In this situation it is recommended that the administrator renames the **cost_per_qty2** to **cost_per_qty4** to **DO NOT USE 2** to **DO NOT USE 4** to ensure there is no confusion about which rate to use on projects, especially when a project is created and a rate has to be selected when running the **Create New Project** wizard

---

17.3.10 Industry Tab

The **Industry Selection** determines the terminology used in some fields. In earlier versions this was set when the software was loaded. It may now be set **Admin**, **Admin Preferences...**, **Industry** tab.

You will need to restart P6 for a change to take effect:

The following table displays the terminology:

Industry Type	Terminology	Name of Project Comparison Tool
Engineering and Construction	Budgeted Units & Cost Original Duration	Claim Digger in earlier versions and now Schedule Comparison
Government, Aerospace, and Defense	Planned Units & Cost Planned Duration	Schedule Comparison
High-Technology, Manufacturing and Others	Planned Units & Cost Planned Duration	Schedule Comparison
Utilities, Oil, and Gas	Budgeted Units & Cost Original Duration	Claim Digger in earlier versions and now Schedule Comparison

Engineering and Construction:

Government, Aerospace, and Defense:

17.3.11 Consent Notice

Consent notices alert users to any corporate policies designed to protect personally identifiable information that may be stored or transmitted when using P6.

There are five **Consent Notices** that may be enabled, and each notice may be edited to suit your organisation:

Add resources consent notice
Add users consent notice
Download data consent notice
Login page consent notice
Visualizer login consent notice

The consent notice should be created to reflect corporate policies and/or government regulations.

A **Consent Notice** is displayed when a user first operates one of the functions enabled as a Consent Notice. The user must accept the consent notice before being allowed to progress.

17.3.12 Status of User Acceptance

This tab shows how many **Consent Notices** have been displayed and accepted by users

This publication is only sold as a bound book, no parts may be reproduced by any means, e.g., electronic, video or print.

© *Hyde Park Solutions Limited*   **280**

17.3.13 Exception Site List

In P6 Version 20 a list of web sites may be added to **Admin Preferences**, **Options**, **Exception Site List.**

The URLs may then be added to Notebook Topics and UDFs and permitted URLs may be launched from P6 by clicking on the URL and selecting Launch.

Other URLs in P6 fields may be copied and pasted into a browser but not run from P6.

NOTE: Any web site may be launched from the **Projects** window, **General** tab, **Project Web Site URL**.

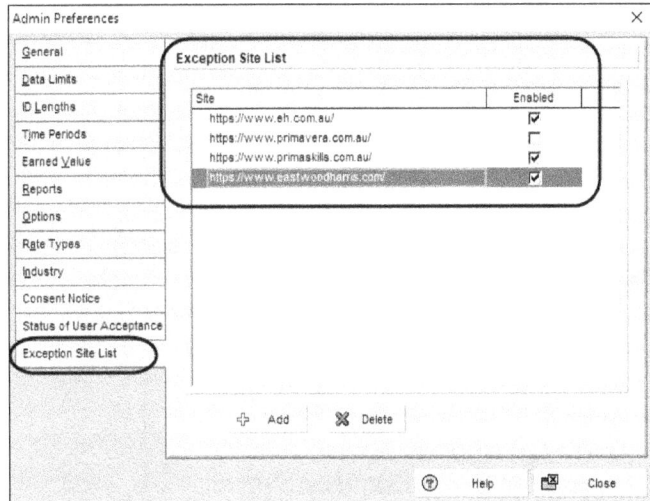

The picture below demonstrates what happens when a URL that has not been enabled has been selected for Launching:

17.4 Admin Categories

The **Admin**, **Admin Categories** form is where the global data items are defined. This form is self-explanatory and will not be explained in detail. The following categories are defined:

- Baseline Types
- Expense Categories
- WBS Categories
- Document Categories
- Document Status
- Risk Categories
- Notebook Topics
- Units of Measure – for Material Resources

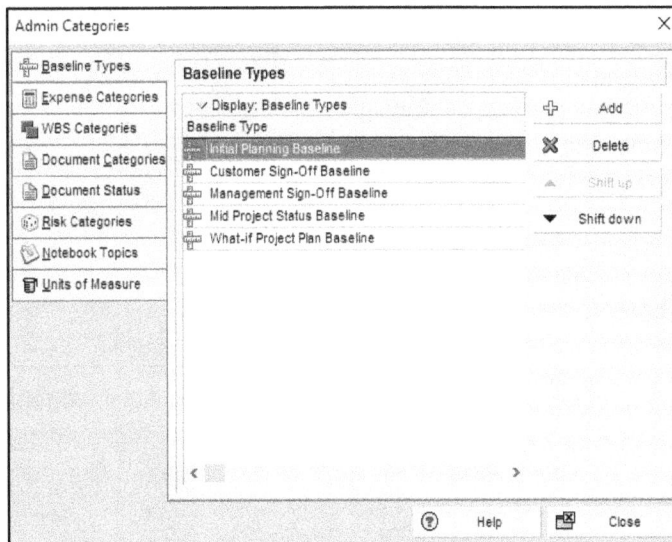

The WBS Category defines a set of codes that may be assigned to WBS Nodes allowing the WBS structure to be reorganized under a different set of codes. See para 6.5 for more information.

17.5   Miscellaneous Defaults

17.5.1   Currencies

The **Currencies** form is used to define system currencies. Currency fields are:

- **Currency ID**
- **Currency Name**
- **Currency Symbol**
- **Exchange Rate**

To make the Base currency into your country's currency you will need to edit the **Currency ID** and **Currency Symbol** as the first currency is permanently checked.

See the warning under Currency earlier in this chapter. The author recommends that all unwanted currencies are deleted and make all Currency Symbols unique.

17.5.2   Financial Periods and Financial Period Calendars

This is where the Financial Periods associated with Storing Period Performance are created.

Additional functionality was added in P6 Version 20 allowing different projects to have different Financial Periods and the function was renamed **Financial Period Calendars**.

For details on this function see the section on Store Period Performance in the **Earned Value** chapter, see para 27.4.4.

Financial Periods have to be used when it is important to have data that reflects how much work was completed or costs spent in each period and not just averaged over the periods to date. Period data is often used to create S-Curves.

17.5.3 Default Project

Select **Project**, **Set Default Project...** to open the **Set Default Project** form.

When multiple projects are opened the **Default Project** settings are used to:

- Schedule and level all open projects.

- All open projects **WILL** have their **Schedule Options** set to the same as the **Default Project** permanently, without telling the user, after the projects have been scheduled.

- New data items, such as **Issues**, are assigned to the default project when they are added to the database.

- The **Default Project** may also be overridden in Version 20 from the **Schedule Options** form and the **Level Resources** form.

When multiple projects are scheduled in Version 19 and earlier all the **Schedule Options** of all the projects are changed to the **Default Project**. This issue must be well understood by the Database Administrator and is covered in more detail in the **Multiple Project Scheduling** chapter.

In Version 20 the **Default Project** selected in the **Set Default Project** form may be overridden by selecting a different project in the **Scheduling Options** form, **Use scheduling options from** drop down box which will not change the selected project in the **Set Default Project** form but will override it and change all the other projects **Scheduling Options** to the one selected in the **Scheduling Options** form, see para 25.3.2 for details.

17.5.4 Set Language

The selection of the menu language is made from the **Tools** menu to the **Login screen**.

P6 Version 20 changed the Login screen format but the content remains the same. Supported languages are:

- English
- French
- German
- Simplified Chinese
- Traditional Chinese
- Russian
- Japanese
- Spanish
- Brazilian Portuguese
- Italian
- P6 Version 20 added Arabic

Note: The menus are in the nominated language but in some P6 versions some languages are not translated in the Help.

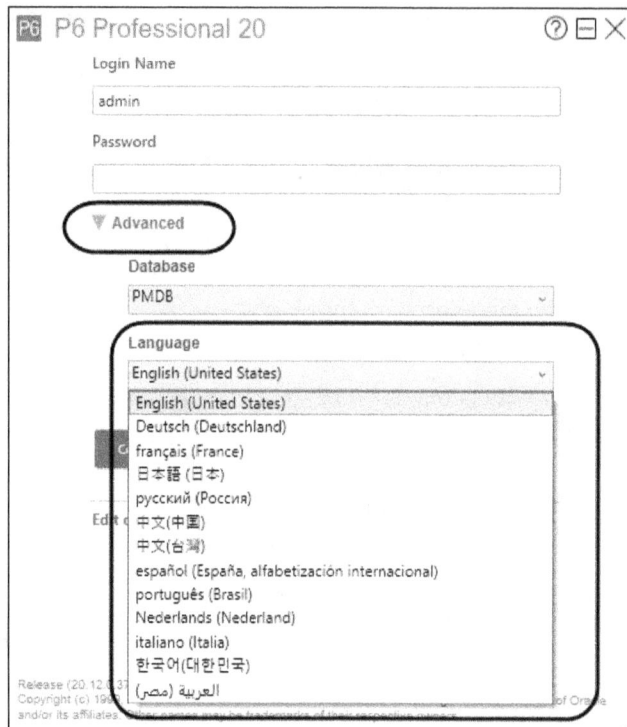

18   CREATING ROLES AND RESOURCES

Traditionally, planning and scheduling software defines a **Resource** as something or someone that is required to complete the activity and sometimes has limited availability. This includes people or groups of people, materials, equipment and money.

Primavera is able to assign Costs, a Calendar, one or more Roles and some personal information to a **Resource**.

Primavera has a function titled **Roles**. A Role is normally used at the planning stage of a project and represents a skill or position. Later, and before the activity begins, a Role would be filled by assigning a specific individual who would be defined as a Resource. Roles may be assigned to both Resources and Activities. A search by Role may be conducted on all the Resources when it is required to replace an Activity-Assigned Role with an individual from the Resource pool. Primavera allows rates to be assigned to Roles.

There are a large number of resource functions available in Primavera. Without getting into too much detail, this publication will outline the important resource-related functions that will enable you to create and assign Roles and Resources to your schedules.

This chapter will concentrate on:

Topic	Menu Command
Creating **Roles**	Select **Enterprise**, **Roles**... to open the **Roles** form.
Creating **Resources**	Open the **Resources Window**: • Select **Enterprise**, **Resources**, or • Click on the ▨ icon on the **Enterprise** toolbar.
Editing **Resource Calendars**	Select **Enterprise**, **Calendars**... to open the **Calendars** form.

The following steps should be followed to create and use resources in a Primavera schedule:

- Create the resources in the **Resources Window**.
- Create the **Roles**, if required, in the **Roles** form.
- Assign Resources to Roles from either the **Resources Window** or the **Roles** form.
- Manipulate the Resource Calendars if resources have special timing requirements.

18.1 Understanding Resources and Roles

There are typically two methods of using the Resource function for resource planning:

- Individual Resources, and
- Group Resources

18.1.1 Individual Resources

These resources are individual people who are often responsible for completing the activity or activities to which they have been assigned. They are identified by name in P6.

This is typically work undertaken in an office environment, such as an IT development project, where timesheets are often completed by the people undertaking the work and the timesheet system is directly linked to the scheduling system.

In this situation, the updating of Activities that are in-progress is completed by the person assigned as a Resource to an Activity, often via the timesheet system, and the scheduler has a review function in the project updating.

18.1.2 Group Resources

These resources represent groups of people, such as trades or disciplines on a construction site. Very large projects gangs or crews, which would be made up of equipment and a number of different trades, could also be considered. The person responsible for the work is not a resource assigned to an activity and individual people doing the work will not be assigning their timesheets directly to activities in the schedule.

Also, in this environment the scheduler normally updates the activities and the resources. In this situation it is recommended that a minimum number of resources be assigned to activities. This is because every resource added to the schedule will need to be updated and as more resources are added, the scheduler's workload will increase.

Resource minimization simplifies a schedule and makes it easier to manage large schedules. This is achieved by not cluttering the schedule with resources that are in plentiful supply or are of little importance, and/or by grouping trades or disciplines into crews and gangs on large projects.

When Group Resources are used the Role function tends to become redundant but could be used to plan the contractor type and/or the actual contractor to be used on the project.

18.1.3 Input and Output Resources

When you create your resources, you may also consider them within the context of the following headings:

- **Input Resources** – These resources are required to complete the work and represent the project costs:
  - Individual people by name.
  - Groups of people by trade, discipline, or skill.
  - Individual equipment or machinery by name.
  - Groups of equipment or machinery by type.
  - Groups of resources such as Crews, Gangs, or Teams made up of equipment and machinery.
  - Materials.
  - Money.

Output Resources – These could be the project deliverables or outcomes and could have a direct relationship to the project income:

- Specifications completed.
- Bricks laid.
- Tons/Tonnes of material loaded with an excavator.
- Lines of code written.
- Tests completed.

This type of resource is often used in the mining environment where the output in tones/tonnes or volume is scheduled and/or leveled.

The analysis of and difference between the Input and the Output resources' value and timing may be used to represent the Cash Flow, Cash Position and Project Profit (or loss).

The type of contract that the work is being conducted under would often determine if the client is more interested in the Input or Output Resources.

18.1.4 Understanding Roles

An evaluation at project or enterprise level in order to understand the long-term demand for resources may be made by a combination of Roles for long term planning and Resources for short term planning.

Roles are assigned to activities for long term planning and Resources represent individual people are assigned to roles for short term planning and would represent activity assignment.

The light area to the right of the histogram below shows the unsatisfied demand of the roles titled **Unstaffed Remaining Units** and the satisfied demand from the resources is in the dark are to the left and are titled **Staffed Remaining Units**.

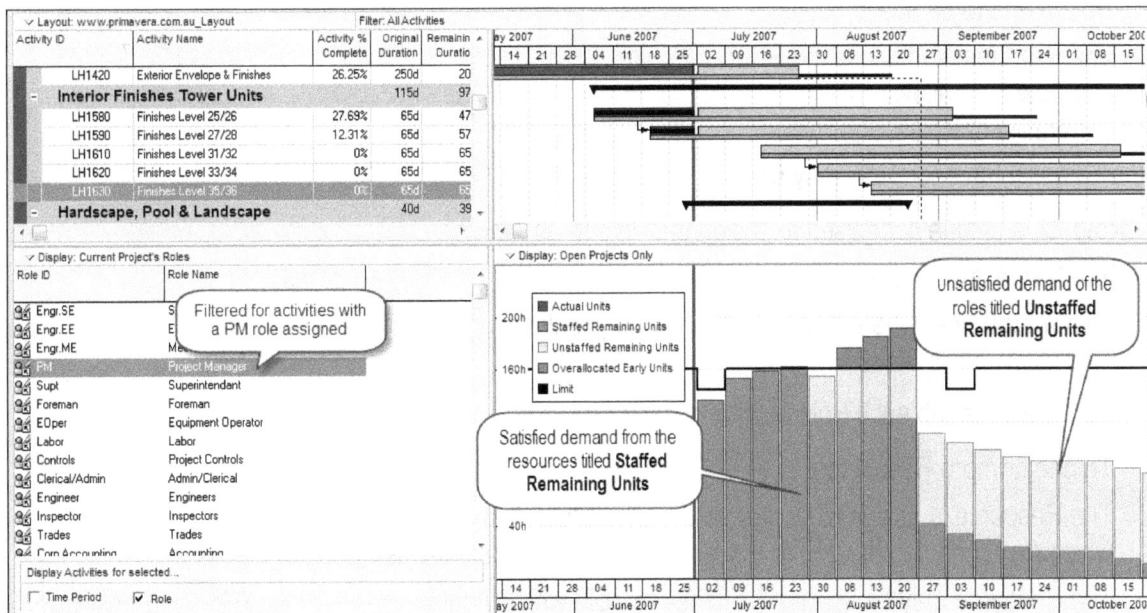

If you are a construction contractor and not assigning work to individual people then you may consider using resources only as they have more functions than roles.

18.2 Creating Roles

18.2.1 P6 Version 19 and Earlier – Roles Rate may not be varied over time

Roles are created, edited, and deleted in a similar method as WBS Nodes.

To create, edit, or delete a **Role** select **Enterprise**, **Roles...** to open the **Roles** form:

The following formatting, filtering, and sorting functions are available in the **Roles** form:

- Click on **Display: All Roles** and then the **Filter By** tab to open a menu where the roles can be filtered by **All Roles** or **Current Projects Roles**.

- Click on the **Role ID** title or the **Role Name** title to sort the Roles by **Role ID** or **Role Name**.

- **Roles** may also be displayed by the **Chart** view. The **Roles** form will have to be resized to use this function effectively.

- The **Find** function (or **Ctl+F**) enables a Role name to be searched.

- The **Print** function opens the **Print Preview** form allowing the printing of the current list of Roles.

In the **General** tab each Role may be assigned a:

- **Role ID**, a unique code used to assign the Role to an Activity.
- **Role Name**, the Name of the Skill or Trade.
- **Responsibilities**, where you may enter text, hyperlinks, and pictures about the Role Responsibility.

In the **Resources** tab each Role may be assigned:

- To one or more Resources.
- The Resource is assigned by default a **Proficiency** of "3 – Skilled" which may then be changed to any of the options shown in the list.
- The Resource may be assigned a **Primary Role** which would represent the activity or job they would normally be assigned.
- The **Primary Role** also links to Role availability when the option in the **Edit**, **User Preferences...**, **Resource Analysis** tab, **Display the Role Limit based** on is set to **Calculate primary resources' limit**.

Primavera supports **Rates for Roles**. Up to 5 rates (the same number of rates as resources) may be assigned to roles which may be used for estimating and cash flow forecasting of projects before the actual resource completing the work is assigned to the activity.

- Click on the **Prices** tab to edit the Role Price/Unit, and

- The **Role Rate** Type is adopted from the **Resource Rate Type** set in the **Admin**, **Admin Preferences…**, **Rate Type** tab.

- In P6 Version 19 and earlier Role rates may not be varied over time or levelled but Resources may be.

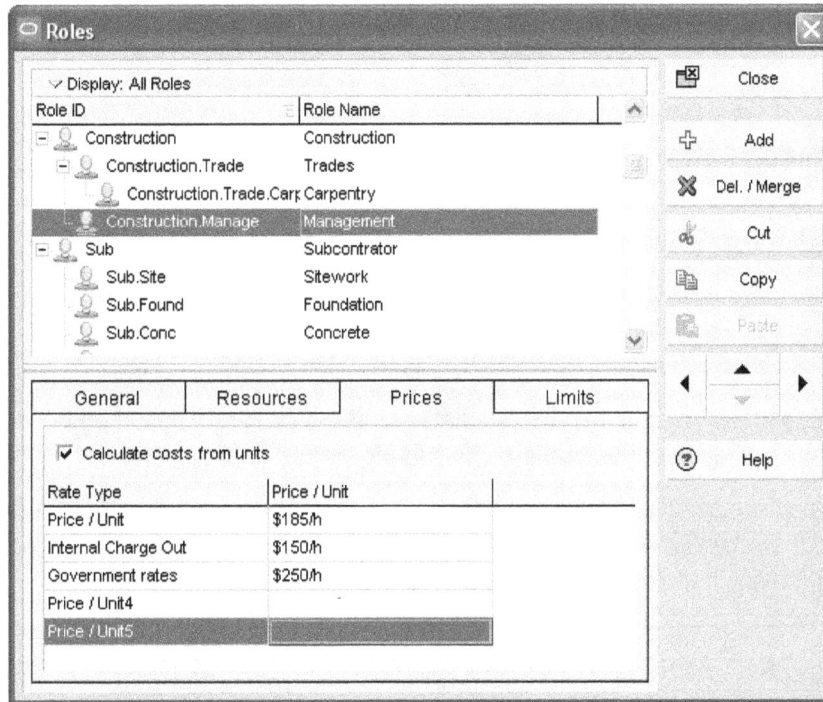

- The data columns in the **Prices** tab and **Limits** tab forms may be sorted by clicking on the column titles.

- The default rate for a project is selected when a project is created and may be changed in the **Projects Window**, **Resources** tab, **Assignment Defaults** area:

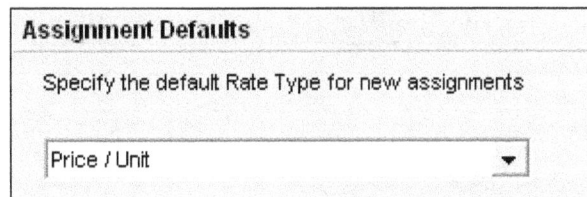

Different rates may be required for different clients such as internal project rates and rates for different types of external clients.

> *i*   Five resource and role rates may not be sufficient when a company has a number of clients. There are some options which include creating a new set of resources for each project, or a new database for each project, or not selecting the option of linking costs and units.

18.2.2 P6 Version 20 and Later – Roles Rate may be varied over time

Resources have always been able to vary their rate over time but Roles were not and this was one of the drivers to use Resources and not Roles in project schedules.

P6 Version 20 now allows Role rates to vary over time:

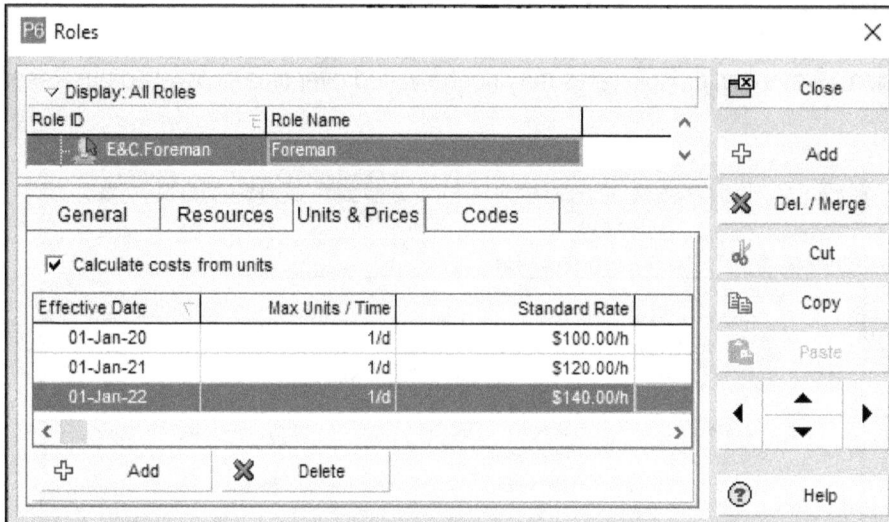

When an activity spans two periods then P6 calculates a proportional rate based on the activity duration in each period. You must use the **Recalculate Cost Assignment** function during or after rescheduling.

The pictures below show the result of assigning the Role Foreman above and has 4 days work in 2020 and 6 in 2021 and then 3 and 7 days. They demonstrate how the cost are calculated which are not entirely correct as the costs should be lower in 2021 and higher in 2022.

Note: This is the same way that resources calculate when an Activity spans an Effective Date.

This issue was fixed in P6 Version 21, see para 18.2.4.

18.2.3 P6 Version 20 and Later – Roles may be assigned a Role Code

P6 Version 20 introduced Role Codes allowing Roles to be assigned Code in the same way as Resources and Activities.

This would be useful to assign attributes such as location or office and may be used to group or filter roles.

- **Role Codes** are created in the **Role Codes** form by selecting **Enterprise**, **Role Code**s:

- **Role Code**s are assigned to Roles in the **Roles** form.

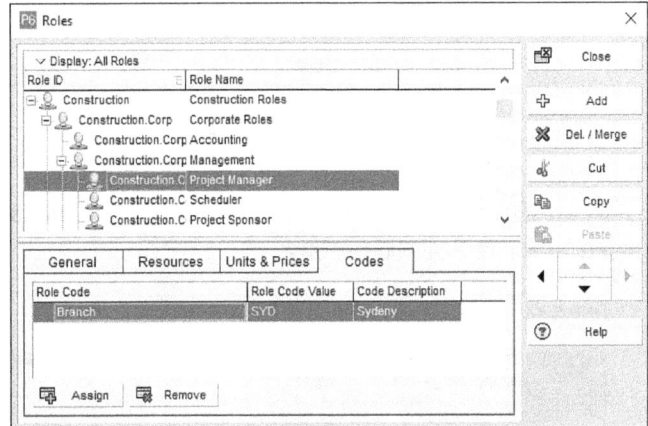

18.2.4 Resource and Role Cost Spreads Consider Rate Changes Over Time

The **Admin Preferences**, **Options** has introduced in Version 21 a **Cost Spread** option.

This changes how the cost spreads for resources and role rates are reflected in the Resource Usage Spreadsheet and Profile, Activity Usage Spreadsheet and Profile, Tracking View, Resource Assignments window, and Activity Usage Spreadsheets and Profiles, Publishing and Reports.

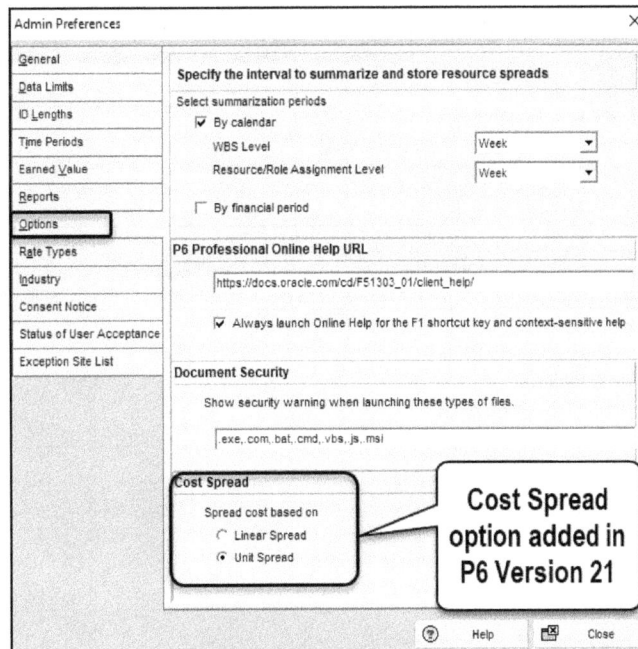

In earlier versions when a resource rate changed during the duration of an activity then P6 took an average rate for the resource over the activity duration which gave an incorrect cashflow.

- In the example below I have created a resource that doubled its unit rate from $20.00 per hour to $40.00 per hour after the first week:

With **Linear Spread** option, which is how older versions calculated, an average rate of $30.00 per hour is used, which is $240.00 per day:

With **Unit Spread** option, the cash flow is calculated correctly:

18.3   Creating Resources and the Resources Window

To create, edit, or delete resources open the **Resources Window**:

- Select **Enterprise**, **Resources…**, or

- Click on the ⊡ icon on the **Enterprise** toolbar,

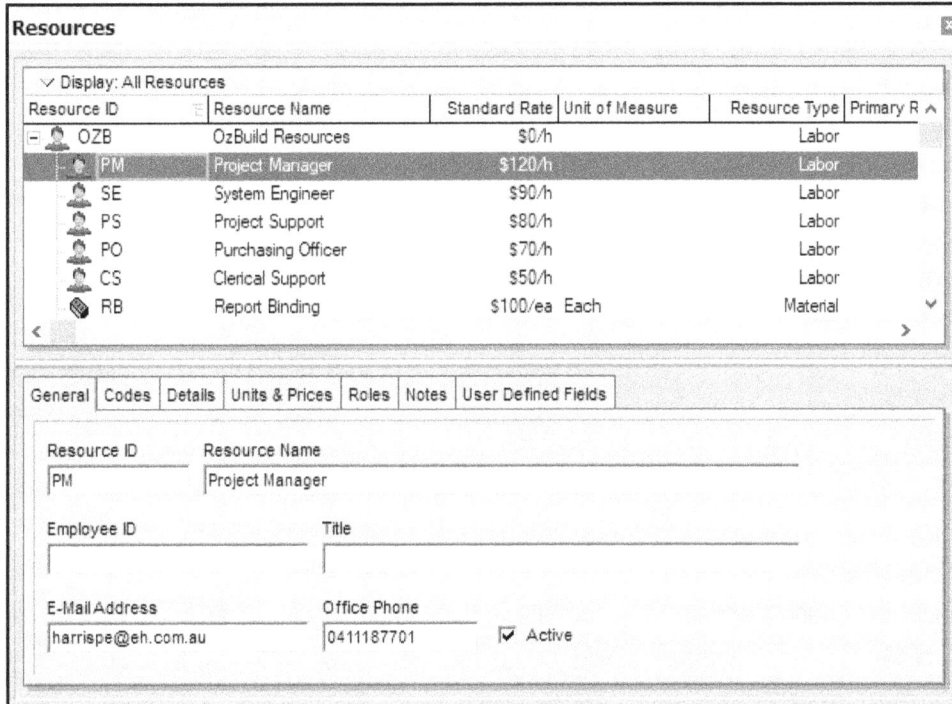

- In the **Resources Window:**

  ➢ ⊡ indicates a **Resource** which is not assigned to an open project,

  ➢ ⊡ indicates a **Resource** assigned to an open project,

  ➢ ⊡ and ⊡ indicate an unassigned and assigned **Nonlabor Resource**, and

  ➢ ⊡ and ⊡ indicate an unassigned and assigned **Material Resource**.

18.3.1   Resource Breakdown Structure – RBS

Resources may be added and organized hierarchically in a similar method to creating a WBS.

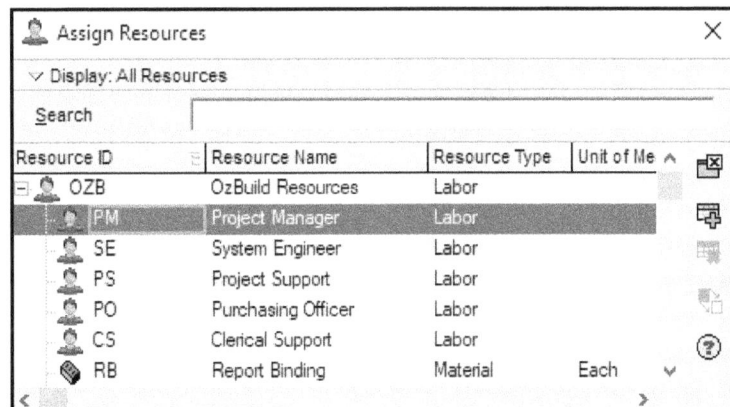

The OzBuild resources in the picture above are listed under a higher-level node titled **OzBuild Resources**. Primavera Systems calls this structure a **Resource Breakdown Structure** or **RBS**.

18.3.2 Formatting the Resources Window

The menu under the **Display: All Active Resources** has many functions that are similar to other forms:

- The **Details** check box displays or hides the **Details** form in the lower pane.

- **Chart View** displays the resources as a Chart. To use this format, **Group and Sort By** must be set as **Default** or have the **Customize...** option grouped by Resources.

- **Columns**, **Table Font and Row...**, **Filter By** and **Group and Sort By** options work in a similar way to the formatting of the **Activities Window**. Click on the menus to see the options available with each.

- When the **Resources** are organized hierarchically, the **Expand All** and **Collapse All** options work in a similar way to other windows and rolls up the Resources.

18.3.3 Adding Resources

New Resources are added and deleted in a similar method to adding Activities in the **Activities Window**. Use the **Insert** key, right-click and select **Add**, or use the Add ⊞ icon on the **Edit** toolbar.

18.3.4 General Tab

The fields in this tab are self-explanatory:

- The **Resource ID** has to be unique within a database and a **Resource Name** is mandatory,

- The **Employee ID**, **E-Mail Address**, **Title** and **Office Phone** are optional, and

- When the **Active** box is unchecked, the Resource is inactive and indicates that the resource is not available. When assigning Resources to Activities there is a filter to display only active Resources.

18.3.5 Codes Tab

Resource Codes are assigned to Resources allowing additional facilities to sort and report on them in the **Resource Usage Spreadsheet** and **Resources Window**.

- **Resource Codes** may be defined in the **Resource Code Definition** form, which is opened by selecting **Enterprise**, **Resource Codes...** and clicking on the [Modify...] icon.

- Individual **Resource Code Values** may be added to a **Resource Code** in the **Resource Codes** form by selecting **Enterprise**, **Resource Codes...**.

- Resource Codes may then be selected in a layout to sort and group Resources.

General	Codes	Details	Units & Prices	Roles	Notes	User Defined Fields

Resource Code	Resource Code Value	Code Description
Office	BRM	Birmingham
Corporate Division	Con	Construction
Gateway - Area	05-ST	05 - Mill Site
Gateway - Trade	Mang.SS.Pipe	SS - Pipe
Department	PM	Project Management Office

18.3.6 Details Tab

General	Codes	Details	Units & Prices	Roles	Notes	User Defined Fields

Resource Type

(•) Labor   (○) Nonlabor   (○) Material

Unit of Measure

Currency and Overtime

Currency
🔲 Australian Dollar   ...
☐ Overtime Allowed

Profile

Calendar
🔲 Trades - 5 Day Workweek   ...   Create Personal Calendar

Default Units / Time
8.0h/d

☑ Auto Compute Actuals
☑ Calculate costs from units

Resource Types

There are three types of Resources:

- **Labor**, intended for people
- **Nonlabor**, intended for equipment used to perform project work
- **Material**, intended for materials/supplies.

Material Resources

May be leveled and have the following differences from other resources:

- They may be assigned a **Unit of Measure**, which is created in the **Admin**, **Admin Categories...**, **Unit of Measure** tab. This is not available to Labor and Nonlabor resources.

- They may not be assigned a Role.
- They may not log Overtime.

Material resources do not display units (quantities) in the **Activities Window**, as with many other products like Microsoft Project and Elecosoft (Asta) Powerproject. These values may be displayed in other views such as the **Resource Assignments Window** and in reports.

Currency

An alternate **Currency** may be associated with a resource. This will not affect how the Resource Unit Rates costs are entered but provides a further tagging mechanism for sorting and reporting. The costs are stored in the default currency but are displayed using the conversion rate in the currency selected for the resource.

Overtime

A **Labor Resource** may be allowed to record **Overtime** in the **Primavera timesheet** system when the **Overtime Allowed** box is checked and the costs derived from the **Unit Rates** are multiplied by the **Overtime** Factor.

Calendar

The Resource is assigned a **Global** or a **Shared Resource Calendar** in this form.

- A **Shared Resource Calendar** may be created and assigned to more than one Resource. This topic is covered in more detail in the next section of this chapter.

- Click on the [Create Personal Calendar] icon to create a **Personal Calendar** for this resource.

NOTE: The **Resource** calendar is used to display the resource limits irrespective of the calendar assigned to an activity.

Default Units/Time

The **Default Units/Time** is the value that a resource adopts when it is first assigned to an activity. In a similar way to Microsoft Project, the **Units per Time Period** may be displayed as a **Percentage** or in **Units/Time**.

- Select **Edit**, **User Preferences...**, **Time Units** tab and select the preferred display from the **Units/Time Format** section:

Units/Time Format

Resource Units/Time can be shown as a percentage or as units per duration

- Show as a percentage (50%)
- Show as units/duration (4h/d)

Default Units / Time
50%

Default Units / Time
4.00h/d

For example, you may have a fleet of 12 trucks and you usually assign four trucks to each loader. In this situation you would assign the **Default Units/Time** as 400%, or 4 d/d, or 32h/d if the trucks are working 8 hours per day.

Resource and Activity Auto Compute Actuals

When a Resource **Auto Compute Actuals** field is unchecked, the work for a resource may be read from the Primavera Timesheet system or manually entered.

But when the **Activity Auto Compute Actuals** field is checked, this makes all the activity resource assignments to be **Auto Compute Actuals** irrespective of their settings in the Resource Window.

When the User uses the **Apply Actuals** function and activities or resources are set to **Auto Compute Actuals** Primavera calculates the Remaining Units based on the Remaining Duration and the Actual Units by subtracting the Remaining Units from Budgeted Units.

There are several places where the Resource **Auto Compute Actuals** field in Primavera is displayed:

- Against each resource in the **Resources Window**, **Details** tab,
- In a column in the **Resources Window**, when displayed, and
- Against each resource after it has been assigned to an activity and is displayed in the **Resources** tab of the bottom window in the **Activities Window**.

The option may **ONLY** be switched on or off against a resource in the **Resources Window** and if changed in the **Resources Window** it will affect all resource assignments for all projects for this resource.

The **Activity Auto Compute Actuals** field may be displayed as a column in the **Activities Window**:

Calculate Costs from Units

With this option checked the costs for a resource are calculated from the **Resource Unit/Time** when a resource is assigned to an activity. When unchecked, the costs remain at zero when a resource is assigned to an activity. This was called **Cost Units Linked** in earlier versions of P6.

When a resource has been assigned to an activity, there is a Resource Assignment field available in the **Resources** tab of the **Activities Window** titled **Calculate Costs from Units**. This is checked to match the **Calculate Costs from Units** field in the **Resources Window**.

The **Activities Window** field titled **Calculate Costs from Units** is not linked to the **Calculate Costs from Units** field in the **Resources Window** and only adopts the setting when a resource is assigned to an Activity.

The following picture shows a resource with the **Calculate Costs from Units** field unchecked; therefore, the costs are not calculated from the **Resource Unit Rate**.

18.3.7   Units and Prices Tab
Effective Date and Rates

Each Resource may have up to five rates (Price/Unit) and these rates may be varied over time.

- The **Effective Date** represents a change in Rate or availability at that point in time.
- To display the other rates their columns should be displayed in the **Units and Prices** tab.
- The column titles of **Price/Unit 1** to **Price/Unit 5** may have their descriptions edited in the **Admin**, **Admin Preferences…, Rate Type** tab. These titles are shared with Roles.
- When a rate is added the effective date is the date from which the rate is applied.

Shifts

Resource Shifts are used in conjunction with leveling and should not be assigned unless they are being used. **Resource Shifts** are covered in the **Resource Optimization** chapter:

- **Resource Shifts** are created in the **Resource Shifts** form, which is opened by selecting **Enterprise**, **Resource Shifts...**,

- The **Resource Shifts** and the number of shifts a resource works are assigned in the **Units and Prices** tab, **Shifts Calendar**.

> *i*   The author does not use the **Resource Shifts** function but finds it far simpler to create a **Task Dependent** activity for the day shift and afternoon and night shifts are created using **Level of Effort** tasks and linked to the day shift activity. See para the end of 20.6.3 for more information.

18.3.8 Roles Tab

- A Resource may be assigned more than one Role, and their **Proficiency** for the Role, in this tab.

- When multiple Roles are assigned, one is assigned as the **Primary Role**.

Role ID	Role Name	Proficiency	Primary Role
Oz.BM	Bid Manager	3 - Skilled	☑
Oz.SC	Scheduler	4 - Proficient	☐

18.3.9 Notes Tab

Notes may be added here but there are no Notebook topics available.

18.3.10 Progress Reporter Tab

Originally called **Progress Reporter** tab then changed to **Timesheets** and now back to **Progress Reporter** and has been removed from P6 Professional.

When Timesheets are implemented, the user must be added as a system user through the **P6 Web Administer**, **User Access** form where the user is assigned to a P6 Resource, thus providing the link from the timesheet user to the Primavera resource. This is covered in the **Admin Menu**, **Users** section.

For timesheets to operate, the **Uses timesheets** box in the **Progress Details** tab must also be checked and the **Timesheet Approval Manager** selected.

18.4 Workshop 15 – Adding Resources to the Database

Background

This workshop will only use Resources and these must now be added to the database.

We have updated our current project, but we need a project that has not been updated for the next activity of assigning resources. Therefore, we will have to restore the Baseline schedule saved prior to updating the current schedule to provide an un-progressed schedule for this exercise.

NOTE: If you are working in a database with other people completing this workshop then each person's Resource ID will have to be unique, say by adding your initials at the end of each Resource ID. A training course leader or database administrator should advise here.

Assignment

1. Select **Project**, **Maintain Baselines…** and copy the **Bid for Facility Extension – Baseline**, which did not have any progress.

2. Restore the copied project using **Project**, **Maintain Baselines…**, **Restore** command.

3. Go to the **Projects Window** where the restored baseline file will be visible.

4. Rename the restored Baseline project **Bid for Facility Extension – Resourced Schedule** and change the Project ID to **OZB-R**.
    NOTE: Users sharing a database will need to use unique Project IDs.

5. Open the restored project.

6. Open the **User Preferences** form, set the **Calculations** and **Time Units** tab as per the following pictures.

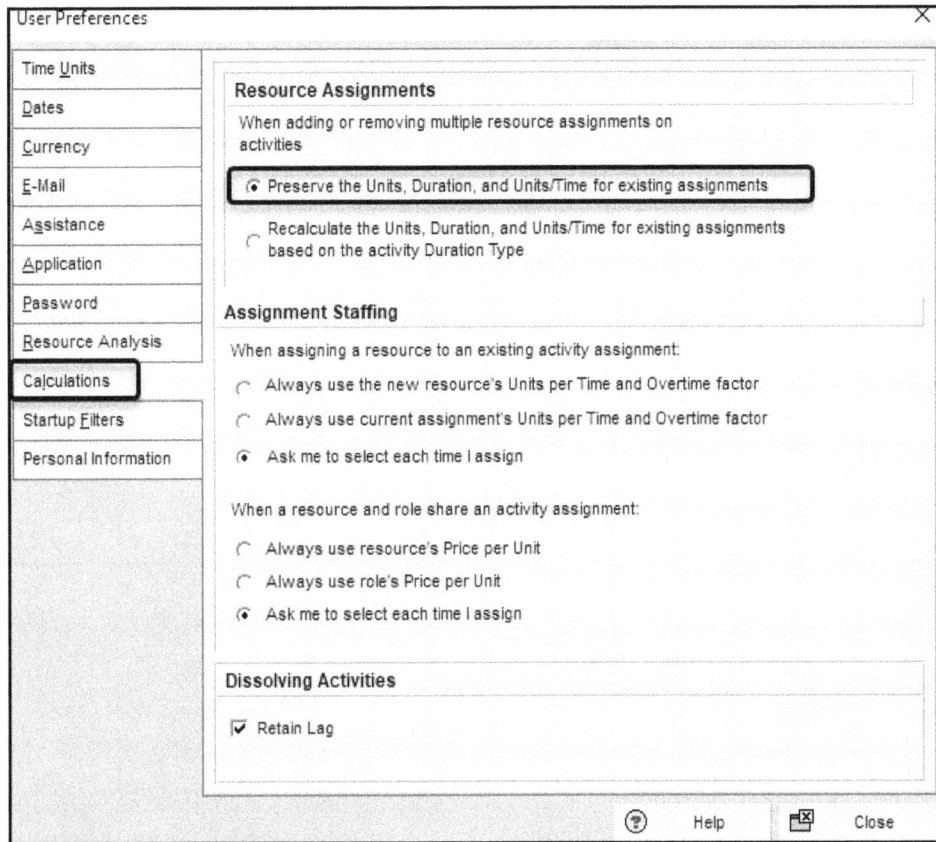

7. Now open the **Resource Window**.

8. If no resources are displayed, then select all resources from the **Display:** menu:

9. Format the columns in the **Resources Window** as in the following picture.

10. Add the resources as in the following picture:

   ➢ If the **New resource Wizard** is displayed then close it and disable it in the **User Preferences** as it is quicker just to type in resources.

   ➢ The **Unit of Measure** may not be available in your database, so either add it in the **Admin**, **Admin Categories…**, or do not assign one if you do not have the access right to create a **Unit of Measure**.

   ➢ **Price/Unit** must be entered in the bottom pane, it may be viewed but not added or edited in a column.

   NOTE: If you are working in a database with other people completing this workshop then each person's Resource ID will have to be unique, say by adding your Initials at the end of each Resource ID.

Resource ID	Resource Name	Resource Type	Price/Unit or Standard Rate	Unit of Measure
☐ 👤 OZB	OzBuild Resources	Labor		
👤 PM	Project Manager	Labor	$120.00/h	
👤 SE	Systems Engineer	Labor	$90.00/h	
👤 PS	Project Support	Labor	$80.00/h	
👤 PO	Purchasing Officer	Labor	$70.00/h	
👤 CS	Clerical Support	Labor	$50.00/h	
🔷 RB	Report Binding	Material	$100.00/ea	Each

11. You may need to use the arrows on the **Move** toolbar to move the resources to the correct indent location:

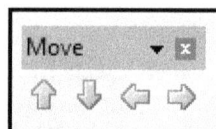

12. Set the **Default Units/Time** to 8 hours per day for all the resources.

13. Set the calendar for all resources to be a Global 5-Day Workweek, with 8 hours per day, yours may be called a Standard 5 Day/Week or similar.

14. Check **Calculate Costs from units** and **Auto compute actuals** for each resource.

15. Ensure that the resource **Effective Date** in the **Units & Prices** tab is set to 1 December 2024 or earlier otherwise the Resource will be delayed beyond this date when Leveling the resources in the Resource Optimization Workshop.

19 ASSIGNING ROLES, RESOURCES AND EXPENSES

During the planning stage, **Roles** may be assigned to Activities to gain an understanding of the long-term resource demand and they are later replaced by a **Resource** when it is known who will be undertaking the work. If you are not using named resources then you should consider not using Roles, as Resources have more functionality than Roles. A Resource may be assigned:

- Directly to an Activity, or
- To a Role which has been assigned to an Activity.

There are three types of resources, **Labor**, **Nonlabor** and **Material**, as discussed in the previous chapter. A Labor Resource has additional functionality including Overtime, Resource Calendars, Shifts and user defined Autocost rules. The **Labor** and **Nonlabor** resources are similar to the Microsoft Project **Work Resources**. A **Material** resource is similar to Microsoft Project **Material Resources** but may not have the units displayed in **Activities Window** columns.

Primavera also has a function titled **Expenses**, where costs may be assigned to activities without resources and may be assigned a quantity and the default quantity is one. This function is similar to the **Cost Resource** function in Microsoft Project. As the project progresses, Actual and To Complete Units and Costs may be assigned to Expenses in the same way as resources. Expense units may not have the units displayed in **Activities Window** columns, may not be assigned Resource Curves, but may have costs assigned before the activity has started, may have Remaining Costs when the activity is complete, and may be assigned to Milestones.

This chapter will cover the following topics:

- Understanding Resource Calculations and Terminology
- Project and Activities Windows Resource and Role Preferences
- Details Status Form
- Activity Types and Duration Types
- Assigning and Removing Roles and Assigning Resources
- Resource and Activity Duration Calculation and Resource Lags
- Expenses
- Suggested Setup for Assigning Resources

	Topic	Menu Commands
•	Set **Units/Time Format** and **Resource Assignments**	Select **Edit**, **User Preferences…** to open the **User Preferences** form and select the **Time Units** tab and **Calculations** tab.
•	Set **Default Duration Type** and **Default Activity Type**	Set these defaults in the **Defaults** tab in the **Projects Window**.
•	Assign a **Role** to an Activity	Select the Resources tab in the Activity Details form and click on the 🔲 icon on the **Assign** toolbar to open the Assign Roles form.
•	To assign a **Resource** to a **Role** that has been assigned to an activity	Select the Role to be assigned a Resource from the **Resources Details** tab and click the 🔲 icon on the **Assign** toolbar to open the **Assign Resources By Roles** form.
•	To assign a **Resource** to an activity without a **Role**	Select the Activity to be assigned the Resource and click the 🔲 icon on the **Assign** toolbar to open the **Assign Resource** form.

19.1 Understanding Resource Calculations and Terminology

A Resource has three principal components after it has been assigned to an Activity:

- **Quantity**, in terms of **Work** in hours or days or **Material** quantities required to complete the activity, which are referred to as **Units** by Primavera,

- The **Resource Unit Rate** is termed **Price/Unit** in Primavera, and

- **Cost**, which is calculated from the **Price/Unit** x **Units**.

Each Resource and Expense has the same four fields for **Costs** and **Units**, which are **Budget**, **Remaining**, **Actual** and **At Completion**. The relationship among these fields changes depending on whether the activity is Not Started, In-Progress or Complete.

- When an activity is Not Started and the % Complete is zero then:

  - **Budget** is normally linked to **Remaining** and **At Completion** and therefore a change to one will change the other two and they will always be equal, and

  - **Actual** will be zero.

- When the activity is marked Started and would normally be In-Progress and the % Complete is between 0.1% and 99.9% then:

  - **Budget** becomes unlinked from **Remaining** and **At Completion**, thus allowing progress and the **At Completion** value to be compared to the **Budget** value (of the current schedule), or a **Baseline Budget** value or a **Baseline At Completion** value, and

  - **At Completion = Actual + Remaining** and have a link to **Units % Complete**, where a change in value to one will result in a change to the other values.

- When the activity is Complete and the **Units % Complete** is 100% then:

  - **Remaining** is set to zero, and

  - **At Completion = Actual**.

The Budget values for Costs and Units are linked to the At Completion values until:

- An Activity has been marked as Started or has a % Complete, or

- The **Link Budget and At Completion for not started activities** in the **Project Window Calculations** tab is unchecked, see the following picture:

i   This function in P6 also unlinks the **Original Duration** from the **At Completion Duration** for un-started activities which adds another complication that should be avoided.

The comparison of the current At Completion Costs is normally made with the Baseline project Budget or Baseline project At Completion values. Therefore, the Budget value in the current schedule is effectively a redundant value and probably should not be displayed.

19.2   Project Window Resource Preferences

Preferences set in the **Activities Window** decide how each individual activity and resource is calculated and are covered in the next section.

Preferences and defaults (which may be changed for each resource assignment) affect how all resources in a project are calculated are set in the **Project Window** and pertain to all activities and resources.

19.2.1   Resources Tab

The **Resources** tab in the P6 Professional **Projects Window** has had the Progress Reporter (called Timesheets in Version 6.2 and earlier) removed.

Assignment Defaults

- There are five Resource Rates available in Primavera. One rate may be set as a project default. After assignment to an activity, the Resource Rate may be changed using the **Rate Type** field in the **Resources** tab of the **Activities Window**.

Drive activity dates by default

- This is covered in more detail in the next section.

Resource Assignments

- Checking the **Resources can be assigned to the same activity more than once** box enables a resource to be assigned to an activity more than once. This is useful if it is required to assign a resource at the beginning of an activity and later at the end of an activity with a lag.

  For example, one may want to assign a crane on the first day of the activity to assist in erecting and one on the last day to assist in dismantling. This check box needs to be checked for a resource to be assigned twice to an activity.

19.2.2   Understanding Resource Option to Drive Activity Dates

A resource has the following fields that are linked and a change to the **Original lag** or **Original Duration** will make a change to one or both dates:

- **Original Lag**. The duration from the Activity Start Date to the Resource Start Date, which is the date the resource commences work.

- **Original Duration**. The duration that a resource is working.

- **Start**. The Resource Start Date=Activity Start Date + the Resource Original Lag.

- **Finish**. This date is calculated by the addition of the Activity Start Date + Original Lag + the Original Duration.

When the **Drive Activity Dates** option is switched off it is possible for a resource to be scheduled outside the activity duration. In the following example the activities are 5 days long and the resources assigned to each activity are working for 10 days. This has resulted in the resource being overloaded. The Resources acknowledge the activity Start date but not the Finish Date.

Now the **Drive Activity Dates** option has been checked against each activity, the activities are now 10 days long, and the resource is not overloaded.

It is recommended that the **Drive activity dates by default** box is always checked, thus Resources will be assigned as **Drive Activity Dates** and this ensures that all work is contained within the duration of an activity.

The Activity Start is controlled by the Activity Calendar, therefore when an activity is Resource Driven it is important to set an Activity Calendar that will allow the resource to start work when it is required to start. Thus, if there is a morning shift starting at 4:00 am, the Activity Calendar should start at 4:00 am or earlier.

In schedules with complex resource calendars may wish to consider placing all the Resource Driven activities on a 24x7 calendar and then all resource work will be controlled by the resource calendars.

19.2.3 Calculations Tab

The **Calculations** tab in the **Projects Window**:

Activities – Default Price/Unit for activities without resource Price/Units.

This rate is also used to calculate the resource costs when an activity is not assigned roles or resources but has been assigned a quantity in the **Activities Window**, **Status** tab.

The other functions in this tab affect the updating of resourced activities and are covered in the **Updating a Resourced Schedule** chapter.

19.3 User Preferences Applicable to Assigning Resources

Select **Edit**, **User Preferences...** to open the **User Preferences** form:

19.3.1 Units/Time Format

Select the **Time Units** tab. The **Units/Time Format** enables Microsoft Project-style formatting of **Resource/Time Format** showing Resource utilization as a percentage or as units per duration.

> **Units/Time Format**
>
> Resource Units/Time can be shown as a percentage or as units per duration
>
> ○ Show as a percentage (50%)
>
> ● Show as units/duration (4h/d)

19.3.2 Resource Assignments

The **Calculations** tab has two **Resource Assignment** options:

> **Resource Assignments**
>
> When adding or removing multiple resource assignments on activities
>
> ● Preserve the Units, Duration, and Units/Time for existing assignments
>
> ○ Recalculate the Units, Duration, and Units/Time for existing assignments based on the activity Duration Type

- **Preserve the Units, Duration, and Units/Time for existing assignments**. With this option, as Resources are added or deleted the total number of hours assigned to an activity increases or decreases. Each Resource's hours are calculated independently.

- **Recalculate the Units, Duration, and Units/Time for existing assignments based on the activity Duration Type**. The total number of hours assigned to an activity will stay constant as second and subsequent resources are added or removed from an activity. Thus, the work assigned against a resource is reduced as more resources are assigned to the activity.

  NOTE: This function does not work when the Activity Type is **Fixed Duration and Units/Time**.

> *i*
>
> The **Recalculate the Units, Duration, and Units/Time for existing assignments based on the activity Duration Type** function is similar to the Microsoft Project Effort Driven function and the **Preserve the Units, Duration, and the Units/Time for existing assignments** is the same as Non Effort Driven.
>
> It is recommended that **Preserve the Units, Duration, and Units/Time for existing assignments** be used as a default as each individual resource assignment does not change as resources are added or removed from an activity.

19.3.3 Assignment Staffing

The **Assignment Staffing** option is self-explanatory and should be considered carefully when resources and roles have different rates. If it is not understood and set correctly the resource may end up with the incorrect unit rate when assigned to a Role or existing Resource.

When two users have different settings, this may result in a schedule having two different rates for the same resource.

19.4 Activities Window Resource Preferences and Defaults

19.4.1 Details Status Form

This form has a section titled **Labor Units** at the right side as seen in the following picture. The drop-down menu enables you to select which data is to be displayed in this section of the form.

There is a link between the entries in this form and the values that are assigned to resources:

- The values in this form are the sum of the values assigned to Resources and Roles.
- When these values are edited, they will change the values assigned to Resources and Roles.

NOTE: It is possible to enter a **Labor Unit** value in the **Status** tab and not assign a resource. When a resource is assigned the resource will adopt this value in the **Status** tab. This rate is set in the **Calculations** tab in the **Projects Window, Activities tab – Default Price/Unit for activities without resource or Roles Price/Units** field.

19.4.2 Activity Type

There are five **Activity Types** assigned in the **General tab** in the **Activities Window**:

Activity Type	Notes
Task Dependent	Activities assigned as Task Dependent acknowledge their **Activity Calendar** when scheduling and the Finish Date is calculated from the Activity Calendar. Resources ignore their Resource Calendar and scheduled on the Task Calendar.
Resource Dependent	Activities assigned as Resource Dependent acknowledge their **Resource Calendar** when being scheduled. This is similar to an Independent Activity Type in P3 and SureTrak and the resources work independently and do not have to be available at the same time.
	The Activity Finish Date is calculated based on the longest Resource Duration when the resource option of **Drive Activity Dates** is checked against the resource assignment.
	NOTE: The activity start date is still calculated on the activity calendar, not the resource calendar, may delay the start of an activity when the resource calendar has longer working hours than the activity calendar.
Start Milestone	This Activity Type is used to indicate the commencement of a Phase, Stage, or a major event in a project.
	• It has only a Start Date and no Duration or Finish Date.
	• It may only have **Start Constraints** assigned.
	• It may not have time-dependent resources assigned but may have:
	➤ An **Owner** assigned from the list of users to indicate who is responsible for the activity. "Owner," enables a user who is **NOT** a resource to be assigned responsibility for an activity.
	➤ A **Primary Resource** assigned from the **Activities Window**, **General** tab who may update the Milestone, but no effort is assigned or recorded.

Activity Type	Notes

Finish Milestone	This Activity Type is used to indicate the completion of a Phase, Stage, or a major event in a project.
	
	• It has only a Finish Date and no Duration or Start Date.
	
	• It may only have **Finish Constraints** assigned.
	
	• It may not have time-dependent resources assigned but may have:
	
	  ➤ An **Owner** assigned from the list of users to indicate who is responsible for the activity. "Owner," the new activity field in Primavera Version 6.0, enables a user who is **NOT** a resource to be assigned responsibility for an activity.
	
	  ➤ A **Primary Resource** assigned from the **Activities Window**, **General** tab who may update the Milestone, but no effort is assigned or recorded.

Level of Effort (LOE)	This Activity Type spans other Activities. Therefore, the Start Date, Finish Date, and Durations may change as the start or finish date of activities that it is dependent upon change during scheduling or updating. There is no equivalent in Microsoft Project. Elecosoft (Asta) Powerproject has **Hammock** tasks and **Buffer Tasks** which calculate differently but may achieve the same results. This type of activity does not create a critical path irrespective of the float calculations that are displayed. The Start Date may be controlled by the following relationships: • Finish-to-Start predecessors • Start-to-Start predecessors • Start-to-Finish successors • Start-to-Start Successors The Finish Date may be controlled by the following relationships: • Finish-to-Finish predecessors • Start-to-Finish predecessors • Finish-to-Start successors • Finish-to-Finish successors Resources assigned to a Level of Effort activity are not considered in calculations when a schedule is **Leveled**. Level of Effort activities may not be assigned a **Constraint**. When creating a **LOE** activity and the bar is not displayed, check the **Bars** form to ensure a LOE bar has been created and is being displayed.

Activity Type	Notes
WBS Summary Activity	The new Primavera Version 5.0 **WBS Summary Activity** is an activity that spans the duration of all activities which are assigned exactly the same WBS Code and, unlike a Level of Effort Activity, do not have any predecessors or successors.

Therefore, a WBS activity will change duration when either the earliest start or latest finish of activities that it spans is changed. This may happen as the project progresses and activities do not meet their original scheduled dates, or the duration of an activity is changed, or logic is changed, or the schedule is leveled.

This function calculates the WBS Activity Duration in the same way as Elecosoft (Asta) Powerproject WBS or Summary activities. This is also similar to the way Summary activity durations are calculated in Microsoft Project and Elecosoft (Asta) Powerproject, except the activities do not need to be demoted below the detailed activities in as Microsoft Project and Elecosoft (Asta) Powerproject.

WBS activities may be used for:

- Reporting at summary level by filtering on WBS activities,

- Entering estimated costs at summary level for producing cash flow tables while the detailed activities are used for calculating the overall duration for the WBS and day-to-day management of the project, and

- Recording costs and hours at summary level when is it not desirable or practical to record at activity level, especially when the detailed activities are liable to change.

It does not matter how activities are Grouped as they always span activities with the same WBS Code.

19.4.3 Duration Type

The Duration Type becomes effective after a resource has been assigned to an activity.

The **Duration** Type for all new activities is set in the **Defaults** tab in the **Projects Window** and all new activities are assigned this Duration Type.

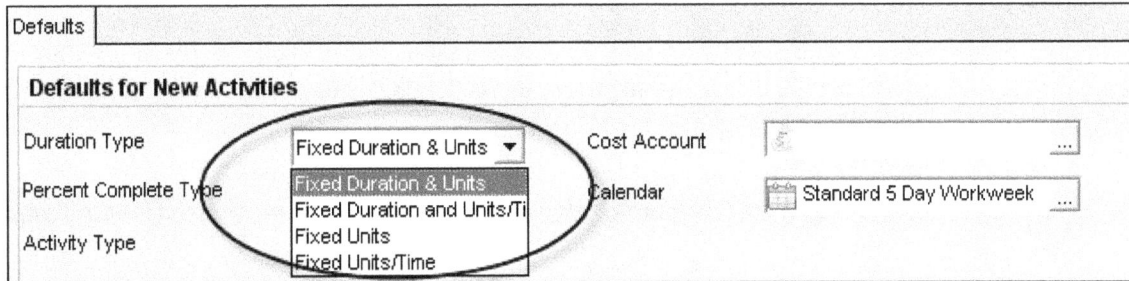

The **Duration Type** for each new activity may be changed in the **General** tab in the **Activities Window** or by displaying the **Duration Type** column:

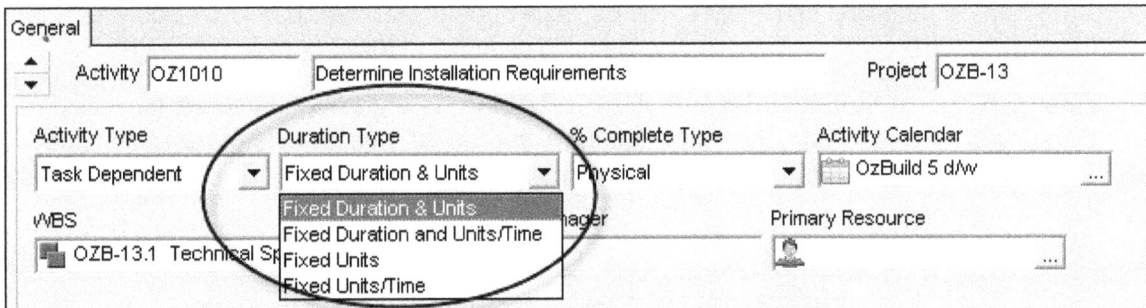

The Duration Type determines which of the following variables change when one of the others is changed in the equation:

- Resource Units = Resource Units per Time Period x Duration

For example, a 40-hour activity with 2 people working 8 hours per day will take 20 hours or 2.5 days:

- 40 hours of work = 2 people per hour x 20 hours

When an activity is in-progress this equation is modified to:

- Remaining Resource Units = Resource Units per Time period x Remaining Duration

Primavera has four options for Duration Type, Microsoft Project has three options.

Primavera terminology that describes the way the software treats the relationship between Durations, Resource Units and Resource Units/Time Period is different from Microsoft Project and Elecosoft (Asta) Powerproject. Primavera has more options than all the other products and this gives the product more flexibility. The following table should clarify these options.

It is unfortunate that unlike earlier Primavera software it is not possible to assign the Duration Type to each individual resource, thus this makes it difficult to model mining and earthworks operations where normally the materials are made Fixed Units and the mobile equipment as Fixed Units/time period.

Purposes of the Duration Types

Duration Type	Purpose
• Fixed Duration & Units	**Option 1** This option is used when the Duration of an activity should not change when Resources are added or removed or Units/Time changed. For example, when the time to complete an activity is fixed, the resources may be manipulated until a satisfactory resource loading is established without the activity duration changing. **Option 2** A change to the Duration will change the Units/Time; however, the Units will remain constant. If one person is assigned to an activity for 8 hours per day and the activity is doubled in duration, there will now be one person working on the activity for 4 hours per day and the activity will require the same number of hours to complete. **IMPORTANT POINT:** The Estimate at Completion **WILL NOT** change when the activity duration is changed and the number of resources **WILL** change.
• Fixed Duration & Units/Time	This **Duration Type** disables the **User Preferences**, **Calculations** tab option **Recalculate the Units, Duration, and Units/Time for existing assignments based on the activity Duration Type**. **Option 1** This option is used when the Duration of an activity should not change when Resources are added or removed or Units/Time changed. For example, when the time to complete an activity is fixed, the resources may be manipulated until a satisfactory resource loading is established without the activity duration changing. **Option 2** A change in the Duration will change the Units; however, the Units/Time will remain constant. For example, when there are two people assigned to an activity and the activity is increased in duration, there will still be two people working but for a longer period of time. **IMPORTANT POINT:** The Estimate at Completion **WILL** change when the activity duration is changed and the number of resources **WILL NOT** change.
• Fixed Units	This option is used when the amount of work required to finish an activity is constant. For example, if there are 8,000 bricks to be laid and a bricklayer is able to lay 100 bricks per hour, there are 80 hours of work for one bricklayer, 40 hours for 2 bricklayers and 20 hours for 4 bricklayers. Changing the Duration or the Units/Time will not change the number of hours required to complete the activity.
• Fixed Units/Time	This option is used when the same number of people are required to complete an activity irrespective of the activity duration. For example, if a machine requires two people to operate it and therefore a Resource is assigned to the Activity at 200%, changing either the Units or the Duration will not change the Units/Time and there will always be two people operating the machine.

> The duration of both **Fixed Units** and **Fixed Units/Time** activities will change if the resource Units/Time Period or Remaining Units are changed. It is the author's preference to use:
>
> - **Fixed Duration & Units** when the estimate at completion must not change, and
> - **Fixed Duration & Units/Time** when the crew size must remain constant.

The following table displays what happens to the relationship in each of the four options when one variable is changed and

- The **User Preferences, Calculations** tab option **Preserve the Units, Duration, and Units/Time for existing assignments** is selected:

Duration Type	Labor Units Change in Status Tab	Activity Duration Change	Resource Units Change	Units/Time Period Change	Add or Remove Resources
Fixed Units/Time	Duration Change	Units Change	Duration Change	Duration Change	Activity Units Change, Resource Units Constant, Duration Constant
Fixed Duration & Units/Time	Units/Time Change	Units Change	Units/Time Change	Units Change	Activity Units Change, Resource Units Constant, Duration Constant
Fixed Units	Duration Change	Units/Time Change	Duration Change	Duration Change	Activity Units Change, Resource Units Constant, Duration Constant
Fixed Duration & Units	Units/Time Change	Units/Time Change	Units/Time Change	Units Change	Activity Units Change, Resource Units Constant, Duration Constant

The following table displays what happens to the relationship in each of the four options when one variable is changed and

- The **User Preferences, Calculations** tab option **Recalculate the Units, Duration, and Units/Time for existing assignments based on the activity Duration Type** is selected:

Duration Type	Labor Units Change in Status Tab	Activity Duration Change	Resource Units Change	Units/Time Period Change	Add or Remove Resources
Fixed Units/Time	Duration Change	Units Change	Duration Change	Duration Change	**Activity Units Constant, Resource Units Change, Duration Change**
Fixed Duration & Units/Time	Units/Time Change	Units Change	Units/Time Change	Units Change	Activity Units Change, Resource Units Constant, Duration Constant
Fixed Units	Duration Change	Units/Time Change	Duration Change	Duration Change	**Activity Units Constant, Resource Units Change, Duration Change**
Fixed Duration & Units	Units/Time Change	Units/Time Change	Units/Time Change	Units Change	**Activity Units Constant, Resource Units Change,** Duration Constant

- Bold descriptions in the right column in the table indicate the differences from the upper table.
- The **User Preferences, Calculations** tab option **Preserve the Units, Duration, and Units/Time for existing assignments** will not freeze the Activity Units when the **Duration Type** of **Fixed Units** is selected.

19.5   Assigning and Removing Roles

To assign a Role to an activity:

- Select the one or more activity to be assigned the Role,

- Select the **Resources** tab in the **Activity Details** form,

- Click on the ⬛ **Roles... Assign** toolbar icon to open the **Assign Roles** form,

- Use the **Display:**, **Filter By** menu to select either:

  ➢ **All Roles**, which will display all Roles in the database,

  ➢ **Current Project's Roles**. This option will only display Roles that have been assigned to this project, or

  ➢ **Customize**, which opens a **Filter** form enabling the user to limit the number of displayed Roles by creating a filter.

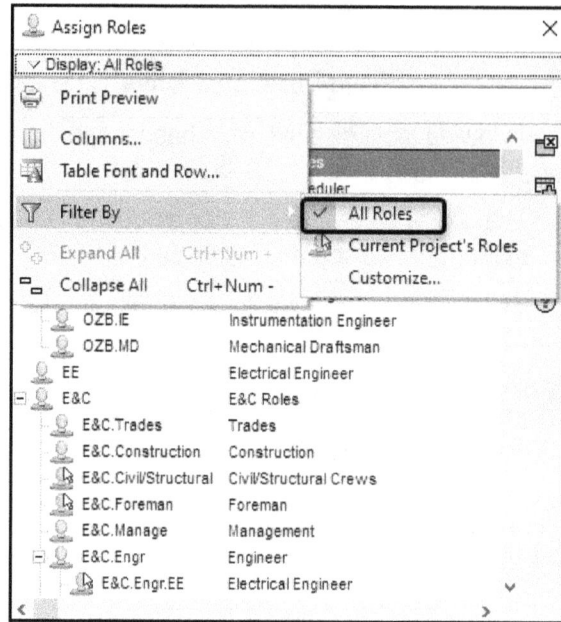

- Select one or more Roles to be assigned to an activity using the **Ctrl**-click function,

- Then to assign a Role:

  ➢ Click on the 🔲 icon, or

  ➢ Double-click one of the Roles.

To achieve the following picture, you may need to format the columns in the **Resources Details** form.

At this point, the Roles hours and costs may be edited as required.

To remove a Role:

- Select the Role, and

- Click on the [🔲 Remove] icon.

19.6   Assigning and Removing Resources

Resources may be assigned directly to:

- An activity that has an Assigned Role, or
- An Activity without a Role.

19.6.1   Assigning a Resource to an Assigned Role

To assign a Resource to a Role assigned to an activity:

- Select the activity to be assigned a Resource,
- Select the Role to be assigned a Resource from the **Resources Details** tab,
- Click on the ▥ **Resources by Role…** **Assign** toolbar icon to open the **Assign Resources By Roles** form,
- Click on the **Display:** menu and select **Filter By** to open the **Filter By** form,
  - ➢ **All Roles Required**: Chooses to view all roles assigned to the activity.
  - ➢ **Staffed Roles:** Displays Roles with an assigned resource.
  - ➢ **Unstaffed Roles Required:** Displays Roles without an assigned resource.
  - ➢ **Unstaffed Roles with Required Proficiency:** Displays Roles without an assigned resource and requires a resource with a specific proficiency level.
- Select which Resources you wish to have displayed in the **Assign Roles** form from the **Filter By** form,
- Select ▣ Apply to return to the **Assign Resources By Role** form,
- From the **Assign Resources By Role** form click the Resource you wish to assign,
- To assign the Resource either:
  - ➢ Double-click the Resource, or
  - ➢ Click on the ▦ icon.

19.6.2 Assigning a Resource to an Activity Without a Role

To assign a Resource to an activity:

- Select the activity to be assigned the Resource,

- Click on the 🔲 **Resources... Assign** toolbar icon to open the **Assign Resource** form,

- Click on the **Display:** menu and select **Filter By** and then select from the three options which resources you wish to display in the **Assign Resources** form,

- To assign the Resource either:
  - ➤ Double-click the Resource, or
  - ➤ Click on the 🔲 icon.

You may now edit the hours or Units/Time Period for each resource.

19.6.3 Removing a Resource

Before you remove a Resource from an activity that has more than one resource assigned to it, you must be aware of your **Resource Assignment** preferences. These preferences determine if the total number of Units assigned to the activity (or work) will be reduced or remain constant as resources are deleted.

To remove a resource, select one or more Resources in the bottom pane Resource tab and either:

- Strike the **Del** key, or

- Click on the 🔲 Remove icon at the bottom of the screen, not the ✖ on the **Edit** toolbar.

After the last resource is removed there will be the message:

- If you select ✔ Yes then the Resource Units values in the **Activities Window**, **Status tab** will be set to zero, and the Resource Costs in the **Activities Window**, **Status tab** will be calculated from the value entered.

If you select [✗ No] then:

- The Units values in the **Activities Window**, **Status tab** will be set to equal the Resource values before they were deleted, and

- The Cost values in the **Activities Window**, **Status tab** will be calculated from the value set in **Calculations** tab in the **Projects Window.**

Calculations	
Activities	**Resource Assignments**
Default Price / Unit for activities without resource or role Price / Units **$50/h**	When updating Actual Units or Cost
	○ Add Actual to Remaining
	◉ Subtract Actual from At Completion
☐ Activity percent complete based on activity steps	
	☑ Recalculate Actual Units and Cost when duration % complete changes
☑ Link Budget and At Completion for not started activities	
	☐ Update units when costs change on resource assignments
○ Reset Original Duration and Units to Remaining	
◉ Reset Remaining Duration and Units to Original	☑ Link actual to date and actual this period units and costs

- At this point you will have Units and Costs assigned to an activity that may be seen in the **Activities Window**, **Status tab** without any assigned resources, which may not be desirable.

∨ Labor Units		∨ Labor Cost	
Budgeted	80h	Budgeted	$4,000
Actual	0h	Actual	$0
Remaining	80h	Remaining	$4,000
At Complete	80h	At Complete	$4,000

⚠ When you assign a resource to an activity in this condition the resource will adopt the Units value from the **Activities Window**, **Status tab**, ignoring the **Default Units /Time Period** set in the **Resource Window**, but normally calculate the resource value from the resource Rate.

19.6.4 Assigning a Resource to an Activity More Than Once

The option in the **Projects Window Resources** tab under the **Resources Assignments** heading enables a resource to be assigned more than once to an activity.

Resources	
Resource Assignments	
☑ Resources can be assigned to the same activity more than once	

A resource could be assigned to work at the start of an activity and then in conjunction with **Resource Lag** work again at the end of an activity.

19.7   Resource and Activity Duration Calculation and Resource Lags

19.7.1   Activity Duration

An Activity Duration (or Activity Remaining Duration of an In-Progress Activity) is adopted from the longest Resource Duration (or Resource Remaining Duration of an In-Progress Activity) when more than one resource has been assigned to an activity.

In a situation where more than one Resource has been assigned to an activity with different Units and/or Units/Time, the Resources may have different durations.

In the following example the Activity Duration is 10 days, which is calculated from David William's **Resource Original Duration** of 10 days:

Activity ID	Activity Name	Original Duration
A1050	Duartion Type - Fixed Units	10d

General | Resources | Status

Activity A1050   Duartion Type - Fixed Units

Role ID	Resource ID Name	Original Lag	Original Duration	Remaining Units	Remaining Units / Time
Oz.SE	ARL.Angela Lowe	0d	5d	40.00h	100%
Oz.BM	DTW.David Williams	0d	10d	40.00h	50%
Oz.CS	MAY.Melinda Young	0d	5d	40.00h	100%

19.7.2   Resource Lag

A Resource may be assigned a Lag, the duration from the start of the activity to the point at which the Resource commences work.

In the following example the Activity Duration is 12 days, which is calculated from Angela Lowe's **Resource Original Lag** of 7 days and **Resource Original Duration** of 5 days:

Activity ID	Activity Name	Original Duration
A1050	Duartion Type - Fixed Units	12d

General | Resources | Status

Activity A1050   Duartion Type - Fixed Units

Role ID	Resource ID Name	Original Lag	Original Duration	Remaining Units	Remaining Units / Time
Oz.SE	ARL.Angela Lowe	7d	5d	40.00h	100%
Oz.BM	DTW.David Williams	0d	10d	40.00h	50%
Oz.CS	MAY.Melinda Young	0d	5d	40.00h	100%

19.8 Expenses

Expenses are intended to be used for one off non-resource type costs and could include, travel costs, insurance costs, and training courses and are deleted when the activity is deleted.

- Expenses may be created using the:
  - ➤ **Project Expenses** window and assigned to an activity in this form, or
  - ➤ The **Activities**, **Expenses** tab.

- Expenses have a **Budget**, **Actual**, **Remaining** and **At Completion** quantity (**Units**) and a unit price (**Price / Unit**), which are linked in the same way as resources and may:
  - ➤ Have an **Actual Cost** assigned before an activity starts, say to represent an upfront mobilization payment,
  - ➤ May be negative, say to represent a contractor charge back,
  - ➤ Have a **Remaining Cost** after an activity is complete, say to represent contract retention.

- Expenses costs may be seen in activity views such as the **Activity Usage Spread Sheet** and **Activity Usage Profile.**

- Expenses costs may **NOT** be seen in any resource vies such as the **Resource Usage Spread Sheet** or **Resource Usage Profile** or **Resource Assignments** window, therefore a complete cash flow may not be obtained from any resource view.

- It is also very difficult to get expense quantities out of P6, one has to create or edit and existing report, but this will not show Baseline Expense quantities and there no way of obtaining a time phased Expense consumption in units.

19.8.1 Expenses Window

The **Expenses Window** is opened by:

Expense Item	Expense Category	Vendor
🏛 Training Manuals	Training	Eastwood Harris Pty Ltd
🏛 Primavera Training Course	Training	Eastwood Harris Pty Ltd

- Clicking in the 🏛 icon on the **Project** toolbar, or
- Selecting **Project**, **Expenses**.

Creating a new **Expense** is similar to creating a new activity:

General | **Activity** | **Costs** | **Description**

Expense Item
Training Manuals

Expense Category
🏛 Training

Vendor
Eastwood Harris Pty Ltd

Cost Account
🔹 Con.11.4 Training

Document Number
110803 P6V81S

- Select **Edit**, **Add**, and
- The **Select Activity** form will then be displayed and the activity the expense is to be associated with is selected.

Enter the following Information in the tabs in the bottom window:

- **General Tab**
  - ➤ **Expense Item** – A free form field to enter the description of the Expense.
  - ➤ **Vendor** – A free form field to enter the vendor or supplier name.
  - ➤ **Expense Category** – These are created in the **Admin Categories** form.
  - ➤ **Cost Account** – Select a **Cost Account** should you wish to see or report the costs against a Cost Account. Costs accounts are created in a similar method to other hierarchical structures in Primavera, such as the WBS, by selecting **Enterprise**, **Cost Accounts**....

> **Document Number** – A free form field to enter the document number that could represent the Purchase Order, Contract, or Invoice Number.

- **Activity** tab displays information mainly adopted from an activity, the Accrual Type, is editable:
  > **Accrual Type** – this enables you to select if the costs are accrued or cash flowed at the beginning, end, or uniformly over the duration of the activity.

- **Costs** tab is mainly self-explanatory. The following information is entered:
  > **Budgeted Units, Actual Units**, **Remaining Units** and **At Completion Units** – the quantity of the Expense item. When an Expense is created it is set a default value of 1. If set to zero then the costs are set to zero and costs may now not be entered.

  > **Price/Unit** – the cost per Expense item,

  > **Unit of Measure** – the units of the Expense; for example, each, foot, meter, etc.

  > Check **Auto Compute Actuals** should allow the software to calculate the Actual and Remaining Costs and Units (quantities) based on the **planned completion percentage** but the author could not make this option operate and always has to manually update Expenses.

  > The remainder of the fields are used when the activity is progressed.

| General | Activity | Costs | Description |

Budgeted Units	Actual Units	Remaining Units	At Completion Units
10.000	0.000	10.000	10.000

Price/Unit	Unit of Measure
$100	each

Budgeted Cost	Actual Cost	Remaining Cost	At Completion Cost
$1,000	$0	$1,000	$1,000

Expense % Complete: 0% ☐ Auto Compute Actuals

- **Description** tab is where you enter an extended description of the Expense item.

19.8.2 Expenses Tab in the Activities Window

This tab may have all the columns of data available in the **Expenses Window** displayed. All the fields may be edited from this tab:

Activity ID	Activity Name		January 2014				February 2014				March 2014			
			06	13	20	27	03	10	17	24	03	10	17	24
P6 Training														
A1000	Primavera Training Course													

Expenses

Activity: A1000 — Primavera Training Course   Project: Training

Expense Item	Accrual Type	Price / Unit	Unit of Measure	Remaining Units	Budgeted Cost
Primavera Training Course	Uniform over Activity	$1,600	day	3.000	$4,800
Training Manuals	Uniform over Activity	$100	each	10.000	$1,000

19.9 Suggested Setup for Creating a Resourced Schedule

The order that topics are introduced in this chapter is also a satisfactory order of actions that should be considered when preparing to assign resources to activities.

The simplest calculation options should be used as a default, and more complex options considered only when there is a specific scheduling requirement.

The table following lists processes and suggested options that could be considered when creating a resourced schedule. It is important to set all the parameters before the activities are added otherwise a lot of time is wasted changing parameters on a number of activities. These are not intended to suit every project but are a starting point for less experienced users.

Step	Suggested Settings
• Set the **Units/Time** format by selecting **Edit**, **User Preferences…** to open the **User Preferences** form and select the **Time Units** tab.	There is a choice of **percentage (50%)** or **units/duration (4h/d)**. This should be set on personal preference. The author prefers **(4h/d)** as this reduces typing. The **User Preferences**, **Time Units** setting affects how these are displayed and 16h/d or 2d/d or 200% is two people.
• Set the **Resource Assignments** option by selecting **Edit**, **User Preferences…** to open the **User Preferences** form and select the **Calculations** tab.	It is suggested that the **Preserve the Units, Duration, and Units/Time for existing assignments** is selected. With this option as Resources are added or deleted the total number of hours assigned to an Activity increases or decreases. Each Resource's hours are calculated independently. The options under **Assignment Staffing** need to be carefully considered and understood so that when Resources are assigned to Roles and resource assignments are changed that the user understands which Unit Rate and which Unit Cost will remain against the activity.
• In the **Project Window**, **Defaults** tab set the default **Activity Type**.	It is suggested that **Task Dependent** is used, as with this option Resource calendars are not used making the schedule simpler.
• In the **Project Window**, **Defaults** tab set the default **Duration Type**.	It is suggested that **Fixed Duration & Units** is used. With this option the Activity Duration does not change when resource assignments are altered, and when an Activity Duration is changed the Units do not change, so your estimate of hours and costs will not change. When you wish the crew size to remain the same when the activity duration is changed then you should select **Fixed Duration & Units/Time**. The cost and units will change proportionally.
• In the **Project Window**, **Defaults** tab set the default **Percent Complete Type**.	The author prefers to use **Physical** as this enables the Activity Percent Complete to be independent of the Activity Durations.
• In the **Project Window**, **Resource** tab set the default **Resource Assignment Defaults**.	Unless multiple Rates are being used then **Price/Unit** should be selected. Check **Drive activity dates by default**.

19.10 Workshop 16 – Assigning Resources and Expenses to Activities

Background

The Resources must now be assigned to their specific activities.

Assignment

Open the OzBuild with Resources project and complete the following steps.

1. Apply the **OzBuild Workshop 10 – Without Float** layout and save as **OzBuild Workshop 16 – Assigning Resources** layout.

2. In the **Activities Window** display the **Gantt Chart** in the top view and **Resources** and **Expenses** tab of the **Activities Details** form in the bottom view.

3. Assign an Expense to the **Create Technical Specification** activity as per the picture below:

Expenses					
Activity	OZ1020		Create Technical Specification		
Expense Item	Accrual Type	Price / Unit	Budgeted Cost	Budgeted Units
Specialists Consultant	Uniform over Activity	$5,000.00	$5,000.00	1.000

4. Format the **Resources** tab with the columns shown in the following picture:

Resources					
Activity	OZ1010		Determine Installation Requirements		
Resource ID Name	Price / Unit	Default Units / Time	At Completion Units	At Completion Cost
PM.Project Manager	$120.00/h	8/d	32	$3,840.00
SE.Systems Engineer	$90.00/h	8/d	32	$2,880.00

5. Set your **User Preferences** as in the picture below:

User Preferences				✕
Time Units	**Units Format**			
Dates	Unit of Time	Sub-unit	Decimals	
Currency	Hour ▼	☐ Minutes	1 ▼	
E-Mail	☑ Show Unit label		Example 40.5h	
Assistance				

continued....

---

6. Add the **Resources** column to the Gantt Chart per the picture below.

7. Assign the following Resources to the Activities using the **Resource** tab [Add Resource] icon:

Activity ID	Activity Name	Resources
Bid for Facility Extension		
Technical Specification		
OZ1000	Approval to Bid	
OZ1010	Determine Installation Requirements	Project Manager, Systems Engineer
OZ1020	Create Technical Specification	Systems Engineer
OZ1030	Identify Supplier Components	Purchasing Officer
OZ1040	Validate Technical Specification	Project Manager, Systems Engineer
Delivery Plan		
OZ1050	Document Delivery Methodology	Project Manager
OZ1060	Obtain Quotes from Suppliers	Purchasing Officer, Project Manager
OZ1070	Calculate Bid Estimate	Project Support
OZ1080	Create the Project Schedule	Project Support
OZ1090	Review the Delivery Plan	Project Manager, Systems Engineer
Bid Document		
OZ1100	Create Draft of Bid Document	Clerical Support, Project Manager
OZ1110	Review Bid Document	Project Manager, Systems Engineer
OZ1120	Finalise and Submit Bid Document	Project Manager, Report Binding
OZ1130	Bid Docuement Submitted	

8. Enter 3 as the Budgeted Units and At Completion Units for the Report Binding.

9. Add the columns per below and your answer should look like this:

Activity ID	Activity Name	Resources	At Completion Labor Units	At Completion Labor Cost	At Completion Expense	At Completion Material Cost	At Completion Total Cost
Bid for Facility Extension			520h	$49,760.00	$5,000.00	$300.00	$55,060.00
Technical Specification			152h	$14,800.00	$5,000.00	$0.00	$19,800.00
OZ1000	Approva		0h	$0.00	$0.00	$0.00	$0.00
OZ1010	Determir	Project Manager, Systems Engineer	64h	$6,720.00	$0.00	$0.00	$6,720.00
OZ1020	Create T	Systems Engineer	40h	$3,600.00	$5,000.00	$0.00	$8,600.00
OZ1030	Identify	Purchasing Officer	16h	$1,120.00	$0.00	$0.00	$1,120.00
OZ1040	Validate	Project Manager, Systems Engineer	32h	$3,360.00	$0.00	$0.00	$3,360.00
Delivery Plan			224h	$21,520.00	$0.00	$0.00	$21,520.00
OZ1050	Docume	Project Manager	32h	$3,840.00	$0.00	$0.00	$3,840.00
OZ1060	Obtain C	Purchasing Officer, Project Manager	128h	$12,160.00	$0.00	$0.00	$12,160.00
OZ1070	Calculat	Project Support	24h	$1,920.00	$0.00	$0.00	$1,920.00
OZ1080	Create tl	Project Support	24h	$1,920.00	$0.00	$0.00	$1,920.00
OZ1090	Review	Project Manager, Systems Engineer	16h	$1,680.00	$0.00	$0.00	$1,680.00
Bid Document			144h	$13,440.00	$0.00	$300.00	$13,740.00
OZ1100	Create C	Clerical Support, Project Manager	96h	$8,160.00	$0.00	$0.00	$8,160.00
OZ1110	Review	Project Manager, Systems Engineer	32h	$3,360.00	$0.00	$0.00	$3,360.00
OZ1120	Finalise	Project Manager, Report Binding	16h	$1,920.00	$0.00	$300.00	$2,220.00
OZ1130	Bid Doc		0h	$0.00	$0.00	$0.00	$0.00

10. Change the **User Preferences, Time Units, Units Format, Units per Time** to **Days** and see the difference:

User Preferences				✕
Time **U**nits	**Units Format**			
Dates	Unit of Time	Sub-unit	Decimals	
Currency	Day ▼	☐ Hours	1 ▼	
E-Mail				
A**s**sistance	☑ Show Unit label		Example 5.1d	

11. You will notice that there is no column to display the Materials quantity at completion.

Activity ID	Activity Name	Resources	At Completion Labor Units	At Completion Labor Cost	At Completion Expense	At Completion Material Cost	At Completion Total Cost
Bid for Facility Extension			65d	$49,760.00	$5,000.00	$300.00	$55,060.00
Technical Specification			19d	$14,800.00	$5,000.00	$0.00	$19,800.00
OZ1000	Approva		0d	$0.00	$0.00	$0.00	$0.00
OZ1010	Determir	Project Manager, Systems Engineer	8d	$6,720.00	$0.00	$0.00	$6,720.00
OZ1020	Create T	Systems Engineer	5d	$3,600.00	$5,000.00	$0.00	$8,600.00
OZ1030	Identify :	Purchasing Officer	2d	$1,120.00	$0.00	$0.00	$1,120.00
OZ1040	Validate	Project Manager, Systems Engineer	4d	$3,360.00	$0.00	$0.00	$3,360.00
Delivery Plan			28d	$21,520.00	$0.00	$0.00	$21,520.00
OZ1050	Docume	Project Manager	4d	$3,840.00	$0.00	$0.00	$3,840.00
OZ1060	Obtain C	Purchasing Officer, Project Manager	16d	$12,160.00	$0.00	$0.00	$12,160.00
OZ1070	Calculat	Project Support	3d	$1,920.00	$0.00	$0.00	$1,920.00
OZ1080	Create tl	Project Support	3d	$1,920.00	$0.00	$0.00	$1,920.00
OZ1090	Review	Project Manager, Systems Engineer	2d	$1,680.00	$0.00	$0.00	$1,680.00
Bid Document			18d	$13,440.00	$0.00	$300.00	$13,740.00
OZ1100	Create C	Clerical Support, Project Manager	12d	$8,160.00	$0.00	$0.00	$8,160.00
OZ1110	Review	Project Manager, Systems Engineer	4d	$3,360.00	$0.00	$0.00	$3,360.00
OZ1120	Finalise	Project Manager, Report Binding	2d	$1,920.00	$0.00	$300.00	$2,220.00
OZ1130	Bid Doc		0d	$0.00	$0.00	$0.00	$0.00

⚠️ In a multi-user environment it is important that all users have the same User Preferences otherwise each person may display different Quantities at completion.

12. Change the **User Preferences, Time Units, Units Format, Units of Time** to **Hours**.

13. Save your layout as **OzBuild Workshop 16 – Assigning Resources**.

20 RESOURCE OPTIMIZATION

The schedule may now have to be resource optimized to:

- Reduce peaks and smooth the resource requirements, thus reducing the mobilization and demobilization costs, or to reduce the demand for site facilities, or

- Reduce resource demand to the available number of resources, or

- Reduce demand to an available cash flow when a project is financed on income.

20.1 Reviewing Resource Loading

There are a number of facilities for reviewing resource loading which consist of either displaying a Layout or running a report. The Timescale interval affects the displays. Layouts will not be covered in detail, as they are self-explanatory.

20.1.1 Activity Usage Spreadsheet

This window is displayed by clicking on the [icon] icon or selecting **View**, **Show on Bottom**, **Activity Usage Spreadsheet**.

- This displays a total of all the resource costs or units assigned to activities:

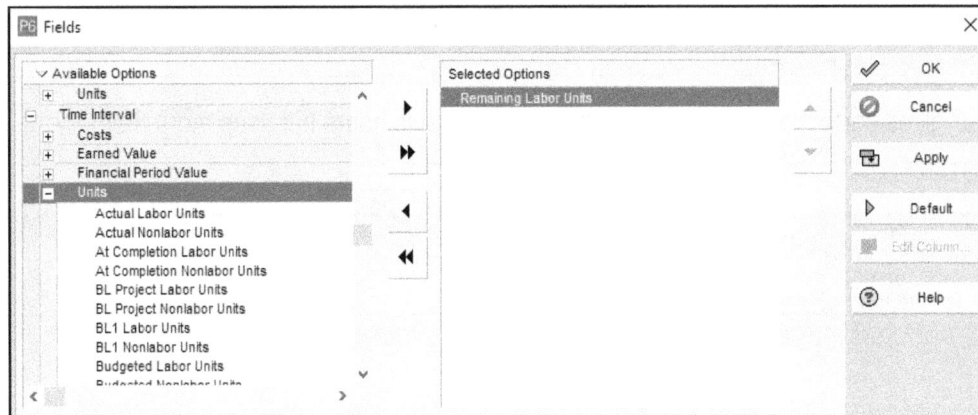

- Right-clicking will display a menu and the **Spreadsheet Fields...** option allows the selection of Cumulative and Time Interval display of Resource and Expenses information.

⚠️ Cumulative **Expense Units** and **Material Resources Units** are not available in this view.

- **Spreadsheet Options...** allows the calculation of the average number of resources:

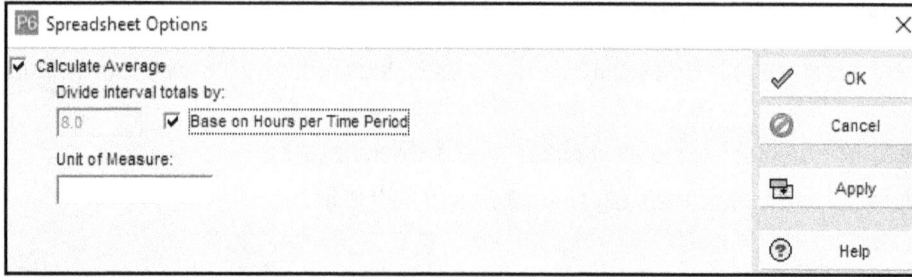

- The **Exclude inactive resources** was added in P6 Version 23 and this option a allows a user to conduct a resource analysis without the inclusion of **Inactive Resources** allowing more accurate reporting when **Inactive Resources** are being used.
  Note: This is a User Preference and thus different users may have different results if they use different Resource Analysis settings.

- The units are formatted using the **User Preferences**, **Time Units** tab. If the minimum time unit is an hour, ensure the **User Preferences**, **Resource Analysis**, **Interval for time-distributed resource** calculations is set to one hour; otherwise, the data will not be displayed correctly when the timescale is opened up to hours,

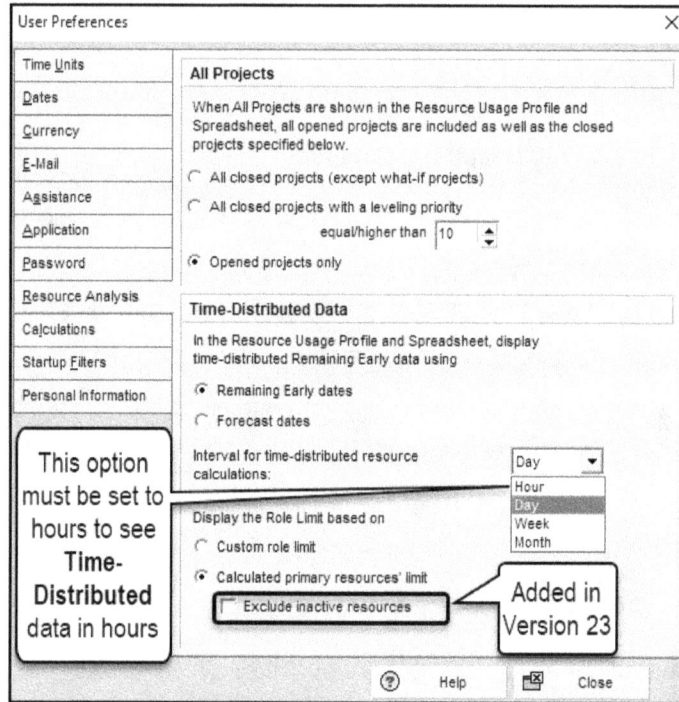

- By **Day** gives incorrect distribution when the time interval is hours but uses less memory:

- By **Hour** gives correct distribution when the time interval is hours but uses more memory:

20.1.2 Activity Usage Profile

This is displayed by clicking on the ⌷ icon or selecting **View**, **Show on Bottom**, **Activity Usage Profile**.

- It displays the total resource histogram for selected or all activities. Right-click the Histogram for the display options:

- The **Activity Usage Profile Options…** menu opens up the **Activity Usage Profile Options** form:

It may not be clear where these options are drawing their information from by reading the descriptions in the **Activity Usage Profile Options** form. The **Earned Value** chapter covers these options in more detail. The following functions affect the graphs display:

- The project Baseline/s,
- **User Preferences**, **Time Units** settings,
- **Projects Window**, **Settings** tab, **Project Settings** section, **Baseline for earned value calculations**,
- **Admin**, **Admin Preferences…**, **Earned Value Tab**, **Earned value calculation** section.

20.1.3 Resource Usage Spreadsheet

This is displayed by clicking on the 🖻 icon or selecting **View**, **Show on Bottom**, **Resource Usage Spreadsheet**.

- This form has three windows showing the resources that are assigned to activities.
- Each window has a menu when right-clicking in the window.
- The units are formatted using the **User Preferences**, **Time Units** tab.
- As with the **Activity Usage Spreadsheet**, when the minimum time unit is an hour, ensure that the **User Preferences**, Resource Analysis **Interval for time-distributed resource** calculations is set to one hour; otherwise, the data will not be displayed correctly.
- When multiple resources are selected on the left-hand window then the corresponding Resource activities are displayed in the center and right-hand side window:

20.1.4 Editing the Resource Usage Spreadsheet – Bucket Planning and Range Copy

This new option in Primavera Version 6.0 enables resource assignment values to be manually edited. This enables more control over the assignment of resources that are working intermittently on an activity.

This is similar to editing a Microsoft Project Resource Usage table and making a resource assignment "Contoured."

The following picture shows the edited values in the **Resource Usage Spreadsheet**.

Each time period, therefore, may contain a different value.

⚠️ It is recommended that you experiment with this function if you plan to progress Bucket Planned Resources as the author has found this process gives some interesting results for the incomplete portion of an in-progress activity.

20.1.5   Range Copy and Paste from Excel and P6 into the Resource Usage Profile

P6 Version 22 introduced the ability to copy and paste a rage of cells using the right click **Range Copy** function (Shift+Ctl+C) and paste somewhere else using the **Range Paste** (Shift+Ctl+V) function and this was enhanced in Version 23 to enable copying and pasting to Excel. Users may copy a range of cell from the **Resource Usage Profile** by selecting a range and then right clicking and selecting **Range Copy**:

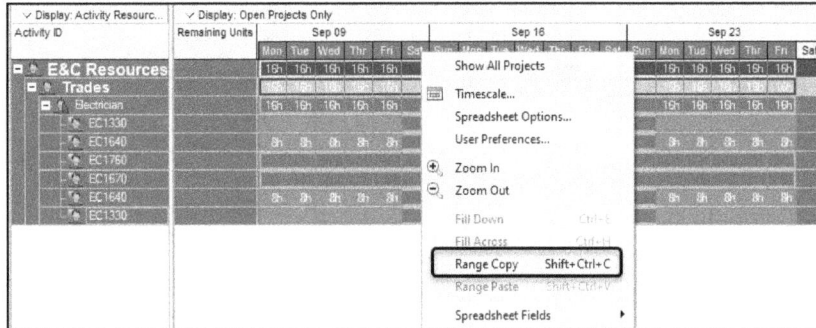

These may then be pasted into Excel.

- The author found that this option did not bring over timescale dates, data names found in columns or summary data, so the data copied in the picture above was pasted as per the picture below.

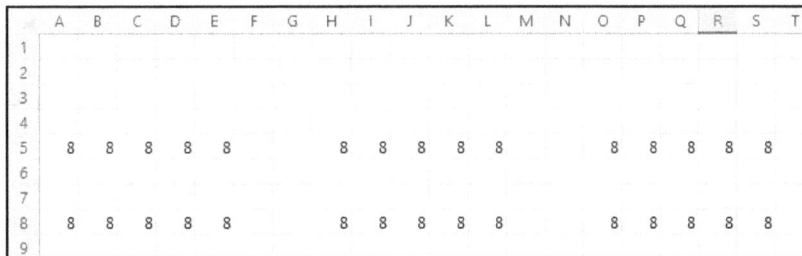

- Also, sometimes the author found the data was all pasted in the first Excel column as comma separated and had to be parsed (Text to Columns) to be useful.

You may also copy and paste values within the Resource Usage Profile and the cells below were copied:

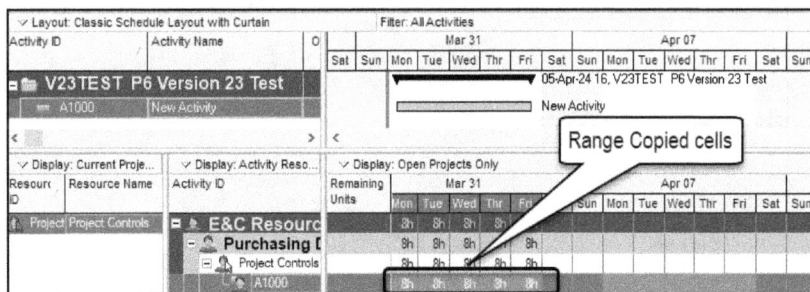

The 5 cells were selected and then **Range Paste** selected to paste the values into the next week:

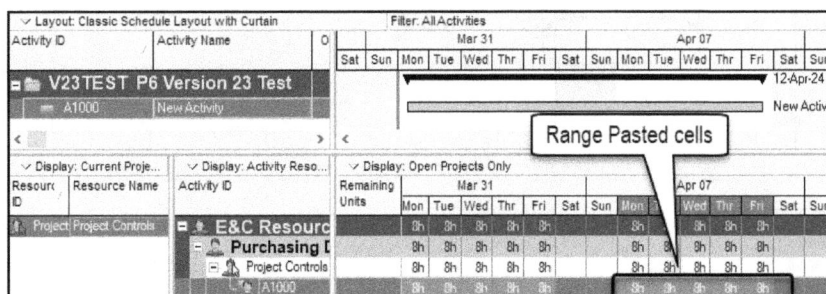

The ability to paste from Excel into a spreadsheet using **Range Paste** was not functioning on the authors system, although the **Oracle Primavera P6 Cumulative Feature Overview** stated it should and this may be fixed with an enhancement.

20.1.6   Resource Usage Profile displaying a Resource Histogram

Click on the ▨ icon or select **View**, **Show on Bottom**, **Resource Usage Profile**.

- The options in this form are similar to the ones covered in the previous paragraphs,

- A **Stacked Histogram**, which require a filter to be created in the **Resource Usage Profile Options** to select the resources to be displayed, or individual histograms are available from the menu:

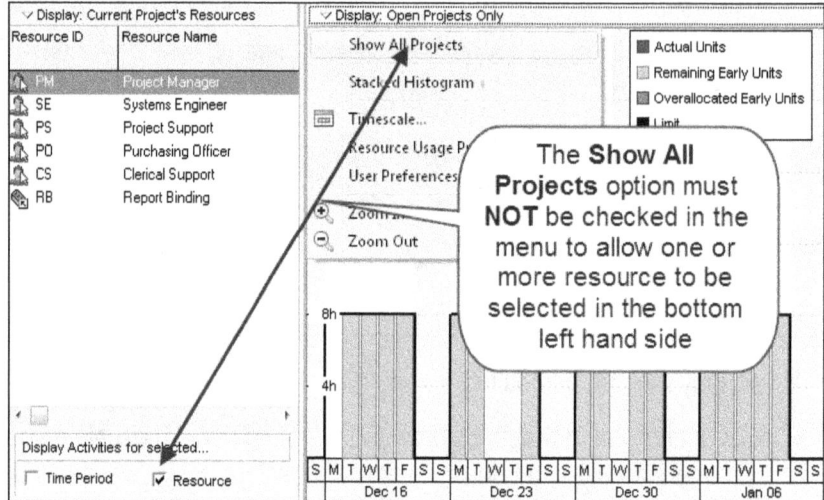

> The **Show All Projects** option must **NOT** be checked in the menu to allow one or more resource to be selected in the bottom left hand side

A **Stacked Histogram** may be created by right clicking in the Histogram area, selecting **Stacked Histogram**, then selecting **Resource Profile Options** and add the resources required to be displayed in the **Resource Profile Options** form.

> ⓘ The resource availability is displayed using the Resource Calendar when the **Activity Type** is set to **Task Dependent** and the activity is scheduled using the Activity Calendar.

In P6 Version 20 value of histograms may be displayed on histograms in the Resource Usage Profile, Activity Usage Profile, and Tracking View by selecting the **Show Values** option in the **Profile Option** form, **Graph** tab:

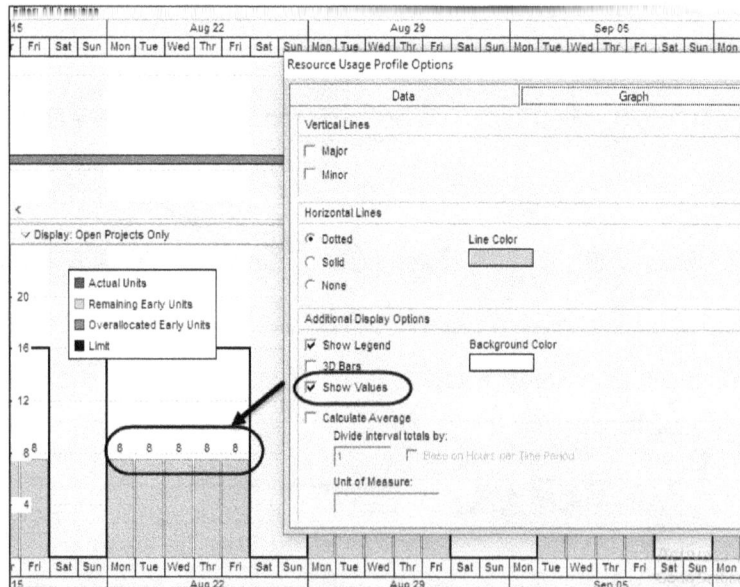

20.1.7 Activity Usage Profile Displaying S-Curves

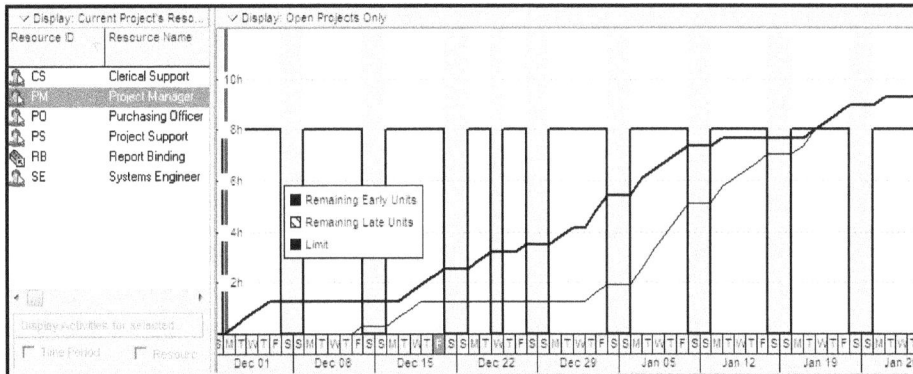

You must be prepared to experiment with the formatting menus by right-clicking in each of the windows of the above displays to understand all the many options, which include:

- Roles or Resources,
- All Resources, All Active Resources and Current Projects Resources only,
- Options to show period and cumulative values, or an average by dividing by a number,
- Options to filter, and
- Options to Group and Sort.

20.2 Resource Assignments Window

The **Resource Assignments Window** has some functions that are very useful especially when you wish to copy and paste data into Excel. It also supports the new P6 Version 22 and P6 Version 23 functions of **Range Copy** (Shift+Ctl+C) and **Range Paste** (Shift+Ctl+V). See para 28.26.13 for more detail.

This view is essentially a time-phased view that is grouped by default by Resource, Role, or Activity and allows the display of:

- Cumulative and Period totals
- Cost of all Resource Types
- Units of all Resource Types

This view does not show either Expense Costs or Expense Units. So, using this view for a cash flowing project with Expenses will not give the full value of the project. Resource Units Totals, say at project level, are only available when one resource type is displayed by using a filter.

20.3 Copying and Pasting into Excel

The following data may be copied and pasted into Excel:

- Activity data from the Activities Window
- Activity Usage Spreadsheet
- Tables in the Tracking Window
- Resource Assignments Window
- The **Range Copy and Paste from Excel and P6 into the Resource Usage Profile** is not very useful, see para 28.26.13 for details.

Data from the Resource Usage Spreadsheet may NOT be copied and pasted into Excel but similar data may be obtained in the Resource Assignments Window and copied and pasted into Excel.

> *i*   You should be aware of the following issues:
>
> - The **User Preferences** need to be appropriate especially for date formatting if you wish the data to be pasted as dates into Excel.
> - Dates that are pasted with an "A" at the end may be removed with the Excel command of **Find and Replace**. You may need to put a space before the "A" so you do not lose the "A" in front of August.
> - To remove the "*" at the end of a date you must use the syntax of "~*" in the Find and Replace command as a "*" on its own will replace all the data in the spreadsheet.

20.4 Other Tools for Histograms and Tables

Oracle Primavera also sells a reporting add-on software package titled **Primavera Earned Value Management** which allows the production of a number of reports such as time-phased table, bubble, and period variance.

Contact your Oracle Primavera distributor or view the Oracle Primavera web site for more information.

20.5 Methods of Resolving Resource Peaks and Conflicts

Methods of resolving resource overload problems are:

- **Revising the Project Plan**. Revise a project plan to mitigate resource conflicts, such as changing the order of work, contracting work out, or using off-site pre-fabrication, etc.
- **Duration Change**. Increase the activity duration to decrease the resource requirements, so a 5-day activity with 10 people could be extended to a 10-day activity with 5 people.
- **Resource Substitution**. Substitute one resource with another available resource.
- **Increase Working Time**. This may release the resource for other activities earlier and is created by working more days per week or hours per day.
- **Split an activity around peaks in demand**. Some software enables the splitting of activities, which in turn enables work to be split around peaks in resource demand. The split function is not available in Primavera, however, an activity may be split in two individual activities to allow the work to cease in times of peak demand. If one needs to relate back to a baseline then two new activities may be created to represent the split and the original activity made into an LOE to span the two new activities, but remember to display the LOE Baseline Bar.
- **Leveling the schedule**. This technique delays activities until resource(s)are available.
- **Resource Curves** or **Manually Editing the Resource Spreadsheet** may assist in some instances.

20.6 Resource Leveling

20.6.1 Methods of Resource Leveling

After resource overloads or inefficiencies are identified with Resource and Tables, the schedule may now have to be leveled to reduce peaks in resource demands. Leveling is defined as delaying activities until resources become available. There are several methods of delaying activities to level a schedule:

- **Turning off Automatic Calculation and Dragging Activities**. This option does not maintain a critical path and reverts to the original schedule when recalculated. This option should not be used when a contract requires a critical path schedule to be maintained, as the schedule will no longer calculate correctly.

- **Constraining Activities**. A constraint may be applied to delay an activity until the date that the resource becomes available from a higher priority activity. This is not a recommended method because the delay of the higher priority activity may unlevel the schedule.

- **Sequencing Logic**. Relationships may be applied to activities sharing the same resource(s) in the order of their priority. In this process a critical path is generated. If the first activity in a chain is delayed, then the chain of activities will be delayed. But the schedule will not become unleveled and the critical path will be maintained. In this situation, a successor activity may be able to take place earlier and the logic will have to be manually edited.

- **Leveling Function**. The software Resource Leveling function levels resources by delaying activities without the need for Constraints or Logic and finds the optimum order for the activities based on user defined parameters. Again, as this option does not maintain a critical path developed by durations and relationships, it should not be used when a contract requires a critical path schedule developed in this way. The Leveling function may be used to establish an optimum scheduling sequence and then Sequencing Logic applied to hold the leveled dates and to create a critical path.

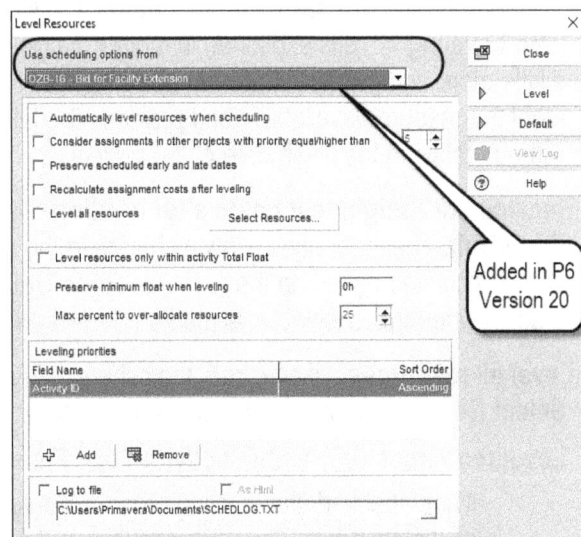

The Resource Leveling function enables the optimization of resource use by delaying activities until resources become available, thus reducing the peaks in resource requirements. This feature may extend the length of a project.

The leveling function should be used by novices with extreme caution.

- It requires the scheduler to have a solid understanding of how the software resourcing functions calculate.

- Leveling increases the complexity of a schedule and requires a different approach to building a schedule. In principle, the sequencing logic is replaced by Priorities but a Closed Network should still be maintained.

Your ability to understand how the software operates is important for you to be able to utilize the leveling function with confidence on larger schedules. It is recommended that you practice with small simple schedules to gain experience in leveling and develop an understanding of the leveling issues before attempting a complex schedule.

20.6.2   Resource Leveling Function

This section outlines the software Resource Leveling functions including:

- **Level Resources** form,

- Leveling Examples, including Resource Shifts,

- Guidelines on Leveling, and

- What to look for if resources are not leveling.

20.6.3   Level Resources Form

The **Level Resources** form enables you to assign most of the Leveling prerequisites. Select **Tools**, **Level Resources…** to open the **Level Resources** form:

- **Automatically level resources when scheduling** – levels the schedule each time the schedule is recalculated and is not recommended.

- **Consider assignments in other projects with priority equal/higher than**. – levels resources and at the same time considers the demands of other projects. The leveling priority is set in the **Projects Window**, **General** tab.

- **Preserve scheduled early and late dates** – in simple terms, when unchecked enables the option of **Late Leveling**. This is explained in more detail in the following paragraphs as the computations are a little more complicated. **Late Leveling** pushes forward in time activities from their late dates to meet the resource availability and provides the latest dates the activities may be started and finished without delaying the finish date of the project.

- **Recalculate assignment costs after leveling** – is used with the resource **Effective date** and **Price/Unit**. These facilities allow a change in the cost of a resource over time. The Resource Costs are recalculated based on the resource **Price/Unit** if an activity is moved into a different price bracket when this check box is marked.

- **Level all resources** – if checked, the schedule levels all the resources; if unchecked, enables the **Select Resources** form to be opened and one or more resources selected for leveling.

- **Level resources only within activity Total Float**

  ➤ When checked, the leveling process will not generate negative float but may not completely level a schedule. Thus, the activities will only be delayed until all float is consumed and leveling will not extend the finish date of the project. This option will also check the **Preserve scheduled early and late dates** option.

  ➤ When unchecked, leveling will allow activities to extend beyond a **Project Must Finish By date**, when assigned in the **Projects Window Dates** tab, or beyond the latest date calculated by the schedule and may create **Negative Float**.

  ➤ **Preserve minimum float when leveling** – works with **Level resources only within Total Float** and will not level activities if their float will drop below the assigned value.

  ➤ **Max percent to over-allocate resources** – works with **Level resources only within activity Total Float** and enables the doubling of the resource availability, although this new limit is not displayed in the histogram limits.

- **Leveling priorities** – sets leveling the priorities, and activities are assigned resources according to the Data item chosen in the first line. If two activities have the same value in the first line then the priority in the second line is used. The Activity ID is the final value used to assign resources. There are many options for leveling priority and the following are some to consider:

> **Activity Leveling Priority** is a field that may be set from 1 Top to 5 Lowest; the default is 3 Normal. Those with a priority 1 Top are assigned resources first.

> **Activity Codes** and many other data fields such as **Remaining Duration**, **Early Start**, **Total Float**, and **Late Start** may be used to set the priority for leveling, but not **User Defined Fields**.

20.7 Leveling Examples

Two simple examples can assist you in understanding how the software works:

- The first will allow the schedule to level with positive float, and
- The second will NOT allow the schedule to level with positive float and may generate negative float.

(i) It is recommended that you set up a small schedule and try the various options until you understand what the software is doing and how it operates before trying your hand with a large schedule.

You should then look at leveling more complex schedules only after you have mastered leveling a small schedule like the examples in this chapter.

20.7.1 Leveling with Positive Float

The following picture displays the schedule unleveled:

- A project **Must Finish By Date** of 27 Feb has been set.
- The histogram shows both the Early and Late resource histogram is overloaded.
- The bars displayed are the **Early**, **Remaining**, the **Late** and **Total Float**:

Early Bar –

Remaining Bar –

Late Bar –

After Leveling with all the Leveling options off except the **Select Resource...** option:

- Early and Late leveling has taken place and the Early and Late histogram are leveled.
- The Early and Remaining Bars have the same dates and are leveled.
- Total Float is the difference between the Late and Early Finish and provides a similar result if there is a relationship between the activities.

With **Preserve scheduled early and late dates** option checked:

- Early leveling of the Remaining dates has taken place and the Early histogram is leveled.
- Late leveling has NOT taken place and the Late histogram is NOT leveled.
- The Early and Late Bar have NOT been leveled.
- The Total Float is the difference between the Late and Remaining Finish dates and provides a similar result if there is NO relationship between the activities.

20.7.2 Leveling without Positive Float

The following picture displays the schedule unleveled:

- A project **Must Finish By Date** of 13 Feb has been set.

- The histogram shows both the Early and Late resource histogram are overloaded.

After Leveling with all the options off except the **Select Resource...** option:

- Early and Late leveling has taken place and the Early and Late histogram is leveled.

- The Early and Remaining Bars have the same dates and are leveled and Negative Float developed.

- The Total Float is the difference between the Late and Early Finish and provides a similar result if there is a relationship between the activities.

With **Preserve scheduled early and late dates** option checked:

- Early leveling has taken place and the Early histogram is leveled.
- Late leveling has NOT taken place and the Late histogram is NOT leveled.
- The Early and Late Bar have NOT been leveled.
- The Remaining Bar has been leveled and Negative Float developed.

With **Preserve scheduled early and late dates** and the **Level resources only within activity Total Float option** checked:

- Early leveling on the Remaining dates has taken place as much as possible without creating Negative Float.
- Activity 2 with the lowest priority has been left on the Data Date.
- Late leveling has NOT taken place and the Late histogram is NOT leveled.
- The Early Bar has NOT been leveled.

20.8   Resource Shifts

Resource shifts enable the modeling of resource availability when a different number of resources may be available on various shifts. Resource shifts should be used with:

- Resource Dependent activities, and
- Resources set to Drive Activity Dates after they have been assigned to activities.

Unlike other products, when an Activity is made Resource Dependent the Activity Calendar is still acknowledged for the start of an activity, but not the finish.

Before attempting to use shifts, a user should have considerable familiarity with the software or work with someone experienced.

20.8.1   Creating Shifts:

Select **Enterprise**, **Resource Shifts…** to open the **Resource Shifts** form:

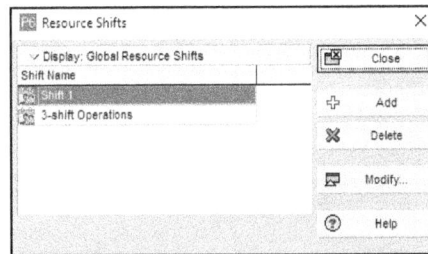

When a shift is added it must total 24 hours:

20.8.2   Assigning Shifts to Resources

A shift may be assigned to a resource in the **Resource Window Units & Prices** tab, with a different availability (**Max Units/ Time**) and rate (**Price/Unit**) assigned for each shift.

This example shows there are no resources assigned to shift 3, therefore representing a two-shift environment.

A Resource will have a little arrow pointing to its head when assigned to an activity of an open project:

20.8.3 Leveling with Shifts

Shifts are acknowledged when the leveling function is used. The following example shows activities on a 24-hour per day, 7-day per week activity calendar, with shifts set up as on the previous page, with all activities set as Resource Dependent and Drive Activity Dates. The situation before leveling with the Resource Limit displayed according to shift availability:

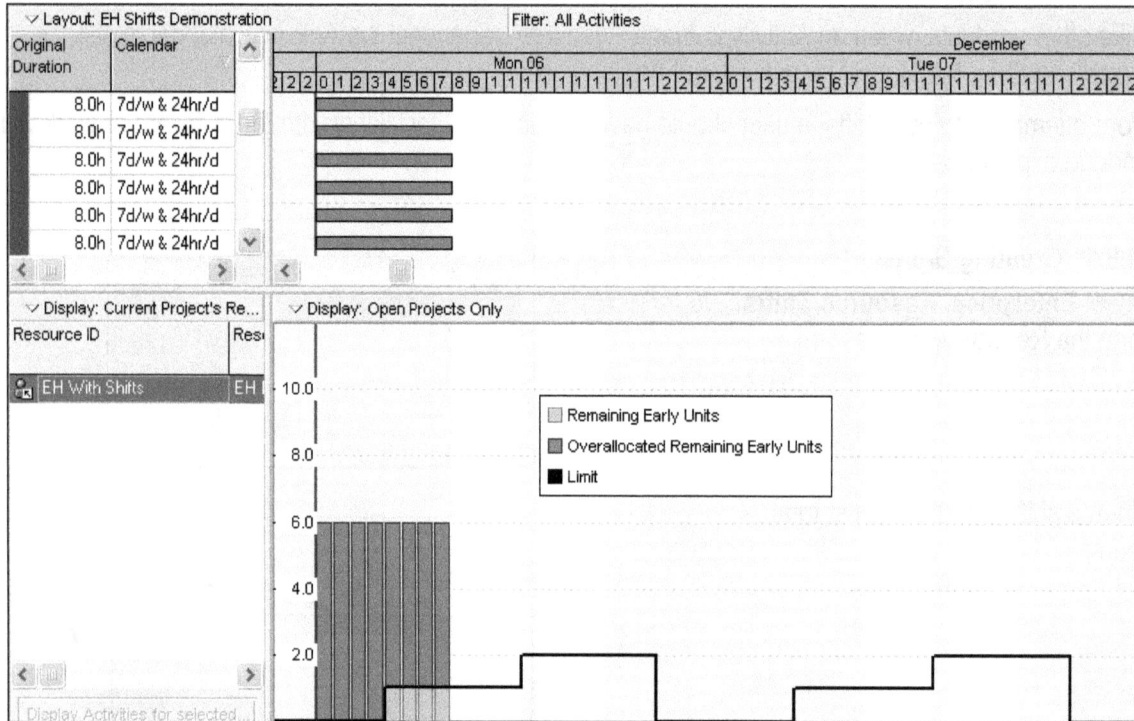

After Leveling with all leveling options **NOT** checked:

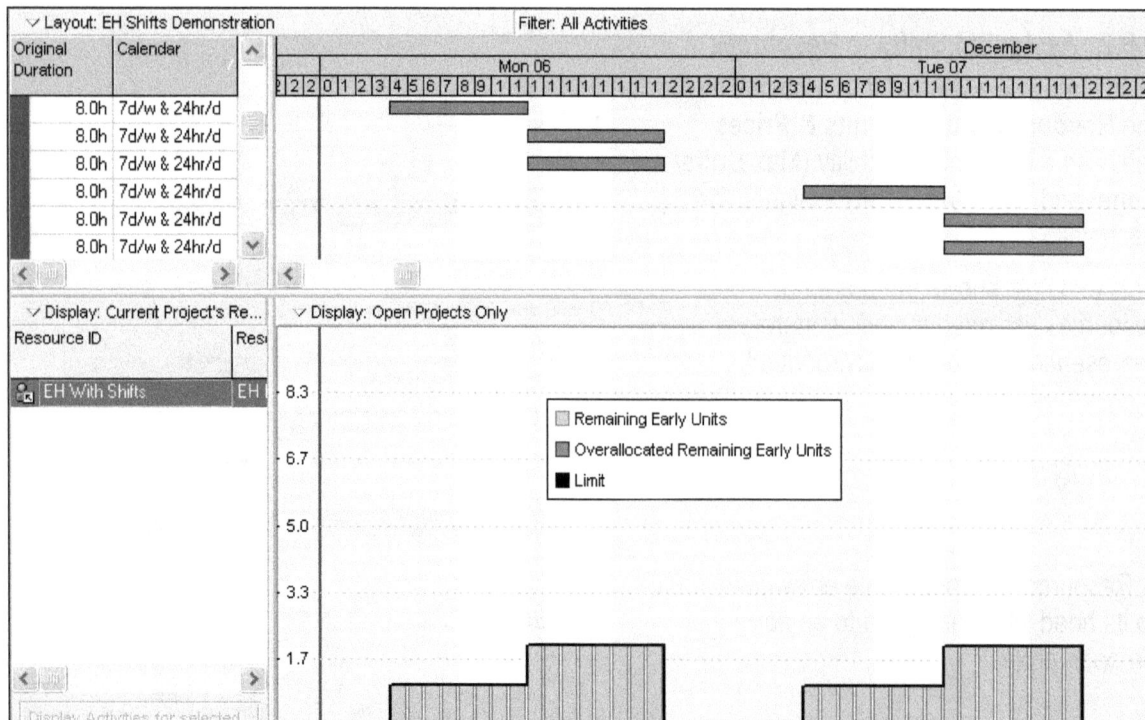

The following example has the activities on an 8-hour per day, 7-day per week calendar:

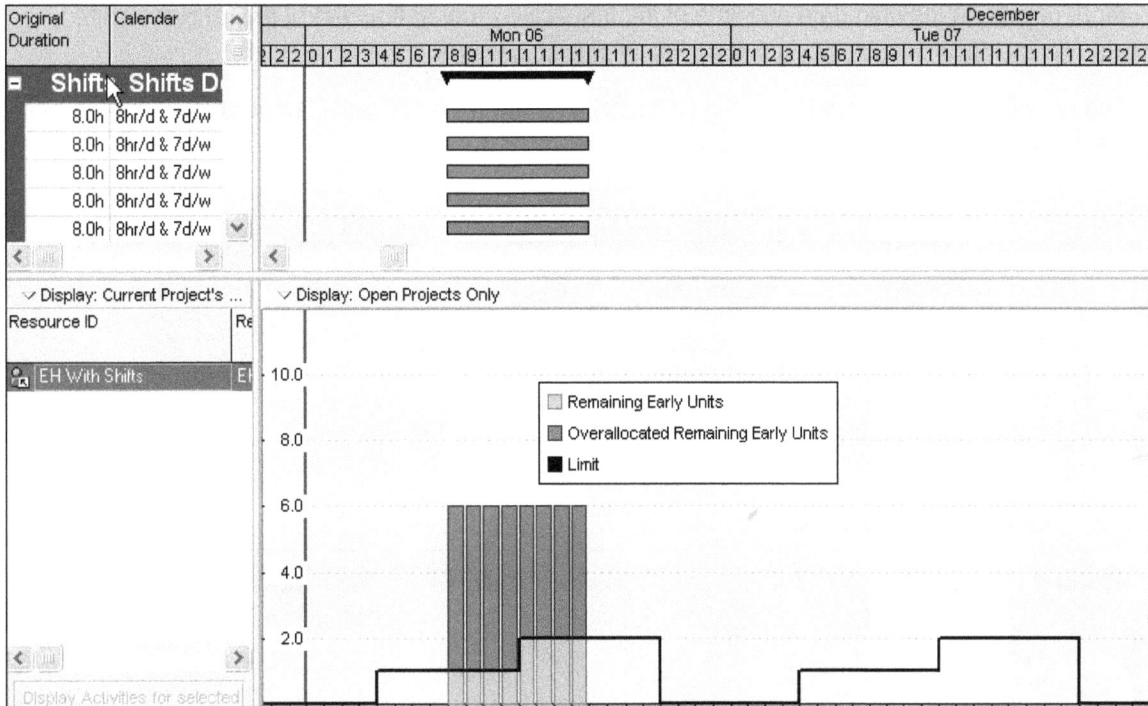

In this situation, the leveling considers the Activity Calendar for each Start of each activity and the Shifts operated after the activity Start time. Even though the activities are Resource Driven:

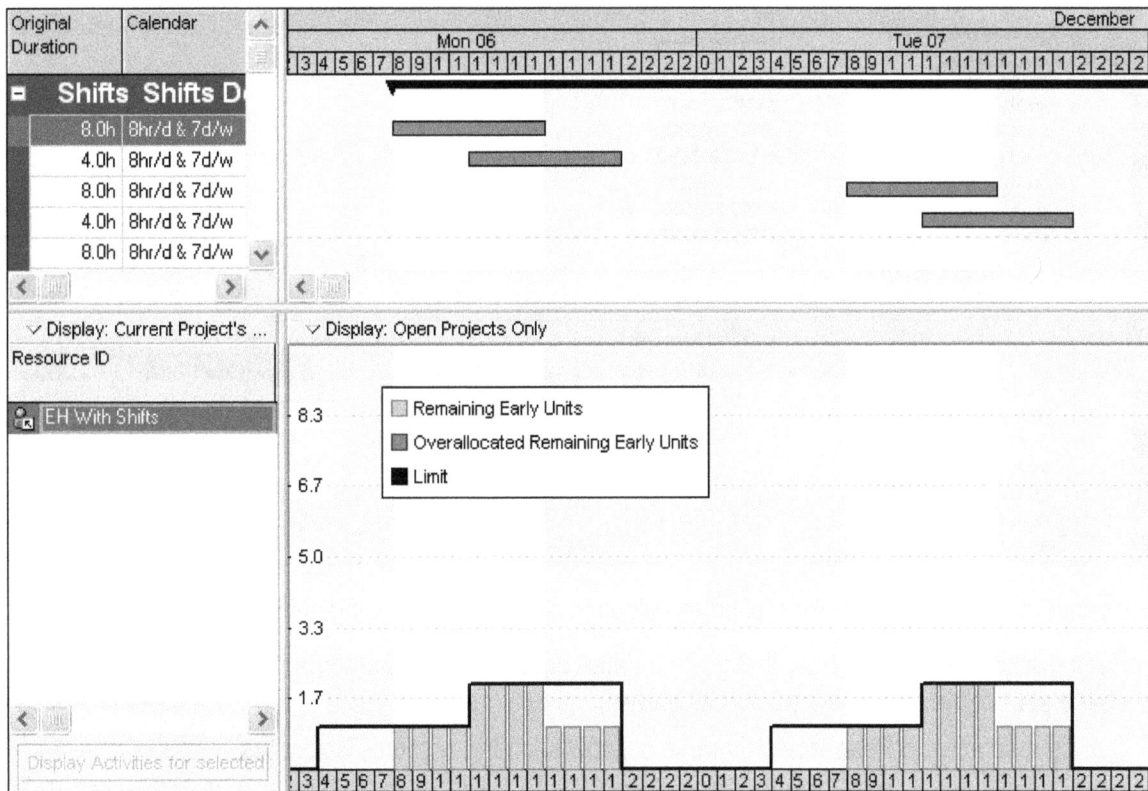

When the Resources are set to **NOT Drive Activity Dates** the resources still level, but:

- Work begins on the start date and time of the first activity, not at the start of the resource shift.
- The Activity Bars do not show when the work is taking place.
- The activities also do not begin on the shift start time when the **Default Calendar** is set 7 days per week, 24 hours per day.

It appears the best option to make resources calculate correctly when using shifts is to:

- Put the activities on a calendar that has the same or greater working hours than the Resource Shifts, so the start of the resource work is not delayed,
- Set the resources to **Resource Driven**, to acknowledge the resource calendars,
- Set the resources to **Drive Activity Dates**, to ensure the Activity Bars move with the Leveled Resources,
- Create a small schedule and experiment to make sure the schedule is behaving the way you think it should and you understand what is happening.

The author does not use the **Resource Shifts** function but finds it far simpler to create a **Task Dependent** activity for the day shift and afternoon and night shifts are created using **Level of Effort** tasks and linked to the day shift activity.

A three-shift situation looks like this:

Activity ID	Activity Name	Activity Type	Original Duration	Calendar	Sun	Mon	Tue	Wed	Thr	Fri	Sat
Shifts			5d								
A1020	Day Shift	Task Dependent	5d	7x8 Day Shift							
A1030	Afternoon Shift	Level of Effort	4d	7x8 Night Shift							
A1040	Nght Shft	Level of Effort	4d	7x8 Morning Shift							

There is a technical paper on this subject titled "Scheduling with Shifts in Primavera P6" at https://primavera.com.au/ under technical papers with some more examples.

20.9 Guidelines for Leveling

Leveling a schedule is a skill that is acquired through practice and experience and there are a few fundamentals that a user must bear in mind before attempting to level a complex schedule.

- If you are not an experienced scheduling software user then it is strongly suggested that you obtain some serious experience in using Primavera with resources before attempting to use leveling on a complex schedule, especially if you are trying to level a progressed schedule. You will need this experience to resolve some of the complex issues that are often present when leveling a schedule.

- You need to approach the structure of the schedule differently at the beginning of schedule construction. Without leveling, schedulers normally apply soft logic (sequencing logic) to prevent a number of activities occurring at the same time. If leveling is your method of scheduling, then soft logic should be omitted from the beginning of the construction of the schedule.

- All users and reviewers of the schedule must understand that a levelled schedule may dramatically change with the addition or removal or change to activities or change in priorities.

- There are some principles that should be considered when leveling:

  ➤ Only level resources that are overloaded and that you are unable to supplement easily or that have an absolute limit.

  ➤ Try leveling one resource at a time and view the histograms to ensure each resource is leveling. If a resource is not leveling and the histograms display overload, you will need to go through the check list on the next page and level again. This process often finds a driving overload resource and leveling that resource levels the whole project.

  ➤ After all resources are leveling individually, you should start leveling with two resources and then three. Do not start leveling with all the resources at once, as the schedule will often do some drastic things and extend the project end date unrealistically.

  ➤ Do not expect a perfect result; be satisfied with an average resource usage that meets your requirements over periods, such as months. Sort out small peaks in future resource requirements nearer to the start of the activity.

To understand how leveling will delay or change durations of activities you will need to be aware of which of the above combinations you have employed in your schedule, and you will then need to understand how each combination calculates under a non-leveling environment.

20.10 *What to look for if Resources are Not Leveling*

It is very frustrating if you have a project that will not level. Try some of these options when your schedule will not level:

- Have you selected a resource to level in the **Select Resources** form? The resources to be leveled must be selected in the **Select Resources** form.

- Have you set the **Limits** in the **Resource Window**? A resource needs a limit to level.

- A resource will not be leveled when you assign a resource to an activity with a Units per time period greater than value set in the resource dictionary. This may occur when:
  - ➤ The **Resource Limit** in the **Resource Window** is reduced, or
  - ➤ An activity has been assigned a resource with a **Unit per Time Period** that is greater than the **Limit**, or
  - ➤ When the activity has **Fixed Units** and the duration of an activity has been reduced, thus increasing the assigned **Units per Time Period** over the maximum available in the **Resource** form.

- Have you assigned a **Mandatory Constraint** to an unleveled activity? Activities with a **Mandatory Constraint** will not be leveled.

- Have you checked **Level resources only within activity Total Float** option? This option enables activities without float to level.

- Have you assigned resources to WBS or LOE activities? These will not be leveled.

20.11 *Resource Curves*

Resource Curves enables a non-linear assignment of resources to schedules in the same way as Microsoft Project and Elecosoft (Asta) Powerproject. These are often used on long activities where there is not a requirement for a linear assignment of resources.

Resource curves are assigned in the **Curve** column in the **Resources** tab of the **Activities Window**:

The Electrical wiring activity in the following picture has a bell-shaped Resource Curve assigned to it:

To create and use **Resource Curves**:

- Select **Enterprise**, **Resource Curves…** to open the **Resource Curves** form:

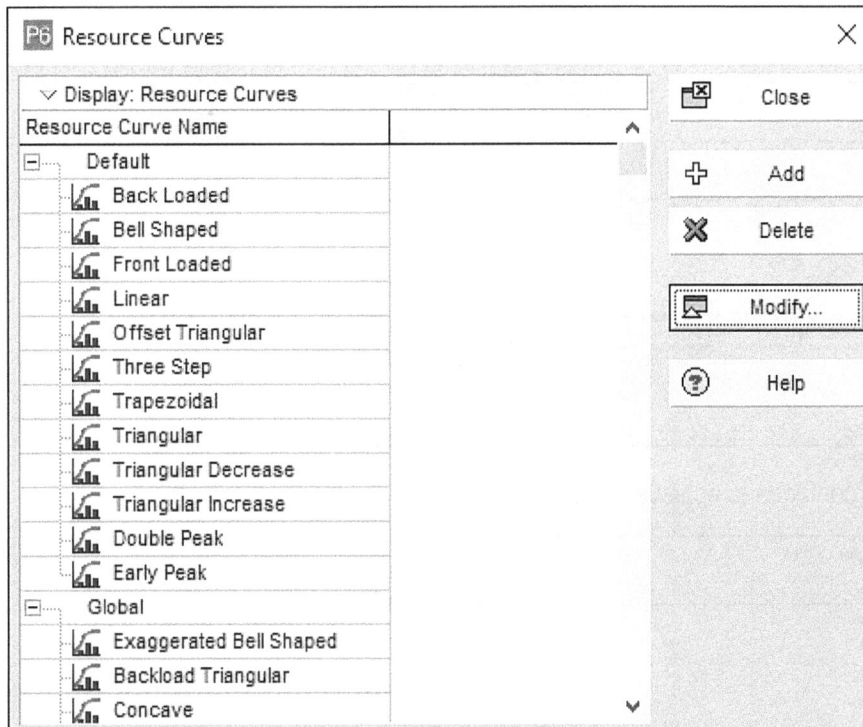

- **Default** curves may not be deleted or edited but may be copied in the **Modify Resource Curves** form.

- **Global** curves may be edited, copied or deleted.

- To create a new curve, select [⊕ Add] to open the **Select Resource Curve To Copy From** form and select a curve to copy.

- You will be returned to the **Resource Curves** form where the title may be edited.

- Click the [🖳 Modify...] icon to open the **Modify Resource Curves** form:

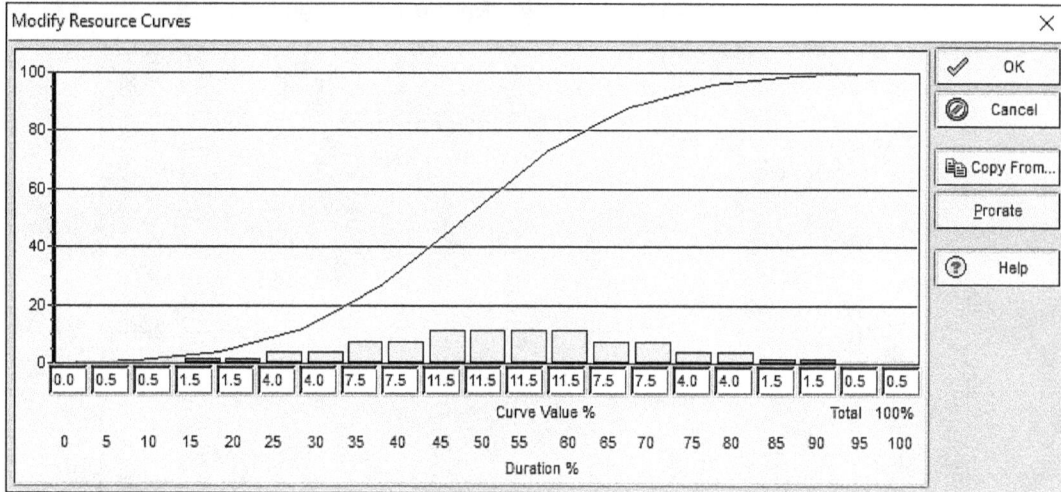

- Edit the percentages to achieve the desired shape:

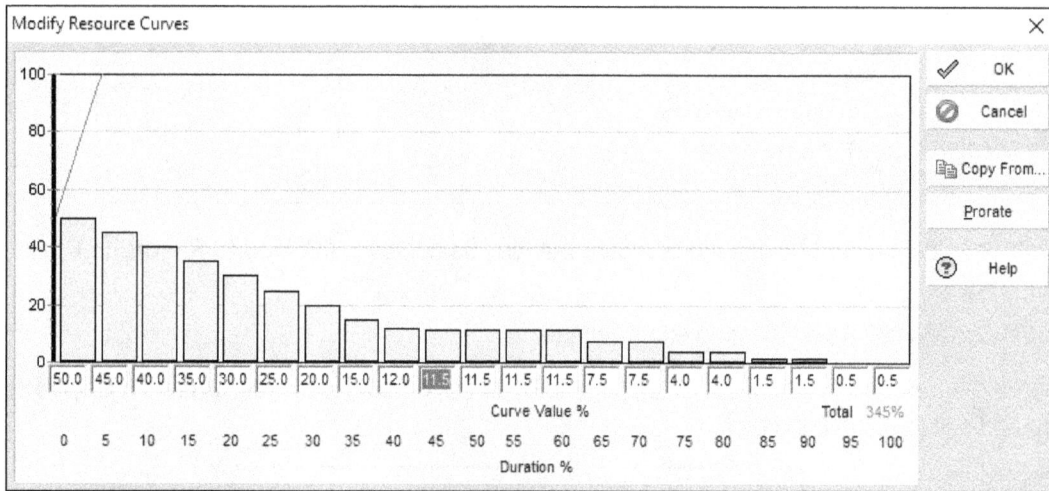

- Click on [Prorate] to make the percentages add to 100%:

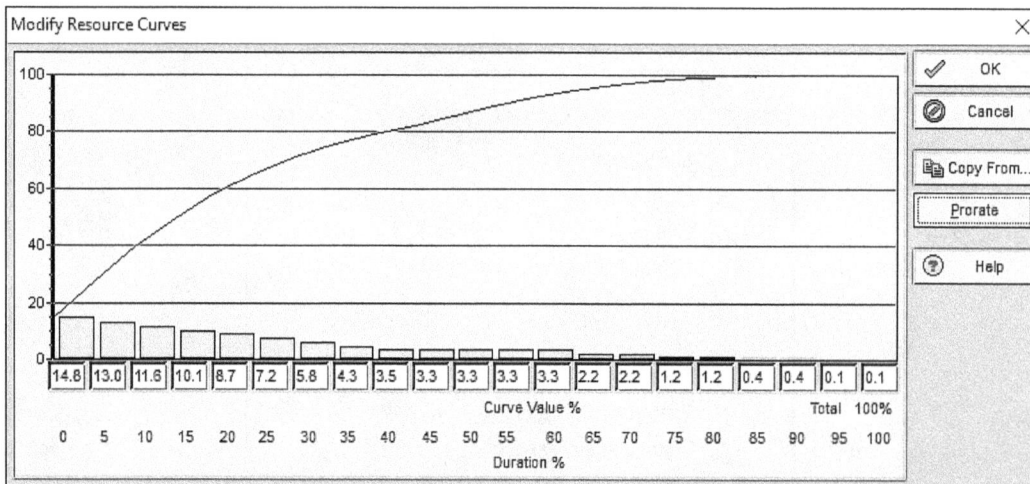

You may now assign this curve to an activity.

20.12 Workshop 17 – Resources Optimization

Assignment

1. Open the OzBuild schedule and apply the **OzBuild 10 – With Float** Layout,

2. Display the **Activity Usage Spreadsheet** by clicking on the ▣ icon. The following picture shows the number of hours per week per activity, adjust the timescale to weeks and change your **User Preferences**, **Time Units**, **Units of Time** as required:

Activity ID	Activity Name	Remainin Labor	December 2024			January 2025				
			09	16	23	30	06	13	20	27
OZB-16	**Bid for Facility Extension**		72h	40h	40h	64h	160h	72h	64h	8h
OZB-16.1	**Technical Specification**		72h	40h	40h					
OZ1000	Approval to Bid									
OZ1010	Determine Installation Requirements		64h							
OZ1020	Create Technical Specification		8h	32h						
OZ1030	Identify Supplier Components			8h	8h					
OZ1040	Validate Technical Specification				32h					
OZB-16.2	**Delivery Plan**					64h	80h	56h	24h	
OZ1050	Document Delivery Methodology					32h				
OZ1060	Obtain Quotes from Suppliers					32h	80h	16h		
OZ1070	Calculate the Bid Estimate							24h		
OZ1080	Create the Project Schedule							16h	8h	
OZ1090	Review the Delivery Plan								16h	
OZB-16.3	**Bid Document**						80h	16h	40h	8h
OZ1100	Create Draft of Bid Document						80h	16h		
OZ1110	Review Bid Document								32h	
OZ1120	Finalise and Submit Bid Document								8h	8h
OZ1130	Bid Document Submitted									

3. Display the **Resource Usage Sheet** by clicking on the ▣ icon.

4. Use the **Display**, **Filter** option in the bottom left window to display the **Current Project's Resources** only,

5. Select **Resource** for the option **Display Activities for selected…** (in the bottom left corner of the screen), this will display only the activities assigned to this resource.

6. Select the **Project Manager** (in the bottom left window), which will display the Project Managers Resource Table,

7. Increase the timescale to a daily interval.

8. The **Projects Manager** is overloaded (16 hours per day) on a number of days where he/she is working two activities at a time:

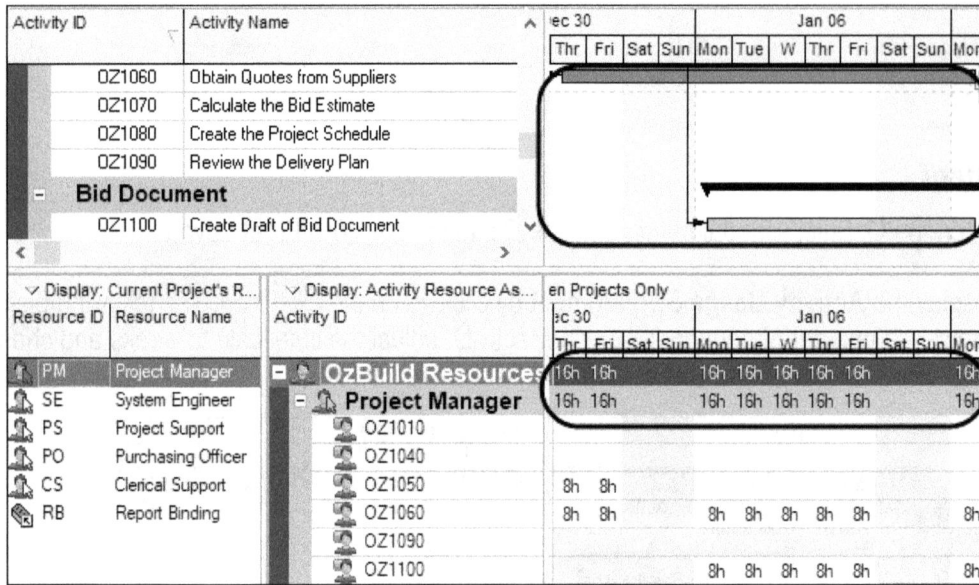

9. Display the **Resource Usage Profile** by clicking on the [icon] icon; you will also see that the Project Manager is overloaded from the end of December to start of January.

10. Check the other resources. Project Support appears overloaded on Saturday 15 January. This is because some activities are on a 6-day per week calendar and the resource calendar is a 5-day per week:

11. At this point in time resources may be optimized by a number of methods including:

> Assigning a different resource, or

> Reducing the assignment against the activities, or

> Adding sequencing logic to level the schedule, or

> Splitting activities, this has to be done by creating two activities in P6, or

> Using the Bucket Planning function, or

> Using the Primavera leveling function.

12. We will try using the leveling function to resolve the Project Managers overload.

13. Firstly, we will create and assign a baseline and display the Baseline bar by:

> Select **Project**, **Maintain Baselines…** and create a Baseline by saving a copy of the existing project,

> Select **Project**, **Assign Baselines…** and select this as both your **Project Baseline** and **Primary User Baseline**, thus ensuring the baseline bar will either be blank or display the **Baseline** and not the **Planned Dates**.

> Apply your **OzBuild Workshop 13 – Baseline** layout and the Baseline bars should be displayed,

> Ensure only the **Project Baseline** bars are displayed by hiding all **Primary Baseline Bars**.

> If there is a yellow vertical band then this is created by the **Progress Spotlight** line. Drag the **Progress Spotlight** line back to the **Data Date**.

14. Display the **Resource Usage Profile** by clicking on the ▨ icon,

15. Select **Current Projects Resources**.

16. Increase the timescale to a daily timescale.

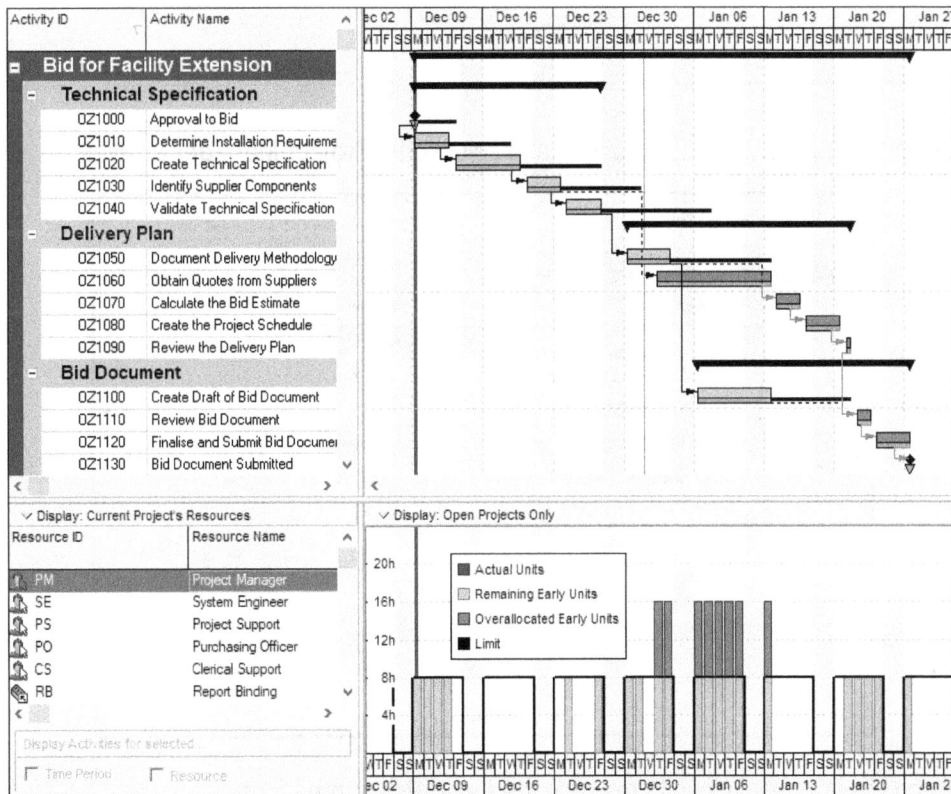

continued…

---

17. Save the layout as **OzBuild Workshop 17 – Leveling**.

18. Select **Tools**, **Level Resources**.

19. Set options as per the picture below:

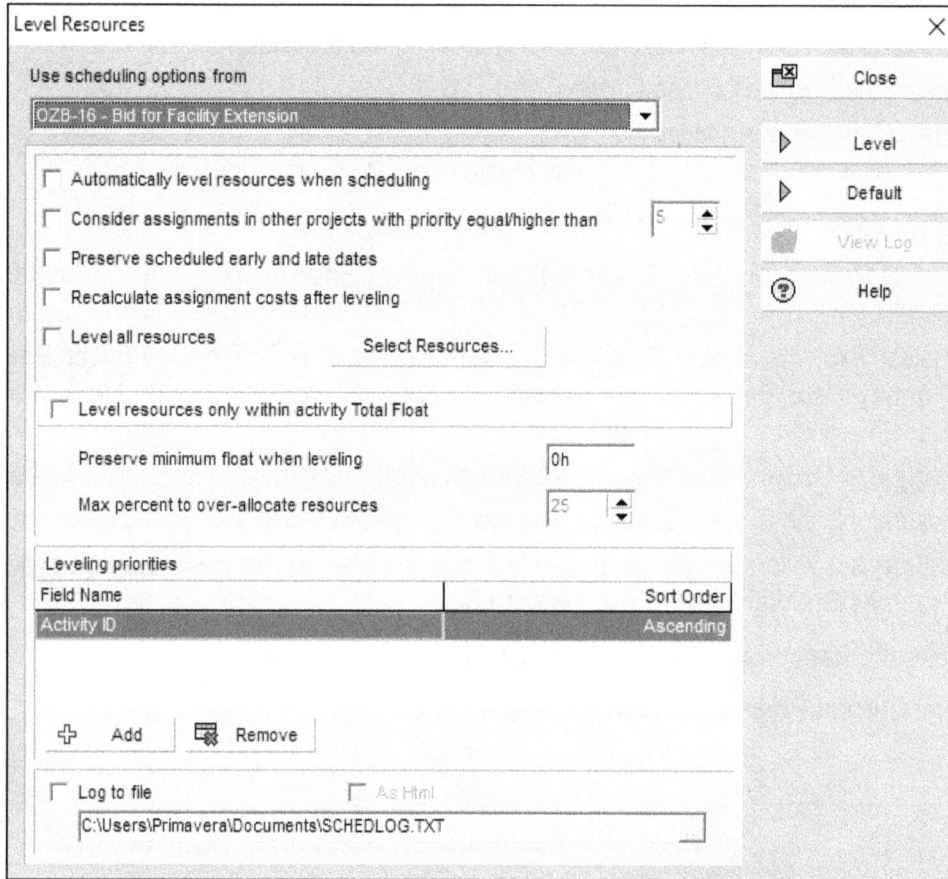

20. Click on the [Select Resources...] icon and select only **Project Manager** to level:

21. Click on the [✓ OK] icon to return to the **Level Resources** form,

22. Click on the [▷ Level] icon to level **Project Manager's** resource assignment:

> ➤ The **Project Manager's** assignment will be leveled,
> ➤ There should be Negative Float as your schedule should have a **Late Finish Constraint** on the last activity, and
> ➤ There will be a Baseline variance.

23. Reschedule and therefore un-level by pressing **F9**.

24. Now try leveling on Early Start, the schedule is levelled with an earlier finish date:

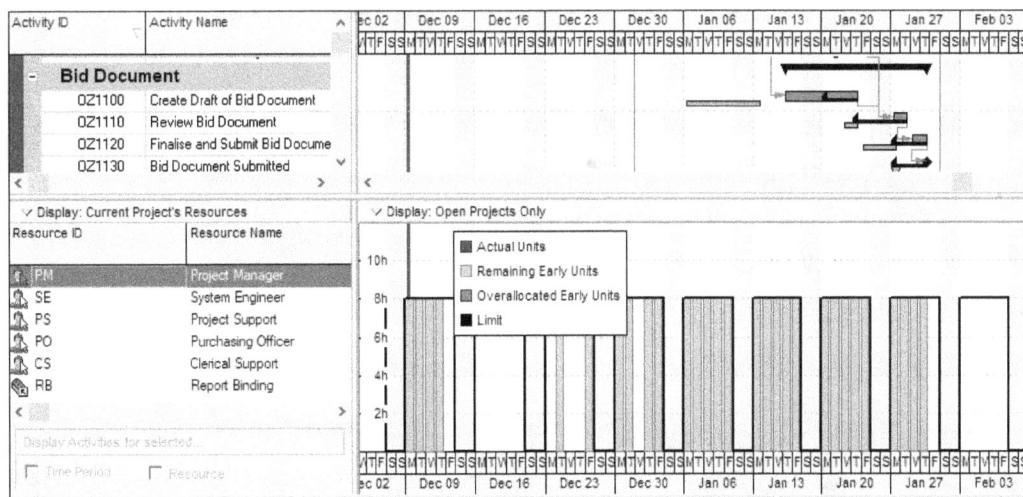

25. At the end of the workshop, schedule so the project so it is not leveled.

21 UPDATING A RESOURCED SCHEDULE

It is often considered best practice to update a project between 10 and 20 times in its lifecycle. Some companies update schedules to correspond with accounting periods, which are normally every month. This frequency is often too long for projects that are less than a year in duration, as too much change may happen in one month. Therefore, more frequent updating may identify problems earlier.

Updating a project with resources employs a number of preferences and options, which are very interactive and will require a significant amount of practice by a user to understand and master them.

After reading this chapter and before working on a live project, inexperienced users should gain confidence with the software by:

- Creating a new project and setting the **Defaults**, **Preferences**, and **Options** to reflect the method in which you wish to enter information and how you want Primavera to calculate the project data.

- Creating two or three activities and then assigning two or three resources to each activity.

- Updating the Activities and Resources as if you were updating a schedule and observe the results.

- Alter the preferences and defaults if you are not receiving the result you require. Re-update and note the preferences and defaults for future reference.

- **Note:** Always update an activity twice as the software performs differently on the second update.

Some of these settings may have been set by your organization and you may not be assigned access rights to change the settings. You should still go through the updating process in a test project with dummy data similar to your real project data and be prepared to change those settings to which you do have access, as required.

Updating a project with resources takes place in two distinct steps:

- The dates, durations and relationships are updated using the methods outlined in the **Updating an Unresourced Schedule** chapter, and

- The Resource, Expenses Units (hours and quantities) and Costs, both the Actual to Date and To Complete, are then updated. These resource values may be automatically updated by Primavera or imported from accounting and timesheet systems or updated by the Primavera Timesheet system.

A decision needs to be made about what data is to be entered or imported into the schedule and what data is to be calculated by the software and the software options set appropriately.

This chapter covers the following topics:

- Understanding **Budget** Values and **Baseline Projects**
- Understanding the **Current Data Date** with respect to resources
- Information required to update a resourced schedule
- Project and Activities Windows Defaults
- Updating Resources and Expenses
- Reviewing the updated schedule

21.1 Understanding Budget Values and Baseline Projects

21.1.1 Cost and Units Budget Values

The **Budget Values** in Primavera are assigned to both Units and Costs for each Resource and Expense at the time the Resource or Expense is assigned to an Activity.

Budget Values reside in the current project and in all **Baseline Projects**.

The **Budget Values** normally by default are linked to the **At Completion** values when an activity has not commenced, but may be unlinked from **Projects** window, **Calculations** tab.

After the activity is in-progress by being marked as Started or having a % Complete these values become unlinked.

> Should you wish to re-estimate the cost of a project and compare it to a previous value when activities have not started you could either:
>
> 1. Create a Baseline Project before re-estimating the project and compare your revised costs to the Baseline, or
>
> 2. In the **Project Window**, **Calculations** tab and uncheck the **Link Budget and At Completion for non-started activities** which will unlink:
>
>   ➢ **Budget Costs** from **At Completion Costs**
>
>   ➢ **Budget Units** from **At Completion Units**
>
>   ➢ **Original (Planned) Durations** from **At Completion Durations**
>
>   This option to unlink Original and At Completion Durations may not be desirable, but this option does not involve setting a baseline. This therefore adds further complications and it is recommended that it is not used except in advanced scheduling.

21.1.2 Baseline Project and Values

A Baseline project is a complete copy of a project including the relationships, resource assignments and expenses.

The creation and assignment of a Baseline Project was covered in the **Updating an Unresourced Schedule** chapter.

- **Baseline Dates** are also known as Target Dates and are normally considered to be the approved Project Early Start and Early Finish dates of a progressed project, which are recorded by saving a Baseline project.

- **Baseline Duration** is the original planned duration of an activity, calculated from the Early Start to the Early Finish of an Activity. This is not the P6 Planned Duration Value.

- **Baseline Costs** are also known as Budgets and represent the original project cost estimate. These are the figures against which the Actual Costs and Cost at Completion (or Estimate at Completion) may be compared.

- **Baseline Units** are also known as Budgeted Quantity and represents the original estimate of the project quantities. These are the quantities against which the consumption of resources may be compared.

The Baseline values are values against which project progress is measured. All these values may be read by and compared with the current project values and show variances from the original plan.

A Baseline would normally be created prior to updating a project for the first time.

The Primavera Variance columns use Baseline data from Baseline Projects to calculate variances.

21.2 Understanding the Current Data Date

The **Data Date** is a standard scheduling term. It is also known as the **Review Date**, **Status Date**, **Report Date**, **As of Date**, **Time Now**, and **Update Date**.

- The **Data Date** is the date that divides the past from the future in the schedule. The **Data Date** is not normally in the future but is often in the recent past due to the time it may take to collect the information required to update the schedule.

- **Actual Costs** and **Quantities/Hours** or **Actual Work** occur before the Data Date.

- **Costs** and **Quantities/Hours to Complete** or **Work to Complete** are scheduled after the Data Date.

- **Actual Duration** is calculated from the **Actual Start** to the **Current Data Date**.

- **Remaining Duration** is the duration required to complete an activity. It is calculated forward from the **Current Data Date** and the Early Finish date or an in-progress activity is calculated from the **Current Data Date** using the:

  - ➤ **Activity Calendar** when the Activity Type is Task Dependent or is Resource Dependent but no Resources have been assigned, or

  - ➤ **Resource Calendar** when the Activity Type is Resource Dependent and uses the longest Resource Duration.

> *i* Primavera has one Data Date, the **Current Data Date**. Microsoft Project has four dates associated with updating a schedule. The Microsoft Project **Status Date** is similar in functionality to the Primavera **Current Data Date** but calculates very differently because Microsoft Project by default does not force incomplete work into the future. Elecosoft (Asta) Powerproject supports multiple Data Dates which are termed **Report Dates**, these are set up at the start of a project and has many schedule options enabling the mimicking of either P6 or Microsoft Project scheduling calculations.

21.3 Information Required to Update a Resourced Schedule

A project schedule is usually updated at the end of a period, such as each day, week, or month. One purpose of updating a schedule is to establish differences between the plan, which is usually saved as a Baseline, and the current schedule.

The following information is required to update a resourced schedule:

Activities completed in the update period:

- **Actual Start** date of the activity.
- **Actual Finish** date of the activity.
- **Actual Costs** and **Quantities** (Units) consumed or spent on **Labor Resources**, **Material Resources** and **Expense**. These may be calculated by the software or collected and entered into the software.

Activities commenced in the update period:

- **Actual Start** date of the activity,
- **Remaining Duration** or **Expected Finish** date,
- **Actual Costs** and/or **Actual Quantities**. Only when these are to be entered into the software,
- **Quantities to Complete** and **Costs to Complete**. Only when these are to be entered into the software,
- **% Complete**.

Activities Not Commenced:

- Changes in Logic, Constraints, or Duration, or

- Changes in estimated **Costs**, **Hours** or **Quantities** and

- Add or remove activities to represent scope changes.

The schedule may be updated after this information is collected.

Other Considerations

Primavera normally by default calculates:

- The Units to Complete and in turn the Actual Units by the relationship between the Remaining Duration and Resource Units.

- The Costs to Complete and the Actual Costs by the relationship between the Resource Unit Rate and Resource Units.

When these relationships are turned off then the Units and Costs may be entered manually.

A marked-up copy of the schedule recording the progress of the current schedule is often produced prior to updating the data with Primavera. Ideally, the mark-up should be prepared by a physical inspection of the work or by a person who intimately knows the work, although that is not always possible. It is good practice to keep this marked-up record for your own reference. Ensure that you note the date of the mark-up (i.e., the data date) and, if relevant, the time.

Often a Status Report or mark-up sheet is distributed to the people responsible for marking up the project's progress. A page break could be placed at each responsible person's band, and when the schedule is printed, each person would have a personal listing of activities that are either in-progress or due to commence. This is particularly useful for large projects. The marked-up sheets are then returned to the scheduler for data entry into the software system.

Other electronic methods, such as the Primavera Timesheet system or an e-mail based system with spreadsheet or pdf attachments, may be employed to collect the data. Irrespective of the method used, the same data needs to be collected.

It is recommended that only one person update each schedule. There is a high probability for errors when more than one person updates a schedule.

21.4 Project Window Defaults for Updating a Resourced Schedule

The **Project Window** settings affect all activities in a project that is being updated. When more than one project is open, then the settings of the **Project**, **Default Project**, which in Version 20 and later may be overridden by the project selected in the **Schedule Options**, **Use scheduling options from**, and the selected project **Schedule Options** are used to calculate all open projects when they are scheduled or leveled. Please read the **Multiple Project Scheduling** chapter for more details.

The **Calculations** tab in the **Projects Window** sets some important resource defaults:

- **Activities**

  - ➤ **Default Price/Unit for activities without resource or role Price/Units**. When an activity is assigned a quantity in the **Activities, Status** tab but no resource is assigned, then this rate is used to calculate the cost against Labor and Nonlabor units.

  - ➤ **Activity percent complete based on activity steps**. The Primavera **Step** function enables activities to be broken down into elements called Steps. Each element earns a designated % Complete when the Step is marked as complete. Physical % Complete Type must be selected to use Steps.

  - ➤ Unchecking **Link Budget and At Completion for not started activities** enable the user to re-estimate the cost or quantities of un-started activities while preserving the **Original Budget** of an activity. This also unlinks the **Original Duration** from the **At Completion Duration** for un-started activities.

  - ➤ The next two options **Reset Original Durations and Units to Remaining** and **Reset Remaining Duration and Units to Original** determine how the Original Duration and Units are set when progress is removed from activities. This was new to Primavera Version 4.1.

- **Resource Assignments**

  - ➤ **When updating Actual Units or Costs**. There are two options:

    Add Actual to Remaining. When Actual Costs are entered, the At Completion increases by the amount of the Actual Costs.

    Subtract Actual from At Completion. When Actual Costs are entered, the At Complete does not change and the To Complete is reduced by the value of the Actual. This is the author's preferred option, as the At Completion does not change until the At Completion is exceeded by the Actual.

  - ➤ **Recalculate Actual Units and Cost when duration % complete changes**. This option links the Duration % Complete to the Budget and To Complete, thus an increase in Duration % Complete will increase the Actual and decrease the To Complete values keeping the At Completion constant.

  - ➤ **Update units when costs change on resource assignments**.

    With this option checked a change in Costs will recalculate the Units.

    With this option unchecked, a change in costs may be made independently of units after units have been changed.

    This allows the importation of Costs from an accounting system and hours from a timesheet system separately.

  - ➤ **Link Actual to date and Actual This Period Units and Cost**. With this option checked, when you enter an **Actual this period**, the **Actual to date** will be calculated by increasing the original value by the value of the **Actual this period**. Alternatively, you may enter the **Actual to date** and Primavera will calculate the **Actual this period**. When unchecked, the two fields are unlinked and you may enter any figure in each field. This option is grayed out if the project is not open and is used to fix errors in data entry.
    This allows the fixing up of data errors when the **Store Period Performance** function is being used.

21.5 Activities Window – Percent Complete Types

There are three **% Complete** types which may be assigned to each activity. The default is adopted from the setting in the **Defaults** tab in the **Projects Window**. The author recommends changing the default to **Physical,** and then when actual units and costs information is entered, the **Activity % Complete** will not change and **Steps** may be used.

- **Physical**
- **Duration**
- **Units**

21.5.1 Assigning the Project Default Percent Complete Type

A project default **Percent Complete Type** is assigned in the **Defaults** tab of the **Projects Window** to each new activity created in a project. This may be changed at any time and only affects new activities created from that time onward:

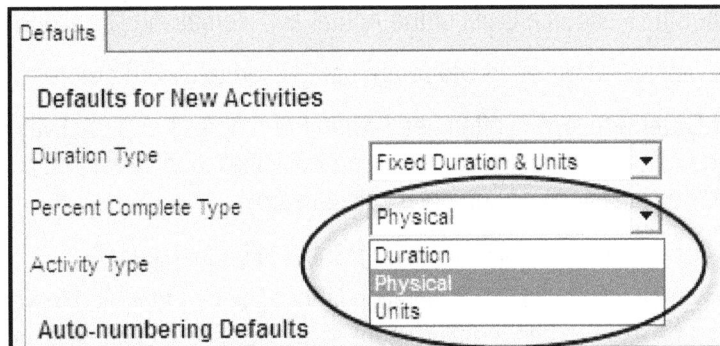

After an activity has been created, the **Percent Complete Type** may be changed in the **General** tab of the **Activities Window**:

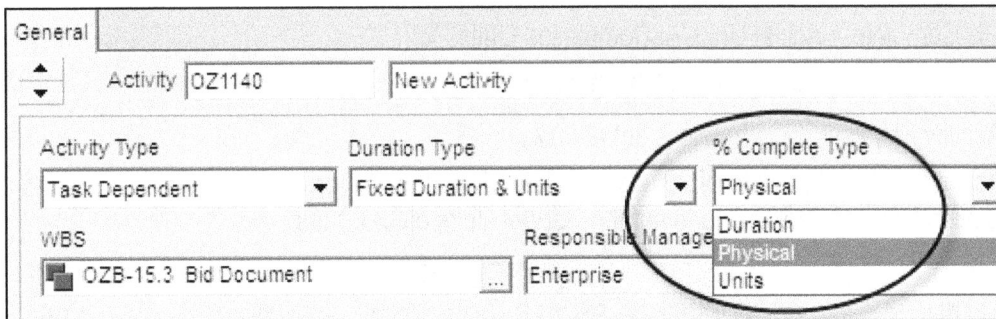

The Activity Percent Complete may be updated in the **Status** tab of the **Activities Window** where the **Percent Complete Type** is also displayed:

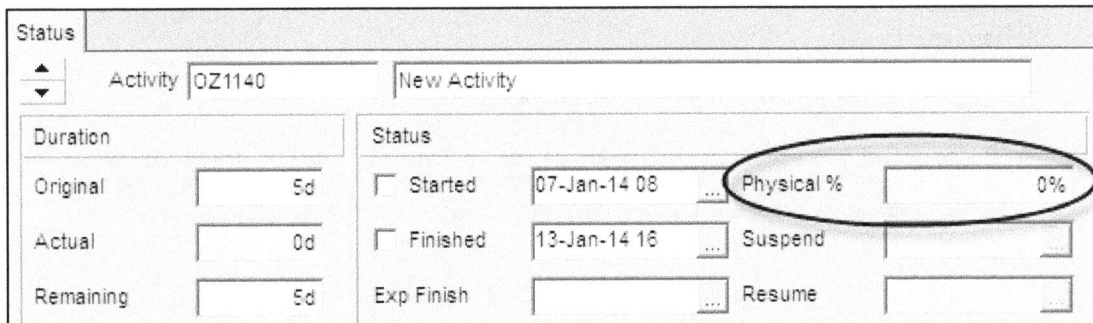

Each **Percent Complete Type** has its own data column and is always calculated.

There is also an **Activity % Complete** column which is linked to and displays the value from the **Percent Complete Type** column that has been assigned to the activity. See the following picture:

Activity ID	Activity Name	Percent Complete Type	Activity % Complete	Physical % Complete	Duration % Complete	Units % Complete
AA1000	% Complete Physical	Physical	50% ◄───►	50%	0%	0%
AA1010	% Complete Duration	Duration	50% ◄───	0% ───►	50%	0%
AA1020	% Complete Units	Units	50% ◄───	0%	0% ───►	50%

The **Activity % Complete** is in turn linked to the Bar Percent Complete, therefore in effect the **Percent Complete Type** determines the way the percent complete is displayed on the bars.

21.5.2 Physical Percent Complete Type

An activity assigned Physical Percent Complete Type may have the % Physical Complete entered in the **Physical % Complete** or the **Activity % Complete**. This field has no impact on schedule calculations and is not linked to either the Resource Units or the Actual and Remaining Durations of the Activity.

Physical % Complete must be used when **Steps** are being used to record progress.

The **Physical Percent Complete** type is often used when the progress of an Activity is being measured outside Primavera. For example, an activity representing the installation cable that is measured by length of cable installed would have the percent complete calculated by:

- % Complete = Qty. of Cable Installed/Total Qty. of Cable to be Installed

For example, the activity may only have the installation labor assigned to it, and therefore the installation labor parameter may not be used for the measurement of the Activity % Complete. In addition, because the percent complete of the activity is based on the length of cable installed, the Activity % Complete (the progress of the work) may be compared to the resource **Units % Complete** (the amount of labor used) which is calculated from the formula:

- Units % Complete = Actual Units/At Completion Units

This example is demonstrated in the following picture:

- The Activity Physical % Complete is set at 50%.
- The Activity Unit % Complete of 20% is calculated from the At Completion Units of 12.00 hrs and At Completion Units of 60.00 hrs and not the Budget Units of 48.00 hrs.

Percent Complete Type	Activity % Complete	Physical % Complete	Duration % Complete	Units % Complete	BL Budgeted Total Cost
Physical	50%	50%	0%	20%	$1,296.00

Resources

Activity	AA1000		% Complete Physical		

Budgeted Units	Actual Units	Remaining Units	At Completion Units	Units % Complete
48.00h	12.00h	48.00h	60.00h	20%

After a second resource is added, the Activity Units % Complete of 40% is calculated from the addition of the two resource Actual Units and At Completion Units:

- Activity Unit % Complete = Actual Labor Units/At Completion Labor Units

- Therefore, 40% = (12 + 36)/(60 + 60)

Percent Complete Type	Activity % Complete	Physical % Complete	Duration % Complete	Units % Complete	Actual Labor Units	At Completion Labor Units
Physical	50%	50%	0%	40%	48.00h	120.00h

Resources

Activity AA1000   % Complete Physical

Budgeted Units	Actual Units	Remaining Units	At Completion Units	Units % Complete
48.00h	12.00h	48.00h	60.00h	20%
48.00h	36.00h	24.00h	60.00h	60%

21.5.3 Duration Percent Complete Type

With Duration Percent Complete there is a link established between:

- **Duration % Complete**
- **Original Duration**
- **Remaining Duration**

A **Duration % Complete** may only be entered after an Actual Start Date has been assigned and should be in the past with respect to the Current Data Date.

A change in one parameter will change one other:

- A change in the **Duration % Complete** will change the **Remaining Duration,** and

- A change in the **Original Duration** or **Remaining Duration** will change the **Duration % Complete**:

Percent Complete Type	Activity % Complete	Physical % Complete	Duration % Complete	Units % Complete	Actual Labor Units	At Completion Labor Units
Duration	40%	0%	40%	50%	16.00h	32.00h

Status

Activity AB1080   Duration % Complete

Duration		Status		
Original	5d	☑ Started	27-Jun-03	Duration %	40%
Actual	1d	☐ Finished	02-Jul-03	Total Float	
Remaining	3d	Exp Finish		Free Float	

The **Actual Duration** is calculated from the duration of **Actual Start** to the **Current Data Date**.

The Activity **Units Percent Complete** is still calculated from the Resource Units.

21.5.4 Units Percent Complete Type

When **Units Percent Complete** type is selected:

- This option creates a link between the **Activity % Complete** and the activity **Units % Complete**, and

- The **Units % Complete** is calculated from the relationship between the **Actual Units** and **At Completion Units**.

21.6 *Using Steps to Calculate Activity Percent Complete*

An activity percent complete may be defined by using steps. A Step is a measurable or identifiable task required to complete an activity. Steps are useful to update activities that have many components, where the order of completion is not important but the measurement of progress is. Examples of the use of Steps:

- Driving of piles, with the **Step Weight** of each pile being the length of the pile,

- Pouring of footings, with the **Step Weight** being the m3 of concrete for each footing,

- Pulling of electrical cable, with the **Step weight** being the weight or length of each cable.

In summary, to use steps:

- A Step template may be created by selecting **Enterprise**, **Activity Step Template…** to open the **Activity Step Templates** form.

- Add as many steps as required and assign their weight which will be used to apportion the percent complete of an activity.

- Check the **Activity percent complete based on steps** check box in the **Projects Window**, **Calculations** tab,

- Select the **Physical** in the **% Complete Type** for each activity that is to be measured by steps in the **General** tab of **Activities Window**,

- Select the **Steps** tab in the **Activities Window**,

- Format the columns you wish to display,

- Add the number of steps you require or import from a Step Template,

- Edit the descriptions as required,

- Edit the **Step Weight** so the **Step Weight Percent** reflects the desired value of the Step,

- Check the **Completed** check box as each step is completed and this will update the percent complete.

- The **Remaining Duration** may be updated from the **Step % Complete** via the **Physical % Complete** using a **Global Change**.

Step Name	% Complete	Step Weight	Step Weight Percent	Completed
Specify Document Composition	100%	10.0	10.0	☑
Document First Draft	100%	40.0	40.0	☑
Final Draft and Internal Approval	0%	25.0	25.0	☐
Client Approval	0%	25.0	25.0	☐

21.7 Updating the Schedule

21.7.1 Preferences, Defaults and Options for Updating a Project

Most Primavera Options are good, but there are some that should be changed. The options to be considered and checked before updating a schedule:

Function	Discussion
• **% Complete Type**	It is the author's preference to use **Physical % Complete** when the resources are **Input** resources, i.e., those doing the work. This allows the % of deliverables complete to be measured independently of the resource(s) doing the work, thus allowing a comparison of the deliverables completed against the resources consumed. **Physical % Complete** must be used with steps.
• **Activity Type**	Activities with known durations should be set as **Task Dependent** and will use the Activity calendar (not the Resource Calendar) for calculating the finish date of the activity. **Resource Dependent** activities should only be used if there are resource availability issues which may only be resolved by the use of **Resource Calendars**. **Level of Effort** and **WBS** activities are useful but should be avoided by the novice user as these add an additional level of complexity that is not required.
• **Project Window Calculations tab**	The **Calculations** tab in the **Projects Window** sets some important resource defaults that should be reviewed, understood, and set so the schedule calculates the desired way. The **Link actual to date and actual this period units and Costs** option found in the **Calculations** tab of the **Project Window** should be checked if it is intended to **Store Period Performance**.
• **Duration Type**	It is the author's preference to use **Fixed Duration and Units** because the estimate to complete is not altered by changing the Activity Duration or Units/Time, but you should use **Fixed Duration & Units/Time** to keep the crew size constant.
• **User Preference, Calculation Tab**	This duration type also sets the **Resource Assignments** option in the **User Preferences, Calculation** tab to **Recalculate the Units, Duration, and Units/Time for existing assignments based on the activity Duration Type**. Thus, adding and removing resources will not change existing resource assignments

Function	Discussion
• **Timesheets**	Timesheets may be used to update actuals for none, some, or all resources. Organizations using timesheets should have procedures managing their use. Timesheets are out of the scope of this publication but if they are being used the actual values should be carefully checked before being applied to ensure they are logical.
• **Resources Cost Calculation**	Resource Costs may be calculated from the Resource Unit Rates for each individual resource assignment. Each resource assignment has a field titled **Calculate cost from units**. When this is checked the resource costs are calculated from the resource units. The **Calculate costs from units** check box in the **Resource Window, Details** tab sets the default value for **Calculate cost from units** for new resource assignments. The two fields are not linked and the resource assignment setting may be changed at any time.
• **Resource Window Details Tab**	• **Auto Compute Actuals** This field is linked to all resource assignments. When this option is checked for a resource Primavera calculates the Remaining Units based on the Remaining Duration and the Actual Units by subtracting the Remaining Units from Budgeted Units. An unchecked resource assignment option may be overridden by applying the **Activity Auto Compute Actuals** option. • **Calculate Costs from Units** There is a field available when a resource is assigned to an activity titled **Calculate cost from units.** With this option checked the costs for a resource are calculated from the **Resource Unit/Time** when a resource is added to an activity and whenever the Resource Units are changed.
• **General Schedule Options**	One of the more important options to review is the **When scheduling progressed activities use** options, as these affect how out-of-progress sequence is handled. These options should be reviewed to ensure that when the schedule is recalculated you will understand what is happening. The author prefers **Retained Logic** as this gives a more conservative schedule and those relationships that need editing may be edited to reflect retained logic as required.
• **Steps**	Should it be decided to use Steps to update a schedule the **Projects Window Calculations** tab should have the **Activity percent complete based on activity steps** option checked and the Activity must be assigned **Physical % Complete Type** in the **General tab** of the **Activities Window** for each activity.

Function	Discussion
• Earned value calculation	The <u>A</u>dmin, Admin <u>P</u>references…, Earned Value tab, **MUST NOT BE SET TO** "**Budgeted values with planned dates**" when a Baseline has progress, otherwise the Planned Dates will be displayed in the Baseline and these may contain irrelevant data when the schedule has progress.
	The author recommends using **At Completion values with current dates**. Then you are comparing the **At Completion** of the current schedule with the **At Completion Values** of the **Baseline** schedule.

21.7.2 Updating Dates and Percentage Complete

The schedule should be first updated as outlined in the **Updating an Unresourced Schedule** chapter. In summary, this is completed by entering:

- The **Actual Start** and **Actual Finish** dates of **Complete** activities.
- The **Actual Start**, **% Complete** and/or **Remaining Duration** of **In-Progress** activities.
- Adjust **Logic**, **Constraints** and **Durations** of **Un-started** activities.

Before updating the **% Complete**, the **% Complete Type** should be checked to ensure that the Actual and Remaining Durations, Costs, and Units calculate as required. This ideally should be done by setting the project defaults at the time the project is created and adjusting the settings as activities are added and resources assigned.

21.8 Updating Resources

There are many permutations available for calculating resource data. Due to the number of options available in Primavera, it is not feasible to document all the combinations available for resource calculation.

Resource units and costs may be updated using one of the following methods:

- Entering Progress Automatically from the timesheets, a process titled **Applying Actuals**, or
- Using the function titles **Update Progress**. This is **NOT** recommended due to the risk that your **Actual Start** and **Early Finish** may be changed by P6 when the schedule has progress, or
- Entering the data using the **Resource** tab in the **Activities Window**, or
- Entering the data using the right section of the **Status** tab in the **Activities Window**, or
- Importing from Excel. Actual dates and Remaining Durations may be imported but Suspend and Resume may not.

21.8.1 Resources Tab

The **Resources** tab may be used to update the resource **Units** (and Costs if the Units and Costs have been unlinked with the **Calculate cost from units** field). An updating layout could be created and the columns in the Resources tab formatted to your updating method; see the following picture:

21.8.2 Status Tab

The right window may be used for updating the resources.

- When there is one resource there will be a direct link between this form and the values assigned to the resource.

- When there is more than one resource there will be a proportional change to all the resource values when a change is made in this form.

21.8.3 Applying Actuals

This functions automatically:

- Statuses activities with resources as if they went according to the Planned Dates (this may change Actual Dates and current schedule dates) and only updates activities in the period from the old to the New Data Date, or

- Applies actuals entered in the Primavera Timesheet system.

To Apply Actuals:

- Select **Tools**, **Apply Actuals...** to open the **Apply Actuals** form,

- Enter the **New Data Date** and click Apply icon.

- If more than one project is open a different data date may be selected for each project.

- The Activity requires the Activity **Auto Compute Actuals** field checked for this function to apply to an Activity and all the Resources assigned to an activity.

- When the Activity **Auto Compute Actuals** field is not checked only the resources that have the Resource **Auto Compute Actuals** field checked in the **Resource Window** will be updated. If one resource is checked and one not, then the checked resource will be updated and the unchecked resource work will be delayed until after the **Current Data Date**.

There are some important issues with using **Apply Actuals** that must be understood:

- P6 Version 19 allows project to use their own **Data Date** when applying actuals. In earlier versions all projects were set to the same **Data Date**.

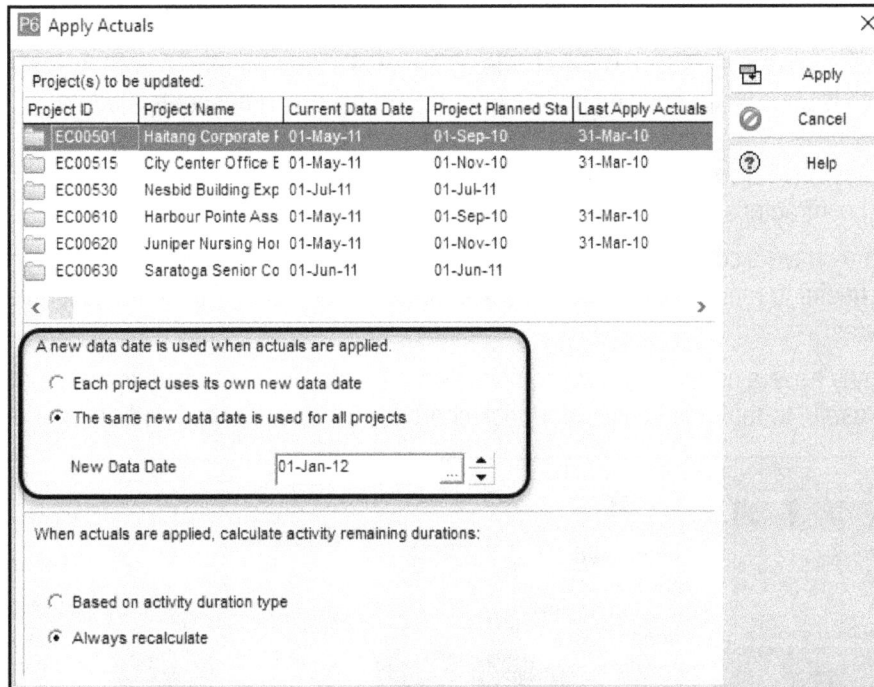

- This function uses the **Planned Dates**, not the current schedule dates, to progress a schedule so Actual Start Dates and the Early Finish dates may be changed by this function. This calculation process makes this function of little use to most schedulers.

- The **Apply Actuals** function does not work in the same way as the Microsoft Project function **Update Project** which updates all activities and resource assignments as if the project progressed exactly according to current schedule. They do not change any existing Actual Dates in the way the Primavera Update Progress and Apply Actual functions change dates to the Planned Dates which may hold irrelevant data.

- When the **Activity Auto Compute Actuals IS NOT** checked only activities with resources that are assigned **Auto Compute Actuals** will have their dates updated to their Planned Dates and resource assignments recalculated. Unresourced activities are scheduled after the Data Date.

- When the **Activity Auto Compute Actuals IS** checked then these activities will have their dates updated to their Planned Dates and resource assignments recalculated.

- With the introduction of **Progress Spotlight** there would initially appear to be no need to use **Apply Actuals** to automatically update a project and **Update Progress** and/or **Progress Spotlight** could be used. But as the **Update Progress** function also resets **Actual Dates** to **Planned Dates** this feature makes this function also of little use to many schedulers.

- A **Global Change** may be run first to set the **Planned** dates to the **Start** and **Finish** dates before Appling Actuals or Updating Progress, but this results in a change to the Original Duration and therefore the % Duration will calculate incorrectly and there is a risk that the user will forget to run the Global Change.

21.9   Updating Expenses

Expenses are updated in a similar way to resources in the **Activities Window**, **Expense** tab. Expenses will not be covered in detail, but here are some notes about Expenses that you may find useful:

- Expenses do not automatically update from any % Complete and have to be manually updated.

  ⚠️ The Expense **Auto Compute Actuals** option works only with the **Apply Actuals** function, which is used when bringing in data from the Primavera Timesheets module.

- Expenses may have a cost assigned before their activity is started; resources may not. This is useful to represent contractor's mobilization costs and are scheduled on the Data Date.

- Expenses may have a cost to complete before their activity is NOT marked started; resources may not. This is useful to represent contractor back charges or retention. These are scheduled on the Planned Dates.

- Expenses may have a negative cost to complete after the activity is marked complete; resources may not. This is useful to represent contractor back charges. These are scheduled on the Planned Dates:

- Expenses must be assigned a quantity and unit rate. The quantity is by default set to a value of one when a cost is entered against an Expense.

- Expense quantities may not be displayed in the:
  - ➢ **Activities Window** columns, or
  - ➢ **Resource Usage Spreadsheet**, or
  - ➢ **Resource Usage Profile**, or
  - ➢ **Activity Usage Spreadsheet**, or
  - ➢ **Tracking Window**, or
  - ➢ **Resource Assignment Window**.

- Expense quantities may be displayed in:
  - ➢ **Reports,** or
  - ➢ **Activity Details**, **Expenses** tab, or
  - ➢ **Expenses Window**.

  ℹ️ Thus, it is simple to get Expense Data into the system but difficult to get **Expense Quantity** data out of the system.

  ⚠️ Remaining Expenses assigned to a complete activity are Cash Flowed on the Planned dates, which would normally result with an incorrect Cash Flow with Remaining Costs in the past.

21.10 Workshop 18 – Updating a Resourced Schedule

Background

We now need to update the activities and resources as of 16 Dec 24.

Assignment

1.   If you did not complete the previous Leveling Workshop you will need to create and assign a baseline and display the Baseline bar:

>   Select **Project**, **Maintain Baselines…** and create a Baseline by saving a copy of the existing project,

>   Select **Project**, **Assign Baselines…** and select this as both your **Project Baseline** and **Primary User Baseline**, thus ensuring the baseline bar will either be blank or display the Baseline and not the **Planned Dates**.

2.   Apply your **OzBuild Workshop 13 – Baseline** layout and the Baseline bar should be displayed.

3.   Ensure only the **Project Baseline** bar is displayed.

4.   Go to the **Project Window**, **Calculations** tab ensure your settings are as per the following picture. These are the standard settings:

5.   Assign the **Project Manager** to the **Create Technical Specification** activity as this resource was missed out at the estimating stage and will give an immediate difference between the Current Schedule and the Baseline Units and Costs.

6.   Update this schedule manually by entering the following data in the **Activities**, **Status** tab or columns. Ensure all activities are **Physical % Complete**.

Activity ID	Activity Name	Actual Start	Actual Finish	Activity % Complete	Remaining Duration
OZ1000	Approval to Bid	10-Dec-24 08:00		100%	0d
OZ1010	Determine Installation Requirements	10-Dec-24 08:00	12-Dec-24 16:00	100%	0d
OZ1020	Create Technical Specification	12-Dec-24 08:00		80%	2d

7. Schedule and move the **Data Date** to 16-Dec-24 08:00.

Activity ID	Activity Name	Activity % Complete	Original Duration	Remaining Duration	Start	Finish	Total Float	Dec 09 / Dec 16
Bid for Facility Extension			33d	28d	10-Dec-24 08 A	27-Jan-25 16	0d	
Technical Specification			11d	6d	10-Dec-24 08 A	23-Dec-24 16	8d	
OZ1000	Approval to Bid	100%	0d	0d	10-Dec-24 08 A			
OZ1010	Determine Installation F	100%	4d	0d	10-Dec-24 08 A	12-Dec-24 16 A		
OZ1020	Create Technical Spec	80%	5d	2d	12-Dec-24 08 A	17-Dec-24 16	6d	
OZ1030	Identify Supplier Compo	0%	2d	2d	18-Dec-24 08	19-Dec-24 16	6d	
OZ1040	Validate Technical Spe	0%	2d	2d	20-Dec-24 08	23-Dec-24 16	8d	

8. OZ1010 is complete so there are no Remaining Costs or Remaining Units and the Actuals have been set to equal the Budget but may be manually adjusted.

Resources

Activity OZ1010 — Determine Installation Requirements

Resource ID Name	Remaining Units / Time	Budgeted Units	Actual Units	Remaining Units	At Completion Units
PM.Project Manager	8h/d	32h	32h	0h	32h
SE.Systems Engineer	8h/d	32h	32h	0h	32h

Resources

Activity OZ1010 — Determine Installation Requirements

Resource ID Name	Price / Unit	Budgeted Cost	Actual Cost	Remaining Cost	At Completion Cost
PM.Project Manager	$120/h	$3,840	$3,840	$0	$3,840
SE.Systems Engineer	$90/h	$2,880	$2,880	$0	$2,880

9. OZ1020 is in progress and the Remaining Units and Costs have been calculated from the Remaining Duration and the Remaining Units/Time but may be manually adjusted.

Resources

Activity OZ1020 — Create Technical Specification

Resource ID Name	Price / Unit	Budgeted Cost	Actual Cost	Remaining Cost	At Completion Cost
PM.Project Manager	$120/h	$4,800	$2,880	$1,920	$4,800
SE.Systems Engineer	$90/h	$3,600	$2,160	$1,440	$3,600

Resources

Activity OZ1020 — Create Technical Specification

Resource ID Name	Remaining Units / Time	Budgeted Units	Actual Units	Remaining Units	At Completion Units
PM.Project Manager	8h/d	40h	24h	16h	40h
SE.Systems Engineer	8h/d	40h	24h	16h	40h

10. Check the expenses for the Specialist Consultant assigned to OZ1020; they do not auto update. Update the Actual Costs to $2,000.00 and the remaining to $4,500.00.

Expenses

Activity OZ1020 — Create Technical Specification

Expense Item	Budgeted Cost	Actual Cost	Remaining Cost	At Completion Cost
Specialist Consultant	$5,000	$2,000	$4,500	$6,500

11. Now create an **OzBuild Workshop 18 – Percentages** layout and display the Percent Complete columns as per the following picture. Ensure Group Totals are displayed:

12. Enter 40% against the Physical % Complete of **Create Technical Specification** and see the Activity % Complete change to 40% as the activity % Complete Type is Physical:

Activity ID	Activity Name	Activity % Complete	Physical % Complete	Duration % Complete	Units % Complete
Bid for Facility Extension				13.89%	20%
Technical Specification				45.45%	58.33%
OZ1000	Approval to Bid	100%	100%	100%	0%
OZ1010	Determine Installation Requirements	100%	100%	100%	100%
OZ1020	Create Technical Specification	40% ⟷ 40%		60%	60%

13. Select the **Create Technical Specification** activity, open the Status tab, and change the Actual Labor Units from 48h to 24h in the box on the right side. Notice the Units % Complete change to 30% as fewer hours have been used, but the Remaining has changed to 56 hours:

Activity ID	Activity Name	Activity % Complete	Physical % Complete	Duration % Complete	Units % Complete
Bid for Facility Extension				13.89%	15.71%
Technical Specification				45.45%	45.83%
OZ1000	Approval to Bid	100%	100%	100%	0%
OZ1010	Determine Installation Requirements	100%	100%	100%	100%
OZ1020	Create Technical Specification	40%	40%	60%	30%

14. Now open the **Resources** tab, both resources now show 12h Actual and 28h remaining each. The **Remaining Units/Time** is now 14 hours/day because the **Activity Type** is **Fixed Duration and Units**:

Resources					
Activity OZ1020		Create Technical Specification			
Resource ID Name	Remaining Units / Time	Budgeted Units	Actual Units	Remaining Units	At Completion Units
PM.Project Manager	14h/d	40h	12h	28h	40h
SE.Systems Engineer	14h/d	40h	12h	28h	40h

15. The Actual Costs and Remaining Costs are also recalculated:

Resources					
Activity OZ1020		Create Technical Specification			
Resource ID Name	Price / Unit	Budgeted Cost	Actual Cost	Remaining Cost	At Completion Cost
PM.Project Manager	$120/h	$4,800	$1,440	$3,360	$4,800
SE.Systems Engineer	$90/h	$3,600	$1,080	$2,520	$3,600

16. Now change the **Remaining Units** of **Create Technical Specification** in the **Status** tab from 56 to 24. Note the change in the Units and Costs against the resources.

Resources					
Activity OZ1020		Create Technical Specification			
Resource ID Name	Remaining Units / Time	Budgeted Units	Actual Units	Remaining Units	At Completion Units
PM.Project Manager	6h/d	40h	12h	12h	24h
SE.Systems Engineer	6h/d	40h	12h	12h	24h

17. The Actual Costs and Remaining Costs should have also been recalculated:

Resource ID Name	Price / Unit	Budgeted Cost	Actual Cost	Remaining Cost	At Completion Cost
Activity	OZ1020		Create Technical Specification		
PM.Project Manager	$120/h	$4,800	$1,440	$1,440	$2,880
SE.Systems Engineer	$90/h	$3,600	$1,080	$1,080	$2,160

18. Create a new View titled **OzBuild Workshop 18 – Baseline Compare** and edit the columns so you are able to see the **At Completion Variances** against activity OZ1020, the Technical Specification WBS Node, and the Project:

Activity ID	Activity Name	Activity % Complete	BL Project Labor Units	At Completion Labor Units	Variance - BL Project Labor Units	BL Project Total Cost	At Completion Total Cost	Variance - BL Project Total Cost
Bid for Facility Extension			520h	528h	-8h	$55,060.00	$58,000.00	($2,940.00)
Technical Specification			152h	160h	-8h	$19,800.00	$22,740.00	($2,940.00)
OZ1000	Approval to Bid	100%	0h	0h	0h	$0.00	$0.00	$0.00
OZ1010	Determine Installation Re	100%	64h	64h	0h	$6,720.00	$6,720.00	$0.00
OZ1020	Create Technical Specifi	40%	40h	48h	-8h	$8,600.00	$11,540.00	($2,940.00)
OZ1030	Identify Supplier Compon	0%	16h	16h	0h	$1,120.00	$1,120.00	$0.00
OZ1040	Validate Technical Spec	0%	32h	32h	0h	$3,360.00	$3,360.00	$0.00
Delivery Plan			224h	224h	0h	$21,520.00	$21,520.00	$0.00
OZ1050	Document Delivery Meth	0%	32h	32h	0h	$3,840.00	$3,840.00	$0.00
OZ1060	Obtain Quotes from Supp	0%	128h	128h	0h	$12,160.00	$12,160.00	$0.00
OZ1070	Calculate the Bid Estimat	0%	24h	24h	0h	$1,920.00	$1,920.00	$0.00
OZ1080	Create the Project Sched	0%	24h	24h	0h	$1,920.00	$1,920.00	$0.00
OZ1090	Review the Delivery Plar	0%	16h	16h	0h	$1,680.00	$1,680.00	$0.00
Bid Document			144h	144h	0h	$13,740.00	$13,740.00	$0.00
OZ1100	Create Draft of Bid Docu	0%	96h	96h	0h	$8,160.00	$8,160.00	$0.00
OZ1110	Review Bid Document	0%	32h	32h	0h	$3,360.00	$3,360.00	$0.00
OZ1120	Finalise and Submit Bid [	0%	16h	16h	0h	$2,220.00	$2,220.00	$0.00
OZ1130	Bid Document Submitted	0%	0h	0h	0h	$0.00	$0.00	$0.00

19. At this point you may experiment with this activity. Uncheck **Auto Compute Actuals** will allow you to change the Costs and they are not recalculated from the Resource Rate.

20. You may also look at some of the other tabs such as the **Summary** tab.

---

22 OTHER METHODS OF ORGANIZING PROJECT DATA

The **Work Breakdown Structure – WBS** function was discussed earlier as a method of organizing projects and activities under hierarchical structures. There are alternative features available in Primavera for grouping, sorting and filtering activities, resources, and project information:

- Activity Codes
- User Defined Fields (UDF)
- WBS Categories
- Resource Codes
- Cost Accounts
- EPS Level Activity Codes
- Assignment Codes – new to Primavera P6 Version 20
- Role Codes – new to Primavera P6 Version 20

> *i* There are no Activity ID Codes in Primavera like the function found in P3 and SureTrak. In Primavera each activity must have a unique Activity ID but no logical code system may be associated with the Activity ID. Some users double-code activities so some Activity ID characters are the same as an Activity Code.

22.1 Understanding Project Breakdown Structures

A Project Breakdown Structure represents a hierarchical breakdown of a project into logical functional elements. Some organizations have highly organized and disciplined structures with "rules" for creating and coding the elements of the structure. Some clients also impose a WBS code on a contractor for reporting and/or claiming payments. The following are examples of such structures:

- WBS **Work Breakdown Structure** breaks down the project into the elements of work required to deliver a project.

- COA **Code of Accounts**, also known as **Cost Breakdown Structure**. Often this contains costs that are not included in a schedule, such as insurances and overheads. The WBS would in this situation represent part of the COA.

- OBS **Organization Breakdown Structure** shows the hierarchical management structure of a project. Primavera has a predefined field for this breakdown structure.

- CBS **Contract Breakdown Structure** shows the breakdown of contracts into elements.

- SBS **System Breakdown Structure**, a **System Engineering** method of breaking down a complex system into elements.

- PBS **Product Breakdown Structure**, a **PRINCE2** term used for the breakdown of project deliverables under two headings of Project Management and Specialist products.

22.2 Activity Codes

Activity Codes may be used to Group, Sort, and Filter activities from one or more open projects.

- **Activity Codes**, such as Phases, Trades, or Disciplines, are often defined in the **Enterprise**, **Activity Codes** , **Activity Codes Definition** form.

- **Activity Code Values** are defined in the **Enterprise**, **Activity Codes...**form, such as:
  - ➢ Phases of Design, Procure, Install and Test,
  - ➢ Trades of Brickwork, Plumbing and Electrical, and
  - ➢ Disciplines of Concrete, Mechanical, Pipework.

- **Activity Codes** are assigned from the **Activities Window** using the **Codes** tab in the lower pane or displaying the appropriate Activity Code column.

  > *i* Microsoft Project 2002 introduced Custom Outline Codes, which is a hierarchical coding structure that may be assigned to activities and enables the activities to be Grouped under these codes. There are 10 Custom Outline Codes available with every project that may be renamed to suit the project requirement. The Primavera Activity Code function operates similarly to both the Elecosoft (Asta) Powerproject Code functions and the Microsoft Project Custom Outline Codes, but in addition enables an unlimited number of Code Dictionaries and Values for each Code Dictionary and may be hierarchical. Elecosoft (Asta) Powerproject codes work in a similar way to P6 but a task may be assigned multiple values from one code dictionary which is very useful and not possible in other products. For example, a column may be assigned all three floors that it is associated with.

22.2.1 Understanding Activity Codes

There are three types of Activity Codes:

- **Global Activity Codes** that may be created at any time and applied to any project.

- **EPS** which are created for projects associated with one EPS Node and may only be assigned to project activities that are associated with that EPS Node. Thus, you may wish to create Railway EPS Activity Codes for projects in the Railway EPS and Software Development EPS Activity Codes for projects in the Software Development EPS.

- **Project Activity Codes** that may only be created when a project is opened and applied only to the project they were created for. These may be made Global by clicking the [ⓢ Make Global] icon in the **Activity Codes Definition – Project** form.

Activity Codes may be added, deleted, or modified in the **Activity Codes** form:

- Select **Enterprise**, **Activity Codes...** to open the **Activity Codes** form,

- Select either **Global**, **EPS** or **Project** radio button depending on whether the codes are for a specific project or available to all projects,

- Select from the drop-down box under **Select Activity Code** which code structure is to be edited.

- The code structure is modified in a similar way to WBS codes.

- Each Activity Code has a Code value and a Description. The length of the Code is defined when the code is created; see the next section.

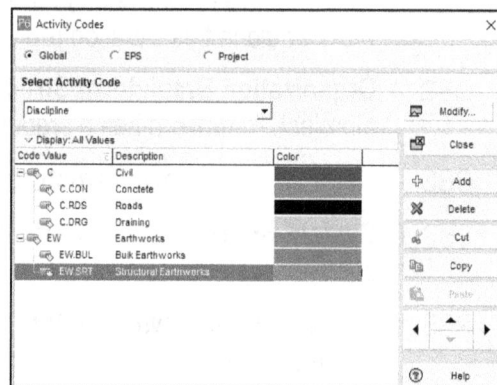

22.2.2 Activity Code Creation

This process creates a field in the database where the Activity Codes may be added.

- Open an **Activity Codes Definition** form from the **Activity Codes** form by selecting either:
  - ➤ **Global**,
  - ➤ **EPS,** or
  - ➤ **Project**,

  Each form is slightly different.

- Click the [🖳 Modify...] icon to open the **Activity Codes Definition** form.

- The Activity Codes may be created, deleted, or made into Global and reordered in these forms.

- The **Maximum Length** is the maximum number of characters a code may be assigned when it is created in the **Activity Codes form**.

- The **Secure Code** allows access to be controlled through the Users Security Profile.

- The **Activity Codes Definition – Project** form has the following icons:
  - ➤ [🌐 Make Global] that makes a Project Activity Code a Global Activity Code, and
  - ➤ [◇ Make EPS] that makes a Project Activity Code an EPS Activity Code.

© **Hyde Park Solutions Limited**   **375**

22.2.3 Defining Activity Code Values and Descriptions

Defining an Activity Code is similar to creating a Codes in and Elecosoft (Asta) Powerproject or renaming a Microsoft Project Custom Outline Code:

- From the **Activity Codes** form select **Global**, **EPS** or **Project**,

- Select the **Activity Code** to edit from the drop-down box,

- Add **Activity Codes Values** and **Descriptions** in the same way as WBS Codes and descriptions.

- The **Activity Code Color** may be used with the **Timescaled Logic Diagram** in **Visualizer.**

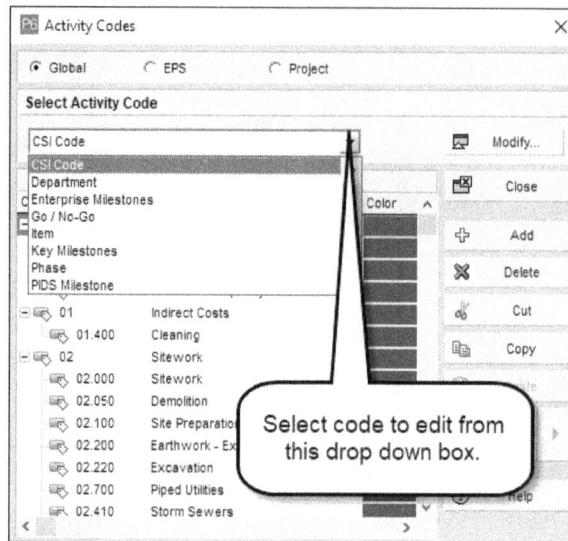

22.2.4 Assigning Activity Code Values to Activities

Activity Codes may be assigned to an activity:

- Select the **Codes** tab in the lower pane by clicking the [Assign] icon to open the **Assign Activity Codes** form and assign an Activity Code, or

- Display the appropriate activity code column and either:
  - ➤ Type in the code, or
  - ➤ Click twice on the Activity Code cell and open the **Select "Code"** form.

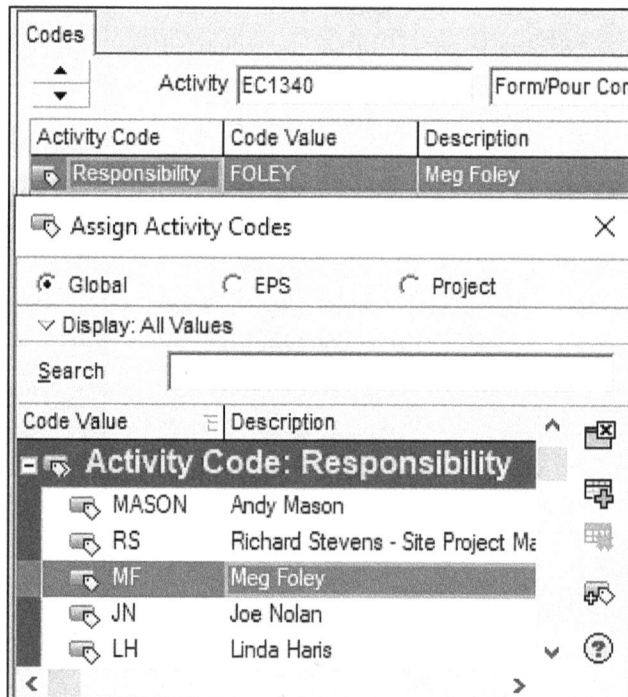

22.2.5 Add Activity Codes When Assigning Codes

Activity Codes may be added on the fly, as there is a new icon titled **New** on the **Assign Activity Codes** form that allows Activity Codes to be created as they are assigned:

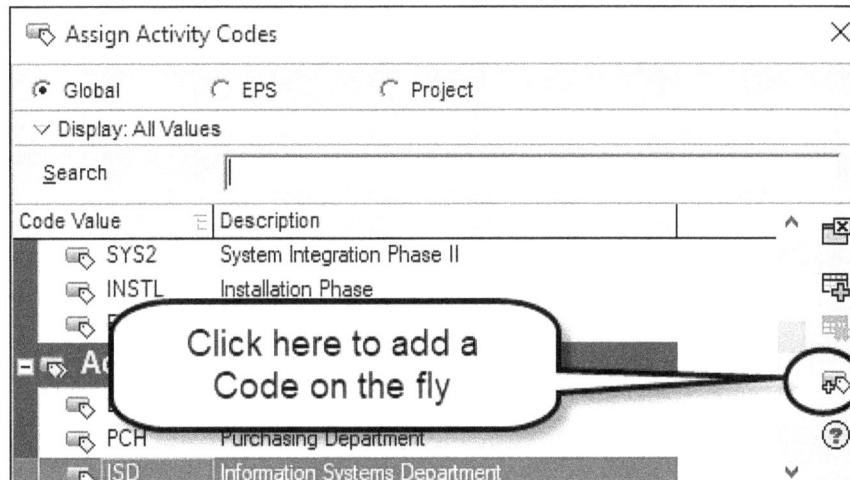

Click on the [icon] icon to open the **Add Code Value** form and enter the new Code Value and Code Value Description.

22.2.6 Grouping, Sorting and Filtering with Activity Codes

When more than one project is open an Activity Code may be used to group activities from all the open projects under one code structure.

Activity Codes are Grouped and Filtered in the same way as WBS codes.

22.2.7 User Preferences, Application, Codes Option

This option was introduced in Version 20.

- P6 normally displays the Code Value in columns and the Code Description in the Bands, as per the picture on the left.

- P6 has an option to display the Activity Code value in bands from the **Group and Sort** form, see the picture on the right.

- This option allows for the either the Code or Code Description to be displayed in columns, see the picture on the right.

Activity ID	Activity Name	OzBuild Department
OzBuild Department		
OZ1000	Approval to Bid	OZD
OZ1130	Bid Document Submitted	OZD
Project Support		
OZ1040	Validate Technical Specification	OZD.PS
OZ1080	Create the Project Schedule	OZD.PS
OZ1090	Review the Delivery Plan	OZD.PS
OZ1100	Create Draft of Bid Document	OZD.PS
OZ1110	Review Bid Document	OZD.PS
OZ1120	Finalise and Submit Bid Document	OZD.PS
Engineering		

Activity ID	Activity Name	OzBuild Department
OZD OzBuild Department		
OZ1000	Approval to Bid	OzBuild Department
OZ1130	Bid Document Submitted	OzBuild Department
OZD.PS Project Support		
OZ1040	Validate Technical Specification	Project Support
OZ1080	Create the Project Schedule	Project Support
OZ1090	Review the Delivery Plan	Project Support
OZ1100	Create Draft of Bid Document	Project Support
OZ1110	Review Bid Document	Project Support
OZ1120	Finalise and Submit Bid Document	Project Support
OZD.EN Engineering		

22.2.8 Importing Activity Codes with Excel

If Activity Codes are to be imported with activities using the Primavera Excel Import function, then they must exist in the database before the codes may be imported; otherwise the code will not be imported.

There are some options for importing Activity Codes and Code Values and other data that is not imported with Excel:

- You may create a project with the Activity Codes defined and one code added, export the project as an XER, open with Excel, add the Code Values and reimport. The is a paper on https://primavera.com.au/ that explains how this is achieved.

- There are several tools available listed on https://primavera.com.au/under Third Party Software that assists in the import of data such as Activity Codes into P6.

22.3   User Defined Fields

User Defined Fields are similar to **Custom Fields** in Microsoft Project or **User Fields in** and Elecosoft (Asta) Powerproject and provide the ability to assign additional information to database records. They may be used for recording information about the data field as an alternative to Activity Codes and other predefined Primavera fields. The type of data that may be assigned to User Defined Fields would be equipment number, order number, variation or scope number; road, railway or pipeline changes; address and additional costs data.

Activity data may be filtered, grouped, and sorted using these User Defined Fields in a similar way to Activity Codes.

Data may be imported into the fields and, unlike Activity Codes, the data item does not have to exist in the database before importing.

There are a number of predefined fields that may be renamed and new ones may be created. User Defined Fields may be defined for:

- Activities
- Activity Resource Assignments
- Activity Steps
- Issues
- Project Expenses

- Projects
- Resources
- Risks
- WBS
- Work Products and Documents

The fields are assigned a **Data Type** from the following list:

- Text – maximum of 255 characters
- Start Date and Finish Date – which may be used to create bars
- Cost
- Indicator – select from ⊗ ▽ ⊘ ★
- Integer
- Number

After some data has been entered against a field in any project, the **Data Type** may not be changed.

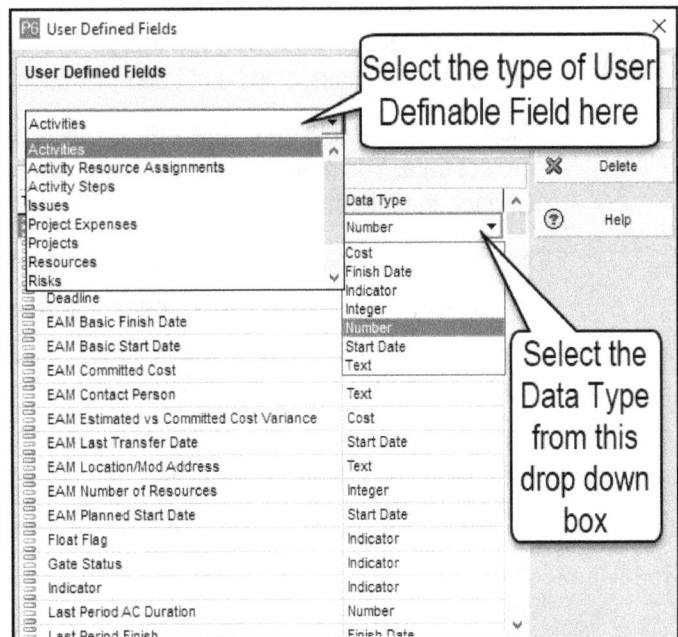

Select the type of User Definable Field here

Select the Data Type from this drop down box

P6 Version 19 added a new **Details**, **User Defined Fields** tab, similar to the **Codes** tab, displaying the assigned User Defined Fields (UDFs). It is available in the following windows: Projects, WBS, Activities, Resource Assignments, Project Expenses, Issues, and Work Products, Risks and Documents.

- The user must add the UDF Field to the **User Defined Fields** tab by clicking on the **Customize User Defined Fields** button.

- The displayed UDF Fields are saved as part of the View, thus the user will not automatically see which UDFs a data item such as a Project or Activity are being utilized.

- The picture below shows that the activity has been assigned a Parts Availability date but this is not displayed in the **User Defined Fields** tab as this UDF field has not been added by clicking on the **Customize User Defined Fields** button.

- The **Hide empty rows** will hide any blank UDF fields, so the Deadline line in the picture below would be hidden if the **Hide empty rows** was checked.

Activity ID	Activity Name	Work Order	Parts Availability	Start
− **Design and Engineering**			13-Jan-16 00:00	18-Jan-16 08:00
EC100	Design Building Addition	8124	13-Jan-16 00:00	18-Jan-16 08:00

User Defined Fields

Activity EC1000   Design Building Addition

User Defined Field	Data Type	Value
Work Order	Text	8124
Deadline	Finish Date	

Customize User Defined Fields   ☐ Hide empty rows

i One advantage of **User Defined Fields** over **Notebook Topics** is that they may be also displayed in columns and be cut and pasted into other programs like Excel.

Also, User Definable Field data may easily be imported from Excel and will not change your project data. You may consider importing data into User Defined Fields and then Global Change the information into the appropriate location as a second step.

- Thus, Resource data needs to be imported into Resource User Defined Fields, and
- Activity data needs to be imported into Activity User Defined Fields.

⚠ You must be careful that you do not make a User Definable Field with the same name as a P6 field, otherwise you will not know which is which when creating filters.

You may consider adding a full stop at the end of each User Definable Field name so it is clear which is a User Definable field and which is a P6 field when creating Filters and Group and Sorts.

Select **Enterprise**, **User Defined Fields…** to open the **User Defined Fields** form:

- Select the **Subject Area** in the drop-down box in the top left-hand side of the form.

- Use the ⊹ Add and ✖ Delete icons to create and delete fields.

- Select the **Data Type** from the drop-down list.

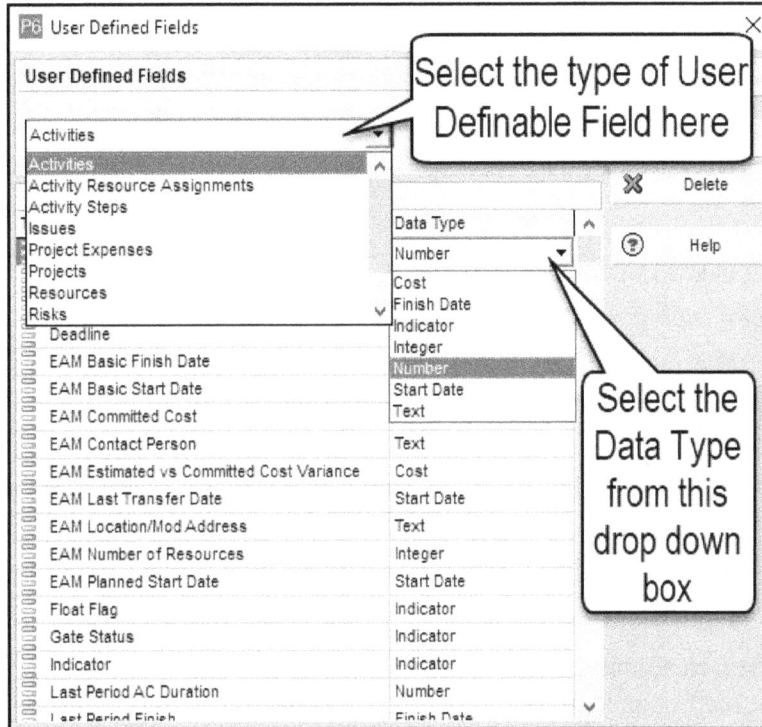

⚠ The list of User Defined Fields will re-sort as soon as a new field is added or the title edited and you may have to scroll up or down to find it in the list

To display or edit data in a User Defined Field the column should be displayed in the appropriate window. For example, if an Activity User Defined Field has been created then the Activities Window should be selected and the field will be displayed under **User Defined**.

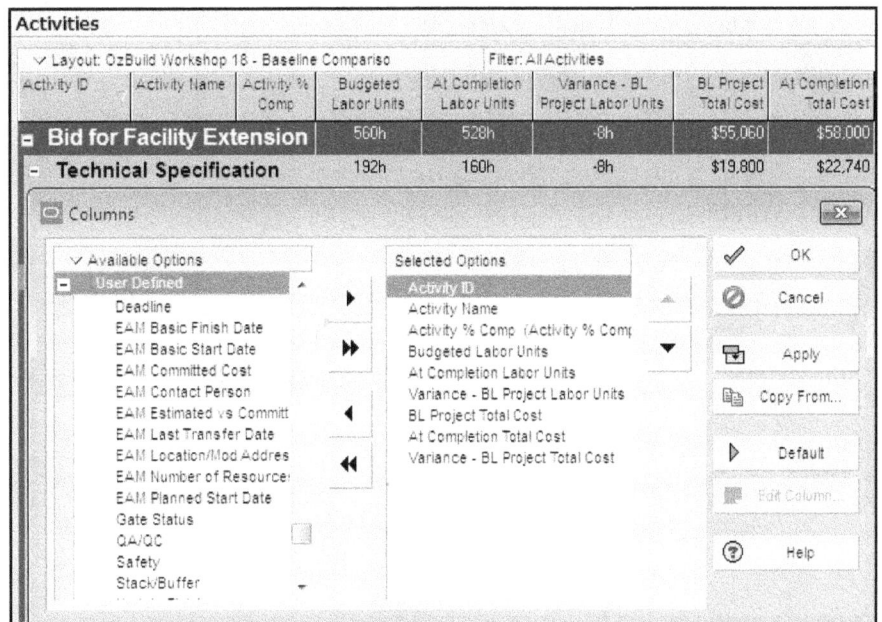

22.4 WBS Category or Project Phase

The **WBS Categories** is assigned to **WBS Nodes** in the **WBS Window** and may be used to Group and Sort WBS Nodes under a different set of headings.

This would enable, for example, all design WBS Nodes that were distributed throughout a project WBS to be grouped together under one heading without assigning an Activity Code to each activity. WBS Codes are to a WBS in same way as Activity Codes are to Activities and Project Codes to Project but there is only one dictionary or set of WBS Codes.

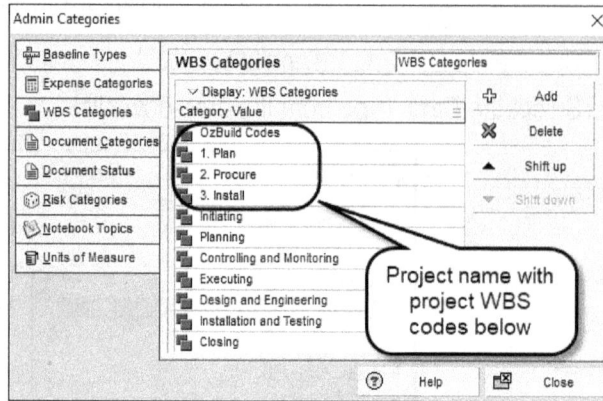

Separate sets of project WBS Codes can be listed under a dummy code as the project name, see para 6.5 for more information.

22.5 Resource Codes

Resource Codes are to resources as Activity Codes are to activities and allow resources to be Grouped, Sorted, and Filtered by these codes. Resources may have codes such as Office, Location, or Employment Status assigned to them.

To create a Resource Code:

- Select **Enterprise**, **Resource Codes...** to open the **Resource Codes** form.

- The Resource Codes are created, edited, and deleted in a similar way to Activity Codes.

Resource Codes may be Assigned to Resources in a similar way to Activity Codes by:

- Opening the **Resources Window**,

- Displaying the appropriate Code Column,

- Opening the **Codes** tab in the **Resources Window**.

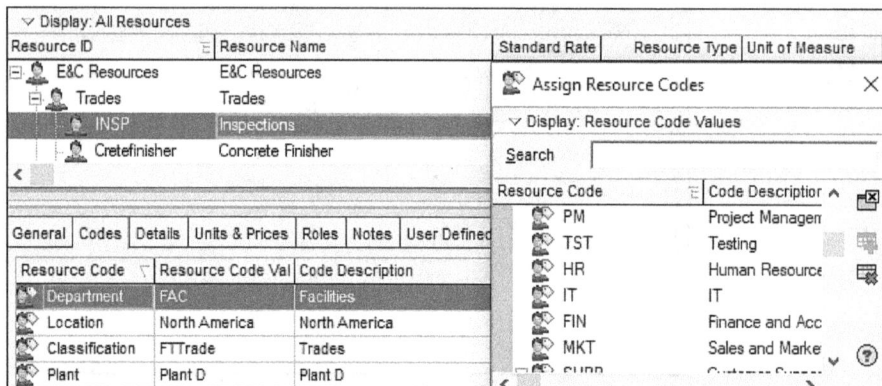

22.6 Cost Accounts

Cost Accounts are to resource assignments as Activity Codes are to activities and are intended to reflect the accounting code structure of a project. Cost Account in Primavera is assigned to a resource. They enable the grouping and reporting of resource data into Cost Accounts, which would allow budgets to be calculated and used to update Corporate Budgets.

Cost Accounts have additional functions that Activity Codes do not have:

- A default Cost Account for each new Resource or Expense may be specified in the **Projects Window**, **Defaults** tab. This is used for each new Resource or Expense and does not affect existing assignments. The **Project Default Cost Account** may be changed at any time:

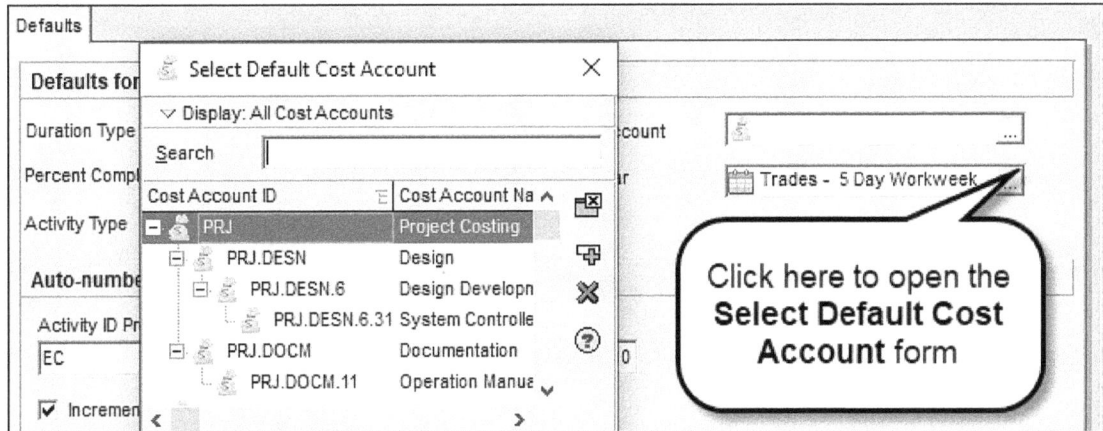

- Cost Accounts may be reassigned and merged.
- Cost Accounts may have descriptive fields when they are created.

Costs accounts are created:

- In the Windows Client **Cost Accounts** form by selecting **Enterprise**, **Cost Accounts…** and opening the **Cost Accounts** form, and
- In the Web Client by selecting **Administer**, **Enterprise Data**, **Activities**, **Cost Accounts**.

Cost Accounts are assigned to Resources or Expenses by displaying the Cost Account column in the **Activities Window** lower pane **Resources** and **Expenses** tabs.

> The drawback of the **P6 Cost Account** function is that all resources are assigned the same value, which is normally undesirable. Cost accounts are normally used to group costs by parameters required by the accounts department, such as permanent or temporary materials, and used for depreciation etc.
>
> It is more normal to assign a Cost Account to a resource and when a resource is assigned to an activity, it automatically has the desired Cost Account. If you wish a more traditional Cost Account set-up then you may wish to consider using a Resource Code to represent a Cost Account.

22.7 Owner Activity Attribute

"Owner," the new activity field in Primavera Version 6.0, enables a user who is not a resource to be assigned to an activity. This now enables the person responsible for an activity to be assigned from the list of users. This function may be used in combination with a Reflection project.

22.8 Assignment Codes

There is a new function titled **Assignment Codes** allowing users to code up assignments so resource assignments may be Grouped or Filtered. This function could be used for:

- Assigning priority to resource assignments against tasks,
- When there is one generic resource in the database that is being supplied by multiple subcontractors and this could be used to identify the subcontractor,
- When there is one generic resource in the database and you require a specific skill or qualification for the resource then this could be identified with an **Assignment Code**.

Assignment Codes are created in the same way as other codes by selecting **Enterprise**, **Assignment Codes**:

Assignment Codes are assigned to Resource or Role Assignments in the:

- **Codes** tab in the **Resource Assignment** window, or

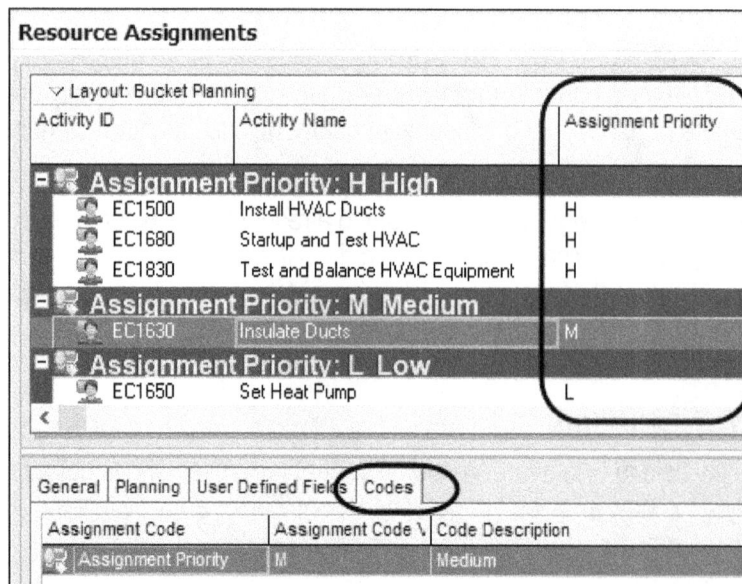

- Displaying the **Assignment Code** column in the **Activities** window **Details** pane, **Resources** tab, or

- Displaying the **Assignment Code** column in center section of the **Resource Usage Spreadsheet**.

22.9   Role Codes

P6 Version 20 introduced **Role Codes** allowing Roles to be assigned a Code in the same way as Resources and Activities.

This would be useful to assign attributes such as location, skill or office and may be used to group or filter roles.

- **Role Codes** are created in the **Role Codes** form by selecting **Enterprise**, **Role Codes**:

- **Role Codes** are assigned to Roles in the **Roles** form.

22.10 Workshop 19 – Activity Codes and User Defined Fields

Background

This workshop will look at creating an Activity Code and some UDFs. In the next workshop you will populate the UDFs using Global Change.

We will create an activity code to represent the departments' responsibilities for the Project.

Assignment – Activity Codes

1. Select **Enterprise**, **Activity Codes...** to open the **Activity Code** form,

2. Click on the **Project** button at the top of the form.

3. Select [Modify...] to open the **Activity Code Definitions – Project** form.

4. Select [Add] to create a new code titled **OzBuild Department** and assign a **Max Length** of 3.

5. Click on [Close] to close the form.

6. Create the Activity Code Values and Descriptions as in the picture on the right.

7. Apply the **OzBuild Workshop 10 – Without Float** layout.

8. Add the **OzBuild Department** column per the picture and save the layout as **OzBuild Workshop 19 – Assign Codes** layout.

9. Assign the **OzBuild Departments** using all the methods available as in the following picture:

10. **Note:** If the **OzBuild Department**'s Code Name and not Code is displayed in the column then this may be changed by selecting **Edit**, **User Preferences**, **Application**, **Codes** and selecting **Code Value**.

Activity ID	Activity Name	OzBuild Department
Bid for Facility Extension		
Technical Specification		
OZ1000	Approval to Bid	OZD
OZ1010	Determine Installation Requirements	OZD.EN
OZ1020	Create Technical Specification	OZD.EN
OZ1030	Identify Supplier Components	OZD.PR
OZ1040	Validate Technical Specification	OZD.PS
Delivery Plan		
OZ1050	Document Delivery Methodology	OZD.EN
OZ1060	Obtain Quotes from Suppliers	OZD.PR
OZ1070	Calculate the Bid Estimate	OZD.PR
OZ1080	Create the Project Schedule	OZD.PS
OZ1090	Review the Delivery Plan	OZD.PS
Bid Document		
OZ1100	Create Draft of Bid Document	OZD.PS
OZ1110	Review Bid Document	OZD.PS
OZ1120	Finalise and Submit Bid Document	OZD.PS
OZ1130	Bid Document Submitted	OZD

11. Now Group and Sort by the **Activity Code: OzBuild Department**, sort by Activity ID. The Milestones are now at the top of the screen.

12. The picture below has the Code Descriptions displayed selecting **Edit**, **User Preferences**, **Application**, **Codes** and selecting **Description**.

13. Save the layout.

14. Now assign the **OzBuild Workshop13** – Baseline layout.

Assignment – UDFs

15. We will create some UDFs which we will populate using Global Change.

NOTE: If you are in a shared database the instructor will create these UDFs.

16. Select **Enterprise**, **User Defined Fields…** to open the **Used Defined Fields** form,

17. Select **Activities** in the drop-down box at the top of the form,

18. Add three UDFs titled:

- **Last Period Start** as a **Data Type** of **Start Date**
- **Last Period Finish** as a **Data Type** of **Finish date**
- **Last Period AC Dur** (Last Period At Completion Duration) as a **Data Type** of **Number**.

19. Display the columns and Group by WBS as in the following picture:

Activity ID	Activity Name	Original Duration	Last Period AC Dur	Start	Last Period Start	Finish	Last Period Finish
Bid for Facility Extension		33d	0.00	10-Dec-24 08 A		27-Jan-25 16	
Technical Specification		11d	0.00	10-Dec-24 08 A		23-Dec-24 16	
OZ1000	Approval to Bid	0d		10-Dec-24 08 A			
OZ1010	Determine Installation F	4d		10-Dec-24 08 A		12-Dec-24 16 A	
OZ1020	Create Technical Spec	5d		12-Dec-24 08 A		17-Dec-24 16	
OZ1030	Identify Supplier Compc	2d		18-Dec-24 08		19-Dec-24 16	
OZ1040	Validate Technical Spe	2d		20-Dec-24 08		23-Dec-24 16	
Delivery Plan		18d	0.00	24-Dec-24 08		21-Jan-25 16	

20. Save the Layout as **Workshop 19 – UDF**.

---

23 GLOBAL CHANGE

23.1 Introducing Global Change

Global Change is a facility for changing more than one data item in one step. Examples of uses of Global Change are:

- Assigning Resources to Roles

- Increasing or decreasing durations of selected activities by a factor

- Creating new activity descriptions by placing activity codes at the beginning or at the end of the original description

- Removing constraints

- Changing Calendars.

At the time of writing this publication, Global Change could not be used in the **Projects Window** as this project data may not be accessed by Global Change.

This chapter is intended as an introduction to **Global Change** and covers the following topics:

- The Basic Concepts of Global Change

- Specifying the Change Statements

- Simple Examples of Global Change

- Selecting the Activities for the Global Change

- Temporary Values and Global Change Functions

- More Advanced Examples of Global Change.

After you understand the basics, you will then develop some interesting ways of using Global Change.

It is very easy to specify a Global Change that will not change data in the way you intended.

You must consider your Autocost rules when using Global Change on resources, percentages complete, and durations. For example, changing Original Durations will have no effect on the Early Finish of activities that have commenced when Remaining Duration and Percent Complete are unlinked.

i Be careful when using Global Change, as the changes may not be undone. Consider copying your project or making a Reflection project if you are using Primavera before making Global Changes. Study the **Global Change Report** to review your changes before making permanent changes.

23.2 The Basic Concepts of Global Change

Select **Tools**, **Global Change…** to open the **Global Change** form:

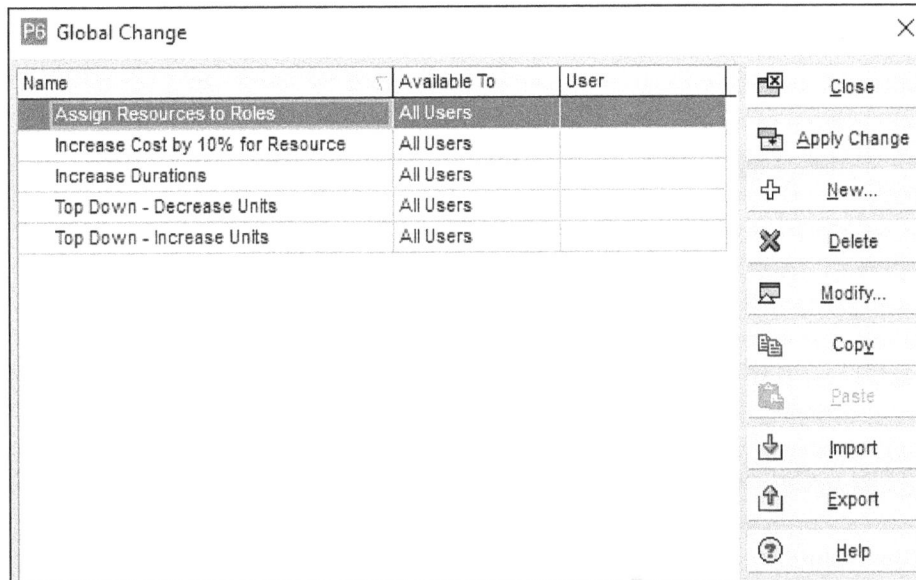

A Global Change may be created, saved, and used at a later date.

A Global Change may not be "Undone."

The **Global Change** form displays the list of Global Changes available in the project.

- [Apply Change] enables the effects of a Global Change in the **Global Change Report** before finalizing changes to the project data by selecting [Commit Changes] in the **Global Change Report.**

- [New…] creates a new Global Change.

- [Modify…] enables you to modify the highlighted Global Change.

- [Delete] deletes the highlighted Global Change.

- [Copy] and [Paste] create a copy of an existing Global Change that may then be edited.

- [Import] and [Export] are used to import from or export to a Global Change from another database in the **Primavera Change File pcf** file format.

It is **STRONGLY** recommended that you always review the **Global Change Report** to review your changes before making permanent changes by running a Global Change.

It is **STRONGLY** recommended that you consider making a copy of your project before using a Global Change, copy the project in the Enterprise Window, make a Baseline or use a Reflection Project.

After creating Global Change using the [✚ New...] option or [▤ Copy] and [▤ Paste] or by selecting [▱ Modify...], you will be presented with the second **Modify Global Change** form. This is where you select the data to be changed and where the operation to the data is specified.

There are boxes at the top of the form:

- **Select Subject Area** enables the option of Activities, Activity Resource Assignments, or Project Expenses, and

- **Global Change Name** is the name displayed in the **Global Change** form.

The form has three lower sections. You will need to click into each area and then use [✚ Add] and [✖ Delete] icons to add or remove criteria or operation lines:

- **If** area is where you create a criterion for selecting the data on which to be operated. This is similar to creating a filter.

- **Then** area is where you specify the operation to be applied to the selected data.

- **Else** area is where you have an option to specify an operation to data that has not been selected.

- [✓ OK] accepts edits to the Change but does not execute it.

- [⊘ Cancel] cancels any edits to the Change.

- [▱ Change] enables you to see the results of your action in a **Global Change Report** before changing the database.

- The other commands are self-explanatory and are used to create and edit lines in the Global Change, but you will need to click into the **If** or **Then** or **Else** sections that you wish to work on.

23.3 Specifying the Change Statements

The basic Global Change in the following picture will add 5 days to the Remaining Durations of activities, where the Original Duration is greater than10 days, and increase all others by 20%.

There are three areas in the **Modify Global Change** form:

- The **If** section has 5 fields and works in the same way as a Filter. It is used to select the data to be changed.

- The **Then** section has 5 fields:

  - ➢ **Parameter** – This is the data field(s) that is(are) to be modified when the **If** statement is satisfied.

  - ➢ **Is** – This is a statement.

  - ➢ **Parameter/Value** – This is the source data for the change and may be the same field as the **Parameter** when it is intended to change the parameter value.

  - ➢ **Operator** – This is how the Parameter Value is to be changed.

  - ➢ **Parameter/Value** – This is the value or other parameter that will be used to make the change. To enter a number, text, or value you will need to select **{Custom}** from the **Parameter/Value** drop-down box:

- The **Else** section operates in the same way as the **If** section when the **If** statement is NOT satisfied.

23.4   Examples of Simple Global Changes

The following examples are very simple Global Changes.

Increase Original Durations

This Global Change will increase the Original Duration field value by 20% by multiplying the original duration by 1.2.

Select Subject Area			Global Change Name	
Activities ▼			Increase Durations by 20%	

If	Parameter	Is	Value	High Value
⊟	(All of the following)			
Where				

Then	Parameter	Is	Parameter/Value	Operator	Parameter/Value
	Original Duration	=	Original Duration	*	1.2

Copying Dates and Durations

This example will copy the Start, Finish, and Original Durations into custom data item fields:

Select Subject Area			Global Change Name	
Activities ▼			Copy Dates and Durations	

If	Parameter	Is	Value	High Value
⊟	(All of the following)			
Where				

Then	Parameter	Is	Parameter/Value	Operator	Parameter/Value
	Last Period Start Date	=	Start		
And	Last Period Finish Date	=	Finish		
And	Last Period AC Dur	=	At Completion Duration		

Removing Actual Dates

Setting a field to be blank will remove data in some situations:

Select Subject Area			Global Change Name	
Activities ▼			Remove Actual Dates	

If	Parameter	Is	Value	High Value
⊟	(All of the following)			
Where				

Then	Parameter	Is	Parameter/Value	Operator	Parameter/Value
	Actual Start	=			
And	Actual Finish	=			

23.5 Selecting the Activities for the Global Change

Often you will want to make a Global Change to data that meets a specific criterion. The **If** statement lines are used to select the data. The operations defined in the **Then** lines will be executed. Data that does not meet the **Then** criteria may be changed with operations defined in the **Else** statement lines.

The following example will double Remaining Durations if the percent complete is greater than 50%.

Select Subject Area			Global Change Name	
Activities ▼			Increase Remaining Durations	

If	Parameter	Is	Value	High Value
⊟	(All of the following)			
Where	Activity % Complete	is within range of	50%	99.9%

Then	Parameter	Is	Parameter/Value	Operator	Parameter/Value
	Remaining Duration	=	Remaining Duration	*	2

The following example will add 5 days to the Original Duration of activities over 10 days and increase by 20% those less than 10 days.

Select Subject Area			Global Change Name	
Activities ▼			Increase Duratiopns by 20% or add 5D	

If	Parameter	Is	Value	High Value
⊟	(All of the following)			
Where	Original Duration	is greater than or equals	10d	
◄ ☐				

Then	Parameter	Is	Parameter/Value	Operator	Parameter/Value
	Original Duration	=	Original Duration	+	5d
◄ ☐					

Else	Parameter	Is	Parameter/Value	Operator	Parameter/Value
	Original Duration	=	Original Duration	*	1.2

23.6 Duration Calculations with Global Change

⚠ When calculating Durations remember that P6 calculates in hours and if you are displaying durations in days then you will need to divide or multiply as appropriate the durations by 8 to obtain the correct duration.

23.7 (Any of the following) and (All of the following)

There are two options under the **Parameter** title in the **If** section, **(Any of the following)** and **(All of the following)**. These are used with the **If** statements in the same way as with filters.

If	Parameter	Is	Value	High Value
Select Subject Area			**Global Change Name**	
Activities ▼			Change Original Durations	
−	(All of the following) ▼			
Where	(All of the following)	equals	2d	
And	(Any of the following)	is under	OZB.2	

When **(Any of the following)** is selected, the Global Change will operate when any of your selection criteria is met.

In the example following, any activity with the Original Duration greater than 2 days, or an activity that is assigned to the WBS Node OZB.2, will be doubled.

If	Parameter	Is	Value	High Value
Select Subject Area			**Global Change Name**	
Activities ▼			Change Original Durations	
−	(Any of the following)			
Where	Original Duration	is greater than	2d	
Or	WBS	equals	OZB.2	

Then	Parameter	Is	Parameter/Value	Operator	Parameter/Value
	Original Duration	=	Original Duration	*	2

Every selection criterion has to be met when **(All of the following)** is selected for the Global Change to operate on the data.

In the example following, only activities with the Original Duration greater than 2 days and an activity that is assigned to the WBS Node OZB.2, will be doubled.

If	Parameter	Is	Value	High Value
Select Subject Area			**Global Change Name**	
Activities ▼			Change Original Durations	
−	(All of the following)			
Where	Original Duration	is greater than	2d	
And	WBS	equals	OZB.2	

Then	Parameter	Is	Parameter/Value	Operator	Parameter/Value
	Original Duration	=	Original Duration	*	2

23.8 Temporary Values

Some calculations require more than one operation to achieve the required change. A **Temporary Value** may be stored in a **User Defined Field**. This **Temporary Value** may then be used on a subsequent line. Any **User Defined Field** may be created and used as a Temporary Value.

The following example is used to calculate Cost to Complete (CTC) based on a unit cost calculated from the Actual Cost divided by the Actual Quantity and the Temporary Value UDF is used to store the unit cost used in the second line calculation.

Select Subject Area			Global Change Name	
Activity Resource Assignments ▼			Calculate Costs to Complete	

If		Parameter	Is	Value	High Value
☐		(All of the following)			
	Where	At Completion Labor U	is not equal to	0h	
	And	Units % Complete	is greater than	30%	

Then	Parameter	Is	Parameter/Value	Operator	Parameter/Value
	Temporary Value	=	Actual Cost	/	Actual Regular Labor Units
And	Remaining Cost	=	Temporary Value	*	Remaining Labor Units

In this example, Actual Costs /Actual Regular Labor Units calculates the actual unit rate in the **Temporary Value** field, and the Remaining Cost is the unit rate x the Remaining Labor Units.

- The percentage complete must be greater than 30%.

- The resource must have a quantity.

- **Temporary Value**, a temporary value, is cost per unit calculated by dividing Actual Cost by Actual Regular Labor Units and represents the resource actual unit rate.

- Remaining Cost is equal to Remaining Labor Units multiplied by the actual unit rate.

It is important that you consider the Autocost rules that you have assigned to the activities and resources, otherwise your Global Change may not work. In this situation you would not want **Cost Linked** checked.

Resource ID Name	Calculate costs from units
🧍 PM.Project Manager	☐

23.9 Global Change Functions

There are some functions that may be used with Global Change in the **Parameter/Value** field under **Then** and **Else**. These functions may be used to populate User Defined Fields from other data fields as part of the process of editing Activity Descriptions and Activity IDs.

Global Change Function	Function Operation
• DayOfWeek (Parameter)	Selects the weekday number of the date.
• LeftString (Parameter,*)	Selects * of characters from the start of a field.
• RightString (Parameter,*)	Selects * of characters from the end of a field.
• SubString (Parameter,a,b)	From character "a" selects "b" number of characters.

23.10 More Advanced Examples of Global Change

At the time of writing this publication, Global Change may be used to assign resources to roles, replace resources, but not assign resources to activities.

Changing Activity ID by Adding a Middle Character

The following Global Change adds a "C" after the second character of the Activity ID:

Select Subject Area				Global Change Name	
Activities ▼				Modify Activity ID's	

If	Parameter	Is	Value	High Value
⊟	(All of the following)			
Where				

Then	Parameter	Is	Parameter/Value	Operator	Parameter/Value
	Temporary 1	=	LeftString(Activity ID,2)	&	C
And	Temporary 2	=	SubString(Activity ID,3,20)		
And	Activity ID	=	Temporary 1	&	Temporary 2

Adding Resources with Global Change

The following example assigns a resource, ARL Angel Lowe, to the Sales Engineer Role when the Start Date is greater than the Current Data Date.

Select Subject Area				Global Change Name	
Activity Resource Assignments ▼				Assign Resources to Roles	

If	Parameter	Is	Value	High Value
⊟	(All of the following)			
Where	Role	equals	Sales Engineer	
And	Start	is greater than	CD	

Then	Parameter	Is	Parameter/Value	Operator	Parameter/Value
	Resource ID Name	=	AR.Angel Lowe		

Other Global Change Uses

Global Changes may be used for the following purposes and you may wish to inspect some of the sample Global Changes provided in the sample database:

- Add a middle character in an Activity ID or other field by using two User Defined fields and the **Concatenation** operator, which is the **"&"** character.

- Add a prefix to an Activity ID.

- Replace a resource with another. Ensure that you check the **Assignment Staffing** setting in the **User Preferences**, **Calculations** tab.

- Update the **Remaining Duration** from a **Step Percent Complete** by setting the **Duration Percent Complete** equal to the **Physical Percent Complete**.

- Edit the Activity Name using Global Change Functions.

- To set the **Planned Dates** to equal the **Start** and **Finish** dates before applying **Update Progress** so **Actual** dates are not changed by **Update Progress**.

23.11 Workshop 20 – Global Change

Background

We wish to copy the current update information to the User Defined Fields created in the previous workshop.

Assignment

1. Apply the **Workshop 19 – UDF** Layout.

2. Create a Global Change titled **Set Last Period Data** and add the following parameters:

> ➢ Last Period Start to equal Start

> ➢ Last Period Finish to equal Finish

> ➢ Last Period AC Dur to equal At Completion Duration divided by 8 as P6 calculates in hours:

Select Subject Area			Global Change Name	
Activities ▼			Set Last Period data	

If	Parameter	Is	Value	High Value
⊟	(All of the following)			
Where				

Then	Parameter	Is	Parameter/Value	Operator	Parameter/Value
	Last Period Start	=	Start		
And	Last Period Finish	=	Finish		
And	Last Period AC Dur	=	At Completion Duration	/	8.00

3. Run the Global Change and commit the changes with the icon at the bottom of the screen:

Activity ID	Activity Name	Original Duration	Last Period AC Dur	Start	Last Period Start	Finish	Last Period Finish
⊟ **Bid for Facility Extension**		33d	40.00	10-Dec-24 08 A	10-Dec-24 08	27-Jan-25 16	27-Jan-25 16
⊟ **Technical Specification**		11d	11.00	10-Dec-24 08 A	10-Dec-24 08	23-Dec-24 16	23-Dec-24 16
OZ1000	Approval to Bid	0d	0.00	10-Dec-24 08 A	10-Dec-24 08		10-Dec-24 08
OZ1010	Determine Installation F	4d	3.00	10-Dec-24 08 A	10-Dec-24 08	12-Dec-24 16 A	12-Dec-24 16
OZ1020	Create Technical Spec	5d	4.00	12-Dec-24 08 A	12-Dec-24 08	17-Dec-24 16	17-Dec-24 16
OZ1030	Identify Supplier Compc	2d	2.00	18-Dec-24 08	18-Dec-24 08	19-Dec-24 16	19-Dec-24 16
OZ1040	Validate Technical Spe	2d	2.00	20-Dec-24 08	20-Dec-24 08	23-Dec-24 16	23-Dec-24 16
⊞ **Delivery Plan**		18d	19.00	24-Dec-24 08	24-Dec-24 08	21-Jan-25 16	21-Jan-25 16
⊞ **Bid Document**		18d	10.00	02-Jan-25 08	02-Jan-25 08	27-Jan-25 16	27-Jan-25 16

You will notice that the WBS and Project Last Period Durations are not correct and are a mathematical addition of the values below. To resolve this, you may either:

- Hide the **Group Total** in the **Group and Sort** form, or
- Use a further Global Change Line to put the Durations in a Text UDF that will not add up in the WBS and Project fields.

---

4. Create and display a gray bar showing from **Last Period Start** to **Last Period Finish** and place in position 3.

Display	Name	Timescale	User Start Date	User Finish Date	Filter	Preview
☑	Last Period	User Dates	Last Period Start	Last Period Finish	All Activities	◁━━━▷

Bar Style		Bar Settings
Shape	◁ ▼	▭ ▼	▷ ▼
Color	▭	▭	▭
Pattern	▼	▬▬▬ ▼	▼
Row	3 ▲▼		

5. Display the Project Baseline, Total Float and Negative Float bars.

6. Adjust the row height as required, say about 27, and your schedule may look like the following picture with three bars.

7. Save the layout as **OzBuild Workshop 20 – Last Period Bars**.

Activity ID	Activity Name	Original Duration	Last Period AC Dur	Dec 09	Dec 16
				un M Tue W Thr Fri Sat Sun M Tue W Thr	
Bid for Facility Extension		33d	40.00		
Technical Specification		11d	11.00		
OZ1000	Approval to Bid	0d	0.00		
OZ1010	Determine Installation Requirements	4d	3.00		
OZ1020	Create Technical Specification	5d	4.00		
OZ1030	Identify Supplier Components	2d	2.00		
OZ1040	Validate Technical Specification	2d	2.00		

8. Create and run a Global Change to multiply the Original Durations of Activities in the Delivery Plan Phase by 2.

Select Subject Area				Global Change Name	
Activities ▼				Increase Durations by 2	

If	Parameter	Is	Value	High Value	
⊟	(All of the following)				
Where	WBS	equals	OZB.2		

Then	Parameter	Is	Parameter/Value	Operator	Parameter/Value
	Original Duration	=	Original Duration	*	2

9. Schedule your project:

Activity ID	Activity Name	Original Duration	Last Period Dur
Bid for Facility Extension		47d	40.00
Technical Specification		11d	11.00
OZ1000	Approval to Bid	0d	0.00
OZ1010	Determine Installation Requirements	4d	3.00
OZ1020	Create Technical Specification	5d	4.00
OZ1030	Identify Supplier Components	2d	2.00
OZ1040	Validate Technical Specification	2d	2.00
Delivery Plan		32d	19.00
OZ1050	Document Delivery Methodology	8d	4.00
OZ1060	Obtain Quotes from Suppliers	16d	8.00
OZ1070	Calculate the Bid Estimate	6d	3.00
OZ1080	Create the Project Schedule	6d	3.00
OZ1090	Review the Delivery Plan	2d	1.00
Bid Document		28d	10.00
OZ1100	Create Draft of Bid Document	6d	6.00
OZ1110	Review Bid Document	2d	2.00
OZ1120	Finalise and Submit Bid Document	2d	2.00
OZ1130	Bid Document Submitted	0d	0.00

10. You will notice that Negative Float has been created and the change in durations is observed in the bars and from the differences in the Duration values.

24 MANAGING THE ENTERPRISE ENVIRONMENT

This section introduces the management of an Enterprise environment and discusses more thoroughly some subjects that have been addressed earlier.

It is important to appoint a database manager who is responsible for security and maintenance of the database for all databases that have more than one user. A database will very quickly degenerate into a mess if it is not strictly controlled. Typical problems include multiple Resources representing the same person, excessive numbers of Layouts, Filters, Calendars and other codes, the deletion of important data, and a misunderstanding or total ignorance of how the software works. The database manager should be responsible for maintaining the database, including but not limited to the following responsibilities:

- Ensuring all users are trained in the software
- Users and Security Profiles
- Enterprise Breakdown Structure
- Organizational Breakdown Structure
- Project Codes
- User Defined Fields
- Global and Resource Calendars
- Roles and Resources
- Global Layouts and Filters
- Creating Projects including setting defaults
- Importing Projects and other data.

Some areas of responsibility that are frequently used by administrators are:

Topic	Menu Commands
• Users	A **User** is created by selecting **Admin**, **Users**....
• Security Profiles	**Security Profiles** are created by selecting **Admin**, **Security Profiles**....
• Enterprise Project Structure (EPS)	Select **Enterprise**, **Enterprise Project Structure...** to open the **Enterprise Project Structure (EPS)** form.
• Portfolios	To create, edit or delete a **Portfolio** select **Enterprise**, **Project Portfolios...** to open the **Portfolio** form. The **File**, **Open** (project) form also allows the selection of a **Portfolio.**
• Organizational Breakdown Structure – OBS	Select **Enterprise**, **OBS**....to open the **Organizational Breakdown Structure** form..
• Project Codes	Select **Enterprise**, **Project Codes...** to open the **Project Codes** form.
• Job Services	A Job Services may be set up by selecting **Tools**, **Job Services** to open the **Job Services** form.

24.1 Multiple User Data Display Issues

The following issues **MUST** be managed by the Database Administrator and have been covered in this publication in other sections:

- Any user, with access rights, may reset the database **Default Calendar** in the **Enterprise**, **Calendar** form, but this option will reset all users to the same calendar. When an organization has projects with different hours per day and days per week then you may wish to select a Default Calendar of 5 days per week and 8 hours per day.

- By default, more than one person may open a project unless the **File**, **Open**, **Read Only** option is used, or access is limited through **Security Profiles**. Thus, two people may make changes and create two versions of a project. Depending on who closes what and when, the final saved version may not be what it is thought to be. The **File, Refresh Data** option enables a user to refresh project data to see what other users changed. Trials by the author indicate that only changed data is saved, thus the final version of the project may be a hybrid of both users' versions.

- When multiple projects are opened together and each project has different **Schedule Options**, then the **Schedule Options** of all the projects will be changed and set to the same as the **Default Project** permanently without warning. If you are intending to open multiple projects together then it is best to ensure all projects have the same Schedule Options.

- **IMPORTANT NOTE:** In Version 20 and later the **Default Project** setting in the **Set Default Project** form may be overridden by selecting a different project in the **Scheduling Options** form, **Use scheduling options from** drop down box which will not change the selected project in the **Set Default Project** form but will override it and change all the other projects **Scheduling Options** to the one selected in the **Scheduling Options** form. See para 25.3.2 for more information.

- **User Baselines** are not **Project Baselines**. When a second user opens a project which has a **Primary User Baseline** set by the first user, then this baseline will not be assigned to the second user. When the same layout is used to display the project, the **<Current Project> Baseline**, which displays the **Planned Dates**, will be displayed as the **Primary User Baseline**. Again, two users opening the same project and using the same Layout may display different data.

- It is possible to have two **Currencies** with the same symbol and if a user selects a different currency, then all costs displayed by the user will be converted to a different value. This option must be carefully monitored and if you do not need multiple currencies then it is suggested that you should delete them all, to avoid any possible problems. If you are using multiple currencies, then make sure that all currencies have a different sign so there is no confusion.

- Users with different **Units Format** in their **User Preferences** will display different values for their unit values which may be confusing when two users report two different resource values for the same project.

  It is critical for organizations to appoint a database manager who understands these issues and keeps an eye on what is being sent to clients and makes sure that any display issues are either hidden or explained to the client in writing. Organizations may wish to consider making the system user and the project the same, as this resolves a number of issues. For example, User Filters and Layouts, including headers and footers, are by default the project's, reducing the possibility of sending out a report with the incorrect header or footer. User defaults become project defaults resolving display issues. Access to the project may be easily restricted to the one user and therefore only one person may have the project open at one time.

24.2 *Enterprise Project Structure (EPS)*

It is likely that your organization has defined an EPS (unless you have a Stand-Alone load of Primavera) that is available for new projects to be created in, but:

- You may need to add an additional EPS Node for your project, or

- If you are starting with a blank database and an EPS has not been defined, you will need to create at least one EPS Node to assign to your projects.

To add, delete, or modify the EPS Node structure:

- Select **Enterprise**, **Enterprise Project Structure…** to open the **Enterprise Project Structure (EPS)** form, or

- **Project**, **EPS**, **Add Sibling EPS** in the Web for Windows Client users.

- The picture shows the EPS of a demonstration database supplied with Primavera.

- The [⊹ Add] icon is used to create a new EPS Node.

- The node is then assigned an:

  - ➤ **EPS ID**,

    - ➤ **EPS Name**, and

      - ➤ Responsible Manager.

- The arrows under the [📋 Paste] icon are used to reorganize the EPS Nodes.

- The remainder of the icons are for modifying the structure, as you require.

24.3 *Project Portfolios*

The **Project Portfolio** function reduces the number of Projects that are viewed in the **Projects Window**:

- To create, edit, or delete a **Portfolio** select **Enterprise**, **Project Portfolios…** to open the **Portfolio** form.

- Create a portfolio and add projects using this form. A **Portfolio** may be **Global** and all users have access or just be available to the assigned user.

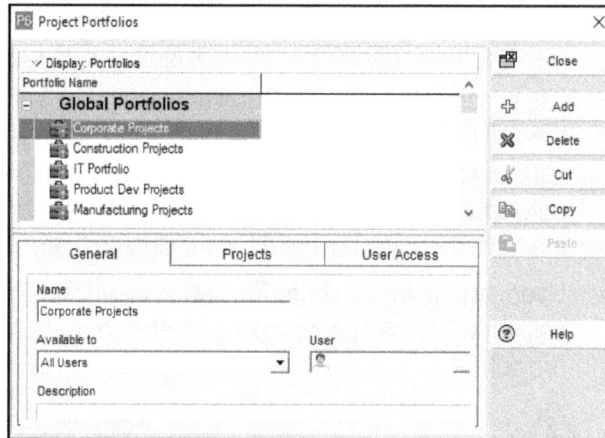

- The **File**, **Open…** (project) form also allows the selection of a **Portfolio**, which reduces the number of projects that are displayed in the **Open** (project) form.

- After a **Portfolio** has been selected using **File**, **Open…**, **Select Project Portfolio…**, only those projects in the Portfolio will be displayed in the **Projects Window**.

- ⓘ This feature is essential when you have a database with a large number of projects.

24.4 Organizational Breakdown Structure – OBS

The OBS is an Enterprise hierarchical structure that is intended to represent the company's OBS.

> *(i)* The OBS function is the security gateway and does not have to mirror your company's OBS. Any structure that enables you to assign user access to projects is usually satisfactory and some companies just duplicate their EPS as the OBS and use a project code for the OBS.

- A user may be assigned to projects or nodes in the EPS or to a WBS Node from the OBS form.

- A user assigned an EPS is normally responsible for projects associated with all elements of the EPS.

- The OBS may also be used to assign access by individual people to projects and WBS Nodes.

24.4.1 Creating an OBS Structure

To create, edit, or delete an OBS:

- Select **Enterprise**, **OBS...** to open the **Organizational Breakdown Structure** form, or

- Select **Administer**, **User Access**, OBS from the Web for the Windows Client users.

- Add, delete, and edit the OBS Nodes in a similar way to a WBS.

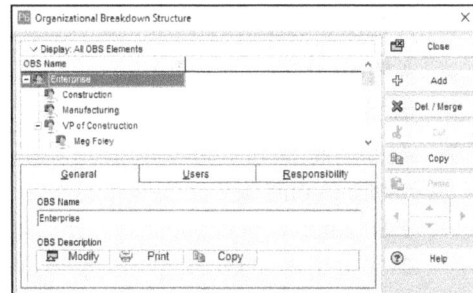

24.4.2 General Tab

The description of the OBS may be added in the **OBS General** tab.

24.4.3 Users Tab

The Login Name is assigned to the OBS in the OBS **Users** tab. Users should therefore be assigned:

- A resource for when they are assigned to work on an activity, and

- An OBS Node for the work they are responsible for or should have access to, and

- A Security Profile assigning their access rights.

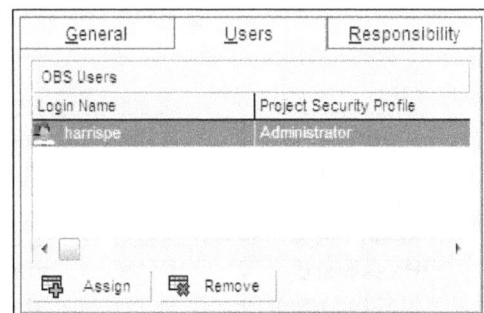

24.4.4 Responsibility Tab

The OBS **Responsibility** tab is used to indicate to which EPS or WBS Node a person has been assigned. The person is assigned to:

- A Project in the **General** tab of the **Projects Window**.

- An EPS Node in the **General** tab of the **Projects Window**.

- A WBS Node in the **General** tab of the **WBS Window**. Assigning responsibility at the WBS Node controls access to the activities under the WBS Node but does not prevent the user from seeing the entire project's data.

24.5 Create Users, Security Profiles and Organizational Breakdown Structure

This section is intended to introduce this topic. Please refer to the Primavera Administration Manual for full details.

The full picture and processes for creating users and assigning access are:

- The **EPS** is created, allowing projects to be created under each Node. This often mirrors the company's network drive hierarchy.

- The **OBS** is created and acts as a security gateway for users to access projects. This may not need to represent your company's **OBS** and often this is set up to mirror the **EPS**.

- A **User** is created by selecting <u>A</u>dmin, <u>U</u>sers... and each User is assigned:

  ➤ A **Global Security Profile** which allows access to Global data such as EPS, OBS, etc.

  ➤ A **Project Security Profile** for each assigned OBS Node which allows access to one or more EPS Nodes, Projects, or WBS Nodes within a project.

  ➤ Access to all or one **Resource Nodes** is assigned to a user from the **Resource Window**. The user can only see and assign resources from this node but may see any resources and their associated costs once they are assigned to activities. P6 Version 19 introduced the ability to allow a user to be assigned up to five resources and the resources underneath the nominated five resources when defining resource access. A user may view and assign the selected resources and the child resources.

  ➤ Access to a software license, allowing the user to login and start the software.

  ➤ The user may be assigned to a resource in the **Resource Window**, thus allowing timesheets to be used.

  ➤ One or more **Resources** may be assigned to one or more **Roles**.

Security Profiles are created by selecting:

- **A**dmin, **S**ecurity Profiles...., or

- **Administer**, **User Access**, **Globa**l or **Project Security** profiles from the Web for Windows Client users.

There are two types of profiles, **Global Profiles** and **Project Profiles**, which are assigned to Users allowing access such as Read Only, Create, Delete, etc.:

- Access to **Global Data** is controlled through **Global Profiles**, and

- Access to one or more **OBS Nodes** is controlled through **Project Profiles** by assigning **Users** to one or more **OBS Nodes** and assigning an applicable **Project Profile**.

A **User** is created by selecting:

- **A**dmin, **U**sers..., or

- **Administer**, **User Access**, **Users** in the Web Client for Window Client users.

Each User is assigned:

- A **Global Profile** that enables access to Global data,

- An optional **Resource Node** thus limiting access to an area of the **Resource Window**, and

- One or more **OBS Nodes** and an applicable **Project Profile** for each **OBS Node**.

Therefore, access to projects is controlled through the **OBS**. Each **OBS Node** that is assigned to a User may be assigned a different **Project Profile**.

As a result, a User may have read-write access to some projects and read-only to others.

The OBS is edited by selecting **E**nterprise, **O**BS....

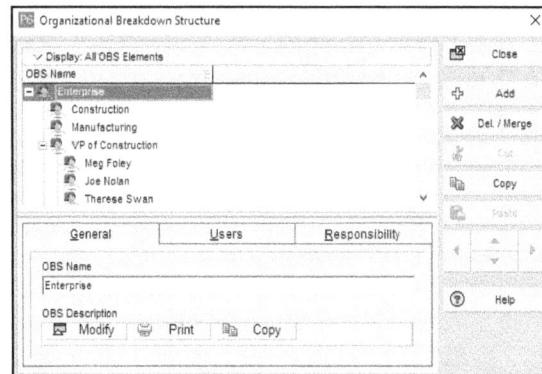

Projects are assigned to an OBS when they are created and the OBS Node must provide the required access rights to the project data.

WBS Nodes may be assigned to individual users which, although does not prevent them from viewing all the project data, will limit their access to just the node they have been assigned to in the **WBS Window**.

24.6 Project Codes

The codes are assigned to projects and enable projects to be Grouped and Sorted under an alternative structure to the EPS.

For example, when an EPS represents the physical location of offices by country, state/county and city, the Project Codes enables projects to be given tags, such as Reason for the Project, Safety, Compliance, New Product, and Increase Production. The Projects may be grouped under these headings.

Therefore, project codes are used to Filter, Group and Sort Projects in a similar way that Activity Codes are used to Filter, Group and Sort Activities.

To create a Project Code:

- Select **E̲nterprise**, **Project Codes…** to open the **Project Codes** form, or

- **Administer**, **Enterprise Data**, **Project**, **Project Codes** from the Web Client for Windows Client users.

  - The Project Codes are created, edited, and deleted in a similar way to Activity Codes.

Project Codes may be assigned to projects in the **Projects Window** in a similar way as Activity Codes are assigned to activities by:

- Displaying the appropriate Code Column, or
- Opening the **Codes** tab in the **Projects Window**.

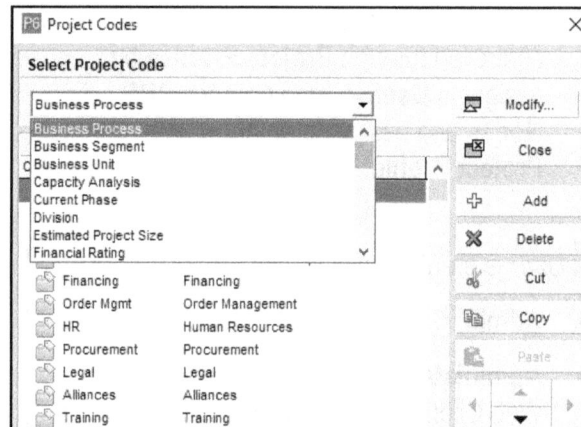

Projects may be Grouped, Sorted and Filtered in the **Projects Window** using the Group and Sort and Filter functions.

24.7 Filtering, Grouping and Sorting Projects in the Projects Window

Projects are Grouped and Sorted and filtered in the **Projects Window** in the same way as activities are in the **Activities Window**. Layouts, Filters, columns and bar formatting work in the same way in both windows.

Projects may be Grouped by fields such as **OBS**, **Responsibility**, **Project Codes** and many other fields. See the **Group, Sort and Layouts** chapter for more detail on this subject.

Projects may be filtered by similar fields, but some of the more useful fields to filter projects by are the **Status**, **Responsible Manager**, and **Project Code** fields.

24.8 Project Durations in the Projects Window

The project durations in both the **Projects Window** and **Activities Window** are calculated based on the Project Default calendar.

The summary durations of bands in the **Projects Window** are calculated on the **Enterprise, Calendars…, Default Calendar**.

24.9 Why Are Some Data Fields Gray and Cannot Be Edited?

If you are unable to edit data then consider the following points:

- You may not have access. Discuss your access rights with your administrator.
- Some data, e.g., the project **Status**, needs the project open before the data may be edited.
- The field may be calculated, such as **Actual Duration**, and cannot be edited.

24.10 Summarizing Projects

All projects should be Summarized. When projects are not **Summarized** then some of the information from unopened P6 projects seen in the **Projects** and **Tracking** windows will be:

- Blank when the project has never been **Summarized**, or
- Out of date if the project has been updated since it was last **Summarized**.

Projects or a database are summarized in the following ways:

- Selecting **Tools**, **Summarize** where you may Summarize either **Open Projects** or all **Projects**,
- Right click on one or more unopened projects and select **Summarize**,
- As a large database takes a significant amount of time to summarize and may be summarized automatically using **Job Services** and this is usually set to run every night.

The following functions control the summarization and availability of data:

- The **Projects** window, **Setting** tab, **Summarized Data** determines how many levels of the WBS is Summarized, a level of zero will summarize all levels,
- The **Admin Preferences**, **Options**, **Specify the interval to summarize and store resource spreads** decides at what time interval that Summarized data is saved.

A project's Summarized data may be deleted by selecting a project, right clicking and selecting **Delete Project Summaries….**

24.11 Job Services

A Job Services may be set up by selecting **Tools**, **Job Services…** to open the **Job Services** form, which can perform the following functions on one or more selected projects or EPS Nodes:

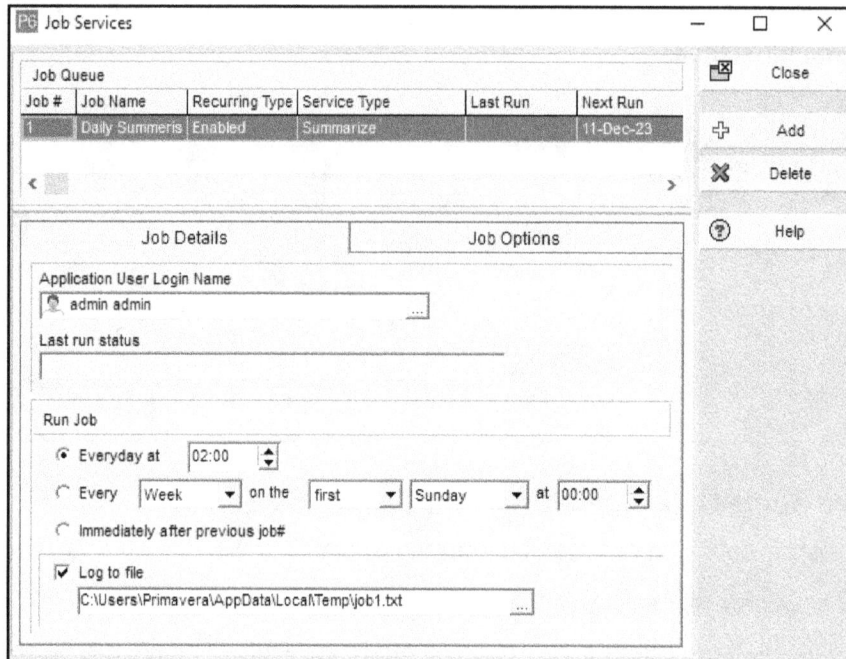

Select **Administer, Global Scheduled Services** in the Web Client for Windows Client users.

- **Apply Actuals** to projects when timesheets are used,

- **Batch Reports**. In the **Reports Window** a **Batch** may be created by selecting **Tools, Reports, Batch Reports…** to open the **Batch Reports** form. This creates one or more reports simultaneously. A Batch may be run on a regular basis using a job service:

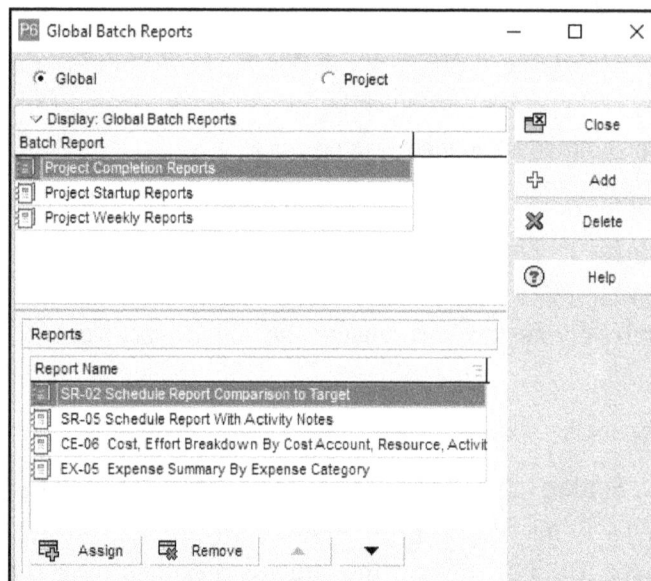

- **Export** one or more projects on a regular basis, or

- **Schedule** one or more projects on a regular basis.

- **Summarize** projects, this should be set up to run nightly.

24.12 Tracking Window

Tracking Layouts are used for resource, cost, and schedule analysis of multiple projects. This section introduces the concepts but does not go into the detail of using this function. You should experiment with the Group, Sort, and Filtering options available, which all function in a similar way to other windows.

- These layouts typically display summarized data to EPS or Project and WBS Node level. The data must be summarized using **Tools**, **Summarize** or using **Job Services** to display the latest current data,

- The **Settings** tab in the lower **Projects Window** allows you to see or reset the WBS level to which data is summarized or to reset the Level to Summarize a project, and

- The time interval that data is summarized at is set in the **Admin Preferences, Options, Specify the interval to summarize and store resource spreads**,

There are four **Tracking Layout** types and a new layout is created by:

- Saving an existing layout, saving with a new name and editing it, or

- Selecting **View, Layout, New Layout…** which opens the **New Layout** form:

The following pictures indicate the type of data a **Tracking Layout** will display:

- **Project Tables** display columns of data for selected Projects or WBS Nodes:

- **Project Bar Charts** display selected projects of WBS Node data in horizontal bars:

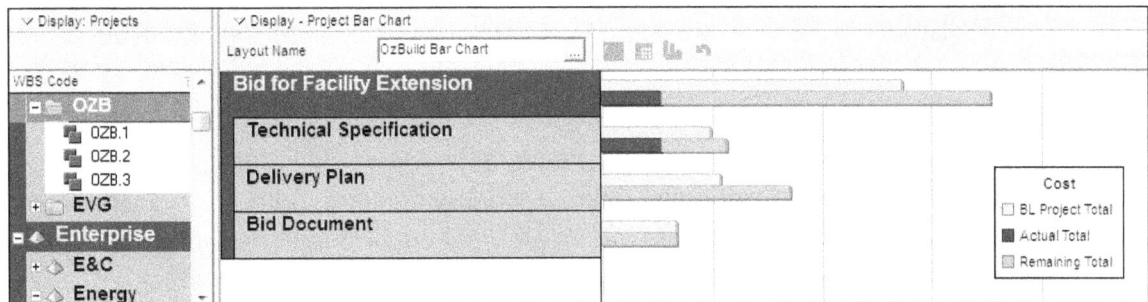

- **Project Gantt/Profiles** display three panes, with bars in the top right pane and either a spreadsheet or a profile in the bottom pane.

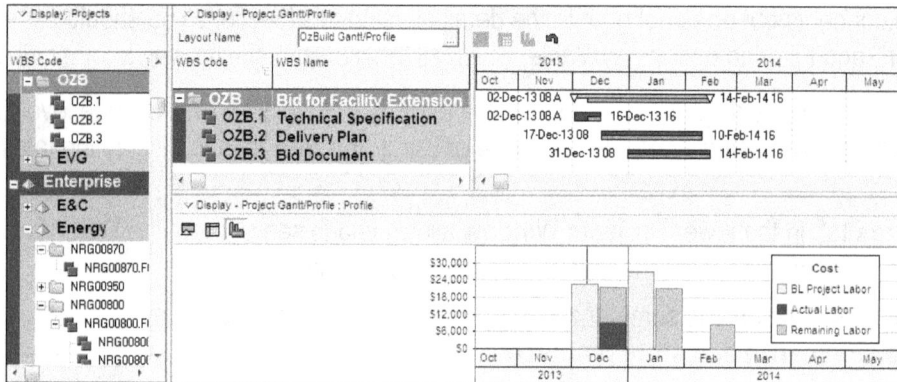

- **Resource Analysis** displays four panes:
  - ➤ The projects to be analyzed are selected in the top left-hand pane,
  - ➤ The resources to be analyzed are selected in the bottom left-hand pane,
  - ➤ Bars, Resource Profiles or a Resource Table may be displayed in the top right-hand pane, and
  - ➤ The bottom right-hand pane may display either a Resource Profile or a Resource Table:

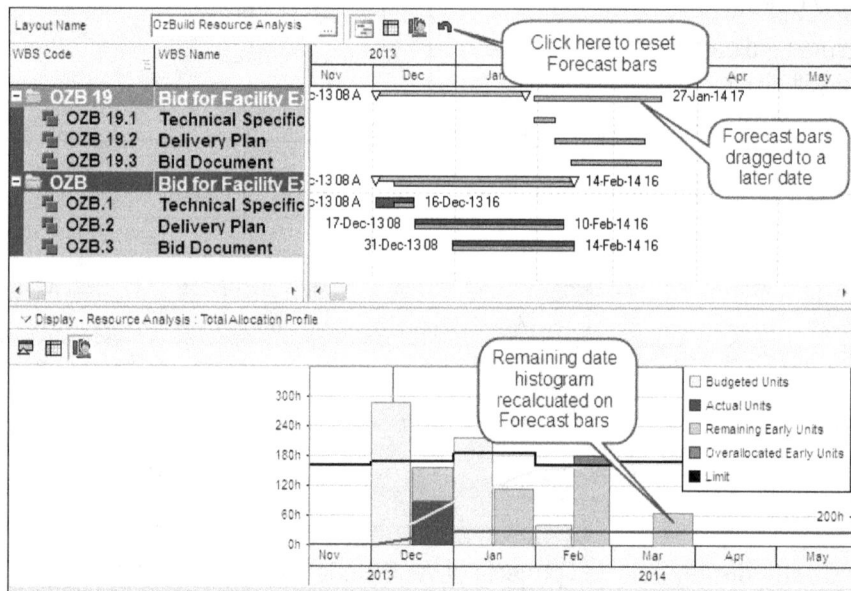

  - ➤ An existing layout may be seen by opening the **Open Layout** form. Select **View, Layout** or click the ⬚ icon in the top right-hand pane.
  - ➤ A **Stacked Histogram** must have a filter created selecting resource(s) to operate,
  - ➤ The **Forecast Bars** have been dragged to a new location and the **Edit**, **User Preferences…**, **Resource Analysis**, **Time-Distributed Data** option set to **Forecast dates** allows the **Resource Remaining Early units/costs** to be recalculated on the **Forecast dates**.
  - ➤ **Forecast Bars** only draw new histograms when the project is open.
  - ➤ The **Reset Forecast Dates** button resets the **Forecast Dates** back to the Start and Finish dates.
  - ➤ The bottom pane of a Tracking Layout may be hidden, as with other windows.
  - ➤ You should experiment by right-clicking in all the panes to see all the display options.

25   MULTIPLE PROJECT SCHEDULING

25.1   Multiple Projects in One Primavera Project

When there are many small projects that need to be managed, it would be logical to create a Primavera Project for each project.

On the other hand, one should also consider putting a number of small projects in one Primavera Project and have the projects identified by the first level WBS Node or some other coding, such as Activity Codes or Project Phase/WBS Category. This is especially practical when there are many projects with a very small number of activities or when an organization only realizes benefits from a number of completed projects when they are all finished. This option is also practical when one scheduler is managing all the small projects. The only problem with this approach is that P6 does not allow partial projects to be Baselined. This issue may be overcome by using User Defined Field Dates and a Global Change to set Baseline Dates for parts of a P6 project.

25.2   Multiple P6 Primavera Projects Representing One Project

Normally, one Primavera Project would be created for each of an organization's projects. There may be a requirement to break a Project down into Sub-projects, these reasons include:

- The project is large enough to require a number of schedulers and therefore a Primavera Project could be created for each scheduler to delineate each scheduler's area of responsibility.

  > Two or more schedulers may open one project and access may be assigned down to WBS Node but the User Access has to be set up to allow them to be able to schedule and they are not able to link to other WBS Nodes.

  There could be a requirement to keep an individual organization's financial information confidential and as security and access is set at project level, information in one project may be hidden from specific users. This situation may exist when there are two or more contractors scheduling parts of a project and they require their cost to be kept confidential from other contractors.

- A project may have separable parts or multiple clients but it is necessary to report the project parts separately yet allow resource management project-wide. Again, a Primavera project could be created for each separate part of the project. In this situation each user may be given access to only one **Resource Node** from the **Global Access** tab of the **Admin**, **Users** form.

- A sub-project could be created as a Primavera Project for the security of sensitive financial information. The cost may be assigned to resources in the financial sub-project with access given to specific individuals. Activities in the financial sub-project may be LOE (Level of Effort) activities, spanning activities in other non-cost sub-projects. This method is generally suitable for high level cost planning and management while allowing the detailed planning of a project in a non-financial sub-project without the burden of managing costs.

When a Primavera Project is created for each sub-project, it would be logical to keep all the Primavera Projects located under one "project" EPS Node and assigned a single Project Code. All the Primavera Projects could be opened at one time for scheduling and reporting by selecting the EPS Node.

The decision to break a project into two or more Primavera Projects must have a sound basis and be well thought out. The environment chosen should be well piloted and tested to ensure the desired results are obtained from the software. Planning and scheduling software is hard enough to use without adding the burden of creating multiple projects. There is a large amount of analysis that may be completed without using multiple projects. Filters may be used to isolate parts of a project and sub-net critical paths may be generated a number of ways, such as using the **Calculating Multiple Paths** function. You must ensure that the requirement to break a project into sub-projects using individual Primavera projects is well-founded.

Some people suggest that sub-contractors should run their own sub-projects within a master schedule. The author's experience is that smaller or new sub-contractors often are very inexperienced at scheduling and many do not know the basics of scheduling. It is therefore unreasonable and risky to expect sub-contractors to drive strange and complex scheduling software and get it right. Some industries are better equipped to manage complex software, with skills found more likely in industries such as IT, but less likely to be found in the construction-related sector.

It is also the author's experience that it is better to reduce the number of schedulers working on a project schedule to the absolute minimum required to manage a project. In large complex projects, these people need to be trained in the use of the software, be reasonably experienced running the software (or working under a person who is experienced) and run the schedule by an agreed-upon and documented set of guidelines.

Managing the inclusion of sub-contractors' schedules always become an issue. Alliances tend to help resolve this problem as the schedules then become a joint responsibility and all located in one database. Another option is to have the contractors create and manage their schedules in your database, but this option is often resisted by IT.

When a single WBS is required for multiple P6 projects representing a project or contract then a Global Activity Code must be used as a WBS may not be shared over multiple P6 projects.

25.3 Setting Up Primavera Projects as Sub-projects

There are a number of issues to be considered when moving to this environment. Be aware that Primavera does not have the sub-project options that are found in other products. For example, there are EPS Activity Codes but there are no EPS Filters, Layouts, Resources or Schedule Options and a WBS may not be shared with more than one P6 project. There is no inbuilt "P3 Project Group" calculation option, which may result in some interesting float calculations that result from inter-project relationships. This section explains some workarounds.

25.3.1 Opening One or More Projects

Enterprise and Project data may be accessed in the **Projects Window**. To access Project activity information, such as activities, resources, and relationships, a project must be opened and the **Activities Window** displayed. One or more projects may be opened at the same time by selecting one or more projects and/or selecting one or more EPS levels and then:

- Right-click and select **Open Project**,
- Select **Ctrl+O**,
- Select **File**, **Open...** to open the **Open Project** form:

The **Open** form enables the options of opening as **Exclusive**, **Shared** or **Read Only**.

> A project may only be opened as **Exclusive** (meaning that only the current user may edit it) by using the **Open Project** form. All other methods will result in the project's being opened in the **Shared** mode and all users with access to the project may open and edit the project(s) at the same time. The **Shared** option may result in one user's edits overwriting another user's edits, depending on who saved what and when. In addition, opening in the **Shared** option may result in different users seeing different values for Activity, WBS Nodes, and Project durations in days or hours if the users have different **User Preferences Time Units**.

25.3.2 Default Project

When multiple projects are opened:

- The system selects the **Default Project** when two or more projects are opened together.

- The **Default Project Schedule Options** are used to calculate all the open projects.

- Select **Project**, **Set Default Project…** to open the **Set Default Project** form where you may change the default project:

- All open projects **WILL** have their **Schedule Options** set to the same as the **Default Project** permanently, without telling the user, after the projects have been scheduled.

- In Version 20 the **Default Project** setting in the **Set Default Project** form may be overridden by selecting a different project in the **Scheduling Options** form, **Use scheduling options from** drop down box which will not change the selected project in the **Set Default Project** form but will override it and change all the other projects **Scheduling Options** to the one selected in the **Scheduling Options** form.

The Help file indicates that the **Default Projects** scheduling and leveling settings are used for scheduling. It is also the default project for new data such as activities or issues when the projects are not grouped by WBS.

> **NOTE:** When more than one Primavera project is opened at the same time and each project has different **Schedule Options**, then the non-default project's **Schedule Options** are changed to be the same as the default project, without warning. These non-default projects may calculate differently when opened with other projects. In addition, the next time a non-default project is opened in isolation it may calculate very differently from the previous time it was opened in isolation. To prevent this it is recommended that all projects in each database have the same **Schedule Options**.

An example of changing the default project when each project has different options is demonstrated in the following picture. The first has retained logic and the second has progress override. Activity PG3-2 has moved forward in time as it is now being scheduled with Progress Override after initially being scheduled with Retained Logic. These types of unexpected changes may significantly affect your project and may occur when two or more projects, each with different Schedule Options, are opened together.

25.3.3 Setting the Projects Data Dates P6 Version 19 and Earlier

The default project does not set the **Data Date** for all projects. In the example following:

- The default project has a **Data Date** of 6 Mar and
- The other two projects have their **Data Dates** set as per their names.

When scheduling, the following message is received:

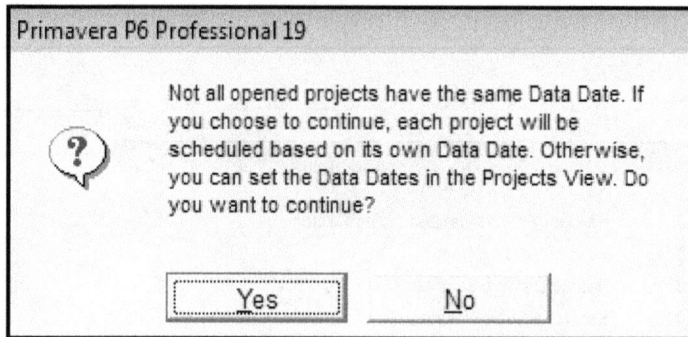

There are unlinked activities, MPS01-30, MPS02-30 and MPS03-30 in each project and it may be seen in the picture:

- All projects are scheduled with their own **Data Dates**,
- The **Data Date** line is shown on the earliest project **Data Date**, not the **Default Project Data Date**.

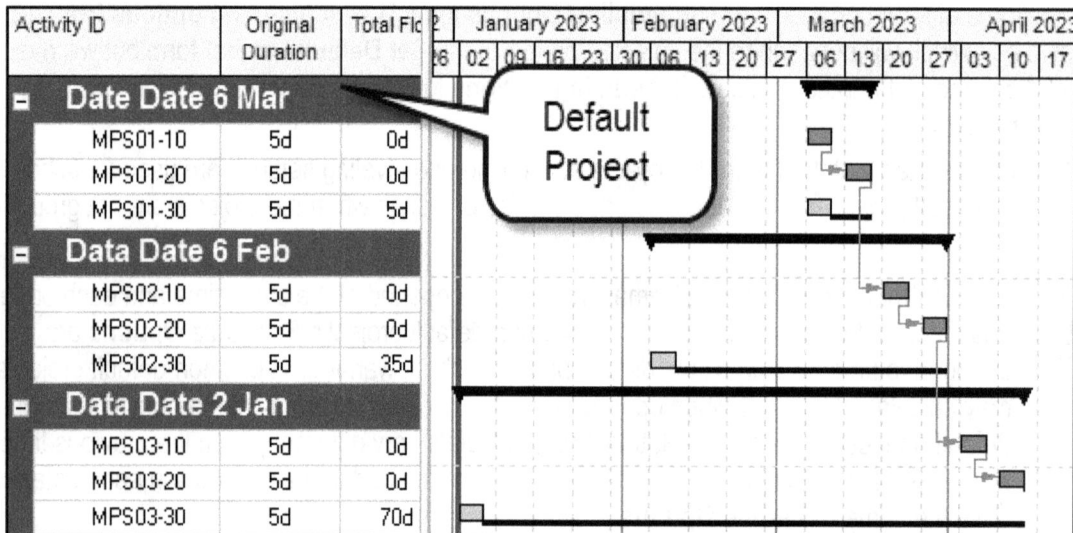

The **Data Dates** of multiple projects may be set using a column in the **Projects Window** and utilizing the **Fill Down** function.

25.3.4 P6 Version 20 Data Date Selection in Multiple Project Scheduling

Primavera P6 Version 20 introduced some additional functions when scheduling multiple projects.

- **All Projects use their own data dates** which is how Version 19 earlier versions calculated, or
- Version 20 added an additional option **Apply selected data date to all open projects** and all projects will have their **Data Date** permanently changed to the selected date.

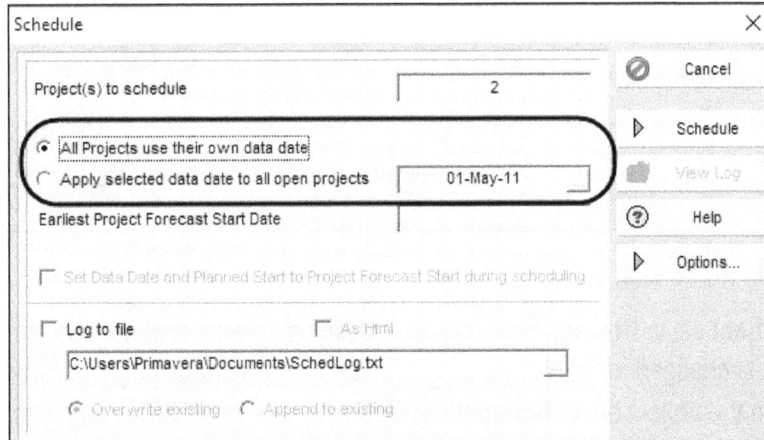

25.3.5 P6 Version 20 Multiple Project Scheduling Options Selection

In the P6 Version 19 and earlier when multiple projects were scheduled together and they had different **Scheduling Options**, which could happen when users change them from default or when you imported a project, then all the different **Scheduling Options** of all the projects being scheduled were changed to the **Default Project** on a permanent basis and changed projects would calculate differently from then on.

The **Default Project** may still be set by selecting **Project**, **Set Default Project**:

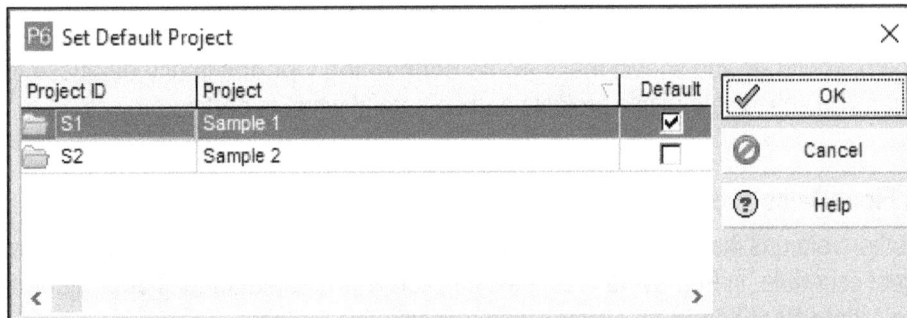

But now you may select which project **Scheduling Options** are used when scheduling multiple project in the **Scheduling Options** form which is opened by selecting **Tools**, **Schedule**, **Options**:

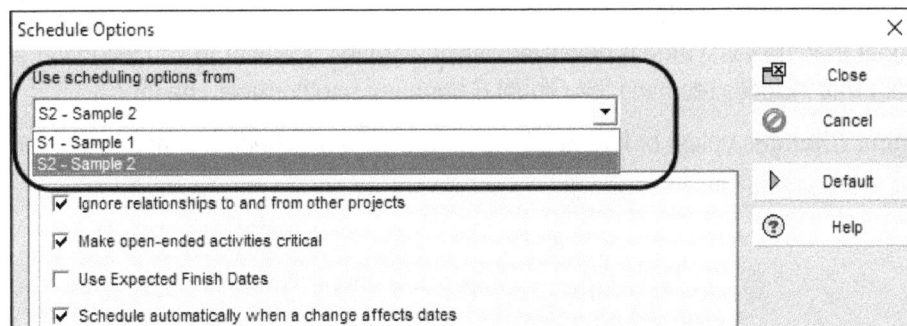

The **Default Project** may also be selected in the **Leveling** form as well:

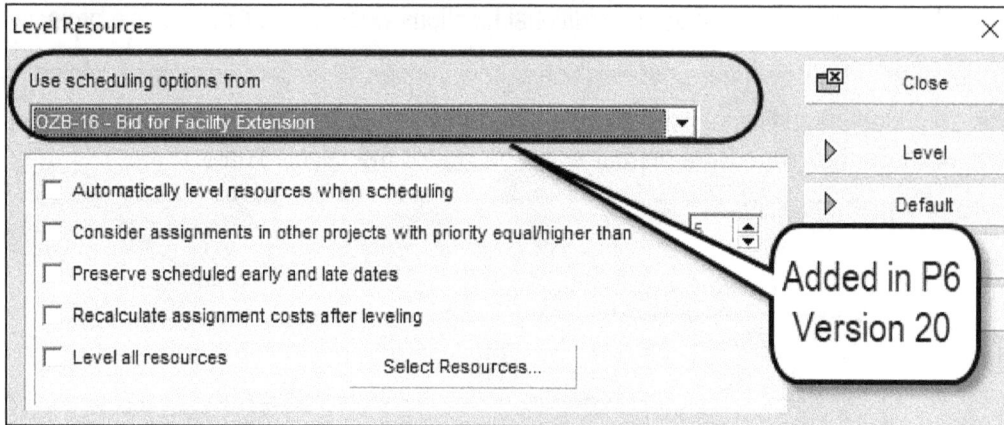

What happens now in P6 Version 20?

- The **Default Project** set in **Project, Set Default Project** is ignored and not changed when the **Default Project** is changed in the **Scheduling Options, Use scheduling options** form,
- The options from the project set in **Scheduling Options, Use scheduling options** form are used to calculate all the projects, and
- The other project(s) **Scheduling Options** are changed permanently to the project selected the **Scheduling Options, Use scheduling options** form on a permanent basis.

> ⚠️ The **Default Project** may now be set in two places, but they are not linked and the project selected in the **Scheduling Options, Use scheduling options** form takes priority.
>
> Thus, the problem of **Scheduling Options** being changed when scheduling multiple projects has **NOT** been solved. You now have two options to mess up your **Scheduling Options** of projects when scheduling multiple projects with different options.
>
> Again, I reiterate you should make all the **Scheduling Options** in one database the same when you schedule multiple projects and be careful when importing projects.

25.3.6 Total Float Calculation

In P6.1 and earlier versions the Total Float of each project is calculated to the last activity of each individual project schedule. In Primavera 6.2 a new function was created under **Tools, Schedule…, Options…, Calculate float based on either** which resolves this problem.

25.4 Refresh Data F5 and Commit Changes F10

The **File, Refresh Data** option or **F5 key** is used when two or more people are working on the same project. It ensures that the latest data is displayed, which enables one user to see the latest edits made by another user. This includes resetting the Global Calendar if another user changes it.

The **File, Commit Changes** option or **F10 key** is used to write any schedule changes to the database.

25.5   Who Has the Project Open?

When a project is opened with Primavera using the **File**, **Open** option the **Open Project** form has Access Mode options to open the project as **Exclusive**, **Shared**, or **Read Only**.

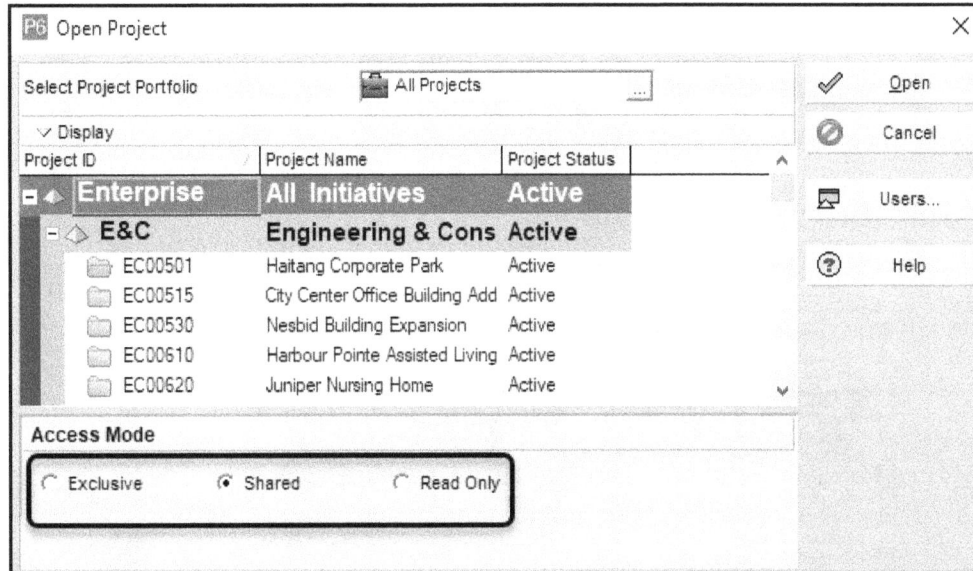

Select [🖳 Users...] to open the **Project Users** form and see who else has the file open.

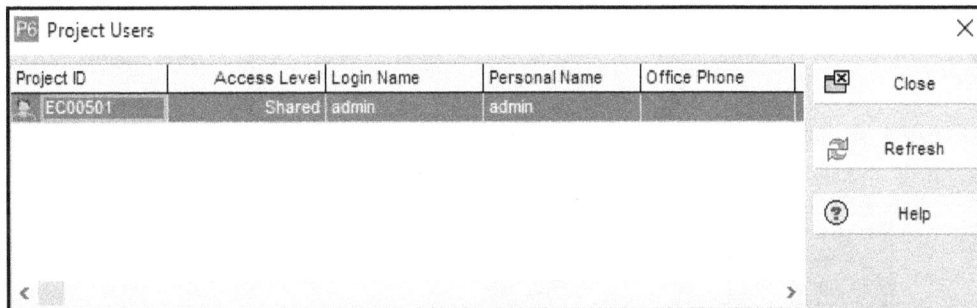

The default option is **Shared** and that means any project that is not opened with the **Open Project** form will be opened as Shared. Anyone who has access may also open the project, calculate and display with their **User Preferences**, and report different data from the same project at the same time.

25.6   Setting Baselines for Multiple Projects

The following process is **NOT RECOMMENDED** because issues covered next when restoring baselines set this way. The Baselines may be set for all the projects using the **Maintain Baselines** form (when multiple projects are open) and the **Assign Baselines** form. The following picture show the process of setting multiple project baselines:

- Open the **Maintain Baselines** form by selecting **P**roject, **Maintain Baselines**…:
  - ➢ Either all projects may be selected and a copy of all projects set as the Baselines at one time, or
  - ➢ Other current projects may be converted from the database one at a time.
- Select [➕ Add] to open the **Add New Baseline** form and create the new baselines,

- Select **P**roject, **Assign Baselines…** to open the **Assign Baselines** form and select one project at a time to assign the baselines.

⚠ Remember, a **User Baseline** set by one user will not be displayed when another user opens the project. The <**Current Project**> **Baseline** displays the **Planned Dates** from the current schedule and will be shown as a baseline.

25.7 Restoring Baselines for Multiple Projects

Schedulers often wish to restore baselines to inspect or review the original schedule.

⚠ The process using **Save a copy of the current project as a new baseline** identified in the previous page results in one interesting issue when Baseline projects are restored. The software creates **Ghost Relationships** between the Current Schedules and Baseline schedules which must be avoided because there is a high risk that neither the Baseline nor Current projects will calculate correctly once Multiple Project Baselines are restored.

The example below explains what happens when three simple projects are baselined together:

- The three projects were opened together and baselined and restored:

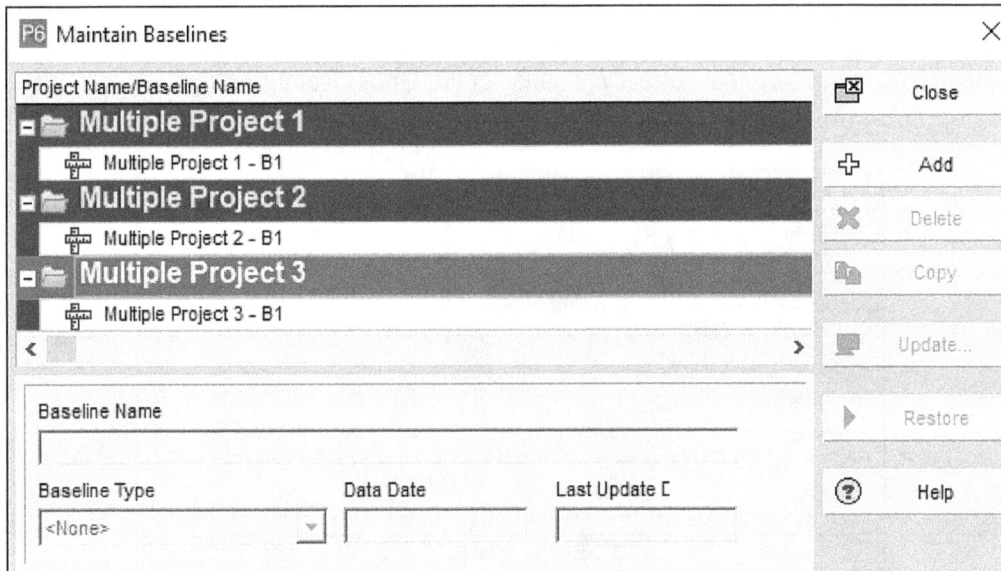

- The baselines were unlinked and restored,

- When the current and baseline projects are opened together there are unwanted **Ghost Relationships** created by the software, without warning, between the Current and Baseline projects:

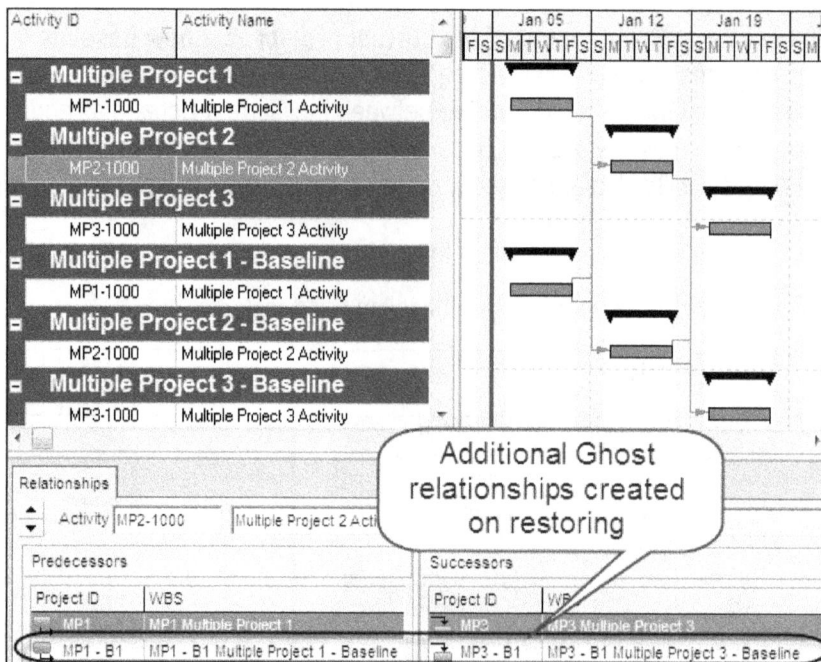

- When the current projects are opened on their own and activity durations shortened you will see that the schedule does not calculate correctly because of the **Ghost Relationships**:

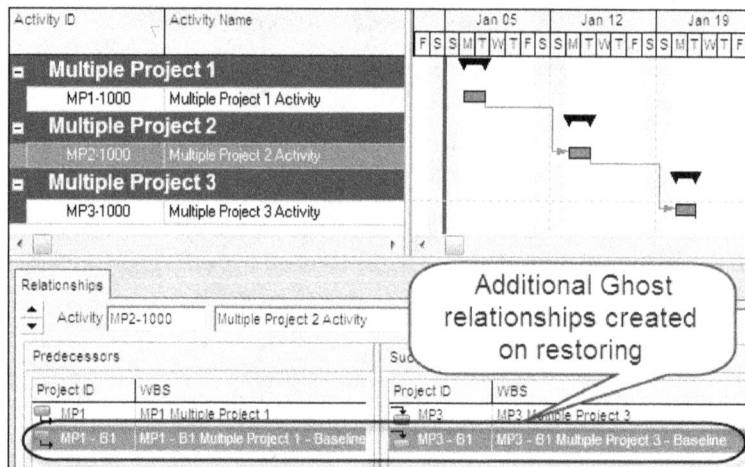

Therefore, if you wish your baseline projects to maintain the relationships to other baselined projects only and not have **Ghost Relationships** created with the current projects when the multiple current projects with relationships amongst them are baselined, then you must:

- Open the **Projects Window**,
- Copy the multiple projects in this view **Projects Window**,
- Then set the baselines using the Convert another project to a new baseline of the current project option in the **Maintain Baseline** form.

Now if the baselined projects are restored there will be no **Ghost Relationships** created.

26 UTILITIES

26.1 Reflection Projects

Primavera Version 6.0 created a Reflection project function. A Reflection is a "What-if" copy of a project that may be edited and then merged back into the original project, as the changes made are required to be kept may be incorporated into the original project and those not required may be ignored.

The **Reflection project** may be shared with a wider audience and people asked to view and make changes to the project. The **Reflection project** may be exported and sent to a customer who may make changes and then imported back into the database.

To create a Reflection:

- In the **Project Window** highlight the project and right-click,
- Select **Create Reflection….**

The Reflection project is created with a new ID and the term Reflection added to the Project Name.

To merge an edited Reflection project:

- Open the Reflection project,
- Highlight the Reflection project and right-click,
- Select **Merge Reflection into source project…,**
- This opens a form that will allow a choice to be made about which changes should be kept, if a backup XER file should be made, and if the Reflection project is to be kept or deleted:

26.2 Advanced Schedule Options

Primavera Version 5.0 has a new option that enables individual critical paths to be banded as in the following picture and is useful when analyzing larger projects that have more than one critical path. This is similar to Grouping by Total Float but this function numbers the Paths and each path contains activities that are linked, whereas banding by Total Float may group unlinked activities.

There are two steps involved, firstly calculating the multiple paths and secondly displaying the multiple paths:

26.2.1 Calculating Multiple Paths

To calculate multiple critical paths:

- Select **Tools**, **Schedule…**, **Options…**, **Advanced** tab,

- Click on **Calculate multiple float paths**,

- Select if you wish the software to use the **Total Float** or **Free Float** to calculate the multiple paths.

- The **Display multiple float paths ending with activity** is used to select an activity that is in the middle of a schedule and the driving paths of this activity are calculated.

- Select the number of paths for the software to calculate in the **Specify the number of paths to calculate** box.

- Select [Close] and schedule the project.

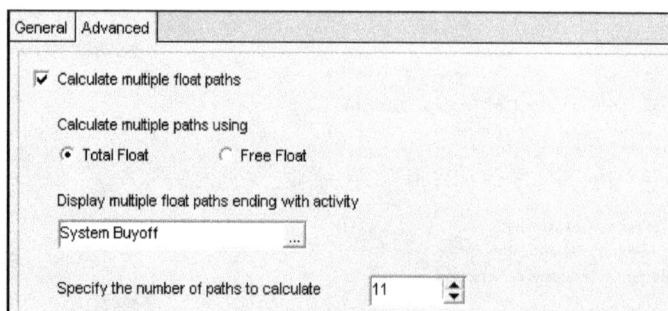

26.2.2 Displaying Multiple Paths

There are two fields that are populated in this process:

- **Float Path**, and
- **Float Path Order**

Either select multiple path Layout or create a Layout that Groups by **Float Path** and Sorts by **Float Path Order**, as in the following examples which show a before and after grouping:

Activity ID	Activity Name	Total Float	Free Float	Float Path	Float Path Order
A1000	Start Milestone	0	0	1	1
A1010	Activity 1	2	0	3	1
A1020	Activity 2	1	0	2	1
A1030	Activity 3	0	0	1	2
A1040	Activity 4	2	0	3	2
A1050	Activity 5	1	0	2	2
A1060	Activity 6	0	0	1	3
A1070	Activity 7	2	2	3	3
A1080	Activity 8	1	1	2	3
A1090	Activity 9	0	0	1	4
A1100	Finish Milestone	0	0	1	5

Activity ID	Activity Name	Total Float	Free Float	Float Path	Float Path Order
Float Path: 1		0	0		
A1000	Start Milestone	0	0	1	1
A1030	Activity 3	0	0	1	2
A1060	Activity 6	0	0	1	3
A1090	Activity 9	0	0	1	4
A1100	Finish Milestone	0	0	1	5
Float Path: 2		1	0		
A1020	Activity 2	1	0	2	1
A1050	Activity 5	1	0	2	2
A1080	Activity 8	1	1	2	3
Float Path: 3		2	0		
A1010	Activity 1	2	0	3	1
A1040	Activity 4	2	0	3	2
A1070	Activity 7	2	2	3	3

The reader may wish to read the Help file or experiment with the software to see the results.

26.3 Audit Trail Columns

Primavera Version 5.0 introduced four basic audit trail columns that may be displayed in the Activities Window, which display the date and user who added the activity and by whom and when it was modified:

- **Added By** – the user who added the activity,
- **Added Date** – the date the activity was added,
- **Last Modified By** – the user who last modified the activity, and
- **Last Modified Date** – the date the activity was last modified.

Primavera Version 6.0 introduced two new resource assignment fields available in the **Activities Window**, **Activity Details**, **Resources** tab:

- **Assigned by**, and
- **Assigned Date**.

26.4   Excel Import and Export Tool

Primavera has a built-in tool for importing to and exporting from Excel the following data when the user is assigned a Superuser security profile in P6 Version 22 and earlier. In P6 Version 23 this right may be assigned to any user:

- Activities
- Relationships
- Resources
- Resources Assignments, and
- Expenses.

To import or export data to Excel select **File**, **Import...** or **Export...** and follow the instructions in the wizards. **Export Templates** may be created and re-used at a later date with this tool.

The following sheets are created upon export and these sheet names must not be changed:

- **TASK** containing Activity data
- **TASKPRED** containing Activity Relationships data
- **PROJCOST** containing Expenses data
- **RSRC** containing Resources data
- **TASKRSRC** containing Resource Assignments data
- **USERDATA** containing user data that should not be changed.

These templates allow the user to specify what data is to be imported and exported; an example is below:

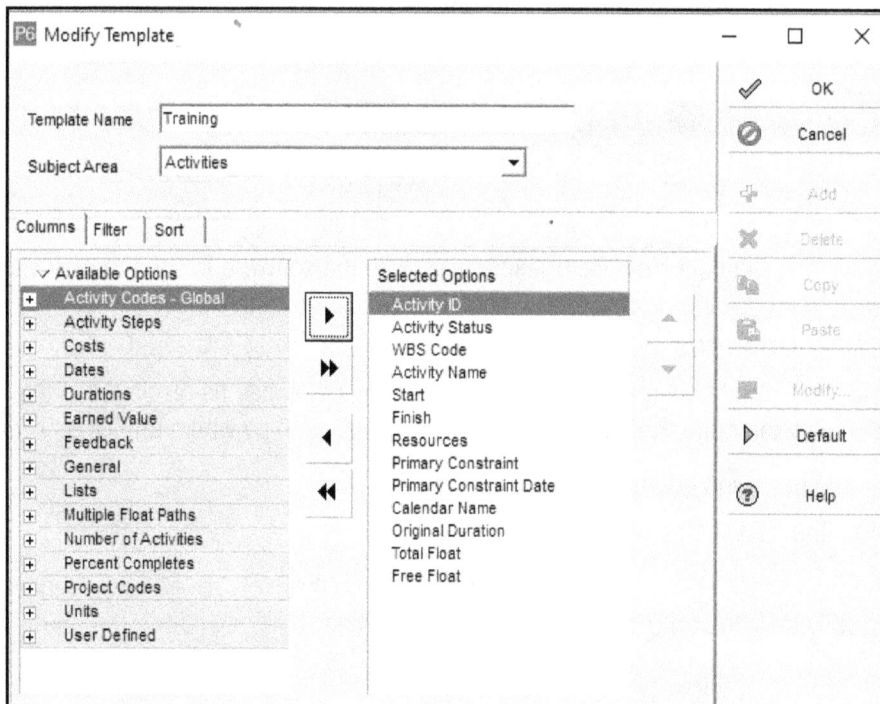

26.4.1 Notes and/or Restrictions on Export

A few points to understand when using the Primavera Excel Import function:

- The following sheets are created on export and these sheet names must not be changed:
  - ➤ **TASK** containing Activity data
  - ➤ **TASKPRED** containing Activity Relationships data
  - ➤ **PROJCOST** containing Expenses data
  - ➤ **RSRC** containing Resources data
  - ➤ **TASKRSRC** containing Resource Assignments data
  - ➤ **USERDATA** containing user data that should not be changed.
- Do not change the language between importing and exporting.
- The first row of data in each sheet that is exported contains the database field name. The first row must not be changed otherwise the data will not be imported.
- The second row in the spreadsheet contains **Captions** that are deleted on spreadsheet import by the **"Delete This Row"** entry in the right column of the spread sheet. The **"Delete This Row"** entry may be copied to and line of data that is to be deleted from the project.
- Dictionary data such as Activity Codes being imported must exist before the data is imported.
- Only Activity Codes may be imported if they exist in the database, if you wish to import the Activity Codes and Code descriptions then you will have to use or a third-party tool, see https://primavera.com.au/ Third Party Software page for a list of software that will work with P6.
- Only a maximum of 200 columns of data may be exported.
- **Sub-units** of time are not supported and the Sub-unit check boxes in the **Edit, User Preferences...**, **Time Units** tab should be unchecked.
- **Percent Completes** must be a value of between 0 and 100.
- Anything listed as a field may be exported.
- The **User Preferences** will affect how your data is exported and may give different values for resources.
- In P6 Version 22 and earlier a user had to be a assigned a **Project Superuser** to import from Excel, and in P6 Version 23 this right may be assigned to any User.

26.4.2 Notes and Restrictions on Import

When attempting to import data using this type of tool there are some guidelines that apply to many applications, not just to this Primavera tool:

- Create a test project and experiment with this function before using it on a live project.
- Export some data first as this exports the correct column headings and sheet names required for import.
- Change or add data to the exported spreadsheet and import new data into the test environment. Then review that the data is importing correctly and that the schedule is calculating as expected.
- Back up or take a copy of your live project before importing into a live project.
- It is often better to import into User Defined Fields to ensure the data gets into the database and then Global Change into the desired place.

- Activity data must have the Activity ID and WBS Code as these are the unique identifiers for each activity within a database.

- The **delete_record_flag**, in the far-right hand column, titled **Delete titled this row** against line 2 of the Excel spreadsheet deletes the line 2 activity on import.

- The **Delete This Row** flag may be placed against any spreadsheet line and the activity will be deleted on import.

- Calculated fields may not be imported and are marked with an (*). See picture below:

	A	B	C	D	E	F	G
1	task_code	status_code	wbs_id	task_name	start_date	end_date	act_start_date
2	Activity ID	Activity Status	WBS Code	Activity Name	(*)Start	(*)Finish	Actual Start
3	OZ1030	Not Started	OZB.1	Identify Supplier Components	17/12/2013 8:00:00 AM	12/12/2013 4:00:00 PM	
4	OZ1040	Not Started	OZB.1		13/12/2013 8:00:00 AM	16/12/2013 4:00:00 PM	
5	OZ1000	Completed	OZB.1		2/12/2013 8:00:00 AM		2/12/2013 8:00:00 AM
6	OZ1010	Completed	OZB.1	ments	2/12/2013 8:00:00 AM	4/12/2013 4:00:00 PM	2/12/2013 8:00:00 AM
7	OZ1020	In Progress	OZB.1		4/12/2013 8:00:00 AM	10/12/2013 4:00:00 PM	4/12/2013 8:00:00 AM

These may not be imported

- To see if the data field you wish to import may be imported, export the field and see if the field has an (*) by the second line description in the spreadsheet. Fields that may not be imported are fields calculated by P6 such as most dates except the Actual Start, Actual Finish and Actual Durations.

- Therefore, if you wish to import dates to create un-started activities without importing the Original Duration then you will have to import the activity with **Actual Start** and **Actual Finish** dates where you want the activity to lie and use a Global Change to take-off the Actual Dates:

	A	B	C	D	E	F
1	task_code	wbs_id	task_name	act_start_date	act_end_date	delete_record_flag
2	Activity ID	WBS Code	Activity Name	Actual Start	Actual Finish	Delete This Row
3	OZ1140	OZB.3	New Activity	5/01/2014 8:00:00 AM	17/01/2014 4:00:00 PM	

Then	Parameter	Is	Parameter/Value	Operator	Parameter/Value
	Original Duration	=	Actual Duration		
And	Primary Constraint	=	Start On		
And	Primary Constraint Dat	=	Actual Start		
And	Actual Start	=			
And	Actual Finish	=			

- When only exporting some data on an occasional basis then it may be easier just to copy and paste the data into a spreadsheet.

  i If you wish to bring across the band headings into Excel then the Activity ID must be displayed in the first column.

There is more information in the Help file under **Reference**, **Importing and Exporting**.

i The P6 Excel Import function does not allow importing of Global data like Activity Codes and you may use a third party tool, there are some listed at https://primavera.com.au/ under Third Party Software.

26.5 Project Import and Export

Whenever you import a project there is a big risk of importing and over writing existing data in your database with values for attributes like resources, roles and calendars, thus there is a risk that importing a file will affect existing data and project in your database. Make sure that you understand the import options when importing a project into a database. Techniques such as:

- Assigning all resources, roles, calendars, codes and UDFs in the imported project unique names not being used in the target database will assist in preventing unintended over writing.

- Using a separate database to import files into for inspection to prevent importing unwanted data into your database could be used.

- Using third party clean-up tools, some listed on https://primavera.com.au/, may be used to remove unwanted data.

- Using products like **Schedule Viewer** to inspect P6 XER and XML files before importing could be considered.

Project data may be imported and exported from and to the following formats:

- **XER**, which is a Primavera proprietary format, used to exchange projects between Primavera P6 databases regardless of the database type in which it was created.
  The XER format is the original format that Eagle Ray, who developed the software, used to export files from one database and import them into another. XER stands for Export Eagle Ray.
  An XER file is a simple text file that does not include Layouts or baselines and therefore is just a simple text file containing project data. Some key points:

  - No Baseline projects may be exported or imported with this tool and Baselines have to be exported and imported separately.

  - A layout (formatting) is not part of an XER file.

  - Baselines are not exported with an XER.

  - The web tool does not import or export XER file.

  - Earlier versions of **XER** files may be imported into later version databases.

  If you try to import a later version of an XER file with an earlier version of P6 you may receive a message stating that the file may not be imported. To resolve this issue, open the XER file with **Notepad** and edit the version number to the version of your version of P6:

  - **XER** file may be opened up either in Notepad or using Excel after changing the file extension to txt. After opening with Excel, then you may data parse it and if you edit it carefully you can add data or remove data before importing the file back into a database. Be careful you do not corrupt your database. This is particularly useful if you want to add a large number of Activity Codes to a project without tying them in. On the other hand, there are a number of tools available to do the same, many listed at https://primavera.com.au/.

- **Primavera Contractor XER**. This is the format produced by Primavera Contractor which is an old single project and cut down version of P6.

- **Primavera PM – (XML)** This tool is continually being developed and different versions of P6 have different functions.

  ➢ It is supported by the web client, where as a XER is not.

  ➢ It allows the import and export of projects with their Baselines and Layouts, both of which are not available with XML files.

  ➢ A Template is used to manage data which may exit in the database and the project to be imported so the user may decide to use the existing database data, import the new project data, update the existing project data or not import the data.

  ➢ After importing an XML you have to recalculate if you wish to see Float values and the critical path.

  ➢ Also, a P6 XML file may recalculate the cost of an imported project when the resource rate in the Resource window of either the source or target project are different to the rate assigned to an activity, thus an imported XML file may change the project costs. See para 26.11 for a full explanation. This has caused issues for contractors submitting projects in XML format to clients when the client's version has different resource rates to the contractor version. P6 Version 22 changed how the resource cost for imported costs but did not resolve the issue.

> ⓘ A P6 and MSP XML file will look the same as both will have the format *.XML. You should consider putting P6 or MSP in the file name so you know which files are P6 XM files and which are MSP XML files.

P6 Version 19 XML format introduced:

  ➢ In Stand-Alone and PPM databases to update baselines when importing Primavera XML file.

  ➢ To export projects in Primavera XML format in a compressed ZIP file.

  ➢ Scheduling and Leveling Options may be imported and exported.

  ➢ Scheduling and leveling options are included and when importing the user may select to import with the Update Existing or Keep Existing import settings for the scheduling and leveling options or Keep Existing import settings for the scheduling and leveling options.

Financial Period Calendar Selection when Importing an XML file.

  ➢ Version 20 introduced the option of different Financial Period Calendars for different projects.

  ➢ Version 21 introduced the option when importing an XER file to select the Financial Period Calendar to be assigned to a project:

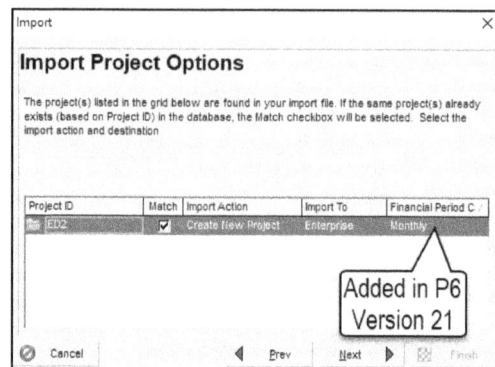

P6 Version 22 XML format introduced:

> ➤ Options for managing **Resources Calendars** and **Responsible Managers** when importing and XML file, and

> ➤ The ability to **Duplicate** an **Import** or **Export** template for all import and export file types.

- **Project (*.XML)**.This is the file format that Microsoft Project now recommends for export and import from other products like Primavera. The P6 routine to import and export a Microsoft Project XML file has been modified over time and does not always operate as one would expect, but some versions have displayed interesting features including:

> ➤ Projects with blank lines will not import.

> ➤ Project with a "/" in fields such as Resource Names and Calendars will not import.

> ➤ Keep Resource names and calendar names to less than 20 characters.

> ➤ In some P6 Versions the Microsoft Project 24 hour per day calendars imported as 1 hour per day in P6 and give gross calculation differences.

> ➤ Milestones in Microsoft Project are calculated as Finish Milestones but are imported into P6 as Start Milestones and give calculation differences.

> ➤ Activity Spits are not supported in P6 and should be removed before importing.

> ➤ As Late as Possible in P6 is calculated as Zero Free Float and as Zero Total Float in Microsoft Project and give calculation differences.

> ➤ A Microsoft Project file is imported into P6 with a Project Must Finish by constraint, this usually has to be removed.

> ➤ A P6 baseline is a complete project, Microsoft Project just records the Start, Finish, Duration, Work and Costs.

Superseded formats, the following formats have been removed from later P6 versions:

- **Project (*.mpp)**.This is the default file format that Microsoft Project uses to create and save files is not supported by recent versions of P6.

- **MPX (*.mpx)**. This is a text format data file created by Microsoft Project 98 and earlier versions. MPX is a format that may be imported and exported by many other project scheduling software packages. The major issue with this format is that it removes activity calendars.

- **Primavera Project Planner P3** and **SureTrak** files saved in **P3** format. A SureTrak project should be saved in Concentric (P3) format before importing. Importing P3 files requires P3 to be installed on the same computer as P6 and later Windows operating systems do not support the loading of P3, effectively making this function inoperable on some operating systems. With Primavera Version 6.0 the importation of P3 files has been improved:

> ➤ One or more individual sub-projects may now be imported, and

> ➤ The import EPS locations specified which may be different for each sub-project.

i To import files saved in **P3** format you need Btrieve loaded on your PC. Btrieve is loaded when P3 is installed. A demonstration version of P3 will load Btrieve onto your machine and enable P3 files to be imported. P3 may not be loaded on more recent operating systems such as Windows 7 make the use of this function difficult without an old operating system. The author maintains a Windows XE Virtual Machine with SureTrak, P3 and an old version of P6 loaded to convert files from P3 or SureTrak to XER format.

Export only Formats

- **UN/CEFACT Format 6 – (XML)**. P6 supports UN/CEFACT XML format. This format is mandated by some US Government agencies.

- **IPMDAR Export Format** introduced in P6 Version 21; an IPMDAR is a project export format required by the US Department of Defence from 2021.
  In P6 Version 21 this option was only available when you open an EEM database and when exporting from a PPM database the option is greyed out. P6 Version 22 PPM may now export IPMDAR format from SQLite and PPM databases.

- **CPP Export Format** introduced in P6 Version 22 and enhanced in P6 Version 23. The US Department of Energy had mandated that the current CSV, and MDB upload formats for PPD (Project Performance Data) upload will be migrated to the JSON (JavaScript Object Notation) format in early 2023. Primavera P6 Version 22 had to be connected to an EPPM to export to a CPP format, now a user may export in CPP format from P6 Professional connected to any database. The mapping for a CPP format must be manually created.

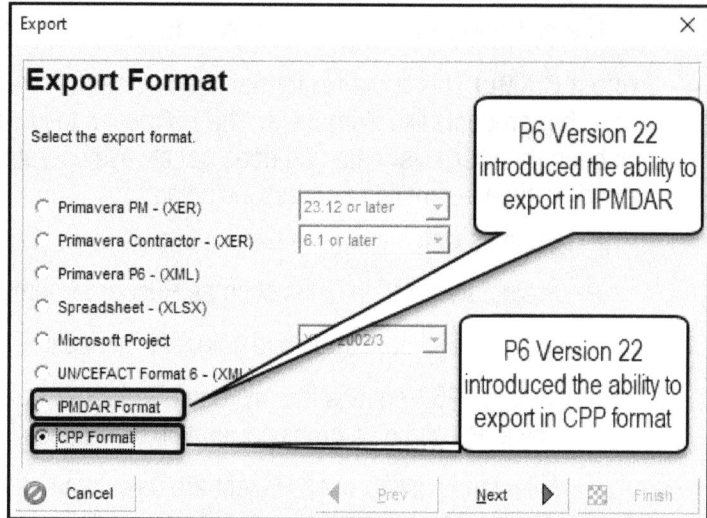

Export Format

Select the export format.

- ○ Primavera PM - (XER) — 23.12 or later
- ○ Primavera Contractor - (XER) — 6.1 or later
- ○ Primavera P6 - (XML)
- ○ Spreadsheet - (XLSX)
- ○ Microsoft Project — 2002/3
- ○ UN/CEFACT Format 6 - (XML)
- ○ IPMDAR Format
- ● CPP Format

P6 Version 22 introduced the ability to export in IPMDAR

P6 Version 22 introduced the ability to export in CPP format

Cancel — Prev — Next — Finish

When projects are imported or exported to other scheduling packages, they will often calculate differently due to the different methods of calculation of each package. Do not expect to import from Microsoft Project or any other software and expect to see the same dates when scheduling.

Importing a file from another Primavera database may give different results depending on the database and user preferences in each database and these should be carefully checked.

Importing a project into a working P6 database must be carefully planned to ensure that existing projects are not impacted by the imported data and the options available on the import wizard are fully understood. Updating or overwriting existing data may affect existing schedules.

A sacrificial database may be the best option for reviewing schedule submitted by subcontractors so as to not corrupt you own working database.

26.6 Check In and Check Out

Check In and **Check Out** function enables a project to be copied from a database, worked on in a remote location such as a client's database, and then be checked in to the original database at a later date and the original schedule updated with the changes.

- Select from the **Project Window**, **General** tab, **File**, **Check Out...** to check out a project:

- The project XER file may then be sent to another person or organization, imported into another database and edited.
- P6 Version 19 introduced the ability **Check In** and **Check Out** projects to XML.
- On import to another database, **External Dates** are created where there are inter-project relationships in the source database.

> These **External Dates** act like Early Start and Late Finish constraints and will affect the schedule calculation. You should always check for **External Dates** when importing a project. See paragraph 15.2.1 for an example of External date.

The file format of a Checked Out file is the same as a project exported in XER format, but checking out a project places a **Read Only** attribute on the project, and then it may be opened but not edited.

To remove the **Read Only** attribute on the project either:

- Select **File**, **Check In...** to check in a project, or
- Select change the status to **Checked In** in the **Project Window**, **General** tab:

> Also ensure you check what has happened to any original external relationships on re-import of a Checked Out project.

- The original inter-project relationships normally get re-linked on import, and
- Then your project may calculate differently when you have Checked In a Checked Out project that now has External Dates and different calculated dates.

26.7   Online HTML Help

The **Admin Preferences**, **Options** tab has a P6 Online Help section which sets the default location for the F1 key. The URL is set to the Oracle Technology Network (OTN):

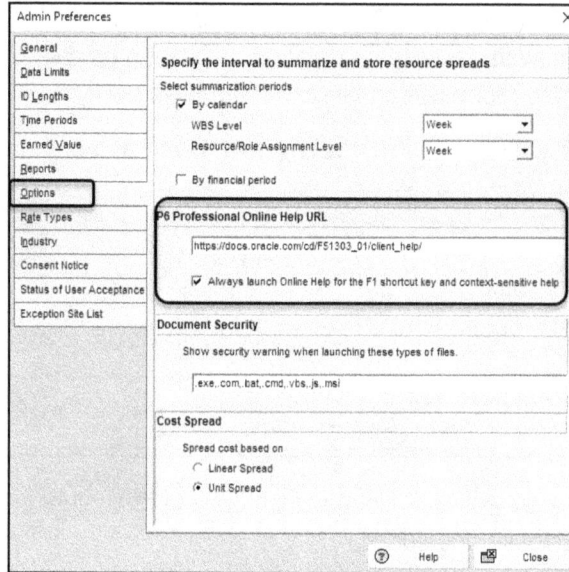

26.8   Activity Discussion Feature

The **Activities Window**, **Discussion** tab enables:

- Users to create a discussion thread for each activity,
- Each entry is saved with the date of entry and user name and the entire thread is recorded allowing and interactive discussion between users who have access to P6,

A new field titled **Unread Comments** has been created so users may identify activities with new comments that they have not read. This may be accessed through Team Member Web, the Team Member for iPhone app, and P6.

i This function has limited use in the environment where only the project scheduler has access to P6.

26.9   Lean Tasks may be imported using an XML file

Primavera Cloud allows activities to be broken down into tasks. **Lean Tasks** are similar to the P6 **Steps** function but with more functionality such as allowing the assignment of tasks to subcontractors. **Lean Tasks** may have the following attributes:

- Assignment of a duration,
- May be made **Private** so other people do not see them,
- **Tasks** may have logic between them which are called **Handoffs**,
- A **Task's Float** is called **Slack**,
- The planning of **Tasks** is completed on a **Planning Board** that may be shared between team members. This is a tool designed for short term planning by the people completing the work.

When you are using an EEPM database you may Import **Lean Tasks** through an XML file from **Primavera Cloud**.

26.10 Maintain Relationships with External Projects

When you import projects from a Primavera XML file, you can choose whether to retain relationships between activities in the project and those in external projects.

P6 Version 20 XML Project Import Options:

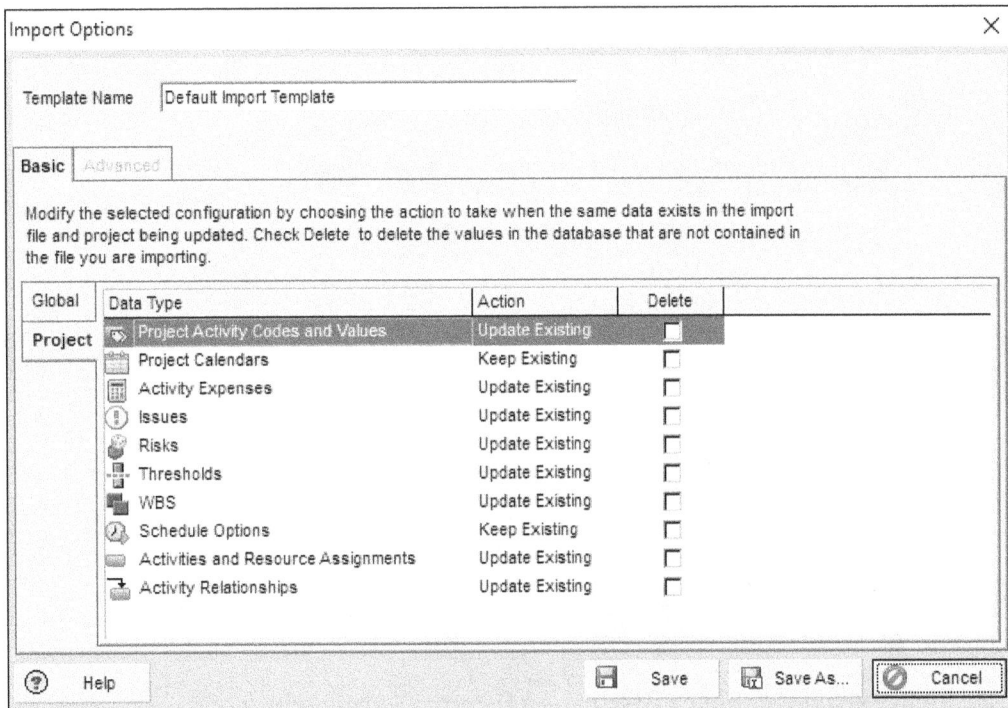

Option added to P6 Version21:

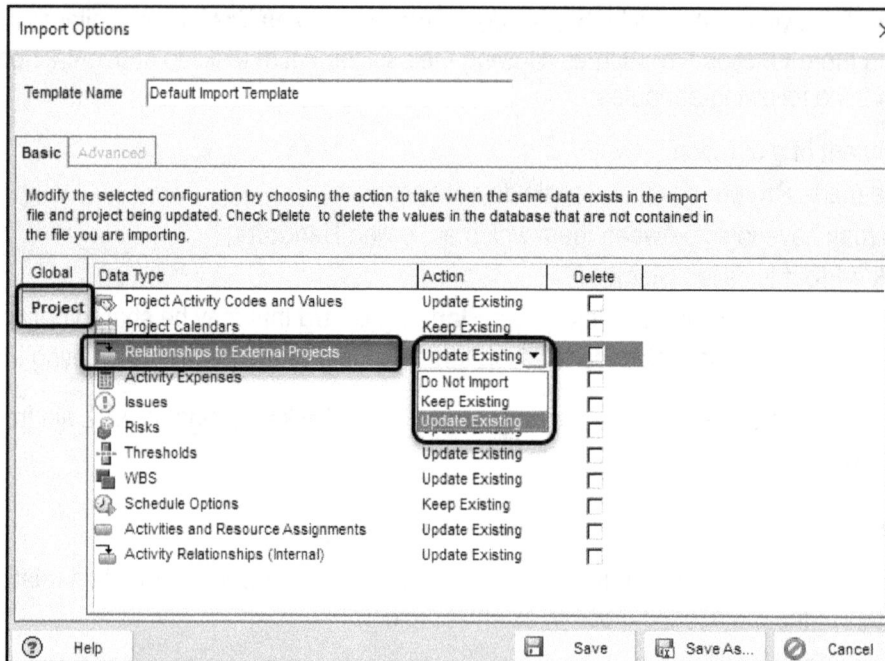

Below are three projects with the activities linked:

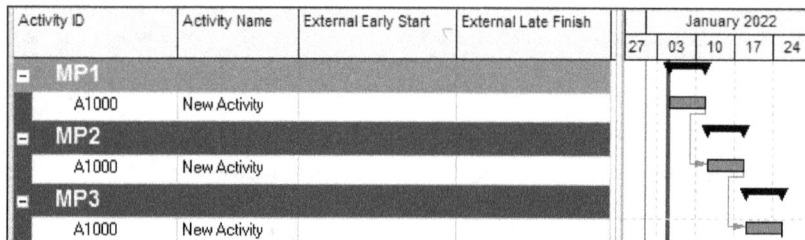

The second project MP2 was exported, deleted and imported and before scheduling.

- With **Do Not Import**, the **External Relationships** and are not reestablished:

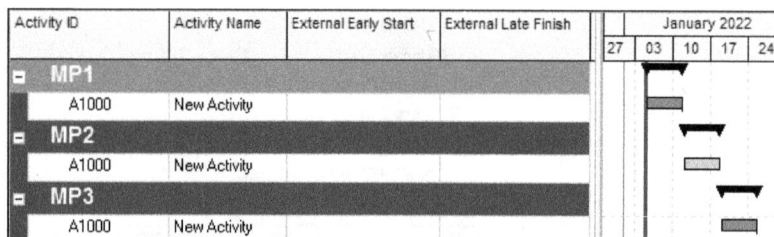

- With **Keep Existing** or **Update Existing** the **External Relationships** and are reestablished:

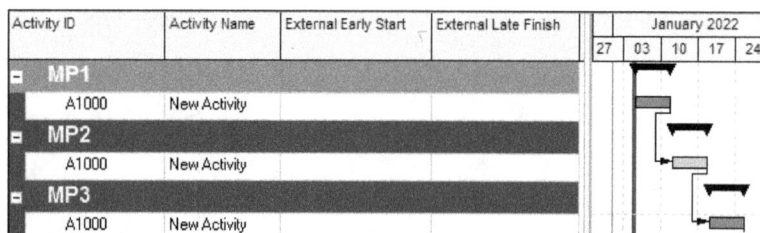

Note: External Early Start and **External Early Finish** dates are not set with this update.

26.11 Assignment Cost are Exported

The Oracle Cumulative Feature Overview for P6 Version 21 file states *"When you export to Primavera XML, Price Per Unit data for assignments is included in the export file."*

This statement is a little misleading and this para will explain what the author discovered with testing. Please note that there are many options that affect how imported data is calculated and the default options were used in the author's tests.

A resource may be assigned to an activity and then the Resource Window Price/Unit may be changed, thus at this point in time there are two resource Price/Unit rates. The resource could exist in the target database with another Price/Unit rate, thus a resource could have three Price/Unit rates.

When the project is exported; the rate assigned to the imported project activity resources are changed to the rate in the Resource Window of the target database and an XML imported project will not calculate the same cost as the exported project.

The change made in Version 21 did not solve the issue, there is one slight change with Version 21 and that is the imported project costs are always calculated based on the exported Resource table Price/Unit rates, but the imported project is still not using the exported assigned activity Price/Unit and the project cost will change.

If you want the costs to remain the same when importing an XML file, then ensure the resource Price per Unit is the same in the export database Resource window, the import database Resource window (or delete it) and the activities do not have their Price per Unit changed. All Price/Unit in all three places need to be the same.

O the other hand you may wish to use an XER file as then the costs will not change unless you recalculate assignment costs for a project.

The authors testing indicates that the Activity Resource assignment Unit Rate being changed on the import of an XML to the Resource table Unit Rate in the has not been fixed with this enhancement.

26.12 Multiple Project Views Displayed Side by Side

With P6 Version 22 there is an additional option in the **Project** menu titled **Additional Activities View**

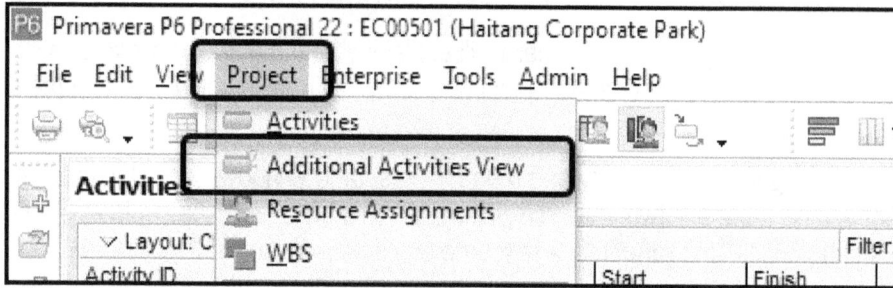

This option will open a second view of the project(s) that are opened. The projects views may then be resized etc:

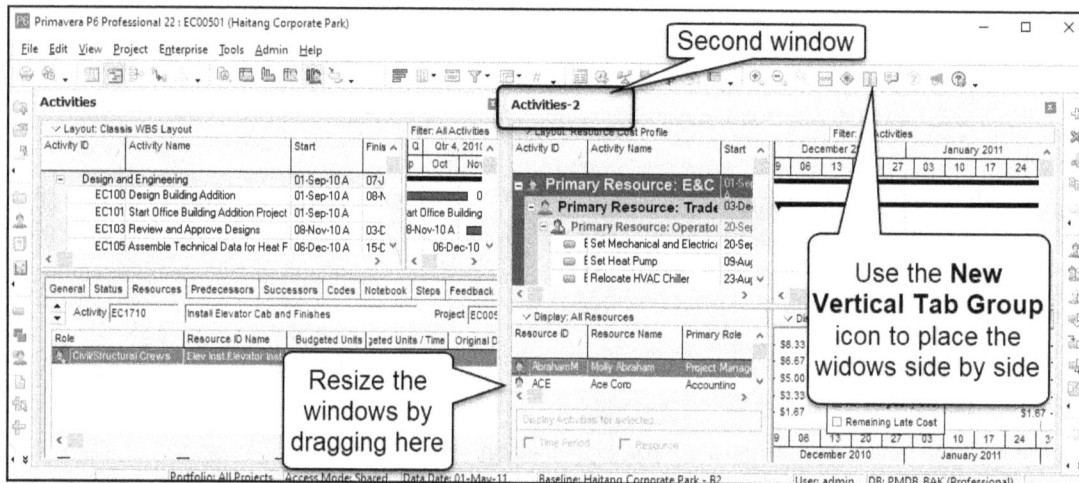

The Oracle description was not clear, but it was found by experiment that:

➢ Each window may be formatted separately,
➢ Each window may be printed separately by clicking in the window that is required to be printed,
➢ The **Schedule Options** and **Schedule Check Report** options may not be different for each view and scheduling one view will schedule both views.

27 EARNED VALUE MANAGEMENT WITH P6

This chapter does not teach Earned Value but it explains how P6 Earned Value functions operate. Therefore, before you read this chapter you will need to have a very good understanding of Earned Value Performance Measurement and the associated terminology. If you do not, then you should consider reading some of the following documents:

- Some current EVM Standards:
  - ➤ ISO 21508 Earned value management in project and programme management
  - ➤ AS 4817 Project performance using Earned Value
  - ➤ Defence Material Supplement to AS 4187
  - ➤ ANSI/EIA-748 Earned Value Management Systems
- Other material:
  - ➤ AACE 82R-13 - Earned Value Management (EVM) Overview and Recommended Practices
  - ➤ PMI Practice Standard for Earned Value Management
  - ➤ Earned Value Management APM Guidelines
  - ➤ Earned Value Project Management – Quentin W. Fleming and Joel M. Koppelman

Furthermore, readers must have a clear understanding of and experience with the following topics:

- The P6 options and preferences associated with resources, and
- Updating a resourced schedule.

This chapter will outline:

- Which P6 functions may be used for EVM,
- What P6 settings are used in these calculations,
- What options are available and how Earned Value calculations may be performed in P6,
- How this information may be reported.

The main Curves that are used in EVM are:

- **Performance Measurement Baseline** (PMB) which is a time-phased BAC.
- **Planned Value** (PV), or Budgeted Cost of Work Scheduled (BCWS), is the value of planned work at a point in time derived from the PMB.
- **Earned Value** (EV), or Budgeted Cost of Work Performed (BCWP), is the value of work completed at a point in time.
- **Actual Costs** (AC), or Actual Cost of Work Performed (ACWP), is the expenditure at a point in time to complete the work.
- **Estimate to Complete** (ETC), a revised estimate of the remaining work.

Some important points:

- No cost or resource data may be held at WBS level. All cost, resource, and expense data is held at Activity Level and summarized at WBS Node.
- If Actual Costs and Units are to be collected at WBS level then it may be appropriate to use a WBS or LOE activity to store this information and detail timing activities created under these.
- P6 will easily create the Planned and Earned values.

- If P6 is used to record Actual Values then your organization will require some mature system to import actual values from other corporate systems (accounting, procurement, time sheeting and contract management) in order that the scheduler does not become a data entry clerk.

> ⚠️ Users should design their system and test their system with P6 to ensure that it is producing the expected results before working on a live project.

27.1 Performance Measurement Baseline

The PMB in Primavera may be read from either the Budget or At Completion values of a Baseline Project.

- At the start of a project the Performance Measurement Baseline (PMB) is usually read from the Baseline project Budget values, which normally are equal to the At Completion values.

- When a project is re-baselined in the mid-point of the project from a project that has progress, then at this point in time some activities will have progress and the At Completion values would normally be different from the Budget values.

> ⓘ Careful consideration needs to be given here as to which Baseline setting is to be used to ensure the correct values are reported as the PMB.

The P6 functions that decide which value is read as the Performance Measurement Baseline:

- The **Project**, **Assign Baselines...** form selects the Baselines projects to be read as the **Project Baseline** and the **Primary User Baseline**:

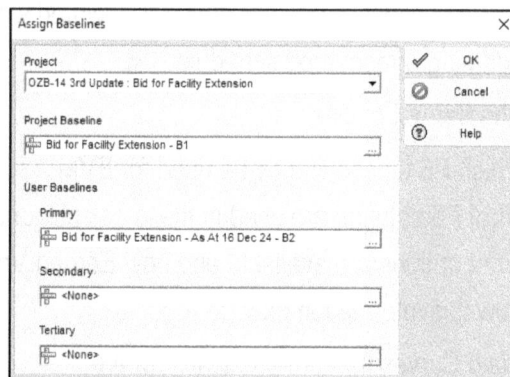

- The **Projects Window**, **Settings** tab, **Project Settings**, **Baseline for earned value calculations** decides which of the **Project baseline** or **User's primary baseline** is read for P6 Planned Values:

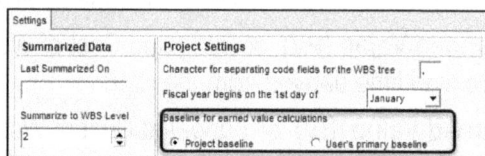

  The **Admin**, **Admin Preferences...**, **Earned Value** tab, **Earned value calculation** section, **When calculating earned value from a baseline use**, you should select either the:
  - ➤ **At Completion values with current dates**, or
  - ➤ **Budgeted values with current dates**.

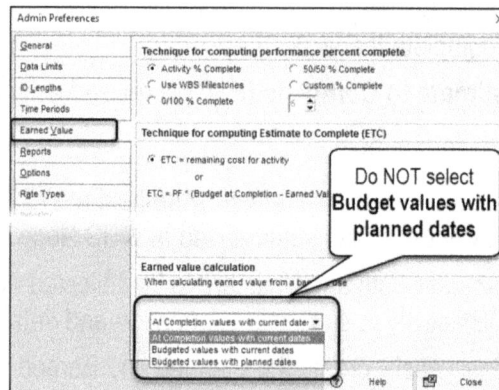

⚠ It is recommended that you do not select or use **Budgeted values with planned dates**, see paragraph 15.1.5 for details of the P6 Planned Dates issues. You should always use the Project Baseline as all users will all see correct data. Using the Primary User Baseline will require each user to set their baseline the same as other users.

27.2 Planned Value

The Planned Value is the value of the work at a point in time that was planned to be completed and is usually represented by the value calculated at the **Current Data Date**.

In P6 there are several options for displaying Planned values that may be confusing. They are:

- **Planned Value Cost** and **Planned Value Units** are read from the Performance Measurement Baseline settings as outlined in the previous paragraph:
  - ➢ These values acknowledge the **Admin Preferences**, **Baseline for earned value calculations**, and
  - ➢ These values acknowledge the **Project Settings**, **Baseline for earned value calculations**

- **BL Project** and **BL1** which may display **Expense**, **Labor**, **Nonlabor**, **Material** and **Total Costs** or **Labor** and **Nonlabor Units**. (**Expense Units** or **Material Units** are usually not available).
  - ➢ These values acknowledge the **Admin Preferences**, **Baseline for earned value calculations**, and
  - ➢ These **DO NOT** acknowledge the **Project Settings**, **Baseline for earned value calculations** and read the **Project Baseline** and **Primary User Baseline** values, respectively.

- **Budgeted Expense Costs**, **Budgeted Labor Costs**, **Budgeted Nonlabor Costs**, **Budgeted Material Costs**, **Budgeted Labor Units** and **Budgeted Nonlabor Units** (**Budgeted Expense Units** or **Budgeted Material Units** are usually not available) are **NOT** read from a Baseline schedule as one might expect but from the **Current Schedule Budget** and the **Current Schedule Planned Dates**.

⚠ All **Budgeted** values should be used with caution as they are always read from the current schedule Baseline and Planned Dates.

The **Planned Value** may be displayed as:

- **Tabulated Data** in locations such as the:
  - ➢ **Activity Usage Spreadsheet**
- **Graphical Data** in locations such as the:
  - ➢ **Activity Usage Profile**
  - ➢ **Tracking Window** by creating a **Project Gantt/Profile**.
- **Columns Data** in locations such as the:
  - ➢ **Tracking Window** by creating a **Project Table**,
  - ➢ **Activities Window** using **Planned Value Cost** or **Planned Value Labor Units**:

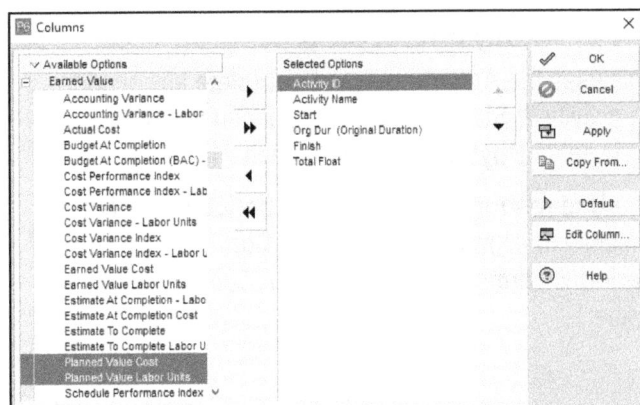

> ℹ️ There are no options for selecting and displaying from a progressed schedule for the following:
>
> - The **Late Baseline** values as a standard option. Many people like to show the Early and Late Baseline curve to display an envelope that progress should stay within.
> - **Planned Material Units**
> - **Planned Expense Units**
>
> Planned data in the following windows or panes display the Budgeted field values which read the **Current Schedule Planned** dates and **Current Schedule Budget** values and should be used with caution:
>
> - **Resource Usage Spreadsheet**
> - **Resource Usage Profile**
> - **Resource Assignments**

27.3 Earned Value

The Earned Value is the value of completed work expressed in terms of the budget. The normal calculation is **Earned Value = Budget x % Complete**.

27.3.1 Performance % Complete

P6 has a field titled **Performance % Complete** which is used to calculate the **Earned Value** for each activity. This may be displayed as a column or a bar in the Gantt Chart.

In P6 there are some options for calculation of the **Performance % Complete** for all activities in each **WBS Node** which is, in turn, used to calculate the **Earned Value**.

- The defaults are set in the **Admin**, **Admin Preferences…**, **Earned Value** tab,
- The options are managed at WBS Node value for all activities assigned to a WBS Node, and each WBS Node may have different values.
- Open the **WBS Window**, **Earned Value** tab to see the options which are mainly self-explanatory:

27.3.2 Activity percent complete

This uses the **Activity percent complete** assigned to an activity. If **Steps** are being used then this will have to be set to **Physical**. See paragraph 21.6.

The **Use resource curves/future period buckets** is checked to allow either **Resource Curves** or **Future Period Buckets** to be used for calculating the Earned Value.

27.3.3 WBS Milestones percent complete

WBS Milestones are created in the **WBS Window**, **WBS Milestones** tab and enable a predefined way of measuring progress against all the work assigned to a WBS Node.

WBS Milestone	Weight	Completed
% Complete	50%	
Start Drafting	1.0	☑
First Draft	4.0	☑
Internal Design Review	3.0	☐
Approved For Construction	2.0	☐

Add   Delete

27.3.4 0/100

The **0/100** option assigns a value of zero for an in-progress activity and assigns 100% when the activity is complete.

27.3.5 50/50

The 50/50 option assigns a value of 50% for an in-progress activity and assigns 100% when the activity is complete.

27.3.6 Custom percent complete

The Custom percent complete allows a further percent complete option if the others do not suit your requirements.

27.3.7 Example of the Calculation of the Earned Value

The example below displays:

- 5 WBS Nodes with their description identifying the option for the **Technique for computing performance percent complete**, i.e., the method of calculating the Earned Value,

- 5 activities, one for each WBS Node each progressed by 50% in duration, hours, and cost,

- The % Complete bar displays the **Performance % Complete**.

Activity ID	Activity % Comp	Performance % Complete	BL Project Total Cost	Earned Value Cost	BL Project Labor Units	Earned Value Labor Units
Earned Value Percent Complete						
Activity % Complete						
A1000	50%	50%	$9,600	$4,800	80h	40h
WBS Milestone Percent Complete 75%						
A1010	50%	75%	$9,600	$7,200	80h	60h
0/100						
A1020	50%	0%	$9,600	$0	80h	0h
50/50						
A1030	50%	50%	$9,600	$4,800	80h	40h
Custom percent complete at 10%						
A1040	50%	10%	$9,600	$960	80h	8h

27.4 Actual Costs

These are the costs actually incurred in performing the work. This is often calculated from the amount paid plus accruals. Actual Costs and Actual Units may be recorded in Primavera and displayed in two methods:

- The total to date, or
- Calculated from the **Financial Periods** values when Period values are stored.

27.4.1 Total to Date

When the total to date is selected then the total cost or units are assigned to each resource or expense and these are spread linearly from the activity **Actual Start** date to the **Data Date**.

Once the total to date has been entered no more action needs to be taken.

27.4.2 Financial Periods

Primavera P6 Version 8 to 19 allowed only one set of Financial Periods to be assigned to all projects, thus if you required some project to have monthly periods and some weekly periods you would have to create two databases. Version 20 enhancements added in the ability to have multiple financial periods.

Thus, there are two sub-sections in this paragraph:

- Version 8 to 19 and
- Enhancements introduced in Version 20

27.4.3 Version 8 to 19 Financial Periods

A more accurate option is to use **Financial Period** values to see a true picture of how much was spent in each period.

> The decision to use **Financial Periods** must be made early as the period values must be saved at each schedule update.
>
> This process takes substantially more time and should have a procedure for people to follow so no steps are missed.

This new function to Primavera Version 5.0 enables:

- The creation of user definable financial periods, say monthly or weekly, and
- The ability to record the actual and earned costs and quantities for each period.

Therefore, actual costs and quantities which span over more than one past period will be accurately reflected per period in all reports. If **Store Period Performance** is not used then the actual costs or units are spread equally over the actual duration of an activity, which may not accurately reflect when the work was performed and what was achieved in each period.

These Periods apply to all projects in the database.

> If one project requires financial periods of months and one of weeks then it would be best to consider setting up two databases, one for each project.

To display **Financial Period data** then two steps are required:

- The **Financial Periods** must be set up using **Admin**, **Financial Periods...**, and
- The period data is stored after each schedule update using **Tools**, **Store Period Performance....**

The steps required to store period performance are:

- Ensure that the user has the necessary privileges to edit **Financial Period Dates**, **Store Period Performance**, and **Edit Period Performance** when past actuals need to be edited.

- Create the **Financial Periods**:
  - ➢ In the Professional Version by selecting **Admin, Financial Periods….** which will open the **Financial Periods** form:

  - ➢ Using **Administer**, **Enterprise Data**, **Financial Data** menu in Web Client for Windows Client users.

- Open the appropriate project, select the **Calculations** tab in the lower pane of the **Projects Window**, and ensure **Link Actual to date and Actual This Period Units and Cost** is enabled by checking the check box. This option is grayed out if the project is not open:

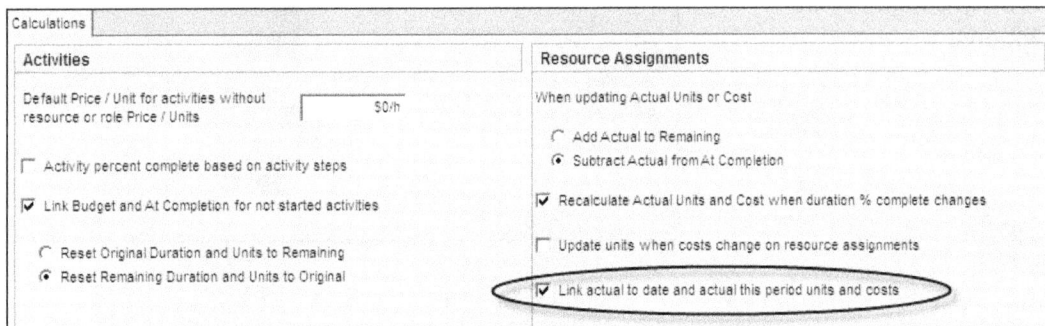

- To store the period performance select **Tools**, **Store Period Performance…** to open the **Store Period Performance** form, select the projects to have the period performance stored and click the

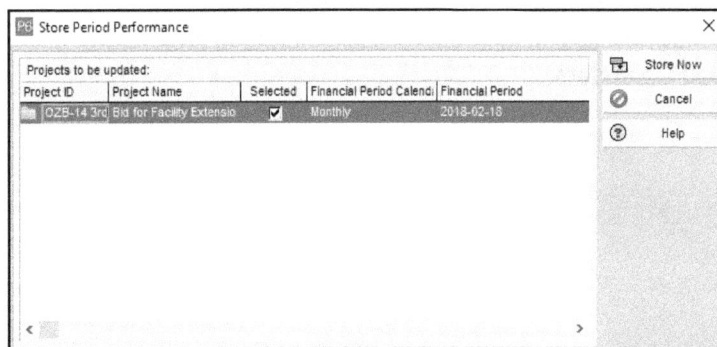 icon.

- The **E̲dit**, **User Preferences**, **A̲pplication** tab, **Financial Period Data** which in earlier version was titled **Columns** section, **Select financial periods to view in columns** enables the user to restrict the number of columns that are displayed in forms such as the **Columns** form, thus reducing the amount of scrolling required to find a specific column:

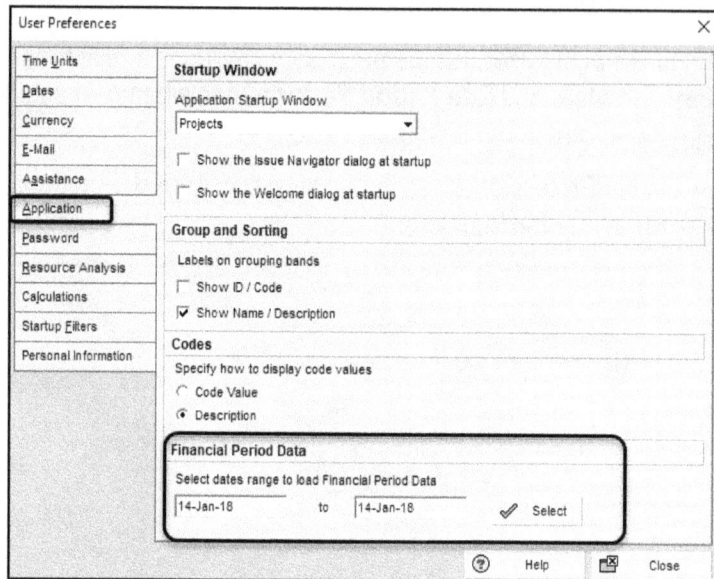

User Preferences		×
Time Units	**Startup Window**	
Dates	Application Startup Window	
Currency	Projects ▼	
E-Mail	☐ Show the Issue Navigator dialog at startup	
Assistance	☐ Show the Welcome dialog at startup	
Application		
Password	**Group and Sorting**	
Resource Analysis	Labels on grouping bands	
Calculations	☐ Show ID / Code	
Startup Filters	☑ Show Name / Description	
Personal Information	**Codes**	
	Specify how to display code values	
	☐ Code Value	
	⦿ Description	
	Financial Period Data	
	Select dates range to load Financial Period Data	
	14-Jan-18 to 14-Jan-18 ✓ Select	
	⑦ Help ⊠ Close	

- Finally, these results may be viewed and edited in the **Past Period Actuals** columns of the **Resources Assignments Window**, **Activity Details Resources** tab, **the Activity Table**, etc.

- The options to display **Financial Period** values is clear in forms like the **Activity Usage Profile Options**:

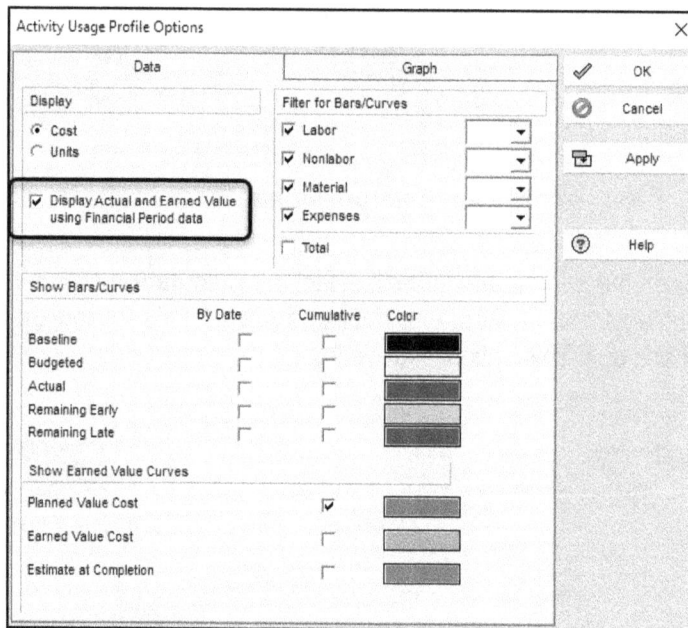

Activity Usage Profile Options		×
Data	**Graph**	✓ OK
Display	Filter for Bars/Curves	⊘ Cancel
⦿ Cost	☑ Labor ▼	
○ Units	☑ Nonlabor ▼	⊡ Apply
	☑ Material ▼	
☑ Display Actual and Earned Value using Financial Period data	☑ Expenses ▼	⑦ Help
	☐ Total	

Show Bars/Curves	By Date	Cumulative	Color
Baseline	☐	☐	▓
Budgeted	☐	☐	░
Actual	☐	☐	▓
Remaining Early	☐	☐	▓
Remaining Late	☐	☐	▓

Show Earned Value Curves		
Planned Value Cost	☑	▓
Earned Value Cost	☐	▓
Estimate at Completion	☐	▓

27.4.4 Version 20 Financial Period Calendars Enhancement

You may now assign different Financial Period to projects in P6 Version 20 by the use of **Financial Period Calendars**.

When you select **Admin**, **Financial Period Calendars** you may create multiple **Financial Period Calendars** and each may have different Financial Periods:

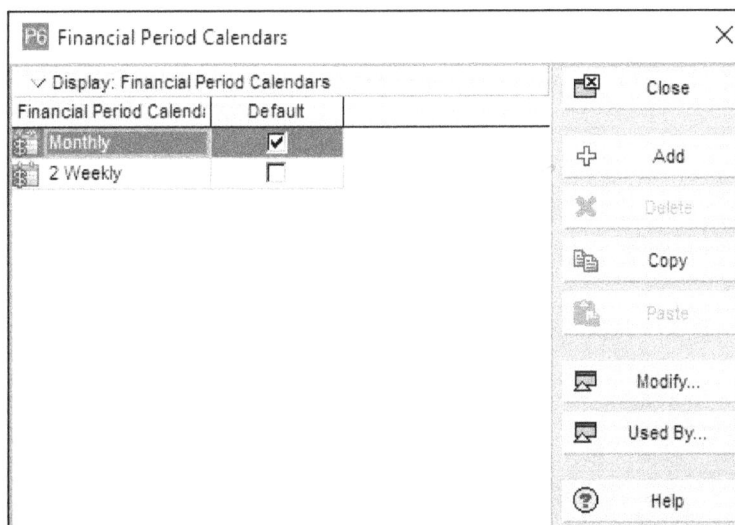

The **Financial Period Calendar** is assigned to a Project in:

- The **Projects Window**, **General** tab, or
- By displaying the **Financial Period Calendar** column:

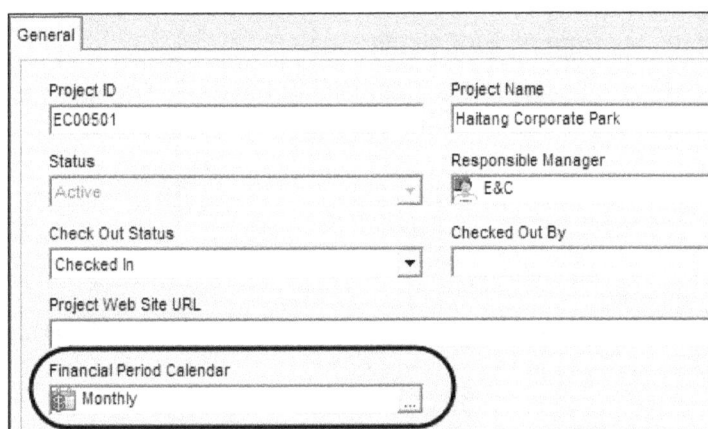

> *i* Version 21 introduced the option when importing an XML file to select the Financial Period Calendar to be assigned to a project.

27.5 Estimate to Complete

P6 has two separately calculated estimate to complete fields:

- Estimate to Complete from Resource and Expense Units and Costs, usually titled **Remaining Costs** or **Remaining Units**.
- Estimate to Complete from P6 Earned Value Calculations, titled **Estimate to Complete** (costs) or **Estimate to Complete Labor Units**.

> *i* It is very important that users understand the differences between these two fields and know which they are using and displaying.

27.5.1 Estimate to Complete from Resource Data

This process calculates the Estimate to Complete directly from Activity Resource Assignments and Expense Remaining Costs and Units.

- The **Remaining Cost** and **Remaining Units** columns read from Resource and Costs values:

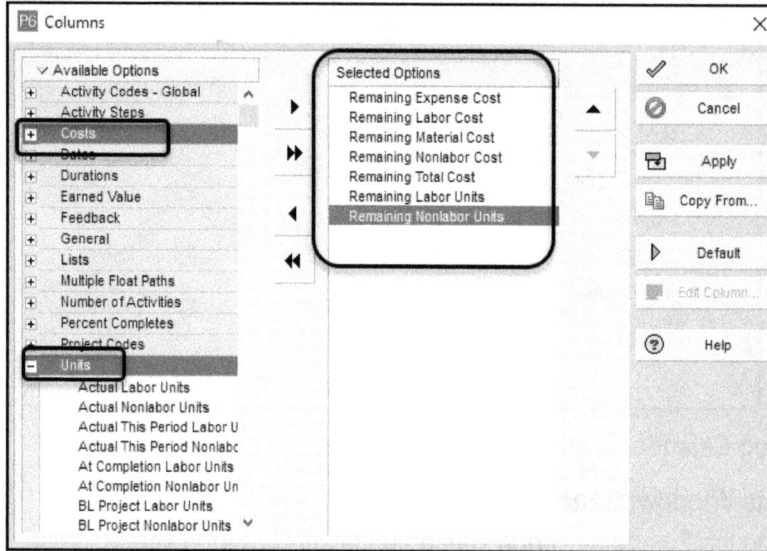

27.5.2 Estimate to Complete from P6 EV Calculations

- The Earned Value **Estimate To Complete** (Cost) and **Estimate To Complete Labor Units**:

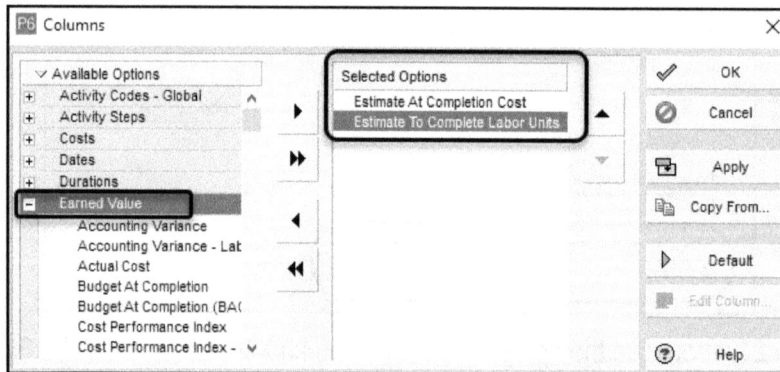

These values are calculated from the **WBS Window**, **Earned Value** tab, **Techniques for computing Estimate to Complete (ETC)** options, which are mainly self-explanatory if you understand Earned Value. **PF** stands for **Performance Factor**.

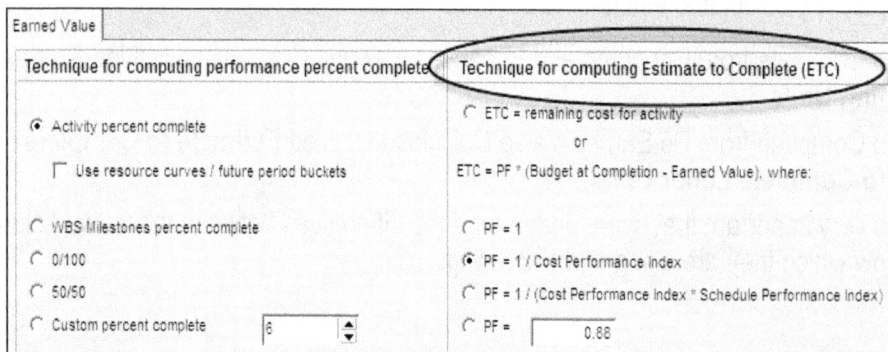

27.6 Activity Usage S-Curves

This section will shed some light on the graphical capabilities of P6 with some examples.

> Users must spend a significant amount of time experimenting with the software so they are confident that the software is doing what they expect it to do. A small schedule with predictable results should be used to gain confidence with the software.
>
> Then write some procedures and follow the procedures on each update.

27.6.1 Activity Usage Profile Bars and Curves

The **Activity Usage Bars** are also commonly called **Histograms** and **Activity Usage Curves** are commonly called **S-Curves**. The activity usage options are displayed in the picture below:

- The **Display** and **Filter for Bars/Curves** are self-explanatory. **Material Units** and **Expense Units** may not be selected and this creates significant reporting restrictions.

- The **Show Bars/Curves** and **Show Earned Value Curves** are not necessarily obvious and will be explained below:

  ➢ **By Date** will display a **Histogram**, and

  ➢ **Cumulative** will display **S-Curves**, in the same color as the Histogram so it may be difficult to read when both sets of data are displayed.

Show Bars/Curves

- **Baseline** uses the Baseline data as specified in the **Admin**, **Admin Preferences...**, **Earned Value** tab, **Earned value calculation** section tab. This is an Early Curve only and drawn from the **Project Baseline** dates.

- **Budgeted** uses the Current schedule Planned dates and Current schedule Budget, not Baseline dates and Budget as might be expected. It is recommended that this is not displayed.

- **Actual** uses the actual Costs and Units as expected. This curve will change shape if **Financial Periods** and **Store Period Performance** are used.

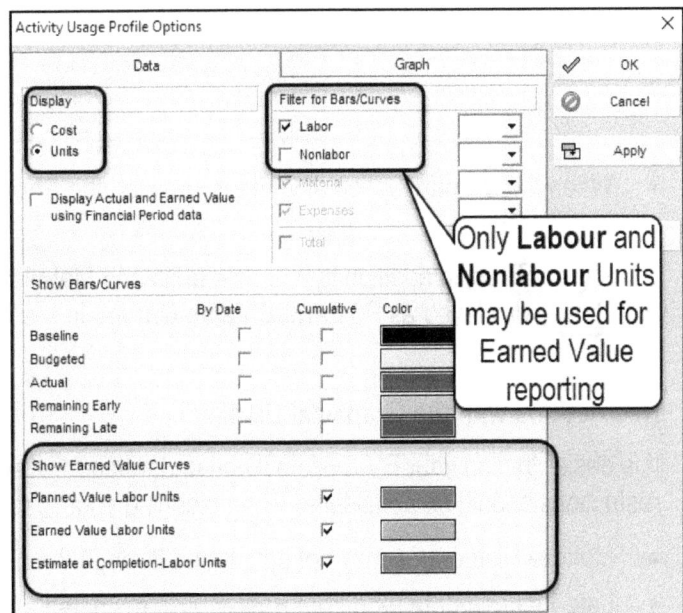

- **Remaining Early** using Current schedule dates and Remaining Costs but are drawn from the zero value of the Y-axis, therefore is of limited value for creating traditional S-Curves where one would draw them from the end of the Actual Curve.

- **Remaining Late** using Current schedule dates and Remaining Costs, but are drawn from the zero value of the Y-axis, therefore of limited value for creating traditional Earned Value S-Curves drawn from the end of the Actual Curve.

27.6.2 Show Earned Value Curves

- **Planned Value Cost** is determined by the combination of two functions:

  - The **Project Window**, **Settings tab**, **Project Settings** section **Baseline for earned value calculations option** selects which Baseline is being read. This curve is usually the same as the **Baseline** curve when the **Project Baseline** is selected but will read different values if the default option is changed to the **User's primary baseline** as shown in the picture below:

  - The Baseline Dates and Costs selected from the **Baseline for earned value calculations option** as set in the **Admin**, **Admin Preferences**, **Earned Value** tab **Earned value calculation** section and may be one of the following options:

- When the **Display** option of **Units** is selected the **Show Earned Value Curves** description changes to Labor units.

  Thus, in addition to Expense units and Material units, **Nonlabor** units may also not be displayed as P6 **Earned Value Curves** in the **Activity Usage Profile**.

Restrictions with the Graphical Display

It is easier to plan your EV System if you understand the system restrictions at the start, the following restrictions should be considered when planning your system:

- Multiple Histograms may not be created through the user interface.

- Late Planned data read from Baselines is restricted and the drawing Late curves difficult to achieve in the user interface.

- Time-Phased Material Resource Units are only available in the Resource Assignment Window where no EV data is available. Thus, the traditional Commodity based EV curves used in the Process Industry are difficult to produce with Material resources. In this situation, users revert to using Nonlabor resources for materials.

- The Bars and Curves functions have some formatting restrictions, such as a low level of control on the vertical axis, colors, and gridline formatting.

27.7 Sample Graphical S-Curves

The following pictures are created from the City Center Office Building Addition project available from the demonstration database available when the software is loaded:

- The curves in the picture below show that the **Remaining** and **Late Remaining** curves are drawn from the zero point not from the end of the **Actual** curve:

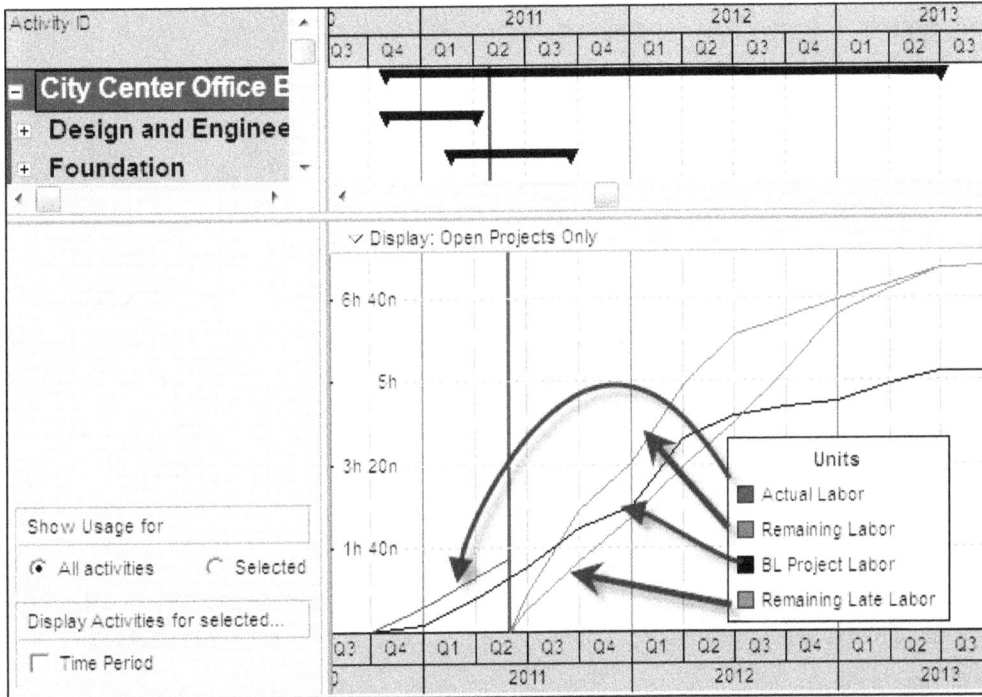

> ⚠ The Remaining may not be drawn from the end of the Actual, thus the Remaining may not be compared Baseline Values.

- The picture below is displaying the traditional Earned Value Curves.

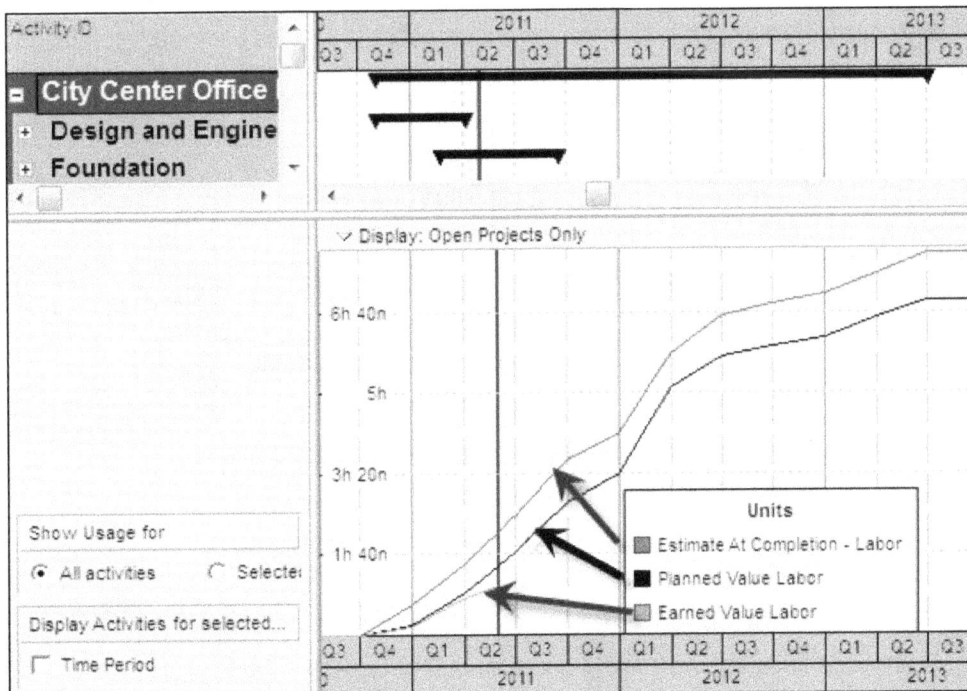

28 WHAT IS NEW IN P6 VERSIONS 18, 19, 20, 21, 22 AND 23

This chapter list the main functional changes in the software since P6 Version 17. Oracle release detailed documents for each release which are available on their web site for all details and a full description of the software changes: https://docs.oracle.com/cd/E64687_01/EPPM/EPPM_CFO.html.

28.1 Databases and Tool

There are essentially three types of databases that the PPM Windows Client may open:

- Stand-Alone, where the database is installed on a PC and only accessed by one user in an organisation.

- PPM, aimed at small companies where all users access the same database and there is limited inbuilt integration with other Oracle products.

- EPPM, aimed at larger companies where all users access the same database. This database may also be opening by the Web Client and has inbuilt integration with many other Oracle tools.

Depending what type of database, you are opening and what version of the software you have, there will be different menu options when using the PPM Windows Client. In summary with later versions of P6:

- When you open a Stand-Alone database, you will not have functions to create users etc.

- When you open an EPPM database you will not have the administration functions.

28.2 Consent Notice and Status of User Acceptance

Consent Notices were introduced in P6 Version 18 and alert users to any corporate policies designed to protect personally identifiable information that may be stored or transmitted when using P6.

A Consent Notice is displayed when a user first operates one of the functions enabled as a Consent Notice. The user must accept the consent notice before being allowed to progress.

Consent Notices are set up in **Admin Preferences**.

Status of User Acceptance shows how many Consent Notices have been displayed and accepted by users.

The **User Preferences**, **Personal Information** tab allows users to see the personal information entered by the administrator when the user was created.

28.3 Stored Images

This function is new to P6 Version 18. This solved the issue of when one user had embedded a picture in a Layout Header and a second user did not have access to the same directory and was thus unable to display the same picture when applying the same Layout.

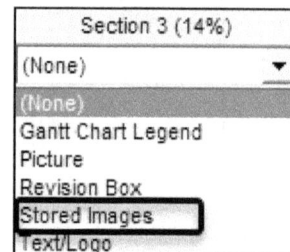

Up to 20 pictures at a max of 500x500 dpi may be saved in a database and are available for any user to access.

- Pictures are uploaded using **Enterprise**, **Store Image….**

- Pictures are inserted into headers and footers from **Page Setup**:

Version 19 introduced the ability to upload multiple images at one time.

28.4 XML Check In and Check Out

P6 Version 19 introduced the ability **Check In** and **Check Out** projects to XML.

28.5   Dissolving Activities with Lag using Retain Lag

This function was new to P6 Version 19 and introduced the ability to retain lag when dissolving activities. When **Retain Lag** is selected from the **User Preferences**, **Calculations** tab then the dissolved activities predecessor and successor lags are be added together in the new relationship. This is covered in detail para 9.10.

28.6   Project Code Maximum Length Increase

P6 Version 19 increased the maximum length in PPM databases for Project Codes to 60 characters.

28.7   Details, User Defined Fields tab

P6 Version 19 added a new **Details**, **User Defined Fields** tab, similar to the **Codes** tab, displaying the assigned User Defined Fields (UDFs). It is available in the following windows: Projects, WBS, Activities, Resource Assignments, Project Expenses, Issues, and Work Products, Risks and Documents.

28.8   Data Date Default for Apply Actuals

P6 Version 19 allows projects to use their own **Data Date** when applying actuals. In earlier versions all projects were set to the same **Data Date**.

28.9   Allow or Restrict Access to Resources from Multiple Parent Resources

P6 Version 18 and earlier only allowed one resource or resource node to be assigned to a user. P6 Version 19 introduced the ability to allow a user to be assigned up to five resources or resource nodes when defining resource access. A user may view and assign the selected resources and the child resources from resources assigned here:

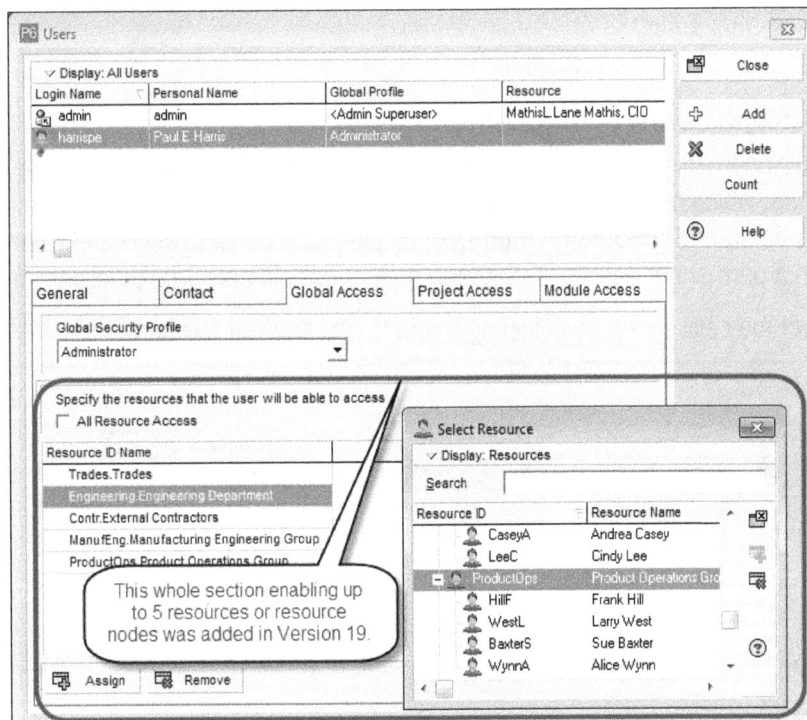

28.10 Relationship Comments

Primavera P6 Version 20 introduced a **Comments** column may be added to the **Activities** window **Relationships**, **Predecessor** and **Successor** tabs, see para 9.12 for more details.

28.11 Roles Rate may now be varied over time

Resources have always been able to vary their rate over time but Roles were not and this was one of the drivers to use resources and not roles on projects.

Version 20 introduced the ability for a Role Rate to be varied over time and is covered in detail in para 18.2.2. This is the same way that resources calculate when an Activity spans an Effective Date and this issue was fixed in Version 21

28.12 Data Date Selection in Multiple Project Scheduling

Primavera P6 Version 20 introduced some additional functions when scheduling multiple projects.

- All **Projects use their own data dates** which is how Version 19 and earlier versions calculated, or

- Version 20 added an additional option **Apply selected data date to all open projects** and all projects will have their **Data Date** permanently changed to the selected date.

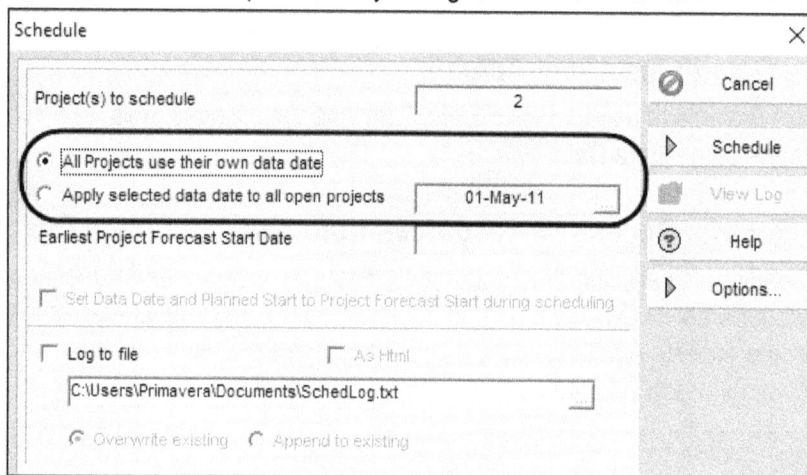

28.13 Multiple Project Scheduling Options Selection

In the P6 Version 19 and earlier when multiple projects were scheduled together and they had different **Scheduling Options**, which could happen when users change them from default or when you imported a project, then all the different **Scheduling Options** of all the projects being scheduled were changed to the **Default Project** on a permanent basis and changed projects would calculate differently from then on.

The **Default Project** may still be set by selecting **Project**, **Set Default Project**:

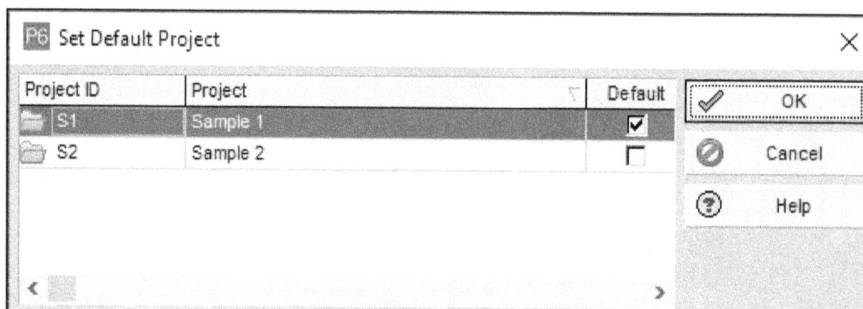

Primavera P6 Version 20 introduced an option where you may select which project **Scheduling Options** are used when scheduling multiple projects in the **Scheduling Options** form which is opened by selecting **Tools**, **Schedule**, **Options**:

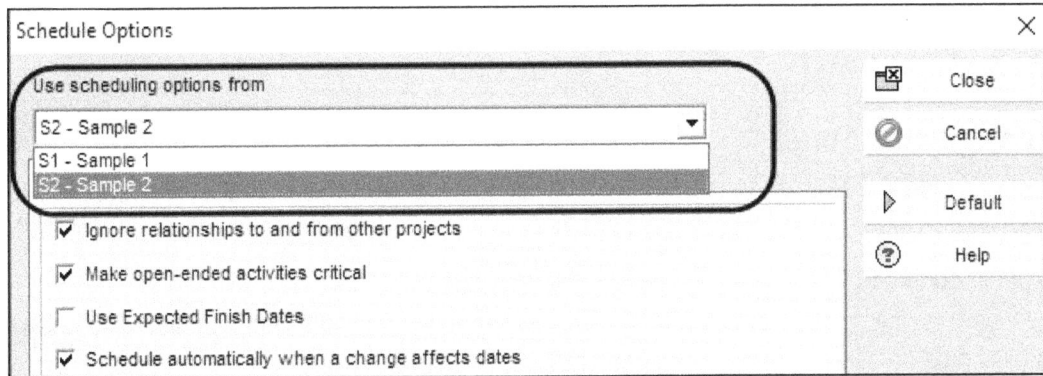

What happens now?

- The **Default Project** is ignored,
- The **Scheduling Options** from the project selected in the **Scheduling Options** are used to calculate all the project, and
- The other project(s) **Scheduling Options** are changed permanently to the project selected the **Scheduling Options** form on a permanent basis.

Thus, the problem of **Scheduling Options** being changed when scheduling multiple projects has **NOT** been solved. You now have two options to mess up your **Scheduling Options** of projects when scheduling multiple projects with different options.

Again, I reiterate you should make all the **Scheduling Options** in one database the same when you schedule multiple projects and be careful when importing projects.

28.14 Lean Tasks may be imported using an XML file

Importing Lean Tasks are a new function in P6 Version 19 allowing users to allow users to VIEW ONLY Tasks created in Primavera Cloud when a project integrated from Primavera Cloud to an EPPM database. Tasks are a function is Primavera Cloud where an activity may be broken down into Tasks which do not drive dates but allow a further granulation of an activity into more detailed work, but they are different to Steps.

Lean Tasks may have the following attributes:

- Assignment of a duration,
- May be made "Private" so other people do not see them,
- Tasks may have logic between them which are called "Handoffs",
- A Task's Float is called "Slack".
- The planning of Tasks is completed on a **Planning Board** that may be shared between team members. This is a tool designed for short term planning by the people completing the work.

Primavera P6 Version 20 introduced an option when you are using an EEPM database you may import **Lean Tasks** through an XML file from Primavera Cloud.

28.15 Different Projects may have different Financial Periods

Primavera P6 Version 20 introduced an option where you may now assign different Financial Period to projects in P6 Version 20 by the use of **Financial Period Calendars**. When you select **Admin**, **Financial Period Calendars** you may create multiple **Financial Period Calendars** and each may have different Financial Periods.

28.16 Assignment Codes

Primavera P6 Version 20 introduced a new function titled **Assignment Codes** allowing users to code up assignments so resource assignments may be Grouped or Filtered. This function could be used for:

- Assigning priority to resource assignments against tasks,
- When there is one generic resource in the database that is being supplied by multiple subcontractors and this could be used to identify the subcontractor,
- When there is one generic resource in the database and you require a specific skill or qualification for the resource then this could be identified with an **Assignment Code**.

This function is covered in detail in para 22.8.

28.17 Histogram Bars Exact Values

In P6 Version 20 value of histograms may be displayed on histograms in the Resource Usage Profile, Activity Usage Profile, and Tracking View by selecting the **Show Values** option in the **Profile Option** form, **Graph** tab:

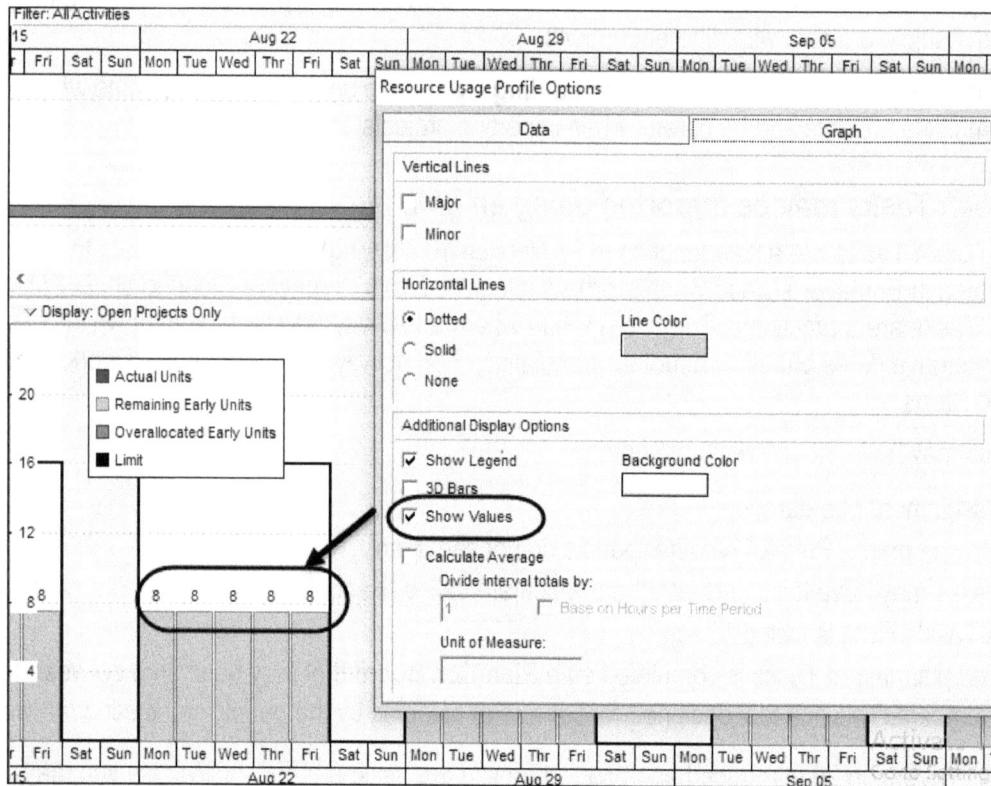

28.18 Other Enhancements in P6 Version 20

28.18.1 Resource Assignment Window now allows Grouping and Filtering by Codes and UDFs

Data in the Resource Assignment window may be filtered and/or grouped using Project, Activity and WBS User Defined Fields (UDFs) and Project Codes in P6 Version 20.

28.18.2 Fill down available in Activities Window Resource Usage Spreadsheet

Fill down is available in the Activities Window Resource Usage Spreadsheet in P6 Version 20.

28.18.3 P6 Continues Working when there is a Network Failure

Users may continue working is some circumstances when connected to an EPPM Cloud Connect database and configured to allow this when there is a network failure.

28.18.4 Prevent Risk Categories being Imported into a PPM Database

When exporting to an XER file Risk Categories are exported but in P6 Version 20 you are able to prevent the Categories being imported into a PPM or SQLite database.

Risk Categories are not imported or exported to an EEPM database.

28.18.5 Reset Locked Users

In the EPPM version users locked out of P6 or Visualizer may be reset.

28.18.6 Uploading of Harmful Files

You may prevent people from uploading harmful files in the **Admin Preferences**, **Options**, **Document Security**. See para 17.3.13 for more detail.

28.18.7 Exception Site List

A list of web sites may be added to **Admin Preferences**, **Options**, **Exception Site List**:

The URLs may then be added to Notebook Topics and UDFs and permitted URLs may be launched from P6 by clicking on the URL and selecting Launch.

URLs not listed or not permitted may not be launched but may be copied and pasted into a browser. See para 17.3.13 for more information.

NOTE: Any web site may be launched from the **Projects** window, **General** tab, **Project Web Site URL**.

28.18.8 Role Codes

P6 Version 20 introduced Role Codes allowing Roles to be assigned Code in the same way as Resources and Activities. See para 18.2.3 for more detail.

28.18.9 User Preferences, Application, Codes Option

This option was introduced in Version 20. P6 normally displays the Code Value in columns and the Code Description in the Bands. This option allows for the either the Code or Code Description, but not both, to be displayed in columns, see para 17.1.6 for more information.

28.19 Assignment Cost are Exported

The Oracle Cumulative Feature Overview for P6 Version 21 file states *"When you export to Primavera XML, Price Per Unit data for assignments is included in the export file."*

This statement is a little misleading and see para 26.11 for a detailed explanation.

28.20 Users may See and Set Activity Start and Finish Times in the Date Picker box when the User Preferences are set only to show the date.

Users may see and set Activity Start and Finish times in the **Date Picker** box operates when the **User Preferences** are set only to show the date without the time.

This is a great enhancement for P6 Version 21 as P6 usually picks the wrong time when setting Actual dates, Constraints, Suspend and Resume dates when the time is not set to be displayed from the User Preferences. See para 3.8.3 for more details.

28.21 Financial Period Calendar Selection when Importing an XML file.

Version 20 introduced the option of different **Financial Period Calendars** for different projects.

Version 21 introduced the option when importing an XML file to select the Financial Period Calendar to be assigned to a project. See para 17.5.2 for more details.

28.22 Maintain Relationships with External Projects.

Introduced in P6 Version 21, when you import projects from a Primavera XML file, you can choose whether to retain relationships between activities in the project and those in external projects. See para 26.10 for more details.

28.23 IPMDAR Format Supported for EEPM Databases only

Introduced in P6 Version 21; an IPMDAR is a project export format required by the US Department of Defence. In P6 Version 21 it is only available when you open an EEM database, when exporting from a PPM database the option is greyed out. P6 Version 22 PPM may now export IPMDAR format from SQLite and PPM databases; Version 21 would only allow export IPMDAR format from an EPPM database.

28.24 Resource and Role Cost Spreads Consider Rate Changes Over Time.

The **Admin Preferences**, **Options** has introduced in Version 21 a **Cost Spread** option.

This changes how the cost spreads for resources and role rates are reflected in the Resource Usage Spreadsheet and Profile, Activity Usage Spreadsheet and Profile, Tracking View, Resource Assignments window, and Activity Usage Spreadsheets and Profiles, Publishing and Reports.

See para 18.2.3 for more details.

28.25 Activity Critical Path Visibility.

There is a new toolbar in Version 21 titled **Activity Critical Path**.

- The Toolbar is displayed by right clicking on any toolbar and checking the **Activity Critical Path** option:

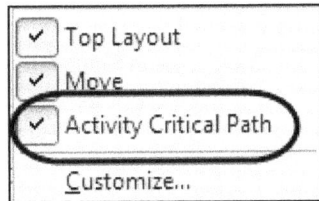

- This will display the toolbar below:

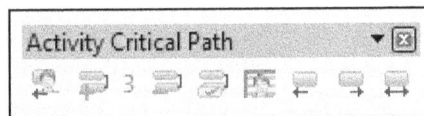

- There is also a new menu item under the **View** command.

- **IMPORTANT NOTE**: Clicking on a button will activate the command and clicking again will deactivate the command,
- This function may be used in conjunction with the **Float Path Order** function,

The Oracle Cumulative Feature Overview file states:

To aid in the resolution of delayed critical paths before they become project over-runs, P6 Professional can show:

- Activities on up to 30 activity-driven critical paths, calculated on the forward pass, backward pass, or forward and backward passes (with or without resource leveling).

- The activities on up to 30 resource driven critical paths, calculated on the backward pass with resource leveling.

This Oracle description is not clear and this topic is explained in para 13.4.

28.26 Other Enhancements in P6 Version 22

28.26.1 Help Menu What's New Command

The P6 Version 22 **Help Menu** has introduced a **What's New** command button:

This button takes users to the Oracle Primavera Website where users may select their old and new software version and obtain a list of enhancements.

28.26.2 Check Schedule Report

P6 Version 22 has added the **Tools**, **Check Schedule Report** option allow the user to conduct a **Quantitative Check** on a schedule which is becoming more popular with a number of organisations. See para 11.6 for more information.

28.26.3 Sort Order Move Up and Move Down Options

P6 Version 22 has added the option of moving the sort order fields up and down in the **View, Group and Sort, Sort** form, see papa 12.1.4 for more details.

28.26.4 Additional Options for Importing XML Data

P6 Version 22 has introduced options for managing **Resources Calendars** and **Responsible Managers** when importing and XML file:

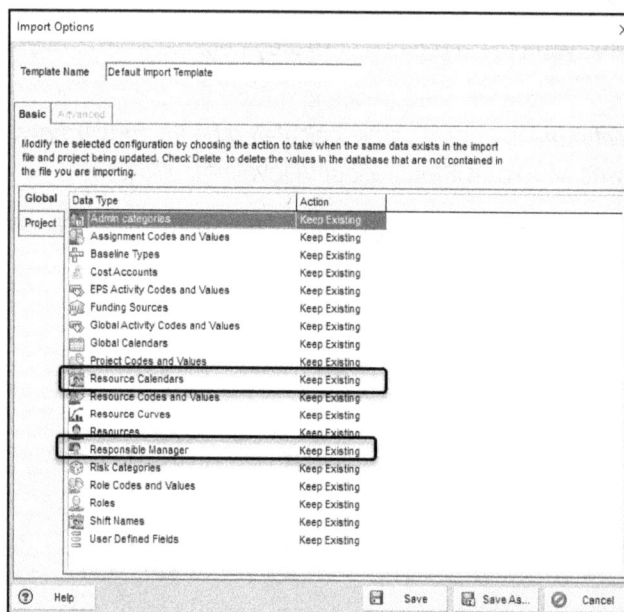

28.26.5 Additional Baseline Data Available when Assigning a Baseline

The **Project**, **Assign Baseline**, **Select Project Baseline** form has customisable columns in P6 Version 22 allowing the user to see more information about a baseline when selecting a baseline project, see para 15.3.6 for more information.

28.26.6 Import and Export Templates may be Duplicated

It is now possible in P6 Version 22 to **Duplicate** an **Import** or **Export** template for all import and export file types as er the picture below:

NOTE: This will save a user a lot of checking time when creating a copy of a template with a small change.

28.26.7 Finish Date Filter Definition

The P6 Version 22 **Admin**, **Admin Preferences**, **General** tab has a new **Data Filters** option which controls which dates are included in a data filter, see para 17.3.1 for more information.

28.26.8 Multiple Project Views Displayed Side by Side

With P6 Version 22 there is an additional option in the **Project** menu titled **Additional Activities View**:

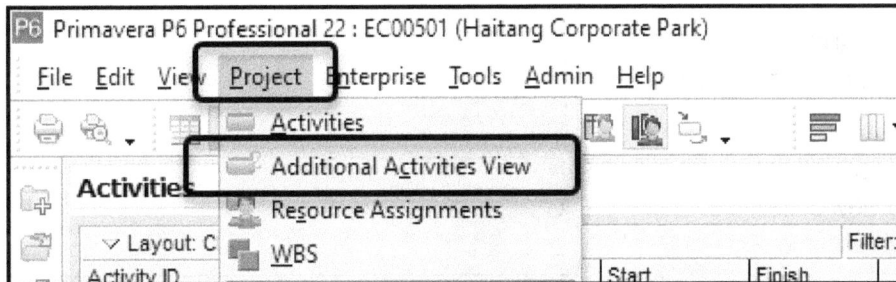

This option will open a second view of the project(s) that are opened. The projects views may then be resized etc:

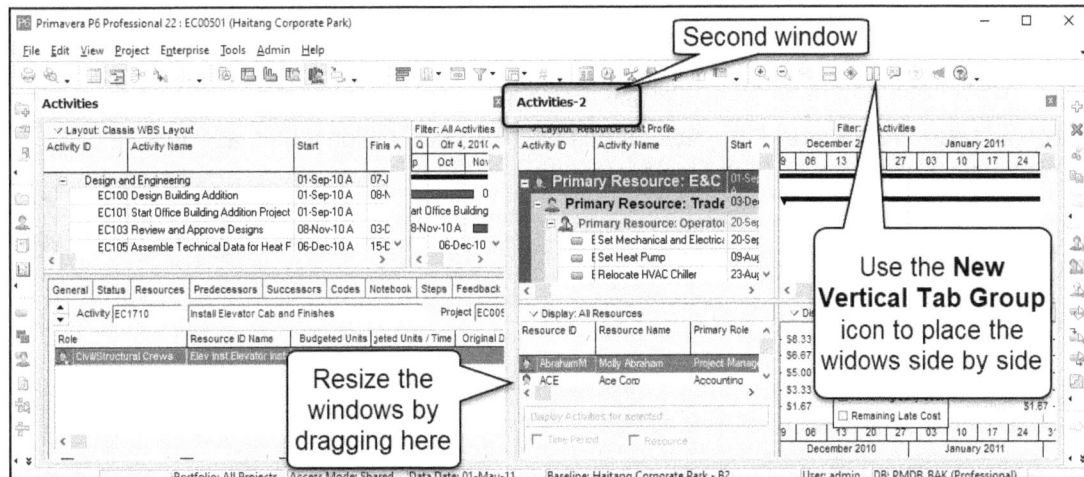

The Oracle description was not clear to me, but I found by experiment that:

> ➤ Each window may be formatted separately,
> ➤ Each window may be printed separately by clicking in the window that is required to be printed.
> ➤ The **Schedule Options** and **Schedule Check Report** options may not be different for each view and scheduling one view will schedule both views.

28.26.9 Colum Header Sort Arrow Direction Reversed

Although not listed as an enhancement in the Oracle documentation the arrow in a column header has been reversed in P6 Version 22 and now when it points up the column is sorted alphabetically down, as in the EPPM Web tool:

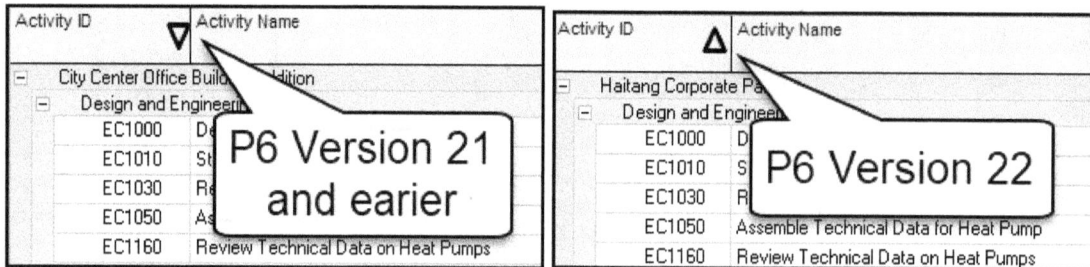

28.26.10   New Earned Value Fields Available

The P6 Version 22 Activity **Details**, **Resources** tab has more fields available as per the picture below, which are calculated using the WBS Node Earned Value settings:

There are also available in the **Resources Assignments** window in columns.

NOTE: It is disappointing that it is still not possible to view baseline data for each individual resource.

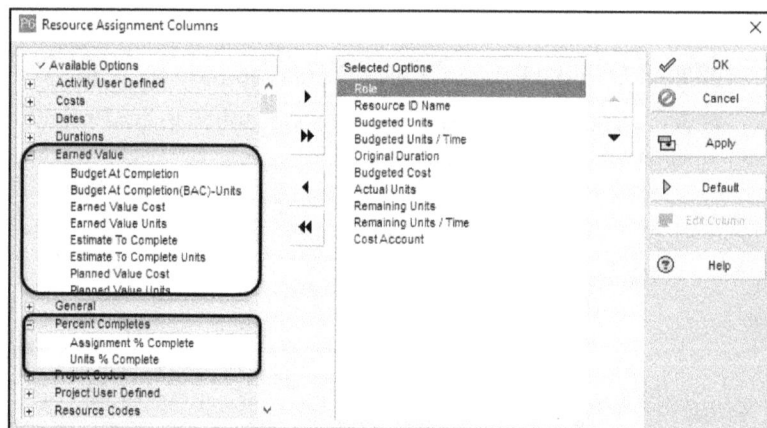

28.26.11   Copy Visualizer Layouts when Copying a Project

There is a new option with P6 Version 22 to copy Visualizer layouts with a project. See para 4.2 for more information.

28.26.12   OBS Assignment when Copying a Project

The P6 Version 22 **User Preferences** form, **Assistance** tab has a new option for the assignment of the OBS to a copied project, see para 17.1.5 for more information.

28.26.13   Copy and Paste a Range of Cells in Spreadsheets

The P6 Version 22 Oracle list of enhancements stated:

"You can copy the values in a range of cells from one row of a spreadsheet and paste the values in those cells elsewhere in the same row or in another row. To copy a range of cells, use the context sensitive right-click menu or use the shortcuts Shift+Crl+C (Copy Range) and Shift+Ctrl+V (Paste Range). Only the values in the cells are copied and pasted, so it is possible to copy and paste between cells with different units of measure. When you paste a range of cells, the data is only pasted into editable cells."

This description is not clear, and this function is explained in detail para 20.1.5

28.26.14   User Preferences, Email Configuration

The **User Preferences**, **Email Configuration** has more email setup options, see para 17.1.4 for more information.

28.27 What's New in P6 Version 23

28.27.1 Resource Analysis Role Limit Calculation Refinement

In the **Edit**, **User Preferences**, **Resource Analysis** for there is now an option to **Exclude inactive resources** for more accurate reporting:

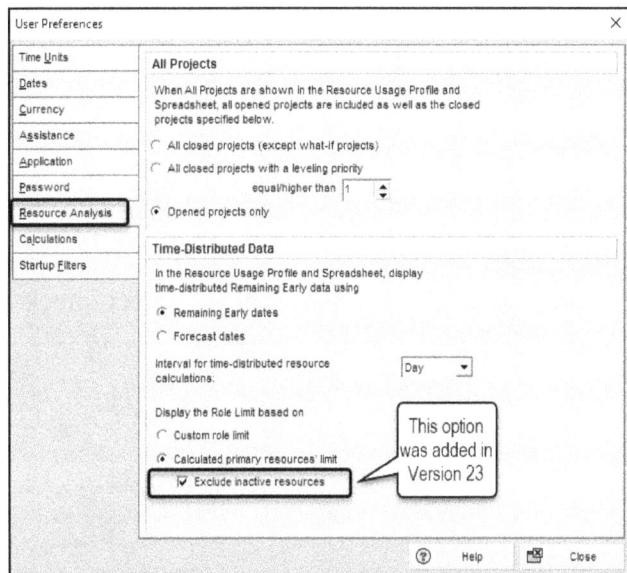

28.27.2 Project Checker Improved

The **Project Checker** asses the health of the project data within a database and conducts check such as ensuring all the Primary Keys within a database table are unique. In other words, makes sure the database tables for the projects being checked are not corrupt.

Admin Superusers, Project Superusers may run the **Project Checker** for projects that they have **Project Superuser** access.

During database configuration **Project Checker** must be enabled for all database types except SQLite database connections by selecting the parameter **Enable Project Checker** on installation. To do this a user must select from the **Login** form **Edit database configuration**, and check the **Enable Project Checker** box:

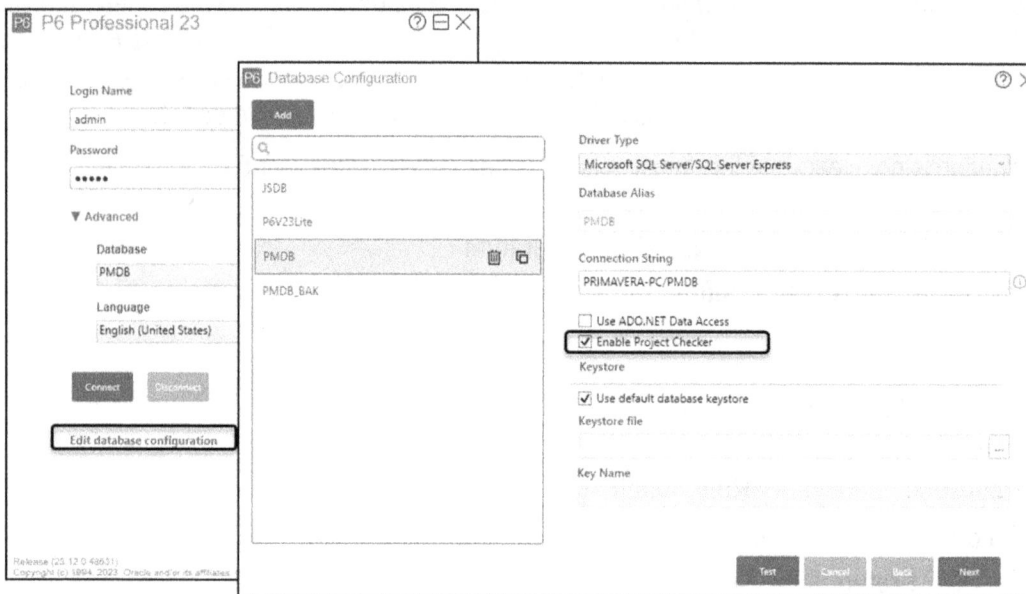

To run the **Project Checker** select **Tools**, **Project Checker**:

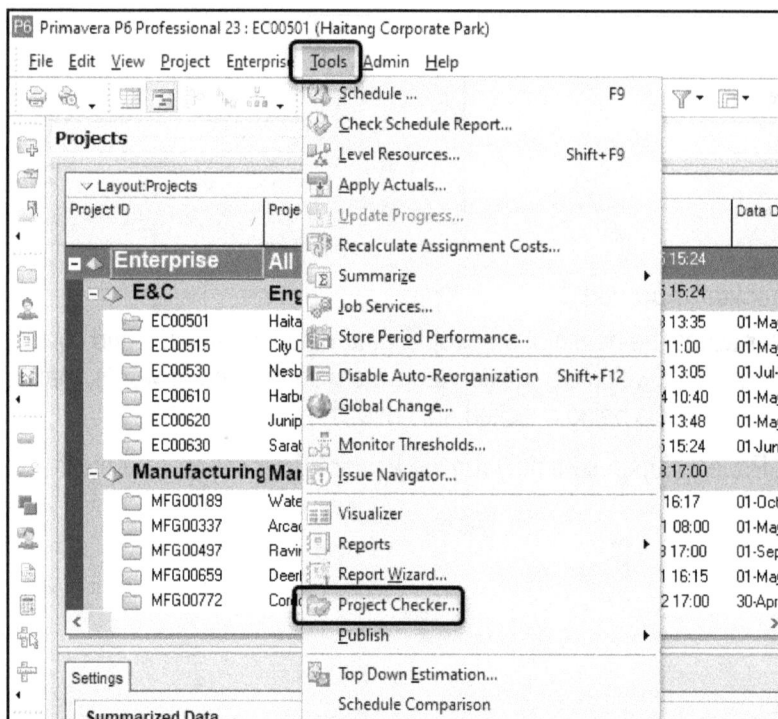

The next form allows the user to select which projects to check, the rules to be checked and report content:

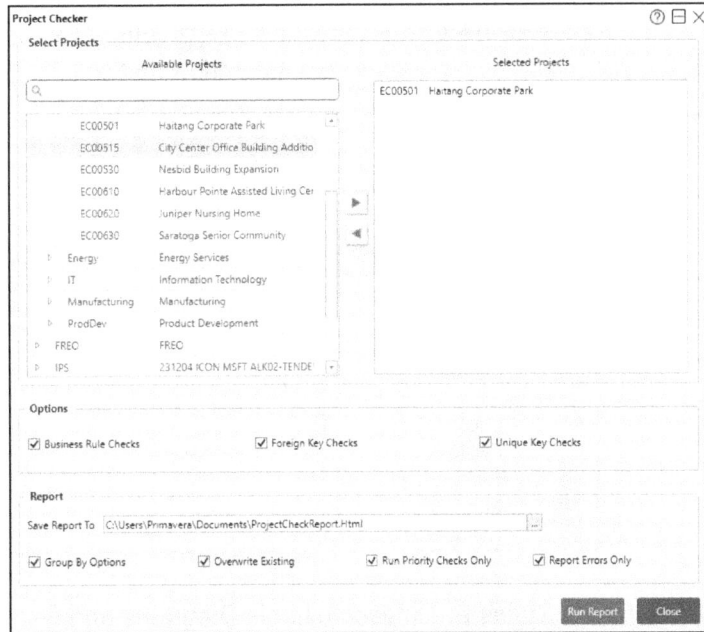

The **Project Checker** dialog box has two new options:

- To restrict the check setting to only severity 1 (important) and 2 (significant) checks, and
- To run a report on the errors.

The report now includes:

- At the top a table allowing report drill down for types and severity and
- You may view the whole report.

The report looks like the picture.

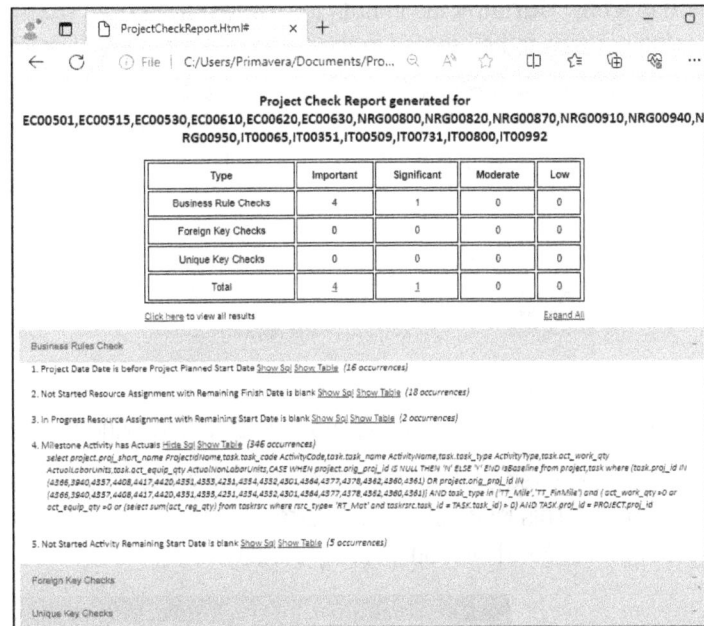

28.27.3 Range Copy and Paste from Excel and P6 into the Resource Usage Profile

Users may copy a range of cell from the **Resource Usage Profile** by selecting a range and then Right Clicking and selecting **Range Copy**, see 20.1.5 for more details.

28.27.4 DOE - CPP Export Feature Enhanced

CPP Format Error! Bookmark not defined. introduced in P6 Version 22 and enhanced in P6 Version 23. The US Department of Energy had mandated that the current CSV, and MDB upload formats for PPD (Project Performance Data) upload will be migrated to the JSON (JavaScript Object Notation) format in early 2023. Primavera P6 Version 22 had to be connected to an EPPM to export to a CPP format, now a user may export in CPP format from P6 Professional connected to any database. The mapping for a CPP format must be manually created.

28.27.5 Projects Window Column to Count the Number of Projects in a Group

A new column is available in the **Projects** window that counts the number of projects in a Group:

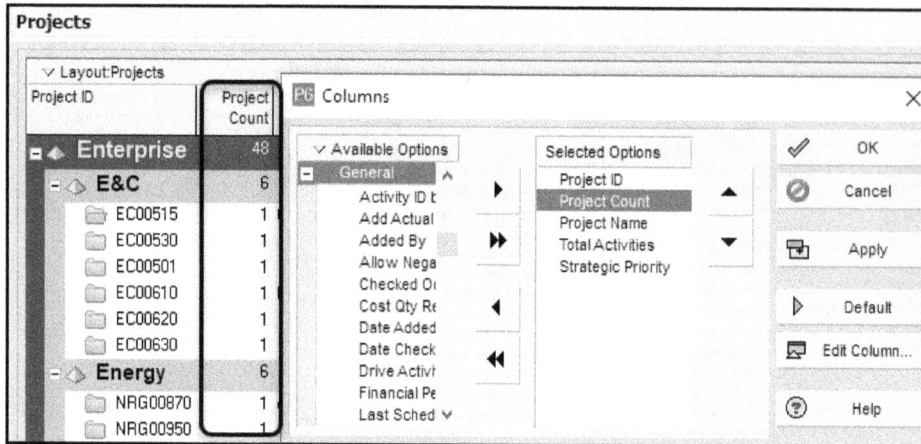

28.27.6 Add Curtains to Timescale Logic Diagrams and Gantt Layouts in P6 Visualizer

There is a new **Curtains** tab in both the **Timescale Logic Diagrams** and **Gantt Layouts** in P6 Visualizer allowing curtains to be created in the same way as in P6:

A curtain is added, deleted and formatted as in t the Windows tool.

The author received an error message and was unable to create a curtain in an existing view in his version of P6. This issue should be corrected in an update and the pictures were created by importing a Layout from P6 PPM with an existing Curtain.

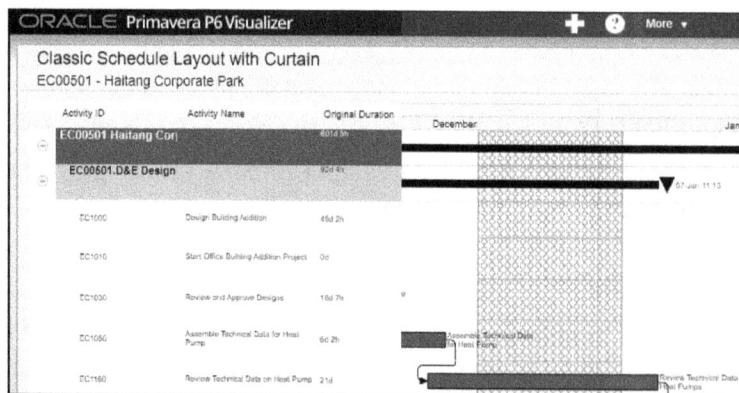

28.27.7 Any User can Import Projects from Excel Spreadsheets

In P6 Version 22 and earlier a user had to be a assigned a Project Superuser to import from Excel, and in P6 Version 23 this right may be assigned to any User.

29 TOPICS NOT COVERED IN THIS PUBLICATION

The following topics are not covered in this publication:

- Budgets, including:
  - ➤ Budget Summary
  - ➤ Budget Log
  - ➤ Funding
  - ➤ Spending Plan
- Issues
- Risks and Risk Calculation
- External Applications
- Timesheets
- Timesheet Date Administration.

30 INDEX

This publication is only sold as a bound book, no parts may be reproduced by any means, e.g., electronic, video or print.

© *Hyde Park Solutions Limited*   480

www.ingramcontent.com/pod-product-compliance
Lightning Source LLC
Chambersburg PA
CBHW081246220326
41597CB00024BB/4460